Roundell P. Selbourne

Ancient Facts and Fictions concerning Churches and Tithes

Roundell P. Selbourne

Ancient Facts and Fictions concerning Churches and Tithes

ISBN/EAN: 9783337162719

Printed in Europe, USA, Canada, Australia, Japan

Cover: Foto ©ninafisch / pixelio.de

More available books at **www.hansebooks.com**

ANCIENT
FACTS AND FICTIONS

CONCERNING

CHURCHES AND TITHES

BY

ROUNDELL, EARL OF SELBORNE

AUTHOR OF
'A DEFENCE OF THE CHURCH OF ENGLAND AGAINST DISESTABLISHMENT'

SECOND EDITION

WITH A SUPPLEMENT CONTAINING REMARKS
ON A
RECENT HISTORY OF TITHES

London
MACMILLAN AND CO.
AND NEW YORK
1892

All rights reserved

TO

MY VERY DEAR BROTHER

EDWIN PALMER, D.D.

ARCHDEACON OF OXFORD AND CANON OF CHRIST CHURCH

THIS BOOK IS

AFFECTIONATELY INSCRIBED

Digitized by the Internet Archive
in 2007 with funding from
Microsoft Corporation

http://www.archive.org/details/ancientfactsfict00selbrich

PREFACE

My purpose is to examine, in the following pages, more fully and critically than was possible in a former work,[1] some historical questions, which, although they have not any real bearing upon controversies of the present day, are sometimes represented as if they had, in a way which makes it desirable that the facts concerning them should be understood. In my former work I preferred, whenever it was possible, to support my statements on those subjects by the authority of other writers, particularly Selden; whose views I regarded as generally, though not on every point, accurate. We have now the benefit of many great collections, made since Selden's time, of ecclesiastical and historical documents; and manuscripts, with which he was not acquainted, have been published or brought to light. The advantages which we so possess leave room for something to be added to his researches, sometimes by way of

[1] *Defence of the Church of England against Disestablishment* (Macmillan, 3rd ed. 1887).

verification or illustration, sometimes by way of correction and supplement.

The period of time which the present work is intended to illustrate is that which preceded the Norman Conquest of England. It is divided into two parts; the first relating to Continental Churches, a knowledge of whose laws and customs (though different from our own) may frequently throw useful light upon those of this country; the second, to the Anglo-Saxon Church. In the second part some space has been necessarily devoted to the criticism of ancient documents; which (although I am sensible that it may make a considerable demand upon the patience of my readers) was indispensable for the purpose which I had in view. The work, in its general conception, may perhaps be best described as an attempt to trace the course of those developments of early ecclesiastical institutions, which resulted in the formation of the modern parochial system, and its general endowment with tithes.

In the preparation of the materials for this work, I have received ready and courteous assistance (for which I desire to return my grateful acknowledgments) from the principal librarian, and keeper of the manuscripts, of the British Museum, and their Assistants; and also from the authorities of the Bodleian Library, particularly Falconer Madan, Esq. And to the Rev. S. S. Lewis, Fellow and Librarian of Corpus Christi College, Cambridge, and the Master and other members of that learned Society, I owe thanks, not only for the facilities given to me while consulting some of the manuscript treasures of their library, but for the more than ordinary personal kindness with which those facilities were accompanied. Nor can I be silent as to my obligations to my brother, the Archdeacon of Oxford (to whom this volume is inscribed), for most valuable help received from him in many ways.

December 1887.

I have been enabled in the present Edition (besides some other new matter) to carry forward, beyond the point which it had reached in the First Edition, my investigation of some of those ancient documents mentioned in the foregoing Preface; particularly the Exeter Penitential, No. 718, in the Bodleian Library,[1] and Bishop Leofric's Rule for Secular Canons (No. 12 of Wanley and 191 of Nasmith), in the Library of Corpus Christi College, Cambridge.[2] As to the former, I had the opportunity, when at Rome in January 1888, of collating with it two manuscripts in the Vatican Library, which had been erroneously supposed to

[1] *Post*, pp. 229, 230, 235-241, and Appendix C.
[2] *Post*, pp. 263-268.

be copies of it, but from both of which all that was material to my subject in the Bodleian manuscript is absent. The latter I have now traced to its source, in the Gallican Rule for Canons, enlarged, after the Council held at Aix-la-Chapelle in A.D. 816, from that given by Chrodegang in King Pippin's time to three churches at Metz.

CONTENTS

INTRODUCTION, pages 1-20

Church and State on the Continent of Europe under the Frank Kingdom and Empire, 1, 2. Legislation, 3, 4. Judicature, 4, 5. Faith and Ritual, 5, 6. Church Appointments, 6, 7. The Papacy, 8. Roman Canon Law, Dionysius Exiguus, 9. Ansegisus, 10. Benedict the Levite, 10, 11. Ingilram, 11-13. Isidore 'Mercator,' 13-18. Letter of Clement to St. James, 14, 15. Donation of Constantine, 15-18. Regino, Burchard, and Ivo, 18, 19. Gratian's *Decretum*, 19, 20. Later Roman Canon Law, 20.

PART I.—CONTINENTAL

CHAPTER I

CHURCH REVENUES AND RULES OF DISTRIBUTION, pages 23-45

Patrimony of the Poor, 23, 24. Episcopal Authority, 24-26. Local Customs, 26, 27. Roman rule of Quadripartite Division, 27, 28. Apportionment not numerically equal, 29. Quadripartite Division beyond Italy, 29-32. Tripartite Division, 32-37. *Capitulare Episcoporum*, 37-45.

CHAPTER II

CONTINENTAL LAWS AS TO TITHES, pages 46-68

Before Charlemagne, 46-49. Legislation of Charlemagne and his Successors, 50, 51. Witnesses and Compulsion, 51-54. Ancient Baptismal Churches, and their Rights, 54-63. Irregular Appropriations of Tithes, 63-68.

CHAPTER III

PRACTICAL WORKING OF THE CUSTOMS OF APPORTIONMENT, pages 69-80

Bishop's Share, 69. Share of Clergy, 70, 71. Fabric Fund, 71-74. Poor's Fund, 74, 75. Houses of Reception, 75-77. 'Matricularii,' 77-79. Participation of the Monastic Orders, 79, 80.

CHAPTER IV

TRANSITION TO THE PAROCHIAL SYSTEM, pages 81-96

Private Oratories, 81-84. Ordinances of Louis the Pious, 84-86. Their results, 87, 88. Subdivision of Rural Parishes, 88, 89. Parochial Revenues not apportioned, 90, 91. Modern Roman Canon Law, 91, 92. Presumption as to Parochial Tithes in the twelfth century, 93. Van Espen as to Parochial Benefices, 93-95. French Jurisprudence on the same subject, 95, 96.

PART II.—ANGLO-SAXON

CHAPTER I

FIRST PERIOD—FROM AUGUSTIN TO THE DEATH OF ARCHBISHOP THEODORE, pages 99-123

Preliminary, 99. Original British Church, 100-102. Gregory the Great, as to Church Revenues in England, 102-105. Archbishop Theodore as to Tithes, 106, 107. Bede, 107, 108. Pope Gregory's Instructions as to Diocesan Organisation, 108, 109. Progress of Diocesan Organisation under Archbishop Honorius, 109, 110; under Theodore, 110-112. Parochial system not introduced by Honorius, 112-116; nor by Theodore, 116-123.

CHAPTER II

SECOND PERIOD—BEDE, BONIFACE, ARCHBISHOPS CUTHBERT AND EGBERT; KINGS INA, WIHTRAED, OFFA, pages 124-143.

Introductory, 124-126. Monastic Baptismal Churches, 126, 127. Secular Laws of King Ina, 127. 'Privilege' of King Wihtraed, 127, 128. Letters of Boniface, 128, 129. Bede's Letter to Archbishop Egbert, 129-133. Archbishop Cuthbert's Canons, 133-136. Episcopal Power as to Revenues, 137, 138. Fictions as to Grant of Tithes by Offa, King of Mercia, 138-143.

CHAPTER III

SECOND PERIOD—LEGATINE INJUNCTIONS OF CHALCHYTH, A.D. 785-787, pages 144-168

Legatine Injunction as to Tithes, 144, 145. Causes of the Legatine Mission, 146-152. Character of the Legatine Injunctions, 152-155. The Legates' Report: known from the Magdeburg 'Centuries,' 153, 154; confirmed by Archbishop Odo's Injunctions in the tenth century, 154, 155. The Legates' Narrative, 155-158. Character and Constitution of the Legatine Synods, 159. Internal Evidence, 160-167. Their Relation to the Constitutions of Archbishop Cuthbert's Council (A.D. 747), 168.

CHAPTER IV

THIRD PERIOD—FROM OFFA TO EDMUND—RETROGRESSION AND DECAY, pages 169-185

Ravages of the Danes, 169-171. Consequent Diocesan Changes, 171. General Decay of Learning, 172. Other Causes of Decay, 172, 173. Effect on the older Church Organisation, 173. Archbishop Wulfred's Canons, 174-177. Opinions of Selden and Lingard as to Parishes in the ninth century, 177, 178. Pope Leo the Fourth's Decretals, 179. Treaty between Edward the Elder and Guthrum, 179-183. King Athelstan's Tithe Ordinance, 183-185.

CHAPTER V

THIRD PERIOD—KING ETHELWULF'S CHARTERS,
pages 186-206

History of the opinion that King Ethelwulf made a Grant of Tithes, 186, 187. Traditions of Chroniclers, 187-192. Selden's Interpretation, 192-195. Extant Charters, 195-206. Enfranchisement of *Folcland* their real object, 196-198. First General Charter of A.D. 844, 199-204. Second General Charter of A.D. 854, 204, 205. Conclusions of recent Critics, 205, 206.

CHAPTER VI

FOURTH PERIOD—PRIMACIES OF ODO AND DUNSTAN,
pages 207-226

New Relations between England and the Continent, 207, 208. Archbishop Odo, 208. The Reforming Triumvirate, 208, 209. Oswald, Bishop of Worcester, and his Foreign Associates, 209-211. Ethelwold, Bishop of Winchester, 211, 212. Dunstan, Archbishop of Canterbury, 212. Council of Winchester and *Regularis Concordia*, 213-216. Dunstan's Canons, enacted under King Edgar, 216-218. King Edmund's Laws, 218, 219. Edgar's Laws, 219-221. Effects of Edgar's Tithe Legislation, 222-226.

CHAPTER VII

FOURTH PERIOD—ECCLESIASTICAL LITERATURE: THE
EGBERTINE COMPILATIONS, pages 227-246

Introductory, 227-230. Worcester 'Excerptions' in the Library of Corpus Christi College, Cambridge, 230-234. Exeter 'Penitential' in the Bodleian Library, 235-241. Fragment, copied from Exeter 'Penitential,' in National Library at Paris, 229, 236. Worcester 'Excerptions' in Cottonian Collection, 241-246.

CHAPTER VIII

FOURTH PERIOD—AELFRIC AND OTHER WRITERS OF THE
GALLICAN SCHOOL, pages 247-270

Canterbury *Statuta Synodorum* (now lost), 247-249. Aelfric 'the Grammarian,' 249-254. Aelfric's 'Canons,' 255-262. Gloss on Dunstan's Canons, 263, 264. Bishop Leofric's Rule for his Chapter at Exeter (falsely attributed to Theodore), 264, 265. Its Contents and History, 266-270.

CHAPTER IX

FOURTH PERIOD—LEGISLATION OF ETHELRED AND CANUTE, pages 271-293

Ancient Latin Translations of Anglo-Saxon Laws, 271, 272. Ordinances of Habam, 272, 273. Council of Enham, and Ordinance of A.D. 1008, 273-278. Ethelred's supposed Law for Partition of Tithes, 278-287. Canute's Laws, 287-293.

CHAPTER X

FOURTH PERIOD—FINAL SETTLEMENT OF THE PAROCHIAL SYSTEM, pages 294-316

Summary of Laws as to Tithes, down to Canute, 294, 295. Course of Transition to modern Parishes, 295-298. Canute's Letter from Rome, 298, 299. 'Ecclesiastical Institutes,' 299, 300. Laws of Edward the Confessor, 300-304. Laws of William the Conqueror, 304-306. Laws ascribed to Henry I., 306, 307. Endowments of Parish Churches with Tithes, 307-316.

APPENDICES

APPENDIX A.—*Capitulare Episcoporum* (Andain and Metz Texts, and those of the Bodleian and the two Worcester manuscripts of 'Egbertine' Compilations, collated), 317-323.

APPENDIX B.—Comparison of corresponding passages in Archbishop Odo's Injunctions and the Legatine Injunctions of A.D. 785-787, 324-326.

APPENDIX C.—Comparison of the Exeter 'Penitential' Volume in the Bodleian Library, No. 718, with the Vatican (Palatine) Manuscript, No. 1352, 327-331.

APPENDIX D.—Comparison of the 'Excerptions' of Canons, etc., in the Worcester Manuscript belonging to Corpus Christi College, Cambridge (No. 265 of Nasmith), with those in the Cottonian Manuscript (Nero A. 1), 332, 333.

APPENDIX E.—Comparison of *Church-Grith* (the document containing the supposed law of Ethelred as to a partition of tithes) with the corresponding provisions of Canute's Laws, 334-346.

APPENDIX F.—Letter of Pope Leo IX. to King Edward the Confessor, urging the removal of the See of Crediton, and its bishop, Leofric, to Exeter, 347.

APPENDIX G.—Clauses in the Exeter Rule of Life for Canons, relating to meals and the dormitory, 348-350.

APPENDIX H.—Consecration Charters of Churches endowed by their Founders at the time of consecration with tithes, 351-352.

APPENDIX I.—Ancient grants of, or compositions as to, tithes, 353-357.

APPENDIX J.—Bishop Kennett and Selden, 358-361.

SUPPLEMENT

REMARKS ON A RECENT 'HISTORY OF TITHES,' 364-402.

INTRODUCTION

As I shall have frequent occasion to refer to the civil legislation of the Frank kingdom and empire concerning ecclesiastical affairs, and to the Roman Canon Law, some preliminary observations on the relations of the Ecclesiastical to the Civil Power down to the end of the tenth century, and upon the gradual development of Roman Canon Law, may be desirable.

§ 1. *Church and State.*

It is unnecessary to inquire whether the patriarchal authority of the Popes in Western Christendom, and the precedence conceded to the See of Rome even in the East, arose out of the tradition which represented the Apostles St. Peter and St. Paul as the original founders of that See, or from the dignity of Rome as the capital of the ancient world. The tradition was certainly ancient; but it is at least as certain that the local distribution of the power of government in the early Church was determined, generally, by the existing civil organisation. Even in the work of the false Isidore, St. Peter[1] is made to instruct his successor,

---

[1] *Decretales Pseudo-Isidorianæ*, etc. (Hinschius, Leipsic 1863, p. 39).

Clement, to place patriarchs and primates of the highest rank and authority in those cities where the heathens had their 'Flamens' and judges of the first order; and archbishops of subordinate rank in smaller cities, where there had been 'Arch-Flamens' of lower degree than the highest. Anacletus (next but one in succession to Clement) and Lucius, nineteenth after Anacletus, are also represented, in supposed decretals (embodied as to this point in Gratian's Code)[1] as re-asserting the same principle. Whatever may have been the cause, the fact is indisputable, that some pre-eminence belonged to the See of Rome; and also, that the authority which accompanied it was less in the Eastern and other Churches which had not, directly or indirectly, derived their Christianity from Rome, than in those nations and races which had.

The influence of the Popes varied with their circumstances and opportunities, and with their personal qualities. On theological questions the influence of a great Pope, such as Leo I., was often very great. But in other respects, and especially during the centuries of decay which preceded the extinction of the Roman Empire in the west,—during the wars and ravages, in Italy and elsewhere, of Goths, Huns, Vandals, Lombards, and Franks,—the Primacy of the Roman See was, for a long time, honorary rather than practical. Its main symbol was the 'Pall,'[2] which it was usual for the Pope to confer upon archbishops or metropolitans, and without which the dignity of those offices was not deemed complete. Even of Gregory the Great it is said by Gibbon,[3] that 'his ecclesiastical jurisdiction was

---

[1] *Decretum*, pars i., dist. 80, cap. 1; and 99, cap 1.
[2] See, as to the *pallium*, *Decretum*, pars i., dist. 100. The citation in cap. 1 from Pelagius is not of that Pope's time.
[3] *Decline and Fall*, ch. 45 (vol. v. p. 479; ed. 1828).

confined to the triple character of Bishop of Rome, Primate of Italy, and Apostle of the West.'

Both in the Frank kingdom and empire, from the conversion of Clovis (A.D. 496), and in the Gothic kingdom of Spain (A.D. 506-711), the civil power interfered in ecclesiastical affairs. It will be sufficient to advert to the manner in which it did so in the greater of those States, the Frank kingdom and empire.

1. *As to Legislation.* — Even under the Merovingian dynasty it was not held lawful to convene ecclesiastical synods without the royal permission. Sigebert II.,[1] a prince of high reputation for sanctity (about A.D. 650), forbade this. Kings and emperors often called together ecclesiastical councils;[2] of which those of the year A.D. 813,[3] and the imperial ordinance[4] confirming twenty-eight of their constitutions, may be taken as examples. Their confirmation was necessary[5] to give force to canons passed by any such synod. They also, in mixed councils of laymen and ecclesiastics (held in the manner usual for the enactment of secular laws), legislated directly for the Church, on disciplinary and other questions. A striking instance is found in the capitulars of A.D. 789,[6] derived in great measure from the Code of Oriental Canons[7] which Charlemagne had six years before (A.D. 773) received at Rome from the hand of Pope Adrian I. Those capit-

---

[1] Baluze, *Capit.*, vol. i. p. 143.
[2] Francis de Roye (*apud* Mansi, *Concil.*, vol. xvii. p. 938).
[3] Arles vi., Tours iii., Chalons, Rheims, Mentz (Mansi, *Concil.*, vol. xiv.)
[4] Baluze, *Capit.*, vol. i. p. 503. (The synods are described in the title as '*Auctoritate Regia nuper habitis.*')
[5] Baluze, Preface (*Capit.*, vol. i. pp. 8, 9).
[6] Baluze, *Capit.*, vol. i. p. 209.
[7] Mansi, *Concil.*, vol. xii. p. 859.

ulars, enacted in the name of and with a preface from Charlemagne himself, are a series of purely ecclesiastical constitutions, extending over important points of doctrine as well as discipline. Some of them were addressed to bishops; some to priests; some to 'all the clergy;' some to 'clerks and monks;' some to 'all men.'

Such legislation as this was not, in the ninth century, regarded as an encroachment by the secular upon the spiritual power. Gratian, in a 'Distinction,'[1] in which he insists upon the principle that secular are subordinate to ecclesiastical constitutions, quotes a letter of Pope Leo IV. to the Emperor Lothair (written about A.D. 847), in which that Pope engaged to observe inviolate and for ever the imperial capitulars and ordinances of Lothair and his predecessors. 'If, perchance' (he added), 'any one may have told or shall tell you otherwise, be "assured that he speaks falsely."'

2. *As to Judicature.*—Charlemagne, by one of his Lombard laws,[2] exempted abbots, priests, deacons, subdeacons, and clerks generally, from secular jurisdiction, referring the decision of causes concerning them to the bishops. That privilege, however, was not without exceptions. Royal Commissioners (*Missi Dominici*) took cognisance of criminal offences[3] against the general public law, though committed by clerks. And the course as to questions of property, private or ecclesiastical, in which the clergy were concerned, was this:[4] the civil judge, before whom a claim was made to any such property, sent the claimant to the bishop with

[1] Dist. 10. Some of these capitulars (so described) are embodied in the *Decretum*.
[2] *Leg. Longob.*, lib. iii., tit. i., cap. 11.
[3] De Roye, *De Missis Dominicis* (*apud* Mansi, vol. xvii. p. 926).
[4] *Ibid.*, pp. 915, 916.

a civil 'advocate,' whose duty it was to see justice done. If the parties still failed to arrive at a settlement, the cause was then remitted to the Count, or civil judge, before whom the bishop, in his turn, was represented by an advocate of his choice, and the matter was determined according to law.

It was not till a later period, after the publication of Ingilram's canons and the false decretals, that the supreme judicial authority of the Pope was acknowledged.

3. *As to Faith and Ritual.*—When the Eastern Church, in the second Council of Nicæa, pronounced in favour of image-worship, Charlemagne took a decided part in opposing its decrees. The 'Caroline books,'[1] composed for that purpose by his order, and published in his name, were sent by him (A.D. 790) to Pope Adrian I.; and, notwithstanding the support which that Pope gave to the Council, he communicated them (A.D. 792) to the Anglo-Saxon bishops,[2] and afterwards (A.D. 794) procured from the Synod of Frankfort[3] an emphatic condemnation of that practice. In A.D. 788 he ordered a revision of the service-books used in the churches of his dominions to be made by Paul the Deacon, of Aquileia;[4] and he 'estab-

---

[1] Moreri's *Dictionnaire Historique*, etc., *voce* 'Carolins.' Gibbon, *Decline and Fall*, cap. 49 (vol. vi. p. 232, note; ed. 1828).

[2] See Symeon of Durham (Savile's *Hist. Angl. Script.*, p. 113, and Haddan and Stubbs, *Councils*, etc., vol. iii. p. 469, note). Alcuin is supposed to have been the writer of the reply sent by the English bishops to the King, and he was probably the bearer of Charlemagne's communication.

[3] Mansi, vol. xiii. p. 99.

[4] Moreri, *Paul, diacre;* Baluze, *Capit.*, vol. i. pp. 204-206. Paul had been secretary to Desiderius, the last Lombard king. Charlemagne's letter, ordering the use of the book, was addressed *religiosis lectoribus* of his kingdom.

lished'[1] the use of a book,[2] in two volumes, with lessons or 'homilies' for readings throughout the year (which Paul had collected from the Fathers), in the churches of his kingdom. In the diocese of Liége, when Emperor, he interposed his authority to postpone the public baptism[3] of certain candidates who were found insufficiently instructed, and he appointed a special fast, and commanded the bishop to give notice of it in all the greater churches of his diocese.[4]

4. *As to Church Appointments.*—The consent of civil rulers to the election of bishops was required[5] from early times. The twelfth Council of Toledo[6] (A.D. 681) authorised the consecration, by the Archbishop of Toledo, of such persons as the King might choose (being judged fit by the archbishop), to fill all vacant sees in any province of the Spanish or 'Gallician' Church. The Frank Kings and Emperors appointed directly to vacant bishoprics and abbacies,[7] until a law qualifying that power, by allowing the 'clergy and people' to elect bishops, by license from the

---

[1] *Quarum omnium textum nostra sagacitate perpendentes, nostra eadem volumina auctoritate constabilimus, vestræque religioni in Christi ecclesiis tradimus ad legendum.*

[2] The book was printed at Spires, A.D. 1472, and extracts from it were reprinted by Mabillon, and in the ninth volume of Martene and Durand's *Amplissima Collectio.*

[3] Martene and Durand, *Ampl. Coll.*, vol. vii. p. 19.

[4] *Ibid.*, p. 21.

[5] See letter of Gregory the Great (A.D. 592), lib. ii., ep. 23 (St. Maur edition of Gregory's works); *Decretum*, pars i., dist. 63, cap. 9.

[6] See *Decret.*, pars i., dist. 63, cap. 25.

[7] See petition, *Cleri plebisque viduatæ civitatis ad Regem* (Baluze, *Capit.*, vol. ii. p. 379); and Sirmondi's note, *De antiquis Episcoporum promotionibus*, in Mansi, *Concil.*, vol. xvi., App., p. 879. The fifth Council of Paris (A.D. 615) had in vain declared for freedom of election (Mansi, vol. x. p. 539).

sovereign, and subject to his approval of the person elected, was passed (A.D. 816) by Louis the Pious.[1] It may be inferred, from a later address of the second Council of Aix-la-Chapelle to the same Emperor[2] (A.D. 836), praying him to be vigilant in the appointment of good pastors and rulers to churches, that the substantial power remained with him. Popes of the ninth century, Leo IV.[3] and Stephen V.,[4] recognised the necessity, in all cases, of the imperial license to elect, and the imperial consent to an election. Adrian I. (according to the history of Sigebert of Gembloux, composed A.D. 1112, and quoted as authentic in Gratian's *Decretum*)[5] conceded to Charlemagne (A.D. 774), in a synod held at Rome, and attended by 153 bishops, the investiture of all archbishops and bishops, in all provinces of his realm, forbidding their consecration until accepted and invested by the King, and threatening excommunication and other severe penalties against all who should contravene that decree. The same concession, under still heavier penalties, was renewed to the German Emperor, Otho I., by Leo VIII.,[6] in A.D. 963; and the system of royal investiture, so sanctioned by Popes, continued to prevail until the time of Gregory VII.

These concessions to the imperial power were accom-

[1] Sirmondi's note, *ubi supra* (and see Baluze, *Capit.*, vol. i. p. 566). Ludovicus Pius is this emperor's Latin, and Louis le Debonnaire his French, designation.

[2] Mansi, vol. xiv. p. 690 (art. 9). See the Forms of Petition and License, etc., in Baluze, *Capit.*, vol. ii. pp. 379, 509, 591, 594, 595, 601. A 'Visitor,' appointed by the Crown, presided at these elections.

[3] *Decretum*, pars i., dist. 63, cap. 16, 17.   [4] *Ibid.*, cap. 18.

[5] *Ibid.*, cap. 22 (and see Richter's note, *Corp. Jur. Canon.*, Leipsic 1839, p. 207). See also on this point the Chronicle of John, Abbot of Peterborough, who places the grant in A.D. 772 (*Chronicon Angliæ*, in *Historiæ Anglicanæ Scriptores Veteres*, London 1724, pp. 8, 9).

[6] *Decretum, ubi supra*, cap. 23 (see Richter's note).

panied by another, greater still. By the same synodical act of Adrian I.[1] which gave Papal sanction to the royal investiture of archbishops and bishops, Charlemagne was constituted patron of the Holy See itself, with authority upon every vacancy to nominate the Pope. His son and grandson, Louis the Pious and Lothair, seem[2] to have declined the exercise of that power, and to have restored the right of election to the Roman people. In the succeeding century (A.D. 918-934, and again in A.D. 962) Henry the Fowler and Otho I. also successively[3] recognised the title to elect freely, and without interference, of 'those Romans, to whom, by ancient custom and the appointment of the Holy Father, it belonged.' But to check the disorders which followed, Pope Stephen[4] (probably the fourth of that name), and Pope John IX.[5] in a council held at Rome (A.D. 898), required the presence of Imperial legates for the validity of a Papal election. The Papacy, during the tenth and the earlier part of the eleventh century, reached its lowest point of degradation. In the next year (A.D. 963), after Otho I. had confirmed the liberty of election acknowledged by his father to belong to the Roman people, he was crowned Emperor by the Pope; and Leo VIII. synodically, and with the general assent of the clergy and people of Rome, renewed in his favour the same powers and privileges which Adrian I. had granted to Charlemagne. That synodical constitution finds (like Sigebert's narrative of the original grant) a place in Gratian's *Decretum*.[6] Until the death of Otho III. in A.D. 1002, the gravest disorders were of frequent recurrence at Papal elections, and the Popes continued to be practically dependent on the Emperors.

[1] *Decretum, ubi supra.*
[2] *Ibid.*, cap. 30, 31.
[3] *Ibid.*, cap. 32 (see Richter's note).
[4] *Ibid.*, cap. 28.
[5] *Ibid.*, Richter's note to cap. 28.
[6] *Ibid.*, cap. 23.

§ 2. *Roman Canon Law.*

1. Towards the close of the fifth century, Dionysius (called *Exiguus*, or 'the Little'), a Scythian monk,[1] at the suggestion of Stephen, Bishop of Salona in Dalmatia, made a collection[2] of 401 Oriental and African Canons, which was accepted and approved at Rome,[3] and afterwards in France, and generally by the Latin Churches. It was, doubtless, to this collection that reference was made by Theodore, Archbishop of Canterbury, at the Council of Hertford,[4] A.D. 673. To this, Dionysius is said afterwards to have added decretals of Popes Siricius and Anastasius I. (A.D. 384-402). At a later date, the same code was enlarged by the addition of other decretals of later Popes down to Gregory II. (A.D. 715).[5] It constituted, as so enlarged, the body of Canon Law which was in force at Rome down to the middle of, or later than, the ninth century. It is the same in substance with that which Adrian I. delivered (A.D. 773) to Charlemagne;[6] and with that which Leo IV. (A.D. 847-855), in a letter addressed to the 'bishops of Britain,'[7] declared to con-

---

[1] See Moreri, *Dictionnaire*, etc., *voce* 'Denys le Petit.'

[2] *Codex Canonum Ecclesiasticorum Dionysii Exigui* (Paris 1628).

[3] The authority for their acceptance is the contemporary historian Cassiodorus, who was minister to Theodoric the Great.

[4] Bede's *Hist.*, lib. iv., cap. 5. (See, as to the particular canons referred to by Theodore, Johnson's *Laws and Canons*, etc., Oxford ed., 1850, vol. i. pp. 90-94.)

[5] See Pithou's edition of this enlarged Code (*Codex Canonum Vetus Ecclesiæ Romanæ, Pithæi*, Paris 1687); also Sirmondi's note, Mansi, *Concil.*, vol. xii. p. 882.

[6] Mansi, *Concil.*, vol. xii. p. 859; and note, p. 882.

[7] See *Decretum*, pars i., dist. 20, cap. 1. Pope Leo IV., however, also mentioned Sylvester, whose spurious 'Acts' had been published before his time.

tain the laws then used by the Popes 'in all ecclesiastical judgments'; by which 'the bishops judged, and themselves, as well as the rest of the clergy, were judged.'

To this body of law ecclesiastical forgery began to make spurious additions before the end of the eighth century. Among the earliest of these forgeries were the supposed 'Acts' of Pope Sylvester[1] (A.D. 314), including the 'Donation of Constantine.'

2. In A.D. 827, Ansegisus,[2] Abbot of Fontenelle, made a collection of capitulars of Charlemagne and Louis the Pious, in four parts: the two first containing ecclesiastical, the two latter secular laws. This, though not always accurate, was an honest collection; and was known and cited before the end of Louis the Pious's reign. It was, however, incomplete; and it did not extend back to any of the constitutions of Charlemagne's predecessors.

3. To supply the deficiencies of that work, Benedict,[3] a deacon of the church of Mentz, at the suggestion of Otgar (the immediate predecessor of Rabanus Maurus in the Archbishopric of Mentz), compiled, from many miscellaneous sources, secular and ecclesiastical, public and private, Roman, Gallican, Gothic, Salic, Ripuarian, and Bavarian, authentic and unauthentic, three additional books of (real or

---

[1] See, as to this, Hinschius, *Commentatio de Collectione Decretalium et Canonum Isidori Mercatoris*, p. 96 (*Decretales Pseudo-Isidorianæ et Capitula Angilramni*, Leipsic 1863); Alcuin's letter of A.D. 800 to Arno, Bishop of Salzburg (ep. 108; Migne's ed., 1831, vol. i. p. 325); and Benedict the 'Levite,' lib. iv., cap. 302 (Baluze, *Capit.*, vol. i. p. 886).

[2] Baluze, *Capit.*, vol. i. p. 691 *et seq.*, and Preface, §§ 39-43.

[3] 'Benedictus Levita.' (*Levite*, in those days, was a common term for deacon.) See his three books (numbered 5, 6, and 7, after the four of Ansegisus) in Baluze, *Capit.*, vol. i. pp. 801-1132; and see Baluze's Preface, §§ 44-46. As to Benedict himself, see Moreri, *Dictionnaire*, etc., under the name 'Benoist, diacre.'

supposed) laws and canons, which he published after leaving the diocese of Mentz on the death of Otgar in A.D. 847.[1] To these he prefixed the four books of Ansegisus, making seven books in all, known from that time under his name. The earliest known citation of that collection in Western France was at a synod or assembly held at Quierzy in Picardy, under Archbishop Hincmar, in A.D. 857.

Baluze, in the preface to his *Capitulars*,[2] after specifying the materials of which Benedict so made use, says that his collection 'is patched together from all these sources, confusedly enough, without attention to any order of time, and with frequent changes in the words of the chapters referred to.' For this Baluze does not blame Benedict, who found his materials in that confused and undigested state. He cannot, however, be absolved from the charge of tampering, to some extent, with the authorities which he followed.

4. The next publication which requires mention is that under the name of Ingilram (or Angilram),[3] who was Archbishop of Metz from A.D. 768 to 791, and chaplain-general and grand-almoner to Charlemagne. It consists of eighty pretended canons, constituting a sort of code of procedure, applicable to charges against bishops, clerks, and laymen; its tendency being to exalt, as supreme and absolute, the power and authority of the Pope, and to invest the clergy with extraordinary immunities. It asserted the invalidity of all constitutions against the canons or decrees of Roman pontiffs, and the right of the Pope to set aside, by his vicars, the proceedings of provincial synods. The Pope himself was to be judged by no man, 'because the disciple is not

[1] Hinschius, *Commentatio*, etc. (*ubi supra*, part iv., cap. 1).
[2] Vol. i., Preface, § 45.
[3] Mansi, vol. xii. p. 904 *et seq.*; Hinschius, *Decretales Pseudo-Isidorianæ*, etc. (Leipsic 1863).

above his master.' Formidable penalties were denounced against all who might make malicious accusations, or fail to establish any charges made by them when brought to trial. A bishop, against whom a charge might be made, might either claim to have the question transferred to the Pope in the first instance, or appeal to the Pope (whose decision was to be final) after judgment by the metropolitan. No charge could be made by a priest against a bishop, or by a deacon against a priest, or by any one in any inferior order against a clerk of an order above him. No lay testimony was to be received against a clerk; and many witnesses (graduated according to the different ranks of clerks, but in the case of a bishop not less than seventy-two, in that of a cardinal priest sixty-four, in that of a cardinal deacon twenty-six) were required to justify an adverse sentence.

According to a title (perhaps not in the original publication, but early prefixed to it),[1] these were represented as 'Articles (*Capitula*) collected from various authorities (*sparsim collecta*)—from Greek and Latin Canons, Roman Synods, and decrees of Roman Pontiffs and Princes; and delivered at Rome, by the Blessed Pope Hadrian, on the thirteenth day before the Kalends of October, Indiction 9, to Ingilram, Bishop of the City of Metz, when he was there upon his own business'—no year being mentioned.

Some of them were taken (more or less exactly) from the work of Benedict the Levite,[2] and cannot be earlier than that work. That they were delivered to Archbishop Ingilram by Pope Adrian I. is incredible. There was nothing resembling them in the code delivered by that Pope to Charlemagne, and afterwards (with the interpola-

---

[1] Hinschius, *Commentatio*, etc. (*ubi supra*, p. cxvii. *et seq.*).
[2] *Ibid.* (*ubi supra*, cap. 3, 4).

tion only of the pretended canons of Sylvester) referred to by Leo IV. as containing the rules of judgment accepted by the Roman See. The theory of those who have regarded the ascription of them to Ingilram as genuine, is not that they were known at Rome, but that he published them to justify himself against certain imputations, and 'that they were almost all taken from the false decretals, which then began to appear;' this being 'the first trace of the use of those fabrications.'[1] Among them are passages from the spurious Epistles of Clement to the Apostle St. James, and of Popes Anacletus, Eleutherius, Victor, Cornelius, Lucius, Sixtus II., and Marcellinus; as well as canons of the spurious synod under Sylvester, which are also found in the fifth book of Benedict.

There are strong grounds for the belief of Hinschius,[2] that Ingilram was not the real author of that publication; that it was not compiled until after his time, and that it may not improbably have been the work of the same man who produced the larger Collection of false decretals, of which it was the precursor.

5. That Collection was fabricated and published between the years A.D. 847 and 853. It is said to have been introduced from Spain by Riculf, Archbishop of Mentz; and it is quoted by Hincmar (not without some apparent doubt of its authority) as passing under the name of St. Isidore, Archbishop of Seville, A.D. 601-636.[3]

The title (as given in Hinschius's edition)[4] is 'A Breviary of the Canons of the Apostles and first Bishops of the Church from Clement to St. Silvester, and of the various

[1] Moreri, *Dictionnaire*, etc., under the name 'Ingelram.'
[2] *Commentatio*, etc. (*ubi supra*, cap. 4).
[3] *Ibid.* (*ubi supra*, pars iv.)
[4] *Decretales Pseudo-Isidorianæ*, etc. (Leipsic 1863).

Councils in their order, whose acts also are collected in this work, their heads being subjoined.'

It contains, first, the (so-called) Apostolic Canons,—genuine, though not of the Apostolic age; and, after these, a series of pretended 'Decretal' Epistles from thirty early Popes, beginning with Clement (the supposed successor of St. Peter) and ending with Melchiades, the immediate predecessor of Sylvester; occupying the whole period from the martyrdom of St. Peter and St. Paul to A.D. 314, and omitting only two of the traditional Popes of that period, viz. Linus (the second) and Clement II. (the fourth).

After these there are added the famous document called the 'Donation of Constantine,' and some canons of the spurious Roman Council under Pope Sylvester; which are followed by other false decretals of Popes Julius, Liberius, and Damasus, and then by the Oriental and African Canons contained in the Code of Dionysius 'Exiguus,' (with some variations), and afterwards by canons of Gallican Councils, ending with the first Council of Orleans, and Spanish and Portuguese Councils, ending with the second Council of Seville.

Of the forgeries contained in this collection, a sufficient idea may be formed from two examples: the fabulous letter,[1] with which the book opens, of Clement to St. James the brother of our Lord; and the 'Donation of Constantine.'[2]

In the former of these, Clement is made to relate to the Apostle St. James the circumstances of his appointment, by St. Peter, before his martyrdom, to succeed him in the Bishopric of Rome, with the power of binding and loosing, 'so that, as he should decree on earth, it should also be

---

[1] *Decretales Pseudo-Isidorianæ*, etc. (Leipsic 1863), pp. 30, 42.
[2] *Ibid.*, p. 249.

decreed in heaven; inasmuch as he would bind only that which ought to be bound, and loose only that which ought to be loosed.' Long addresses from St. Peter to Clement himself, to the priests, the deacons, and the laity, are reported as following that commission; and the Apostle is said to have then consecrated him before them all by imposition of hands, and to have compelled him (overwhelmed with diffidence) to sit in his own chair. Then Clement repeats, in the most formal and scientific terms of post-Nicene theology, the doctrine which he has received from St. Peter; and informs St. James that he has ordained bishops, and will ordain others, for Gaul, Spain, Italy, and Germany. The rules according to which patriarchs and archbishops are to be appointed, according to the relative secular importance of cities (which have been already mentioned) are then laid down; and St. Peter is quoted as saying that bishops are to have rule in the Apostles' place, and priests in place of the other disciples; that no accusation should be received against bishops and priests except from persons of good report and of equal dignity; that laymen should not be permitted to make such charges; that all should be subject to Clement; that he (St. Peter) forbade secular men to resist spiritual; and that no priest should do anything in any diocese without the bishop's permission.

The decretal letters of the other early Popes are conceived in the same spirit.

The 'Donation of Constantine' begins with a long profession of faith, made by that Emperor upon his conversion and baptism, and an exhortation by him to all nations to hold the same faith; after which, an account of his conversion is given. Afflicted with leprosy, and persecuting the Christians, he had compelled Pope Sylvester to fly from Rome, and to take refuge in a cavern in Mount Soracte. The Apostles St. Peter and St. Paul (at once recognised by the Pope, from the Emperor's description of their forms and lineaments) then appeared to Constantine in a vision, and revealed to him the truth of Christianity, and that Sylvester (for whom they commanded him to send) was 'Universal Pope.' At his request the Pope came, cured him of his leprosy, instructed and baptized him. I translate the material parts of the Act of Donation, said to have been made four days afterwards, and dated at Rome the 31st March, 'in the Fourth Consulship of our Lord Flavius Constantinus Augustus':

'We, together with all our Rulers of provinces (*satrapis*), and the whole Senate, and all our Nobility, and all the Roman people, have judged it expedient, that as the Blessed Peter appears to be appointed Vicar of the Son of God on earth, so the Pontiffs also, who stand in the place of the same Prince of the Apostles, should obtain by grant from us, and from our Empire, a princely power, exceeding that which the earthly graciousness of our Imperial Serenity seems to have; choosing the same Prince of the Apostles, and his successors, to be our sure advocates with God. And, as our earthly Imperial Power, so have we decreed that the Holy Roman Church should be reverently honoured, and that the most Holy See of the Blessed Peter should be gloriously exalted above our Empire and earthly throne; giving to it the power, and glorious dignity and strength, and honourable estate, which belong to Empire. And we decree and ordain that it shall hold the Primacy, as well over the four Principal Sees of Alexandria, Antioch, Jerusalem, and Constantinople, as over all other Churches of God throughout the world; and that the Pontiff for the time being of the Holy Roman Church shall be higher than, and Prince over, all the priests of the whole world; and that according to his judgment all matters relating to the worship of God, and to the establishment of the Christian Faith, shall be settled.'

Then, after mentioning large endowments, as granted to the see of Rome in Judea, Greece, Asia, Thrace, Africa, Italy, and different islands, it proceeds:

'And we do presently deliver up to the Blessed Silvester, our Father, and Pope of the Universal City of Rome, and to all the Pontiffs his successors, who shall sit in the chair of the Blessed Peter, even to the end of the world, the Lateran Palace of our Empire, and with it the diadem or crown of our head, and the cap, the Imperial collar, the purple mantle, the scarlet tunic, and all other our Imperial robes; together with the rank and dignity of our presidents of the Imperial horsemen, and the Imperial Sceptres, and all signs and badges and Imperial ornaments of every kind, and the whole pomp of Imperial pre-eminence, and glory of our power.'

Then follow grants of privileges to the Roman clergy of all orders. They are to have senatorial rank, to be made 'patricians,' and 'consuls,' and adorned with the other dignities of the empire; to wear military decorations; to ride on horses, with white linen reins and trappings; and to wear, like senators, sandals covered with white linen. The Pope's diadem is to be of the purest gold and precious stones. The document proceeds:

'But since the most Blessed Pope has not endured at all to use the golden crown above the crown of his clerical tonsure, which he wears in honour of the Blessed Peter, We have, with our own hands, placed on his most Holy Head a cap of dazzling whiteness, symbolising the Resurrection of the Lord; and holding the bridle of his horse for reverence of the Blessed Peter, have ourselves performed for him the office of groom; appointing that, in imitation of our Imperial state, his successors shall have the sole privilege of using the same cap in their Processions.—Wherefore, that the Pontifical Eminence may not be degraded, but may be adorned with more glory and power than the dignity of the earthly Empire, lo! we do give up and relinquish to our aforesaid most blessed Pontiff, Silvester, the Universal Pope, both our Palace (already mentioned) and the City of Rome, and all our provinces, places, and Cities of Italy and the regions of the West; and we decree, by this our "Dival" and "Pragmatic" Constitution, that they shall be at the disposal of him and his successors; and we grant them to remain for ever in right to the Holy Roman Church. And for this reason, we have thought it convenient to transfer our Empire and the power of our Kingdom to the regions of the East, and that a city should be built, after our own name, on a fair site in the Byzantine province, and our Empire there established; because it is not right that any earthly Emperor should have power where the Heavenly Emperor has established the Prince of Priests, and the Head of the Christian Religion.'

The Emperor then declares his will, that all the powers, privileges, and rights thus granted shall endure in all their fulness, without disturbance, until the end of the world; and he adjures his successors, and all his lords, ministers, senate, and people, and all who at any future time, in any part of the globe, may be subject to any of his successors, to preserve them inviolate under the penalty of his curse:

'But if any one (which we do not believe) shall be found in this matter a scorner or despiser, let him lie under the sentence of eternal condemnation, and have for his adversaries, in this and in the future life, the saints of God, the Princes of the Apostles, Peter and Paul; and let him perish in the fire of the lowest hell with the Devil and all the wicked. And so, confirming with our own hands the scroll of this our Imperial decree, we have placed it over the venerable body of Peter, the Prince of the Apostles.'

6. The 'Isidorian wares,'[1] of which these are, perhaps, the most remarkable specimens, found in those times a ready market and little or no criticism. They were largely relied on by the canonists of the tenth and eleventh centuries—

[1] See Van Espen, *Jus Univ. Canon.*, pars ii. sect. 4, tit. i. cap. 6, § 7.

Regino, Abbot of Prüm (who died A.D. 915); Burchard, Bishop of Worms (A.D. 1008-1026); and Ivo, Bishop of Chartres (A.D. 1091-1116).

7. The work of Gratian, which (under the name of *Decretum*)[1] enters into and constitutes the first part of the modern Body of Roman Canon Law, is a systematic digest of the most important parts of the works of his predecessors, with further collections of his own. The title by which he himself called it was *A Concordance of Discordant Canons*. He was a Benedictine monk of Bologna, and his compilation is full of those errors into which a compiler, who either did not or could not verify his authorities, was liable to fall. It contains numerous extracts from the false decretals of the early Popes,[2] including the letter of Clement[3] to St. James of which I have given an account. All that part of Constantine's pretended Act of Donation[4] which I have translated or abridged is contained in it. It was published about A.D. 1151, and is said to have been approved by Pope Eugenius III., who died in A.D. 1153.[5] It soon became the received text-book of Canon Law. This may

---

[1] The *Decretum* of Gratian constitutes the whole first volume of the *Corpus Juris Canonici* (Richter's ed., Leipsic 1839).

[2] In the first 483 alone, out of 1249 pages of the *Decretum* (Richter's ed.) there are 9 citations from Clement, 24 from Anacletus, 4 from Evaristus, 4 from Alexander I., 1 from Sixtus I., 2 from Telesphorus, 2 from Vigilius, 3 from Pius I., 3 from Anicetus, 3 from Eleutherius, 2 from Victor I., 9 from Zephyrinus, 10 from Calixtus I., 1 from Pontianus, 1 from Anterius, 15 from Fabianus, 4 from Cornelius, 4 from Lucius, 4 from Caius, 4 from Marcellus, 1 from Marcellinus, 8 from Eusebius, 1 from Melchiades, 7 from the Acts of Sylvester, 6 from Julius I., 8 from Damasus.

[3] Dist. 80, cap. 2; dist. 93, cap. 1, 6, 7; causa ii., quæst. vii., cap. 8, 9; causa vi., quæst. i., cap. 5, etc.

[4] Dist. 96, cap. 14.

[5] See Moreri, *Dictionnaire*, etc., *in nom.* 'Gratien.'

have been partly due to its systematic form, and partly to the reputation of the law school of Bologna; but the chief cause (according to Van Espen)[1] was that 'Gratian, in this work, not only repeated those fictions of the false Isidore, and of the sources from which he drew, which were directed to the aggrandisement of the authority of the Popes, but added much more of the same tendency, beyond what even the false Isidore could venture to write.' Pope Innocent III. was in his day reputed a great canonist; but Van Espen[2] says, that he regarded the *Decretum* as the purest fountain of Canon Law, and relied upon it in his decretals and decisions; that he was contented to take what he found there, indiscriminately and without hesitation; never inquiring into its genuineness or spuriousness, or whether it presented its authorities in a pure or in a garbled form.

8. The rest of the modern Roman Canon Law, which in the *Corpus Juris Canonici* follows the *Decretum*, consists of successive digests of canons of councils and decretals of Popes later than Gratian's time. It ends with the decrees of the Council of Trent, and the bulls of Pope Pius IV. confirming them.

[1] *Works*, vol. iii. p. 493 *et seqq.* (*Comment. in Decretum Gratiani*).
[2] *Ibid.*, vol. iv. p. 69.

ANCIENT FACTS AND FICTIONS

PART I.—CONTINENTAL

CHAPTER I

CHURCH REVENUES AND RULES OF DISTRIBUTION

§ 1. *Church Revenues the Patrimony of the Poor.*

NOT tithes in particular, but all Church property, of every kind, was from early times, and down even to the fourteenth century, described as 'the patrimony of the poor.'[1] The poor were always, and always must be, in an especial degree, objects of the Christian ministry. To them 'the Gospel' was to be 'preached.' The provision needful for the different orders of a settled ministry, and for churches in which they might meet for prayer and sacraments, was at least as beneficial to them as anything which might be specially devoted to the relief of their temporal wants. The relief, however, of the temporal as well as the spiritual wants of the destitute and the sick, the aged and afflicted, of strangers and foreigners, of prisoners and captives, was also, from the beginning, part of the office and work of the Church. The words of the Apostle:[2] 'Let brotherly love continue; be not forgetful to entertain strangers: remember them that are in bonds, as bound with them, and them which suffer adversity, as being yourselves also in the body,' —contain the germ of all later ecclesiastical ordinances

---

[1] Van Espen, *Jus Univ. Canon.*, pars ii. sect. 4, tit. i., cap. 3, §§ 1-16.
[2] Hebrews xiii. 1-3.

and practice on this subject. There is not a hospital or charitable institution in Christendom which is not, directly or indirectly, the fruit and a monument of the preaching of the Gospel.

This was the principle which regulated the use and application of Church revenues when those revenues were brought into one treasury and were subject to one general diocesan administration. The ancient customs and laws on that subject were as much applicable to offerings made at the altars of churches, and revenues arising from landed or other estates given to the Church, as to anything else. Of tithes, there is no mention at all in the Western Church until the beginning of the fifth century; none, indeed, in this particular connection, until much later.

§ 2. *Episcopal Authority.*

In the early diocesan administration everything depended upon the bishop. That was the rule laid down in the canons called 'apostolical,'[1] and in those of Antioch;[2] the former giving the bishop full power of disposition over all the goods of the Church, 'for the benefit of the poor;' the latter, according to the bishop's judgment, for himself and others, as the wants of each might require. Those Eastern canons were adopted into the original[3] ecclesiastical law of the Roman Church and of the Western Churches generally. The first Council of Orleans,[4]

---

[1] Canons 35, 37.   [2] Canons 24, 25.
[3] *Codex Canonum Ecclesiasticorum Dionysii Exigui* (Paris, ed. 1628). It contains 50 'apostolical' canons, 20 Nicene, 24 Ancyran, 14 Neo-Cæsarean, 29 Gangrian, 25 of Antioch, 59 Laodicean, 3 Constantinopolitan, 9 of Chalcedon, 21 Sardican, 33 of Carthage, and 105 other African canons.   [4] Mansi, *Concil.*, vol. viii. p. 347.

·assembled in A.D. 511 under the first Christian King of the Franks, laid it down as an ordinance (which they followed) of 'the more ancient canons,' that the general property of the Church was to be in the bishop's power.' The same thing was often[1] repeated in the legislation, civil as well as ecclesiastical, of the eighth and ninth centuries; and, as late as the eleventh century, Pope Gregory the Seventh[2] (as to tithes) endeavoured to restore that power to bishops.

Even as to the local endowments of 'oratories' on private men's estates, the bishops (for a long time successfully) claimed the same power. 'There are many' (said a canon[3] of the third Council of Toledo, A.D. 589, repeated[4] from time to time in later Acts both of Spanish and of German Councils), 'who, against the canonical rule, seek to get their own churches consecrated upon such terms as to withdraw their endowment (*dotem*) from the bishop's power of disposition. This we disapprove in the past, and for the future forbid. Let all things be done according to the ancient rule, under the bishop's power and control.' The first Council of Châlons[5] (A.D. 649), after taking notice that some powerful laymen opposed the exercise of the episcopal authority as to oratories built by them on their estates, and their endowments (*facultates ibidem conlatas*),

---

[1] See, *e.g.*, Charlemagne's capitulars of Frankfort, A.D. 794, of A.D. 813, and of uncertain date (Baluze, vol. i., *Cap. Reg. Franc.*, pp. 270, 503, 527); also canons of Arles (A.D. 813), of Mentz (A.D. 813 and 841), and of Pavia (A.D. 850 and 855)—Mansi, *Concil.*, vol. xiv. p. 60, etc., and pp. 905, 936; vol. xv. p. 18.

[2] *Decretum*, pars ii., causa xvi., quæst. i., cap. 1.

[3] Mansi, *Concil.*, vol. ix. p. 998.

[4] *Ibid.*, vol. xi. p. 25; vol. xv. p. 870; vol. xviii. p. 62. Also Baluze, *Capit. Reg. Franc.*, vol. i. p. 527; vol. ii. p. 352. And *Decretum*, pars ii., causa x., quæst. i., cap. 2-8.

[5] Mansi, *Concil.*, vol. x. p. 119.

decreed that the bishops, in all such cases, ought to have power over the endowments as well as over the clergy.

§ 3. *Local Customs.*

In the application of these principles a variety of usages grew up in different Churches. Van Espen[1] says that the Apostolic practice of supplying out of a common fund all the wants of the Church, without any definite rule of distribution, prevailed for at least four centuries; and that all definite rules were of later date. Augustin of Canterbury (as to a question of ritual) asked Pope Gregory the Great how the variety in the customs of Churches was to be reconciled with the unity of the faith. That wise man,— the same who reproved[2] a Patriarch of Alexandria for calling him 'Universal Pope,'—answered:[3]

'You are familiar with the custom of the Roman Church, in which you were brought up. But my judgment is, that you ought to choose whatever is most likely to be pleasing to Almighty God, whether you find it in the Roman, or in the Gallican, or in any other Church; introducing into your rules for the English Church, while yet new in the faith, the best things which you may be able to collect from many Churches. Things are not to be loved for the sake of places, but places for the good which is to be found in them.'

A local liberty, acknowledged as to ritual, could not be denied as to temporalities. And, accordingly, the authority of local custom, in the administration of Church revenues, was recognised by the third Council of Orleans[4] (A.D. 568) —which made a distinction between the churches of

[1] *Jus Univ. Canon.*, pars ii., sect. 4, tit. i., cap. 6, §§ 1-5.
[2] Gregory's Epistles, lib. i., cap. 36; and see *Decretum*, pars i., dist. 99, cap. 8.
[3] Bede's *Hist.*, lib. i., cap. 27.   [4] Mansi, *Concil.*, vol. ix. p. 13.

cathedral cities, where the bishop was to have full power over all offerings, etc., and those of towns and villages elsewhere in the diocese; in which the custom of each place was to be observed.[1] And, by a capitular of Louis the Simple[2] (A.D. 819) relating to tithes, the imperial commissioners—civil officers—were instructed to see that tithes were paid by every one, 'according to the ascertained custom or usage.'[3]

§ 4. *The Roman rule of Quadripartite Division.*

The Roman custom, from at least the time of Pope Gelasius (A.D. 501), was to divide the general diocesan revenues into four portions—one for the bishop; one to be distributed by him among his clergy, according to their respective degrees and merits; one for the poor and strangers (*peregrinis*); one for the fabrics of churches. In a decretal letter to the 'bishops of Dardania,' Pope Gelasius[4] ordered that every bishop should be charged, on his consecration, so to divide all the Church revenues. In two other decretal Epistles,[5] addressed to officers[6] of the Church of Volterra (in which abuses requiring correction had occurred), the same Pope directed that the bishop should associate with those officers a third, as his own special representative; and that the three should bring to him the full amount of all rents and payments from all the landed estates (*prædia*)

---

[1] '*De facultatibus vero parochiarum vel basilicarum in pagis civitatum constitutis, singulorum locorum consuetudo servetur.*'

[2] Baluze, vol. i. p. 620.

[3] *Sicut mos vel sacra consuetudo esse dignoscitur.*

[4] Mansi, *Concil.*, vol. viii. p. 12: '*Ut de reditu ecclesiæ vel oblationibus fidelium quatuor fiant portiones*,' etc.   [5] *Ibid.*, pp. 114, 115.

[6] The Archdeacon and 'Oeconomus.'

of the Church, both urban and rural; which the bishop, after deduction of expenses, and reserving a fund for contingencies, was to divide into the same four portions. The Church officers were to be cognisant of the distribution of the portion allotted to the poor, and, under the bishop's direction, were to make the necessary expenditure on the church fabrics. The portion allotted to the clergy was to be distributed according to the sole discretion of the bishop himself.

These decretals of Gelasius were often, in countries where the Roman rule of fourfold division was followed, referred to as the authority for it.[1] It was mentioned,[2] as the custom (*mos*) of the Apostolic See, with respect to every sort of Church revenue (*de omni stipendio quod accedit*), in the answer of Pope Gregory the Great to the first of Augustin's questions; and he enforced it, on several occasions,[3] in Italy and Sicily. Some of the bishops of Sicily had sought to confine it to ancient revenues (*antiquorum redituum*) of the Church, and had dealt with the fruits of later acquisitions on a different footing. But Gregory[4] refused to allow that distinction. He did not, however, consider the same rule applicable to the condition of the nascent Anglo-Saxon Church, advising Augustin to follow the primitive practice of the Apostolic Church.

[1] See, *e.g.*, Mansi, *Concil.*, vol. xiii. p. 428; vol. xviii. p. 139. A pretended decree of the (fictitious) Roman Council under Pope Sylvester (A.D. 324), enjoining the same division of all Church revenues (*de reditibus ecclesiæ*), has been sometimes alleged as an earlier authority. As to this, see Van Espen, *Jus Univ. Canon.*, pars ii., sect. 4, tit. i., cap. 6, §§ 6, 7; also *Jus Nov. Canon.* (ed. 1777), pars ii., p. 470.
[2] Bede, lib. i., cap. 27.
[3] See his *Works* (Bened. ed. of St. Maur, 1705), tom. ii., pp. 691, 737, 774, 899, 1249.
[4] *Ibid.*, p. 691 (Letter to Bishop of Syracuse).

§ 5. *Apportionment not numerically equal.*

Neither the Roman, nor any other mode of division ever used in the Church, contemplated (generally) an apportionment of the divisible funds into so many shares, numerically or by valuation equal. 'An arithmetical or equal proportionate division,' says Van Espen,[1] 'was neither appointed nor made; it varied according to the customs and circumstances of different places, which suggested the expenditure, now of a larger portion upon the poor, and at another time upon the clergy, according to the numbers and wants of the one or the other class. . . . It is clear that, out of the revenues of the Church, the clergy were paid and supported, the sustenance of the poor provided for, and the sacred buildings repaired, by a reasonable, and not by an arithmetical distribution.'

§ 6. *Quadripartite Division beyond Italy.*

It is said, by the same canonist, that the custom of quadripartite division was not received and in express terms established [2] in many places out of Italy; though the general principle of employing the ecclesiastical revenues for the purposes contemplated in that division was universally recognised. And he cited [3] (apparently without dissent) a statement by one of the earlier editors of the works of Gregory the Great, that the quadripartite division prevailed 'in few, if any, parts of France.' That statement (which I do

---

[1] *Jus Univ. Canon.*, pars ii., sect. 4, tit. 1, cap. 6, §§ 10, 14.
[2] '*Accepta vel stabilita verbis expressis*' (Van Espen, *Jus Univ. Canon.*, ubi supra, § 15). [3] *Ibid.*

not find adopted or repeated by the Benedictine editors of A.D. 1705 [1]) cannot be accepted as correct. The quadripartite division, according to the Roman rule, prevailed in the ninth century in both the great dioceses of Paris and Rheims, and also in the diocese of Soissons; as clearly appears from the Acts of the sixth Council of Paris [2] (A.D. 829), from the capitulars of Archbishop Hincmar of Rheims,[3] addressed to the priests of his diocese in A.D. 858, and from the constitutions of Riculf, Bishop of Soissons [4] (A.D. 889). Nor is there any reason to suppose that it was confined to those dioceses. In Germany, also, it largely prevailed; and was restored by bishops and councils in some places where it had been departed from. Thus, at the Council of Salzburg [5] (A.D. 807) the question arose, and was determined from 'the ancient canons' in favour of the quadripartite division; and certain abbots, then present, who had received tithes without accounting for the episcopal one-fourth share, made restitution to their respective bishops. At Basle, in A.D. 821, the bishop[6] (named Ahyto) considering himself entitled under a canon of the fourth

---

[1] The St. Maur edition of Gregory the Great's works is, by universal consent, better than any which preceded it.

[2] Mansi, *Concil.*, vol. xiv. p. 550 (lib. i., cap. 15, of the Acts of the Council, referring to '*Gelasius in decretalibus*, cap. 27;' and relating to Church revenues, '*ecclesiasticæ res*' and '*facultates*' generally).

[3] Mansi, *Concil.*, vol. xv. p. 480 (pars ii., art. 16, of Hincmar's capitulars): '*juxta institutionem canonicam*,' as to tithes in particular.

[4] Mansi, *Concil.*, vol. xviii. p. 85 (art. 11): '*canonica auctoritate*,' as to all the '*facultates ecclesiæ*.' The quadripartite division is also directed in some (though not the best or most) of the manuscripts of the Acts of the Council of Thionville, A.D. 803 (Mansi, vol. xiii. p. 428).

[5] Mansi, *Concil.*, vol. xiv. p. 13. (The question there was as to tithes.)

[6] *Ibid.*, p. 390. (As to tithes: '*Nos vero hac potestate uti nolumus, sed tantum quartam partem, juxta constitutiones Romanorum Pontificum, et observantiam sanctæ Romanæ ecclesiæ, habere volumus.*')

Council of Toledo to one-third, elected, in preference, to take a fourth part only, 'according to the ordinances of the Roman pontiffs, and the usage of the Holy Roman Church.' The Council of Mentz,[1] held (A.D. 841) under Archbishop Rabanus Maurus, decreed 'that the tithes given to the several churches be dispensed by the priests, according to the bishop's judgment, for the use of the Church and the poor;' and 'that both of the rents of land and of the offerings of the faithful, four portions be made, as the means of each church may allow, according to what was long since reasonably ordained: one part for the bishop, another for the clergy, another for the poor, and the fourth to be laid out as the bishop may appoint on the fabrics of the Church.'

The Councils of Worms[2] (A.D. 868), and of Tribur[3] and Martzen[4] (both A.D. 895), and Walafrid Strabo,[5] much of whose life was spent in the monastery of Fulda, and who became Abbot of Reichenau in the diocese of Constance (writing in the earlier half of the ninth century), all laid down the same rule of quadripartite division, as canonically binding on their several churches. Every royal and imperial capitular which speaks of any division at all, whether Transalpine or for Lombardy, and every canon or law mentioning it in the collections of Ansegisus and of

[1] Mansi, *Concil.*, vol. xiv. p. 906 (art. 10).
[2] Mansi, *Concil.*, vol. xv. p. 871 (art. 7): '*De reditu ecclesiæ et de oblatione fidelium*,' etc.; in the exact words of Gelasius, though not naming him, and not mentioning tithes.
[3] Mansi, *Concil.*, vol. xviii. p. 139. (Art. 13, as to tithes.)
[4] *Ibid.*, p. 169. (Art. 10, as to tithes.)
[5] Cap. 27 : '*De decimis dandis*' (Migne's ed., 1852, p. 961). He lays down the rule of division, not as to tithes only, but more generally: '*Quatuor enim partes juxta canones fieri de fidelium oblationibus debent*,' etc.

Benedict the Levite,[1] relates to the quadripartite division only.

§ 7. *Tripartite Division.*

For the statement of Bishop Kennett[2] (followed by Blackstone[3] and others) that 'when sees began to be endowed with lands, etc., the bishops, to encourage a quicker foundation of churches, did tacitly recede from their quarter part, and were afterwards by canons forbid to demand it if they could live without it,' there does not seem to be any good foundation. The customs, both of quadripartite and of other modes of division, were local; I find no trace of a transition anywhere from the quadripartite to a tripartite division, or of canons 'forbidding bishops to demand' their share. It was, indeed, suggested by some bishops[4] and councils,[5] that the case might happen of a bishop who did not need his share being willing to forego it; but of any compulsion to do so, or of any such renunciation by a bishop for his successors as well as himself, I have found no example.

There is much more ground for saying that direct proofs of the prevalence, either in France or elsewhere, of a tripartite or any other mode of division different from the Roman,

---

[1] Baluze, *Capit.*, vol. i. p. 691 *et seq.* As to Benedict, see Introduction, *ante*, p. 10.

[2] *Case of Impropriations* (1704), p. 15.

[3] *Comm.*, vol. i. pp. 384, 385 (book i., cap. 11).

[4] Bishop Riculf of Soissons (A.D. 889): '*Scire debetis, quia facultates ecclesiæ in quatuor partes canonica auctoritate sunt divisæ; ex quibus una est, si voluerit, episcopi; alia ad luminaria,*' etc. (Mansi, *Concil.*, vol. xviii. p. 85).

[5] Toledo xvi. (A.D. 693): '*Si eas* (sc. *tertias, quas antiqui canones de parochiis suis habendas episcopis censuerunt) maluerint reddere*' (Mansi, *Concil.*, vol. xii. p. 72).

are few and scanty, than for affirming such a proposition as to the quadripartite division in Continental Churches west and north of the Alps. I will first speak of the usages of the Spanish Peninsula, of which the influence extended to parts of France bordering on the Mediterranean, and was even felt north-eastward (as we have seen in Bishop Ahyto's case) as far as Basle.

In Spain there is evidence, in the sixth and seventh centuries, of a particular form of tripartite division; not, however, of one from which the bishop was excluded. On the contrary, the bishop took one-third share, subject to the repair of those churches to which a fourth would have been assigned by the Roman rule; and this would seem, from Bishop Ahyto's case, to have been more profitable to him than if he had taken one-fourth. This mode of division was established by the Council of Tarragona[1] (A.D. 516), which threw upon the bishop the burden of those repairs, expressly on the ground of his canonical right to one-third of all church revenues. The fourth[2] and ninth[3] Councils of Toledo (A.D. 633 and 657) recognised that right, but were silent as to the burden; the sixteenth[4] Council of Toledo (A.D. 693) reinforced the obligation which that of Tarragona had imposed, giving the bishop an option to relieve himself from it at the expense of the worshippers in the churches, if he waived his one-third; which, however, he was to be at all times free to take, when repairs were not necessary.

[1] Mansi, vol. viii. p. 543. (This, and the other Spanish and Portuguese canons mentioned, relate to church revenues generally, and not to tithes in particular.)

[2] *Ibid.*, vol. x. p. 627. (This council and the next gave the bishop one-third both of oblations and of the rents and profits of lands.)

[3] *Ibid.*, vol. xi. p. 26.   [4] *Ibid.*, vol. xii. p. 72.

In Portugal the first Council of Braga[1] (A.D. 567) laid down the rule that the ecclesiastical revenues should be divided into three *equal* portions—one for the bishop, one for the clergy, and one for church repairs and lights. The second Council of the same place[2] (A.D. 610) forbade the bishop, on his visitations, to take a third of the offerings made by the people in 'parish churches' (*ex quacunque oblatione populi in ecclesiis parochialibus*); appointing a third of those offerings to be given to the repair fund, and (apparently) leaving the rest to the clergy of those churches. And the Council of Merida[3] (A.D. 666) directed all the offerings of the faithful *in the churches of cathedral cities* to be divided into three equal parts; one for the bishop, one for the priests and deacons of those city churches, and one for the sub-deacons and other clergy in minor orders; while, in country churches (here also called parochial),[4] two-thirds were to be divided among the clergy of different orders, as in cathedral cities; but the other third was to go, not to the bishop, but for repairs. In this Portuguese mode of division no share was specially assigned for the poor.

Passing now to France, the Benedictine editors of Gregory the Great's Works (1705) referred[5] to the first

---

[1] Mansi, vol. ix. p. 773. [2] *Ibid.*, xi. 835. [3] *Ibid.*, p. 83.
[4] *Parochitanæ ecclesiæ*, having *parochitanos presbyteros*. These were, apparently, collegiate or conventual churches, having each a *familia*, which was a nursery for clerks; and having deacons, as well as priests, and lower clerks, among whom the division was to be made. The Council spoke of the bishop as entitled, under the former canons, to a third part of the revenues of this class of churches also—which it took away, thinking him otherwise amply endowed: '*Priscis quippe canonibus erat decretum, ut episcopus de parochitanis ecclesiis tertiam sequeretur; cui sua plenissime sufficere possunt.*'
[5] Tom. ii., p. 691 (note to Gregory's Epistle to Bishop of Syracuse).

Council of Orleans[1] (A.D. 511), as having laid down the Roman rule for Gallican Churches. This is not accurate, unless the Acts of that Council, as printed in the great collections of Mansi and his predecessors, are corrupt. Several of its canons relate to the distribution of different kinds of church revenues; and they are not easy to reconcile with each other. They laid down, first, a special rule, not for a tripartite division, but for the application, generally, to 'the repair of churches, the sustenance of priests and the poor, or the redemption of captives,' of the fruits and profits of certain royal gifts (given, doubtless, by Clovis after his conversion), of lands privileged from secular services, and of any similar gifts which might at any future time be made to the Church. Then, as to offerings at the altars of churches, another canon assigned *half* of them to the bishop, and the other half for distribution among the clergy: adding, that *prædia* of every kind were always to remain in the bishop's power. A third canon said that all the offerings of the faithful to the diocese, consisting of lands, vineyards, or other private property, should be in the bishop's power; and (which seems inconsistent with what had gone before) that a *third* part of what was offered at the altar should go to the bishop. And, lastly, the bishop was enjoined, 'as far as possible,' to give food and clothing to the poor and infirm who were incapable of manual labour.

These were special and intricate provisions. There was no quadripartite division. There was either a tripartite or a bipartite division of offerings, from which the bishop was *not* excluded; and there was a general appropriation of the revenues arising from *royal* gifts of land to the other

[1] Mansi, vol. viii. p. 347.

usual purposes, in which the bishop was to take no share. How far, and how long, these canons of Orleans were acted upon, may be doubted. By a letter of Abbo,[1] the celebrated Abbot of Fleury, who at the close of the tenth century defended monastic claims to tithes against his own diocesan (of Orleans) and other bishops, it appears, that the bishops of Orleans and other neighbouring parts of France were then in the habit of claiming, and taking for themselves, one-third of the general ecclesiastical revenues; and that, in Abbo's view, their right was to one-fourth, according to the Roman rule.

No Acts of any ancient Gallican Councils, either earlier or later than this first of Orleans—no royal or imperial capitular or law—can be cited in support of the proposition advanced by some respectable writers,[2] that a tripartite division, either of all ecclesiastical revenues, or of tithes in particular, was at any time the general custom of France.[3] The document, to which Ducange refers for that purpose (known as the *Capitulare Episcoporum*),[4] is interesting, and

---

[1] Gallandii *Bibliotheca Veterum Patrum* (Venice 1781), tom. xiv. p. 151; Bouquet, *Recueil des Histoires*, vol. x. p. 440.

[2] Ducange (Gloss in v. 'Dismes'): '*Tantum moneo, Decimas Ecclesiæ in tres partes divisas,*' etc.; referring to Charlemagne's capitular of A.D. 779, which says nothing about any division; to the *Capitulare Episcoporum;* and to De Lauriere's *Glossarium Juris Gallici*, v. 'Dismes,' where, also, there is nothing in point.

[3] The fourth article of the Ordinances of Aix-la-Chapelle, of A.D. 816 (see *post*, p. 85), provided for a division different from either the quadripartite or the tripartite; giving a larger share to the poor than either one-fourth or one-third, and no share to the bishop. But this division was to take place only as to gifts to the Church, later than A.D. 813, of which no appropriation might be made by the donors.

[4] Baluze, *Capit.*, vol. i. p. 357; Mansi (from Baluze), vol. xiii. p. 1069. See both texts of this document, from the Metz and Andain MSS., in Appendix A.

may be accepted as evidence that in some districts of France and the Low Countries (including, probably, Brabant, Luxemburg, the Ardennes, and parts of the adjoining provinces of Lorraine to the south-east, and Artois and Picardy to the west), tithes were in the ninth century divided into three portions;[1] one for the Church, one for the poor, and one for the priests. But it has been already seen that, to the immediate south of that region, the limits of that custom were so circumscribed that it did not extend to Soissons or Rheims; the quadripartite division, which was the rule in those dioceses, prevailed in the metropolitan diocese of Paris also; and at Orleans, in the tenth century, Abbo knew nothing of the *Capitulare Episcoporum*, or of any practice corresponding with its article as to tithes.

As a document, identical for this purpose (though not so entitled) with the *Capitulare Episcoporum*, will elsewhere in this work be shown to have been the true source of every passage in certain Anglo-Saxon compilations of the tenth and eleventh centuries which mentions a tripartite division of tithes, it seems desirable to collect such information as is accessible about it.

§ 8. *The 'Capitulare Episcoporum.'*

This title is in one only of three ancient Gallican manuscripts of the document in question, which were extant (I am not aware that any others were then, or are now, known) in the seventeenth century—that preserved at Metz, in the library of the monastery of St. Vincent, and first

---

[1] One of its articles directed such a division to be made '*according to canonical authority, before witnesses.*' See *post*, p. 228.

published by Sirmondi in A.D. 1629, in his *Gallican Councils*;[1] from which work it was copied by Baluze,[2] in his *Capitulars of the Frank Kings*. It is from those publications that it is best known. Of this Metz text there is another ancient copy (without the title *Capitulare Episcoporum*) in the Vatican Library,[3] which is supposed to be of the ninth or tenth century, and which, having originally belonged to the church of St. Martin at Mentz, was transferred in the fifteenth century to the library of the Elector Palatine at Heidelberg, and from thence to Rome in A.D. 1623, after the conquest of the Palatinate by Maximilian, Duke of Bavaria. The third manuscript was in the library of the monastery of St. Hubert, at Andain in the Ardennes; and was published by Martene and Durand[4] in A.D. 1733, in their *Amplissima collectio* of ancient ecclesiastical documents; being considered by them to be then 800 years old,[5] and to belong to the earlier part of the tenth century. The Metz manuscript was, probably, not less ancient; it is described as one of very high quality. The originals, from which both were copied, must have been a century or more older.

A singular heading—singular, because it is difficult for a man of ordinary intelligence to find all that follows in Holy Writ—is common to all three manuscripts:

'*These are the articles (capitula) from the writings of the Holy Scriptures, which the chosen priests have thought fit to be kept and observed.*'

[1] *Concilia Antiqua Galliæ*, vol. ii. p. 249.   [2] Vol. i. p. 357.
[3] The volume containing it is numbered 582, in the recently published catalogue of the Latin Palatine MSS. now in the Vatican. It contains an imperfect collection of Frank Capitulars, followed by the four books of the Abbot Ansegisus.
[4] *Veterum Scriptorum et Monumentorum*, etc. *Amplissima Collectio*, Paris 1733, vol. vii. p. 26.   [5] *Ibid.*, p. 16.

There is nothing to show who 'the chosen priests' were, or when, where, or by what authority they were chosen. The Metz title, *The Bishops' Capitular*, implies, not that those who drew up the paper were bishops, but that the authority by which it was promulgated was episcopal, not secular. It did not obtain a place in any Gallican or other Continental code of laws or canons; and the source of those copies of or extracts from it which were made by Anglo-Saxon scholars or divines remained unknown to the learned until after Sirmondi's publication.

The first step towards a probable conclusion as to the character and true date of the original document is to ascertain the relative value of the Metz[1] and Andain texts.

The Metz text contains twenty-two articles, of which one (the seventeenth) is absent from the Andain; the rest correspond, with only a few clerical variations. In the Metz manuscript each article has prefixed to it a sub-title; the corresponding articles in the Andain text, and in the Vatican manuscript also, have no sub-titles. In all three texts the thirteen last articles (exclusive of that which is not common to them) occur in the same order; but the order of the eight first is different. Both in the order, and in the omission of the seventeenth (Metz) article, the Anglo-Saxon copyists followed the Andain, and not the Metz text. All the twenty-one articles which occur in both relate to the duties of priests, and were (perhaps for that reason) called 'Sacerdotal Laws' (*jura sacerdotum*) by the Anglo-Saxon copyists. The word 'sacerdos,' 'sacerdotes,' or 'presbiterus,' occurs in every one of them. But it does not occur in the seventeenth article of the Metz text, which is an incongruous

---

[1] The Vatican text (except where any difference is noted in Appendix A) is the same as the Metz.

interpolation, relative not to any priestly duty, but to the rule of thirty years' prescription in cases of disputed ecclesiastical titles. Nor is this the only indication of the superior claim of the Andain manuscript (clerical errors excepted) to represent the original text. Its seventh and eighth articles, enjoining upon priests the duty of praying 'for the life and empire of the Lord Emperor, and for his sons and daughters,' and for bishops, stand there in an order which the context makes natural and probable. If they had stood first, it is not probable that any later copyist would have degraded them to a lower place. But in the Metz text those two articles are made to precede all the rest; and there is no difficulty in understanding such a transposition of the original order by ecclesiastical courtiers.

The force of these considerations is not weakened by the fact that, in the Andain manuscript, six other articles (not in the Metz text) are added. They are added in such a manner as to distinguish them from the twenty-one, and to show that they were not derived from the same original source; a sub-title of its own being prefixed to each of them. Their addition is consistent with the date to which the twenty-one 'Sacerdotal Laws' (only one of the added articles referring to the duties of priests) ought probably to be assigned.

What is that date? Sirmondi (and Baluze following him), finding none on the face of the document, beyond the proof (afforded by the injunction to pray for the 'Lord Emperor,' etc.) that it must have been later than the assumption of the imperial dignity by Charlemagne (A.D. 800), placed it—for that reason only—immediately after the capitulars of the first year of his empire.[1]

---

[1] Its place in the Vatican manuscript is after the Capitulars of Pippin,

But Selden[1] observed (not indeed upon that document, for he was ignorant of it, but upon the articles which were copied from it, as he found them in the Cottonian manuscript of what are generally called 'Egbert's Excerptions') that it could not be earlier than the 'canonical authority' for the division of tithes 'before witnesses,' to which the article on that subject referred; and he found no such 'canonical authority,' earlier than an imperial capitular really belonging (as will be seen in a later chapter) to A.D. 830.[2] There was, however, an earlier capitular of the last year of Charlemagne's reign (A.D. 813), confirming a canon of the third Council of Tours (one of the several Gallican Councils held by the Emperor's command in that year), which seems more likely to be the 'canonical' authority so referred to. The canon of Tours[3] is in these words: 'The bishops are to have power, in the presence of the priests and deacons, out of the treasure of the church, to take for the family and poor of the same church, according to the institution of the canons, agreeably to their need.' The imperial ordinance[4] confirming it is: 'That every bishop have power, out of the treasure of the church, in the presence of witnesses

and before those which follow under the title '*Capitular. Karoli Imperatoris.*' Mansi (vol. xiii. p. 1073), after saying, in his note to the reprint from Baluze (p. 1069), '*Ad annum* 802 *viri docti revocant,*' prefixes to a number of documents reprinted by him from Martene and Durand, including those from the Andain MSS. (of which this is one), a preface in these words: '*In calce conciliorum ad ætatem Caroli Magni pertinentium, collocandas duxi sanctiones has ecclesiasticas ejusdem Imperatoris, et aliorum; non quod omnes vel saltem ex iis aliquas sub exitum vitæ Caroli datas censeam, sed eo usus consilio, quod cum incerti sint temporis, ideo illis omnibus canonicis constitutionibus, de quarum epocha certi sumus, subjiciendas duxerim.*'

[1] Selden's *Hist. of Tithes*, ch. 8, § 1, ed. 1618, p. 197.
[2] *Post*, pp. 53, 54.   [3] Mansi, vol. xiv. p. 85.
[4] Baluze, *Capit.*, vol. i. p. 503.

(*cum testibus*), to take what is needful, according to the canons, for the support of the poor.' This is the first enactment as to witnesses in connection with any distribution of church revenues, which is anywhere to be found; and, taking this to be the 'canonical authority' referred to in the 'Sacerdotal Laws' of the Metz, Vatican, and Andain manuscripts, it follows that they were not earlier than A.D. 813. That conclusion is confirmed, as to the Andain manuscript, by one (that numbered 23) of those six articles, which (in that manuscript only) are added. This is taken, almost *verbatim*, from a canon as to the rights of 'ancient churches,' first enacted in the same year (A.D. 813) by two others of Charlemagne's synods (those of Mentz[1] and Arles),[2] and also confirmed by the nineteenth article of the same imperial capitular.[3]

As to the occasion for the work of 'the chosen priests,' and the place or places for which its rules were prepared and published, the mere situation (in the Ardennes and in Lorraine and at Mentz) of the monasteries in whose libraries it was preserved, might be inconclusive; but it is not without weight. For it was certainly probable that transcripts of such a document would be preserved in those dioceses in or near which it was, or had been, in force, rather than elsewhere; and the two Benedictine monasteries of Metz and Andain were places in which (assuming it to have been in force in those parts of the Frank territory) it would have been likely to be found. They were famous among the greatest and most ancient religious houses of the Gallican Church. That of Andain was founded by one of the earliest Bishops of Liege. The remains of St. Hubert, the founder

---

[1] Mansi, vol. xiv. p. 55 (art. 41).   [2] *Ibid.*, p. 60 (art. 20).
[3] Baluze, vol. i. p. 503.

of that see, were solemnly translated to it in A.D. 825, from which time it was called by his name. That of St. Vincent of Metz was founded by Theodoric or Thierry, son of Clovis, and King of Austrasia (of which Metz was the capital), in the sixth century. From Metz it might naturally pass to other places, such as Mentz on the Rhine. The situation of those monasteries, however, is not the only clue to the history of the document. In the Andain manuscript it did not stand alone, but was associated with a series of other documents relating to the diocese of Liege, and to the period between A.D. 800 and A.D. 808, which may be reasonably believed to have had some connection with it.

Charlemagne, as Emperor, and under that title (therefore after A.D. 800), addressed to Ghaerbald, then Bishop of Liege, a letter,[1] which is the first in that series of documents. He took notice that certain children, presented at the preceding Epiphany for public baptism, had been examined by his order as to their knowledge of the Lord's Prayer and the Creed; and that, being found wanting, he had caused their baptism to be deferred till they should be better prepared. He urged the bishop to impress upon his clergy the necessity of paying more attention to that part of their duty; and the letter ended with an admonition to the bishop 'to be mindful concerning the duties of the priestly ministry, and for that purpose to convene an assembly of the priests of his diocese, and carefully search into and examine the truth of that matter.'

On this the bishop addressed two pastoral letters,[2] suitable to the occasion (which follow next in the series),—the one to his 'flock' in his seignories of Condros, Loortz,

---

[1] Martene and Durand, *Ampliss. Coll.*, vol. vii. p. 19.
[2] *Ibid.*, pp. 16, 20.

Hasbain, and Ardennes; the other to the priests of his diocese. To the former he mentioned, to the latter he sent copies of, the Emperor's communication; taking to himself some share of the reproof which it conveyed, but intimating that he feared there must have been neglect of duty by many of his clergy.

The fourth document, which succeeds this, is another letter[1] from the Emperor to the same bishop, appointing a special fast to be observed, for the calamities of famine, pestilence, and war, then afflicting the empire; and directing notice of it to be given in all the 'baptismal churches' and monasteries of the diocese. To this was subjoined (not in a separate, but in the same manuscript) an episcopal charge,[2] by the same prelate, under seventeen heads; and after that, the 'Sacerdotal Laws' of 'the chosen priests,'[3] with the six articles added to them. Among the other topics specially dealt with by the bishop's charge are the duty of teaching children the Lord's Prayer and the Creed, the observance of the Lord's Day and festivals and fasts, and the payment of tithes. All these are the subjects of different articles in the Sacerdotal Laws,' the first being that to which the Emperor had particularly directed the bishop's attention. As to tithes, the bishop ordered that all defaulters, of whatever degree, should be brought before him, and should cause their occupying husbandmen (*familias*) to appear at such places as he should appoint. The charge concluded with a declaration of his readiness and desire to reform all abuses which might be brought to his notice.

Charlemagne had suggested that the bishop should con-

---

[1] Martene and Durand, *Ampliss. Coll.*, vol. vii. p. 21.
[2] *Ibid.*, p. 23.   [3] *Ibid.*, p. 26.

vene a synodical assembly, to 'search into and examine the truth of the matter' 'concerning the duties of the priestly ministry;' and it is at least probable, that the bishop, or his successor (for he died in A.D. 808), acted upon that suggestion; and that some priests, qualified by their learning and piety, may have been chosen to draw up a short code of rules for the instruction and use of priests in that and, perhaps, some other dioceses. If this was done, the twenty-one articles of 'Sacerdotal Laws,' which in the Andain manuscript follow Bishop Ghaerbald's charge, are of just such a nature and character as might be likely to have arisen out of that occasion. Various causes (perhaps, among others, the necessity for consideration by the bishops on whose authority they were to be issued), may have caused their final settlement, in the form in which they were published, to be delayed for five or more years after Bishop Ghaerbald's death. In the whole series of documents there is so much appearance of connection and mutual relation, as to make it at least probable, that their association together in the Andain manuscript was not the arbitrary act of the monk or clerk who transcribed them in a later century. That they all belong to the first quarter of the ninth century is certain. Until some more reasonable account is given of the matter, it seems to me to be a probable conclusion, that these 'Sacerdotal Laws' were prepared and issued primarily for the bishopric of Liege and churches dependent upon it, and for the dioceses of such bishops of other neighbouring parts of the Frank empire as may have concurred in their adoption; and that this was done within a short time after the death of Charlemagne.

CHAPTER II

CONTINENTAL LAWS AS TO TITHES

§ 1. *Before Charlemagne*

In the preceding chapter I have spoken of the ecclesiastical rules and customs which, from the time of Pope Gelasius to the tenth century, governed, upon the continent of Europe, the episcopal administration of diocesan revenues, including tithes. Of tithes, particularly, I propose now to speak.

In the *Decretum* of Gratian, several passages, now admitted to be spurious, are cited, as from works of St. Augustine,[1] St. Jerome,[2] and St. Ambrose,[3] to prove the assertion by those Fathers of a canonical obligation to pay tithes. But in the works of two at least of them, St. Augustine[4] and St. Jerome,[5] there are genuine passages, which,

---

[1] *Decretum*, pars ii., causa xvi., quæst. 1, cap. 66: '*Decimæ tributa sunt egentium animarum*,' etc. And *ibid.*, quæst. 7, cap. 8: '*Majores nostri*,' etc.

[2] *Ibid.*, quæst. 1, cap. 68: '*Liberum est clericis decimas monachis concedere*,' etc.

[3] *Ibid.*, quæst. 2, cap. 5: '*Nam qui Deo non vult reddere decimas*,' etc. And quæst. 7, cap. 4: '*Fideliter decimas dat*,' etc.

[4] *Sermo* 85 (on Matt. xix. 17), *Opera*, vol. vii., Venice 1802, p. 454.

[5] Comm. on Malachi, cap. 3 (*Opera*, vol. vi., Venice 1768), pp.

reasoning from the analogy of the Levitical law, and from our Lord's saying, that the righteousness of His disciples ought to exceed that of the Scribes and Pharisees, urge upon Christians the dedication, for religious and charitable purposes, of at least a tithe of their means. Cæsarius,[1] Archbishop of Arles from A.D. 503 to 544, appears to have been the first writer who more distinctly placed the claim of the Church to tithes on the footing of right. 'Tithes,' he said, 'are not ours, but appointed for the Church' (*ecclesiæ deputatæ*).

There is no mention of tithes in any part of the ancient canon law of the Roman Church, collected towards the end of the fifth century by Dionysius Exiguus.[2] Two Gallican Councils of the sixth century—the second Council of Tours[3] (A.D. 567), and the second Council of Macon[4] (A.D. 585)—are the earliest synodical authorities commonly cited for the requirement of tithes as payable of right to the Church. But the genuineness of the supposed Acts of that second Council of Macon is too doubtful to make it, for this purpose, a satisfactory authority. If genuine, they would seem to prove that the Mosaic law, as to the payment of tithes, was then regarded not only as binding from the first upon Christians, but as having been for centuries universally observed. For the fifth of the canons attributed to that Council (after a preamble as to the necessity of restoring to their former state all matters concerning the Catholic faith which had fallen into decay), runs thus :—

976-977. Cited also by Gratian (*Decret.*, pars ii., causa xvi., quæst. 1, cap. 63).

[1] *Homil.* 9, 21 (see Thomassinus, *De Beneficiis*, cap. 6, p. 29, Mentz 1787).   [2] *Ante*, p. 9.
[3] Mansi, vol. ix. p. 807.   [4] *Ibid.*, p. 951.

'The laws, therefore, of God, providing for the priests and ministers of churches, commanded all the people to render the tithes of their fruits to the holy places, as the lot of their (the priests') inheritance; so that, without hindrance from any kind of labour, they might have leisure for their spiritual duties. Which laws the whole body of Christians for a long space of time observed inviolate: but now, by degrees, nearly all Christians are seen to be gainsayers (*prævaricatores*) of the laws, while they refuse to fulfil those things which are divinely commanded. Wherefore, we ordain and decree, that the ancient custom be restored by the faithful; and that all the people bring their tithes to those who serve in the sacred offices; which being applied by the priests either for the use of the poor, or for the redemption of captives, they may obtain for the people, through their prayers, peace and salvation.'

A witness who proves too much is generally discredited; and this canon seems to prove too much for that time, and may therefore reasonably be suspected of spuriousness.[1]

As to the second Council of Tours, there is no mention of tithes in its canons or recorded Acts. But there is extant a pastoral letter[2] from four bishops, who were present at that Council, to the people (*plebem*) of their province, written after the synod, in a time of pestilence. That pastoral epistle cannot properly be said to place the payment of tithes on the footing of canonical obligation. It is an urgent exhortation to the people to 'follow the example of Abraham, by paying tithes of all their means, in order to save and to obtain God's blessing upon the rest, if they wish to be received into Abraham's bosom, and to reign with Christ'; and, beyond this, on account of the then threatened mortality, to give the Church the tenth of their *slaves;* or, if they have none, but have children, to pay something for each child towards the redemption of captives.

[1] See Selden, *Hist. of Tithes*, ch. 5, §§ 5, 6 (ed. 1618), pp. 57, 58, 65.
[2] Mansi, vol. ix. p. 809.

An early Spanish Council (that of Seville, A.D. 590) has also been quoted by some writers,[1] not only as enjoining the payment of tithes, but as enumerating titheable matters in considerable detail. But the genuine Acts of that council[2] contain nothing about tithes. Such a canon was, indeed, attributed to it by Ivo, who (like other canonists of his class) has much apocryphal matter under false descriptions. That 'fragment' (as Mansi calls it[3]) is in part taken from a capitular made at Aix-la-Chapelle by the Emperor Louis the Pious,[4] in A.D. 816.

That the payment of tithes, not long after the date of the second Council of Tours, acquired in the Western Church (if it did not previously possess) the character of a recognised ecclesiastical duty, is certain. But I have met with no canon enforcing it under ecclesiastical penalties earlier than that of the Council of Rouen (A.D. 630), quoted in the second part of Gratian's *Decretum*;[5] which, after saying that 'all the tithes of the earth, whether of corn or of the fruits of trees, belong to the Lord,' took notice, that 'many were found unwilling to give tithes;' and ordered that all such persons should be three times admonished, and, if those admonitions should fail, placed under anathema, until they might make satisfaction and suitable amends. There was no mention of tithes in any ancient code[6] of canon law before Charlemagne's time, nor in the collection of canons given to that emperor by Pope Adrian I.[7]

---

[1] Prideaux, *Original and Right of Tithes* (ed. 1736), p. 92.
[2] Mansi, *Concil.*, vol. x. p. 450; and see Selden, *Hist. of Tithes* (ed. 1618), p. 61.   [3] *Ibid.*, p. 453.   [4] *Post*, p. 85.
[5] Causa xvi., quæst. 7, cap. 5.
[6] Not in the Code of Dionysius Exiguus (*ante*, p. 9), nor in that published by Pithou (*Codex Canonum Vetus Ecclesiæ Romanæ*, Paris 1687).
[7] The '*Compendiosa traditio*' (of Oriental and African Canons)

E

§ 2. *Legislation of Charlemagne and his Successors.*

Civil legislation on this subject, upon the Continent, began with the celebrated ordinance of the eleventh year of Charlemagne's reign as King of the Franks, made in a general assembly of his Estates, spiritual and temporal, A.D. 778-779 :[1]

'Concerning tithes, it is ordained that every man give his tithe, and that they be dispensed according to the bishop's commandment.'

This was followed (A.D. 789) by another capitular, for Saxony,[2] appointing tithes to be paid out of all public property (*de omni re quæ ad fiscum pertinet*), enjoining all men 'whether noble, or gentle, or of lower degree (*tam nobiles et ingenui, similiter et liti*) to give according to God's commandment, to the churches and priests, of their substance and labour : as God hath given to each Christian, so ought he to repay a part to God.' A capitular of

---

given by Pope Adrian I. to Charlemagne, A.D. 773 (Mansi, vol. xii. p. 861). Sirmondi says that the Pope not only gave Charles this 'Epitome,' but also the text of the same canons in full, with a collection of Papal decretals, from Siricius (A.D. 318) to Gregory II. (A.D. 715); which was first published at Mentz (under the same title as by Pithou), in A.D. 1528, with a letter from the Pope, in Latin acrostic verses, to the king (see Mansi, *ubi supra*, note at p. 882). This is confirmed by the contents of Charlemagne's own ecclesiastical constitutions, eighty in number, of A.D. 789 (Baluze, *Capit.*, vol. i. p. 209). Of these, the forty-nine first are from the Oriental and African Canons, the nine next from decretals of Popes Siricius, Innocent I., Celestine I., Leo I., and Gelasius; and the rest either from the Holy Scriptures, or from royal capitulars. There is no mention of tithes in any of them.

[1] Baluze, vol. i. pp. 196, 197. Selden, *Hist. of Tithes*, ch. 6, § 7.
[2] Baluze, vol. i. p. 253.

A.D. 800,[1] applicable to the whole Frank kingdom, directed the payment of tithes to churches within the 'fiscal' domains.

For Lombardy, the Roman quadripartite division, of tithes expressly, was established by a capitular[2] made in the first year of Charlemagne's empire, A.D. 801; and in the Bavarian edition of the capitulars of Thionville, A.D. 808, there is an article directing the same quadripartite division, 'according to the decree of Pope Gelasius.'[3] This, however, is of doubtful authority; it was not found in six better texts of those capitulars, collated by Baluze. In the Salz capitular[4] of the same emperor, A.D. 804, and in that of A.D. 813,[5] confirming various constitutions of the synods held in the same year, there are articles on the subject of the churches to which tithes ought to be paid; to which I shall refer particularly, in another part of this chapter.

§ 3. *Witnesses and Compulsion.*

The earliest law as to witnesses, in connection with the receipt or distribution of ecclesiastical revenues, is the capitular of A.D. 813,[6] confirming a canon of the third Council of Tours. This, as has been seen in the preceding chapter, related, not to tithes particularly, but to the treasure of the Church generally. But in another canon[7] of the same Council of Tours, there was a direction that tithes were to be dispensed by the priests, under the bishop's direction, for the use of the Church and poor; and to this distribution

---

[1] Baluze, vol. i. p. 331 (art. 6.): '*Volumus, ut Judices decimam ex omni conlaboratu pleniter donent ad ecclesias quæ sunt in nostris fiscis.*'
[2] *Ibid.*, vol. i. p. 356.   [3] *Ibid.*, p. 428.
[4] *Ibid.*, p. 415.   [5] *Ibid.*, p. 503.
[6] *Ibid.*, p. 503 (art. 16).   *Ante*, p. 41.
[7] Mansi, vol. xiv. p. 85 (art. 16).

the canon as to witnesses would be applicable. The sixth Council of Paris[1] (A.D. 829), referring to a quadripartite division of the general church revenue, said that, however clearly a bishop might think himself able to prove his dispensation of the portion allotted to the poor to be in accordance with the principles of the Divine law, yet, agreeably to the Scripture, that 'they may see your good works, and glorify your Father which is in Heaven,' this ought to be established by testimony (*præsenti testificatione*), 'and published by the voice of good fame' (*bonæ famæ præconiis non taceri*). Archbishop Hincmar,[2] thirty years later, required the presence of witnesses for the division into four portions; as in the *Capitulare Episcoporum*, or 'Sacerdotal Laws,' spoken of in the last chapter, it was required for a tripartite division :

'Of the tithes,' he said, 'let four portions be made, according to the canonical rule; and let them, under the testimony of two or three faithful men (*sub testimonio duorum aut trium fidelium*), be studiously and carefully divided.'

The witnesses required by the canon of the third Council of Tours were 'priests and deacons;' but the language of the confirmatory ordinance of Charlemagne (A.D. 813) was general (*cum testibus*). Archbishop Hincmar, when speaking of 'two or three faithful men,' may be presumed to have had in view the civil legislation as to witnesses (in connection with the receipt and payment rather than the distribution of tithes) which had taken place in A.D. 830, and which Selden[3] believed to be the earliest

---

[1] Mansi, vol. xiv. p. 550 (lib. i., cap. 15, of the Council's Acts).
[2] *Ibid.*, vol. xv. p. 480 (*Capit. ad Presbyteros*, etc., part ii., art. 16).
[3] *Hist. of Tithes*, ch. 8, § 1.

'canonical authority' on that subject. Of this I shall now speak, in connection with the compulsory laws, of which it forms part.

In A.D. 829 (the year in which the sixth Council of Paris was held), the Emperor Louis the Pious, by his capitular at Worms,[1] gave a civil remedy, by distraint, for the recovery of tithes from persons who were unwilling to pay them except on some terms of redemption (*de decimis quas populus dare non vult, nisi quolibet modo ab eo redimantur*). This enactment was at the same time extended to Lombardy by Lothair,[2] whom his father had associated in the empire, and to whom he had assigned the government of the Lombard kingdom; and it fixes, by internal evidence, the date of that which follows (about which there has been some controversy);[3] which was also a law, both of Louis the Pious, and of Lothair for Lombardy. That law begins: 'As to tithes, the ministers of the Commonwealth are to compel them to be given, even by those who are not willing to give them, *as was declared last year*' (*de decimis*,

---

[1] Baluze, *Capit.*, vol. i. p. 664 (art. 7).
[2] *Ibid.*, vol. ii. p. 340 (*Excerpta ex lege Longobardorum*, art. 39).
[3] '*De decimis ut dentur et dare nolentibus*,' etc. (*ibid.*, p. 333). Auerbach, in his *Præcipuæ Constitutiones Caroli Magni* (A.D. 1545, p. 3, cap. 7), printed this among his selected laws of Charlemagne, but noted in the margin that it was ascribed (in the *Lombard Laws*, lib. iii., tit. '*De decimis*') to the Emperor Lothair. Martene (vol. vii. pp. 5-10), on the authority of a Chigi MS. (published by Mabillon), ascribed to Charlemagne, and to a time earlier than his accession to the empire, all the laws contained in that MS.; which is a miscellaneous collection, supposed to be of the ninth century, of laws, including some on their face Imperial. Muratori (*Rerum Italicarum Scriptores*, tom. ii. p. 133; *Ludovici Augusti Leges*, cap. 34) determined the law in question to belong to the reign of Louis the Pious, on the authority of an Este MS.; and with him agrees Mansi (vol. xiii. p. 1073).

ut dentur ei dare nolentibus, quod anno præterito denuntiatum est, a ministris Reipublicæ exigantur). It was made, therefore, in the year after A.D. 829; that is, in A.D. 830.

After that sentence, it proceeds thus:—

'And let either four or nine men, of good reputation, or as many as shall be needful, be chosen out of each body of laity of the Public Churches (*de singulis plebibus*), according to the quality of each such Body, to be witnesses between the priest and the people (*ut ipsi inter sacerdotem et plebem testes existant*), where the tithes have, or have not, been given—our object being to avoid the necessity for oaths in such cases. We do not, however, mean that all the persons so chosen as witnesses need always be present when tithes are given;—we have fixed so large a number, to diminish the burden upon each. The actual presence of two will be enough.'

That law went on to provide means for compelling payment;—first, by priestly admonition; then, by exclusion from the Church; then, by the intervention of the civil power, and the infliction of fines; then, by a sort of interdict against defaulters' houses; and last, if the use of all those means failed to produce the desired effect, by taking the defaulters into custody, and bringing them before the Imperial or Royal Courts.[1]

§ 4. *Ancient Baptismal Churches, and their Rights.*

Although the early canon law attributed to the bishops

---

[1] Milman (*Hist. of Latin Christianity*, vol. iii. p. 87) cites this as a Lombard law of A.D. 803, and also of Lothair (A.D. 825), and of Louis II. (A.D. 875). As to Louis II., Milman followed Baluze (vol. ii. p. 339), but for the other dates he had not that, or (as far as I know) any other authority. Muratori (*ubi supra*) observed that it was easy to confound Louis I. with Louis II., and preferred the authority of the Este MS. It is remarkable that neither Baluze, nor Martene, nor Muratori, nor Mansi, said anything of the internal evidence, by which that question seems to be decided.

a very wide discretion as to the disposal and employment of diocesan revenues, it was not possible that such a power should be exercised without some local organisation, or without the aid of subordinate officers and ministers. As early as A.D. 451, the Council of Chalcedon,[1] by a canon which passed into all the Roman codes, ordered that in the diocese of every bishop there should be a treasurer (*oeconomus*) chosen out of the diocesan clergy, to dispense the Church funds according to the bishop's direction; so that there might be evidence of the manner in which that dispensation was made (*ut ecclesiæ dispensatio præter testimonium non sit*), and any waste of the revenues of the Church, and consequent scandal, might be prevented. The second Council of Seville[2] (A.D. 619), by a canon also adopted into the modern (though it does not appear to have found a place in the ancient) Roman canon law, required the strict observance of this rule; and forbade the substitution of lay for clerical treasurers, which had been introduced by some Spanish bishops.

Although there were not, in those times, parishes in the modern sense, the principal[3] and more ancient[4] churches became local centres of administration; and these, at an early date, obtained recognised rights and privileges, within districts[5] over which they exercised some sort of authority.

[1] Mansi, vol. vi. p. 1228 (Canon 26); Gratian, *Decret.*, pars ii., causa xvi., quæst. 7, cap. 21.
[2] Gratian, *Decret.* (*ibid.*), cap. 22.
[3] '*Majores*' (see *post*, capitular of Louis II., A.D. 855).
[4] '*Antiquitus constitutæ*' (*post*, capitular of Charlemagne, A.D. 813).
[5] Although the word '*parochia*' may sometimes have been applied to these districts (as, *e.g.*, by the Portuguese Councils of Braga and Merida, A.D. 567 and 666, *ante*, p. 34), they were more generally called '*dioeceses.*' They were certainly not parishes of the modern kind; and to call them by that name (as seems to be done by Dean Milman, *Latin*

They were called 'Mother Churches' (*matrices*),[1] because private oratories and chapels within their circles were dependent upon them; those who worshipped in such oratories and chapels were bound, according to the canons of several Councils, to resort to the mother church three times a year; which rule did not become obsolete until the eleventh century.[2] They were called 'People's Churches' (*plebes*),[3] on account of the public character by which they were distinguished from those built on private men's estates. An imperial capitular of A.D. 806 prohibited the solemn celebration of festivals elsewhere than in public townships (*vicis publicis*);[4] that is, places within the royal or public domain, not granted to be held as *beneficia*, or fiefs, by private persons. Many of those churches were called *monasteria*,[5] or, in Saxon, *minsters*, because they were usually of a collegiate character, with a more or less numer-

---

Christianity, vol. iii. p. 87, note) might lead to misconception. The distinction is well marked in Gratian's *Decretum* (pars ii., causa xiii., quæst. 1), where, in a controversy as to tithes between two churches, this position is stated as clear: '*Constat, unamquamque Baptismalem Ecclesiam habere dioecesim sibi legitime assignatam: sicut et parochiales ecclesiæ habent parochias sibi distributas.*' The words '*parochia*' (of which the leading sense is *neighbourhood*), and '*dioecesis*' (of which the leading sense is *administration*), were flexible; both originally signifying the bishop's diocese.

[1] See Ducange, *in voc*. 'Matrica,' 'Matrix Ecclesia.' Archbishop Hincmar's Articles of Inquiry, A.D. 858 (Mansi, vol. xv. p. 480) were to be executed '*per singulas matrices ecclesias, et per capellas*' of his province.

[2] See Baluze's note, *Capit.*, vol. i. p. 1063.

[3] Ducange, *in voc*. 'Plebes'; capitular of Charles the Bald, A.D. 876 '*Ecclesias baptismales, quas plebes appellant*' (Baluze, vol. ii. p. 242); Leo IV., in *Decretum*, pars ii., causa xiii., quæst. 1, § 1; and Walafrid Strabo.

[4] Baluze, vol. i. p. 457; and see Ducange, *in voc*. 'Vicus Publicus.'

[5] See Ducange, *in voc*. 'Monasterium.'

ous body of clergy, either secular canons or monks, living together within their precincts.

These phrases were rather popular than technical. 'Baptismal' churches (*baptismales*)[1] was their most proper designation; which meant churches having public baptisteries, in which, at the great feasts of Easter and Pentecost (sometimes Epiphany[2] also), the sacrament of baptism was solemnly and publicly administered for the people of their several districts. Sometimes they were themselves called baptisteries (*baptisteria*),[3] and the titles to them were called baptismal (*tituli baptismales*). It was decreed by the Synod of Verneuil,[4] held under Pepin, the father of Charlemagne, in A.D. 755, that 'no public baptistery should be established except by the bishop's command, or in any places, except such as he should appoint; but this was not to prevent any priest from administering the sacrament of baptism elsewhere in cases of emergency.' It was at the Epiphany celebration of baptism, in the chief baptismal church of the diocese of Liege, that Charlemagne took the part mentioned in his first letter to Bishop Ghaerbald;[5] and it was doubtless to such solemn celebrations of that sacrament at the appointed times that the *Capitulare Episcoporum*[6] referred, in the article numbered ten in both the Andain and the Metz manuscripts: 'That the law and time of

[1] See, on this whole subject, the note of Baluze, *Capit.*, vol. i. p. 1063. As to the great public baptisms at Easter and Pentecost, and also Epiphany, see note of Martene and Durand in *Amplissima Collectio*, vol. vii. p. 20.

[2] Walafrid Strabo (*de ecclesiasticarum rerum exordiis et incrementis*), cap. 26. (Migne's *Patrologiæ Cursus*, vol. cxiv. p. 959.)

[3] Baluze's note, *ubi supra*.

[4] Baluze, *Capit.*, vol. i. pp. 167, 171.

[5] Martene and Durand (*Ampliss. Collect.*), vol. vii. p. 20; *ante*, p. 43.

[6] *Ante*, p. 37, and Appendix A.

baptism, at the proper seasons, according to the canonical institution, be most carefully observed by all priests'; (with a qualification, as to time, in the next article, like that as to place in the canon of Verneuil, viz. 'That all priests should with the greatest diligence administer baptism, at whatever hours, to those who by reason of ill-health might stand in need of it').

It was in all the 'baptismal churches'[1] of the diocese of Liege that Charlemagne commanded notice to be given by Bishop Ghaerbald of the special fast which he had appointed. The rights and privileges of 'baptismal churches' (by that name) are among the subjects of examination by Gratian[2] in the second part of his *Decretum*.

Of such churches there was at first only one (the cathedral)[3] in each diocese; but when dioceses became large the number was increased. The most important of them were conventual, served by many priests and clerks; and it was canonically necessary[4] that they should be served by at least one priest, with the assistance of one or more deacons and inferior clerks.

Walafrid Strabo[5] (writing in the early part of the ninth century) speaks of the priests of baptismal churches as

---

[1] Martene and Durand (*Ampliss. Collect.*), vol. vii. pp. 21-23 : '*Per singulas ecclesias baptismales.*' *Ante*, p. 43.

[2] *Decret.*, pars ii., causa xiii., xvi., and xxv.

[3] Baluze's note, vol. i. p. 1064, quoting and approving the statement of Joseph Visconti (*Josephi Vicecomitis*).

[4] Baluze's note, *ubi supra*, p. 1065 : '*Cum in reliquis sufficeret unus Presbyter, in istis necessarius erat unus diaconus cum Presbytero.*' And see Baluze, *Capit.*, vol. ii., App. p. 1575 : '*Capitula data Presbyteris,*' cap. 8; and Bishop Riculf's *Constitutions for Soissons* (A.D. 889), art. 11 (Mansi, vol. xviii. p. 85).

[5] *Ubi supra*, cap. 31 (Migne's *Patrol.*, vol. cxiv. p. 964).

having authority over priests of lower degree (*presbyteri plebium, qui baptismales ecclesias tenent, et minoribus presbyteris præsunt*), and as qualified, for that reason, to be 'vicars,' or 'centenarions' (*centenariones*), of the bishop; an office, for the oversight of country churches, superior to that of rural dean (*decuriones, vel decani*).

When these greater and more ancient churches, or minsters, first acquired the right to receive and administer tithes, or other diocesan revenues accruing within their districts, does not clearly appear. A canon of the Council of Chalcedon[1] (A.D. 451), establishing, as between diocese and diocese, in cases of disputed titles, a rule of thirty years' prescription, was afterwards by analogy extended to them. Selden[2] quotes from Cassian the hermit (who died about A.D. 430) a passage, showing that 'in Egypt some holy abbots had tithes of all fruits offered them,' accepting the dispensation of them as 'treasurers for the poor.' In the eighth and ninth centuries (according to Lupus, Abbot of Ferrieres, as quoted by Van Espen),[3] bishops and laymen preferred paying their tithes to canons, rather than rural priests (*presbyteris pagensibus*), on account of the greater

[1] Mansi, vol. vi. p. 1228 (Canon 16). See Gratian's *Decretum*, pars ii., causa xiii., quæst. 2, cap. 1.

[2] *Hist. of Tithes*, ch. 5, § 1, ed. 1618, p. 47; and 'Review,' *ibid.*, p. 465.

[3] *Jus Univ. Canon.*, part ii., sect. 4, tit. i., cap. 3, § 18. '*Eorum sanctitati creditum fuit totum decimarum onus; et honesta Presbyteri alimentatio, et ecclesiasticæ fabricæ reparatio, et cura pauperum et peregrinorum.*' Lupus was a pupil of Rabanus Maurus. He became Abbot of Ferrieres (where Alcuin was one of his predecessors) A.D. 842. He took a leading part in the Councils of Verneuil, A.D. 844, and of Soissons, A.D. 855, and he was a correspondent of the Anglo-Saxon King Ethelwulf, and of Wigmund (archbishop), and Altsig (abbot), of York. (See Haddan and Stubbs, *Councils*, etc., vol. iii. pp. 634, 635, 648, 649).

reputation of the former for sanctity, and the greater confidence felt in the integrity of their administration. It was probably through causes such as these, that baptismal churches acquired such rights as they claimed to tithes. Another authority of the ninth century, Amulo, Archbishop of Lyons, in a letter to Theobald, Bishop of Langres (quoted by Baluze),[1] mentions those rights, among other instances of 'the dignity and authority of baptismal churches.'

'Let the lay-people (*unaquæque plebs*) everywhere abide quietly in their own dioceses and churches (*parochiis et ecclesiis, quibus attributa est*), and let them offer willingly their vows and oblations at those Sanctuaries where they receive holy Baptism, where they partake of the Lord's Body and Blood, where they may hear solemn Masses, and obtain from their priest penance for sin, visitation in sickness, and burial in death; where, also, they are commanded to offer their tithes and first-fruits, where they rejoice in the initiation of their children into the grace of baptism, where they continually hear God's Word, and are instructed in what they ought and what they ought not to do.'[2]

A decretal epistle of Pope Leo IV. in the same century, (quoted by Gratian),[3] laid it down as a rule approved, not by that pontiff only, but by his predecessors, that tithes ought to be paid 'only to those public churches where the holy baptisms are administered' (*plebibus tantum, ubi sacro-*

---

[1] Note on Baptismal Churches, *Capit.*, vol. i. p. 1065. Amulo was Archbishop of Lyons from A.D. 841 to A.D. 853.

[2] That these were the greater, and not the seignorial churches, is evident from the capitular of Louis II. (A.D. 855): '*Quidam vero laici, et maximè potentes ac nobiles, quos studiosius ad prædicationem venire oportebat, juxta domos suas basilicas habent, in quibus divinum audientes officium, ad majores ecclesias rarius venire consueverunt*' (art. 3, Baluze, vol. ii. p. 352).

[3] *Decretum*, pars ii., causa xiii., quæst. 1, § 1. Leo IV. was Pope from A.D. 847 to A.D. 855.

sancta baptismata dantur). And as to sepulture, a canon of the Council of Tribur[1] (A.D. 895), also cited in the *Decretum*,[2] ordered that it should take place, whenever possible, in the burial-ground of the principal church of the diocese (*apud majorem ecclesiam, ubi sedes est Episcopi*); or, if that were not possible, in the burial-ground of the church of some religious house of canons, monks, or nuns, living together conventually. If this, too, could not be done, then a man was to be buried where he had paid his tithes while living.

Every 'baptismal' church had its district (sometimes called 'diocese')[3] assigned, or presumed from usage to have been assigned, by competent authority; and in each such district there could be only one such church, with its dependent chapels.[4] The older organisation of these 'sub-dioceses' (if I may so call them) may have been in some respects the model on which the modern parochial system grew up.

Charlemagne, by his capitular *de villis*[5] (A.D. 800), while reserving generally the tithes of royal or public lands to the public churches on the royal domain (*in nostris fiscis*), made an exception in favour of churches elsewhere, having ancient titles to them (*ad alterius ecclesiam nostra decima data non fiat, nisi ubi antiquitus institutum fuit*). And by

[1] Mansi, vol. xviii. p. 139.
[2] Pars ii., causa xiii., quæst. 2, cap. 6.
[3] *Ibid.*, causa xvi., quæst. 1; and causa xxv.
[4] '*Plures baptismales ecclesiæ in unâ terminatione esse non possunt; sed una tantummodo, cum suis capellis; et si contentio fuerit de terminatione duarum matricum, plebes utrarumque discernant, et, si non convenerint, lis Dei judicio discernatur*' (Grat., *Decret.*, pars ii., causa xvi., quæst. 1, cap. 54, where that canon is ascribed erroneously to a Council of Toledo. Other canonists had, before Gratian's time, attributed it to a Council of Aix). [5] Baluze, *Capit.*, vol. i. p. 331.

his imperial ordinance at Salz[1] (A.D. 804) he established, generally, the right of ancient baptismal churches to tithes bestowed upon them with the consent of their diocesan Bishops (*ubi antiquitus fuerint Ecclesiæ Baptismales, et devotio facta fuit, juxta quod Episcopus ipsius parochiæ ordinaverit*); adding, that 'if, by gifts of kings or other good and God-fearing men, anything from which the older churches had been accustomed to receive tithes, under ancient titles, should have been granted to bishoprics or monasteries, the earlier gift or devotion should continue in force, and the tithes should be paid by those in possession of the land.'

One of the articles of the capitular of A.D. 813[2] (confirming canons made in almost identical terms by two of the synods of that year, those of Mentz and Arles) was for a like purpose; and was repeated,[3] in terms or substance, in many later laws.

'Churches established of old time are not to be deprived of tithes, or of any other possessions, so as to give them to new churches (*Ecclesiæ antiquitus constitutæ nec decimis, nec aliis possessionibus, priventur, ita ut novis ecclesiis tribuantur*).'

In some of the repetitions of that law, as well as glosses of canonists, after A.D. 816, it was qualified so as to reconcile it with the legislation of Aix-la-Chapelle[4] in that year, of which I shall hereafter make mention; in others it was not. The Council of Mentz, held under Archbishop Rabanus Maurus[5] (A.D. 841), allowed exceptions to be made to it

---

[1] Baluze, *Capit.*, vol. i. p. 415.

[2] *Ibid.*, p. 503. (The Canons of Mentz and Arles are in Mansi, vol. xiv.)

[3] *E.g.*, A.D. 899 (Baluze, vol. ii. p. 18), 888 (Mansi, vol. xvii. p. 62), 895 (*Ibid.*, vol. xviii. p. 139), 958 (*ibid.*, pp. 463-467).

[4] Baluze, *Capit.*, vol. i. p. 565.   [5] Mansi, vol. xiv. p. 905.

'with the consent and advice of the bishop;' and Herard, Archbishop of Tours[1] (A.D. 855-870), allowed them 'on very strong grounds of practical utility.' Gratian, in his *Decretum*,[2] produced an apocryphal decree of Pope Anastasius, in which those who, 'without their bishop's knowledge, might bestow their tithes on any other than the baptismal church,' were threatened with excommunication; and, in a gloss[3] upon a canon ascribed by him (erroneously) to a Council of Toledo, he said that the rights of those churches were to be understood as secured to them against diminution or encroachment, not absolutely, but 'unless they should be assigned, by the bishop's disposition (*episcopo disponente*), to other churches.'

§ 5. *Irregular Appropriations of Tithes.*

Many encroachments on the ancient rights of baptismal churches did in fact take place, not only for purposes authorised by the laws of Aix-la-Chapelle (the effect of which will be the subject of a later chapter), but for others, always condemned by the law of the Church; such as grants of tithes to monasteries by laymen,[4] without episcopal concurrence; and the feudalisation of tithes in the hands of laymen,[5] under tenures often created by the bishops themselves, or by other ecclesiastical tithe-owners. The baptismal churches long struggled for their privileges; and were supported at the Council of Pavia[6] (A.D. 855, under the

[1] Baluze, *Capit.*, vol. ii. p. 129.
[2] Pars ii., causa xvi., quæst. 1, cap. 55.
[3] *Ibid.*, gloss on cap. 54.
[4] See numerous authorities, cited by Gratian (*Decret.*, pars ii. causa xvi., quæst. 7). [5] *Ibid.*
[6] Mansi, vol. xv. p. 18; Baluze, *Capit.*, vol. ii. p. 257.

Emperor Louis II.), and by a capitular of Charles the Bald,[1] A.D. 869. Canons and laws were passed for the punishment, by ecclesiastical censures and civil penalties, of laymen who, 'for reward or favour,' took upon themselves to divert their tithes from the churches entitled to receive them;[2] or, who, 'despising the direction of their bishops, gave their tithes, not to the churches where they received baptism, preaching, imposition of hands, and the other Christian sacraments, but to private churches on their own estates and fees, or to clerks of their own choice, at their pleasure.'[3] It was not, however, by laymen only, that the ancient rights of baptismal churches were subverted. When they were in the hands of canons, or other secular priests, the monastic orders[4] were constantly invading them; sometimes by getting grants of tithes, and sometimes by procuring exemptions, which it was their policy in every possible way to extend, and which the Popes were afterwards[5] obliged to curtail. Van Espen[6] says that, 'when in the tenth and eleventh centuries laymen were willing to restore to ecclesiastical uses tithes and churches of which they or their ancestors had taken possession, they preferred, generally

---

[1] Baluze, *Capit.*, p. 212.

[2] Capitular of Worms, A.D. 829 (Baluze, vol. i. p. 664); Synod of Pavia, A.D. 850 (Mansi, vol. xiv. p. 936); Archbishop Herard's Constitutions (Baluze, vol. ii. p. 129).

[3] Synod of Pavia, A.D. 855 (Mansi, vol. xv. p. 18; Baluze, vol. ii. p. 357). See *ante*, p. 60.

[4] See letter of Paschal II. (A.D. 1099-1113) to Victor, Bishop of Bologna, in Grat. *Decret.*, pars ii., causa xvi., quæst. 1, cap. 9; also *ibid.*, quæst. 7, cap. 2, 39; *Decret. Greg. IX.*, lib. iii., tit. xxx., cap. 3, 4, 9, 10, 11, 27, 30, 34, 35; *Sexti Decret.*, lib. iii., tit. xiii., cap. 2.

[5] *Decret. Greg. IX.*, lib. iii., tit. xxx., cap. 8, 9, 10; *Sexti Decret.*, lib. iii., tit. xiii., cap. 2.

[6] Van Espen, *Opera* (ed. 1753-59), vol. iii. p. 596.

(*passim*), to give them to monks or canons,[1] rather than to the churches from which they had been taken away; although this had been denounced as unauthorised by many ecclesiastical laws, and monks and canons had been forbidden to receive tithes or churches from lay hands without the bishop's consent.' That they obtained them very early with the consent or by the act of bishops, is clear from a charter of a bishop of Le Mans,[2] dated in A.D. 649-650 (under Clovis II.), by which he granted for ever to a convent of nuns all the tithes arising within ten townships belonging to his see. In A.D. 997 a synod of bishops was held at St. Denis near Paris, in order to take measures for the restitution to the Church of such tithes as might be uncanonically possessed by laymen or monks. This council was attended by the Abbot of Fleury, Abbo, a man of great fame, and very zealous for monastic institutions. He offered to the intended resumption a strenuous resistance; which had the effect (although his biographer, Aimonius,[3] threw the blame on the bishops whom he resisted) of so exciting the lay people, that an angry mob invaded the synod, and broke it up in disorder.[4] A controversy followed between Abbo and his own bishop, Arnulph of Orleans. The abbot addressed a public defence[5] of his conduct to Robert and John, Kings of the Franks, in

[1] See citation from Abbot Lupus (*ante*, p. 59, note).

[2] '*Omnes decimas de supradictis villulis, tam de annonis, quam agrario, vinum, fænum, omnium pecudum seu farmatico, vel undecunque decimari debetur . . . ipsam decimam omni tempore ipsi monasterio habeat concessam*' (Mabillon, *Vetera Analecta*, tom. ii., p. 278).

[3] See Mabillon, *Vetera Analecta*, tom. ii.

[4] Baronius, *Annales*, vol. xvi. p. 434.

[5] '*Apologeticus Abbonis adversus Arnulphum Episcopum Aurelianensem, et aliquot Epistolæ*' (App. to Pithou's *Codex Canonum Vetus Ecclesiæ Romanæ*, Paris 1687, pp. 398-400, 417, 418).

F

which he accused bishops of avarice and corruption, and appealed to the civil power to exercise the authority in these matters, which (he said) had been admitted by the most ancient councils to belong to emperors and consuls. And in a letter to a brother monk named Gerald,[1] he inveighed against the covetousness, 'which was not satisfied with a third, or a fourth at least, of the revenues of their own churches;' citing Gregory the Great for the proposition, that 'monasteries ought not to be disquieted by bishops;' and inquiring what Scriptural authority there was for requiring yearly accounts of church endowments or tithes to be rendered to bishops?

Gregory VII.,[2] in his Lateran Council of A.D. 1078, made a canon forbidding the possession of tithes by laymen, and declaring them guilty of sacrilege unless they restored them to the Church, whether received from bishops, or kings, or any other persons. And, after affirming the obligation of all to pay tithes, he thus endeavoured to restore the bishop's power over their distribution:

'Our judgment is, that the tithes should be under the bishop's hand; that he who is set over the rest should distribute them justly to all, without showing more honour to one than to another, so as to disturb scrupulous hearts; but all things ought to be common; for it seems wrong that some priests should have, while others suffer loss: and, as there is one Catholic faith, so it is needful, that he who has the care of the whole diocese, although there are in it many churches, should yet faithfully distribute to them all.'

It was found, however, that this canon could not be put in force; and the question was soon again raised, at the Council

---

[1] App. to Pithou's *Codex Canonum Vetus Ecclesiæ Romanæ*, Paris 1687, pp. 398-400, 417, 418; also Bouquet, *Recueil des Histoires*, vol. x. p. 440; and Galland, *Bibliotheca Veterum Patrum*, vol. xiv. p. 151.

[2] Grat. *Decret.*, pars ii., causa xvi., quæst. 7, cap. 1.

of Clermont¹ (A.D. 1095) 'as to churches and ecclesiastical possessions, acquired without the sanction of bishops from clerks and monks.' Pope Urban II. found it necessary, 'for the sake of peace, and to avoid scandal,' to confirm all such titles, acquired (however irregularly) from clerks, monks, *or other persons*, in favour of those who were then in possession under them;—at the same time prohibiting their creation for the future without the bishop's consent.

Even this did not stop those alienations. In A.D. 1100, a Council of Poictiers² denounced, as no better than heretics and antichrists, certain bishops who were reported to have bestowed the tithes and oblations of their people, 'not on the priests of their dioceses, but on lay persons—soldiers, servants, and (worst of all) their own kindred.' Pope Alexander III.,³ confirming a canon of a Council of Tours (A.D. 1163), took notice that, bad as it was for laymen to usurp ecclesiastical revenues which properly belonged to the priests, they were sometimes encouraged in that error by the clergy themselves: bishops and other prelates giving them permission to dispose at their will of tithes, and even of churches. And he decreed that any one who should grant to a layman, continuing such (*alicui laico, in sæculo remanenti*), any tithe or oblation, should be degraded from his office, until he made amends. The same Pope had, shortly before,⁴ declared a grant of tithes made in perpetuity to a layman by the Abbot of Montreuil to be void; and had ordered its recipient to be excommunicated, until he should

---

¹ Grat. *Decret.*, pars ii., causa xvi. quæst. 7, cap. 2.
² *Ibid.*, cap. 3, where the canon of this council is attributed to Gregory VII. See Richter's note, *Corpus Juris Canonici*, Leipsic 1839, vol. i. p. 689.
³ *Decret. Greg. IX.*, lib. iii., tit. xxx., cap. 17. See Richter's note.
⁴ *Ibid.*, cap. 15.

release his claim 'freely and absolutely' to the Church. In the third Lateran Council (A.D. 1179), the same Pope made a celebrated constitution,[1] often afterwards referred to by English common lawyers, as having put an end to the free appropriation of their tithes by laymen, which (in practice) until then existed. The form of that constitution varied in different manuscripts. According to some it ran thus: 'We forbid laymen, detaining tithes at their soul's peril, to transfer the title to them, by any means, to others: and if any one shall receive, and not restore them to the Church, let him be deprived of Christian burial.' This form of prohibition may, or may not, justify the construction placed upon it by English lawyers. Other manuscripts, however, confined it to grants of tithes to laymen;[2] and qualified it by the exception of gifts to which the bishop might have consented. It is not improbable that it may have been known, in this country, in its more unqualified form.

[1] *Decret. Greg. IX.*, lib. iii. tit. xxx., cap. 19. See various readings in Richter's notes (*Corp. Jur. Canon.*, 1839, vol. ii. p. 341). Selden agreed with the English lawyers: 'Whoever' (he says) 'observes the practice of the preceding time only, and the words both of that council, and to the same purpose of the other held under Calixtus II., may well enough be persuaded that the intent of those canons was not otherwise.' And, after referring to the narrower construction of Innocent III. and later Roman canonists, he adds, 'They may, as they will, understand it by judicial application; but you may, at least, doubt still that the historical understanding of it is to be had out of arbitrary consecrations before practised' (*Hist. of Tithes*, ch. 4, § 7 *ad finem*).

[2] See, as to feudalised tithes, which had become so before the Lateran Council of A.D. 1179, and the lay titles to which were recognised by Continental Jurisprudence, Jouy, *Principes et Usages*, etc., ch. i.

CHAPTER III

PRACTICAL WORKING OF THE CUSTOMS OF APPORTIONMENT

THE practical working of the apportionment of church revenues under the older organisation invites attention, before tracing the transition from the system of ancient baptismal churches to that of modern parishes.

§ 1. *The Shares of Bishop and Clergy.*

Of the bishop's share, either of tithes or of other diocesan revenues, not much needs to be said. It was intended to provide him with the means, not only of supporting himself and his *familia* (his ecclesiastical household, however constituted), and meeting other necessary expenses, but also[1] of maintaining the hospitality becoming his office. The manner of doing this was left to his own conscience. Unless in Spain (where, as has been seen, the burden of church repairs was thrown upon it), the bishop's share does not appear to have been interfered with, except when his functions as diocesan were temporarily in abeyance. On one such occasion, in the diocese of Rimini, Gregory the Great[2] directed the shares of the

[1] See Gregory the Great's letter to Augustin (Bede, *Hist.*, lib. i., § 27): '*Una episcopo et familiæ propter hospitalitatem atque susceptionem.*'
[2] Ep. 44, lib. v., indict. 13 (Benedictine ed. of St. Maur, Paris 1705, tom. ii. p. 774).

bishop and the fabric to be added together, and divided into three parts; one for the support of the incumbent of the see, another for the bishop appointed by Gregory himself to administer the diocese, and the third for repairs. On another, during a visitation of the diocese of Girgenti, by a bishop acting as his Commissary, the whole fourth share of the diocesan bishop, accruing while the visitation lasted, was ordered by the same Pope[1] to be paid to the visitor.

As to the share of the clergy, the rule of Pope Gelasius[2] was, that the bishop should distribute it, having regard to the ranks and merits of those who were to participate, according to his own judgment. Gregory the Great[3] recommended a bishop (of Palermo) to appoint annually a *tabularius*, or steward, of the clergy's portion, to make distribution among those clergy whose names were inscribed on lists or tablets to be kept by him. But Gregory, like Gelasius, acknowledged no other rule of distribution than the bishop's reasonable discretion. An appeal was made to him by certain priests of the diocese of Catania, who were dissatisfied with what their bishop had done; but the only direction given by Gregory[4] was, that the fourth portion of all revenues which might come to the Church from the rents or profits of land, or by any other title, should be set apart without deduction, and divided 'dis-

[1] Ep. 12, lib. v., indict. 13 (Benedictine ed. of St. Maur, Paris 1705, tom. ii. p. 737).
[2] In his letter to the Bishops of Dardania, '*clericis pro officiorum suorum sedulitate distribuat;*' and in the first letter to the Church officers of Volterra, '*clericis pro suo judicio et electione dispertiat*'—qualified in the second letter to those officers, by reference to the bishop's 'knowledge of the place and merit of each of them' (Mansi, *Concil.*, vol. viii. pp. 121, 114, 130).
[3] Ep. 44, lib. xiii. indict. 6 (ed. 1705, tom. ii. 1249).
[4] Ep. 7, lib. viii. indict. 1 (ed. 1705, tom. ii. p. 899).

creetly, and in the fear of God,' among the priests, deacons, and clerks in minor orders; with full liberty for the bishop to determine how much each ought to receive, according to his own opinion of the quality and value of their respective services. Later canons of Councils[1] affirmed the same principle, down to the end of the ninth century; though, doubtless, in each *familia* or body of clergy, the course of precedent and practice had its usual effect, and tended to establish an ordinary proportionate rate of dividend, as between different ranks and orders. All participated, unless excluded by some fault of their own; but those higher in office received more than those who were lower: priests received more than deacons, and deacons more than sub-deacons, acolytes, exorcists, readers, or doorkeepers.

§ 2. *The Fabric Fund.*

The fabric fund, according to the rule of Gelasius, was to be laid out by the church officers, under the bishop's direction; and any surplus from the expenditure of any year was to be kept in store for the enlargement or improvement of fabrics, or invested in some property productive of revenue 'for the common good.'[2]

The uses of this fund were for repairs; for lighting the churches, with *luminaria* of wax or oil; and for supplying necessary vestments, vessels, and other 'ornaments.'

The churches for which it was provided were the 'greater' or 'baptismal,'[3] and not those on private men's

---

[1] *E.g.*, the sixth Canon of Worms (A.D. 868), which states the rule of quadripartite division in the exact words of the letter of Pope Gelasius to the Bishops of Dardania (Mansi, *Concil.*, vol. xv. p. 871).

[2] Letters to the Church officers of Volterra (*ibid.*, vol. viii. pp. 114-130).

[3] Capitular of Pavia, A.D. 877, art. 11 (Baluze, *Capit. Reg. Franc.*, vol. ii. p. 242). See *post*, pp. 73, 74.

estates. Even the greater or baptismal churches, within the limits of 'benefices' or lands held by noblemen under the Church, were to be kept in proper repair and condition by them;[1] relieving, to that extent, the diocesan fabric fund. Those 'benefices' were granted upon the terms of paying, by way of rent-service, what were called 'ninths and tenths'[2] to the bishops or ecclesiastical corporations who granted them; and bishops receiving 'ninths and tenths' were bound[3] to see that this duty of their grantees, as to church repairs and lights, was properly performed.

With respect to churches or oratories built by private persons on their own lands, the rights of patronage and other proprietary rights conceded to the founders were subject to the condition, that they should not be destroyed, but should be reverentially preserved.[4]

As to the public churches, it was the duty of every

---

[1] Frankfort capitular, A.D. 794, art. 24: '*Ut ecclesiæ per eos restaurentur, qui beneficia habeant*' (Baluze, vol. i. p. 267); and canon of Mentz, A.D. 813, art. 5 (Mansi, *Concil.*, vol. xiv.) The word *beneficium*, as used in the Middle Ages, meant *prædium fiscale, quod a Rege vel Principe, vel ab alio quolibet, ad vitam viro nobili utendum conceditur* (Ducange, *in verbo*).

[2] See Thomassinus, *De Beneficiis* (Mentz 1787, tom. iii., lib. i. cap. 8, entitled *Nonæ et decimæ*): '*Qui jure beneficiario fundos ecclesiæ obtinebant laici, decimas ei et nonas solvere tenebantur.*' Also Selden, *Hist. of Tithes*, ch. 6, § 6. The law of Pepin, of A.D. 764, quoted by Prideaux (*Origin and Right of Tithes*, p. 96), relates, not to tithes generally, but to these '*ninths and tenths.*'

[3] See Lombard capitular of A.D. 801, art. 43 (Baluze, vol. i. p. 356): '*Ut vos episcopi, qui in omnibus nonas et decimas accipitis, in vestra providentia sit, quatenus ecclesiæ vel capellæ quæ in vestra parochia sunt emendentur, et luminaria eis præbeatis, ut in eis presbyteri vivere possint.*'

[4] Frankfort capitular, A.D. 794, art. 52 (*ibid.*, p. 269): '*De ecclesiis quæ ab ingenuis hominibus construantur, licet eas tradere, vendere, tantummodo ut ecclesia non destruatur, sed serventur quotidie honores.* As to the power of alienation and sale, see *post*, pp. 81-83.

bishop, under the Frankfort capitulars and the Salz[1] capitular of A.D. 804, to see that those within his diocese were well built and repaired, and also to look after their 'offices and lights.' By the capitulars of Thionville[2] (A.D. 805) reformation was directed to be made of neglected churches, 'without offices or lights;' and also of those 'who received tithes without taking care of the churches.' The Council of Toul[3] (A.D. 859) decreed that 'the churches should be repaired and restored by those who had the use of their possessions; and that all members of the clerical or monastic body belonging to each of them (*ex earum familia*[4]) should assist, as far as possible, in their re-edification.' The capitulars of Charles the Bald at Pavia[5] (A.D. 877), in which Archbishop Hincmar of Rheims, and other Transalpine bishops present concurred, directed the baptismal churches, called *plebes*, to be repaired by 'the sons of the church,' according to ancient custom (*ut ecclesias baptismales, quas plebes appellant, secundum antiquam consuetudinem, ecclesiæ*

---

[1] Baluze, vol. i. p. 415 (art. 1): '*Ut ecclesiæ Dei bene constructæ et restauratæ fiant, et episcopi, unusquisque infra suam parochiam, exinde bonam habeant providentiam, tam de officio et luminariis, quam et de reliqua instauratione.*'

[2] *Ibid.*, p. 421 (art. 6): '*De ecclesiis sine honore manentibus, absque officiis et luminariis, et de his qui decimas quidem adsumunt, et de ecclesiis non curant, ut omnimodis emendetur.*'

[3] Mansi, *Concil.*, vol. xv. p. 539 (art. 11): '*Ut ecclesiæ sarciantur et restaurentur in ædificiis ab his qui earum rebus utuntur, aut ab unoquoque tale ex earum familia præbeatur adjutorium, per quod, si fieri potest, reædificetur.*'

[4] Ducange explains '*familia ecclesiæ*' as including all who owe service to the Church; and, as used with respect to monasteries, all who share the conventual life. Examples of that use of the word, as to cathedral chapters and other religious houses in the Anglo-Saxon Church (of the years 813, 824, and 844, etc.), will be found in Haddan and Stubbs, *Councils*, etc., vol. iii. pp. 515, 575, 580, 581, 582, 595, 617, 629.

[5] Baluze, vol. ii. p. 242.

filii instaurent);—the canonical power of the bishop over tithes being mentioned in the same context.

Archbishop Hincmar,[1] and Bishop Riculf[2] of Soissons, in their constitutions of A.D. 858 and 889 (both enjoining the quadripartite division), directed yearly accounts of the expenditure of the fabric fund to be rendered to the bishop or his officers; showing how much had been laid out for oil or wax-lights, how much for structural repairs, and how much for 'ornaments.'

§ 3. *The Poor's Fund.*

With the poor, widows and orphans, sick and infirm, were associated strangers (*hospites*), foreigners or pilgrims (*peregrini*), and captives. In some laws the poor only, in some (*e.g.*, in Bishop Riculf's[3] constitutions) strangers (*hospites*) only were mentioned. But, when one of these classes was mentioned, all might be understood as comprehended.

Van Espen[4] says, that the portion of the poor, as well as that of the clergy, was distributable according to the bishop's discretion, having regard to the greater or less indigence and merits of particular persons. For this, he quotes an Epistle of Pope Gregory[5] the Great, recommending larger gifts to honest and poor men who were not common beggars, and smaller to those who were. The first Council of

---

[1] Mansi, vol. xv. p. 480.

[2] *Ibid.*, vol. xviii. p. 85 (art. 11): '*Ex ipsa parte, quæ fabricis debetur ecclesiæ, volumus aut per nos, aut per nostros comministros, rescire quid annuatim, tam in luminaribus olei vel ceræ, quam etiam in restauratione tectorum, vel in ornamentis, inde in ecclesia pareat.*' The '*comministri*,' here mentioned, were (probably) the *oeconomus* and the archdeacon.

[3] (*Ubi supra*): '*Quarta hospitibus deputata.*'

[4] *Jus Canon. Univ.*, pars ii., sect. 4, tit. i., cap. 6, § 13.

[5] Ep. 29, lib. ix.

Orleans,[1] in the same spirit, directed the bishop, as far as he could (*in quantum possibilitas habuerit*), to give food and clothing to those who, by reason of infirmity, could not labour with their own hands. Poor persons of the bishop's own kindred were not excluded. A canon, attributed to a Council of Worms[2] (A.D. 868), said that 'the bishop was to have the care of all Church temporalities, and to dispense them as in God's sight, not for himself or for his relations; but that, if any of his relations were poor, he might give them aid. He might dispense to all who were in need; he might himself, if in need, supply out of them his own necessary wants, and also the wants of those brethren who lived with him (*fratrum, qui ab eo suscipiuntur*).'

Poor clerks were admitted to participate in this share, as is plain from a sentence in Hincmar's ordinances of A.D. 874, excluding from such participation priests degraded for certain causes. Of monks, bound by vows of poverty, and often called 'Christ's poor,' I shall afterwards speak.

All these charitable objects were provided for in the Eastern Church, by organised institutions — *ptochia* or '*ptochodochia*'[3] (poor-houses); '*orphanotrophia*' and '*gerocomia*'[4] (houses for orphans and aged persons); and '*xenodochia*'[5] (guest-houses or hospices). They were all under ecclesiastical superintendence, and had churches or

[1] Mansi, vol. viii. p. 347.

[2] *Ibid.*, vol. xv. p. 871. This canon (art. 46) is not in the older copies of the Acts of that council.

[3] Eighth Canon of Chalcedon (*ibid.*, vol. vi. p. 1227), and see Van Espen's quotation from Zonaras (*Opera*, vol. iii. p. 248).

[4] See Van Espen's quotation from Balsamon, Patriarch of Antioch in the twelfth century (*Opera*, ed. 1753-59, vol. iii. p. 249).

[5] Mansi vol. ii. p. 947.

chapels in or near them. Canons,[1] received in some parts of the East as Nicene (not, however, really made by the Council of Nicæa), directed that there should be in every cathedral city a *xenodochium*, 'set apart for strangers, infirm, and poor,'[2] and that the bishop should choose and set over it a 'brother';—if possible, an anchorite; who was to be called the guardian of the poor (in the Latin translation, *procurator pauperum*); also, that collections should be made for them from all Christians, if the goods of the Church were not sufficient.

The principles of those arrangements were followed in the Western Church. At Rome there was an officer called by the same name, *procurator pauperum*; an office which continued to exist, at least in name, until recent times.[3] Othelon,[4] who wrote in the twelfth century the *Life of St. Boniface*, lamenting over the departure, then general, from the ancient rules for the distribution of Church revenues, said: 'The holy canons, by authority of which tithes are paid, required not that only, but that they should be distributed among the various uses of the Church; and that there should be in some cities and towns guest-houses (*xenodochia*) established, for the support of poor men and foreigners (*peregrini*).' In the eighth century there were houses of entertainment provided for the alms-people of baptismal churches, usually adjoining them; which, from one of the titles of those churches (*matrix ecclesia*), were

[1] These canons were translated from Arabic into Latin, and published A.D. 1551, by the Spanish Jesuit Francis Turrianus.
[2] Canon 70. '*Ut sit in omnibus civitatibus locus separatus peregrinis, infirmis, et pauperibus, qui vocetur xenodochium, id est, hospitium peregrinorum.*'
[3] See Mansi's note, *Concil.*, vol. ii. (to the canons of Turrianus, just cited): '*Sic Romæ vocatur hodie procurator pauperum.*'
[4] Quoted by Kemble, *Saxons in England* (1876), vol. ii. p. 479, note.

called *matriculæ*;[1] and the same name, *matricula*, was also applied to a book,[2] in which the names of those admitted as alms-people of the Church were inscribed. In the ninth century those persons only who had been regularly admitted, or 'matriculated,' as alms-people or bedesmen of the particular church, were recognised as having claims to relief upon the ground of poverty.

The statutes of Corbey, and of some other monasteries, ordered lodging, food, and clothing to be given to those whose names were in the matriculation book; requiring from them in return services to the house, of which they were (in effect) lay brethren.[3] They were to be treated on the same footing with the other servants of the house, and were (with them) to have the first share in every distribution of food. The monks belonging to the house were often themselves called *matricularii*.[4] Alcuin, when Abbot of St. Martin's at Tours, in a letter to Charlemagne[5] (written in A.D. 801), so styled himself. There was an officer of each baptismal church or monastery, like the *procurator pauperum*, charged with the care of the matriculated poor.[6]

Archbishop Hincmar's ordinances of A.D. 858[7] gave injunctions to his commissaries and rural deans, as the foundation of annual inquiries to be made by them in all the mother churches and chapels of the province,

---

[1] Ducange, *in voce* 'Matricula.'   [2] *Ibid.*

[3] Ducange, *in voce* 'Matricularii' (quoting Adelard and Guerard): '*In matriculam ecclesiæ inscripti, sub servitiis quibusdam in monasterio præstandis, inibi tectum, victum, vestitum invenerunt.*'

[4] Hence the modern use of the term 'matriculation,' for admission to universities.

[5] See Haddan and Stubbs, *Councils*, etc., vol. iii. p. 533.

[6] From the name of this office the modern French term for church-wardens (*marguilliers*) is derived.

[7] Mansi, *Concil.*, vol. xv. p. 481 (art. 16, 17).

and of reports to himself. One of these injunctions (already quoted) prescribed the quadripartite division of tithes before witnesses. The next enjoined the priests of the churches to which tithes were payable to admit to matriculation persons suitable to the quality of the place (*ut matricularios habeant juxta qualitatem loci*); 'not cowherds or swine-herds, but infirm and poor persons, and of the same lordship' (*de codem dominio*); with an exception in favour of any brother or other relative of the priest, who might be infirm or very poor, whom he was permitted to maintain out of the tithe (*qui de eadem decima sustentetur*).

The same prelate returned to that subject in a charge to the priests of the province, in his synod held at Rheims A.D. 874.[1]

'I have often' (he said) 'admonished you concerning the matriculated, what sort of persons you ought to admit, and how you ought to dispense to them their portion of the tithe. But I have found that there are some who take little heed to our admonition, which indeed is God's own, through our instrumentality, small as we are. Wherefore it is necessary to repeat what I know some to neglect. I forbade you, speaking by God's authority, that any priest should presume, in return for an entry of any name in the book, to require or accept any present (*xenium*), or harvest-work, or other kind of service to himself; or that any one should presume to sell that part of the tithe which is due to the matriculated, and which the faithful, as ransom for their sins, offer to the Lord.'

It appears, therefore, that in Hincmar's time the poor, who had the benefit of a share in the quadripartite division of tithes, were only those whose names were inscribed for that purpose in the 'matriculation' book of the dispensing Church. And from Eadmer's narrative of St. Oswald's life[2]

---

[1] Mansi, vol. xv. p. 494.
[2] Wharton's *Anglia Sacra*, vol. ii. p. 195.

when in the monastery of Fleury, in the succeeding century, it may be collected that the practice of the diocese of Orleans was then the same; and that this was the mode of administering the 'poor's share' of Church revenues, with which foreigners, visiting the greater Gallican Churches and religious houses (such as Fleury and Corbey), in the ninth century, would naturally become acquainted. 'Before the doors of a certain crypt (at Fleury) twelve poor men were wont, according to ancient usage, to assemble and receive the supply of their daily needs from the church; men of such dispositions, that all were associated together in the study of learning, all were clerks (*ut omnes literarum socii, omnes clerici essent*).' One of these alms-men was selected by Oswald to wait upon and assist him at mass.

It has been intimated that the monks, as 'Christ's poor,'[1] might themselves advance claims to participate in, even to absorb, the 'poor's share;' and it is not doubtful that they did so. The Eastern monks of the fifth century were ordinary sharers in the alms distributed by the bishops:[2] and the same principle was recognised in the West. In the *Decretum* of Gratian,[3] a chapter entitled '*The Clergy are free to grant Tithes to Monks*,' is represented as taken from a letter of St. Jerome to Pope Damasus; though no such letter was really written by that Father. I translate the material parts of it :

---

[1] Ducange, *in voce* 'Pauperes Christi'; and Selden : 'The distribution of tenths also to the poor according to the owner's free will (which I take to be consecrations or grants to monasteries, for the monks were usually called *pauperes*, and were so indeed by their vow) was expressly complained of, as a great fault of the time, by Pope Innocent III.' (*Hist. of Tithes*, ch. 6, § 2, p. 78, ed. 1618).

[2] See Moreri, *Dictionnaire, in voce* 'Moines.'

[3] Pars ii., causa xvi., quæst. 1, cap. 68.

'Inasmuch as whatever the clergy have belongs to the poor, and their houses ought to be common to all, it is their duty to attend diligently to the entertainment of foreigners and strangers (*peregrinorum et hospitum*). Especially should it be their care to lay out as much as they are willing and able, out of the tithes and oblations which they receive, upon convents and guest-houses (*coenobiis et xenodochiis*). For they are free to grant their tithes and oblations and all other benefits (*remedia*) to monks and spiritual persons fearing and worshipping God, and to transfer both the ownership and the use of them from themselves to such religious men (*de jure suo in dominium illorum et usum transferre*); and in the poor to consider not so much poverty as religion (*nec tam in pauperibus paupertatem quam religionem attendere*). As to the question which your Holiness has asked, whether it be possible for secular persons to acquire a right to the use of tithes and oblations, your Holiness knows that it is quite unlawful; the divine authority of the canons of our fathers forbidding it. Wherefore, if things which are known to be of divine right shall have at any time been wrongly detained by such persons, and afterwards have passed to the use of monks and servants of God with the consent of the diocesan bishop, they should all be secured to them, and sustained by firm and sure titles for ever.'

It may be added, that after the time of Gratian the preaching friars regarded so jealously the receipt of tithes or other endowments by the secular clergy, that Gregory IX.[1] found it necessary to forbid them to encourage their hearers to refuse payment of tithes and other things due to churches.

[1] *Sexti Decret.*, lib. iii., tit. xiii., cap. 1: '*Fratribus Prædicatoribus et Minoribus:—Discretioni vestræ mandamus, districtius inhibentes, ne talia, quæ audientes a decimarum, seu aliarum rerum ecclesiæ debitarum, solutione retrahant, vel alias animas corrumpant audientium, in sermonibus vestris vel alibi proponere de cætero præsumatis.*' The Dominican and Franciscan friars (says Selden) 'falsely taught them' (*i.e.* tithes) 'not at all payable but arbitrarily as alms, even since parochial right in them established' (*Hist. of Tithes*, ed. 1618, Preface, p. xiv.) 'By this doctrine' (he adds, in ch. 7, p. 166), 'the Mendicants especially often got them to themselves.'

CHAPTER IV

TRANSITION TO THE PAROCHIAL SYSTEM

§ 1. *Private Oratories.*

FROM an early date, private oratories or chapels were built and consecrated upon the estates of powerful laymen.

The rule was, that no one should build such a church before the bishop of the diocese came and publicly set a cross on the ground, and marked out the intended precinct (*atrium*); and the founder was required, by an instrument of gift to be produced before consecration, to make reasonable provision for its lighting and due care, and for the wages of those (*custodes*), who should be put in charge of it.[1]

Such oratories were, for some purposes, private property, of which the proprietor might dispose as he pleased. The Frankfort capitulars[2] (A.D. 794) permitted them to be bought and sold. It was not until a late period, when their character had been changed, that the restrictions upon the rights of founders of churches, stated in very wide terms by Pope Gelasius, and by the ninth Council of Toledo (A.D. 657), were held to be applicable to them. Gelasius[3] had said

---

[1] Note, Burchard, lib. iii.; Canon of Orleans, A.D. 511 (Mansi, *Concil.*, vol. viii., 363); and see *ibid.*, vol. xv. p. 563, and Baluze, *Cap. Reg. Franc.*, vol. i. p. 1570.   [2] (Art. 52), *ibid.*, vol. i. p. 267.
[3] See extracts from two of his decretal epistles, in Gratian's *Decretum*, pars ii., causa xvi., quæst. vii., cap. 26, 27.

that the builder of a church should not, after consecration, have any private right in it, except that of access to public worship, due to every Christian (*præter processionis aditum, qui omni Christiano debetur*). The canon of Toledo[1] is long and special; but its effect is summarised in the gloss of Gratian:[2] 'The founders of churches have the right of protecting them, of taking counsel for them, and of finding priests to serve them: but they have no right to sell them, nor to give them away, nor to use them as their own property.' The canon of the Roman Council held under Leo IV.[3] (A.D. 848-854), which forbade the taking away of a monastery or oratory, canonically erected, 'from the dominion' of the founder (*a dominio constructoris*), against his will, and which recognised his right of patronage, might be reconcilable with either the larger or the more restricted power. Pope Innocent III. (who was in the habit of taking from Gratian his rules of judgment,[4] and who exalted to the highest point ecclesiastical against lay authority), in his decretal[5] to which the rubric, '*Laymen, even Kings, cannot give churches or tithes, nor can a prescription be founded on such grants,*' is prefixed, held that if, in the grant of a church, a layman used such words as 'I give you such a church,' they must be understood only of his right of patronage; and that nothing more would pass.

[1] Mansi, *Concil.*, vol. ii. p. 26.
[2] *Decretum*, pars ii., causa xvi., quæst. vii., cap. 30.
[3] *Ibid.*, cap. 33.
[4] That Pope had a high reputation as a canonist. Van Espen (*Opera*, vol. iii. p. 69) says that he used the *Decretum* of Gratian, as 'the purest fountain of canon law.'—'*Atque in Gratiano contenta sine discrimine aut examine, num sincera vel supposititia sint, integra an mutilata, in decisionum quarum fundamenta assumat, et secundum ista sine ulla hesitatione resolvat,*' etc.
[5] *Decret. Greg. IX.*, lib. iii., tit. xxx., cap. 31. (About A.D. 1212.)

In the ninth century, and later, when the system of lay investitures prevailed, and the see of Rome itself was to a great extent under lay control, the founders of this class of churches practically exercised larger rights. Such churches were liable, like other inheritances, to be divided among co-heirs. At the Council of Chalons[1] (A.D. 813) a complaint was made of scandals resulting from that cause. There were sometimes three or four co-proprietors of the same altar, who quarrelled, and each appointed his own priest. To remedy those evils, the council decreed that in such cases the performance of masses should be interdicted, until all the co-heirs were so far reconciled as to agree in the appointment of one priest, who might do the duty of his office without disturbance. Another ordinance (of uncertain authorship), found in the collections of Benedict the Levite,[2] Regino,[3] Burchard,[4] and Ivo,[5] and which was ascribed by Gratian[6] to Gregory the Great, provided that if, in any case of division and dispute among co-heirs, the bishop's interposition should prove fruitless, it should be competent to him to determine whether he would allow the churches to remain open, or would remove from them the 'relics' by which they were (supposed to be) sanctified. This was converted into a peremptory law by the Council of Tribur[7] (A.D. 895); decreeing that, 'if co-heirs should be in contention concerning a church belonging

---

[1] Mansi, *Concil.*, vol. xiii. p. 98.
[2] Lib. v., cap. 99 (Baluze, *Cap. Reg. Franc.*, vol. i.)
[3] *De disciplinis Ecclesiasticis*, etc., lib. i., cap. 242.
[4] *Magnum volumen Canonum*, lib. iii., cap. 41.
[5] *Exceptiones Ecclesiasticarum Regularum*, part iii., cap. 45.
[6] *Decretum*, pars ii., causa xvi., quæst. 7, cap. 35. (See, as to all these canonists, Introduction, *ante*, pp. 10 and 19.)
[7] Cap. 32 (Mansi, *Concil.*, vol. xviii. p. 139).

to them in common, the bishop shall order the holy relics to be taken away, and the church to be shut up, until, by common consent, with the bishop's concurrence, they appoint a priest to do the duty, with sufficient provision for his subsistence.'

By Charlemagne's capitular of Salz[1] (A.D. 804), it was enacted, that whoever desired to build a church upon his own property might do so, with the bishop's consent; but under the condition (repeated in later laws)[2] that 'the more ancient churches should not, on that account, lose their tithes or any other rights.'

The great men who built those oratories and chapels, and their vassals or 'villeins' (for whose benefit and convenience they were usually built), frequented them in preference to the older and more distant churches.[3] There was a constant tendency to demand for them increased privileges, and greater independence of episcopal control; and this pressure, long opposed by the bishops, proved at last too strong to be resisted. But the change did not take place until after the death of Charlemagne.

§ 2. *Ordinances of Louis the Pious, and their Results.*

On the accession of Louis the Pious to the empire, the foundations of the future parochial system were laid at Aix-la-Chapelle, in the great Council of A.D. 816.[4] The ordinances there made were agreed to 'for the benefit of the

---

[1] Baluze, *Capit.*, vol. i. p. 415.   [2] *Ante*, p. 62.
[3] Capitular of A.D. 855 (Baluze, vol. ii. p. 352).
[4] Baluze, *Capit.*, vol. i. p. 565; and see his note, vol. ii. p. 1149: '*Ante constitutionem istam decimæ non pertinebant ad ecclesias noviter fundatas, sed ad antiquiores ecclesias.*'

whole church' (*pro utilitate totius ecclesiæ*), by an assembly of bishops, abbots, counts, and heads of great Frank families (*majorum natu Francorum*), from all parts of the empire.

By the fourth article of those memorable laws it was provided that, whatever, since the accession of the Emperor Louis, might have been voluntarily given to the Church by the faithful, and not specially appropriated by the donors, should be divided, in the richer places, into three parts— two for the poor, and one for the clerks or monks; in smaller places, into two equal parts—one for the clergy, the other for the poor. But this division was not to be made when the will of the donors had been expressed to the contrary (*nisi forte a datoribus, ubi specialiter dandæ sint, constitutum fuerit*);—when the donors had given their gifts a particular destination, that destination was to prevail.

The ninth article prohibited the appointment of priests to, or their removal from, the churches of lay founders, without the bishop's authority. But it guarded that prohibition by another, forbidding the rejection by the bishop, on any pretext, of a clerk of good life and sound doctrine, presented by a lay patron for ordination to his own church.

The tenth article required, 'that to every church one entire manse, free from all service, should be assigned; and that the priests appointed to the churches should do ecclesiastical service only for their tithes, for the offerings of the faithful, for their houses of residence, for the precincts or gardens adjoining the churches, and for the necessary manse.' For any endowment in land beyond these, they were to render the same services to the lord of the seignory, as would in any other case be due.

Subject to those requirements, the eleventh article

directed, that every church should have its own priest, if means for his support were provided to the satisfaction of the bishop.

And by the twelfth article (the most important in its consequences, and the greatest innovation upon the earlier laws of all) it was enacted, that *the tithes* arising within new townships, in which new churches were founded, *might be granted to those churches; (sancitum est, de villis novis, et ecclesiis in eis noviter constitutis, ut decimæ de illis villis ad easdem ecclesias conferantur).*

Even in Charlemagne's time, episcopal founders[1] of new churches had, in some cases, granted the tithes of lands belonging to their sees, by way of endowment, to such churches. But, until these capitulars of Aix, there was no legal power for founders, even with the consent of bishops, to do so to the prejudice of older churches. It was forbidden by the Imperial laws[2] already mentioned.

After this new legislation at Aix-la-Chapelle, the endowment of new churches with manses and with tithes by lay founders, with the consent of the diocesan bishops, gradually became common. Districts were assigned to the churches so endowed; and those districts, before the end of that century, acquired the name of 'rural parishes' (*rusticanæ parochiæ*). Under that name Archbishop Hincmar, in A.D. 874,[3] laid down rules for their visitation by his archdeacons.

---

[1] See the 'Form,' No. 11, of Marculfus (Baluze, *Capit.*, vol. ii. p. 442), by which a bishop, in the seventh year of Charlemagne's empire, with the consent of his chapter, endowed with two manses, and with arable land and a vineyard, a church built and consecrated by him for four specified townships (*villæ*) which were to regard that as the church to which they were to resort for hearing masses and for baptism and preaching, *and to which they should pay their tithes.* See *post*, Appendix II.   [2] *Ante*, p. 62.

[3] Mansi, *Concil.*, vol. xv. p. 494 (art. 1-4 and 7).

By degrees the celebration of all the sacraments and rites of the Church in the churches of those rural parishes, and burials in their consecrated precincts, were allowed by episcopal authority. This change made further legislation necessary, as to conflicting claims to tithes; as to seignorial rights claimed over those endowments of rural parishes which were not expressly exonerated from them by the capitulars of Aix; and as to the subdivision of those parishes themselves.

In the Lombard Laws of Lothair[1] (A.D. 830) there is a provision, that the townships, from which each church was to receive tithes, should be defined by boundaries: (*'Ut terminum habeat unaquæque ecclesia, de quibus villis decimam accipiat'*).

Rodolph, Archbishop of Bourges[2] (A.D. 850), reciting that 'there were some who neglected to give their tithes to their own churches, where they and their servants heard mass,' decreed that 'all should there give their tithes where their children were baptized and where they heard masses, as should appear, in the bishop's judgment, to be suitable to the circumstances of each case.'

The appropriation of the tithes of newly cultivated lands was the subject of a capitular of the Emperor Louis II.[3] (A.D. 867), which provided that the tithes of such lands, when adjacent to those already in cultivation, should be paid to the older church; (which I understand, in this place, to mean the baptismal or other church already existing, which received the tithes of the lands already in cultivation). But if, at a distance of more than four or five miles, any 'worthy person' (*digna persona*) should have recently re-

---

[1] Baluze, *Capit.*, vol. ii. p. 340.   [2] Mansi, *Concil.*, vol. xiv. p. 954.
[3] Baluze, *Capit.*, vol. ii. p. 364.

claimed wild or forest land, and should have built a church there with the bishop's consent, he was to be at liberty, when the new church was consecrated, or afterwards, to provide for it a priest, and to endow it with the tithes of the newly reclaimed lands. A canon to the like effect was made by the Council of Tribur[1] (A.D. 895).

There were in those days some churches, for the maintenance of which, with a priest to serve in them, no adequate provision had been made when they were consecrated. Walter, Bishop of Orleans,[2] in A.D. 858, made an ordinance in his diocesan synod, that the priests of any churches which had not received the endowments required by the capitulars of Aix-la-Chapelle should represent their cases to the bishop, in order that the lords of the seignories (*seniores*) might be prevailed upon to make good that neglect.

The same ordinance recognised the title of those 'seignors' to feudal services, for such lands as might be given to churches in excess of any legal requirements; and two constitutions, one attributed to the Council of Worms[3] (A.D. 868), and the other made by the Emperor Charles the Bald[4] in the following year, made the bishops arbiters between the parochial clergy and their lords, in any case of difference between them as to such seignorial rights.

The subdivision of rural parishes was regulated by the capitulars of Toulouse[5] (A.D. 844). The bishops were forbidden to divide 'the parishes of priests' (*parochias presbyterorum*) for any other consideration than the people's good. If there were a population so distant from the 'principal

---

[1] Mansi, *Concil.*, vol. xviii. p. 139. [2] *Ibid.*, vol. xv. p. 505.
[3] Art. 58 (which is not in the older manuscripts of the Acts of that Council), *ibid.*, p. 879.
[4] Baluze, *Capit.*, vol. ii. p. 212 (art. 9). [5] *Ibid.*, p. 24 (art. 7).

church' (*ecclesiam principalem*) that women, children, and infirm people could not safely and conveniently resort to it, and yet not so far but that the priest of that church might go there to minister to the people, the parish might remain undivided, and it would be enough, in such a case, to set up an altar (*statuatur altare*) in that place. But if the people did not desire this, or if it could not conveniently be done, the bishop might, after due consideration, divide the parish; making a proper apportionment of duties and charges between the priests of the old parish and the new.[1]

The Gallican bishops appear to have acted in matters of this kind by their archdeacons. Archbishop Hincmar,[2] in A.D. 874, instructed his archdeacons 'not to unite or divide rural parishes for the friendship, or on the solicitation, of any persons; nor to put those churches which were accustomed from old time to have priests of their own, (*quæ ex antiquo presbyteros habere solitæ fuerunt*), under other churches, as if they were chapels; nor to transfer chapels from those churches on which they had been from old time dependent, to other churches.' And he desired a return to be made to him in writing of all those older churches (*quæ antiquitus presbyteros habuerunt*), and of the chapels which had been from old time dependent on them (*capellas antiquitus illis subjectas*).

Decrees of the Synods of Ravenna[3] (A.D. 877), and of

---

[1] In the modern French law, before the Revolution, when such a division of parishes took place, by the erection of an *église succursale* into the church of a new parish (*paroisse*) or title (*titre*), the whole burden of church repair, including the choir or chancel, was thrown upon the parishioners of the new parish, and not upon the tithe liable to the repairs of the old church (Jouy, *Principes et Usages*, etc., pp. 330-333.)   [2] Mansi, *Concil.*, vol. xv. p. 494 (art. 7).
[3] *Ibid.*, vol. xvii. p. 340 (art. 48).

Metz[1] (A.D. 888), make it clear, that the tithes with which rural parishes were endowed were enjoyed beneficially by the priest-incumbents, and did not fall under any rule or custom of quadripartite, or tripartite, or other proportionate division.

The Synod of Ravenna ordered that every one should pay his tithes 'to that priest, in whose parish, and under the jurisdiction of whose bishop, he lived; he being appointed by the bishop to receive them' (*quia ad hoc recipiendum ab episcopo suo est constitutus*); and that no stranger, priest, or deacon (*levita*), should either carelessly or wilfully seek or accept any gift of these things, which by canonical right belonged to another (*alteri jure canonum debita*).

The Synod of Metz forbade the lord of any seignory (*nemo seniorum*) to take for himself any portion of tithes, (*de decimis aliquam portionem*); 'the priest alone, who served in that place to which of old time the consecration of the tithes had been made (*ubi antiquitus decimæ fuerunt consecratæ*), was to receive them without deduction, 'for his own support, and for keeping in good order the lights and buildings of the church, and providing himself with the priestly vestments, and other things of necessary use for his ministry;' (*in sui sustentationem, et ad luminaria concinnanda et basilicæ ædificia, vestimenta quoque sacerdotalia, et cætera utensilia suo ministerio congrua, obtinenda*).

Here we observe two things;—first, the use by that council of the term *consecration*, in the same sense in which Selden used it, to signify the endowment of particular churches with tithes; and, secondly, the Continental rule[2]

---

[1] Mansi, *Concil.*, vol. xviii. p. 78.
[2] See Coke, 2nd *Institute*, p. 653. Van Espen, *Jus Univ. Canon.*, pars ii., sect. 2, cap. 6, §§ 7, 10 *et seq.*

of throwing upon the parish priest, who received the tithes, the obligation to keep the church in repair and find himself in vestments, etc.; which rule in England[1] never prevailed, except so far as the rectors of parishes, receiving great tithes, were liable for the repair of the chancels of their churches.

§ 3. *Modern Roman Canon Law.*

In the modern canon law of the Roman Church (the *Decretum* of Gratian, and the constitutions of later Councils and Popes), the ancient quadripartite[2] division of tithes or other Church revenues is hardly (I think only twice[3]) mentioned; and then incidentally or argumentatively, and not as still in practical force and operation. When the churches of rural parishes became endowed with tithes, and those tithes were subtracted from the diocesan funds dis-

---

[1] Coke, 2nd *Inst.* p. 653; and Selden, *Hist. of Tithes*, Preface, p. v., ed. 1618. The modern French law, before the Revolution, threw upon the tithe-owner (where there was no sufficient fabric fund arising from endowments) the repair of the chancel or choir only of the fabric of the church of an ancient parish, and the obligation of supplying lights, vestments, and ornaments;—an ecclesiastical corporation, if *gros decimateur*, being liable in priority to a lay improprietor, owner of 'feudalised tithes.' (See Jouy, *Principes et Usages concernant les Dîmes*, Paris 1775, cap. 10, § 2, p. 297.) The repairs of the nave of the church were a burden on the parishioners.

[2] Of tripartite or any other mode of division than the ancient Roman, there is no mention at all.

[3] *Decret.*, pars ii., causa xvi., quæst. 1, cap. 63; and causa xxv., quæst. 1 (Initial position of the First Party). And see Van Espen, *Jus Univ. Canon.*, pars ii., sect. 2, tit. i., cap. 6, § 4: *Quamvis hodie non fiat ea reddituum ecclesiasticorum divisio in partes, quarum tertia aut quarta cedat fabricæ*, etc. In Dauphiné there was in force, as late as A.D. 1768, a special custom to apply one twenty-fourth part of the tithes for the benefit of the poor of the parishes in which the tithes arose. (Jouy, *ubi supra*, cap. 10, § 37, p. 337.)

tributable under the ancient system, the old baptismal churches naturally sought exoneration, as to the tithes and other endowments which they still retained, from deductions and charges which might have left the wants of their clergy and religious services insufficiently provided for. And, accordingly, they obtained from Rome grants of privileges, authorising them to retain for their own uses the tithes which they received. The validity and effect of such Papal grants to baptismal churches was examined by Gratian in the *Decretum*,[1] under the form of a controversy between a monastery, setting up a Papal exemption from tithes, and a baptismal church, claiming tithes for its own benefit out of lands belonging to that monastery. In the argument for the monastery, the rule of quadripartite division was insisted on; no one (they contended) was more bound than the Pope to observe 'the decrees of the holy canons;' and the conclusion was drawn, that the privilege granted to the clergy of the baptismal church did not entitle them to claim the tithes for themselves (*quod auctoritate illius privilegii decimas sibi ex integro vendicare non valeant*).[2] But Gratian's determination[3] of the point was, that the ancient canonical rules, as to tithes or other church property, were subject to change, dispensation, and exception, according to the judgment of the Holy See; and, therefore, that 'the clergy of this baptismal church, by virtue of their privilege, might make good their claim to the whole tithes of their "diocese"' (*clerici ergo hujus baptismalis ecclesiæ, privilegii auctoritate muniti, suæ dioecesis decimas sibi ex integro vendicare valent*), except in the possible case of a bishop being compelled by 'some

[1] Pars ii., causa xxv.   [2] Initial position of the First Party.
[3] Conclusion of quæst. 1, cap. 16.

extreme necessity' (*summa necessitate*) to take his fourth part, and of proof being made that the clergy of the baptismal church had more than they wanted; (*et illi superabundare monstrentur*).

Before the end of the twelfth century, the endowment of parish churches with tithes had become so general, that the burden of proof was thrown upon those claiming against them. In the diocese of Beauvais a question arose as to the tithes of newly-cultivated lands in parishes, in which some churches (baptismal or conventual), or other ecclesiastical persons, had from ancient time a right to the perception of tithes; (*ad quasdam ecclesias vel personas ecclesiasticas ab antiquo pertineat perceptio decimarum*). The determination of Innocent III.[1] was, that, 'inasmuch as, of common right, the perception of tithes belonged to the parochial churches' (*perceptio decimarum ad parochiales ecclesias de jure communi pertineat*), their title to the tithes of lands newly brought into cultivation was clear, unless reasonable proof could be made, by those who received the other tithes, that their title did extend to the newly-cultivated lands.

The system, therefore, of modern parishes, endowed (generally) with tithes, had then become well established. I cannot better conclude this narrative, than by a summary of the course and results of this change, taken from the work of Van Espen; to which I shall add an opinion, given in France early in the eighteenth century, to the Chancellor d'Aguesseau, by magistrates learned in this branch of law, whom that great jurist had thought fit to consult. Van Espen says:

'As time went on, and as the fidelity and integrity of the bishops and their officers in the dispensation of church revenues

---

[1] *Decret. Greg. IX.*, lib. iii., tit. xxx., cap. 29.

declined, many dissensions and quarrels arose between the clerks to whom distribution was to be made, and those to whom the duty of making the distribution belonged. The earliest claim asserted by the priesthood was to the offerings made in their own churches; and when the right to receive and retain these for his own use had devolved upon the priest, separate titles to other kinds of church property began also to be generally acquired; and a particular portion of lands, of which he was to receive the profits for his own use, began to be assigned to the priest of each church. This, however, did not happen all at once everywhere; nor was the practice introduced by the decree of any council; it passed gradually from one to another church.[1]

'In the end it became a legal axiom, that the parish priests had a valid claim to the tithes, oblations, and other church revenues arising within the bounds of their respective parishes; and, in this way, the right to receive those profits became annexed, not to particular persons, but to churches, and the titles to them. He who had the title acquired also the right to receive the profits of all that belonged to that title. This system, at last, became universal. A further consequence was, that the title acquired the name of *benefice*, because he who obtained it obtained at the same time the right to receive and enjoy its fruits; and also, because the ecclesiastical office or ministry was regarded as the principal thing, and the right to receive and enjoy the fruits and profits as its accident. Canonists, retaining the old designation of "benefice" (which signified an usufructuary right granted to the clergy as "soldiers of the Church"), were accustomed to define it as "a perpetual right granted by the authority of the Church in respect of a spiritual office, to receive and enjoy the fruits, of whatever kind, of ecclesiastical property or things dedicated to God." Divines preferred to say, "A perpetual right of ministering in the Church, granted by the bishop's authority, and having, as incident to it, the right of receiving and enjoying the fruits."'[2]

In another place [3]—'The word *peculium* probably came to

---

[1] Van Espen, *Jus Univ. Canon.*, pars ii., sect. 3, tit i., cap. 1, § 8.
[2] Pars ii., sect. 3, tit. i., cap. 1, §§ 11-14.
[3] Pars ii., sect. 4, tit. i., § 2.

be applied to church property granted to clerks for their own use, after the goods of the church had become, by the erection of benefices, divided into certain portions, annexed to particular titles, and separated from the general mass. It acquired that name by analogy to the *peculium* of the Roman law, which signified property acquired by a slave separately from that of his master, by the master's leave. . . . And since, under this modern system, every beneficed clerk has as ample power of administration, and as free a use, in respect of the portion of goods annexed to his title, as bishops ever had over the estates and goods of their churches, it is not strange that the beneficed clerk should be regarded as the owner (*dominus*) of his ecclesiastical revenues, and should be commonly spoken of as having the ownership (*dominium*) of them, or as taking them for his own; although, in truth, he is but put in charge of them. He obtains over them a power of disposition (including the right to apply them to his own use), so absolute, as to make him accountable for his stewardship to God alone.'[1]

A question arose before the Chancellor d'Aguesseau, between a bishop entitled to the great tithes of a certain parish and the *curé* of that parish, as to the tithes of lands within the parish, newly brought into cultivation. The magistrates, consulted by the Chancellor, gave their opinion in the bishop's favour, for these reasons:[2]

'In the ancient state of the Church all ecclesiastical goods were in the power of the bishop, who distributed them to the priests and other ministers of the Church. The division which succeeded to that ancient state of things irrevocably assigned to each ecclesiastical function and office certain portions of the goods which had composed that common mass; and this introduced what at the present day are called *titles to benefices*. At the time of that division the bishops, to form their separate estates (*leur manses particuliers*), reserved to themselves certain domains and tithes, which they continued to possess by

---

[1] Pars ii., sect. 4, tit. i., § 23.
[2] Jouy, *Principes et Usages*, etc., cap. 7, § 9, pp. 226-228.

the same title as when the division was made. It is impossible, under these circumstances, to say that the *curés*, who got their own proper share (*leur partie contingente*) of the common goods, can establish against the bishops a right, by reason of their churches (*de leur clocher*), to receive all the tithes of their parishes. That original state of things assures to the bishops a right in perpetuity, as against the *curés*, to the tithes of each parish so situated. This right of the bishops is not an exemption; for the right of a tithe-owner not to pay the tithe of his own landed property cannot be called exemption from tithes.'

ANCIENT FACTS AND FICTIONS

PART II.—ANGLO-SAXON

CHAPTER I

FIRST PERIOD—FROM AUGUSTIN TO THE DEATH OF
ARCHBISHOP THEODORE

§ 1. *Preliminary.*

I SHALL refer to the general history of the Anglo-Saxon Church so far only as it throws light upon the particular subjects which it is my object to examine. That history may be divided into four periods. The first (to which the present chapter relates) occupies nearly a century, from the coming of Augustin in A.D. 597 to the death of Archbishop Theodore in A.D. 690. It is that of the first plantation of the Church by Augustin and his successors,—all but one of them sent, like himself, from Rome. The second begins with Brihtwald, the first of a long line of native Anglo-Saxon primates; and ends with the restoration of the see of Canterbury, in A.D. 803, from the position of diminished authority to which it had been reduced by King Offa. This was a period of vigorous, independent growth. The third and longest period, extending over nearly 140 years, from the Council of Cloveshoo (where that restoration was effected) to the primacy of Archbishop Odo (A.D. 941), was one of decay. The fourth and last, from A.D. 941 to the Conquest (A.D. 1066), was marked by a revival of learning, and the establishment of monastic ascendency.

§ 2. *The Original British Church.*

If I may seem to pass by the history and the labours of the original British Church, it is not because I am insensible to the interest of that subject; but because the questions of ecclesiastical organisation, customs, and laws, with which I wish to deal, are Anglo-Saxon, not British. Speaking generally, the local succession and organisation of the Anglo-Saxon Church was from Augustin; it was not a continuation of the succession or organisation of the ancient British Church. It arose out of the conversion, by missionary enterprise, of new heathen nations, which had obtained possession of the greater part of England, and had driven into the remoter parts of the island that portion of the British race which they did not exterminate or enslave. And at the outset there was a difference, not of organisation and succession only, but also of rite; the British Church having its peculiar customs,[1] of which there was on both sides a disposition to exaggerate the importance.[2] By degrees, the natural law, by which the weaker is attracted to the stronger, prevailed.[3] The organisation which had for its centre the see of Canterbury was the stronger, ecclesiastically, from its nearer relation to the metropolis of Western Christendom; and temporally, because, according to the measure of the success of its missionary efforts, it acquired the support of

---

[1] See Haddan and Stubbs, *Councils*, vol. i. pp. 152-155.

[2] *Ibid.*, pp. 108, 126, notes; and see Theodore's 'Penitential,' lib. ii., cap. 9 (*ibid.*, vol. iii. p. 197).

[3] 'In A.D. 731, all the Scottish and Pictish, and probably the Cornish, Churches had yielded; but the Welsh still retained their own Easter' (*ibid.*, p. 62, note). The Welsh Churches began to adopt the Roman Easter, etc., between A.D. 768 and 777 (*ibid.*, vol. i. p. 204).

the governing races. The result, when distinctions of rite had disappeared, was not to make the new organisation fall into the old, but the old into the new.

On the other hand, there is no reason to doubt that the influence of the two converging traditions of historical Christianity in this island was to some extent reciprocal; especially when the communications[1] of both with the Scottish and Irish Churches (kindred to the British) are taken into account. Some customs of the Anglo-Saxon Church seem to have been borrowed[2] from the British; and bishops of the older churches took part in the conversion, or reconversion after relapses into heathenism, of some of the Anglo-Saxon kingdoms; and also in consecrations,[3] by which, in particular dioceses, the succession of the Anglo-Saxon episcopacy was kept up. These relations to the British, Scottish, and Irish Churches contributed to give to the Anglo-Saxon Church a character of its own, and to modify or retard the assimilation of its customs and institutions to those of Continental Churches.

As to the revenues and territorial arrangements of the ancient British Church, little is known. There was a Welsh custom,[4] when Giraldus wrote his 'description of Wales' in the twelfth century, of paying an extraordinary tithe, which was divided between the bishop and the 'baptismal church' (*ecclesiæ suæ baptismali*), in the proportion of one-third to the former and two-thirds to the

[1] Haddan and Stubbs, *Councils*, vol. i. pp. 115, 116, note; p. 121, note; and see Bede, *Hist.*, lib. v., cap. 22.
[2] Haddan and Stubbs, *Councils*, vol. i. p. 140.
[3] *Ibid.*, p. 124; and vol. iii. p. 106 note, 109.
[4] *Descr. Wall.*, lib. i., cap. 18 (quoted by Baluze, *Capit.*, vol. ii. p. 1065, note). See, as to Welsh baptismal churches, the Laws of Howel the Good (Haddan and Stubbs, *Councils*, vol. i. pp. 241, 247).

latter, on certain special occasions, such as marriages, journeys, or a change of life undertaken by advice of the Church. As to the antiquity of that custom, or as to other customs of the ancient Welsh Church, relating either to tithes or to parochial arrangements, before the end of the eleventh century, we have no certain information. In the 'Laws of Howel the Good,' which belong to the tenth century (and were later than the cessation of the ritual differences which had estranged the Welsh Church from the Anglo-Saxon), tithes are mentioned; in a manner, however, from which we derive little light. In two of the three forms of that code, the 'priest of the household' (second in rank of the royal officers) was to have a third of the king's tithe,[1] and the 'priest of the queen' a third of the queen's tithe;[2] the 'priest of the household' was also to have the tithe of the household.[3] The code of the south-western province,[4] imposing fines by way of penalty upon any persons 'fighting within the churchyard,' gave all those fines to 'the abbot' and 'the priests and canons' of the church—from which the inference arises, that at the time when those laws were made, the churches in Wales which had churchyards or burial-grounds were conventual.

§ 3. *Gregory the Great, as to Church Revenues in England.*

Augustin and several of his coadjutors were monks; not, however, of the Benedictine order founded in Italy during the earlier part of the sixth century, as has often been asserted. Before that time there were monks and monasteries, and monastic vows; there were famous monasteries in

---

[1] Haddan and Stubbs, *Councils*, vol. i. pp. 227-231.
[2] *Ibid.*, p. 235.   [3] *Ibid.*, p. 227.   [4] *Ibid.*, p. 243.

CHAP. I *FIRST PERIOD OF ANGLO-SAXON CHURCH* 103

Wales, in Scotland and its islands, and in Ireland. But Benedict was the first founder of a regular order of monks, living apart from others, and governed by one definite system of positive rules. The Roman missionaries, when they effected their settlement at Canterbury, did not found a Benedictine monastery;[1] they lived together as a college of clergy, the germ of the future chapter of Canterbury Cathedral; which, until a time later than Dunstan, consisted of canons, under rules less austere and more flexible than that of St. Benedict. Augustin stated to Gregory several questions on which he desired instructions; one of them, as to the diversity of the customs of churches; and Gregory's answer allowing that diversity, and advising Augustin to decide for himself what might be best and most suitable for the edification of his converts, without holding himself bound by the rules or customs of Rome, has been elsewhere mentioned.[2] The answer given to Augustin's first question,[3] which related to the distribution of the offerings of the faithful, was in conformity with that principle.

'As to bishops' (it was asked), 'how should they live with their clerks? Into what portions should the offerings made by the faithful at the altar be divided? How should the bishop conduct himself in the church?' The answer (after referring to St. Paul's Epistle to Timothy as to the conversation and behaviour suitable to bishops) was:

'It is the custom of the Apostolic See to instruct bishops at the time of their consecration, that of all revenues of every kind (*de omni stipendio quod accedit*) four portions should be made: one for the bishop and his "family," for hospitality's

---

[1] See Hook's *Lives of Archbishops*, vol. i. p. 34 (3rd ed. 1875).
[2] *Ante*, p. 26.   [3] Bede, *Hist.*, lib. i., cap. 27.

sake, and the entertainment of others; one for the clergy; a third for the poor; the fourth for repair of churches. But inasmuch as you, my brother, who have been trained in the monastic rules, ought not to be separate from your clergy, you should institute in the English Church, brought so lately by God's help to the faith, the same manner of administration (*conversationem*) which was in use by our fathers in the very first infancy of the Church (*initio nascentis ecclesiæ*), in which "no man of them said that ought of the things which he possessed was his own; but they had all things common." But if there are clerks not in holy orders who cannot live single, they should take to themselves wives, and receive stipends outside. For we know that of the same fathers, of whom we have just spoken, it is written that "distribution was made to every man according as he had need." Their payment should be considered and provided for, and they should be kept under ecclesiastical rule, so as to live good lives, and attend to psalm-singing, and keep, by God's help, heart, tongue, and body from all things unlawful. But as for making portions, or showing hospitality, or performing deeds of mercy, what need can there be to speak of such things to those who live in community, when all that they have, beyond their own needs, ought to be applied to pious and religious uses, as the Lord the master of us all teaches? "But rather[1] give alms of such things as ye have" (*quod superest date eleemosynam*), "and all things are clean unto you."

To suggest[2] that Gregory by this answer intended to recommend to Augustin the Roman rule of quadripartite division is to contradict his words. The offerings in question were those made at the altar of a church, served by a body of men living together as monks in community, with inferior clergy not bound by monastic vows under them. They were first to provide out of their offerings for their common wants and those of their dependent clergy. Everything beyond what might be necessary for these purposes was to be used as they should judge most convenient, without

[1] Luke xi. 41.
[2] See Kennett's *Parochial Antiquities* (ed. 1818), vol. i. p. 107.

any partition, for hospitality and works of charity and mercy. It would not indeed have been inconsistent with that advice, if at some later period, and under altered circumstances, the Anglo-Saxon Church had adopted either the quadripartite or any other rule of division. On that point Gregory's instructions left them free; they might either permanently retain the same latitude of discretion which had prevailed generally in Christendom for more than four hundred years from the time of the Apostles, or they might introduce the Roman or some other definite rule. That they did so, is not a thing to be presumed without evidence. As to the quadripartite division, there is no documentary or historical evidence of any kind which can be alleged as showing its acceptance anywhere or at any time in England. That some other definite rule should be adopted in preference was not, perhaps, *à priori* probable; but there are documents (belonging to the fourth and last period of the Anglo-Saxon Church) which will require examination when we come to that period; from which some have concluded that there was in this country, then or earlier, a tripartite rule of division. In that opinion I do not agree; but for the present it is sufficient to say, that nothing of that kind can be alleged of earlier date than King Edgar's (or, more probably, King Ethelred's) reign. Whelock,[1] the Cambridge editor of Bede in the seventeenth century, connected the name of Theodore, seventh Archbishop of Canterbury, with one of the documents to which I have referred. On that point it is not necessary, and it would not be convenient, to anticipate here what may be proper to be said hereafter.

[1] Bede's *Hist.* (Cambridge 1644), p. 358; Whelock's note.

§ 4. *Tithes.*

The earliest notice of tithes in any document belonging or relating to the Anglo-Saxon Church is in the 'second book'[1] of a collection of answers or precepts, said to have been given to inquirers by Archbishop Theodore, on a series of ecclesiastical questions. That collection appears to have been made after Theodore's death by a compiler calling himself 'a disciple of the Umbrians,'[2]—probably a student of theology in one of the Northumbrian schools, at Wearmouth or elsewhere in the province of York. Wasserschleben[3] and the late Mr. Haddan and Bishop Stubbs[4] have agreed in accepting it as authentic; I shall, on their authority, assume it to be so. It is divided into two 'books,' each containing chapters arranged according to subjects — the first book 'Penitential,' the second of a different character. The precepts so ascribed to Theodore make no pretension to the character of laws or canons: they represent at the most his pastoral teaching upon the points to which they relate. Some of them (as to re-baptism,[5] divorce, and re-marriage[6]) appear to be at variance with the received doctrine of the Roman and other churches.

The effect of the articles as to tithes (in bad Latin, and perhaps corrupt) is this—(1) That no priest is bound to

---

[1] Haddan and Stubbs, *Councils*, etc., vol. iii. pp. 191, 203.
[2] *Ibid.*, pp. 173, 175 (and see vol. i., Preface, xiv.)
[3] *Die Bussordnungen*, etc. (Halle 1851).
[4] *Ubi supra.*
[5] Lib. ii., cap. 2, § 12 (Haddan and Stubbs, *Councils*, vol. iii. p. 192); and compare lib. i., cap. 10, § 1 (*ibid.*, p. 185).
[6] Lib. ii., cap. 12, §§ 5, 8, 19-24 (*ibid.*, pp. 199-201). Compare Howel's Welsh Marriage Laws (*ibid.*, vol. i. pp. 249, 251).

pay tithes (*presbitero decimas dare non cogitur*);[1] (2) That in gifts to the Church (*tributum ecclesiæ*) the custom of the province should be observed; but so, that no force be put upon the poor as to tithes or anything else (*ne tantum pauperes inde, in decimis aut in aliquibus rebus, vim patientur*);[2] (3) That it is not lawful to give tithes, except to the poor and strangers, or laymen to their own churches (*decimas non est legitimum dare nisi pauperibus et peregrinis, sive laici suas ad ecclesias*).[3]

The first of these articles occurs in a chapter relating to the powers, duties, and obligations of bishops, priests, and deacons, and headed, '*Of the three principal degrees of the Church*'; the other two in the concluding chapter, '*Of divers questions.*' They are negative rather than positive: they put the payment of tithes on the footing of custom, depending for its observance upon episcopal or clerical influence rather than ecclesiastical censures. Of a division into portions between bishop, clergy, fabrics, and poor, or for any of those objects, they afford no indication;—rather the reverse. What were the churches described as those of laymen, to which tithes might be paid by them, is not clear; they might be oratories built upon their estates, or (as I should rather be disposed to think) those conventual or baptismal churches whose public ministrations they ought properly to have attended.

In the *History* of Bede there is only one passage making mention of tithes. This occurs in the account which he gives of Bishop Eadbert,[4] St. Cuthbert's successor at Lindisfarne; 'a man remarkable for his knowledge of the

---
[1] Haddan and Stubbs, *Councils*, vol. iii. p. 191 (lib. ii., cap. 2, § 8).
[2] *Ibid.*, p. 203 (lib. ii., cap. 14, § 9).
[3] *Ibid.* (lib. ii., cap. 14, § 10).   [4] Bede, *Hist.*, lib. iv., cap. 29.

Scripture, and his observance of the divine commandments, and (most of all) for his alms-deeds, which were such that, in every year, he gave to the poor a tithe, not only of his beasts, but of all his corn and fruits of trees, and of his garments also.' Bede evidently regarded this as an instance of more than ordinary virtue.

§ 5. *Ecclesiastical Organisation.*

Gregory the Great considered it to be within his power (whether as founder of the Anglo-Saxon Mission or as Patriarch of the West, for he repudiated the title of 'Universal Pope') to regulate for all Britain the future episcopal organisation.[1] This he did by conferring on Augustin himself, during his lifetime, the primacy over the whole island, directing him to ordain for his own province twelve bishops, and to consecrate and send to York another bishop, who, after the conversion of that city and the country near it, should himself ordain twelve other bishops, and become a metropolitan, receiving the pall, but being subject, as long as Augustin lived, to his superior authority. After Augustin's death, London was to become the metropolitan see of the southern province, without any superiority over the metropolitan of York; each metropolitan taking precedence of the other according to the date of his consecration.

These instructions were not acted upon. The see of Canterbury, if not by the positive appointment of later Popes, by a practice to which they gave such sanction as was implied in sending the pall to Augustin's successors,

[1] Letter of Gregory to Augustin (22nd June A.D. 601), sent with pall (Bede, *Hist.*, lib. i., cap. 29; Haddan and Stubbs, *Councils*, vol. iii. pp. 29, 30).

retained its metropolitan character, which was never transferred to London; and it also retained (though without any practical assertion until Theodore's time [1]) the primacy over all England. The scheme of two archbishops and twenty-four bishops was not capable of being at once realised; the heathen must first be converted, and some *modus vivendi* must be arrived at with the remnants of the British Church; which was never done at all as to the regions north of the Forth and Clyde, nor (in Anglo-Saxon times) as to Wales; and was only done gradually in other parts of England. The only bishoprics established by Augustin himself (besides Canterbury) were Rochester and London. It was not till the time of his fellow-labourer and third successor, Justus, that the first steps were taken for the conversion of the country beyond the Humber. Paulinus [2] was then (A.D. 625) consecrated to York, and, after he was forced to leave the northern province for Kent, he received the pall (which was not sent to any of his successors in that see before Egbert, in the middle of the next century); but he consecrated no other bishops for the northern province.

On the accession of Honorius to the archiepiscopate in A.D. 627, there were thus four bishoprics only of the Anglo-Saxon rite in the island; and even of these, one (London) was practically in abeyance, for the kingdom of Essex had relapsed into heathenism, and had expelled its bishop, Mellitus, some years before; [3] and the same thing not long afterwards happened in Northumbria, from which Paulinus also was expelled.[4] Of the kingdoms of the (so-called) Heptarchy, East Anglia, Wessex, Mercia, and Sussex were still heathen. Under Honorius, the Kings of East

---

[1] Bede, *Hist.*, lib. iv., cap. 2.
[2] Haddan and Stubbs, *Councils*, vol. iii. p. 75.
[3] *Ibid.*, p. 66.   [4] *Ibid.*, pp. 86-88.

Anglia and Wessex were converted, and two new sees[1] were erected, at Dunwich in Suffolk, and Dorchester in Oxfordshire; the latter see being soon afterwards, during the same primacy, removed to Winchester.[2] The conversion of Mercia was begun in the time of the next primate; not, however, under his authority, but by Finan of Lindisfarne, who was of the British succession,[3] and it was during the vacancy of the see of Canterbury, after that archbishop's death, that another new bishopric was established for Mercia.[4] Thus, when Theodore succeeded to the primacy, there were five suffragans only under Canterbury, and one bishop only of the Anglo-Saxon Church in the northern province.[5]

Theodore was the first to assert and exercise, with the assent and support of the rulers of the professedly Christian kingdoms on both sides of the Humber, and their subjects of the Anglo-Saxon rite, the authority of primate and metropolitan of all England;[6] and he formed the design of subdividing the greater sees. He assembled at Hertford[7] (A.D. 673) a general synod of the Church, and proposed for

[1] Haddan and Stubbs, *Councils*, vol. iii. pp. 88-91.
[2] *Ibid.*, p. 127, note.
[3] *Ibid.*, pp. 93-98; and Hook, *Lives of Archbishops*, vol. i. p. 120.
[4] Bede, *Hist.*, lib. iv., cap. 3; Haddan and Stubbs, vol. iii. p. 96. Dean Hook says that the first Mercian see was at Repton, and that it was removed to Lichfield under Theodore (*Lives of Archbishops*, vol. i. p. 121).
[5] 'The whole of England, except Kent, East Anglia, Wessex, and Sussex, was, at the beginning of A.D. 664, attached to the British Communion, and Wessex was under a bishop, Wini, ordained in Gaul, and in communion with British bishops (Bede, lib. iii., cap. 28). Sussex was still heathen. So that Kent and East Anglia alone remained completely in communion with both Rome and Canterbury.' (Haddan and Stubbs, vol. iii. p. 106, note.)
[6] Bede, *Hist.*, lib. iv., cap. 2.   [7] *Ibid.*, cap. 5.

its acceptance, amongst other things, a resolution to the effect 'that the number of bishops should be augmented as the number of believers increased.'[1] This, after discussion, was left undecided; probably because it encountered opposition from the Bishop of Lichfield, who was present, and was known to be unacceptable to Wilfrid of York (a man of great zeal and energy, and tenacious of power), who was absent, but represented by proxies. Theodore, however, did not relinquish his design. He procured the removal[2] of both those bishops from their sees; and with the concurrence of the civil rulers of Northumbria, East Anglia, and Mercia, he established in the north two new bishoprics, Hexham and Lindisfarne,[3] and in the south five (if not six)—Elmham, Lindsey, Hereford, Worcester, and Leicester.[4] Whether he did or did not then revive the see of Dorchester in Oxfordshire is a controverted point.[5] In Wessex he did not himself divide the see of Winchester; but it is probable[6] that he contemplated its division after the death of the then bishop, Heddi, who was his friend, and who survived him; dying in, or shortly before, A.D. 705; when the see of Sherborne was established.[7] The kingdom of Sussex continued heathen till A.D. 684–86, when its king and many of the people were

---

[1] Bede, *Hist.*, lib. iv., cap. 5 (art. 9); Haddan and Stubbs, *Councils*, vol. iii. pp. 120-122.

[2] As to Winfrid, the deposed Mercian bishop, see Wharton, *Anglia Sacra*, vol. i. p. 423; and Bede, *Hist.*, lib. iv., cap. 5. As to Wilfrid of York, *ibid.*, cap. 12; and see his *Life*, by Eddius (Gale, *Script. XX.*, cap. 24-33); and Bede, *Hist.*, lib. v., cap. 19.

[3] *Ibid.*, lib. iv., cap. 12; Haddan and Stubbs, vol. iii. pp. 125, 126.

[4] Wharton's *Anglia Sacra*, vol. i. *ubi supra* (A.D. 676, 678, 679); Haddan and Stubbs, vol. iii. pp. 127-130; Bede, *Hist.*, lib. iv., cap. 5; Florence of Worcester, *App. ad Chron.*

[5] Haddan and Stubbs, *Councils*, vol. iii. p. 130, note.

[6] *Ibid.*, pp. 126, 127, note. [7] *Ibid.*, pp. 267, 275, 276.

converted by Wilfrid,[1] who took charge of it at that time as bishop; but it was not till A.D. 711, after Theodore's death, that Selsey became the seat of a settled bishopric for that kingdom.[2]

The history thus summarised will enable any one to judge of the probability of the statements, for which there is no ancient authority, but which were made by chroniclers of later ages, and have been repeated by more recent writers, as to the introduction into England of what is now known as the parochial system,—by Honorius according to some; according to others by Theodore;—in either case, more than a century before the foundations of that system were laid on the other side of the Channel, by the capitulars of Louis the Pious at Aix-la-Chapelle.[3]

The author of the tradition ascribing the origin of that system to Honorius appears to have been Archbishop Parker, or Josceline his secretary, to whom Selden[4] ascribed the authorship of the work commonly attributed to that archbishop; rightly calling it a 'History of the Archbishops of Canterbury'; though its title is 'Of the antiquity of the Church of Britain.'[5] It is not improbable, that the archbishop may have prepared the materials for that work, from the great collection of monastic and historical manuscripts which the dissolution in his time of the religious houses enabled him to make, and which he bequeathed to Corpus Christi College, Cambridge; and that he may have employed in their arrangement the hand of Josceline, which is seen in marginal and other annotations on some of those manuscripts, and also on others belonging to the Cottonian

---

[1] Bede, *Hist.*, lib. iv., cap. 13. [2] *Ibid.*, lib. v., cap. 18.
[3] *Ante*, p. 85. [4] *Hist. of Tithes*, ch. 9, § 3.
[5] First published A.D. 1572 (three years before the archbishop's death).

collection. The passage as to Honorius,[1] in this work (whether Parker's or Josceline's), is:

> 'He not only placed bishops over the Church, as chief keepers of its bulwarks, but he was also the first who, dividing his province into parishes, appointed ministers unto them (*neque solum episcopos, tanquam superiores turrium custodes, ecclesiæ superimposuit, sed etiam provinciam suam primus in parochias dividens, inferiores ministros ordinavit*); whom also he frequently instructed and exhorted, that they should teach God's people, gently and patiently, not by their doctrine only, but also by the goodness of their lives; knowing that unbelievers are thus more easily converted, than by severity of reproof or austerity of manners.'

To the same source may, with great probability, be traced a statement to the same effect in Stow's *Annals*,[2] a work published soon after that of the archbishop or his secretary. Stow was, like Josceline, a learned antiquary, and made large collections from ancient documents; and Archbishop Parker was his patron. Under the year A.D. 640 (when Ercombert, King of Kent, is stated by him to have 'first suppressed the temples of the idols'), he said:

> 'It is recorded in the antiquities of Christ's Church in Canterbury, that about this time Honorius, Archbishop of Canterbury, divided his province into parishes.'

Camden,[3] in the chapter of his *Britannia* which relates to 'the division of Britain,' has a passage to the like effect:

> 'As to the Ecclesiastical Government, after the Bishop of Rome[4] had assigned to each presbyter his church, and set them

---

[1] *De Antiquitate*, etc., p. 52 (ed. 1605).
[2] Page 59 (Howes' ed. 1631).   [3] Vol. i. p. ccxxviii. (ed. 1722).
[4] It has been seen, in the first part of this work, that the modern system of parishes, on the Continent of Europe, did not grow up till much later.

over distinct parishes, Honorius, Archbishop of Canterbury, about the year of our Lord 636, first began to divide England into parishes, as we read in the Canterbury History.'

The *Britannia* was published soon after the works of Parker (or Josceline) and of Stow; and Camden purchased Stow's collections from ancient manuscripts, etc. Whether, by the *Canterbury History*, he meant the work of Parker or Josceline, or the record of 'the antiquities of Christ's Church in Canterbury,' to which Stow referred, may be doubtful. Bishop Godwin,[1] in his work on 'the Bishops of England' (published A.D. 1611), followed these authorities.

Selden, in his *History of Tithes*,[2] made observations upon these statements, which (but for the disposition of later writers of different political and ecclesiastical sentiments to disregard his authority) might have been sufficient to prevent their repetition afterwards. After speaking of the community of life, and of goods, between the bishops and clergy in Augustin's time (Honorius had been one of Augustin's own companions), he said:

'Yet it is commonly received that Honorius, about the year 630, first divided his province into parishes. And in the late history of the Archbishops of Canterbury, written by Mr. Josceline, it is thus delivered of him' (quoting the passage). 'And according to this have some of our greatest and most learned writers[3] related. But I doubt much how it can stand with truth. For, if *parochiæ* be here meant only for such as were assigned limits for those which were sent arbitrarily from the bishop, out of the number of his

---

[1] *De Præsulibus*, etc., p. 40 (ed. 1611).
[2] Ch. 9, § 3. Bishop Kennett, in A.D. 1704 (*Case of Impropriations*, p. 4) took the same view with Selden.
[3] Evidently referring to Stow, Camden, and Godwin.

chaplains or his *clerus*, residing for the most part in those elder times with him at his bishopric, then, clearly, Honorius was not the first that made division of them. *Such* kind of *parochiæ* are even near as ancient as bishoprics; and, questionless, in Augustin's time. How could, otherwise, God's service be orderly had in the infancy of the Church? And, whenever several churches for Christian service, or other places for holy assemblies began, then began such *parochiæ*. . . . If, on the other side, *parochiæ* be taken for what it is usually understood, that is, for such limits as now make parishes, bounded as well in regard of the profits received from the parishioners (due only to the minister of that church), as of the incumbent's function and residence,—how will that stand with the community of ecclesiastical profits, and the bishop's and his clergy's living together, that may be without much difficulty discovered also, out of Bede, to have continued after Honorius also? But, wherever that testimony of his dividing parishes was first found, I doubt it was misunderstood, through the various signification of *parochia*. For, in those ancient times, *parochia* usually denoted as well a bishopric or diocese, as a less parish. . . . And the truth is, that it may be said, properly enough, that Honorius was the first under whom his province was divided into such *parochiæ* or bishoprics; that is, no other bishoprics, except Canterbury, London, and Rochester, were in his province until his time; these three being almost of one antiquity.'

Notwithstanding this criticism of Selden, Sir Henry Spelman,[1] in his *Councils* (published A.D. 1639) repeated in terms Stow's statement, referring expressly to Stow; and Hume[2] in the first part of his *History of England* (published A.D. 1761) repeated that of Josceline or Parker. Dr. Lingard,[3] a more critical writer than Hume, thought the tradition as to Honorius reconcilable with the statement which the editors of Bede, Whelock and Smith, had extracted from the

[1] *Concil.*, vol. i. p. 152 (ed. 1639).
[2] *History of England*, vol. i. p. 65 (Oxford ed. 1826).
[3] *Antiquities of Anglo-Saxon Church*, vol. i. pp. 92, 93.

chronicler Elmham as to Theodore; saying (in his *Antiquities of the Anglo-Saxon Church*, published A.D. 1806) that—

'The inconvenience of the desultory method of instruction was soon discovered; and Honorius of Canterbury is said to have first formed the plan of distributing each diocese into a proportionate number of parishes, and of allotting each to the care of a resident clergyman.[1] To Archbishop Theodore belongs the merit of extending it to the neighbouring churches, from which it was gradually diffused over the remaining dioceses.'[2]

It is probable, that no one will now be found to refer the origin of our modern parishes to Honorius; but it is otherwise as to Theodore; though if such a question depended on modern authority, those in favour of the tradition as to Honorius are as weighty as any who can be appealed to for that as to Theodore. We cannot now verify the reference of Stow and Camden to the 'antiquities of Christ Church in Canterbury;' but they can hardly have been less ancient than the monastic chronicle of St. Augustine's Abbey in Canterbury, written by Thomas of Elmham, a monk of that house, in A.D. 1414, 724 years after Theodore's death; which was quoted from a manuscript (then in the library of Trinity Hall, Cambridge, and published for the first time in A.D. 1848 by the late Archdeacon Hardwick) by Whelock[3] in his edition of Bede's *History*, published A.D. 1644, without, however, mentioning Elmham's name; and this is the sole foundation upon which later writers have

---

[1] He refers for this to Godwin and Spelman.

[2] He refers to Smith's *Bede*, p. 189, note; and Whelock's *Bede*, p. 399 note, of which he repeats the substance as taken by Whelock from Elmham. Smith's note follows Whelock's; naming, however, Elmham as the authority.

[3] Bede, *Hist.* (Cambridge 1644), p. 399; Whelock's note.

attributed the origin of modern parishes to Theodore. Elmham[1] wrote thus :

> 'The most pious Theodore, with the consent of the rest of the bishops and other holy fathers, conferred the power in all the cathedral cities of whatever province (*in quarumlibet provinciarum civitatibus*) and in all townships (*necnon villis*) of building churches and making separate parishes (*paroecias distinguendi*), obtaining also for them the royal assent, so that all men of sufficient estate, whose devotion led them to build churches in God's honour upon their own lands, might for ever enjoy the patronage of those churches ; but if any built them within the limits of other men's lordships, such churches were to be in the patronage of the lord of the land on which they were built.'

The words, 'with the consent of the rest of the bishops and other holy fathers,' suggest synodical action; and we are in possession of the Acts, well authenticated, of the only two synods held under Theodore; for Bede, who preserved these, would certainly have preserved any others, if such there had been. The Acts of the Council of Hatfield[2] (the later of the two), subscribed by all the bishops present, relate to doctrine only. Those of the Council of Hertford[3] (A.D. 673) relate to church government and discipline; and their tendency, so far from confirming, is to discredit Elmham's statement. The word *parochia* is used in two[4] of the 'canons' or articles of that Council; the one providing that no bishop is to invade another bishop's diocese (*parochiam*); the other that no foreign bishop or clerk is to perform any priestly office without the permission of the diocesan bishop (*episcopi in cujus parochia esse cognoscitur*). The *word*, therefore, in the Acts of that Council, meant only a diocese; and, as we have already seen, one of the sub-

[1] Hardwick's ed. (1858), pp. 285, 286.
[2] Bede, *Hist.*, lib. iv. cap. 17, 18.
[3] *Ibid.*, cap. 5.   [4] The second and sixth.

jects then discussed, though not decided, was as to the increase of the diocesan organisation (*ut plures episcopi, crescente numero fidelium, augerentur*).[1] In the other articles there is no hint of any territorial subdivision of duty among the clergy of the priestly order. The article [2] which most nearly approaches that subject has a contrary aspect :

'Let no clerk, leaving his own bishop, go about everywhere as he may please, or be received wherever he may come, without commendatory letters from his own bishop. If, after being so received, he is unwilling to return, he who receives him, as well as himself, shall be liable to excommunication.'

There are two[3] articles as to monasteries; one of them is against the unauthorised migration of a monk from monastery to monastery.

Besides these synodical Acts, we have Archbishop Theodore's collected precepts, if the 'Penitential,' published by Wasserschleben,[4] and the 'second book' appended to it, are really his. In the Penitential, penances are prescribed for monks, priests, and other clerks; but nothing is there which implies such a distinction as that between parish priests and others; no penalty of deprivation or suspension, as distinguished from degradation. The only article[5] which refers to a priest's assigned sphere of local duty (such as Selden truly says there must always have been) calls it his 'province' (*provincia*), not parish :

'If any priest, either in his own province or in another's, or anywhere, shall be found guilty of refusing, even on the ground of his having to go a long way, to baptize a sick person recommended to him for that purpose, and so that person die unbaptized, let him be degraded' (*deponatur*).

---

[1] The ninth article.   [2] Fifth article.   [3] Articles 3 and 4.
[4] *Die Bussordnungen der Abendländischen Kirche* (Halle 1881).
[5] Lib. i., cap. 9, § 7 (Haddan and Stubbs, *Councils*, vol. iii. p. 185).

There is also an article[1] in this Penitential, showing that the ecclesiastical organisation of the province of Canterbury (the word *provincia* is there used in that sense) did not, in Theodore's time, admit of public penances; and, for that reason, there was to be no public reconciliation of penitents.

The 'second book' of the same compilation contains chapters on 'the service of the church, and its rebuilding;'[2] on 'the three principal degrees of the church;'[3] on 'the ordination of divers persons;'[4] (which extends to the consecration of abbots, abbesses, and monks); on 'baptism and confirmation;'[5] on 'the mass of the dead;'[6] on 'abbots and monks, or monasteries;'[7] (which extends to the election and deprivation of an abbot, the obligation of an abbot to allow the advancement of a monk of his house to the episcopate, and the obligation of a monk ordained priest to return to the monastery); and on 'various' other[8] ecclesiastical 'questions.' Not one of the articles, in any of those chapters, deals with the position or duties of a parish priest, or implies that a definite office and charge of that kind then existed.

Two recent writers who have accepted Elmham's statement as evidence of the formation of parishes of the modern sort by Theodore — Mr. Soames[9] and Dean Hook[10] — have embellished that statement by some additions; such as, that the institution was founded on something similar, with which Theodore 'had been familiar

---

[1] Lib. i., cap. 13, § 4 (Haddan and Stubbs, *Councils*, vol. iii., p. 187).   [2] *Ibid.*, p. 190.
[3] *Ibid.*, p. 191.   [4] *Ibid.*, p. 192.   [5] *Ibid.*, p. 193.
[6] *Ibid.*, p. 194.   [7] *Ibid.*, p. 195.   [8] *Ibid.*, pp. 202, 203.
[9] *History of Anglo-Saxon Church* (2nd ed. 1838), vol. i. p. 119.
[10] *Lives of Archbishops* (3rd ed. 1875), vol. i. p. 152.

in the Greek Church;' that it was 'an oriental system,' following the principle of laws enacted by the Emperor Justinian. Mr. Soames saw, in the mere fact of the consecration of two noblemen's churches by John, a northern bishop of that time, which Bede mentions (and I see no reason to doubt that there were at the same time other such churches, built by other private landowners on their own estates), evidence that 'this judicious policy had' (in those cases) 'proved effective;' though he added, 'that the system had been in operation for ages before every English estate of any magnitude had secured the benefit of a church within its boundary;' and that 'this very lingering process has thrown much obscurity around the origin of parishes.' It might have been supposed, by a reader unacquainted with Bede's text,[1] that there was in Bede some reference to the 'judicious policy' ascribed to Theodore, or something in Bede's narrative of the consecration of those churches to connect them with territorial arrangements identical with, or similar in principle to, those of parishes, in the modern sense of that word. But it is not so. They were instances of consecrated oratories, built by Northumbrian noblemen on their estates, and nothing more. There is nothing, in Bede's mention of them, by which they could be distinguished from the churches of that class, which were common under the Frank kingdom and empire before the introduction of the parochial system. The silence of Bede, who devoted a considerable space in his *History* to the acts of Theodore, appears to me to be strong negative proof that no such novelty in the organisation of the Church as Elmham ascribed to him was introduced by that prelate.

[1] *Hist.*, lib. v., capp. 4, 5.

Lappenberg[1] appears to have thought that 'the earliest parish churches' in England were 'first erected in the south, under Archbishop Theodore; and about a century later, that is, before and during the time of Egbert, Archbishop of York, in the northern parts of England.' I shall not here consider what was done in the eighth century;[2] but for Lappenberg's distinction between the north and south there is no warrant. The two instances mentioned by Bede,[3] on which Mr. Soames laid stress, were in the north (in Yorkshire), not in the south. Mr. Haddan and Bishop Stubbs say[4] that there 'were no settled parishes in Northumberland in the time of Cuthbert, A.D. 670; nor in the beginning of Egbert's pontificate, A.D. 734.' Elmham, on whom alone the tradition rests, makes no such distinction; and, as to some churches on the coast of Essex (to which Bede's statement[5] that Cedda 'set up churches, and ordained priests and deacons for them in some places among the East Saxons,' relates), Lappenberg[6] himself thinks that they were similar to four baptismal churches founded in Holstein, soon after its conversion, by the Anglo-Saxon Willehad, '*from the districts of which the later parochial division was established.*' That the modern parochial system may have been developed by some modification and adaptation of the principle on which districts were assigned to the old baptismal churches, I have myself suggested, in the former part of this work;[7] and it is not to be doubted that the churches of the great monasteries which were founded in England in

---

[1] *History of England under the Anglo-Saxon Kings* (Thorpe's translation, 1845), vol. i. p. 196.

[2] See *post*, p. 129.   [3] *Hist.*, lib. v., capp. 4, 5.

[4] Haddan and Stubbs, *Councils*, vol. iii. p. 122, note.

[5] *Hist.*, lib. iii., cap. 22.   [6] *Ubi supra*, p. 197.   [7] *Ante*, p. 61.

and shortly before Theodore's time were baptismal churches, similar (generally) to those of the Continent. But, although the parish system may have been a development, springing out of the older system of baptismal churches, it is nevertheless very remote from the truth to describe the two systems as the same.

My conclusion is, that Mr. Haddan and Bishop Stubbs were certainly right, when they set aside Elmham's statement (as Selden set aside those of Josceline or Parker and Stow), as having grown 'out of a confusion between the ancient and modern senses of the word *parochia*. 'Theodore,'[1] (they say) 'who certainly constituted dioceses,—the identical dioceses, with a few exceptions and subdivisions, that exist at the present day,—may have been thence inferred to have constituted parishes.' The conception of the modern parochial system is unsuitable to any other than a settled church, in a settled country. The completion of the diocesan system must come first. That was Theodore's work. The country was unsettled. Mercia had been converted only just before the commencement of his primacy. Northumbria and Essex had very recently required reconversion from relapses into heathenism; and, in[2] those cases, the work had been done by missionaries of the British and not of the Anglo-Saxon Church. Sussex[3] was not converted until Theodore's own time; this also was done, not by any regular, but by an irregular missionary effort. It is not reasonable to believe, on evidence no better than the statement of a monk of the fifteenth century (who, if he had

---

[1] Haddan and Stubbs, *Councils*, vol. iii. p. 122, note. (See also *ibid*, p. 114, note.)
[2] *Ibid.*, pp. 91, 93, 94, 96, 109 (from Bede).
[3] *Ibid.*, p. 167 (from Bede).

access to Canterbury records, may have honestly misunderstood them, as Josceline and Stow did in the succeeding century), that Theodore anticipated, under circumstances so little suggestive of them, developments, which in older Churches of the Continent were reserved for a later age.

CHAPTER II

SECOND PERIOD—BEDE, BONIFACE, ARCHBISHOPS CUTHBERT AND EGBERT; KINGS INA, WIHTRAED, OFFA

§ 1. *Introductory*

THE primacy of Theodore introduced a new era in the Anglo-Saxon Church. By him the metropolitan authority was firmly established; the diocesan organisation was all but completed; the practice of holding national synods was introduced. Under him, and his coadjutor Abbot Adrian, schools, not of ecclesiastical only but of classical learning, were successfully planted in the great religious houses, which, during and just before that time, began to arise. Canterbury,[1] York, Peterborough,[2] Malmesbury,[3] Abingdon,[4] Wearmouth,[5] Glastonbury,[6] Evesham,[7] and Crowland,[8] became centres of light to the Church, and to people of all ranks cities of refuge, fortresses of humanity and civilisation. It was in Theodore's time that Bede, a child seven years old, was placed under the care of the first Abbot of Wearmouth; there, or in the affiliated monastery of Jarrow, he received his education. Ald-

---

[1] There was a school at Canterbury as early as the time of Honorius (*Bede*, lib. iii. 18).

[2] Founded about A.D. 650.   [3] About A.D. 675.   [4] About A.D. 675.

[5] Founded, about A.D. 673, by Benedict Biscop, who came with Theodore from Rome, and was for some time Abbot of Canterbury.

[6] Anglo-Saxon foundation (there had been an earlier British) about A.D. 680.   [7] A.D. 709.   [8] A.D. 716.

helm,[1] the first Bishop of Sherborne (whom Lappenberg and others have regarded as Bede's equal in scholarship, and his superior in practical wisdom), was a pupil in the schools of Malmesbury and Canterbury. These men, and others like them, handed on the lamp of learning to Egbert, Prince-Archbishop of York, Alcuin's teacher, and founder of the famous library at York which Alcuin has celebrated in verse,[2] where were found the works of Aristotle, Cicero, Pliny, Virgil, and Lucan, as well as a large store of ecclesiastical literature. The Anglo-Saxon Church stood no longer in need of foreign rulers; from the death of Theodore to the Conquest it was governed in both provinces by native prelates, and acquired a national character. Its light and influence extended to the continent of Europe,[3] where the Gallican and other Churches had for a short time fallen behind it in the race. Early in the eighth century it sent missionaries to the pagan races of Friesland and other parts of Germany,[4] the greatest of whom was Boniface. It gave Alcuin to the Frank kingdom, to be the restorer of letters in France, and the instructor, minister, and friend of the hero of the age. The writings

[1] See his Life, by William of Malmesbury (reprinted in Wharton's *Anglia Sacra*, vol. ii. pp. 1-49). See also Hook, *Lives of Archbishops*, vol. i. p. 180.

[2] William of Malmesbury, *Gesta Regum* (Hardy's ed. 1840), p. 93; and see Hook's *Lives of Archbishops* (3rd ed.), vol. i. pp. 165, 166. Archbishop Egbert was brother to one of the Kings of Northumbria, who, after an honourable reign of some years, retired and adopted the monastic life.

[3] See Alcuin's verses (A.D. 793) in Haddan and Stubbs, *Councils*, vol. iii. p. 478; King Alfred's Preface to his translation of Pope Gregory's *Pastoral* (Wise's edition of Asser, Oxford 1722, pp. 87-90); Wasserschleben, Preface to *Bussordnungen*, etc., p. iv.

[4] See Hook, *Lives of Archbishops*, vol. i. (3rd ed.) pp. 235-237; Haddan and Stubbs, *Councils*, vol. iii. pp. 302, 303, etc.

of Anglo-Saxon scholars and divines, from Theodore downwards, became (probably by Alcuin's means) well known to and highly esteemed by Continental Churches.

§ 2. *Monastic Baptismal Churches.*

I postpone the subject of tithes (which in this second period does not emerge till towards its close) to deal first with the question, whether there were parishes, of the modern sort, in England during the eighth century? There is evidence in my judgment sufficient to justify the conclusion that there were not. As on the Continent 'baptismal churches,' generally conventual, were an institution intermediate, in order of time as well as in ecclesiastical functions, between dioceses and parishes of the modern sort, so in England were the monasteries [1] of canons or monks, and their churches. It was upon these (which included cathedral churches) that the administration of the offices of religion to the lay people practically depended during the eighth century, and for a considerable time afterwards.

Of laws, during the primacy of the first Saxon archbishop, Brihtwald (A.D. 693-731), we have the code of Ina in Wessex (about A.D. 690), and of Wihtraed in Kent (about A.D. 694). Under the three next primates, Tatwine, Nothelm, and Cuthbert (A.D. 731-758), we have the letters of Boniface and Bede, and the Acts of the Provincial Synod of Cloveshoo, held under Archbishop Cuthbert in A.D. 747. All these contain evidence—direct or indirect, scanty or full—of the actual state of things; and neither there, nor in any other part of the ecclesiastical literature of that time which has been preserved to us, is there any trace of a

[1] Lappenberg (Thorpe's translation, 1845, pp. 191-195).

parochial system, or of the existence of parishes, in the modern sense. Whenever the word *parochia* is used, it is for a diocese, not a parish; not even (as far as I have been enabled to observe) for any district of which a baptismal church, other than the cathedral of the diocese, may have been the immediate ecclesiastical centre.

§ 3. *Secular Laws.*

The laws of Ina,[1] King of Wessex, were made (about A.D. 690) in a witenagemot of that kingdom, at which the two bishops whose sees were then subject to Ina's dominion (Winchester and London) were present. Some of these relate to ecclesiastical subjects; but there is only one which bears, even indirectly, upon the question of territorial organisation. That is the sixth article, '*Of Fighting.*'[2] It imposes penalties on those who fight in different places—the king's house; a *minster* (mynstre); an ealdorman's house, or the like; a land-renter's or boor's house; in a field, or at a feast;—graduated according to the character of the place. A 'minster' must here mean a monastery, or a monastic church; and, from the absence of any penalty for fighting in any other consecrated building, it may be inferred that all the churches then in existence, or, at all events, all the public churches, as to which public legislation was thought necessary, were of that character.

Another famous enactment, in favour of the Church, was the 'grant of privileges' by Wihtraed,[3] King of Kent (about A.D. 694), in a Kentish witenagemot, at which both

---

[1] Thorpe's *Ancient Laws and Institutes*, vol. i. p. 102.
[2] *Ibid.*, p. 107.
[3] Anglo-Saxon Chronicle; *sub* A.D. 694 (see Haddan and Stubbs, *Councils*, vol. iii. pp. 238-246).

the Kentish prelates, the Archbishop and the Bishop of Rochester, were present. In the preamble they are said to have treated of, and anxiously examined into, 'the state of the churches of God or monasteries in Kent,' of which the king's predecessors or near relatives were founders. All kings, princes, and other laymen were by that law forbidden to usurp 'dominion over any church or family of a monastery' (*alicujus ecclesiæ vel familiæ monasterii dominium*) so founded; the exclusive right to fill vacancies in the office of abbot or abbess was reserved to the diocesan bishop (*propriæ parochiæ episcopus*); it was declared to be for the metropolitan bishop 'to govern the churches of God, and to choose, appoint, ordain, establish, and correct (*ammonere*) abbots, abbesses, priests, deacons, so that no one of the sheep of the Eternal Shepherd might be lost'; and it was immediately added, that 'this precept is for the monasteries whose names follow: Upminster, Reculver, Southminster, Dover, Folkestone, Lyminge, Sheppey, and Hoo.'

Exemptions from public burdens were by the same law granted to the cathedral churches of Canterbury and Rochester.—It is at least a reasonable inference that these were, at that time, all the public churches in the kingdom of Kent, on which 'the sheep of the Eternal Shepherd,'[1] in that kingdom, were dependent for pastoral care.

§ 4. *Letters of Boniface.*

In the letters of Boniface (then Archbishop of Mentz) to the English Church, and to Archbishop Cuthbert, there is little which has a direct bearing on English church organisation, but much as to abuses connected with monasteries.

---

[1] '*Ne quis ovis de ovibus æterni pastoris erret*' (Haddan and Stubbs, *Councils*, vol. iii. p. 239).

That to the English Church generally[1] (written probably before A.D. 741) has an address, to all the then known orders and degrees of ecclesiastics: 'To all the most reverend bishops, the venerable white-robed members of the presbyterate (*venerabilibus presbyteratus candidatis*), the deacons, canons, clerks, the true flock of Christ, prelates, abbots, and abbesses, the most humble monks, servants of God, virgins consecrated and devoted to God, and all other the maidens of Christ, and generally all Catholics fearing God, of the English stock and race.' Of the rank or office of parish priest there is here no indication. In his letter to Archbishop Cuthbert,[2] the word *parochia* is used as to the bishop's diocese, which he ought to visit once a year, and as to nothing else.

§ 5. *Bede's Letter to Archbishop Egbert.*

Lappenberg,[3] on grounds which do not support his inference from them, treated Bede as an authority for the opinion that parish churches were 'first erected before and during the time of Egbert, Archbishop of York, in the northern parts of England':

'St. Cuthbert, Abbot of Melrose, wandered from place to place to confirm and animate believers by his preaching; yet, when Bede subjoins to this narrative that *such was the custom of the clergy at that time*, it would follow, that in his own days the case was otherwise in those northern parts.'

I am far from clear (considering what we know to have been Bede's opinion as to the corruption and degeneracy of many of the northern clergy between the time of St. Cuthbert's preaching and that at which he wrote), that the

---

[1] Haddan and Stubbs, *Councils*, vol. iii. p. 313.   [2] *Ibid.*, p. 376.
[3] *History of England*, etc. (Thorpe's translation), vol. i. pp. 196, 197.

conclusion would legitimately follow, if the premiss had been correct. But Bede[1] did *not* subjoin to his account of St. Cuthbert's preaching, 'that such was the custom of the clergy at that time.' The passage is this:

'He was wont often to leave his monastery, sometimes on horseback, but more frequently on foot, and to go to the surrounding townships and preach to wanderers the way of truth. . . . For indeed it was at that time the manner *of the English people* (*erat quippe moris eo tempore populus Anglorum*) all to collect together, when a clerk or priest came into their township, at his call, to hear the Word; and to hear gladly those things which were spoken to them; and, still more gladly, to put in practice those things which they could hear and understand.'

He added, that St. Cuthbert went chiefly to the poorest places, and those which were far away in rough and high mountain districts, 'a horror generally to other men.'

Bede, therefore, spoke of the 'custom at that time,' not of the clergy, but of those to whom they preached; and if there be an implied comparison with his own later time, it was not that the people had now the benefit of a settled ministry, under a different system, but that they were less desirous of hearing, and less attentive in practice to what they heard.

If Bede had written as Lappenberg represented him, and if Lappenberg's inference were sound, it would prove too much; viz. that so many parish churches existed in Bede's time, as to have superseded, in the northern province, the need for itinerant preaching, even in wild and outlying places, according to the older custom. This Lappenberg himself evidently did not think. He referred, in a note, to Bede's letter to Archbishop Egbert;[2] but that letter, written

---

[1] *Hist.*, lib. iv., cap. 27.
[2] Haddan and Stubbs, *Councils*, vol. iii. pp. 314-325.

in the last year of Bede's life, is far from supporting, and really repels his inference from the passage in the *History*. It is a document of great interest, for the light which it throws on the state of the Northumbrian Church at that time, and also upon the character of the writer and his correspondent. Egbert had just been made archbishop; he had, according to tradition, been the pupil, and appears plainly by this letter to have been the friend, of Bede. The letter is full of advice—which might be called fatherly but for the rank of the person addressed—to the archbishop personally, as to the conduct and demeanour befitting his high office, and also as to the affairs and wants of the Church.

Bede suggested to the archbishop to follow the example of the Apostles Paul and Barnabas, who, wherever they went, as soon as they entered into cities or synagogues, preached the Word of God. This (he said)[1] 'is the work to which you are called, and for which you were consecrated.'

'And this you will do if, wherever you go, you collect round you the inhabitants of the place, and deliver to them the word of exhortation, and also, as a leader in the heavenly warfare, with all who come with you, set them an example of good living.'

'And since the places which belong to the government of your diocese occupy too wide a space to make it possible for you alone to go through them all, and preach the Word of God in each of the smaller villages and hamlets (*solus per omnia discurrere, et in singulis viculis atque agellis verbum Dei prædicare*), even in the course of a whole year, it is necessary that you should associate with yourself many helpers in this holy work, by appointing priests and teachers to go through all the villages, constantly preaching the Word of God, and consecrating the heavenly mysteries, and especially administering the office of holy baptism, as opportunity may be found.'

---

[1] Haddan and Stubbs, *Councils*, vol. iii. pp. 315, 316, §§ 2, 3.

He then advised that those preachers should teach all the people the Apostles' Creed, and the Lord's Prayer, in the vulgar tongue; not laymen only, 'but also clerks and monks who do not know Latin.'

A little further on [1] he said:

'We have heard, and it is commonly reported, that many townships and villages of our nation are situated among mountains hard of access or in thorny woodlands, where for many years past no bishop has been seen, to confer any of the gifts of the heavenly ministry; and yet no man there can be free from the payment of dues to the bishop; nor is the destitution of those places confined to the want of a bishop to confirm the baptized by laying-on of hands; they have no teacher to instruct them in the true faith, or in the difference between right and wrong.'

These evils he exhorted the archbishop to correct to the best of his power; and expressed his belief that in so doing he would be supported by Ceolwulf, then King of Northumbria; suggesting that the king should be exhorted to put the ecclesiastical state of his people on a better footing than it had ever yet been, which he thought could only be accomplished by an increase in the number of bishops. He referred to Pope Gregory's desire, that twelve suffragan bishops should be consecrated for the province of York, and urged the archbishop to fulfil it (notwithstanding difficulties arising from improvident grants of public land by former kings), by erecting a sufficient number of monasteries into episcopal sees.[2]

He then proceeded to speak[3] of abuses prevailing in many of the monastic houses of the province (*quibus nostra provincia miserrimè vexatur*),[4] and reminded the archbishop that

---

[1] Haddan and Stubbs, *Councils*, vol. iii. p. 417, § 4.
[2] *Ibid.*, pp. 318, 319, § 5.   [3] *Ibid.*, pp. 319-322, §§ 5-8.
[4] *Ibid.*, end of § 7, p. 322.

it belonged to his office to look carefully into all that was done, right or wrong, in the monasteries of his diocese (*in singulis monasteriis tuæ parochiæ*). After dwelling much on this topic, he returned[1] to that with which he began:

'Of those, too, who are still living in the world, it is needful for you to have care, as was said in the outset of this epistle: you should send to them sufficient teachers of the life by which they may be saved, and make them, among other things, learn by what works they may most please God, from what sins those who desire to please God must abstain, with what sincerity they must believe in God, with what devotion they must pray for the Divine mercy, how diligently they should strengthen themselves against the wiles of unclean spirits by the sign of the Lord's cross, how salutary to all Christians is the daily partaking of the Body and Blood of the Lord, according to the constant practice of the Church of Christ in Italy, Gaul, Africa, Greece, and throughout the East.'

And he complained, that, through the negligence of those who ought to teach them, this sort of religion was a thing so far from and foreign (*peregrinum*) to nearly all the laity of the province, that even the more religious only communicated at the three feasts of Christmas, Epiphany and Easter; although there were many persons of pure life, of both sexes, old and young, fit (if they were but properly instructed) to communicate on every Lord's Day and at other festivals.

The tenor of this letter appears to me to be very adverse to the supposition, that the parochial system had been in Bede's time introduced even partially in the Northumbrian province.

§ 6. *Archbishop Cuthbert's Canons.*

As to the south, the evidence of the synod held under Archbishop Cuthbert in A.D. 747[2] is not less strong.

[1] Haddan and Stubbs, *Councils*, vol. iii. p. 323, § 9. [2] *Ibid.*, p. 340.

How far the 'canons' (as they are called) of that synod may have been founded on suggestions made by Pope Zacharias, from whom a letter[1] was read at the opening of the proceedings, it is impossible to say. There are various matters as to which adherence to the Roman usage is enjoined,[2] probably in consequence of those suggestions; but there is much, which does not speak a foreign origin. As I have said of Bede's letter, so I say of those 'canons,' that they are extremely interesting; they breathe a genuine Christian spirit, and leave a favourable impression of the virtues of Archbishop Cuthbert.

At that synod, besides the primate, eleven suffragans of the province of Canterbury were present. I shall refer to those only of its canons which bear upon my immediate subject.

The third[3] directed a visitation of his diocese (*parochiam suam*) by every bishop, in every year; he was to call before him, at convenient places, the people of all conditions, and both sexes, and publicly to teach them 'as those who seldom hear the Word of God' (*utpote eos, qui raro audiunt verbum Dei*); warning them particularly against certain heathen superstitions.

The fourth[4] enjoined the bishops to admonish the abbots and abbesses of their dioceses (*episcopi in suis parochiis abbates atque abbatissas moneant*) properly to perform their duties. Other[5] canons also related to religious houses and their inmates.

The canons which relate to priests[6] imply, not that they,

---

[1] Not now extant.   [2] Canons 13, 15, 16 (Haddan and Stubbs, *Councils*, vol. iii. pp. 367, 368).   [3] *Ibid.*, p. 363.   [4] *Ibid.*, p. 364.

[5] The fifth, seventh, nineteenth, twentieth, twenty-eighth, and twenty-ninth (*ibid.*, pp. 364, 368, 369, 374).

[6] The sixth, eighth, ninth, tenth, eleventh, and twelfth (*ibid.*, pp. 364, 365, 366).

or any of them, were or might be in charge of country parishes, but that they belonged to conventual establishments. Thus, in the eighth [1] (entitled, '*That priests attend carefully to the duty of their office*'),—after mentioning the service of the altar, the care of the church (*oratorii domum*) and its accessories, reading, prayer, masses, and psalm-singing, it is added : 'and to give aid, whenever need may be, diligently and faithfully *to their abbots or abbesses*.' By the fourteenth [2] (as to 'the honour and observance of the Lord's Day'), 'all abbots and priests were required to remain,' on the Lord's Day, 'in *their own monasteries and churches*,'[3] without travelling, etc., unless for some necessary cause, and to preach to the inmates or dependents of each house (*subjectis famulis*).

By the fifteenth,[4] they were ordered to perform the offices and sing the appointed hymns for all the canonical hours of day and night, 'so as to follow everywhere the same rule of monastic psalmody' (*monasterialis psalmodiæ parilitatem*); and to pray, 'ecclesiastics or monks' (*ecclesiastici sive monasteriales*), not for themselves only, but also for their kings and the whole Christian people. The seventeenth canon[5] provided for the observance of certain days, in commemoration of Pope Gregory the Great, and Augustin of Canterbury, as holy days, 'by ecclesiastics and monks' (*ab ecclesiasticis et monasterialibus*). The twenty-first

---

[1] Haddan and Stubbs, *Councils*, vol. iii. p. 365.   [2] *Ibid.*, p. 367.
[3] The twenty-ninth canon (entitled, ' *Ut nullus servorum Dei inter laicos habitet*'), forbids all *clerks* (*clericos*), as well as monks or nuns, to dwell among laymen in secular houses (*apud laicos habitare in domibus sæcularium*); ordering them to return to the monasteries where they first took the monastic habit (*repetant monasteria, ubi primitus habitum sanctæ professionis sumpserant*). *Ibid.*, p. 374.
[4] *Ibid.*, p. 367.   [5] *Ibid.*, p. 368.

canon[1] warned 'monks or ecclesiastics' (*monasteriales sive ecclesiastici*) against drunkenness; the twenty-second[2] exhorted them (by the same description) to frequent communion. The ninth[3] article, as to the employment of priests by the bishops in country places, I translate fully:

'That priests be careful diligently, and according to due order, to fulfil the duty of evangelical and apostolical preaching, by baptizing, teaching, and visiting, through those places and regions of the lay people, which have been suggested and enjoined to them by the bishops of the province (*per loca et regiones laicorum, quæ sibi ab episcopis provinciæ insinuata et injuncta sunt*); so that, according to the Apostle's word, they may be held worthy of double honour; and be very careful, as becomes God's ministers, to set no examples of discreditable or evil conversation, either to secular men or to monastics (*sæcularibus sive monasterialibus*); that is (to mention nothing else), either in drunkenness or for filthy lucre's sake, or by filthy speaking, or the like.'

Throughout this body of canons, from first to last, there is nothing implying the existence of, nothing applicable to, a parochial system. Nor is anything of that kind, during the rest of the same period down to the close of the century, elsewhere to be found. Neither in Archbishop Egbert's 'Penitential,'[4] nor in his answers to certain questions, known as his 'Dialogue of Ecclesiastical Ordinances,'[5] is there anything on that point.[6]

[1] Haddan and Stubbs, *Councils*, vol. iii. p. 369.
[2] *Ibid.*, p. 370.   [3] *Ibid.*, p. 365.
[4] *Ibid.*, pp. 416-431. The 'Penitential' (as given by Wasserschleben, and by Haddan and Stubbs), and the 'Dialogue,' are the only works ascribed to Egbert, which may really have been his.
[5] *Ibid.*, pp. 403-413.
[6] *Respons. ad Interrogat.* 12 (*ibid.*, pp. 408, 409).

§ 7. *Episcopal Power as to Revenues.*

From Theodore's time until the legatine councils of A.D. 785-787, we have no information as to tithes in England, except one incidental allusion[1] in the letter of Boniface to Archbishop Cuthbert, written between A.D. 746 and 749. Quoting from Ezekiel (xxxiv. 25), 'Woe be to the shepherds of Israel that feed the flock: should not the shepherds feed the flock? Ye eat the fat, and ye clothe you with the wool,' etc.,—he translated 'shepherds' into 'bishops,' and 'the flock' into 'Christian people' (*per pastores episcopos significat; greges Domini, id est, fideles populos ad pascendum*); and continued: 'In daily offerings and tithes of the people, they receive the milk and wool of the sheep (*lac et lanas ovium Christi oblationibus quotidianis ac decimis fidelium suscipiunt*); but they take no care of the Lord's flock.'

Boniface was Archbishop of Mentz; but he was an Englishman; and writing on matters concerning the English Church to the English primate, he must have thought what he said applicable to England. His words, therefore, may be accepted as evidence, that tithes were paid in England at that time, and that they went into a diocesan treasury, the revenues of which were at the bishop's disposal.

Bede's letter to Archbishop Egbert does not anywhere mention tithes; but it speaks[2] of the bishop as the receiver of those church dues which were paid as of obligation, even in places which the ordinary ministrations of the church did not reach. Of the administration of church revenues

---

[1] Haddan and Stubbs, *Councils.*, vol. iii. p. 380.
[2] Sect. 4 (*ibid.*, p. 317).

by a good Anglo-Saxon bishop at the end of that century (so far as relates to hospitality and almsgiving), some opinion may be formed, from a letter written in A.D. 796, by Alcuin[1] to Archbishop Eanbald of York, in which he urged the importance of choosing suitable places for 'guest-houses or hospitals (*xenodochia, id est hospitalia*), for the daily entertainment of poor persons and strangers;' (*in quibus sit quotidiana pauperum et peregrinorum susceptio, et ex nostris substantiis habeant solatia*). Alcuin was Abbot of Ferrieres in France.

§ 8. *King Offa.*

A few modern writers (whom some persons even now accept as authorities) have ascribed to Offa, King of Mercia (who died, after a long reign, in A.D. 796), a grant of tithes to the Church. The story is thus told by Dean Prideaux[2] in his book about Tithes:

'About the year 794, Offa made a law whereby he gave unto the Church the tithes of all his kingdom, which the historians tell us was done to expiate for the death of Ethelbert, King of the East Angles.'

Dean Prideaux seems to have persuaded himself, not only that this was true, but that, in making such a law, Offa intended to imitate Charlemagne's capitulars; of which he supposed Charlemagne to have sent him copies.

What historians tell us this? There are fables enough about King Offa in some of the Chronicles; and for this fable, the Chronicle of John Bromton, Abbot of Jorvaulx

---

[1] Haddan and Stubbs, *Councils*, vol. iii. p. 504.

[2] *The Original and Right of Tithes*, published in A.D. 1709 (2nd ed., London 1736, pp. 101-103).

in Yorkshire, is cited. That work belongs to the latter part of the fourteenth century, and is of no credit, except when derived from earlier sources.[1] No statement of that 'historian' would be worth anything, as proof that Offa 'gave unto the Church the tithes of all his kingdom,' if he had said so. But neither Bromton, nor any other historian, did say so. What Bromton[2] said is this:

'This Offa, by the wicked advice of his wife, treacherously put to death St. Ethelbert, King of the East Anglians, when visiting him as a suitor to his daughter: in atonement for which sin, he brought down his pride to such a degree of humility and penitence, that he gave to Holy Church *a tenth of all that belonged to him (decimam omnium rerum suarum sanctæ ecclesiæ dedit)*, and also conferred, as it is said, many lands upon the Church of Hereford, in which the same glorious martyr Ethelbert lies; which lands that church possesses to this day.'

He went on to speak of the translation, by the same king, of the relics of St. Alban to Verulam; of his foundation of St. Alban's Abbey; of his journey to Rome; and of his gift of Peter's pence to the Pope.

Only two later chroniclers followed Bromton in that statement;—Polydore Vergil,[3] in the time of Henry VIII., and Holinshed,[4] in the time of Elizabeth. Polydore Vergil's

---

[1] See Mr. Thorpe's 'Literary Introduction' to his translation of Lappenberg, p. lix. The Chronicle is supposed to have been written under Abbot Bromton's name, not by himself.

[2] Twysden's *Hist. Angl. Script. X.* (1651-52), p. 775.

[3] *Hist. Angl.*, lib. iv., ed. 1649, p. 99. Polydore Vergil was an Italian, of Urbino, who, having come to England to collect 'Peter's pence' for the Roman see, remained in this country, and was made Archdeacon of Wells. He published his History of England, with a dedication to Henry VIII., in A.D. 1533.

[4] *History of England*, book vi. cap. 6. Holinshed was a bookseller, and not the author of the 'History' which he published.

words are, that 'for fear of the punishment due to his sins, he determined to appease the wrath of God, and gave *the tenth part of all his goods* to priests and other poor men (*decimam partem omnium bonorum sacerdotibus aliisque inopibus hominibus condonavit*). Polydore added, that, being truly penitent, he did not consider that he had by this, or by his foundation of St. Alban's and Bath Abbeys, and the church which he built at Hereford, done enough; but that he also went to Rome to obtain absolution, and there 'made his realm tributary,' by the grant of Peter's pence, to the Pope. Holinshed translated Polydore: 'Finally, King Offa, as it were for a means to appease God's wrath, which he doubted to be justly conceived towards him for his sin and wickedness, granted *the tenth part of his goods* unto churchmen and to poor people.'

If this story had been true, it would not have been to the purpose. A gift of the tenth part of a man's own goods or property has nothing, beyond the principle of decimation, in common with a law for the payment of tithes. Selden[1] referred (among other things) to this story, as told by Polydore Vergil, when he was discussing the question (with which I shall deal in its proper place) of a later supposed grant of tithes by King Ethelwulf, the father of Alfred.

'Should it' (he said) 'be understood only for a particular consecration to the Church of one time, and of the land itself, to be employed to other good uses of charity, then had it no more place here among the laws of tithes, than the story of Robert, Earl of Gloucester, his giving every tenth stone of his provision for the building of a tower near to Bristol, to the erecting of a chapel; or Edward the Confessor, his building

---

[1] *Hist. of Tithes*, ch. 8, § 4, p. 208 (ed. 1618).

Westminster Abbey with the tenth of one year's revenue; *or Offa's giving the tithe of his estate to the clergy and the poor.*'

I must not omit to add that, except as to the murder of King Ethelbert, and the grant of Peter's pence (of which, if really made by Offa, the date and the occasion were misrepresented), the story is mythical. Neither the alleged gift of a tenth of Offa's estate or goods to the Church, nor his alleged journey to Rome, is mentioned by the author of the Anglo-Saxon Chronicle, or Asser, or Ethelward (who wrote before the Conquest); nor by Florence of Worcester, or the author of the history current under the name of Ingulph (who wrote in the eleventh century); nor by William of Malmesbury, Henry of Huntingdon, or Symeon of Durham (who wrote in the twelfth century); nor by Diceto, or Gervase of Canterbury, or John of Wallingford, or Roger Hoveden, or John, Abbot of Peterborough, or the Melrose Chronicle (which belong to the thirteenth century). All those writers spoke more or less of Offa; all, except Symeon, the Abbot of Peterborough, and the Melrose Chronicle, spoke of the murder of King Ethelbert; and several of them (Asser, Malmesbury, Hoveden, and the Melrose Chronicle) told or repeated a romantic story, as to the crimes, adventures, and miserable end of one of Offa's daughters.[1]

In the latter part of the thirteenth century, the mythical element which had gathered round the memory of King Offa received great development in the *Flowers of Histories* of Roger of Wendover (Prior of Belvoir), and in the *Lives of the Two Offas*, by a monk of St. Albans, generally

[1] *Asser* (Wise's ed., Oxford 1722), p. 16; and Giles' *Six Old English Chronicles* (1848), p. 47; *Malmesbury* (Hardy's ed. 1840), *De Gestis Regum*, vol. i. pp. 169, 170; *Hoveden* (Riley's transl. 1853), p. 19; *Melrose* (in Fulman's *Rerum Anglic. Scriptores*, Oxford 1684, p. 140.)

identified with Matthew Paris. It is to the imagination or credulity of those writers (who in the succeeding century were followed by Matthew of Westminster and Bromton), that we owe Offa's supposed journey to Rome,[1] and the attempt to excuse[2] him from the guilt of being a principal actor in King Ethelbert's murder, by representing his queen (a lady commended by Alcuin,[3] in Offa's lifetime, for her virtue and piety) as performing in that transaction a part not unlike that of a Jezebel or Lady Macbeth.[4] But even Wendover and the monk of St. Albans (though the latter, in his enthusiasm for the founder of that monastery, calls him 'magnificent,' 'most glorious,' 'most religious,' and omits nothing which might be supposed to do

---

[1] *Wendover* (Coxe's ed. 1841), p. 254; *Lives of Offas* (Matt. Paris, *Historia Major*, etc., London 1640, p. 28); *Matt. Westminster* (Frankfort ed. 1601), p. 169; *Bromton* (Twysden, *Hist. Angl. Script. X.*), pp. 775, 776.

[2] *Wendover* (*ubi supra*), p. 249; *Lives of Offas* (*ubi supra*), pp. 23-25; *Matt. Westminster* (*ubi supra*), pp. 147, 148.

[3] Alcuin's Letters in Migne's *Patrologiæ cursus*, ep. 50. The date assigned to it there (A.D. 796) is manifestly wrong. Prince Ecgfrid was crowned king in his father's lifetime, A.D. 786 or 787; and this letter was evidently written on that occasion.

[4] Florence of Worcester also (a more trustworthy authority), though he did not excuse Offa, or relate the extraordinary tale of Wendover and the monk of St. Albans, said that Queen Cynethryth suggested the murder. Lappenberg, who was more disposed than seems quite reasonable to give credence to romantic passages in the chroniclers, repeats (p. 237 of Mr. Thorpe's translation) a story that Queen Cynethryth was, three months after the murder of Ethelbert (*i.e.* in or soon after A.D. 792), 'thrown by robbers into her own well;' which (he says), 'if void of truth, may nevertheless serve to show what her contemporaries thought of her.' How such a story, told in a book written more than 400 years afterwards, could be evidence of what *contemporaries* thought, it is not easy to see. As a matter of fact, Queen Cynethryth survived Offa: she attested two charters of her son Ecgfrid during his short reign in A.D. 796 (Kemble, *Cod. Diplom.* A.D. 796).

him honour) are silent as to any gift by him of tithes of any sort or kind; as also is Matthew of Westminster, who followed them. Of the story, therefore, on that subject, such as it is, the author of Bromton's Chronicle seems to have been the inventor; and, as that story says nothing about any 'law made by Offa, whereby he gave to the Church the tithes of all his kingdom,' and as the report of the proceedings of the Legatine Council of Chalchyth in A.D. 785-787 was unknown to the world until its publication in the latter part of the sixteenth century, it is impossible to search for an explanation of it in those proceedings.

CHAPTER III

SECOND PERIOD—LEGATINE INJUNCTIONS OF CHALCHYTH,
A.D. 785-787

§ 1. *Article as to Tithes*

NOTHING which bears upon the history of tithes in England, beyond the simple inculcation of their payment as, in the view of the Church of that day, a religious duty, is to be found in the twenty Injunctions or Articles,[1] delivered in the name of Pope Adrian I. by his legates, at the Legatine Councils held in this country in A.D. 785-787. Before entering into the question of the general nature and character of those Injunctions, it may be convenient to give a translation of the particular article (the seventeenth),[2] in which alone tithes are mentioned, and which also relates to some other subjects:

'The seventeenth Article :—Of giving tithes, as it is written in the law, "Thou shalt bring the tenth part of all thy crops or first-fruits (*frugibus seu primitiis*) into the house of the Lord thy God." Again, by the prophet, "Bring (he says) all the tithes into my barn, that there may be meat in mine house; and prove me now herewith, if I will not open unto you the windows (*cataractas*) of heaven, and pour you out a blessing,

---

[1] Haddan and Stubbs, *Councils*, vol. iii. pp. 447-459. (The number of these Injunctions is stated as twenty-nine, by an error overlooked in correction, in *Defence of the Church*, etc., p. 129.) [2] *Ibid.*, p. 456.

even to abundance (*usque ad abundantiam*); and I will rebuke the devourer for your sakes, who eateth and spoileth (*qui comedit et corrumpit*) the fruit of your ground, and your vineyard shall no more be barren (*et non erit ultra vinea sterilis*) in the field, saith the Lord." As saith the wise man : " No man can give a true alms of that which he possesseth, unless he hath first separated to the Lord what He from the beginning has appointed for man to render Him." And through this it commonly happens that he who does not give a tenth is himself reduced to a tenth. Wherefore also we solemnly lay upon you this precept, that all be careful to give tithes of all that they possess, because that is the special part of the Lord God (*quia speciale Domini Dei est*); and let a man live on the nine parts, and give alms; and we advised, that this should rather be done secretly, because it is written, " When thou doest thine alms, do not sound a trumpet before thee."

'We also forbade usury; for the Lord said to David that the man should be "worthy to dwell in His tabernacle who had not given his money upon usury." Augustine also saith : " No one has unjust gain without just loss. Where gain is there is loss; it is gain in the chest, but loss in the conscience."

'We ordained also (*statuimus*) that men should set forth (*statuant*) equal measures and equal weights for all, it being said by Solomon, " Weight and weight, measure and measure, the Lord hateth"; that is, that no man do sell to another by a different weight or measure from that wherewith he buys, because everywhere God "loveth justice," and "His countenance beholdeth equity."'

I should have thought that the terms of this article were sufficient to speak for themselves; that their character is evident; being that of pastoral precept, not legal enactment. But a disposition has been manifested in certain quarters to claim for this Injunction (accepted, as in some sense it undoubtedly was, by the kings of Northumbria and Mercia) the character of a civil enactment for the payment of tithes. An authority which I hold in much respect has been supposed to give some countenance to that view. The subject, therefore, of the Legatine Mission, Synods, and Injunctions, of A.D. 785-787, ought to be fully examined.

§ 2. *Causes of the Legatine Mission.*

The causes which led Pope Adrian I. to send George, Bishop of Ostia, and Theophylact, Bishop of Todi, as his legates to this country, may be collected from known facts with reasonable certainty. For nearly a century the Anglo-Saxon Church had been governed by native prelates, some of whom visited Rome; and letters from the Roman see (*e.g.* that of Pope Zacharias[1] in Archbishop Cuthbert's time) were from time to time received by the English Church. But no Papal legate had visited England since the time of Augustin; and the English Church was practically independent. Pope Adrian was a statesman; he had obtained from Charlemagne protection, friendship, and large territorial possessions. And he had paid his price for them. He knew, probably, that the relations of Charlemagne and Offa, whatever professions might be made on either side, were not very cordial; he may have felt a doubt how far his own security might be affected by any policy intended to improve them, unless he could succeed in conciliating to himself the goodwill of both kings. That he was seriously apprehensive, down to A.D. 784 or 785, of intrigues on the part of Offa to depose him from the Papal throne, and to obtain Charlemagne's consent to the substitution of a Frank Pope, is clear from a letter[2] which he wrote about that time to Charlemagne, from whom he had received reassuring messages upon the subject. This was the position and the state of mind of the Pope.

[1] Haddan and Stubbs, *Councils*, vol. iii. p. 360.   [2] *Ibid.*, p. 440.

On the other hand, King Offa had an object of his own to accomplish, in which the Pope's assistance was important to him, if not indispensable. He was jealous of a primacy over the churchmen of his kingdom, the seat of which was beyond his own border, and easy of access from the continent of Europe. He desired to deprive the see of Canterbury, not of precedence, but of power; and to make Mercia ecclesiastically independent, with a metropolitan of its own, whose primacy should extend to the bishoprics of East Anglia, which, though not yet annexed to Mercia, was under its influence. It is not necessary, for an explanation of this policy, to suppose (as one of the chroniclers[1] says), that Offa feared an invasion of England by Charlemagne, and distrusted the fidelity of Jaenberht, then Archbishop of Canterbury; or (with Dean Hook[2]) that Archbishop Jaenberht was intriguing with the Frank king, and aspiring, in imitation of the Pope, to civil sovereignty in Kent, the direct line of whose kings had become extinct. The contests for supremacy, and the changes in the balance of power, within England itself—Mercia aiming at, and seeming at that time likely to obtain, the position which, under Egbert, was not long afterwards obtained by Wessex,—and Kent being a small kingdom, never likely to be again independent, yet not in acknowledged dependence on

---

[1] The author of the *Lives of the Two Offas*.(Matt. Paris, ed. 1640, p. 21). Other chroniclers (Diceto, Wendover, and Matthew of Westminster) speak of enmity on the part of Offa towards the Kentish men; and the language of the letter of Offa's successor, Kenwulf, to Pope Leo III., in A.D. 798, asking for the restoration of the see of Canterbury to its former rights, is to the like effect: '*Cujus dignitatis honorem primum Rex Offa, propter inimicitiam cum venerabili Janberto et gente Cantuariorum acceptam, avertere, et in duas parochias dissipare, nisus.*' (Haddan and Stubbs, *Councils*, vol. iii. p. 522.)

[2] *Lives of Archbishops*, 3rd ed., vol. i. pp. 245, 246.

Mercia, and liable, from its situation, to fall at any time under West Saxon influence,—these were sufficient reasons for Offa's wish that the ecclesiastics of his kingdom should be placed under an archbishop of his own at Lichfield. The opportunity was favourable, because of the preponderance at that time of his power; he could reckon upon the acquiescence, if not support, of the other kings south of the Humber; and Kent, without any acknowledged king, could not offer an effectual resistance. The Pope, however, must give the pall, to place a new archbishop in Mercia upon an equality with other metropolitans; and for that it was necessary to obtain the concurrence of Rome. Offa therefore (as we know from that letter of Pope Adrian to Charlemagne, which has been already mentioned) sent a special mission[1] to Rome, accompanied and recommended by messengers from Charlemagne; and the Pope (as he said), to please Charlemagne, agreed to comply with the wishes which, on Offa's part, they expressed. The legatine mission to England soon followed; which again was accompanied by a French abbot,[2] sent by Charlemagne to give such aid to the legates as might be in his power.

[1] William of Malmesbury (*Gesta Regum*, Hardy's ed., p. 119) and the author of the *Lives of the Two Offas* (Matt. Paris, ed. 1640, p. 21) speak of this mission from Offa to Rome, and of its object.

[2] Wigbod, of whom nothing else is known (Haddan and Stubbs, vol. iii. p. 448; and see *ibid.*, p. 461, note). He accompanied the chief legate (Bishop George) into Northumbria, and it is probable that he may have been a friend of Alcuin's, sent at his instance to secure for the legates a favourable reception in the northern kingdom, with which Alcuin was more closely connected by birth, education, and friendship than with other parts of England. Eanbald, then Archbishop of York, was succeeded in A.D. 796 by another prelate of the same name, who was a friend and correspondent (perhaps a pupil) of Alcuin; (see Haddan and Stubbs, *Councils*, vol. iii. pp. 500 note, 501, 505, 507, 534).

It may be concluded, under these circumstances, that the understanding arrived at in Rome was this. The Pope was to send representatives to England, with a commission authorising them to inquire into the state and condition of the English Church, and to give such pastoral counsels as might seem to him necessary. Friendly relations between the Roman see and that Church already existed, but they were to be more firmly established; and the legates were to be empowered, on the Pope's behalf, to assent to the King of Mercia's wishes for the creation of a new province, separate from Canterbury, with a metropolitan see at Lichfield, if the concurrence of a provincial synod could be obtained.

For the conclusion of this arrangement, King Offa's ambassadors doubtless employed such means as they and their master considered likely to be effectual. The use of questionable means is alleged in the solemn Act of the Council of Cloveshoo,[1] by which the see of Canterbury was restored to its former authority in A.D. 803; (Pope Leo III. and Kenwulf King of Mercia then reversing the policy of their predecessors); and the chroniclers tell us, that large sums of money were spent on the negotiation. The monk of St. Alban's,[2] Offa's biographer and encomiast (though in names and other particulars certainly incorrect), was probably not far from the mark, when he said that Offa did not rely only on his confidence in the Pope's 'pre-eminent sanctity,' or upon the 'discretion and elo-

---

[1] Haddon and Stubbs, *Councils*, vol. iii., p. 543: '*Cartam a Romanâ Sede missam per Adrianum Papam de palleo et de Archiepiscopatus Sede in Liccedfeldensi monasterio, cum consensu domini Apostolici Leonis Papæ præscribimus* [non] *aliquid valere, quia per subreptitionem et male blandam suggessionem adipiscebatur.*'

[2] *Lives of the Two Offas* (Matt. Paris, ed. 1640, p. 21).

quence' of his own ambassadors; but that he 'knew what it was that the Romans wanted' (*noverat erim Rex desideria Romanorum*); and carried his point by means of gifts.

The impost called 'Peter's pence' may, not improbably, have been part of the price paid for the Pope's assistance on that occasion. This indeed is not mentioned by any chronicler older than Henry of Huntingdon[1] (A.D. 1135-1184); and he assigns to it an earlier date. Supposing dates to be mistaken, he and the chroniclers who followed him (in this respect) in the thirteenth and fourteenth centuries—Diceto,[2] Hoveden,[3] and Higden[4]—are all the more credible, because none of them spoke of any journey of Offa to Rome. That impost was certainly subsisting in and before Edward the Elder's time.[5] It is said, by some writers,[6] to have been imposed in Wessex by King Ina, early in the eighth century; and to have been in the ninth century confirmed and extended by King Ethelwulf.[7] If the story as to Ina's grant of Peter's pence was true, there is no reason for disbelieving the like story as to Offa; and it is not improbable, that his ambassadors, who conducted the negotiation at Rome which led to the legatine mission, may have offered that contribution, on Offa's part, to the Papal treasury.

[1] Book iv.; under A.D. 755 (Forester's translation, 1883, p. 133).

[2] Savile's *Hist. Angl. Script. X.*, p. 446. (Diceto connects the gift with the later foundation of St. Alban's Abbey, as do also Wendover, the author of the *Lives of the Two Offas*, Bromton, and Matthew of Westminster.)

[3] Riley's transl., 1853, p. 24.

[4] Gale's *Rer. Angl. Script. XV.*, p. 250. (Hardyng and Polydore Vergil also mention Offa as author of the impost.)

[5] See Thorpe's *Ancient Laws and Institutes*, vol. i. p. 171.

[6] *E.g.* Higden (Gale, *Script. XV., supra*, under A.D. 728).

[7] *E.g.* Higden (Gale, p. 253); Bromton (Gale's *Script. XX.*, Oxford 1691, p. 808).

The fact of the legatine mission, and its object, as declared on the Pope's part, are attested by two of our earliest and most trustworthy chroniclers—the 'Anglo-Saxon Chronicle,'[1] and Symeon of Durham.[2] Of the object, both speak in almost the same words :—' to renew the faith and the peace which St. Gregory had sent us by the Bishop Augustin,' is the phrase of the former; 'renewing among us the ancient friendship and Catholic faith which the holy Pope Gregory taught by the blessed Augustin,' of the latter. Symeon mentions ' the Venerable Bishop George,' as holding the first place in the legation. He assigns A.D. 786 as the date: the Anglo-Saxon Chronicle gave A.D. 785. Henry of Huntingdon[3] put it in the second year of Beohrtric, King of Wessex, (successor of Kenwulf of Wessex); which could not be earlier than A.D. 787. The Anglo-Saxon Chronicle, and Florence of Worcester,[4] mention, under the same date (A.D. 785), a 'contentious,' or 'litigious,' synod at Chalchyth, at which ' Jaenberht gave up some portion of his bishopric, and Higbert was elected by King Offa, and Egferth (Offa's son) was consecrated king.' Those writers do not speak of the legates as present at that synod : but Huntingdon says[5] that it was held by the legates. There is a letter extant from Pope Leo III.[6] to Offa's successor, Kenwulf of Mercia, in which that Pope spoke of a vow made by Offa to

---

[1] Under A.D. 785. (The passage is extracted in Haddan and Stubbs, *Councils*, vol. iii. p. 444.)

[2] Savile's *Hist. Angl. Script. X.*, p. 110 (Haddan and Stubbs, *Councils*, vol. iii. p. 443).

[3] Forester's translation, 1853, p. 137 (see Haddan and Stubbs' extract from the original, *Councils*, vol. iii. p. 445).

[4] A.-S. Chron., *ubi supra*. Florence, under A.D. 785 (Thorpe's ed. 1848, p. 61).   [5] *Ubi supra.*

[6] Dated A.D. 798 (Haddan and Stubbs, *Councils*, vol. iii. p. 523; see p. 525).

send a certain sum yearly to Rome for charitable purposes, 'in the presence of a synod, as well of all the bishops, princes, and great men, and the whole people dwelling in the island of Britain, as of our most trusty messengers, the most holy Bishops George and Theophylact.' Higbert of Lichfield assumed the style of Archbishop (in charters still extant,[1] which he signed) during the course of the year A.D. 788; having waited, probably, until that time for the pall from Rome. He continued to hold the same dignity during the rest of Offa's life, and for several years afterwards; retiring from the episcopate,[2] when Pope Leo III. reversed the action of his predecessor, and restored to the see of Canterbury its former pre-eminence.

§ 3. *Character of the Legatine Injunctions.*

It is not an uncommon thing for questionable propositions to be advanced as admitting of no doubt,—sometimes by persons whose judgment is entitled to great respect. It becomes those who call them in question to avoid mere strength of assertion, and to rely on the force of their reasons.

I find it stated, as the opinion of two learned and excellent scholars,[3] to whose labours all students of English ecclesiastical history are deeply indebted, that the decrees of the councils held under Pope Adrian's legates 'were accepted as binding by the Kings and Witan of Mercia and Northumbria, and probably by the Witan of Wessex also;' and (as to the article relating to tithes) that 'there can be no doubt that the legatine canon, as approved by the

---

[1] Haddan and Stubbs, *Councils*, vol. i. p. 446, note (and see the charters in Kemble's *Cod. Diplom.*, there referred to).

[2] He signed the Acts of the Synod of Cloveshoo in A.D. 803, as *Abbot*, after Aldulf, then Bishop of Lichfield. (See Haddan and Stubbs, *ibid.*)

[3] Haddan and Stubbs, *Councils*, vol. iii. p. 637, note.

Kings and Witan, had the force of law; although it is uncertain by what means the law was enforced, or whether it was enforced at all.'

The word *canon* is very flexible, when applied to the Acts of ecclesiastical synods; it would be idle to demur to that phrase if it stood alone. If, by 'law,' canon law only were meant, I might content myself by saying that sanctions, of some kind, seem practically necessary to the idea of law; and that the matter of these (so-called) 'canons' does not agree with my conception, even of canon law. But if (as some have understood) more than this is meant by the words which I have quoted,—if the 'law' intended be a civil enactment, or a civil confirmation of an ecclesiastical law by a secular legislature—then I not only doubt, but I am obliged to dispute the proposition. I think I can show good reasons for my belief that it is erroneous and untenable :—reasons depending partly on external, and partly on internal evidence.

§ 4. *The Legates' Report: how known.*

The external evidence is that contained in the report made by the legates themselves (or rather by George, Bishop of Ostia, the head of the mission) to the Pope.

It is remarkable, that our knowledge of this document is derived entirely from the *Magdeburg Centuries*,[1] published in A.D. 1567 at Basle by an association of Protestant writers, in a voluminous compilation, relative to the church history of the twelve first centuries. They have told us nothing about the manuscript which they used; what was its antiquity, or its place of custody; or how it

[1] *Ecclesiastica Historia, per aliquot studiosos et pios viros in urbe Magdeburgica*' (Basileæ, 1567, Centuria VIII., cap. 9, pp. 574, 575, under the heading '*Alia Synodus Anglica*').

came to their knowledge. Its proper place of custody would seem to have been in the archives of the Vatican, to which they were not likely to have access. If it (or any original or copy of it) were now in the Vatican, the research of later scholars would (I suppose) long since have traced it out, and placed it, in a complete form, and with all the aids of criticism, before the world; but there is no reason[1] to believe that it has ever been seen or known since the time of the Magdeburg 'Centuriators.' I have said this, not as doubting its genuineness; for I concur without hesitation in the opinion,[2] that it contains sufficient internal proof of authenticity; but because it is not probable that, if the Injunctions which we now know from this source only had entered into the body of the public law of the three greatest Anglo-Saxon kingdoms of the eighth century, they would, in this country, have entirely disappeared.

I ought not to be understood as suggesting, that no copies of these Injunctions were formerly in the hands of Anglo-Saxon ecclesiastics and men of learning. From the nature of the case, that could hardly be; and it is clear, as the matter stands, that they were in the hands of Archbishop Odo in the tenth century; who said that he compiled those Injunctions of his own, which have been miscalled *canons*,[3] 'from the former injunctions of illustrious men.' In that compilation there is one article (the tenth, as to tithes[4]) which is an abridgment of the corresponding part of the seventeenth article of the legatine synods; and in the second article (as to kings), the third (as to bishops), the seventh (as to marriages), and the

---

[1] Haddan and Stubbs, *Councils*, vol. iii. p. 461 (first note). [2] *Ibid.*
[3] Spelman's *Concilia*, vol. i. p. 415; Wilkins' *Concilia*, vol. i. p. 212; Johnson's *Laws and Canons*, vol. i. p. 358 (Oxford ed. 1850).
[4] Johnson's *Laws and Canons*, vol. i. p. 363 (Oxford ed. 1850).

eighth (as to unity), other things[1] are also taken directly from the same legatine Injunctions. Not only did Archbishop Odo so partially reproduce (without naming) them; but he is a witness to their character, as lessons of spiritual admonition and instruction, not laws. He prefixed to his compilation (after an invocation of the Holy Trinity) this preamble :[2]

'Though it be a bold presumption to give documents of pious exhortation, without having any merits of my own; yet, because a spiritual prize is promised to them that strive and take pains in the race of this life, by the Author of gifts, the Spirit; therefore I, Odo, the lowly, and meanest of those promoted to the honour of a pall, and of being a chief prelate, have resolved to put together in this paper some institutions not unworthy of any worshipper of Christ, which I found to be of the greatest authority, from the former injunctions of illustrious men, to the consolation of my lord the king, that is Eadmund, and of all the people subject to his most excellent empire. Therefore I most devoutly beseech, and with clemency exhort the minds of the hearers, that they inwardly graft them in their hearts by frequent meditation, whenever they hear them rehearsed; and thus, at the time of harvest, gather for themselves the most peaceable fruit, by the manifold exercise of good works.'

§ 5. *The Legates' Narrative.*

I pass to the narrative of the legates, which is not, in my judgment, imperfect; neither does its termination seem to me abrupt.[3] If it has no formal conclusion, neither has it any formal commencement; the 'Centuriators' omitted

[1] See Appendix B for a collation of the Latin passages in Odo's and the legatine Injunctions.

[2] Johnson's *Laws and Canons*, vol. i. p. 358.

[3] See Haddan and Stubbs, *Councils*, vol. iii. p. 462 (last note, in which it is suggested, that the report is imperfect, because it ends abruptly, without any formal conclusion; and that, if perfect, it might have been expected to contain all the other proceedings of the Synod of Chalchyth).

both; and it was consistent with their method to do so. In all other respects the document is complete in itself. The date which the 'Centuriators' assigned to the mission is A.D. 786; they described its objects very much as the English chroniclers did: 'To travel through and visit this island, and to confirm the authority of the Roman pontiff, acquired there formerly through the mission of Augustin'; and they introduced the report with the words, 'What they did and effected, they themselves thus explain.'[1]

The material points in the narrative are, that, having landed in England, and having seen Archbishop Jaenberht at Canterbury, and given him such information as they thought necessary, they went to Offa's palace, where they were well received; meeting him, and also Kenwulf,[2] King of Wessex, who both promised the amendment of some matters of which the Pope had spoken in his letters accrediting the mission. A consultation followed, not with those kings only, but also with the bishops and lords of the land (*pontificibus et senioribus terrae*); which resulted in Theophylact following the court of Offa into Mercia, with the intention to visit Wales; and in George (with Charlemagne's Abbot Wigbod[3]) going to York, from

[1] *Ecclesiastica Historia*, etc., pp. 574, 575.

[2] Kenwulf was assassinated A.D. 786. But, even if that (and not A.D. 785, as stated in the Anglo-Saxon Chronicle) was the year of the legates' arrival in England, the meeting recorded by the legates might well take place before his assassination. The mention of his name, therefore, creates no difficulty. He is not stated to have been present at either Council.

[3] See *ante*, p. 148. It is worth noting that Offa did not send any ambassadors with the legates to the King of Northumbria, but the latter king sent ambassadors to Offa on Bishop George's return. It may be conjectured, that Theophylact remained with Offa to complete the negotiations as to that king's own business; and that, until that was settled to his satisfaction, Offa was not disposed to give active assistance to the Pope.

whence, through Archbishop Eanbald, messengers were sent to Aelfwald, King of Northumbria. He convened a council, which was attended by all the principal people of those parts, clergy and laymen; and the legate then read the Injunctions prepared (as the report said), as to all the matters which were understood to need correction. All the several points were explained in their order; and those who were present, professing submission to the Pope, as represented by the legates, unanimously promised obedience (*tam admonitionem vestram, quam parvitatem nostram, amplexantes, spoponderunt se in omnibus obedire*). The Pope's letters were then read; the legate exhorting (*contestantes*) his hearers to keep, and to cause those under them to keep, the Pope's 'decrees.'[1]

The text of the Injunctions (twenty in number) follows,[2] after which the narrative is resumed:

'These decrees, most blessed Pope Hadrian, we propounded (*proposuimus*) in public council, before King Aelfwald and Archbishop Eanbald, and all the bishops and abbots of that region, and the senators, dukes, and people of the land, who (as we have already said) vowed that they would keep them in all points to the utmost of their power, the Most High in His mercy helping them;' and this vow they confirmed by signing the sign of the Cross, both on the legate's hand as representing the Pope, and on the paper containing the Injunctions, which they subscribed.[3]

The names of the subscribers are given at length. They were the king, and all the bishops of the province of York; also an Irish bishop (of Mayo), and another bishop, whose see was not specified (he is supposed to have been

---

[1] Haddan and Stubbs, *Councils*, vol. iii. pp. 447, 448 (where the introductory statement of the Magdeburg 'Centuriators' is omitted.
[2] *Ibid.*, pp. 448-459.   [3] *Ibid.*, pp. 459, 460.

Welsh), and who signed by proxy. Two abbots and three lay noblemen also signed.

'This done,' the legates returned southward, accompanied by two 'readers,'[1] envoys of King Aelfwald and his archbishop, who are stated to have brought 'the same decrees' with them 'into the council of the Mercians, where the glorious King Offa and the senators of the land had met together with Archbishop Jaenberht of Canterbury and the other bishops of those parts.' There, 'in the presence of the council,' all the articles (*capitula*) were read through and explained, both in Latin and in Saxon; and all with one voice thankfully promised, 'in answer to the Pope's apostolical admonitions (*apostolatus vestri admonitionibus*), that by God's help they would in all things observe those constitutions (*statuta*) according to the degree of their strength' (*juxta qualitatem virium*);—confirming that promise (as in the north) by the sign of the Cross upon the legate's hand as the Pope's representative, and also before their names subscribed to the paper; which were those of King Offa, and of the archbishop and all the bishops of the province of Canterbury, four abbots, and four lay noblemen; all (in the report) set out at full length, with the forms of subscription.[2] The sees of the Archbishop of Canterbury, and of the Bishops of Lichfield, Lindsey, and Leicester, were mentioned after their names; those of the other bishops were not; but they are all sufficiently identified[3] by their signatures to contemporaneous charters, still extant.

---

[1] Those 'readers' (*lectores*) are in the report called 'illustrious men.' The 'reader' was the lowest but one of the five degrees of clerks in minor orders. [2] Haddan and Stubbs, *Councils.*, vol. iii. pp. 460, 461.
[3] *Ibid.*, p. 462, note. In Johnson's *Laws and Canons*, vol. i. p. 282 (Oxford ed. 1850), there is a note, by John Johnson, saying that 'no regard is to be had to these subscriptions; the few names that are

§ 6. *Character and Constitution of the Synods.*

In these proceedings there seems to be nothing inconsistent with the nature of legatine synods, at which the active part was that of the Pope by his legates, others who were present being passive, and merely promising dutiful obedience. For such a purpose, bishops who were strangers to the province might very well be present, or might be represented by proxies, as happened at the northern council. But how could those strange bishops take part in an act of civil legislation for the kingdom of Northumbria? How could bishops of Kent, East Anglia, and Wessex take part in a witenagemot, passing secular laws for the kingdom of Mercia? How could Wessex be bound by secular laws passed at an assembly presided over by the Mercian king and the Kentish archbishop, and containing East Anglian and Mercian bishops, without any representation of Wessex, except by the Bishops of Winchester, Sherborne, and Selsey? What evidence is there that, for all or any of those kingdoms, properly constituted witenagemots were held, to give the 'force of law' to what was then done?

_{genuine are yet so spelt that the men, if they were now alive, would scarce own them.' If the names, or any of them, were forgeries, it would be a strong argument against the authenticity of the whole document; if, on the other hand, they are all capable of being identified with the names of persons who were really English bishops (and one Irish) at that time, notwithstanding the transformation of the Anglo-Saxon names into Latin, this seems conclusive in favour of the document, even if its credit had not been otherwise supported. I had myself, before reading Mr. Haddan and Bishop Stubbs' note, gone carefully through the episcopal signatures to all the charters from A.D. 780 to 803 in Kemble's *Codex Diplomaticus*, and had arrived at the same identification of the signatures, except that of the Irish and the (supposed) Welsh bishop.}

§ 7. *Internal Evidence.*

I pass to the consideration of the internal evidence; which appears to me to prove conclusively, what might have been inferred from the narrative;—that those Injunctions had, and claimed, the authority of the Pope as a spiritual monitor and teacher, and that alone; and that the assent given to them by the kings, bishops, and laymen, to whom they were synodically delivered, had nothing in common with legislation or ratification on the part of civil lawgivers. The character of the Injunctions is, from first to last, pastoral; sometimes it is more, sometimes less, authoritative; the tone is that of an apostolical charge or a pulpit exhortation; they are admonitions and precepts, not laws. Of this character, the seventeenth article itself, which relates to tithes, etc., is an example. The first, third, eleventh, and twentieth, relating to faith, the duties of bishops, the duties of kings, confession, and penitence, are still more so. All these, and some others, consist chiefly of Scripture texts, with a few quotations from the Fathers. There is not one article which deviates in substance from this general character; not one which is enforced by temporal sanctions or penalties. The motives held out, the encouragements and threatenings, the rewards and punishments, are all spiritual.

The form and style of address is that of a chief pastor to his flock. Most of the articles were obviously brought, ready prepared, from Rome; it is not difficult to distinguish the additions made in this country, in consequence of what the legates saw or heard.

1. The first[1] article begins: '*Admonishing* in the first

---

[1] Haddan and Stubbs, vol. iii. p. 448.

place' (*Primo omnium admonentes*). It relates to the Nicene faith, and directs, that all priests be examined as to their faith every year by their bishops in diocesan synods, 'so that they may in all things confess, hold, and preach the apostolical and universal faith of the six councils, approved by the Holy Spirit, as it has been delivered to us by the holy Roman Church; and, if occasion be, may not fear to die for it; and that they receive all whom the holy universal councils have received, and reject and condemn from their hearts all those whom they have condemned.' This is no secular law. Was it ever law in the Anglo-Saxon kingdoms, even canon law, that every priest should be examined annually by his bishop, in a diocesan synod, concerning his faith?

2. The second[1] article begins: 'In the second article *we taught*' (*Secundo capitulo docuimus*), 'that baptism be administered according to the ordinance of the canons, and at no other time, except for great necessity; and that all, generally, should know the Creed and the Lord's Prayer.' It proceeds to instruct sponsors in their duties, and it ends: 'It is, therefore, our precept to all the people generally, that this should be committed to memory' (*generaliter omni vulgo præcipimus hoc memoriæ mandari*).

3. The third[2] article, a long exhortation to the bishops as to their duties, begins: 'In *our third discourse*, we insisted' (*Tertio sermone perstrinximus*).

4. The fourth[3] article begins: '*The fourth discourse*,' (*Quartus sermo*). It orders the bishops to see that all canons live canonically, and monks regularly, and wear proper habits, not dyed with Indian colours, or costly; and it ends, 'As to which matter *we advise* (*suademus*) that the synodal

[1] Haddan and Stubbs, vol. iii. pp. 448, 449.
[2] *Ibid.*, pp. 449, 450.   [3] *Ibid.*, p. 450.

edicts of the six universal councils, with the decrees of the Roman pontiffs, be often read,' etc.

5. The fifth[1] article relates to the election of abbots and abbesses from the inmates of the house, whenever fit persons may be found there, with the bishop's advice (passing over all royal or other patronage). It begins: 'The fifth article *admonishes*' (*Quintum caput admonet*).

6. The sixth[2] article (prohibiting the ordination of unfit persons as priests or deacons by bishops, etc.) is short, and in form authoritative. Its opening words are: 'The sixth *decree*' (*Sextum decretum*).

7. The seventh[3] is shorter still. 'In the seventh article' (*septimo capitulo*): 'That all public churches have their proper course of services reverently performed at the canonical hours.'

8. The eighth[4] is another short article, which cannot well be supposed to have had 'the force of law' in this country. 'In the eighth *constitution*' (*Octavo statuto*): 'That the ancient privileges conferred upon all churches by the holy Roman see be observed. But if, by the consent of wicked men, any should have been granted in writing against the canonical institutions, let them be plucked up' (*avellantur*).

9. And will any one be found to say that it was made an offence against secular law in this country for an ecclesiastic to take food secretly, when in good health? This, however, is forbidden 'by the ninth[5] *head*' (*Nono capite*); 'because it is hypocrisy and Saracenic' (*quia hypocrisis et Saracenorum est*).

---

[1] Haddan and Stubbs, vol. iii. pp. 450, 451.
[2] *Ibid.*, p. 451.   [3] *Ibid.*   [4] *Ibid.*
[5] *Ibid.* This was, obviously, a rule of discipline for monks or clerks living together in community.

10. By the tenth [1] article (*Decimo capitulo*), mass priests are forbidden to minister at the altar with bare legs. The faithful are enjoined to make such offerings that there may be bread and not a mere crust (*ut panis sit, non crusta*). And '*we forbade*' (*vetuimus*) the use of ox-horn for the chalice or paten. The legates also were offended at *seeing bishops in England judging secular matters in their councils, which they forbade* (*Vidimus etiam ibi episcopos in conciliis suis sæcularia judicare, prohibuimusque eos voce apostolica*); quoting St. Paul (2 Timothy ii. 4); and they made it their entreaty (*obsecravimus etiam*) that continual prayers should be offered for the Church.

Was this, also, a law enacted and brought into force for England? Was it from that time an offence against the laws of Northumbria, and of Mercia, and of Wessex, that bishops should judge in councils and courts of law (as they always did) as to secular matters?

11. The eleventh [2] '*discourse*' was to kings and princes (*Undecimus sermo fuit ad reges et principes*) : and a 'sermon' it certainly was, such a sermon as could have come from Rome only. 'We admonished (*admonuimus*) the kings and princes to obey their bishops from the heart with great humility, because the keys of heaven are given to them, and they have the power of binding and loosing;'—an admonition enforced by numerous extracts from Scripture. Did that injunction make it the law of Mercia that Offa should humbly obey his bishops?

12. In the twelfth [3] '*discourse*' they laid it down (*Duodecimo sermone sanximus*), that, in the appointment of kings, no one should permit the consent of the wicked to prevail

---

[1] Haddan and Stubbs, vol. iii. pp. 451, 452. The part of this article beginning '*Vidimus*' etc., was doubtless added in England.
[2] *Ibid.*, pp. 452, 453.   [3] *Ibid.*, pp. 453, 454.

(*nullus permittat pravorum prævalere assensum*); but that kings should be lawfully chosen by the priests and lords (*senioribus*) of the people, of those who were not born in adultery or incest:

'Because, as in our times, no one of adulterine birth can, according to the canons, be ordained priest; so neither can any one not born in lawful wedlock be the anointed of the Lord, king of all the kingdom, and his country's heir' (quoting the not very relevant text of Daniel iv. 17). 'Therefore we admonished (*admonuimus*) all the people, generally, to pray God to give grace to the king whom He himself chooses, and who is to be honoured of all (quoting several texts). No man is to take any counsel for the king's death, because he is the Lord's anointed; and if any one is privy to such a crime, if a bishop or a priest, let him be degraded, and cast down from his sacred heritage, as Judas was from the apostolate; and every one who shall have assented to such sacrilege shall perish under the eternal bond of our anathema, and, in the society of the traitor Judas, shall be burned with everlasting fires.' This, again, is enforced with Scripture texts and examples; and the article ends thus: 'It has often been proved by instances among yourselves,[1] that those who have caused the death of their masters, have prematurely ended their own lives, and lost both civil and spiritual rights (*utroque jure caruerunt*).'

Now, whatever may have been the constitutional law of any of those Anglo-Saxon states as to the qualifications necessary for the royal office (in which I do not doubt that legitimate birth was the rule, though there were notable exceptions to it); it was certainly not by this legatine injunction that it was enacted; nor was regicide less a civil offence before, than after this injunction. Even as to regicide, the penalties of which this injunction speaks are

[1] The part of this article as to regicide (perhaps the whole article) may have been added in England, where regicide had been frequent; the most recent instance being the murder (A.D. 786) of Kenwulf, King of Wessex, after the legates had seen him on their first arrival.

spiritual—degradation from the episcopal or priestly office, the Church's anathema, the pains of hell-fire.

13. The thirteenth[1] *admonition* was (*Decima tertia admonitio fuit*) against unjust judgments, respect of persons in judgment, and taking gifts against the innocent; for which also many texts of Scripture were quoted. Whatever may have been the state of the Anglo-Saxon laws as to unrighteous judgments, nothing can have been added to them by this article.

14. The fourteenth[2] head (*Decimum quartum caput*) deserves quoting fully:

'Fraud, violence, and rapine are forbidden; and let no unjust or greater tributes than those established by the Roman law and the ancient customs of former emperors, kings, and princes, be imposed upon the Church of God; and let every one who desires to communicate with the Holy Roman Church, and the blessed Peter, the Prince of the Apostles, be careful to keep himself wholly clear from this fault of violence. Let there be concord everywhere, and unanimity between kings and bishops, ecclesiastics and laymen, and the whole Christian people, so that there may everywhere be unity of the Churches of God, and peace continuing in the One Church, in one faith, hope, and charity, having One Head, which is Christ, etc.'

Will any one contend that the acceptance of this article at the legatine councils, and the subscriptions of those who subscribed to it, gave it 'the force of law' in the Mercian and Northumbrian kingdoms?

15. The fifteenth[3] 'head' (*caput*) is against incest and adultery; the anathema of the Church (that only) being denounced against those guilty of such acts, until they repent, and are reconciled to their bishops.

16. The sixteenth[4] 'head' (*caput*) says: 'The sons of har-

---

[1] Haddan and Stubbs, vol. iii. pp. 454, 455. [2] *Ibid*
[3] *Ibid.*, p. 455.   [4] *Ibid.*, pp. 455, 456.

lots are by decree (*decreto*) debarred from lawful inheritance. For we judge by the apostolical authority, that sons born of adultery, or of nuns, are spurious and adulterine.' Nuns are stated to be spouses of Christ; and texts are quoted as to the heinousness of marrying with or corrupting them. Then the legates suppose some 'adulterine' person to be arguing with them: 'he will say, my mistress is not a slave, but free.' 'To these we reply, by the Apostle's authority' (*his autoritate apostolica respondemus*); quoting St. Paul (Romans vi. 16). And the article concludes: 'But, as it is written, either in Scripture or the evangelical doctrine, or in the decrees of the apostolical decisions (*decretis apostolicorum dogmatum*), concerning lawful marriages, and appointed times for marriage or abstinence therefrom,—we presume neither to add anything to, nor to take away anything from, those decrees: "But if any man seem to be contentious, we have no such custom, neither the Church of God."'

17. The seventeenth[1] article (*caput*) as to tithes, usury, and just measures and weights, has already been extracted.

18. The eighteenth[2] begins: 'The eighteenth head (*Decimum octavum caput*): Concerning the vow of Christians, that they perform it.' What follows consists entirely of Scriptural examples: Abel, Enoch ('*Remember* Enoch,' etc.), Abraham ('Why should I speak'—*quid loquar*—of Abraham, etc.), Jacob, Manoah ('Remember Manoah,' etc.), David, Solomon; and appropriate texts.

19. The nineteenth[3] appears to have been added by the legates, in consequence of information given them at York, 'that there were still remaining (in those parts) some faults,

---

[1] Haddan and Stubbs, vol. iii. pp. 456, 457; *ante*, p. 144.
[2] *Ibid.*, pp. 457, 458.   [3] *Ibid.*, pp. 458, 459.

by no means small, of which the correction was necessary;' and the fact that it was so added seems to be denoted by its introductory words : '*We annexed* the nineteenth head' (*Decimum nonum caput annexuimus*), 'that every faithful Christian should take example from Catholic men ; and, 'if there be any remnant of pagan rites (*si quid ex ritu paganorum remansit*) it should be plucked up, scorned, and rejected.' They proceed to condemn the practices of (1) tattooing—quoting a verse from Prudentius ; (2) a pagan fashion of dress ; (3) splitting the nostrils, tying up the ears, and docking the tails, of horses ; (4) settling controversies by casting lots ; and (5) eating horse-flesh. These customs are stigmatised as evil, and unfit to be practised by Christians ; they seem to be condemned by the introductory words of denunciation ; but not even under spiritual penalties.

20. The twentieth,[1] and last 'head' (*Vigesimum caput*) is introduced by the words, 'We *intimated* to all generally' (*omnibus generaliter intimavimus*). It consists wholly of an exhortation, enforced by texts, to conversion and repentance, confession of sins, and Holy Communion.

I think I have established, by the simple process of showing what the form and substance of these Injunctions, from beginning to end, really is, their true nature and character ; and that further argument against the proposition that they, or any of them, were legislative enactments by kings and witenagemots of any Anglo-Saxon kingdom or kingdoms, would be superfluous.

[1] Haddan and Stubbs, vol. iii. p. 459.

§ 8. *Relation of the Legatine Injunctions to those of Cloveshoo,* A.D. 747.

It remains to correct an error into which the late Dean Hook[1] fell, when he described these Legatine Injunctions as 'little more than a repetition of the regulations made at the Council of Cloveshoo in the time of Archbishop Cuthbert.' They did, on one or two points, enjoin things which were also enjoined by those regulations; and an explanation of this may be found in the probability, that those injunctions of Archbishop Cuthbert's Council were based upon the letter of Pope Zacharias,[2] then read, but not now extant. Pope Adrian on those few points did, probably, repeat and renew the admonitions of his predecessor. But there is nothing in common between the rest—all, that is, but an insignificant part—of the legatine Injunctions, and the Acts of Archbishop Cuthbert's Council of Cloveshoo.

[1] *Lives of Archbishops,* vol. i. (3rd ed.), p. 251. Dean Hook also says, that the body of canons produced (by the legates) at Chalchyth was '*very similar to those that had been accepted in the kingdom of Northumbria.*' They were not *similar,* but the *same.*

[2] Haddan and Stubbs, *Councils,* vol. iii. p. 360.

CHAPTER IV

THIRD PERIOD—FROM OFFA TO EDMUND—RETROGRESSION AND DECAY

§ 1. *Ravages of the Danes*

To understand the change which passed over the Anglo-Saxon Church during the ninth century, and the condition in which it remained for a considerable part of the tenth, it is necessary to realise the effect of the Danish invasions.

The first serious havoc wrought by those invaders was in A.D. 792-793, when Lindisfarne was ruined, and a state of disorder introduced into Northumbria from which that kingdom never recovered. Alcuin's letters[1] to the churches of Lindisfarne, Wearmouth, and Jarrow, to Ethelred the Northumbrian king, his princes and people, and to King Offa, show the magnitude of that calamity, and the demoralisation consequent on it. 'See the holy places laid waste by the pagans; the altars defiled by perjuries; the monasteries violated by adulteries; the land foul with the blood of kings and princes.' He turned with hope to Offa, who had asked for a teacher, and to whom he sent one of his pupils: 'the light of wisdom, which in many places had been extinguished, might still flourish in Mercia.'

---

[1] Haddan and Stubbs, *Councils*, vol. iii. pp. 470, 472, 492; Migne's *Patrolog.* (Alcuin, vol. i. ep. 14, 15, and 49).

Offa was 'the ornament of Britain; the trumpet of preaching; a sword against the foe; a shield against the enemy.'[1] Offa died three years afterwards, and Alcuin, before long,[2] followed him. His hope was not to be fulfilled. The Danes returned, and continually gathered strength. Repelled for a short time by Egbert, they became terrible during the reign of Ethelwulf. They made their way to Canterbury and to London; they began to winter in Kent. The preamble to Ethelwulf's charter of A.D. 844[3] is a sharp cry of distress:

'We see that in these days, through the conflagrations of wars, the pillage of our wealth, the most cruel depredations of barbarous enemies laying waste the land, and the manifold tribulations, threatening us even with extermination, which we suffer from the pagan tribes, perilous times have come upon us.'

Under Ethelbert, his successor, the Danes ravaged Winchester, destroying its cathedral and other churches, and putting all the monks of the chapter to death. Under Ethelred I. they occupied York, and became masters of Northumbria. Then it was that those calamities occurred, of which Symeon of Durham[4] speaks:

'They went about everywhere, filling the whole country with blood and mourning; destroying the churches and monasteries far and wide with fire and sword, leaving nothing beyond bare walls.'

A few years afterwards they destroyed Lindisfarne (for the second time), Wearmouth, Jarrow, and other monasteries. The consequence of their ravages was that the see of Hexham was suppressed; Lindisfarne also (towards the

---

[1] Migne's *Patrolog.* (Alcuin, vol. i. ep. 49).   [2] A.D. 804.
[3] See *post*, p. 200. (The date of this charter, as given generally in the Chronicles, is wrong, probably through confusion with that of A.D. 854.)   [4] *Hist. Dunelmensis Ecclesiæ*, cap. 6, etc.

close of the century) was removed to Chester-le-Street, and afterwards to Durham. The same chronicler[1] says:

'Christianity was all but extinguished; very few churches were rebuilt; no monasteries were refounded for about two hundred years; the country people never heard the name of a monk, and were frightened at his garb, till some monks from Winchelcomb brought again the monastic way of living to Durham, York, and Whitby.'

The havoc wrought in Mercia, and especially in East Anglia, was not less. In 869-871 the great monasteries of Bardney, Crowland, Peterborough, Ely, and Repton were utterly destroyed, their libraries burnt,[2] their charters torn up, their inmates exterminated. The power of the Danes became absolute in East Anglia; and it extended (before Alfred's great victory in A.D. 878) as far west as Gloucester and Chippenham. The sees of Lindsey (for some time before in abeyance) and of Leicester were suppressed, being united nominally with Dorchester in Oxfordshire. The monasteries of Abingdon, Evesham, and Malmesbury were brought very low. Of the bishoprics left in the south, four were vacant at the time of Alfred's death;[3] there had been no West Saxon bishop for seven years; and some chroniclers add (what must be fabulous) that Pope Formosus published, or threatened, an interdict against England on that account. It was to apply a remedy to this state of things that Archbishop Plegmund, in A.D. 905, consecrated seven bishops in one day: four for vacant sees, three more for new sees, then erected, at Wells and Crediton, and for Cornwall —to which, in the following year (A.D. 906), another was

[1] *Ubi supra.*

[2] '*Ecclesiæ cum bibliothecis suis a Danis combustæ fuerant*' (Gervase of Canterbury, Stubbs' ed. 1880, vol. ii. p. 48).

[3] See Mansi, *Concil.*, vol. xviii. p. 111; and *note* (*ibid.*), as to the impossibility of the supposed interdict.

added at Ramsbury, for Wiltshire. This was in the time of Edward the Elder. What the state of England south of the Humber generally was in Alfred's time, he has himself described, in the preface to his translation of Gregory's *Pastoral*:[1]

'So utterly has learning perished in the English nation, that there are very few (*paucissimi*) on this side the Humber who can understand their common prayers in the English tongue, or translate any Latin writing into English. So few, indeed, have there been, that I cannot remember so much as one on the south side of the Thames, at the time when I succeeded to the kingdom.'

He contrasted this with the state of things which he had seen 'before everything was destroyed and burnt': 'churches, throughout the nation, well furnished with ornaments and books, and served by a multitude of the servants of God;' foreigners resorting to England 'for wisdom and learning,' instead of 'going, as they now did, to seek them abroad.'

§ 2. *Other Causes of Decay.*

There were other causes which contributed to produce this change. Even in the prosperous times of Boniface and Bede, many of the smaller houses, which had the name and the privileges of monasteries, were resorted to rather as sanctuaries or asylums from the insecurity of secular life, than for purposes of religion. In many of them there was sloth, ignorance, self-indulgence, and worse corruption.[2] These, if they escaped the ruin of the greater houses, probably sank into a worse state than before. And these

---

[1] Wise's ed. of *Asser* (Oxford 1722), p. 87. Alfred named, as exceptions, his own instructors, Archbishop Plegmund, Asser, and Grimbald, and his chaplain, John [Scotus Erigena].

[2] See Haddan and Stubbs, *Councils*, vol. iii. pp. 320, 321, 381.

evils were aggravated by the insular character of the Anglo-Saxon Church. Wasserschleben,[1] observing that 'throughout two centuries, English literature offers us no trace of an independent work,' such as the 'Penitentials' of Theodore and Archbishop Egbert, attributed this, 'in part, to the circumstances of dependence in which the English Church more and more stood towards the kings:'

'Ecclesiastical action was, in various and many ways, ruled and determined by peculiar laws. That union with Rome, which might have given protection to the Church, was very loose; and the influence of the Pope in the ecclesiastical affairs of England was, consequently, extremely small.'

§ 3. *Church Organisation.*

I have had occasion to speak of the suppression of some, and the establishment of other, bishoprics during this period. To that subject it will not be necessary to revert. It may be concluded, with reasonable certainty, that the destruction of so many monasteries by the Danes, depriving the Christian people of the means of receiving baptism and other ordinances of religion in the 'baptismal' churches, so destroyed, made laymen generally more dependent than they had previously been upon the priests and the services of private chapels or oratories; and that it was found necessary by the bishops to enlarge the powers and functions of such rural priests, and to consecrate, as burial-grounds, the precincts of some of those chapels or oratories. We shall find, in King Edgar's time,[2] proofs that this step towards the creation of the modern parochial system had then been taken.

[1] *Die Bussordnungen*, etc. (Halle 1851), preface, p. xlix.
[2] *Post*, p. 220.

§ 4. *Archbishop Wulfred's Canons.*

Of this, however, there is no trace in anything which remains to us of the ecclesiastical documents of the ninth century. There is, I think, proof that no such change had taken place before or during the first quarter of that century, in the canons of the only ecclesiastical council held during the whole third period—that of Chalchyth, under Archbishop Wulfred, in A.D. 816.[1] Five of those canons —the second, fifth, ninth, tenth, and eleventh—have a bearing, more or less direct, upon the point.

The second[2] of those canons relates to the form and manner of proceeding in the consecration of churches— called in it by the several names of *ecclesiæ*, *basilicæ*, and *oratoria*—all applicable to any buildings dedicated for the worship and service of God. The word *parochia* does not occur in that canon; nor is there anything in it from which the idea of a parish church (in any sense of the term) can be collected.

In the fifth canon,[3] the word *parochia* is used to include any assigned sphere of local duty, from the diocese of a bishop to any mission-field of a priest acting under proper authority. The object of that canon was to prevent Irish clergy (*Scoti*) from officiating in English churches. This it interdicted, on the ground of the impossibility of ascertaining that they had been properly ordained. And then followed (argumentatively) the passage in which the word *parochia* occurs:

'We know how the canons enjoin that no one of the bishops or priests attempt to invade another's "parish" (*paro-*

---

[1] Haddan and Stubbs, *Councils*, vol. iii. p. 579.
[2] *Ibid.*, p. 580. [3] *Ibid.*, p. 581.

chiam), without the consent of the bishop having authority there (*proprii episcopi*). So much the more are men of alien races to be repelled from the exercise of the sacred offices of the ministry (*sacra ministeria*), who are under no metropolitans, and pay them no respect.'

The reference here to 'the canons' is sufficient proof that, by *parochia*, a parish of the modern kind was not meant.

The ninth [1] canon (relating to synodical judgments, and to the manner of their authentication and publication, by archbishops and bishops in their several dioceses) used the word *parochia* twice, in both instances unequivocally for the diocese of an archbishop or bishop.

The tenth [2] related to the funerals of deceased bishops:

'It is commanded, and we appoint this firmly to be observed, both in our own days, and in future times by all our successors, who after us shall be appointed to the same sees, that as often as any one of the bishops shall depart this life, then we enjoin (*præcipimus*) the division and distribution of the tenth part of his substance, of whatever it consists, among the poor for the benefit of his soul,—whether flocks or herds, or sheep and swine, or even what is in the cellars (*in cellariis*); and further, that liberty be given to every English-born man (*Angliscum*), who in his days has been brought under slavery; so may he earn the reward of his labour, and the remission of his sins. Let there be no contradiction, in any point, by any person, to this article (*capitulo*); but let it rather, as is most meet, receive augmentation from our successors; and let it be honoured and held in remembrance for ever hereafter, throughout all the churches subject to our rule:—at all events, the prayers and alms, upon which we have specially agreed among ourselves (*condictam habemus*)—that at once, in every diocese, and in all the churches (*per singulas parochias, singulis quibusque ecclesiis*), the whole company of God's

---

[1] Haddan and Stubbs, *Councils*, vol. iii. p. 583.   [2] *Ibid.*

servants (*omnis famulorum*[1] *Dei coetus*) shall assemble at the sound of a bell in the church, and there all together (*pariter*), sing thirty psalms for the soul of the dead; and, after that, each bishop and abbot is to cause 150 "psalteries" (*psalterios*), and 120 masses, to be celebrated; and to set free three men, distributing to each of them three shillings (*solidos*): and all the servants of God (*singuli servorum Dei*) are to keep fast that day; and for thirty days, at the canonical hours, after the full course of the prescribed services, the Lord's Prayer is to be sung for him:—all of which being done, on the thirtieth day from his death they are to have a refection, as good as that which they are wont to have on the birthday of each of the apostles. And let them, through all the churches, pray as faithfully for him as they would for those of the household of faith among them (*pro eorum domesticis fidei*): that so, by the grace of such common intercession, they may earn for themselves a common share with all the saints in God's eternal kingdom.'

It is manifest that, in this canon, *parochia* means *diocese;* and that the churches spoken of were conventual, having bishops or abbots at their head, with bodies of monks or clergy (*famulorum*, or *servorum Dei*)[2] living together in community; such as there were (generally) in the old 'baptismal' churches, and such as there would not be in any parish churches of the modern kind. And it is to be observed, in the same connection, that three other canons of this series related to monasteries, while there were none applicable to parish churches of the modern kind, or to the appointment or the duties of priests in charge of them.

The remaining canon (the eleventh[3] and last), in which

[1] This expression, and '*servorum Dei*,' signifies the monks, etc., of convents (see Sharon Turner's *History of the Anglo-Saxons*, 5th ed. 1828, vol. i. p. 493).
[2] The terms of King Ethelwulf's charter of A.D. 844 are similar, and lead to the same inference, as still applicable to Anglo-Saxon churches generally, at that time (see *post*, p. 201, note). [3] *Ibid.*, p. 584.

the word *parochia* also occurs, uses it distinctly for diocese :

'No bishop is to invade the diocese (*parochiam*) of another, or to draw to himself anything belonging to the ministry of another bishop, in the consecration of churches, or the ordination of priests or deacons, except the archbishop only, who is the head of all the bishops of his province. The rest are to be content with their own, or to minister by the consent or license of the bishop in whose diocese (*diocesi*) any one of them may be ; and if any do otherwise, they are to be corrected by the archbishop's judgment.'

§ 5. *Opinions of Selden and Lingard.*

If, in thus arriving at the conclusion that at the beginning of the ninth century there was no approach to parishes of the modern sort in England, I may appear to differ from Dr. Lingard, and perhaps (in a less degree) from Selden,[1] the reason is that those eminent men relied for this purpose upon authorities now discredited. Dr. Lingard[2] assumed that the 'Excerptions,' ascribed to Egbert (Archbishop of York in the preceding century), were a genuine work of that prelate ; and as in those 'Excerptions' there was contained what I may describe as the 'manse' ordinance of the capitulars made by Louis the Pious at Aix-la-Chapelle in A.D. 816, he drew from this, taken in connection with the later laws of Edgar and Canute, conclusions which might have been reasonable enough, if his premiss had not been erroneous. But nothing is more certain than that those 'Excerptions' were not from the hand of Archbishop Egbert, and that they really belong to a much later time. Selden,[3] when

[1] *Hist. of Tithes*, ch. 9 (ed. 1618), p. 261.
[2] *Antiquities of Anglo-Saxon Church*, vol. i. p. 93, note. His references in that note to '*the many regulations* in Wilkins, pp. 103, 245, 300, 302,' are to portions of Egbert's 'Excerptions' and the laws of Edgar and Canute.   [3] *Ubi supra.*

he wrote that by the beginning of the ninth century, 'lay foundations were grown very common, *and parochial limits also of the parishioners' devotions,*' relied upon a number of lay appropriations of churches to Crowland Abbey, which he found recorded in the chronicle of Ingulph, or of the writer who assumed that name. The true character of that chronicle was not then so well understood as it is now; and this is not the only instance (as will be afterwards seen) in which Selden attributed to it more weight than it deserved. That many charters to Crowland Abbey, earlier than A.D. 800, should have been preserved after the total destruction of that monastery and the slaughter of all its monks in A.D. 869-871, is highly improbable. Ingulph, in the Conqueror's time, carried to London all the charters (real or pretended) of that monastery, and they were read before the king in council. Those (says the chronicler) 'which were written in the Saxon hand, down to the last Mercian king, were treated with contempt'; while those of Edred, Edgar, and the succeeding kings, 'being written wholly or in part in the Gallican hand, were allowed;' the king confirming, by a charter of his own, Edred's grant.[1] Mr. Thorpe[2] says that 'almost all the charters' in Ingulph's work 'are forgeries'; and not only so, but that 'the narrative of Ingulph abounds in gross errors and anachronisms with regard to contemporary events.' Mr. Haddan and Bishop Stubbs say,[3] as to the Acts of two pretended Councils of Benningdon and Kingsbury, recorded by the same chronicler, that they 'are unblushing

---

[1] Ingulph, pp. 80-82. See Dugdale's *Monastic* (Caley, Ellis, and Bandinel's ed.), vol. ii. pp. 98, 118.

[2] Thorpe's *Literary Introduction* (to his translation of Lappenberg's *History of England under the Anglo-Saxon Kings*, 1845), p. li.

[3] *Councils*, vol. iii. p. 633, note.

forgeries.' No conclusion, even by the most learned men, can be worth more than the premises on which it is founded; and as to this matter, the premises both of Dr. Lingard and of Selden were unsound.

§ 6. *Pope Leo the Fourth's Decretals.*

The inferences which I have drawn from the canons of Archbishop Wulfred's council receive confirmation from two rescripts or decretals of Pope Leo IV., the one in the form of a complete epistle[1] addressed 'to the Bishops of Britain' (probably sent by the hand of those messengers from King Ethelwulf who accompanied Prince Alfred on his first visit to Rome), and the other[2] without that address, but said by Walafrid Strabo to have been written for the Anglo-Saxon Church. In the former the Pope spoke of the provision for the offices of religion throughout every diocese as to be made by the bishop, 'by such priests and other clerks as he should provide.' By the latter (following, as he said, the rule laid down by his predecessors) he directed that tithes should be paid to 'baptismal' churches only.

§ 7. *Tithes: Treaty between Edward and Guthrum.*

Passing from the subject of organisation to that of tithes, we obtain no new light till the beginning of the tenth century. The celebrated charters of King Ethelwulf do not (as will hereafter be shown) relate to tithes; and (unless the decretal of Pope Leo IV., just mentioned, be an exception) there is nothing else on the subject in this third period, earlier than A.D. 906. King Alfred was a legislator; but

[1] Migne's *Patrologiæ Cursus*, vol. cxv. p. 667.
[2] *Ibid.*, p. 674: '*De decimis, justo ordine, non tantum nobis, sed majoribus visum est, plebibus tantum, ubi sacrosancta dantur baptismata, dari debere.*'

in his laws there is nothing about tithes. He made a treaty of peace with Guthrum (the first Danish king who professed Christianity and was baptized), by which the government of the eastern parts of England was, on terms then agreed upon, conceded to the Danes. In that treaty [1] there was nothing about tithes. But after the death of both those kings war again broke out between their successors; and that war was terminated by a second treaty of peace, confirmed (more than once) by English witenagemots, under which the same territory was again left in the possession of the Danes. I am disposed, with Mr. Kemble,[2] to distinguish a treaty of that kind (though confirmed by the English national legislature) from a municipal law. It was a compact between the King and State of England and the Danish ruler, as to the government of certain parts of England conceded to him. It did not (in my judgment) impose any reciprocal obligation upon Edward as to the government of his own kingdom, or any new law upon his subjects beyond the Danish territory. Its interest, however, with respect to the present subject is considerable, because one of its stipulations related to tithes and other church dues. 'If any one withhold tithes, let him pay *lah-slit* among the Danes, *wite* among the English'; the same thing, in the same terms, being also provided as to (1) Peter's pence (*Rom-feoh*); (2) 'light-scot'; (3) 'plough-alms'; and (4) any other 'divine dues.' *Lah-slit* and *wite* were the Danish and Saxon mulcts or penalties (the one, according to Selden, equivalent to twenty, and the other to thirty shillings) for ordinary misdemeanours.

Selden,[3] after citing that provision of the treaty as to

---

[1] Thorpe's *Ancient Laws*, etc., vol. i. p. 153.
[2] *Saxons in England*, vol. ii. p. 476.
[3] *Hist. of Tithes*, ch. 8, § 3 (ed. 1618), p. 203.

tithes, said : 'It may seem by this that some other law preceded, for the payment of tithes, or else that the right of them was otherwise supposed clear.'

On looking into the earlier national legislation, I think it is reasonably certain, that there was no preceding secular law for the payment of tithes. Alfred,[1] in the preface to his own code, said that he had collected everything which he had approved out of the laws of earlier legislators, mentioning by name his ancestor Ina, '*Offa, king of the Mercians*,' and Ethelbert, the first Christian king of Kent. Among the laws of Ina, which he republished, there are two articles[2] relating to 'church-scots,' viz. :

'§ 4. Let Church-scots be rendered at Martinmas. If any one do not perform that, let him forfeit sixty shillings and render the church-scot fourfold.'

'§ 61. Church-scot shall be rendered according to the healm and to the hearth that the man is at in mid-winter.'

There is nothing as to any other kind of church dues, except church-scot,—nothing, therefore, as to tithes, in any of the earlier laws republished by Alfred, or in those under his own name. And that he would not have been likely to disapprove of an earlier law for the payment of tithes, if he had met with it, may be inferred with certainty, not only from his maintaining those laws of Ina as to 'church-scot,' but from the fact that the preface to his code begins with a

[1] Thorpe's *Ancient Laws*, etc., p. 59.
[2] *Ibid.*, pp. 105-141. *Church-scot* was 'originally a certain measure of corn paid to the Church' (note, *ibid.*); mentioning claims to it by the monasteries of Worcester, Pershore, and Glastonbury ; and adding that 'the definition given by White Kennett seems best suited to the generality of the Anglo-Saxon term : "It was sometimes a general word, and included not only corn, but poultry or any other provision that was paid in kind to the religious."' It was quite distinct from tithe.

summary of Levitical laws ('the dooms which the Almighty God Himself spake to Moses, and commanded him to keep'); among which is the Levitical commandment as to tithes: 'Thy tithes, and thy first-fruits of moving and growing things, render thou to God.'[1]

I conclude, that there was no secular law before the time of Edward the Elder for the payment of tithes. What, then, is the proper explanation of the article as to tithes and other church dues in the treaty of peace with the second Guthrum?[2]

Any one who examines the whole treaty (which method should be observed by all who wish to avoid risks of error in the interpretation of ancient, or indeed any, documents) must perceive that there is in it only one article —the last[3]—which does not relate to ecclesiastical matters; and also that it enforces religious and ecclesiastical obligations in a manner and to an extent for which there had been, down to that time, no precedent in Anglo-Saxon legislation. The reason (as it seems to me) is this; —that the Danes were, many of them, still heathens, and of those who were nominally converts to Christianity not a few remained, and were likely long to remain, in a state of semi-paganism. They were the same people who not very long before made havoc with churches and monasteries; they had, by their recent insurrection, violated the former treaty; and it is, at least, probable that during that war churches had again suffered. It is easy to understand that under those circumstances strong guarantees for the continuance of Christian usages, and for the customary rights of the clergy and the Church (whether previously

[1] Thorpe's *Ancient Laws*, etc., vol. i. p. 53 (art. 38 of Levitical Laws).
[2] *Ibid.*, pp. 159-177 (see art. 6, p. 171).   [3] *Ibid.*, p. 175.

secured to them by law or not), might be thought necessary. In the parts of England under Danish government there would be a mixed population of Anglo-Saxon Christians—the more numerous, but the weaker class—and Danes, the ruling, military, and powerful class, of whom many were pagans, or not much better. It was to be expected, with this state of things in prospect, and with the experience which they had of the past, that the bishops and clergy of (what I may call) the ceded provinces should look to Edward, as lord paramount of all England, for special protection; that his ecclesiastical counsellors should use their influence with him to obtain a treaty of this character; and that he should consider it a duty incumbent upon him to stipulate for the protection which they desired.

It was natural that such stipulations, in such a treaty, for the benefit of the Church in dioceses under Danish government, should before long be followed by corresponding legislation for other parts of the Anglo-Saxon kingdom. The political power of ecclesiastics was on the increase. The observances and church dues in question were customary, and were recognised as of canonical obligation; custom, in certain states of society, passes easily into law; and the line of separation between civil and ecclesiastical legislation was not then clearly drawn.

§ 8. *King Athelstan's Tithe Ordinance.*

A royal injunction for the payment of tithes, although not made or confirmed in the manner necessary to give it the force of a national law, was a step of much importance in that direction. That step was taken by Athelstan, Edward's successor, about A.D. 927,—whether at the time when the Council of Greatanlea was held, or not, seems to me un-

certain. I do not understand, from the text of the first
'Ordinance of King Athelstan,'[1] as printed by Mr. Thorpe,
that the Council of Greatanlea is mentioned in the Anglo-
Saxon manuscript of that ordinance. It is distinguished,
both by a separate title and by internal evidence, from the
laws which follow (headed Athelstan's Ordinances),[2] and
which are on subjects really secular. The Tithe Ordinance
was a royal injunction, addressed to the king's reeves, and to
the bishops and ealdormen; it purports to have been made,
not with the concurrence of the ecclesiastical and lay
'witan,' but by the king, *with the counsel of Wulfhelm,
archbishop, and of my other bishops.* It was communicated,
as a royal message, to 'the bishops, thegns, counts, and
villeins of Kent;' who acknowledged it in a dutiful reply,[3]
thanking the king for 'his admonition,' and stating their
willingness and desire to comply with it. They called it by
its proper name; it was not (as Dean Hook calls it) a
'Canon;' it was a Royal Admonition—conceived under
ecclesiastical advice, and in ecclesiastical style.

It is in these terms:[4]

'I, Athelstan, king, with the counsel of Wulfhelm, archbishop, and of my other bishops, make known to the reeves
at each burgh, and beseech you, in God's name, and by all
His saints, and also by my friendship, that ye first of my own
goods render the tithes, both of the live stock and of the year's
earthly fruits, so as they may most rightly be either meted, or
told, or weighed out; and let the bishops then do the like from
their own goods; and my ealdormen and my reeves the same.
And I will, that the bishops and the reeves command it to all
who ought to obey them, that it be done at the right term.
Let us bear in mind how Jacob the Patriarch spake: "I will

---

[1] Thorpe's *Ancient Laws*, etc., vol. i. pp. 195-199.
[2] *Ibid.*, p. 199. (Both these distinct titles are in the Anglo-Saxon manuscripts.)   [3] *Ibid.*, p. 216.   [4] *Ibid.*, p. 195.

offer to Thee tithes, and sacrifices of peace;" and how Moses spake in God's law: "Thou shalt not delay to offer thy tithes and first-fruits to the Lord." It is for us to think how awfully it is declared in the books: If we will not render the tithes to God, that He will take from us the nine parts when we least expect; and moreover, we have the sin in addition thereto.

'And I will, also, that my reeves so do, that there be given the church-scots and the soul-scots, at the places to which they rightly belong; and plough-alms yearly, on this condition: that they shall enjoy it at the holy places who are willing to serve their churches, and of God and of me are willing to deserve it; but let him who will not, forfeit the bounty, or again turn to right.

'Now ye hear, saith the king, what I give to God, and what ye ought to fulfil under the penalty of contempt of my authority. And do ye also so, that you may give to me my own, what ye for me may justly acquire. I will not that ye unjustly anywhere acquire aught for me; but I will grant to you your own justly, on this condition that ye yield me mine; and shield both yourselves, and those whom ye ought to exhort, against God's anger, and against the penalty of contempt for my authority.'

This is not, in form, a public legislative act. It is a command, authoritative indeed, but only an exercise of the king's authority over his own reeves, and the bishops and ealdormen, to whom it was addressed; and who, on their part, were to use such an authority over others 'who ought to obey them,' as they possessed by law. The penalties to which it referred, and to which those who neglected to obey it might be liable, were those of contempt against the royal authority—not fine or punishment for non-payment of tithes.

I shall now revert to a subject earlier in date, which it has been convenient to postpone for separate consideration —that of King Ethelwulf's charters; once supposed to have operated as a public grant of tithes to the Church throughout the united Anglo-Saxon kingdom.

CHAPTER V

THIRD PERIOD—KING ETHELWULF'S CHARTERS

§ 1. *History of the opinion that Ethelwulf made a grant of Tithes*

SELDEN, after examining some of the authorities, and particularly Ingulph, whom he trusted, interpreted a charter of King Ethelwulf, passed in a witenagemot of his kingdom in A.D. 844, of which the text (differently reported, under wrong dates, and more or less corrupted) was found in several chronicles, as a grant of prædial tithes of the fruits of all lands, as to which that king could legislate, to the Church for ever. After Selden's time it became common for historians and ecclesiastical writers to speak of such a grant of tithes by King Ethelwulf as an undoubted fact. It is sufficient to name Dean Comber,[1] Dean Prideaux[2] (who insisted much upon it, as the true legal foundation of the right of the clergy to tithes throughout England), Hume,[3] Rapin,[4] Echard,[5] and Milman.[6]

I am not sure that I understand—certainly I do not adopt—the argument, that Ethelwulf did not make a gift

---

[1] *Historical Vindication of the Divine Right of Tithes* (1682), p. 169.
[2] *Original and Right of Tithes* (ed. 1736, pp. 104-124).
[3] *Hist. of England* (ed. 1826), vol. i. pp. 64, 65.
[4] Book iv., vol. i. p. 86.   [5] Book i., cap. 4, pp. 65, 66.
[6] *Hist. of Latin Christianity*, vol. ix. p. 10.

of the tithe, 'because it was not his to bestow.'[1] The charter by which that gift was supposed to have been made was a legislative act, assented to by the witenagemot of his kingdom. Such an act might operate upon all the property in the kingdom, though not belonging to the king. Even if the same thing had been already done, it would not have been unprecedented in those times to confirm an old grant (without mentioning it) by a new.

§ 2. *Traditions of the Chroniclers.*

How the chroniclers referred to by Selden (to whom others must be added) understood the matter, is (as Selden justly said) 'best known by the words wherein they sum it.' These witnesses, whatever their value, may be classified under five divisions—(1) those whose language seems to import a grant, not of tithes, but of lands; (2) those who use the verb *tithed* (*decimavit*); (3) those who speak of a grant of lands released from services or burdens; (4) those who speak of release from services or burdens as the substance of the grant; and (5) those who speak, unequivocally, of tithes.

I. To the first class belong the Anglo-Saxon Chronicle (as to this part, of the ninth century), and Hoveden (of the thirteenth).

1. *The Anglo-Saxon Chronicle.*[2]—'A.D. 855. In this year King Ethelwulf chartered the tenth part of his land and also of his whole kingdom, for the glory of God and his own eternal salvation.' Whelock's Latin translation is: *decimam*

---

[1] Haddan and Stubbs, *Councils*, vol. iii. p. 637, note; and see Hook, *Lives of Archbishops*, vol. i. p. 288.

[2] Thorpe's *A.-S. Chron.* (1861), vol. i. pp. 124, 125; vol. ii. p. 57. The original of the material words is, '*gebocade Aethelwulf cyning teothan dael his landes ofer eal his rice.*'

terræ suæ et regni quoque totius partem libro inscribens, in laudem Dei, suæque etiam æternæ saluti consulens, dicavit).[1]

2. *Hoveden.*[2]—'Ethelwulf, the illustrious King of Wessex, in the nineteenth year of his reign, set apart a tenth of all the lands in his kingdom, and bestowed it upon the Church for the love of God, and for his own salvation.'

II. To the second class belong Ethelward (tenth century); Henry of Huntingdon, Symeon of Durham, and Ailred of Rievaulx (twelfth century); Robert of Gloucester (thirteenth); and a French Annalist, cited by Selden.

1. *Ethelward.*[3]—'A.D. 855. In this year King Ethelwulf tithed all his possessions to be the Lord's portion, and so appointed it to be in all the government of his kingdom' (*decumavit de omni possessione sua in partem Domini; et in universo regimine principatus sui sic constituit*).

2. *Huntingdon.*—'A.D. 854. In the nineteenth year of his reign, Ethelwulf tithed all his land to the use of churches, for God's love and his own redemption' (*totam terram suam ad opus ecclesiarum decumavit, propter amorem Dei et redemptionem sui*).

3. *Symeon.*[4]—'A.D. 855. At this time King Ethelwulf tithed all the empire of his kingdom (*decimavit totum regni sui imperium*) for the ransom (*redemptione*) of his own soul, and the souls of his ancestors.'

4. *Ailred.*[5]—'So great was his zeal in almsgiving, that he tithed all his land for Christ, and divided the tenth part among monasteries and churches' (*ut totam terram suam pro Christo decimaret, et partem decimam per ecclesias et monasteria divideret*).

---

[1] Whelock's *Bede* (Appendix, p. 530).   [2] Riley's transl. (1853), p. 38.
[3] Book iii., cap. 3 (Transl. in Giles, *Six Old English Chronicles*, 1848, pp. 23, 24).
[4] Savile's *Hist. Angl. Script. X.*, p. 121.   [5] *Ibid.*, p. 351.

5. *Robert of Gloucester:*[1]
'The king hereafter to holy Chyrche ys herte the more drou,
And tethegede wel and al ys lond, as he agte wel ynou.'

6. *The French Annalist.*[2]—'He tithed the tenth ploughland of all Wessex to feed and clothe the poor' (*dismast la dime hide de tute West-Saxe . . . pur pestre et vestre les pouvres*).

III. To the third class belong William of Malmesbury (twelfth century); Roger of Wendover (thirteenth); Matthew of Westminster, and Bromton (fourteenth); and Stow (sixteenth century).

1. *Malmesbury.*[3]—'Turning himself to God's worship, he granted to Christ's servants the tenth part of all the ploughlands within his kingdom, free from all duties, and discharged from all liability to disturbance' (*ad Dei cultum versus, decimam omnium hydarum infra regnum suum Christi famulis concessit, liberam ab omnibus functionibus, absolutam ab omnibus inquietudinibus*).

2. *Wendover.*[4]—'A.D. 854. In this year, the magnificent King Ethelwulf conferred upon God, and the blessed Mary, and all the saints, the tenth part of his kingdom, free from all secular services, exactions, and tributes' (*decimam regni sui partem Deo beatæ Mariæ et omnibus Sanctis contulit, liberam ab omnibus servitiis sæcularibus, exactionibus, et tributis*).

---

[1] Hearne's edition (Oxford, 1724), p. 261. Selden thus gives the lines:
'The king to holye Chirche thereafter ever the more drough,
And tithed well all his lond, as he ought, well enough.'
(*Hist. of Tithes*, 1618, p. 206).

[2] Cited by Selden (*ibid.*, p. 205) from a fragment at the end of a manuscript of Nicholas of Gloucester, in the Cottonian Library.

[3] *Gesta Regum* (Hardy's ed. 1840, p. 149).

[4] Coxe's ed. 1841, p. 288.

3. *Matthew Westminster*[1] (*verbatim*, as in Wendover).

4. *Bromton.*[2]—' It is written, that King Ethelwulf gave to God and the Church the tenth ploughland of the whole land of Wessex, free and quit of all secular services, for the food and clothing of the poor, weak, and infirm' (*decimam hidam terræ totius West-Saxiae Deo et ecclesiæ contulit, ab omnibus servitiis sæcularibus liberam et quietam, ad pascendum et vestiendum pauperes, debiles, et infirmos*).

5. *Stow.*[3]—' This Athelwulfus did make the tenth part of his kingdom free from tribute and service to the king, and gave it to them that did serve Christ in the Church.'

IV. To the fourth class belong Asser (ninth century); Florence of Worcester (eleventh); and Ralph de Diceto, Dean of St. Paul's (twelfth).

1. *Asser.*[4]—' A.D. 855. In this year, Ethelwulf, the worshipful King of the West Saxons, released the tenth part of his whole kingdom from all royal service and tribute; and by a perpetual inscription offered it as a sacrifice on the cross of Christ to the Triune God, for the ransom of his own soul, and the souls of his ancestors' (*decimam totius regni sui partem ab omni regali servitio et tributo liberavit, et in sempiterno grafio, in cruce Christi, pro redemptione animæ suæ et antecessorum suorum, Uni et Trino Deo immolavit*).

2. *Florence*[5] (*verbatim*, as in Asser).

3. *Diceto.*[6]—' A.D. 849. Ethelwulf, King of the English, released the tenth part of his whole kingdom from all

---

[1] Frankfort ed. 1601, p. 138.   [2] Gale, *Script. XX.*, p. 808.
[3] *Annals* (Hawes' ed. 1631), p. 77.
[4] Gale (*Script. XX.*), p. 156. Asser was tutor to King Alfred, Ethelwulf's son; and also his biographer. He is, therefore, the best witness on this subject.   [5] Thorpe's ed. 1848, p. 74.
[6] Savile (*Hist. Angl. Script. X.*), p. 450.

royal service; and went to Rome,' etc. (*decimam totius regni partem ab omni regali servitio liberavit: Romam perrexit*, etc.)

V. To the fifth class belong Ingulph (or whoever wrote under his name, not earlier than the eleventh century); John, Abbot of Peterborough (thirteenth); Langtoft (fourteenth); Hardyng (fifteenth); and Holinshed (sixteenth century).

1. *Ingulph.*[1]—'A.D. 855. It added to the prosperity of the old age [of Guthlac, Abbot of Crowland], that Ethelwulf, the famous King of the West Saxons, soon after his return from Rome (whither he had gone abroad with his youngest son Alfred to visit, with great devotion, the thresholds of the Apostles Peter and Paul, and the most holy Pope Leo), with the free consent of all his prelates and princes, who presided under him over the various provinces of all England, then first endowed the whole English Church throughout his realm with the tithes of all his lands and goods and chattels by a writing under his royal hand, in this form': (*cum decimis omnium terrarum ac bonorum sive catallorum universam dotaverat Anglicanam ecclesiam per suum regium chirographum confectum*, etc.) The charter is then set forth; after which the narrative is resumed. 'But King Ethelwulf, for fuller assurance, laid this written charter (*hanc chartulam scriptam*) on the altar of the church of the Apostle St. Peter [at Winchester]; and the bishops, for God's faith, received it, and afterwards transmitted it for publication throughout all the churches of their dioceses' (*per omnes ecclesias postea transmiserunt in suis parochiis publicandam*).

5. *John, Abbot of Peterborough.*[2]—'A.D. 855. Ethelwulf

[1] Fulman (*Rer. Angl. Script.*, 1684), p. 17.
[2] *Hist. Angl. Script. Varii* (London, 1724), p. 14.

was the first of the English who gave tithes to God' (*decimas primus Anglorum Deo dedit*).

3. *Langtoft*—[1]

'He was first of England, that gaf God his tithe
Of issue of bestes, of londes, or of tilth.'

4. *Hardyng*—[2]

'He graunted the Church tythes of corne and haye,
Of bestial also, through West-Sex, for aye.'

5. *Holinshed.*[3]—'In the nineteenth year of his reign, King Ethelwulf ordained that the tenths or tithes of all lands, due to be paid to the Church, should be free from all tribute, duties, or services royal.'

§ 3. *Selden's Interpretation.*

Selden[4] acknowledged the difficulty of reconciling the divergent statements of these chroniclers; and also that 'out of the corrupted language of the charter it was hard to collect what the exact meaning was.' But he thought the difficulty might be overcome by understanding 'the granting of the tenth part of the hides or plough-lands' to 'denote the tenth of all profits growing in them'; and he compared such a mode of expression with 'the tenth acre as the plough shall go' (*decima acra sicut aratrum peragrabit*), which, he said, was 'used for tithing of the profits, in the laws of Kings Edgar, Ethelred, and Knout.' And, thinking that construction also supported by the language of those chroniclers who spoke of

---

[1] Hearne's ed. (Oxford, 1725), p. 19.
[2] Page 193.   [3] Book vi., cap. 10.
[4] *Hist. of Tithes*, ch. 8, § 4 (ed. 1618, p. 205).

decimation of the lands of the kingdom, he arrived at the conclusion thus expressed :

'If we well consider the words of *the chiefest of these ancients, that is, Ingulphus,* we may conjecture that the purpose of the charter was to make a general grant of tithes, payable freely, and discharged from all kinds of exactions used in that time.'

This reasoning is not satisfactory; and perhaps it might not have appeared so to Selden, if he had esteemed the authority of Ingulph less highly than he did. It is doing no small violence to the natural sense of words to interpret '*inscribing in a book the tenth part of his land and also of his whole kingdom,*'—'*gave the tenth part of his kingdom,*' —'*gave to God and the Church the tenth plough-land of all the land of Wessex,*'—'*released the tenth part of his whole kingdom from royal service,*—as relating to tithes of the produce of land, and not to land itself. Nor is such a construction of such words, without any context to justify it, warranted by the analogy of any phrases used in the laws of Edgar, Ethelred, or Canute. In the laws of Edgar the phrase mentioned by Selden does not occur; his own[1] Latin translation of the only law of Edgar in which the plough is mentioned is—'*Reddatur omnis Decimatio ad Matrem Ecclesiam cui parochia adjacet de terra Thainorum et Villanorum sicut aratrum peragrabit,*' manifestly relating to the *render* of tithes. The phrase does occur in Ethelred's 'Ordinances of Habam,' which we know only from the Latin of Bromton, and which I again take as Selden[2] gives it :—' Let every man . . . give his church-scot and proper tithe (*rectam decimam*), as in the days of our ancestors, when he did it best; that is, as the plough shall go through the tenth acre' (*sicut aratrum peragrabit decimam acram*). It is not

---

[1] *Hist. of Tithes* (ed. 1618), p. 219.   [2] *Ibid.*, pp. 222, 223.

the tenth acre which is the subject of the payment directed; it is the tithe, to be collected *from* every tenth acre. And in Canute's[1] law the same language occurs, in a similar context, if possible still more clear.

As for the word *decimation*, it is not less appropriate to a gift, or to a release from tribute or service, of the tenth part of lands, than to a gift of the tenth part of the produce of lands. Selden himself mentions instances (to which I have elsewhere referred)[2] of decimal gifts, which had nothing to do with tithes. In those cases, and in others, —such as the extraordinary tithe spoken of by Giraldus Cambrensis,[3] the special tithes levied by Boniface VIII.[4] on ecclesiastical persons for the prosecution of his wars in Sicily, and the Crusaders' or 'Saladin' tithe[5] levied in A.D. 1188 under the Le Mans Ordinance of Henry II. in Anjou, and the articles of the Council of Geddington in England,—the decimal measure was suggested, doubtless, by the same principle, derived from patriarchal and Levitical precedents, with tithes paid for the support of the ministry and charities of the Church. But they had nothing, beyond that principle, in common with prædial tithes. And there is nothing more than this in the verb 'decimated,' used by Chroniclers of my second class as to Ethelwulf's charter. Their language is the same with that of those whom I have placed in the first, third, and fourth classes, except that, where the other Chroniclers use a noun, they use the corresponding verb.

If Selden's is a great name, so is that of the earliest

---

[1] *Hist. of Tithes* (ed. 1618), pp. 223, 224.
[2] *Ibid.*, p. 208 (*ante*, p. 149).
[3] *Ante*, p. 101.   [4] *Extrav. Decret.*, lib. iii., tit. vii., cap. 1.
[5] See *Gesta Henrici II.* (Stubbs), vol. ii. p. 31; and *Gervase of Canterbury* (Stubbs), vol. i. p. 409.

writer after him, who touched on the same matter—John Milton. In his *History of Britain before the Conquest*,[1] Milton placed upon the language of the older Chronicles its natural construction. Ethelwulf, he says, 'in hope of divine aid, registered in a book, and dedicated to God, the tenth part of his own lands and of his whole kingdom, eased of all impositions, and consecrated to the maintenance of masses and psalms weekly to be sung for the prosperity of Ethelwulf and his captains; as appears at large by the patent itself in William of Malmesbury.'

§ 4. *The Extant Charters.*

It is obvious that, unless all the Chronicles can be reconciled in the way which Selden thought possible, the choice (so far as the question depends upon, or may be affected by, their traditions), lies between Asser, the Anglo-Saxon Chronicle, and Malmesbury on the one hand, and Ingulph on the other. The later writers may all be regarded as following one or other of these.

But the charters which have come down to us, if genuine, are surer guides than any such tradition. Their genuineness has been doubted;[2] and their text may be (as Selden thought it) more or less corrupted. But I do not think it possible to explain their number, and their form, on any other supposition, than that of the genuineness of some, if not all, of them; nor do I think it necessary to except from that favourable presumption the charter which Ingulph has recorded; which is, evidently,

---

[1] Milton's Prose Works (Fletcher's ed. 1834), book v., p. 530.
[2] See Haddan and Stubbs, *Councils*, vol. iii. pp. 638, 639, 640, notes.

an abridgment (with some corruption) of the earlier of the two mentioned by Malmesbury.[1]

Since Selden's time much additional light has been thrown on this subject, by the collection and arrangement of many documents bearing upon it. Most of them have been collected and classified in the learned works of Mr. Kemble,[2] and of Mr. Haddan and Bishop Stubbs.[3] Mr. Birch, in his *Cartularium Saxonicum*,[4] mentions twenty-eight in all. Without entering into the question which (if any) of them are spurious, the result confirms Malmesbury's statement, that there were two governing (or, as they might be called in modern phrase, parliamentary) charters, passed by Ethelwulf with the concurrence of witenagemots—the one in the earlier, the other in the latter part of his reign; and they show, by a number of instances, how the benefit of those governing charters was applied to particular lands, in favour of religious houses and of public servants of the realm. To understand their true effect, little more is necessary than attention to the difference, in Anglo-Saxon law, between the two kinds of landed property, called *folcland* and *bocland*.

'*Folcland* was the property of the community. It might be occupied in common, or possessed in severalty. . . . But, while it continued to be *folcland*, it could not be alienated in perpetuity; and therefore, on the expiration of the term for which it had been granted,[5] it reverted to the community, and was again distributed by the same authority. *Folcland* was subject to many burdens and exactions from which *bocland* was

---

[1] The charter given (in an abridged form) by Wendover, and after him by Matthew of Westminster, is also the same.

[2] *Codex Diplomaticus Ævi Saxonici* (1840), vol. ii.

[3] Haddan and Stubbs, *Councils*, vol. iii. pp. 625-645.

[4] Vol. ii. pp. 5-93 (London 1885).

[5] It was, generally, granted for life only.

exempt. The possessors of *folcland* were bound to assist in the reparation of royal vills and in other public works. They were liable to have travellers and others quartered upon them for subsistence. They were required to give hospitality to kings and great men in their progresses through the country; to furnish them with carriages and relays of horses, and to extend the same assistance to their messengers, followers, and servants, and even to the persons who had charge of their hawks, horses, and hounds. Such, at least, are the burdens from which lands were liberated, when converted by charter into *bocland.*'[1]

The learned author, from whose work this extract is taken, goes on to refute some erroneous notions into which Spelman, Lambarde, Somner, and in more recent times Blackstone, had fallen, when they supposed *folcland* to have been always held by serfs in villenage, or only by the common people. It might be, and it was, 'held by freemen of all ranks and conditions;' by noblemen of the highest rank (of which he mentions an instance in King Alfred's time); it was 'assignable to the thegns, or military servants of the State, as the stipend or reward for their services'; and it was often bestowed on monasteries and the Church.

Those who held *folcland* on these conditions of tenure were, for breach of them, liable to forfeiture, or to penalties called *wite-ræden*,[2] that is, fines or mulcts, exigible in addition to the performance of the principal obligation.

[1] Allen's *Inquiry into the Rise and Growth of the Royal Prerogative in England*, pp. 143-149.
[2] See the use of this word in Ina's laws, §§ 50, 71 (Thorpe's *Ancient Laws and Institutes*, vol. i. pp. 135, 149; and 'Glossary,' *ibid.*, vol. ii., *voce* 'Wite'). In the grant by Ethelwulf to the Thegn Duda (A.D. 840) this term is evidently rendered into Latin by the words *poenalium rerum;* and in the remarkable instance of that king's conversion of *folcland* into *bocland* in his own favour (A.D. 847), with the 'consent and license of his bishops and princes,' it is comprehended in the words *vi exactorum operum sive poenalium causarum*' (Birch, *Cartularium*, vol. ii. pp. 5 and 33).

'*Bocland* (or land held by book or charter) had been severed by an act of government from the *folcland*, and converted into an estate of perpetual inheritance. It might belong to the Church, to the king, or to a subject . . . *Bocland* was released from all services to the public, with the exception of contributing to military expeditions, and to the reparation of castles and bridges. These duties or services were comprised in the phrase, *trinoda necessitas;* which were said to be incumbent on all persons, so that none could be excused from them. The Church, indeed, contrived in some cases to obtain an exemption from them : but in general its lands, like those of others, were subject to them.'[1]

The release of *folcland* from the services, duties, exactions, penalties, and forfeitures thus incident to its tenure,—in other words, its enfranchisement, and conversion into *bocland*,—could not be effected, even in his own favour, by the king,[2] without the authority or consent of the national legislature. It became a frequent practice so to enfranchise particular lands, in favour of particular persons, by charters to which witenagemots consented.[3] By the celebrated 'privilege'[4] of Wihtraed, King of Kent (confirmed by Ethelbald of Mercia in A.D. 742), this had been done in a more general way, as to all the lands of the cathedral churches of Canterbury and Rochester, and eight other monasteries there mentioned. But when Ethelwulf succeeded to the crown, lands not so enfranchised were, to a large extent, in the hands of religious houses, and also of powerful laymen.

[1] Allen's *Inquiry*, etc., pp. 143-151.
[2] See the charter in Ethelwulf's own favour in Birch, *Cartularium*, vol. ii. p. 33.
[3] See Kemble's *Codex Diplomaticus*, vol. i. ; charters numbered 138, 140, 141, 142, 161, 162, 163. And Ethelwulf's own grants with assent of the Witenagemot before A.D. 844, in Birch's *Cartularium* (numbered 431, 438, 442), pp. 5, 13, 17, etc.
[4] Haddan and Stubbs, *Councils*, vol. iii. pp. 239, 340, 341.

The copies or abridgments of the first of the two governing charters which are the subject of our present inquiry, found in the pages of Ingulph, of Malmesbury's *Gesta Regum*, of Wendover and of Matthew of Westminster (and also the abridgment of the second, extracted by Selden[1] from the chartularies of Abingdon Abbey), contain no specification of particular lands. But there can be no doubt, that in the originals from which they were taken (and which were preserved as title-deeds in the monasteries to which they belonged) a specification of particular lands in every instance followed; as we learn from Malmesbury himself with respect to his own copy.

His statement on that point is in the *Gesta Pontificum*;[2] where, after mentioning certain quantities of land in seven townships (of which the names are given[3]), as enfranchised (*in libertate posita*) under the charter passed at Wilton on Easter Day A.D. 854, he adds:

'The same king had before, in the first [?*fifth*] year of his reign, made another charter of enfranchisement (*chartam libertatis*), to churches only, of which I have here omitted to make mention, because I have set it forth in the *Acts of the Kings;* wherein he had specified these lands belonging to Malmesbury Abbey:—*Ellendune*, 30 hides; *Elmhamstede*, 15; *Wdetune*, 10; *Cerlstane*, 20; *Toccanham*, 5; *Minti*, 5; *Reodburna*, 10.' (These denominations of land being different from the seven, enfranchised under the later charter.)

The charter thus stated by the annalist of Malmesbury

---

[1] *Hist. of Tithes*, ch. 8 (ed. 1618), p. 208.
[2] 'Fecerat autem solis ecclesiis cartam libertatis, quam hic praetermisi, quia in Gestis Regum posui, anno primo regni sui, Incarnationis DCCCXL^mo iiii⁰, a transitu beati Aldelmi centesimo tricesimo quinto; ubi has terras ad Maldumesburg pertinentes nominaverat: Ellendune, etc.' (Hamilton's ed. 1870, from the original MS. of William of Malmesbury, in Magdalen College Library, p. 390).
[3] *Piretune*, 35; *Lacot*, 15; *Suttune*, 5; *Corsaburn*, 5; *Cridanville*, 10; *Cemele*, 10; *Domcisie*, 11.

Abbey to have been made in the first (? fifth)[1] year of King Ethelwulf's reign is manifestly the same with that abridged by Ingulph, and again abridged by Wendover, except that in the case of each monastery, the particular lands enfranchised (which these chroniclers omitted to mention) would be different. The Malmesbury charter has been printed by Mr. Kemble, and also by Mr. Haddan and Bishop Stubbs, from a Malmesbury cartulary, preserved in the Bodleian Library at Oxford, to which this rubric is prefixed :—'*How King Ethelwulf decimated his land to God and Holy Church, and with what proportion of that tenth he enriched the Church of Malmesbury.*' (*Quomodo Æthelwulfus Rex decimavit terram suam Deo et Sanctæ Ecclesiæ, et quota parte hujus decimæ Meldunensem Ecclesiam ditaverit.*)

As so printed, I now give the substance (and, so far as material, the form) of that document.

It begins with the words (too common, as words of style in public charters, etc., of that period, for anything to turn upon them) 'Our Lord reigning for ever.'[2] It then speaks (in terms which I have elsewhere[3] quoted) of the ravages and depredations of the Danes, and the danger of the times; and it proceeds:

'Wherefore I, Ethelwulf, King of the West Saxons, with the consent of my bishops and princes, have resolved on a salutary counsel and uniform remedy, and have determined to make a gift of a certain portion of land heritably to those of all degrees who are already in possession of it, whether monks or nuns serving God, or lay people, in all cases of the tenth "mansion," or at the least the tenth part, perpetually enfranchised so as to be free and protected from all secular services, royal dues,

---

[1] The text of Malmesbury is faulty as to the date; probably the words *anno primo* ought to be *anno quinto*. Ethelwulf came to the throne A.D. 839, and the date of the charter in the Bodleian MS. is A.D. 844.

[2] '*Regnante Domino nostro in perpetuum.*'   [3] *Ante*, p. 170.

tributes greater and less, or impositions called in our language "*Witereden*," and that it be free from all things for the deliverance of our souls and the forgiveness of our sins, for the service of God only (so that there be not military expedition, bridge-building, or fortification of castles[1]); that so they may the more diligently and without ceasing pour forth their prayers to God for us, because we thus in some degree lighten their secular service.'

After this, it is recited that Ahlstan, Bishop of Sherborne, and Helmstan, Bishop of Winchester (evidently in consideration of the benefit which would result from this Act to the Church), had agreed with their abbots and monastic brethren, that all their 'brethren and sisters' should, in each church, assemble and sing fifty psalms, and every priest celebrate two masses, on every Wednesday, one for King Ethelwulf, and another for his 'dukes' consenting to this gift (*huic dono*) for the ransom and remedy of their faults

[1] '*Quamobrem ego Athelwulfas Rex Occidentalium Saxonum cum consilio episcoporum ac principum meorum, consilium salubre atque uniforme remedium affirmavi, ut* [*? et*] *aliquam portionem terrarum hæreditariam antea possidentibus, gradibus omnibus, sive famulis et famulabus Dei Deo servientibus, sive laicis, semper decimam mansionem, ubi minimum sit tum decimam partem, in libertatem perpetuam perdonare dijudicavi, ut sit tuta et munita ab omnibus sæcularibus servitutibus, fiscis regalibus, tributis majoribus et minoribus, sive taxationibus quæ nos dicimus Witereden ; sitque libera omnium rerum, pro remissione animarum et peccatorum nostrorum, Deo soli ad serviendum, sine expeditione, et pontis instructione, et arcis munitione,*' etc. The word *mansio* is considered by Mr. Kemble equivalent to *hide ;* perhaps it might mean a hamlet or homestead with a certain quantity of *folcland* attached to it. See the Latin rendering of Article 37 of Alfred's laws 'Of a *bold-getæl.*'—'*De mutatione mansionis:—Siquis ab una mansione in aliam transire velit, faciat hoc testimonio aldermanni, in cujus comitatu prius folgavit.*' The word *sine* before the *trinoda necessitas* was understood by Selden to mean a release from those burdens ; but it was probably in this place a word of saving. (Thorpe, *Ancient Laws,* etc., vol. i. p. 87 ; vol. ii. p. 455. Selden, *Hist. of Tithes,* p. 207.)

(*pro mercede et refrigerio delictorum suorum*); prescribing particular psalms for each while living, and also for the continuance of those solemnities after their deaths. Then follows the date:

'This charter (*cartula*) was written, A.D. 844, on the seventh Indiction, on the day of the Nones of November, in the city of Winchester, in the Church of St. Peter, before the High Altar : and this they did for the honour of St. Michael the Archangel, and St. Mary, the glorious Queen, the Mother of God, and at the same time of the Blessed Peter, Prince of the Apostles, and of our Holy Father Pope Gregory, and all the saints; and then, for fuller assurance, King Ethelwulf placed the charter upon the altar of St. Peter, and the Bishops, for God's faith, received it from him: and afterwards they sent it through all the churches in their dioceses, as is aforesaid. *But this land, which we shall enfranchise, belongs to the Church of Malmesbury (terra autem ista quam in libertatem ponamus ad Meldunesburgensem ecclesiam pertinet). Dæt is at Ellendune thrity hyde, and æt Elmhamstede fyftene hyde, æt Wttune tien hyde, et Cherltune tuentig hyde, et Minty vif hyde, at Rodburne tien hyde.*'

The document ends with a blessing on any who might increase, and a curse on any who might infringe or diminish the grant; of which (being a matter of common style) nothing need be said. And then are appended the signatures of the king, the two bishops Helmstan and Ahlstan, six dukes, three abbots, and sixteen royal officers (*ministri*).

A construction of this document which would make it operate, not as an enfranchisement or authority for the enfranchisement of *folcland*, but as a grant of the tithes of the produce of the lands, is not reasonably possible. Laymen, as well as monasteries and churches, were to be benefited by it; and all those on whom that benefit was to be conferred were already in possession (*antea possidentibus*). The benefit to the Church was probably greater than to laymen; the Church in return was to sing psalms and offer masses for the donors while living, and for their souls when dead; and in this way the donors hoped on their side to obtain some profit from their munificence. It was evidently an act of enfranchisement, and nothing else.

We do not know how the tenth 'mansion,' or part enfranchised to each participator in this 'privilege' (*Privilegium Æthelulfi Regis*, as the similar grant of A.D. 854 was called in the Abingdon Cartularies),[1] was ascertained. But the earliest annalist who spoke of it (or rather of that of A.D. 854) described all the privileged lands as chartered by Ethelwulf; and from that language (consistent with the *grafio sempiterno* of Asser), taken in connection with the *quam in libertatem ponamus* of the Malmesbury document itself, and the statement that the bishops 'sent it through all the churches in their dioceses,'—my inference is, that there was a book or terrier of the lands to be enfranchised as the quota of each church, annexed or appended to the governing charter; and that the bishops sent to each a copy of the charter, with that part only of the annexed book or terrier in which it was directly concerned, in the manner appearing by the two[2] Malmesbury examples. This, however, applies only to such lands as were apportioned to the tenth 'mansion,' or part, contemporaneously with the governing charters. There are examples

[1] Selden, *Hist. of Tithes* (ed. 1618), p. 208.
[2] The Malmesbury abridgment of the later charter of A.D. 854 is, on this point, exactly like the Malmesbury copy of the earlier charter, of which the tenor has been stated. The enumeration of the seven denominations of land, containing together eighty-two 'hides,' with which the abridgment ends, is also introduced by the words: '*Terra autem ista quam in libertate ponimus ad ecclesiam pertinens Maldubesburg est*,' etc. (Will. of Malmesbury, *De Gest. Pontif.*, Hamilton's ed., p. 390).

extant of later grants of land in Wessex, founded (apparently) on the governing charter of A.D. 844, one to a layman, the king's *apparitor*,[1] dated in A.D. 845; and one to Malmesbury Abbey,[2] of A.D. 850.

Of the second governing charter (the true date of which seems to have been Easter Day A.D. 854, though referred by most of the Chronicles to 855) it will be sufficient to give such an account, as may explain its points of difference from the first, and why it should have been passed at all. The first, as has been seen, was an act of enfranchisement (*antea possidentibus*), to those already in possession; it applied only to lands so possessed. But the second had a larger operation and effect upon all the *folcland* of Ethelwulf's kingdom. Its difference from the first is marked in many ways. It was passed in the king's palace at Wilton, after St. Swithun had become Bishop of Winchester in the place of Helmstan; the introductory part was not the same, there being here no mention of public calamities, but only of the transitory nature of this life. There was no solemn deposit of the document upon the altar of the cathedral church; no transmission of copies by the bishops to all the churches of their dioceses. The psalms and masses promised by the bishops were the same; but, while these were to be sung and said under the first charter on Wednesday, under the second they were to be repeated on Saturday also. Three full contemporaneous copies[3] of it, introducing by way of preamble grants of enfranchisement (*ista est autem libertas quam Æthelwulf Rex in perpetuam libertatem concessit habere*) of particular parcels of land defined by boundaries,

---

[1] Birch's *Cartularium*, No. 449, vol. ii. p. 30.
[2] *Ibid.*, No. 457, vol. ii. p. 45.
[3] Numbered 1054, 270, and 271 in Mr. Kemble's work. And see Haddan and Stubbs, *Councils*, vol. iii. pp. 638, 640.

—two to thanes, named Hunsige and Wiferth, the third to Malmesbury Abbey,—are printed in Mr. Kemble's *Codex Diplomaticus.*

The material part of that charter of A.D. 854 is thus expressed:

'I have taken and carried into effect, with my bishops, and counts, and all my nobles, a salutary counsel, to grant a tenth part of the lands throughout my kingdom, not only to the holy churches, but have also granted to my servants, that they should hold it enfranchised for ever; so that this donation shall remain fixed and unchangeable, discharged from all royal service, or other secular services.'[1] [Then follows the agreement of Bishops Ahlstan and Swithun, about weekly psalms and masses.]

Of this charter, the royal officers or servants appear to have been especially favoured objects. If it had been otherwise, it would still have been impossible to understand *decimam partem terrarum* of prædial tithes. In later charters, made by virtue of this, and in which the authority given by it is referred to (of which there are several,—two to Winchester Cathedral,[2] and one to a king's officer named Dunne[3]), the subject of the grants was unequivocally land, not tithes.

All the best historical critics of the present century, who have paid any attention to these charters of Ethelwulf, are agreed in conclusions not differing in substance from my own

---

[1] '*Consilium salubre cum episcopis, et comitibus cunctis que optimatibus meis perfeci, ut decimam partem terrarum per regnum meum, non solum sanctis ecclesiis darem, veram etiam et ministris meis in perpetuam libertatem habere concederem; ita ut talis donatio fixa incommutabilisque permaneat, ab omni regali servitio et omnium sæcularium absoluta servitute.*' (*De Gestis Pontificum:* Hamilton's ed., p. 390.)

[2] See Haddan and Stubbs, *Councils*, vol. iii. pp. 641-643.

[3] *Ibid.*, pp. 644, 645.

—Dr. Lingard,[1] Mr. Sharon Turner,[2] Mr. Kemble,[3] the late Mr. Haddan and Bishop Stubbs.[4] The policy of those charters was, perhaps, not so purely ecclesiastical as might at first sight appear. The times were such as to make the subtraction of large quantities of *folcland* from the distributable public estate, out of which soldiers and civil servants might be rewarded, inconvenient. Bishop Ahlstan was a statesman and a soldier, as well as a churchman. Swithun was also a trusted minister of the king. The enfranchisement of a certain proportion of the folkland in ecclesiastical hands might make the resumption of other parts for State uses more easy; and it might check the frequency of applications to the king and Witenagemot, in particular cases, for privileged grants of such land. Nor is it to be assumed, that because, by the second charter, the king took power to grant in *bocland* as much as a tenth part of the folkland of the whole kingdom of Wessex, that power was fully exercised. The charter was potential, not imperative; it may have had (like the first) a 'book' or terrier of grants already determined upon appended to it: but the extant subordinate charters prove that these did not exhaust the power.

[1] *Antiquities of the Anglo-Saxon Church* (1806), vol. i. p. 126; and note (A) at p. 303.
[2] *History of Anglo-Saxons* (5th ed. 1828), vol. i. p. 493.
[3] *Saxons in England* (1876), vol. ii. pp. 480-485.
[4] *Councils,* vol. iii. pp. 637, 638, 642, note.

CHAPTER VI

FOURTH PERIOD—THE PRIMACIES OF ODO AND DUNSTAN

§ 1. *New Relations between England and the Continent*

IT has been seen that in Alfred's time learning was so utterly lost in England, that, with a few exceptions (such as Archbishop Plegmund, Asser, Grimbald, and his own chaplain John),[1] hardly any priest could be found who knew Latin; and those who desired instruction had to go abroad for it. The monastic libraries had been destroyed; it was on the Continent, and not here, that ecclesiastical literature, even of Anglo-Saxon origin, was still known and preserved.

Alfred's son, Edward, was an unlearned man; but he advanced the cause of learning through the alliances by which he sought to strengthen himself in his kingdom. Four of his daughters married French or German kings and princes.[2] The way was thus opened for more frequent intercourse between this country and the Continent. Athel-

---

[1] Gervase of Canterbury (Stubbs' ed. 1879; vol. ii. pp. 44, 45) adds to the exceptions enumerated by Alfred the name of Wenefrid, 'Bishop of the Wiccians.' '*Ecclesiæ*' (he says) '*cum bibliothecis suis a Danis combustæ fuerunt, et propterea in tota insula studium litterarum abolitum est, quod quisque magis vereretur capitis periculum, quam sequeretur librorum exercitium.*'

[2] See Lappenberg, *Hist.* (Thorpe's transl.), vol. ii. pp. 99, 107, 109, 110.

stan, Edward's son, sent presents to foreign monasteries;[1] and in foreign monasteries, from the latter days of Alfred, many English youths destined for the service of the Church received their education.

§ 2. *Archbishop Odo.*

Among these was Odo (or Oda), by birth a noble Dane,[2] who, in the year after the accession of Edmund, Athelstan's half-brother, to the throne, became Archbishop of Canterbury. He had taken the monastic habit[3] in the Benedictine monastery of Fleury, near Orleans. He governed the Church of England for seventeen years, with a constant view to its revival or reformation upon monastic principles. It was under his primacy that Dunstan, and his colleagues Ethelwold and Oswald, rose to power; and if the fame and the honours of canonisation with which the Benedictine party rewarded their successful champions fell to the lot of the disciples rather than the master, the policy which triumphed was that of Odo.[4]

§ 3. *The Reforming Triumvirate.*

Of the men who completed the revolution for which Odo had been preparing the way, Bishop Stubbs[5] says, that 'Ethelwold was the moving spirit; Oswald tempered zeal with discretion; Dunstan may be credited with such little moderation and practical wisdom as can be traced.' From that estimate of their characters I see no reason to

---

[1] See Lappenberg, *Hist.* (Thorpe's transl.), vol. ii. p. 111.

[2] Hook, *Lives of Archbishops*, vol. i. p. 361.

[3] See Eadmer's Life of St. Oswald (Wharton's *Anglia Sacra*, vol. ii. p. 194).

[4] Stubbs, *Memorials of Dunstan*, Introd., p. xxxvii. See *ante*, p. 415, and Appendix B.   [5] *Memorials of Dunstan*, Introd., p. xcviii.

differ. Dunstan was the eldest, Oswald the youngest of the three; all rose to positions of influence early in life. Dunstan had the largest mind, and the most statesmanlike qualities; Oswald had seen most, and Ethelwold least, of the Church and the world beyond England. But they were men of one purpose, and of equal resolution and courage. It is important, with reference to some questions which remain to be examined, that the influence of foreigners, and of foreign Church literature, upon them, and upon the Anglo-Saxon Church in their time, should be understood.

§ 4. *Oswald, Bishop of Worcester, and his Foreign Associates.*

I will speak of Oswald first, Archbishop Odo's nephew, who when young became a monk at Fleury,[1] as his uncle had been before him; passing there through minor orders and the diaconate to the rank of priest. He returned to England, and in King Edred's time went abroad again, with a company whose destination was Rome; but he turned aside to Fleury, upon some mission (as is supposed) from his ecclesiastical superiors.[2] When Dunstan became archbishop in A.D. 960, he was made Bishop of Worcester, and in 972 Archbishop of York. He was very active in the expulsion of the married clergy from the greater monasteries of Mercia, and in bringing those houses under the Benedictine rule. Bishop Stubbs[3] says that 'while the monastic movement had taken its rise at Winchester, it was received with most favour in Mercia.' He brought over from France[4] several learned men to instruct the inmates

---

[1] Eadmer's Life of Oswald (Wharton's *Anglia Sacra*, vol. ii. p. 194). At Fleury he is said to have been a disciple of Abbo.
[2] *Ibid.*, p. 195.   [3] *Memorials of Dunstan*, Introd., p. xcvii.
[4] Eadmer's Life (*ubi supra*), pp. 200, 201.

P

of some of those monasteries in the Benedictine discipline, and in grammar and the liberal arts. Among these was Abbo[1] of Fleury, a man afterwards famous, who, after passing some time at Paris and at Rheims,[2] had returned to his native diocese of Orleans. Oswald, in A.D. 985, made him chief instructor to the monks of Ramsey Abbey, and ordained him priest. Abbo, while in England (perhaps before), was intimate with Dunstan,[3] and composed, at Dunstan's request, and from materials furnished by him, a Life of St. Edmund of East Anglia. On his return to France, he became abbot of his own monastery of Fleury; and in that character attended the council held at St. Denis towards the end of the century, and entered into a controversy about monastic tithes, which I have elsewhere mentioned, with his own diocesan, Arnulph of Orleans, and other French bishops.[4] He lost his life in some affray arising out of the enforcement of monastic discipline, in A.D. 1014; and was reckoned among martyrs and saints by the Gallican Church.[5]

Oswald also sent to the Continent, at his own expense, a monk of Worcester, of his own name, who returned after visiting most of the great monasteries of France and the

[1] Eadmer's Life (*ubi supra*), p. 201.
[2] See Moreri, *Dictionnaire, in nom.* 'Abbon, de Fleuri.'
[3] Stubbs, *Memorials of Dunstan*, Introd., p. xix.; and see Life of Oswald (Wharton's *Anglia Sacra*, vol. ii. pp. 201, 202). Moreri says, 'His merit was recognised and honoured by King Ethelred, and the great men of the kingdom of England.'
[4] *Ante*, pp. 65, 66; and see his *Apologeticus*, etc., in the Appendix to Pithou's *Codex Canonum Vetus Ecclesiæ Romanæ* (Paris 1687); in Mabillon's *Vetera Analecta;* and Gallandii, *Bibl. Veterum Patrum* (Venice 1781), vol. xiv. p. 141 *et seq.*; also Baronius, *Annales*, vol. xvi. p. 434.
[5] Moreri, *ubi supra;* and see Wharton's *Anglia Sacra*, vol. ii. pp. 201, 202.

Low Countries, among others Corbey and Fleury. He died in A.D. 1010.[1]

§ 5. *Ethelwold, Bishop of Winchester.*

Ethelwold[2] was a Benedictine monk of Glastonbury, when Dunstan was abbot there. In King Edred's time he wished to cross the sea with a view to self-improvement; but his presence in England was thought of sufficient importance for leave to be refused him by the king. Soon afterwards he was made Abbot of Abingdon, described by its chronicler[3] as then a small monastery, much impoverished, and the only house in England (except Glastonbury) under the Benedictine rule. There he gathered round him, from all parts of England, men accustomed to different usages of reading and chanting; and, to bring them all to one uniform method, he prevailed on some of the monks of Corbey to come over from France[4] and teach them. He also sent Osgar,[5] who had followed him from Glastonbury, and who succeeded him in the abbacy when he

---

[1] Pitseus (Paris, 1619), *Ætas undecima;* p. 181 : '*In Galliam Belgicam navigavit; et in transmarinis partibus pleraque celebriora monasteria studiorum causa visitavit, liberalitate Oswaldi Episcopi Vigorniensis in tota illa peregrinatione sustentatus. Invisit autem, inter cætera, monasteria S. Bertini, S. Vedasti, et Corbeiam ; deinde S. Dionysii cœnobium non longe a Parisiensi civitate situm, et Latiniacum Fursæi Collegium ;—tandem Floriacense monasterium.*'

[2] See his Life, by Wulfstan (Migne's *Patrolog.*, vol. cxxxvii. p. 82, etc.) ; *Hist. Cœnob. Abendon.* (Wharton's *Anglia Sacra*, vol. i. pp. 163, 164).

[3] *Hist. Cœnob. Abendon.* (Wharton's *Anglia Sacra*, vol. i. pp. 163, 164).

[4] *Ibid.*; and see the Abingdon memoir, *De sancta Athelwoldo*, in Dugdale's *Monastic.* (Caley, Ellis, and Bandinel), vol. i. p. 516.

[5] *Ibid.*; and Wharton's *Anglia Sacra (ubi supra)* ; also Migne's *Patrolog.*, vol. cxxxvii. pp. 82-92 (cap. 14 of Wulstan's *Vita*, etc.)

was advanced to the bishopric of Winchester in A.D. 963, to Fleury for further instruction. Among the pupils of Ethelwold was Aelfric, the 'grammarian,' of whom more will hereafter be said.

§ 6. *Dunstan, Archbishop of Canterbury.*

Dunstan[1] began life as a courtier in King Athelstan's reign, but retired from court in disappointment or disgust. King Edmund (A.D. 942) made him Abbot of Glastonbury. He was the chief minister of Edmund's brother and successor, Edred. He affronted and incurred the enmity of Edwy, the most unfortunate of Anglo-Saxon kings, and in consequence fled to Flanders. There he remained for a year, a guest in the monastery of St. Peter at Ghent,[2] then in the highest repute among the religious houses of the Low Countries for good discipline and learning. The revolution of the succeeding year, A.D. 957, brought him home again; and Edgar made him, by quick steps, Bishop of Worcester and of London, and (in A.D. 960) Archbishop of Canterbury. After this elevation he was for twenty-eight years chief governor of the kingdom. To his policy, ecclesiastical and civil, it was due that Edgar 'the Peaceful' became celebrated by the monastic historians, as among the greatest and most fortunate of kings; as the compeer in glory of Romulus and Cyrus, of Alexander and Arsaces, of Charlemagne and Arthur.[3]

[1] See his Life, by Osbern, in Stubbs' *Memorials*, and in Migne's *Patrolog.*, vol. cxxxvii. p. 410 *et seq.*

[2] *Ibid.*, cap. 27 (Migne, *ubi supra*, p. 437); Stubbs' *Memorials*, Introd., p. lxxxix.

[3] '*Incomparabilis*,' he is called by Ralph Higden; Hoveden compares him to *all* the kings above named; Symeon of Durham and the Melrose Chronicle to all but Arsaces.

§ 7. *The Council of Winchester*—'*Regularis Concordia.*'

It is to the year A.D. 969 that Symeon of Durham [1] refers the commission given by King Edgar to Dunstan, Ethelwold, and Oswald, to eject the married clergy or secular canons from the greater monasteries of Mercia, and to put monks in their places. Others [2] assign a different date to that mandate. Abbot Ailred of Rievaulx [3] (writing in King John's time) put a long and highly rhetorical speech into King Edgar's mouth, as delivered to the three bishops upon that occasion. I extract from it a sentence :

'Thou didst say, O Dunstan, that almsgiving endures for ever ; and that none is more fruitful than that which is bestowed upon monasteries and churches, wherewith God's servants may be sustained, and all that is not wanted for that purpose laid out upon the poor (*quo Dei servi sustententur, et quod superest pauperibus erogetur*).'

Whatever may be thought of this, there can be no doubt that a council was held at Winchester, under King Edgar's authority, at which a rule for all the Benedictine monasteries in England was drawn up and agreed to, in twelve articles.[4] It is commonly ascribed to Dunstan; and is entitled 'The *Regular Concord* (*Regularis Concordia*) of the monks and nuns of the English nation.' The narrative with which it is introduced recites the destruction of many

---

[1] *Gesta Regum Angl.* (Savile's *Hist. Angl. Script. X.*, p. 158).

[2] The charter for expelling the married clergy from Worcester (printed by Mansi, *Concil.*, vol. xviii. p. 479) is dated in A.D. 964.

[3] Savile, *Hist. Angl. Script. X.*, p. 360. (Also in Mansi, *Concil.*, vol. xviii. p. 527); and, translated into English, in Stow's *Annals;* (Howes'.ed. 1632, p. 84, A.D. 963).

[4] Reyner, *Apostolatus Benedictinorum in Anglia* (1626), append., pars iii. pp. 77-92 (and see Migne's *Patrolog.*, vol. cxxxvii. pp. 476-490).

of the English monasteries, and the deficiency of the means for keeping up Divine service in others; and that the king, having restored them,[1] had called the council together to agree upon this uniform rule. It then proceeds:

'Thereupon, cheerfully and with all the energy of their minds obeying this royal command, and remembering how our holy patron, St. Gregory, admonished the blessed Augustin to appoint for the ornament of the then rude English Church any good usages, not of the Roman Church only, but of the Gallican Churches also: They [the bishops, abbots, and abbesses], *having called to their aid monks from the Benedictine house of Fleury, and also from the chief monastery of the famous city named Ghent,* and collecting what is excellent out of their good customs, as bees store their honeycomb in one hive, from the different flowers of the fields,—have put into this small scroll (*hoc exiguo apposuerunt codicillo*) those manners and customs adapted to good living and to the sweetness of the regular discipline; that, by means thereof, those who walk in the royal road of the Lord's commandments may be refreshed as with a welcome draught, and filled with most sweet devotion.'

The twelve articles (*capitula*) of the *Concordia* were preceded by a decree as to the election of bishops (as well as abbots and abbesses), intended to place the monastic system upon a footing of absolute security. The royal consent was required to every election; and no one was to be eligible to any bishopric except a regular monk of the Benedictine order, who, when consecrated bishop, was to be the head of his conventual chapter, and 'to observe in all things the same rule with his monks, like a regular abbot.'

Of the articles constituting the rule, nine are occupied with the order of the church services, at all the different

---

[1] More than forty monasteries are said to have been restored by King Edgar.

hours, times, and seasons; one with a regulation as to weekly cleansing; another with the sickness of any brother, and his burial after death. The tenth article[1] regulated the distribution of the alms of the monastery; and it deserves the more attention, because of the sentiment put into Dunstan's mouth in the speech ascribed to King Edgar, and the statements of his biographers as to his great care, during his primacy, 'for the due application of the revenues of the Church to the relief of widows, orphans, and strangers':

'Let there be in every monastery places set apart for the entertainment of the poor (*singula loca, ad hoc constituta, ubi pauperum fiat susceptio*): and *on each day* let *three* of the poor who are constantly fed in the monastery be chosen, to have the benefit of this mandate, and to be fed with the same victuals which the brethren use. And attendance is to be given there in this course. On Saturday, the boys of the right side of the choir are to do it, with one of the choir-masters; on the Lord's day following, the other boys of the left side, with the other choir-master: and for every other day in the week, so many brethren are to be told off, from holyday to holyday, for this service, that no one of them except the abbot shall be excused from that duty: and he is to do it when he can.

'For the rest, when poor strangers arrive (*supervenientibus peregrinis pauperibus*), the abbot, with brethren chosen by him according to the precepts of the rule, is to see that they have the benefit of this mandate; and so the Father himself (if by any means he can), or one of the brethren, must zealously perform towards them in the hospice all the offices of humanity, and no attention to them which the rule requires is to be omitted through any temptation of pride or error of forgetfulness. . . . And when the strangers go forth, let a supply of victuals be given them, as the means of the place may allow.'

This rule of the *Concordia* affords, in my judgment, strong, though indirect, evidence against the idea, that in

[1] Reyner, p. 92; Migne (*ubi supra*), p. 490.

the English Benedictine monasteries of Dunstan's time any custom of tripartite, or quadripartite, or other definite division of tithes, or of any other part of their revenues, was known. It agrees well with the primitive practice recommended by Gregory the Great to Augustin; and it was adopted (as has been seen) by a council which had directly in view Gregory's answer given at the same time to Augustin upon another point, and which was assisted by foreigners conversant with the customs of the Gallican churches.

§ 8. *Canons enacted under King Edgar.*

Not only was the *Concordia* silent as to any proportionate rule of distribution, but the like silence was preserved in the canons[1] made under King Edgar during Dunstan's primacy, one of which (the fifty-fourth [2]) enjoined all priests to remind the people to pay tithes and other church dues at the usual times and seasons (mentioning them); and another (the fifty-fifth [3]) enjoined 'that the priests so distribute the people's alms that they do both give pleasure to God and accustom the people to alms.'

The implication from the generality and indefiniteness of these provisions, in the *Concordia* and in the canon, is the more forcible when they are contrasted with a later document [4] containing a scheme of rules for a college of secular clergy, into which the article of the *Capitulare*

---

[1] Thorpe's *Ancient Laws*, etc., vol. ii. p. 245 *et seq.*

[2] *Ibid.*, p. 257. The *Law of the Northumbrian Priests* (*ibid.*, p. 301, art. 60), imposed pecuniary mulcts for non-payment of tithes; on a 'king's thane,' ten half marks; on a landowner, six; on a *ceorl*, twelve sous.

[3] Thorpe's *Ancient Laws*, etc., vol. ii. p. 257. [4] *Post*, p. 263-268.

Episcoporum as to a tripartite division of tithes, was introduced; and with a gloss [1] upon the canon itself, demonstrably belonging to, or not earlier than, the latter years of King Ethelred. Those documents will be described in a later chapter. There are parts [2] of Dunstan's canons from which it may reasonably be inferred, that he was not unacquainted with the *Capitulare Episcoporum*. It must certainly have been known to some of the foreigners consulted at the Council of Winchester, or who were brought into England by Oswald and Ethelwold; and it may (not improbably) have come to Dunstan's own knowledge when he was at Ghent. There were certainly afterwards (if not then) some who would willingly have seen it followed in England. But probability is much against the supposition that Dunstan or his colleagues were among that number. The foreign monastery whose principles and practice, of all others, had most weight with them, was Fleury; and nothing can be more certain, than that at Fleury the *Capitulare Episcoporum* (if known at all) was not accepted as law or acted upon in practice, and that it was not there regarded as of authority. Abbo knew nothing of it; he objected [3] to a different form of tripartite division, in which the bishop took a third share. He thought that, as to the church revenues under the bishop's administration, the quadripartite rule (received at Paris and Rheims) ought to be followed at Orleans; and that as to those revenues, whether tithes or anything else, which were in the possession of monasteries, they ought to be disposed of according

---

[1] *Post*, p. 262.

[2] *E.g.*, Canons 26, 45, 54, 65, 66, 67 (Thorpe's *Ancient Laws*, etc., vol. ii. pp. 251, 253, 257, 259).

[3] See his letter to the monk Gerald, in Bouquet, *Recueil des Histoires*, vol. x. p. 440, §§ 2, 3.

to the rules of the house, without episcopal interference.¹ In his controversy with Bishop Arnulph he put forward in aid of his arguments a collection of canons,² in which the rule of the *Capitulare Episcoporum* found no place; but, on the contrary, several of the canons of the first Council of Orleans, and of the Councils of Braga and Toledo, were relied on, together with passages from decretal letters of Popes Gregory the Great and Simplicius laying down the Roman or quadripartite rule.

§ 9. *King Edmund's Laws.*

The secular legislation on ecclesiastical subjects during the primacies of Archbishops Odo and Dunstan (doubtless passed under their influence) consists of the laws of Kings Edmund and Edgar.

Those of Edmund³ are three in number, and short, but not unimportant.

The first (on which it is not material to dwell) imposed a penalty on persons 'in holy orders' (an expression which there appears to include nuns) if guilty of incontinence.

The second made the non-payment of tithes and other church dues punishable by excommunication: 'A tithe we enjoin to every Christian man by his Christendom, and church-scot, and *Rom-feoh* (Peter-pence), and plough-alms. And if any will not do so, let him be excommunicated.' This, proceeding upon the ground of recognised religious obligation, was a step in advance, beyond anything previously contained in Anglo-Saxon secular laws.

[1] App. to Pithou's *Codex Canonum Vetus*, etc. (Paris 1687), pp. 417, 418.

[2] Gallandii *Bibl. Veterum Patrum* (Venice 1781), vol. xiv. pp. 160, 169. See Canons 27, 30, 31, 35, 38.

[3] Thorpe's *Ancient Laws*, etc., vol. i. pp. 245-247.

The third related to the repair of churches:

'We have also ordained that every bishop repair the houses of God in his own district, and also remind the king that all God's churches be well conditioned, as is very needful for us.'

This relates to the repair, out of the funds at the bishop's disposal, of the public baptismal churches of the diocese; and it seems to indicate, that no part of these funds was then separated by any customary mode of division from the rest, and appropriated for the repair of churches.

§ 10. *King Edgar's Laws.*

The ecclesiastical ordinance, made by King Edgar and his witenagemot at Andover,[1] was the first step taken in England, so far as law is concerned, towards the transition from the old baptismal churches and their districts to modern parish churches and parishes. Selden[2] (who seems to have considered the canon passed under Archbishop Wulfred, as to the proceedings to be taken upon a bishop's death, capable of a construction,[3] which I have elsewhere given my reasons for rejecting) rightly observed that

'The first express mention of limitation of profits (other than of the endowing), to be given to this or that church, is in those laws of King Edgar, made about A.D. 970, where a threefold division is of churches. The first is called *ealdan mynstre*, that is *senior ecclesia*, which name anciently was given to cathedral churches; the second, a church that hath *legerstowe*, or place for burial; the third, a church that hath no *legerstowe*.'

Blackstone,[4] rejecting the tradition about Honorius, and also (if he knew it) that about Theodore, referred the

---

[1] Thorpe's *Ancient Laws*, vol. i. pp. 263-265 (see p. 273 as to Andover).   [2] *Hist. of Tithes* (ed. 1618), ch. 9, § 4, p. 262.
[3] *Ibid.*, pp. 261, 262.   [4] *Comment.*, vol. i. p. 113.

origin, or at least the earliest public recognition, of parishes of the modern sort, to these laws of Edgar.

Their first article [1] recognised the general right of the old 'baptismal' churches to tithes:

'That God's churches be entitled to every right; and that every tithe be rendered to the old minster, to which the district belongs; and be so paid, both from a thane's *in-land* (*i.e.* land in the lord's own hands), and from *geneat-land* (*i.e.* land granted out for services), so as the plough traverses it.'

The second article [2] introduced a qualified exception, in favour of manorial churches with burial-grounds:

'But if there be any there who on his *bocland* (*i.e.* his private estate) has a church at which there is a burial-place, let him give the third part of his own tithe to his church. If any one have a church at which there is not a burial-place, then, of the nine parts, let him give to his priest what he will; and let every church-scot go to the old minster, according to every free hearth; and let plough-alms be paid when it shall be fifteen days over Easter.'

The third article [3] fixed the times for payment of each description of tithes, and also of 'church-scot,' on peril of the legal 'wite' (a pecuniary penalty); and it provided, for the first time, a further remedy and penalty, in case of non-payment:

'And if any one will not then pay the tithe, as we have ordained, let the king's reeve go thereto, and the bishop's, and the mass-priest of the minster, and take by force a tenth part for the minster to which it is due; and assign to him the ninth part, and let the eight parts be divided into two; and let the landlord take possession of one half, and the bishop the other half; whether it be a king's man, or a thane's.'

---

[1] Thorpe's *Ancient Laws*, etc., vol. i. p. 263.
[2] *Ibid.*
[3] *Ibid.*, pp. 263-268.

The next article related to Peter-pence; the fifth, and last,[1] to the proper observance of the Lord's Day, and of other festivals and fasts; directing '*soul-scot*' (a burial fee) to be 'paid for every Christian man to the minster to which it is due'; and 'church-grith' (*i.e.* the privileges of churches) to be maintained.

There was no other law of King Edgar, bearing either on tithes or on church organisation. But there was a 'supplement'[2] to his laws, in the nature partly of a royal proclamation, and partly of an archiepiscopal charge. It seems to have been issued on occasion of a pestilence; and it commanded various things, which were regarded as within the proper scope of the executive power. It contained[3] this mandate:

'I and the archbishop command, that people shall not anger God, nor merit either the sudden death of this present life, nor, still more, the future one of eternal hell, by any diminution of God's dues: but that both rich and poor, who have any tilth, render to God His tithes with all joyfulness and without any grudge, as the ordinance teaches, that my *witan* ordained at Andover.'

The king's reeves were then commanded to execute that ordinance strictly; and there is this reference[4] to priests serving in royal or manorial churches or chapels:

'Then will I, that these, God's dues, stand everywhere alike in my dominion; and that the servants of God, who receive the moneys which we give to God, live a pure life: that, through their purity, they may intercede for us with God; *and that I and my thanes direct our priests to that which the pastors of our souls teach us, that is, the bishops*, whom we ought never to disobey in any of those things which they teach us on the part of God!'

---

[1] Thorpe's *Ancient Laws*, etc., vol. i. p. 265.
[2] *Ibid.*, p. 271 *et seq.*   [3] *Ibid.*, pp. 271-273.   [4] *Ibid.*, p. 273.

This legislation, with the illustration which it receives from the 'supplement,' presents several points for inquiry and remark.

What were the 'old minsters,' to which, subject to the exception made by the second article, tithes were generally to be paid? I think the probable answer to that question is, that the word 'minster' had not then departed from its original sense of a conventual or collegiate church;[1] and that those 'old minsters' were 'baptismal' churches; cathedrals, or churches of secular canons or monks. Selden[2] interpreted the words in the first article, which Mr. Thorpe translates '*the old minster to which the district belongs*,' as equivalent to '*the ancientest church or monastery where he hears God's service.*'

He observed, that the monasteries, both when filled with secular clerks before Edgar's time, and (after the change then made) by Benedictines, 'were in many places the only oratories and auditories that the near inhabitants did their devotions in,' and that they had special privileges in respect of burial. The earliest place in any later laws, in which I find the word '*minster*' clearly extended to churches of King Edgar's second class, viz. manorial churches with cemeteries, is the third article of Canute's ecclesiastical ordinances;[3] where there is a graduated scale of penalties

---

[1] See *Institutes of Polity*; (Thorpe's *Ancient Laws*, vol. ii. pp. 321, 323, 325), as to abbots, abbesses, and monks, '*within their minsters;*' and priests and nuns, '*dwelling in a minster.*' Those 'Institutes' were later than Edgar's time (*ibid.* p. 321).

[2] *Hist. of Tithes* (ed. 1618), ch. 9, § 4, p. 263.

[3] Thorpe's *Ancient Laws*, etc., vol. i. p. 361. This article is also contained in the preliminary scheme, entitled *Of Church-Grith*, commonly reckoned among the laws of Ethelred (but as to which see *post*, pp. 276-287), on which most of Canute's ecclesiastical laws were founded. (Thorpe, *ubi supra*, pp. 341, 343, art. 5.)

for violation of the privileges of churches;—so much for a '*chief minster*'; so much less for '*a minster of the middle class*'; less still for '*one yet less, where there is little service, provided there be a burial-place*'; and least of all, for '*a field church, where there is no burial-place.*' Here I understand the 'chief minster' to be the cathedral of the diocese; a 'minster of the middle class' to be a conventual or collegiate baptismal church, of less dignity than the cathedral; '*one yet less*' to be a manorial church, entitled to one-third of the local tithes under Edgar's law; and a 'field-church' to be a private oratory or chapel, not so entitled.

The next question which suggests itself is, as to the condition and rights of those manorial churches (with burial-grounds), and of their priests? They certainly did not immediately after the passing of Edgar's laws become fully developed parish churches, or their priests parish priests. Their parishes (a word which came gradually to be applied to them) appear to have been for a long time called '*shrift-districts*;'[1] explained by Selden to mean 'circuits within which the priests exercised their shriving.' In the supplement to Edgar's laws[2] it seems also to be implied, that they had not what we now call a freehold tenure of their offices; but that the lords, within whose *bocland* their churches stood, had more control over them, and the bishops (without the lords' assistance) less, than under the modern parochial system. With respect to emoluments, their position seems to have been not unlike that of modern

[1] Selden, *Hist. of Tithes*, ch. 9, § 2 (ed. 1618), p. 252. See laws of Ethelred of A.D. 1008, Act 12 (Thorpe's *Ancient Laws*, etc., vol. i. p. 309); *Laws of Northumbrian Priests*, Act 42 (*ibid.*, vol. ii. p. 297); *Institutes of Polity*, Arts. 7 and 19 (*ibid.*, pp. 315, 327), etc.

[2] Thorpe's *Ancient Laws*, etc., vol. i. p. 273.

vicars; the old minster standing towards them in a relation similar to that of those monasteries of later times, to which appropriations of churches or tithes were made; and the one-third of local tithes which they received being like the reasonable stipend (*congrua portio*[1] of the modern canon law) moderated or assigned by the bishop, which the ecclesiastical appropriator (or, on the Continent, the lay owner[2] of feudalised tithes) had to pay the curate or vicar. The one-third, under Edgar's ordinance, was a *congrua portio*, fixed by law for all those consecrated churches on private estates to which cemeteries were attached.

Selden[3] thought, that when in this way the formation of rural parishes had once begun, there would be a natural tendency to the subdivision of such parishes, through the erection of new churches, with cemeteries attached to them, by the owners of *bocland* within their limits; and that, when these 'afterwards became whole parishes, they, by connivance of the time, took (for so much as was in the territory of that *bocland*) the former parochial right that the elder and mother church was possessed of.' That process, however, would rarely take place, unless the title to a tract of *bocland*, originally belonging to one person, had become by some means divided; for it cannot be doubtful that the original 'shrift-district' of every church of King Edgar's second class consisted of adjoining property of the lord on whose land the church stood. And no such process is sufficient to account for the subsequent enlargement of the one-third part of the local tithes of any such 'shrift-district' (or parish), conceded by Edgar's law, into the whole, excluding the 'older minster.' The explanation of such a change as this must be sought in

---

[1] See Jouy, *Principes et usages*, etc., cap. xi; pp. 344-422.
[2] *Ibid.*, p. 352.
[3] *Hist. of Tithes* (ed. 1618), ch. 9, § 4, p. 265.

the power or practice of appropriating tithes (notwithstanding these laws), which I reserve for consideration in my concluding chapter.[1] Meanwhile, it may be here observed, that the limited endowment of these parishes with one-third of the tithes established under Edgar's laws, did in many places long remain; and that it constituted a precedent, which, in the early days of appropriations and vicarages, was often acted upon by bishops, when settling the amount of stipend to be allowed by the appropriators to the vicar. Of both these facts proofs, sufficiently numerous, may be found in Bishop Kennett's *Case of Impropriations*.[2]

To those who believe, or think it probable, that in or before King Edgar's time a tripartite division of tithes, such as that of the *Capitulare Episcoporum*, was customary in England, the theory of Bishop Kennett, that the apportionment of one-third to the earlier parish churches arose out of that rule of division, may, perhaps, recommend itself. Kennett thought that the priest to whom one-third of the local tithes was conceded took that one-third for his own sustenance only, freed and discharged from all other obligations and burdens; and that the whole duty of hospitality and almsgiving to the poor (I presume, also, of providing for the repairs of churches) was thrown upon the other two-thirds payable to the monasteries.[3] To imagine, with-

[1] *Post*, pp. 305-314.
[2] *The Case of Impropriations and of the Augmentation of Vicarages and other Insufficient Cures*, etc. (1704). See pp. 27, 28, 29, 31, 41.
[3] *Case of Impropriations*, etc., pp. 16, 17, 27, 28, 29, 31, 32, 41. Bishop Kennett wrote with the practical object of throwing upon impropriated tithes a liability to augment the endowments of poor Vicarages, according to a doctrine (now exploded, and never tenable in law), which Noy, and some other lawyers of the seventeenth century, had maintained, and according to the analogy of the law of France. (See Jouy, p. 352, etc.)

out proof, that the one-third assigned to the priest of a manorial church was itself subjected to the rule of tripartite division, would, indeed, be extravagant; and that hypothesis, which Bishop Kennett certainly did not entertain, may be dismissed. But, on the other hand, there are many proofs, in that learned writer's own pages,[1] that there never was a time when a parish priest, whether rector or vicar, having cure of souls, was held to be exonerated from the general ecclesiastical duty of hospitality, according to his means, to the poor and to strangers; however scanty his endowment might be, and however free from apportionment into any definite shares. It is equally certain, that the conventual or baptismal churches, which retained two-thirds of the tithes under King Edgar's laws, did not retain them as trustees for the poor and for church repairs without any interest of their own, and did not use or apply them otherwise than as part of the common stock and general revenue of their several monasteries.[2] No reasonable presumption in favour of the existence of a definite proportionate rule for the distribution of tithes (as to which not only this law itself, but every other law as to tithes, ecclesiastical as well as civil, of the same or any other time, is absolutely silent) can be founded upon the fact that the proportion in which, under this law, the local tithes were divided between the greater and the smaller churches, was as two to one.

[1] See, as to Vicars, *Case of Impropriations*, etc., pp. 21, 58 (quoting the twenty-first article of the *Gravamina* of the University of Oxford in Henry V.'s time; and Lyndwode's *Provinciale; de officio Vicarii*, fol. 64).

[2] *Ibid.*, p. 63 (art. 20 of the *Gravamina* of the University of Oxford), p. 68; (Archbishop Peccham's letter, in A.D. 1282, to the Bishop of Hereford, against the Prior of Wenlock).

CHAPTER VII

FOURTH PERIOD—ECCLESIASTICAL LITERATURE:
THE EGBERTINE COMPILATIONS

§ 1. *Introductory*

IF, in examining that ecclesiastical literature of the tenth and eleventh centuries which has been the source of the idea that a tripartite division of tithes, or other church revenues, was anciently customary in England, I give the precedence to certain compilations with which the name of Archbishop Egbert is commonly associated, it is because these, more than anything else, have had a chief influence in establishing that notion in the minds of learned men, both of past and of recent times. If, indeed, it were once granted that those compilations contained canons for the government of his own diocese, codified by a great Northumbrian prelate in the middle of the eighth century, there must be an end of all controversy on the subject. For the 'Sacerdotal Laws,' which passed, from the Frank original described in a former chapter,[1] into all those compilations, contained these injunctions :[2]

[1] The *Capitulare Episcoporum*; see *ante*, pp. 37-39, and Appendix A.
[2] There are a few clerical variations in the different copies I have followed here the Andain text (Martene and Durand, *Ampliss. Coll.*, vol. vii. p. 26).

(*a*) 'That every priest teach all under his charge, so that they may know how duly to offer to God's churches the tithes of their whole means': (*Ut unusquisque sacerdos cunctos sibi pertinentes erudiat, ut sciant qualiter decimas totius facultatis ecclesiis divinis debite offerant*).

(*b*) 'That the priests themselves receive the tithes of the people, and write down their names, and what they have given, and divide it, according to canonical authority, in the presence of witnesses; and choose the first part for the "ornament" of the church; and dispense the second, by their own hands, compassionately and with all humility, for the use of the poor and strangers; and the priests alone are to reserve the third part for themselves': (*Ut ipsi sacerdotes populi suscipiant decimas, et nomina eorum, et quæcunque dederint, scripta habeant; et secundum autoritatem canonicam coram testibus dividant; et ad ornamentum ecclesiæ primam eligant partem, secundam autem ad usum pauperum atque peregrinorum per eorum manus misericorditer cum omni humilitate dispensent. Tertiam vero partem sibimetipsis soli sacerdotes reservent*).

That these injunctions formed part of a compilation made in the eighth century by Archbishop Egbert, or in his time under his name, was the belief of Spelman, Wilkins, and John Johnson, in whose collections of canons, etc., they were published from the Cottonian manuscript, now in the British Museum. Those learned men were followed by Bishop Kennett,[1] and Dr. Lingard,[2] in the same belief; and, in our own day, by such eminent Anglo-Saxon scholars as Kemble[3] and Thorpe.[4] And yet it had been pointed out, as far back as A.D. 1618, by Selden[5] (as it was

---

[1] *Case of Impropriations*, etc., p. 10, note. Southey, in his *Book of the Church*, and the late Mr. Brewer, evidently derived their views as to the division of tithes, and on some other points, from Bishop Kennett.

[2] *Antiquities of Anglo-Saxon Church*, vol. i. p. 93, note.

[3] *Anglo-Saxons in England*, vol. ii. p. 478.

[4] *Ancient Laws*, etc., vol. ii. pp. 97-127.

[5] *Hist. of Tithes* (ed. 1618), ch. 8, § 1, pp. 196-198.

afterwards by Baluze[1] and Mansi)[2] that the 'Excerptions,' with these articles as to tithes in them, could not have been compiled before the ninth century, and therefore could not possibly have been the work or of the time of Archbishop Egbert, who died in A.D. 766. Few who pay attention to literary criticism would now dispute the conclusions of Wasserschleben,[3] and of Mr. Haddan and Bishop Stubbs,[4] that none of these compilations (except the 'Penitential' part of two of them, of which I shall presently speak) have any pretension to be associated at all with Egbert's name; not only that they are not his, or of his time, but that there 'is not sufficient evidence to make it probable that they are even based upon anything which he compiled.'[5] Having examined the manuscripts at Cambridge and Oxford, and in the British Museum, from which they are derived, I do not think it superfluous to give a more particular account of them, than has yet been done in any publication that I have seen.

The twenty-one 'Sacerdotal Laws' of the Andain text occur in four of those 'Egbertine' manuscripts, which I arrange thus, in what I am led by internal evidence to think the true order of the works they represent: (1) That bequeathed by Archbishop Parker to the library of Corpus Christi College, Cambridge (marked K. 2 in Wanley's, and 265 in Nasmith's catalogue); (2) that numbered 718 in the Bodleian Library at Oxford; (3) that published by the Surtees Society[6] from a MS. in the National Library at Paris, in which it is a fragment preceding a 'Pontifical' ascribed to Archbishop

---

[1] *Capit. Reg. Franc.*, vol. ii. (ed. 1780) p. 1055, note.
[2] *Concil.*, vol. xii. pp. 411, 412.
[3] *Die Bussordnungen* (Halle 1851).
[4] *Councils*, etc., vol. iii. pp. 413-416, note.   [5] *Ibid.*, p. 415.
[6] Publications of Surtees Society, vol. xxvii. (*Egbert's Pontifical*).

Egbert; and (4) that marked 'Nero, A1,' which forms part of the Cottonian collection in the British Museum. Of these, the third is copied from the second, or from the work which the second represents. There is not, as far as I know, any other copy of that part of it. It has been said[1] that there are two complete copies of the Bodleian volume, No. 718, in the Vatican library; but this is a mistake. The Vatican manuscripts meant to be referred to are two in the Palatine collection, numbered 1347 and 1352. But the former of these contains only the fourth, and the latter only the three last of the four books into which the Bodleian treatise is divided. Of the two other Egbertine manuscripts, I do not know that any copies exist except those at Cambridge and in the British Museum.

§ 2. *The Worcester Manuscript at Cambridge.*

The first of these four manuscripts belonged before the Reformation to the church of Worcester.[2] It is of the eleventh century, and its date (at all events the date of the earlier part of it) must be referred to some time during the episcopate of Wulstan, the second of that name, who was

---

[1] In this statement, Mr. Haddan and Bishop Stubbs (*Councils*, vol. iii. p. 414) follow Mansi (*Concil.*, vol. xii. p. 411), who has incorrectly represented the account of these two Vatican MSS., given by the brothers Ballerini. See their text in the '*de vetustis canonum collectionibus dissertationum sylloge*' of Gallandius (Venice, 1778), pp. 93-266. They, and also Wasserschleben (*Beitrage*, etc., p. 4), correctly described the Vatican MSS. The Bodleian volume, No. 718, they evidently never saw.

[2] K2 of Wanley, No. 265 of Nasmith. 'Codex membranaceus in 4to; sæculo xi. scriptus. In protocollo habetur forma voti castitatis a monachis faciendi, in hæc verba :—*Ego frater N. promitto, etc. etc., domino præsule Wlstano præsente*' (Nasmith: *Catalogus Librorum*

Bishop of Worcester from A.D. 1003 to A.D. 1023; for the volume opens with a form of the monastic vow of chastity, beginning thus: 'I, brother N., promise, etc., in the presence of the Lord Bishop Wulstan.' The volume contains a collection of many pieces, not all copied by the same hand. It has prefixed to it (in a handwriting much more modern than any part of the book, and therefore not attributable to the original compiler) this general title:

'The penitential book of Egbert, the seventh Bishop of York from Paulinus, who was the first after him to receive the pall, in the seventh year of King Ceolwulf, A.D. 730.'

Among the contents of the volume, there are several works which the compiler could not possibly intend to ascribe to Egbert, because they are attributed by name to other persons, their true authors. There are two letters of Alcuin, to Archbishop Ethelhard of Canterbury and Archbishop Eanbald of York; the pastoral charge of Theodulph, Bishop of Orleans, to his diocese; and some of those homilies of Ælfric, which have often been quoted as proof that the doctrine of transubstantiation was not taught by the Anglo-Saxon Church.[1] I find nothing attributed to Egbert by any rubric of this manuscript except the 'Penitential,' which, after careful research, has been accepted as his genuine work by Wasserschleben, and by Mr. Haddan and Bishop Stubbs.

MSS. *quos Collegio Corporis Christi in Academia Cantabrigiensi legavit Reverendissimus Matthæus Parker, Archiepiscopus Cantuariensis*, Cambridge, 1777). As to this MS. having belonged to the church of Worcester, see Strype's *Life of Parker*, vol. ii. p. 509, and Wanley's *Antiquæ Literaturæ Septentrionalis liber* (1715), p. 109.

[1] See Nasmith's Catalogue (as to pp. 159 and 174 of the manuscript book, No. 265); Whelock's *Bede*, p. 471; Strype's *Life of Archbishop Parker*, vol. ii., book iv., p. 509.

The twenty-one 'Sacerdotal Laws' of the Andain manuscript, under the rubric, *Jura quæ sacerdotes debent habere*, constitute the sixth piece in this collection. Setting aside the later title on the fly-leaf of the book (which, as I have said, is not attributable to the compiler or his scribes), there is no representation that there was any connection between those 'Sacerdotal Laws' and Archbishop Egbert. Of the seventh piece, which follows them, the rubric is: '*Here begin Excerptions from Canonical books*' (*Incipiunt Excerptiones de libris Canonicis*). It consists of 102 extracts from canons of councils and sayings of Fathers (with appropriate sub-titles), of which I shall say more when I speak of the Cottonian manuscript. Here, again, there is nothing to represent that Egbert was the collector of those extracts, or had anything to do with them. The eighth piece, which follows, is distinctly ascribed to Egbert by this rubric: '*Here begins the Excerption from the Canons of Catholic Fathers, and Penitential and Remedy for souls, of the Lord Egbert, Archbishop of the See of York*' (*Incipit Excerptio de Canon. Catholicorum Patrum et Pœnitentia et Remedium Animarum Dni Echberhti Archiepi Eborace Civitatis*). The piece thus introduced is identical with that which (according to the judgment of Wasserschleben, and of Mr. Haddan and Bishop Stubbs) was the genuine work of Archbishop Egbert.

I cannot but think that the internal evidence here points to the library of St. Hubert's monastery at Andain as the probable source from which the author of this compilation may have derived that part of his materials which is relevant to my present inquiry. Among the manuscripts in that library (manuscripts of the tenth century) were the 'Sacerdotal Laws,' and also the genuine 'Penitential' of Archbishop Egbert. Of the 'Sacerdotal Laws,' as published by Martene and Durand (and of the differences between them and the *Capitulare Episcoporum* of the Metz manuscript), I have spoken in an earlier chapter.[1] The Worcester compiler copied them evidently from the Andain, and not from the Metz text. But Martene and Durand also published other manuscripts, equally ancient, from the same library, among which were two Penitentials of Anglo-Saxon origin— the one entitled, *A little book on remedies for sins* (*libellus de remediis peccatorum*); (which Wasserschleben and Mr. Haddan and Bishop Stubbs believe to be Bede's),[2] the other entitled *Another little book on remedies for sins*, which is Egbert's.[3] The fact that both the 'Sacerdotal Laws' and Egbert's 'Penitential' passed into the collection of the Worcester compiler, under the rubrics which I have mentioned, is suggestive of a common source. The works of Bede and of Egbert (the letters of Alcuin also) were in the tenth and eleventh centuries much more likely to be recovered by English scholars from Gallican libraries, than to be known to them from originals or copies preserved in England. This compilation also contains the pastoral epistle of Bishop Theodulph[4] to his diocese of Orleans; who was a great prelate, made abbot of Fleury, and afterwards Bishop of Orleans, by Charlemagne, and in A.D. 818 deprived and exiled by Louis the Pious, and who died in A.D. 821. This seems sufficient to show that the Worcester compilation was the work of a man who had studied theology abroad.

[1] *Ante*, pp. 39, 40. And see Appendix A.
[2] Haddan and Stubbs, *Councils*, vol. iii. p. 326.
[3] *Ibid.* p. 416.
[4] See *Biographie Universelle* (Brussels 1845-47), *in nom.* 'Théodulphe, évêque d'Orleans.'

I am bold enough to offer a conjecture as to who that compiler may, probably, have been. It is certain that he was a monk of Worcester; the first entry in the book points to the time of Bishop Wulstan; he was evidently a learned man, and a foreign traveller. These indications all agree with what we know of Oswald,[1] that monk of Worcester, who was sent abroad to visit the Gallican monasteries by and at the expense of Oswald the famous bishop; he visited the monasteries of Corbey, St. Bertin, St. Vedast, and St. Denis, and others not named by his biographer; he studied grammar at Fleury under Constantine, a learned monk of that time; and he lived till A.D. 1010, eighteen years after the death of Bishop Oswald, and seven after the succession of Wulstan to the see of Worcester. At Fleury he would naturally become acquainted with the pastoral epistle of Theodulph.

It does not appear that in the Andain manuscripts the 'Penitential' *libellus alter*, which in the rubric of the Worcester compilation is expressly attributed to Egbert, was inscribed with that name; the contrary is to be inferred. But if it was really his (as the best critics believe), it was doubtless known or reputed to be his in the monasteries where it was preserved; and it would be of especial interest to an Anglo-Saxon monk and student, the author's countryman. The works of Theodore, Egbert, and Bede were certainly brought into France by Alcuin, and into the northern part of the then Frank territory; for Alcuin had a cell at St. Josse in Ponthieu, a dependency of his abbey of Ferrieres; and it was to that place that his books from England came by sea.

Whatever may be thought as to the authorship of this

[1] See *ante*, p. 211, note.

Worcester compilation, it is at least certain, that the 'Sacerdotal Laws' contained in it came from France; and to infer, from their being found in such a collection or in any later members of the same literary family, that the tripartite division of tithes prescribed by one of their articles prevailed in England, would be no more reasonable than to infer from another article of the same series, which directed prayer to be offered for 'the Lord Emperor, and his sons and daughters,' that there were Emperors to be prayed for in England. There is not a word in the volume, representing that the 'Sacerdotal Laws' had, or were supposed by the compiler to have, authority in England; any more than there is a like representation as to the pastoral epistle of Bishop Theodulph.

§ 3. *The Exeter Penitential in the Bodleian Library at Oxford.*

The Bodleian manuscript volume (No. 718) has been usually regarded[1] as belonging to the tenth, but may, perhaps, really belong to the earlier part of the eleventh century. It was among the books given by Leofric,[2] the last Bishop of Crediton and first of Exeter, to the church of Exeter. That see was removed from Crediton to Exeter in A.D. 1050; and Leofric died shortly before A.D. 1074. He was by birth or education a Burgundian of Lorraine, and

[1] Haddan and Stubbs, *Councils*, vol. iii. p. 415.
[2] *Ibid.*; and see Dugdale's *Monasticon* (ed. Caley, Ellis, and Bandinel, 1819), vol. ii. p. 514, and app. iv. at 527. On the *last written page* of the Bodleian MS. volume is a letter from Pope Leo IX. to Edward the Confessor, objecting to Leofric's position at Crediton, as holding '*sine civitate sedem Pontificalem*'; and urging upon the king, '*ut de Credionensi villulâ ad civitatem Exoniæ sedem Episcopalem possit mutare.*' A copy of it is printed in Appendix F.

he signalised his government of the church of Exeter by reversing there the policy of Dunstan and his colleagues; ejecting nuns, and supplying their places with secular canons,[1] under a rule of life borrowed from Lorraine.

The volume given by him to that church, with which we are now concerned, may be described as a Manual of Pastoral Theology upon the doctrine, practice, and casuistry of Confession and Penitence, divided into four books, made up from different sources. The preface to the third, and the prologue and postscript to the fourth 'book,'[2] would seem to represent that this whole work was composed by a monk or clerk, at the request of an ecclesiastical superior (probably his bishop), for the instruction of others, under that Superior's authority. But this representation is true of the three latter books only (which are irrelevant to our present inquiry), and is inapplicable to the first, with which only we are concerned. The complete work, to which that preface, prologue, and postscript belong, is contained in the Vatican manuscript, No. 1352; on comparison[3] of which with the Exeter volume it is seen that the Anglo-Saxon compiler, leaving out the general introduction and the first book of that work, has substituted for it the same genuine 'Penitential' of Egbert which is found in the Worcester manuscript, with the twenty-one articles of the (Andain) 'Sacerdotal Laws,' interpolated in a singular manner between the prologue and the body of the 'Penitential;'—down to which point (that is, to the end of the 'Sacerdotal Laws') it is copied in the Paris manuscript, published by the Surtees Society;[4] which there breaks off.

---

[1] See *post*, pp. 264-269.   [2] See Appendix C.
[3] See *post*, Appendix C.
[4] Vol. xxvii. of the Surtees Society's publications.

At the end, however, of this substituted first book, there are certain other additions, to be presently described, which form no part of Egbert's 'Penitential.'

At the beginning of this Exeter volume a slip of paper has been pasted in, containing this title in a modern hand —'*The Penitential Book of Egbert, Archbishop of York*' (*Liber Penitentialis Egberti Aepi Ebor*);—which may be disregarded. Three pages of extracts from Papal decrees, irrelevant to the general subject of the volume, follow. These, also, are in a different and later hand from the rest, and they precede the proper paging. On the next page is a rubric, '*Here begin the Articles of the Penitential Book*' (*Incipiunt Capitula libri Poenitentialis*), introducing an epitome of the different matters which, in Archbishop Egbert's genuine 'Penitential,' follow the prologue;—no mention being made in it of the 'Sacerdotal Laws.' After this comes another rubric, which seems to be taken almost literally from that which in the Worcester manuscript introduces Egbert's genuine 'Penitential'—'*Here begins the Excerption from the Canons of Catholic Fathers of the Penitential Book for Remedy of Souls of Egbert, Archbishop of the See of York*' (*Incipit Excerptio de Canonibus Catholicorum Patrum Poenitentialis Libri ad Remedium Animarum Ecgberhti Archi Epi Eburacæ Civitatis*). Then comes Egbert's prologue; and, immediately after it, are interjected the twenty-one 'Sacerdotal Laws' of the Andain and the Worcester manuscripts, preceded by a rubric almost identical with that in the Worcester manuscript, '*These are the Priests' Laws, which they ought to observe*' (*hæc sunt jura Sacerdotum, quæ tenere debent*). Then succeeds the body of the genuine 'Penitential'; divided under nineteen heads, each preceded by its appropriate rubric. A prayer is added, and, after that (introduced by a rubric, '*Here begins the order of Confession according to Jerome; how a Christian ought to confess his sins*'), is a penitential formulary, consisting of litanies first,—prayers by the penitent,—questioning by the confessor,—several forms of confession,—the confessor's answer,—prayer by both together,—the priest's parting admonition; and, finally, a direction to the penitent to return to his home, praying for grace, that he may observe the priest's injunctions.

After all this, the first book ends with the rubric, '*The end of the Penitential Book of Archbishop Egbert*' (*Fin. lib. Poenitential Ecgberhti Archi Epi*).

Nothing in the volume, except this first book, is ascribed, by any title or rubric which really belongs to the compiler's work, to Archbishop Egbert. But the 'Sacerdotal Laws,' and the formulary of the 'order of confession according to Jerome' at the end, do appear, according to the letter of the initial rubric before the prologue, and of the final rubric which closes the first book, to be attributed to him.

I doubt, however, whether this was the compiler's intention. I think it probable, that the matter which was not Egbert's was added, by way of supplement, as germane to the matter of the book, and practically useful for its application; and that it did not seem to the compiler inconsistent or improper still to describe the book as Egbert's, without noticing the interpolation of the 'Sacerdotal Laws' (taken, as the 'Penitential' itself probably was, from the Worcester collection) or the addition of the formulary. The formulary (expressly said to be according to St. Jerome) speaks for itself. Of the interpolation of the 'Sacerdotal Laws' between the prologue and the body of the 'Penitential,' I will state what seems to me to be the probable explanation.

For this purpose it is necessary to describe shortly the nature of the prologue, and of the body of Egbert's 'Penitential.'[1]

The prologue is an exhortation to those priests who are to act as confessors to penitents, and prescribe medicines (an analogy dwelt upon with much earnestness) for moral and spiritual diseases. It urges upon them the duty of discrimination, and attention to what (following the same analogy) may be called the diagnosis of spiritual casuistry. It enforces those precepts by citations from Gregory Nazianzen, and from the prophet Ezekiel; and it refers to 'the apostles and holy fathers, and, afterwards, Paphnutius' (an anchorite of Upper Egypt, a man of much influence and reputation for sanctity in the fourth century,[2] whose name is here written *Penufius*), 'and after him the canons of the holy fathers, and many more, such as Jerome, Augustine, Gregory, and Theodore,' as the founders and expounders of this method of discipline; adding (which explains the reference to the 'canons of the Catholic fathers,' and the use of the word 'Excerption' in the rubric) that the writer had faithfully written down what he found in the sayings and opinions of all those authorities; (*ex quorum omnium ista descripsimus dictis et sententiis veraciter*).

As to the character of the body of the work, it is sufficient to mention a few of the titles or headings of its nineteen articles; such as (1) *What are deadly crimes;* (3) *Of lesser sins;* (5) *Of covetousness*, etc.; (6) *Of homicides*, etc.; (17) *Of the redemption of penance;* (18) *How penance*

[1] See them printed in Haddan and Stubbs, *Councils* (vol. iii. pp. 416-431) from Wasserschleben's text, after a Vienna manuscript.
[2] See the Acts of the first Council of Nicæa, in Mansi, *Concil.*, vol. ii. p. 906.

may be abridged, and (19) *How the priest ought to receive penance.* It is a graduated code of penances, for different offences against religion and morals; in its first aspect severe, but relaxed by allowing the principle of commutation.

Towards the middle of the prologue, this exhortation is addressed to candidates for the priesthood :

> 'Now, therefore, O my brethren, let him who desires to receive the sacerdotal authority first think for the sake of God upon his arms, and prepare them before the bishop's hand touches his head: that is, the psaltery, the lectionary, the antiphonary, the missal, the baptismal office (*baptisterium*), the martyrology through the whole course of the year for preaching, and the cyclical reckoning[1] of time (*compotum cum cyclo*); *that is, the sacerdotal law (hoc est, jus sacerdotum); and, after that, his " Penitential,"* ' etc.

It has been seen, that the twenty-one 'Sacerdotal Laws,' with the rubric before them, '*Hæc sunt jura sacerdotum quæ tenere debent,*' are interjected between the prologue and the practical part of the 'Penitential.' The explanation seems to me to be, that the compiler, finding in the prologue this direction, and also finding in the monastic collection before him (if it was the Worcester collection or any similar text from which he copied), these 'Sacerdotal Laws,' thought it convenient to put them in, by way of supplement to the enumerated service-books and offices of the Church, which would be otherwise accessible to his readers. And he put them into the particular place where they are found, because, forming no part of the 'Penitential' itself, they nevertheless seemed to him germane, as Sacerdotal Law, to the preliminary course of study recommended.

---

[1] *I.e.* of Easter, and the other movable feasts, etc.

The verbal correspondence of the rubrics which I have mentioned with those of the Worcester text, as well as a clerical error, not found either in the Andain or in the Metz manuscript, but which occurs in a contracted form in the Worcester text, and is here expanded without contraction, leads me to think it probable, that the compiler of the Exeter manual may have had before him, and copied from, that Worcester text. The error in question is in the article as to the division of tithes, which was to be made (according to both the Gallican texts) '*before witnesses*' (*coram testibus*). The word *testibus*, if written in a contracted form, might be miscopied by a rapid transcriber, so as to be read *timentibus;* and *timentibus* (contracted) is the word in the Worcester text. It is *timentibus* at full length in the Exeter text, and in the fragment copied from it, which the Surtees Society [1] published; it is also *timentibus* (contracted) in the later Cottonian text. The participle *timentibus* (*fearing*), without any noun to be governed by it—and there is none in any of these texts—left the sense imperfect; it could not (standing alone) be, and it was not in fact, correct. For supplying after it (as most of the English editors did) the word *Deum* (God) there is no authority in any manuscript. Such an error, repeated as it is throughout this particular family of documents, is indicative (as it seems to me) of a common origin; and, if so, that origin may have been in the Worcester collection. Nor is it improbable that Bishop Leofric might have obtained the manual, which he gave to the church of Exeter, from the conventual church of Worcester, then famous for learning. Leofric's immediate predecessor at Crediton, Livingus, had been translated to Worcester.

---

[1] Vol. xxvii. of the Surtees Society's publications.

§ 4. *The Worcester 'Excerptions' in the Cottonian Collection.*

The manuscript volume from which the compilation commonly known as the 'Excerptions of Egbert' was printed by Spelman, Wilkins, and Thorpe (which formed part of Sir Robert Cotton's library, and is now in the British Museum), also belonged to the church of Worcester.[1] It does not contain Egbert's 'Penitential,' or any part of it. It is a mixed collection of Anglo-Saxon laws, etc., and ecclesiastical documents, beginning with the laws, etc. (in Anglo-Saxon) of Canute, Edgar, Alfred, Athelstan, Edmund, and Ethelred, mixed with and followed by other things, some Latin; and, farther on, the 'Excerptions,' also in Latin. Mr. Thorpe[2] says of the 'part of the volume containing Anglo-Saxon laws,' that it was written, 'apparently,' in the beginning and middle of the eleventh century. Of the 'Excerptions,' Selden[3] considered the writing to be of about the time of Henry I. They are preceded by a short preface, about church canons; after which follows a rubric, in the body of the text: '*Here begins the sacerdotal law*' (*Inc. jus sacerdotale*); and opposite to it, in the margin, another rubric (a thing unusual in the volume): '*Here begin the Excerptions of Egbert, Archbishop of York, concerning Sacerdotal Law*' (*Incipiunt Excerptiones Ecgberhti Arcipi Eburace civitatis de Sacerdotali Jure*). I infer, that this marginal title was not found in the book or books (whatever they may have been) from which those 'Excerptions' were

---

[1] Thorpe's *Ancient Laws*, etc. (vol. i., MS. G. in his 'List of Manuscripts,' etc., preceding table of contents; 'Nero A. 1' of the Cottonian collection). [2] *Ibid.*
[3] *Hist. of Tithes* (ed. 1618), ch. 8, § 1, p. 196.

taken; and this seems to have been the view of the framer of a comparatively modern table of contents prefixed to the whole volume, in which notice is taken of the fact that some of them were derived from Frank 'capitulars.' If the marginal rubric was meant to apply to *all* the 'Excerptions' which follow, the description was not happy; for a large number of them relate to other subjects, and not to the law or duties of the priesthood.

I will now state what those 'Excerptions'[1] are. First come the twenty-one 'Sacerdotal Laws' of the Andain manuscript. Then seven more[2] (all taken from Frank capitulars or Gallican canons), which, from their subject matter, might be considered to belong to the same category. One of these[3] is Charlemagne's capitular of A.D. 813 (confirming canons to the same effect made in the same year at the Synods of Mentz and Arles), directing that 'churches established of old should not be deprived of tithes or of any other possessions, so as to give them to new churches.' This (which is also one of the articles following the twenty-one in the Andain manuscript, and not in the Metz), is here given in the words of the Council of Mentz. Two others are from the capitulars of A.D. 816, made by Louis the Pious at Aix-la-Chapelle,—the 'manse ordinance,' and the first part of the ordinance against the appointment or removal of priests without the authority of the bishop; both which have been stated in an earlier chapter of this work.[4] These seven are succeeded by a long series of extracts, 135 altogether,[5] from the (so-called) Apostolical canons, and from Oriental, African, Roman, Peninsular, Gallican, and

[1] Thorpe's *Ancient Laws*, etc., vol. ii. p. 97.
[2] *Ibid.*, pp. 100, 101 (arts. 22-28).   [3] Art. 24.
[4] *Ante*, p. 85.   [5] Beginning with art. 29 (*ibid.*, p. 101).

Irish councils, passages of Scripture, and writings of Fathers and Popes; seventy-two of which are also found in the Worcester manuscript at Cambridge.[1] And, although the order of the extracts common to both collections is, in the Cottonian collection, often changed, it corresponds to an extent sufficient to prove that the author of the later Worcester 'Excerptions' borrowed from the earlier work; which (if he was a Worcester monk) was in the library of his own monastery. There are (for example) eleven extracts together in one part of the series, and nine more in another, which are not only the same, but in the same order.[2] The preface,[3] also, of the Cottonian 'Excerptions' contains a passage attributed to 'Augustine, Bishop of Orleans,' which is the first of the 'Excerptions' in the Cambridge manuscript after the twenty-one 'Sacerdotal Laws.'

Further comment on these Cottonian 'Excerptions,' upon the ascription of which to Archbishop Egbert so many learned men have founded conclusions, seems to be superfluous. I may mention, however, as indicative of their late date and true character, certain things. The article numbered by Mr. Thorpe 133 [4] is (as Mansi [5] has pointed out) taken *verbatim* from the biography of Gregory the Great, by John the Deacon,[6] a monk of Monte Cassino, who wrote about A.D.

---

[1] See Appendix D.
[2] The fifty-second to the sixty-second (both inclusive), and again, the seventy-first to the seventy-ninth (both inclusive) of the Cambridge 'Excerptions,' are the same with the sixty-third to the seventy-third (both inclusive), and the eighty-third to the ninety-first (both inclusive), of the Cottonian 'Excerptions.'
[3] Thorpe's *Ancient Laws*, etc., vol. ii. p. 97.
[4] *Ibid.*, p. 118.
[5] *Concil.*, vol. xii. pp. 411, 412.
[6] *Vita S. Gregorii*, lib. ii., cap. 38. See Mansi, *Concil.*, vol. xii. p. 411.

875 (above a hundred years after Egbert's death) and dedicated his work to Pope John VIII. There are articles (*e.g.* those numbered 141 and 144 by Mr. Thorpe[1]) taken from the 'decretals' of the early Popes fabricated by the false Isidore, and from the spurious Acts of the pretended Roman Council under Pope Sylvester. Another (the 102d[2]) attributes to Augustine the passage, quoted as his in the *Decretum* of Gratian, in which tithes are described as 'the tributes of churches and of needy souls,' and are commanded to be paid from the soldier's wages, the merchant's gains, and the artisan's earnings. Another (the 124th[3]) allowed the husband of a woman who had left him and would not be reconciled to marry again, with his bishop's consent, after five or seven years; declaring, at the same time, that this would be adultery, to be expiated by penance for three years, or for the man's whole life.

Into the question, whether these 'Excerptions' were, as some writers have thought,[4] the work of Hucarius, a deacon of St. German's, in Cornwall, who is said to have lived in the reign of Harold Harefoot (A.D. 1035-1039), I do not think it necessary to enter. It seems hardly probable, that the work of a Cornish deacon would be preserved in the library of the church of Worcester, and not elsewhere, and would bear the relation which this work does to another and earlier compilation, also in that library. If Hucarius was concerned in any of these compilations, it may have been the second in date—that which Bishop Leofric presented to the

[1] Thorpe's *Ancient Laws*, etc., vol. ii. pp. 120, 121.
[2] *Ibid.*, p. 112 (see *ante*, p. 46).   [3] *Ibid.*, p. 116.
[4] See Johnson's *Laws and Canons* (Oxford ed. 1850), vol. i. p. 181 (editor's note); and Bale (p. 152) and Leland, there referred to. Also Mansi, *Concil.*, vol. xii.; *Præmonitio*, p. 411; and Wasserschleben, *Die Bussordnungen*, etc., preface, pp. 44, 45 (Halle 1851).

church of Exeter. But it is enough for my purpose to have exhibited the real nature and character of all these documents, and to have traced, as far as possible, their connection with each other, and with the 'Sacerdotal Laws' of Andain.

CHAPTER VIII

FOURTH PERIOD—AELFRIC AND OTHER WRITERS OF THE
GALLICAN SCHOOL

§ 1. *The Canterbury 'Statuta Synodorum.'*

THE compilations spoken of in the preceding chapter made no claim to authority. They were collected from miscellaneous sources, without special reference to England, or to English laws or customs. Of the canons and other precepts which they brought together, some were, others were not, generally received in the Western Churches. They were composed for the information and edification of priests or clerks, by men who had been students in foreign schools. They contain some things which could not possibly have been meant to be acted upon in England; for example, an Irish canon,[1] directing lots to be cast whether a man who had stolen goods from a church should have his hand cut off, or be thrown into gaol, 'there long to fast and mourn.'

A manuscript, now lost, which Selden[2] has described, and which formerly belonged to St. Augustine's Abbey at Canterbury, and was afterwards in Sir Robert Cotton's library, must have been of the same character. It was entitled,

[1] Art. 74 of *Excerptiones Ecgberti* (Thorpe's *Ancient Laws*, vol. ii. p. 108).   [2] *Hist. of Tithes*, ch. 8, § 5 (ed. 1618, pp. 210-213).

'*Statuta Synodorum*' (*Synodical Constitutions*); and, in its original form, was a collection, made in King Athelstan's time (A.D. 924-940), of Roman, Gallican, and Irish canons, with extracts from St. Augustine, St. Jerome, Gregory the Great, and Isidore of Seville, and some from Gildas and St. Patrick; whence Selden inferred, that the compiler was of British or Irish origin. As to tithes, that collection contained one paragraph; in which no council or canon was referred to, but only the Levitical laws, and a passage attributed to St. Augustine.

To this account of the original collection Selden[1] adds, that there was appended to it, in a later hand of uncertain date, a supplement, with this inscription: '*Incipiunt pauca judicia, quæ desunt de supra-dictis,*'—in which the ancient code of the Roman Church, and some other authorities from the same fathers, and from a few of the older councils, were cited. 'But' (he proceeds)—

'No denominated Pontifical or Synodal is remembered there for tithes; only the texts of Moses for tithes, first fruits, the first born, and such more, are numbered together. And then follows a chapter, "*De divisione decimarum,*" with this declaration: "*Lex dicit, ipsi sacerdotes populi suscipiant decimas, et nomina eorum, quicquid dederint,*[2] *scripta habeant, et secundum autoritatem canonicam,*" etc.,—in the self-same words as are attributed to the "Excerptions" of Egbert.'

'That *Lex dicit*' (he added) 'may be referred to the canon related out of the "Excerptions" of Egbert; but whence that canon is originally, I have not yet learned.'

We know what Selden did not: that the 'Law,' to which

---

[1] *Hist. of Tithes*, ch. 8, § 5 (ed. 1618), p. 211.

[2] The '*quicquid dederint*' (*whatever they have given*), coincides in sense with a clerical error of the Andain text, which the other Anglo-Saxon copyists corrected into '*quicunque dederint*' (*whoever have given*), —the Metz reading.

the compiler of the *pauca judicia* referred, was a local constitution of the bishops of a particular district in the Netherlands or France,—the fifth article of the Andain 'Sacerdotal Laws.' Its occurrence, in such a supplement to a work of King Athelstan's time, confirms the conclusion, that it had become known in this country by means of that intercourse between English ecclesiastics and Gallican monks and monasteries, which in so many ways took place during the days of Oswald, Ethelwold, and Dunstan.

§ 2. *Aelfric 'the Grammarian.'*

There was a period, of perhaps about twenty years, falling within the latter and most troubled part of King Ethelred's reign, during which the influence of the Andain 'Sacerdotal Laws,' upon some persons of reputation belonging to the Benedictine party in England, became very manifest. Among these was Aelfric 'the grammarian,' who composed a Pastoral Epistle or Charge[1] for a bishop named Wulfsin, of which it is now necessary to speak.

Concerning this Aelfric, there has been great controversy.[2] Wharton,[3] the author of *Anglia Sacra*, identified him with Aelfric Putta, Archbishop of York from A.D. 1023 to 1052; Mores[4] (who was followed by Dean Hook)[5] identified him with Aelfric, Archbishop of Canterbury from A.D. 995 to 1005. Both opinions are certainly

[1] See Thorpe's *Ancient Laws*, vol. ii. p. 342; Johnson's *Laws and Canons*, vol. i. p. 382 (ed. 1880).
[2] The arguments of Archbishop Ussher, and other writers earlier than the eighteenth century, are stated by Wharton, '*De duobus Aelfricis*' (*Anglia Sacra*, vol. i. pp. 125-132); and by E. R. Mores, *Aelfric*, ed. 1789, pp. 3-18.
[3] *Anglia Sacra*, vol. i. pp. 125-132.   [4] Mores, pp. 18-42.
[5] *Lives of Archbishops*, vol. i. pp. 436, 437.

erroneous.[1] The document in question (miscalled 'Aelfric's Canons'), must have been composed between A.D. 992 and 1001; in the former of which years Wulfsin, who had been made Abbot of Westminster by Archbishop Dunstan, was advanced to the see of Sherborne.[2] There was no other bishop, of the same or the like name, for whom it could have been written. Wulfsin lived till A.D. 1001;[3] he was, like Aelfric, zealous for monasticism; and in A.D. 998,[4] under a charter of that year from King Ethelred, he expelled secular clerks from his conventual chapter of Sherborne, and established Benedictines in their places.

The preamble to the (so-called) Canons is expressed in terms which show clearly that the writer was not, at the time when it was written, a bishop. But the Aelfric who in A.D. 995 became Archbishop of Canterbury was already, in A.D. 992, Bishop of Ramsbury, to which see he

---

[1] Dean Hook (*Lives of Archbishops*, vol. i. p. 436) accepted Mr. Thorpe's view, that 'the real question lies between Elfric, Archbishop of Canterbury, and Elfric, Archbishop of York'; adding, that, 'if this point be conceded, the question is at once settled by internal evidence':—for which purpose he relied upon historical proofs of the arrogant worldly character of that Archbishop of York. But the question is not so limited. Aelfric was in those days a very common name. Within about a hundred years, from A.D. 941 to 1038, it was the name of eight bishops; it was borne by secular persons of note also, to identify and distinguish whom is hardly less difficult than in the present instance. (See Freeman's *Norman Conquest*, vol. i. p. 627, App. cc.) Mr. Baron, the learned editor of Johnson's *Laws and Canons*, in his note to vol. i. p. 387, justly relies upon William of Malmesbury, as showing that the 'grammarian' was not either of those archbishops.

[2] Stubbs' *Registrum Sacrum Anglicanum*, p. 17.

[3] *Ibid.* (His successor, Ethelric, was consecrated in that year.)

[4] See King Ethelred's charter of A.D. 998 (granted 'on the advice of Archbishop Aelfric'), in Wharton's *Anglia Sacra*, vol. i. p. 170; and see Mores, *Aelfric*, p. 32.

had been consecrated in A.D. 990.[1] The author of the Canons, after he had translated that work (which seems to have been first composed in Latin) into Anglo-Saxon, as we have it, described himself as a 'monk and mass-priest;'[2] and at another time, which could not have been earlier than A.D. 1002, he addressed an Anglo-Saxon translation of another document, of the same character, as 'Abbot Aelfric' to 'the Venerable Archbishop Wulstan'[3] (*Aelfricus Abbas, Wulstano Venerabili Archiepiscopo*). Wulstan, so addressed, was Bishop of Worcester and Archbishop of York from A.D. 1003 to 1023.[4]

The author of the Canons was not, therefore, Aelfric, Archbishop of Canterbury. Neither could he have been Aelfric Putta, Archbishop of York. The 'grammarian' had been a pupil of Ethelwold,[5] at Abingdon or Winchester, and was afterwards Abbot of Malmesbury. A charter of King Edgar, preserved by William of Malmesbury,[6] shows that he was placed in charge of that Abbey before A.D. 974, on account of his great knowledge of ecclesiastical 'manners and offices.' The same chronicler (William of Malmesbury) speaks of him in his Life of Aldhelm,[7] as 'a very learned man, and especially a most elegant translator' (*peritum litterarum, præsertimque elegantissimum interpretem*); as having shown

[1] Stubbs, *Reg. Sacr. Anglic.*, p. 17.
[2] Preface to *Sermones Catholici*, to which the (so-called) Canons were appended. See Wharton, *De duobus Elfricis* (*ubi supra*), p. 130; and Mores, *Ælfric*, p. 8.
[3] See Thorpe, *Ancient Laws*, vol. ii. p. 364.
[4] Stubbs, *Reg. Sacr. Anglic.*, p. 17. He was consecrated to Worcester and York in A.D. 1003.
[5] Wharton's *Anglia Sacra*, vol. i. pp. 129, 130.
[6] A.D. 974. See Wharton, *Anglia Sacra*, vol. i. p. 128; Johnson's *Laws and Canons*, vol. i., ed. 1880, p. 387, note.
[7] Wharton, *Anglia Sacra*, vol. ii. pp. 32, 33.

architectural skill in additions which he made to the buildings of the monastery; as having been appointed in his old age to the see of Crediton, which he held for four years; and as having left behind him excellent works (*codices, non exigua ingenii monumenta*). It cannot be supposed that he would have been made Abbot of Malmesbury before he was thirty years old (the age necessary at that time for priest's orders). If, therefore, he had lived till the death of Aelfric Putta, Archbishop of York, he would have been more than a centenarian.

With respect to his other writings, the *Institutes of Polity*[1] (which belong to Ethelred's reign) correspond closely with the 'Canons,' in several passages;[2] so closely, as to suggest one authorship; and the Pastoral Epistle addressed to Archbishop Wulstan,[3]—a work of the same nature, also written with a view to its delivery as a charge by a bishop to his clergy,—is plainly by the same hand. It is animated by the same monastic zeal; it enforces the rule of clerical celibacy by the same assertions and arguments;[4] it assumes in the same manner ignorance on the part of the secular clergy of the elements of ecclesiastical knowledge[5]; and it instructs them on the same points.[6] In one respect, however, there is a noteworthy difference. The *Institutes* and the Pastoral Epistle do not (although the charge written for Bishop Wulfsin does) borrow from the Metz or Andain 'Sacerdotal Laws' the injunction for a

---

[1] Thorpe's *Ancient Laws*, vol. ii. pp. 305-341.
[2] *E.g.*, art. 22 (as to second marriages of laymen), and art. 23 (as to the Nicene and other Oecumenical Councils), *ibid.*, pp. 333, 335.
[3] *Ibid.*, pp. 364-393.
[4] Articles 9-12, 21, 32, 38-40 (*ibid.*, pp. 369, 373, 377).
[5] Articles 6-8, 34-37 (*ibid.*, pp. 367, 379).
[6] Articles 23-31, 42, 43, 49, 50 (*ibid.*, pp. 374-377, 387).

tripartite division of tithes. They are wholly silent as to any such division; although in the *Institutes*, among other invectives against married priests, is one[1] which imputes to them neglect of their churches and of the poor, and of charitable works.

The times had changed much since the 'peaceful' days of Edgar, and the ascendancy of Dunstan. The Church had once more to contend with heathenism; and within the Church monasticism was no longer all-powerful. The *Institutes of Polity* and the two pastoral epistles or charges written for Wulfsin and Wulstan, as well as some of the documents commonly classed among the secular acts of King Ethelred's reign, reflect that change, and show a disposition to withdraw from the rural secular clergy the rights which in the time of Edgar had been conceded to them. 'Beloved' (said the pastoral epistle addressed to Archbishop Wulstan),[2] 'we cannot now forcibly compel you to chastity; but we admonish you,' etc. And, at the end of the *Institutes*,[3] there is something very like a denunciation of King Ethelred himself:

'No one should injure a church or wrong it in any way. But now churches are, nevertheless, far and wide, weakly *grithed*, and ill served, and cleanly bereft of their old rights,

---

[1] Art. 19 (Thorpe, *Ancient Laws*, vol. ii. p. 329). It speaks of priests 'who will not, or cannot, or dare not, warn the people against sins, and correct sins, but desire, nevertheless, their monies for tithes, and for all church dues,' etc. . . . 'It is all the worse when they have it all, for they do not dispose of it as they ought, but decorate their wives with what they should the altars, and turn everything to their own worldly pomp, and to vain pride, that they should do for the honour of God, in ecclesiastical things, or for the advantage of poor men, or in the buying of war-captives, or in some things that might be for lasting benefit both to themselves and also to those who give them their substance for the favour of God.'

[2] Art. 33 (Thorpe, *Ancient Laws*, vol. ii. p. 377). [3] *Ibid.*, p. 341.

and within stript of all decencies; and ministers of the Church are everywhere deprived of their rank and power. And woe to him who is the cause of this, though he may not think so! Because every one is certainly the foe of God Himself, who is the foe of God's churches, and who impairs or injures the rights of God's churches: as it is written, "*Inimicus enim Christi efficitur omnis, qui ecclesiasticas res usurpare injuste conatur.*" And awfully spake St. Gregory concerning him, when he thus said, "*Siquis ecclesiam Christi denudaverit, vel sanctimonia violaverit, anathema sit: ad quod respondentes omnes dixerunt Amen.*" Great is the necessity for every man that he strenuously secure himself against these things; and let every friend of God constantly take care that he do not too greatly misuse the Bride of Christ. It is the duty of us all to love and honour one God, and zealously hold one Christianity, and with all our might renounce every heathenism.'[1]

Aelfric was a monk, endeavouring in those times and under those circumstances to support or restore monastic institutions and principles, which he identified with those of the Church and of true religion. The bishops for whom he wrote were like-minded with himself. From the time of the *Regularis Concordia* and Dunstan's Council of Winchester they were Benedictine monks, identified in feeling and interest with the conventual bodies of which they were (in most cases) heads; and at this time Wulfsin at Sherborne, and Archbishop Aelfric at Canterbury, were completing Dunstan's work, by substituting in the chapters of their cathedral churches Benedictine monks for secular canons.

[1] This concluding sentence, '*It is the duty*,' etc., corresponds *verbatim* with article 34 of the ordinances of A.D. 1008 (Thorpe, *Ancient Laws*, vol. i. p. 313).

§ 3. *Aelfric's Canons.*

I pass now to the consideration of the document called 'Aelfric's Canons.'[1]

The preamble shows, that the bishop had asked Aelfric to compose for him an address or visitation charge, to be delivered by him to his clergy:

> 'The humble brother Aelfric to the venerable Bishop Wulfsin, health in the Lord. We have willingly obeyed thy command, but have not presumed to write anything of the episcopal degree, because it is yours to know how you ought, by excellence of manners, to become an example to all, and by continual admonitions to exhort those under your charge to the salvation which is in Christ Jesus. Yet I say, that you ought oftener to have addressed your clergy and reproved their negligence; inasmuch as, through their perverseness, the canonical laws and the religion and doctrine of Holy Church are well nigh abolished. Therefore deliver thy soul, and tell them what things ought to be observed by the priests and ministers of Christ, lest thou also perish like them, if thou be accounted a dumb dog. But we write this letter which follows in the English tongue, as if dictated out of thine own mouth, and as if thou hadst spoken to thy clergy, beginning thus,' etc.

What is here said as to the general departure of the clergy from 'the canonical laws, and the religion and doctrine of Holy Church,' excludes the supposition that the injunctions which follow are evidence, not only of what the writer thought proper to recommend, but of the practice at that time of the clergy of the Anglo-Saxon Church.

The nine first articles[2] relate to marriage. Their intention is to enforce upon the secular clergy the strictest

---

[1] Thorpe, *Ancient Laws*, vol. ii. pp. 343-363.
[2] *Ibid.*, pp. 343-347.

rule of celibacy, and upon those who were married the duty of forsaking their wives.

'I say to you, priests' (so the bishop is made to open his charge), 'that I will not bear your negligence in your service, but I will truly say to you how it is constituted [1] concerning priests. Christ Himself established Christianity and chastity, and all those who walked with Him, in His way, forsook all worldly things, and society of women. Wherefore, He Himself said in one of His gospels, "He who hateth not his wife is not a disciple worthy of Me."'

An account follows of the synod of 318 bishops, held at Nicæa against Arius, and of their decree,[2] that 'neither bishop, nor mass-priest, nor deacon, nor any regular canon, should have in his house any woman,' except those in certain specified degrees of very near relationship.

In the sixth article, married priests are supposed to argue, first, from the reason and necessity of the case,—which is denied;—and then from the example of St. Peter;—the reply to which is, that St. Peter had a wife 'by the old law, before he turned to Christ; but he forsook his wife, and all worldly things, after he had turned to Christ, who established chastity.'

The seventh article distinguishes, as to marriage, between the Levitical and the Christian priesthood; the eighth quotes a spurious prohibition [3] of the Nicene Council against the ordination of persons twice married,

[1] Mr. Thorpe's translation is followed, even when it might seem capable of improvement.

[2] Canon 3 of first Nicene Council (Mansi, *Concil.*, vol. ii. p. 670). They did *not* forbid a priest or other clerk to live with his wife. On the contrary, they refused to do so, by the advice of Paphnutius (*ibid.*, p. 906). The third canon was against having *introductam* (συνείσακτον) *mulierem*.

[3] There is no such matter in the Nicene canons.

or who had married widows; the ninth states a canonical ban[1] put upon the second marriages (though tolerated) of laymen.

Then follow nine articles,[2] in which the clergy are informed that 'seven degrees are established in the Church;' which degrees are enumerated, with a statement of the office and duty of each order. As to bishops, the seventeenth article says:

'There is no difference betwixt a mass-priest and a bishop, save that the bishop is appointed for the ordaining of priests and confirming of children, and hallowing of churches, and to take care of God's dues; for it would be too multifarious if every mass-priest so did; but they have one order, though the latter have precedence.'

A series of fourteen articles,[3] almost entirely as to the duties of priests, succeeds. Of these I shall speak particularly.

The thirty-third article[4] enumerates the four first general synods, which (it says) 'are to be observed, so as the four books of Christ, in Christ's church. Many synods have been held since, but these four are, nevertheless, the principal,' etc.

The thirty-fourth article[5] charges the secular clergy with 'despising all their ordinances'; 'while monks hold the ordinances of one man, the Holy Benedict, and live according to his direction,' etc. . . . 'Ye also have a rule if ye would read it; . . . but ye love worldly conversations,

---

[1] See seventh canon of Neo-Cæsarea; and Gratian, *Decretum*, pars ii., causa xxxi., quæst. i., § 8. The nuptial benediction was not to be given; and no priest was to be present at the marriage feast. Some canons added penance.
[2] Thorpe's *Ancient Laws*, vol. ii. pp. 347-349 (arts. 10-18).
[3] Arts. 19-32 (*ibid.*, pp. 351-355).
[4] *Ibid.*, pp. 355, 356.   [5] *Ibid.*, p. 357.

S

and will be reeves, and neglect your churches, and the ordinances, totally.'

'But' (pursues the thirty-fifth article [1]) 'we will recite the ordinances to you.' Then follow injunctions against certain unseemly proceedings at and with respect to funerals, against gay clothing, and against the assumption of the monastic habit; and (in the thirty-sixth article [2]) a very long discourse as to the observances of Good Friday and Eastertide, of the Lord's Day, and of other festivals and fasts; with much instruction about the Holy Sacrament (the *housel*), which is said to be 'Christ's body, not bodily, but spiritually; not the body in which He suffered, but the body about which He spake, when He blessed bread and wine for housel one day before His passion.' [3] The whole document ends (in the thirty-seventh article [4]), with a few admonitory words.

I return to those fourteen articles which relate to the duties of priests. These are not, like the twenty-one 'Sacerdotal Laws' of the Egbertine compilations, transcribed from the Metz or Andain manuscripts, or from any other copy of the same original. Aelfric put the matter which he adopted from that source into his own words, enlarging some things, abridging others; and he did not adhere exactly to the arrangement which he found there. But, nevertheless, the matter of those articles, together with the order and sequence of most of them, and the correspondence of thought and phrase in some with the Gallican original, prove unequivocally that the *Capitulare Episcoporum* was the fountain-head from which all but two of them were derived. Of those two, one has a striking

---

[1] Arts. 19-32 (*ibid.*, pp. 357, 358). [2] *Ibid.*, pp. 359-363.
[3] *Ibid.*, p. 361. [4] *Ibid.*, p. 363.

correspondence with that sentence[1] of the prologue to Egbert's 'Penitential,' which (as I suppose) led the compiler of the Exeter 'Penitential' book, now in the Bodleian Library, to interpolate, between the prologue and the body of Egbert's work, the Andain 'Sacerdotal Laws.'

Art. 19[2] relates to the duty of 'mass-priests, and all God's servants, to officiate in their churches with holy service, and to sing the seven canonical hours therein'—the hours being enumerated. (This corresponds in substance with the *second* Andain article.)

Art. 20[3] enjoins prayers 'for the king and for their bishop, and for those who do good to them, and for all Christian people' (corresponding in substance, as to the king and the bishop, with the seventh and eighth Andain articles).

Art. 21[4] corresponds with the passage in Egbert's prologue, as to the *arms*, which 'he who desires to receive the sacerdotal authority,' should 'prepare before the bishop's hand touches his head':

'*He shall also have for the spiritual work, before he is ordained, these weapons:* psalter, epistle-book, gospel-book, and mass-book, book of canticles, and manual, numeral, and pastoral, penitential, and reading book. These books the mass-priest should necessarily have, and he may not be without them, if he will properly observe his order, and rightly inform the people who look to him; and let him be careful that they are well directed.'

Art. 22[5] relates to mass-vestments, and sacred vessels, etc. (There is nothing corresponding to this in the 'Sacerdotal Laws.')

Art. 23[6] (as to preaching on the Lord's Day and holi-

[1] *Ante*, pp. 239, 240.   [2] Thorpe's *Ancient Laws*, vol. ii. p. 351.
[3] *Ibid.*   [4] *Ibid.*; and see *ante*, p. 239.
[5] Thorpe's *Ancient Laws*, vol. ii. p. 351.   [6] *Ibid.*, pp. 351, 352.

days, and teaching the Lord's Prayer and the Creed), corresponds, in substance, with the third and sixth Andain articles; adding texts from Scripture.

Art. 24[1] is that as to tithes:

'The holy fathers appointed also, that men pay their tithes unto God's church. And let the priest go thither and divide them into three; one part for the repair of the church, and the second for the poor, the third for God's servants who attend the church.'

This corresponds, both in substance and in the order of the prescribed division, with the fourth and fifth Andain articles; but it is shorter, and omits the mention of *witnesses.*

Art. 25[2] (against celebrating mass in unconsecrated houses) corresponds with the ninth Andain article; introducing an exception for cases of great need or sickness, which is not there.

Art. 26[3] (as to the baptism of children suddenly brought to a mass-priest), corresponds, in substance, with the eleventh Andain article.

Art. 27,[4] against the receipt of money by a priest for holy offices, agrees closely with the twelfth Andain article. It is in these words:

'And that no priest do his holy ministry for money, nor demand anything, neither for baptism nor for any ministry; that he be not like to those whom Christ himself drove with a

---

[1] Thorpe's *Ancient Laws,* vol. ii. p. 353.   [2] *Ibid.*   [3] *Ibid.*
[4] *Ibid.* The words of the twelfth Andain article are: '*Ut nullus presbyter sacrum officium, sive baptismale sacramentum, aut aliquid bonorum spiritualium, pro aliquo pretio vendere præsumat, ne vendentes et ementes in templo columbas imitentur; ut pro his quæ adepti sunt gratia divina non pretia concupiscant terrena, sed solam regni coelestis gloriam promereantur accipere.*'

whip from the temple, because they wickedly trafficked therein. Let not the servant of God do God's ministry for money, but to the end that he may merit eternal glory thereby.'

Art. 28[1] also corresponds, almost verbally, with the thirteenth Andain article:

'Nor let any priest, for any covetousness, go from one minster to another; but ever remain in that to which he was ordained, as long as his days continue.'

Art. 29,[2] forbidding any priest to drink immoderately, or to force any man to much drink, corresponds exactly with the fourteenth Andain article. It adds reasons for the prohibition, which are not there.

Art. 30[3] begins with interdicting priests from some secular occupations (this is not in the 'Sacerdotal Laws'); and it then proceeds, deviating but little from the words of the seventeenth, eighteenth, and nineteenth Andain articles:

'Nor let him wear weapons, nor work strife; nor let him drink at wine houses, as secular men do; nor let him swear oaths, but, with simplicity, ever speak truly as a learned servant of God.'

---

[1] Thorpe's *Ancient Laws*, vol. ii. p. 353. The words of the thirteenth Andain article are: '*Ut nullus presbyter a sede propriâ sanctæ ecclesiæ, sub cujus titulo ordinatus fuit, ammonitionis*' [the Metz MS. reads here, *ambitionis*] '*causa ad alienam pergat ecclesiam; sed in eadem devotus usque ad vitæ permaneat exitum.*'

[2] *Ibid.* The fourteenth Andain article is: '*Ut nullus ex sacerdotum numero ebrietatis vitium nutriat, nec alios cogat per suam jussionem inebriari.*'

[3] *Ibid.*, p. 355. The three corresponding Andain articles are: (17), '*Nemo ex sacerdotum numero arma pugnantium unquam portet nec litem contra proximum ullam excitet*'; (18), '*Ut nullus presbyter edendi vel bibendi causa ingrediatur in tabernis*'; (19), '*Ut nullus sacerdos quicquam cum juramento juret, sed simpliciter cum puritate et veritate omnia dicat.*'

Art. 31 [1] relates to hearing confession, and giving the Holy Communion to the sick; corresponding, in substance, with the twentieth Andain article; but adding a caution, which is not there.

Art. 32,[2] as to unction with hallowed oil, corresponds, in its first sentence, with the twenty-first Andain article; to which it adds the words of St. James on that subject, and other matter arising out of them.

There can be no mistake as to the source from which Aelfric derived his precept for the division of tithes. He must have been well acquainted, either with the Worcester 'Excerptions' (now in the library of Corpus Christi College, Cambridge), or with the same Gallican literature of which the compiler of those '·Excerptions' made use: for he made that translation of Theodulph's *Capitula* into Anglo-Saxon, which has been published by Mr. Thorpe under the title of *Ecclesiastical Institutes*.[3] Neither that precept as to tithes, nor anything else in his 'Canons,' was authoritative; it was (if I may borrow the appropriate phrase of Bishop Stubbs [4]), 'a tentative recommendation.' No doubt, Aelfric wished the Bishop of Sherborne to bring into use in his diocese, so far as he could, the rule, as to tithes, of the *Capitulare Episcoporum*. But that could not be done compulsorily, any more than the secular clergy could be compelled to put away their wives, which Aelfric also desired. And it is remarkable (as has been already said) that no similar precept is found in the other pastoral epistle of the same author, written for or addressed to Archbishop Wulstan.

[1] Thorpe, *Ancient Laws*, vol. ii. p. 355.   [2] *Ibid.*
[3] *Ibid.*, pp. 394-443. And see Johnson's *Laws and Canons* ('Theodulf's Capitula'), vol. i., ed. 1850, pp. 450-479; see preface, p. 450, and editor's note, p. 452.
[4] *Letter to a Rural Dean of the Diocese of Chester* (12th December 1885).

§ 4. *Gloss on Dunstan's Canons.*

I referred, in a former chapter, to a gloss not earlier than King Ethelred's time on that article of Archbishop Dunstan's Canons, which directed the priests 'to so distribute the people's alms, that they do both give pleasure to God, and accustom the people to alms.' The gloss,[1] in these words, recommended a tripartite distribution :—

'And it is right, that one part be delivered to the priests, a second part for the need of the Church, a third part for the poor.'

This is found in a manuscript copy of Dunstan's Canons, considered by Mr. Thorpe to be of the tenth century,[2] but which could not be so early. For another gloss[3] upon the sixtieth canon of that series, which follows shortly afterwards, is evidently taken from the twenty-eighth and two succeeding articles of the document called *Church-Grith*,[4]

[1] Thorpe, *Ancient Laws*, vol. ii. pp. 256, 257, note 4.

[2] A Bodleian manuscript (Junius, 121), which Mr. Thorpe distinguishes by the letter X. (See his list of MSS. in *Ancient Laws*, vol. i. xxvi.—between the Preface and the Table of Contents.)

[3] Thorpe, *Ancient Laws*, vol. ii. pp. 256, 257, note 8. It is in these words: 'And it is right, if a minister of the altar direct his own life by the instruction of books, then he be worthy of full thaneship, both in life and in the grave: if he misdirect his life, let his dignity wane, according as the deed may be; let him know if he will, that neither women nor temporal warfare are befitting him, if he will rightly obey God, and rightly observe God's law. Dunstan decided that a mass-priest, if he had a wife, was entitled to no other *lad* than belonged to a layman of equal birth, if he were charged with an accusation. And it is right, if a minister of the altar conduct himself rightly, then he be entitled to full *wer* and worship.'

[4] *Ibid.*, vol. i. p. 347: '§ 28. If a servant of the altar, by the instruction of books, his own life rightly order, then let him be entitled to the full *wer* and dignity of a thane, both in life and in the grave.

certainly not earlier than A.D. 1014. And it refers to a 'decision' of Dunstan, that a married mass-priest was, for the purpose of 'purgation' when he was charged with a crime, to be treated as a layman.

Whoever this commentator upon Dunstan's Canons may have been, he belonged, doubtless, to Aelfric's school; and he would have applied a rule of distribution, similar to that of the Andain 'Sacerdotal Laws,' not to tithes only (as was proposed in *Church-Grith*), but to the voluntary offerings of the people, made at the altars of the Church or to its ministers or to religious houses.

§ 5. *Bishop Leofric's Rule for Secular Canons.*

There is, in the library of Corpus Christi College,[1] Cambridge, a manuscript book, on the inner fly-leaf of which are these words, in a modern hand:

'This book appears to have been first written in Latin by Theodore, seventh Archbishop of Canterbury, and translated into English by Aelfric, and contains 170 pages' (*Hic liber videtur esse scriptus primo Latine, per Theodorum Archiepiscopum septimum Cantuariensem, et per Aelfricum translatus Anglice, et continet paginas* 170).

Whelock[2] (referring, doubtless, to that note on the fly-leaf) quoted the seventy-third article of the text of this book (which is, in fact, the rule of the 'Sacerdotal Laws' as to the

§ 29. And if he misorder his life, let his honour wane, according as the deed may be. § 30. Let him know, if he will, that it befits him not to have any concern, either with women or with temporal war, if he desire uprightly to obey God, and observe God's laws, as is properly becoming to his order.' (See Appendix E.)

[1] 3, 12 of Wanley's *Antiquæ Literaturæ Septentrionalis liber*. (p. 130). No. 191 of Nasmith's *Catalogus*, etc.
[2] Bede, *Eccles. Hist.* (Cambridge 1644), p. 358, note.

partition of tithes), as 'a canon ascribed to Theodore of Canterbury.' The manuscript is stated, by both Wanley[1] and Nasmith, to have belonged to the church of Exeter, and to have been written about the time of the Norman Conquest. Wanley described it as containing 'a collection, if it may be so called, of ecclesiastical canons, in Latin and Saxon,' with a preface (which he transcribed); and he added, after giving the Saxon titles of the chapters:

'It is clear, from the rubrics of these canons, that the volume contains, not (as some learned men represent) the canons of the Nicene Council translated by Archbishop Theodore into Latin, and afterwards into Saxon by Aelfric; but a sort of rule, patched up (*consarcinatam*) out of the Benedictine rule, for the use of priests (*presbyterorum et sacerdotum*).'

Nasmith[2] repeated what Wanley had said.

No learned man, who even looked at this document, could have supposed it to contain a translation of canons of the Nicene Council. That Council is not mentioned at all, except in a marginal rubric to the opening words of the preface, in which it is said, that the work would have been unnecessary, 'if the authority of the 318 holy fathers, and of the rest, had always remained inviolate;'—which the rubric rightly interprets of 'the canons of the Nicene Council, where there were 318 bishops.' It need hardly be added, that the connection of this work with the name of Theodore is an anachronism, still more gross than that which connected the 'Excerptions' with that of Egbert. For supposing the Anglo-Saxon version (which in the manuscript follows the Latin of each article) to have been from the hand of Aelfric, there is no authority. It is not so much, even, as a probable conjecture.

[1] *Antiq. Literat. Septentr. lib.*, p. 130. [2] *Catalogus*, etc., No. 91.

I will describe the contents of the manuscript, before speaking of its history.

It is introduced by a preface, written as by a bishop in a tone of authority, of which the following is the material part:

'If the authority of the canons of the 318 and the rest of the holy fathers always remained inviolate, and the bishops and clergy lived according to that rule of rectitude, it might seem superfluous for us, small as we are, to treat again or say anything new of this matter, which has been in such good order set forth (*rem tam ordinate dispositam*). But since, in these times, the negligence both of pastors and of those under them has too much increased, what else can be done by us, who live in so grave a condition of things, except to bring back our clergy, God giving us grace (*Deo inspirante*), to the line of rectitude, if not so much as we ought, at least as much as we can? Therefore, sustained by the Divine help, let us endeavour to make a small decree (*adgrediamur parvum decretulum facere*), by means whereof the clergy may restrain themselves from what is unlawful, and lay aside what is idle (*otiosa deponat*), and forsake those evils which have too long and too widely prevailed, for His love, who according to the Gospel has redeemed them by His own holy and precious blood. Let us therefore, with watchful care, study to put together a form of instruction which shall plainly set forth how prelates (*prælati*) ought to live and govern those under them, and to constrain them in the Lord's service, and to stimulate to still better things those who do well, and to correct the refractory and the negligent, so far as this Rule of Life can do so (*quatenus formula hæc vivendi spectat*).'

The 'Rule of Life' follows, in a code of eighty-four articles; to each of which a rubric, by way of title or 'argument,' is prefixed. The 'Rule' is for a college of canons of secular clergy;—regulating their morals, subordination, and discipline; their assemblies, officers, and duties; their prayers and church-services, reading and singing; their school teaching and pastoral service; their almsgiving to the poor; the employment of their time; their stipends, meals, dress, dormitory. Canons (*canonici*), or clerks (*clerici*), is their designation throughout. There is an article (the fifty-first) expressly forbidding them to wear the cowls of monks (*ut canonici cucullas monachorum non induant*).

To the sixty first articles, which thus regulate the conventual or collegiate life, are added twenty-five more, concerning duties of clerks and priests, not distinctly cœnobitic; among which is the seventy-third article, relating to the division of tithes. To understand its practical operation in this code, the forty-third, regulating the almsgiving of the chapter, should be stated.

'It is needful' (says that article), 'that the prelates of the Church (*prælati ecclesiæ*), following the examples of the fathers who have gone before us, prepare a place of reception (*aliquod receptaculum*) where poor persons may be gathered together, and appoint out of the goods of the Church as much as will enable them to meet, as far as they possibly can, the necessary expenses—the tithes being excepted which are thereunto contributed from the townships belonging to the Church (*exceptis decimis, quæ de ecclesiæ villis ibidem conferantur*). The canons also themselves should most willingly contribute to the same hospital (*hospitale*), for the use of the poor, tithes both of the fruits of their land and from all offerings of alms made to them. And let a brother of good report be appointed to entertain strangers and foreigners (*hospites et peregrinos*), regarding them as Christ Himself; and let him willingly minister to them all those things which are needful. And moreover, let no one by any means convert to his own uses those things which ought to go to the uses of the poor.' [The washing of the feet of the poor in Lent is then enjoined.]

The article as to the division of tithes[1] is (with the

[1] Art. 73, *de decimis dividendis*.—'*Sacerdotes populi suscipiant decimas, et nomina corum quicunque dederint scripta habeant super altare. Et ipsas decimas secundum auctoritatem canonicam coram*

following qualifications) a literal copy of that in the *Capitulare Episcoporum*:—(1) It directs the scroll, containing the names of those who have paid tithes, to be kept upon (or over) the altar of the church (*super altare*); (2) it repeats expressly, as the subject governed by the verb *divide*, the words 'the same tithes' (*ipsas decimas*), where the Gallican text implies them; and (3) instead of directing (as the Gallican text does) the distribution to be made by the priests' own hands, it says that this is to be done by the hands of 'faithful men' (*per manus fidelium*).

Only one of the remaining twelve articles of the 'Rule' requires notice — the seventy-sixth — which is an extract from the ninth article of the capitulars of Aix-la-Chapelle[1] of A.D. 816 (repeated in the capitulars of Charles the Bald of A.D. 869), against the appointment of priests to, or their expulsion from, churches, without the authority or consent of their bishops.

This description of the manuscript, together with its date (about the time of the Conquest), and the place from which it came—the cathedral church of Exeter—seems to point irresistibly to the conclusion, that the rule of life contained in it was intended by Bishop Leofric, who then governed that cathedral church (first erected by and under him into an episcopal see), for the regulation of the college of secular canons which he founded and placed there. He himself came, as William of Malmesbury[2] tells us, from Lorraine—'*apud Lotharingos altus et doctus.*' By the same historian we are told, that he 'expelled the nuns (*sancti-*

testibus dividant; et ad ornamentum ecclesiæ primam eligant partem; secundam autem per manus fidelium ad usum pauperum atque peregrinorum misericorditer cum omni humilitate dispensent: tertiam vero partem sibimet ipsis soli sacerdotes reservent.'   [1] *Ante*, p. 85.

[2] *De Gestis Pontificum*, lib. ii. (ed. 1596), fol. 145 (cited in Dugdale's *Monast.*, vol. ii. p. 514; Caley, Ellis, and Bandinel's edition).

moniales) from the monastery of St. Peter, and placed there canons, who after the manner of the Lotharingians, but contrary to that of the English, were to eat at one table, and sleep in one chamber' (*canonicos statuit, qui contra morem Anglorum, ad formam Lotharingorum, uno triclinio comederent, uno cubiculo cubitarent*).[1] Malmesbury adds, that, although the rule so given by Leofric to his chapter descended to posterity, much of it had, in his own time, through the increase of luxury, fallen into disuse.

The whole of this document is, in fact, a copy (with the omission of two articles, and with some merely clerical variations) of a Gallican Rule for Canons (*canonici*), compiled by an unknown hand, to which the name of Chrodegang,[2] nephew of King Pippin and Bishop of Metz in his time, was commonly, but erroneously, given. It contains eighty-six articles; twenty-three of which, with the prologue, were taken from the genuine Statutes[3] of Chrodegang, given by him to the clergy of three churches at Metz. Of the rest, thirty-three are from a much larger code (into which some of those Statutes of Chrodegang are incorporated), which was enacted for canons (*canonici*) by the Council of Aix-la-Chapelle in A.D. 816.[4] The remaining thirty are from miscellaneous sources; the article as to tithes, from the *Capitulare Episcoporum*, being one of them.[5]

That Bishop Leofric—educated in Lorraine, in the chief

[1] The articles of the Rule as to meals and the dormitory are consistent with what is said of them by Malmesbury. (See Appendix G.)
[2] See, as to Chrodegang and his statutes, the extracts from Sigebert of Gembloux and Paul the Deacon, in Mansi (*Concil.*, vol. xiv. p. 314).
[3] These genuine statutes of Chrodegang are in the Vatican (Palatine) Manuscript, No. 555, from which they are printed by Mansi (*ibid.* pp. 313-331).   [4] Mansi (*ibid.* pp. 153-226).
[5] The whole collection is in Mansi (*ibid.* p. 232 *et seq.*); and see Labbé's note (*ibid.* p. 314).

city of which province, Metz, the *Capitulare Episcoporum* was well known, and the donor [1] to the library of his church of the Penitential volume (now in the Bodleian Library) which contained, as we have seen, the Andain text of that document—should have given to his Chapter precepts borrowed from the Gallican Churches with which he was most familiar, is easily understood. As founder of that chapter, he could give its members such lawful statutes or rules as he pleased. The practical acceptance of the tripartite division elsewhere in England is no more proved by the place which it found in such a rule, than the acceptance here of the Roman rule of quadripartite division, in the twelfth century, is proved by the fact that, in A.D. 1186, Pope Urban III.[2] directed Baldwin, Archbishop of Canterbury, to divide the offerings made at the shrine of St. Thomas of Canterbury into four parts; one for 'the monks,' one for the 'fabrics of the Church,' one for 'the poor,' and one for such good uses as the archbishop in his discretion should think fit.

[1] *Ante*, p. 235.
[2] Matthew Paris, *Hist. Major.*, vol. ii. p. 325 (Luard's ed. 1874).

CHAPTER IX

FOURTH PERIOD—LEGISLATION OF ETHELRED THE
UNREADY, AND CANUTE

§ 1. *Ancient Latin Collections of Anglo-Saxon Laws*

THE distraction and incoherence of the civil polity during the latter part of Ethelred's unhappy reign left its impress upon the public documents of that time.

Bromton [1] (whatever may be his defects in other respects as a historian) did posterity the good service of collecting to the best of his power the laws of Ina, Alfred, Edward the Elder, Athelstan, Edmund, Edgar, Ethelred the Unready, and Canute. He knew no laws of the reign of Ethelred, except those of Woodstock [2] and Wantage,[3] the treaty [4] with the Norwegian kings Anlaf, Justin, and Guthmund (all purely secular), and the Ordinances of Habam,[5] which he only preserved.

An earlier collection of the Anglo-Saxon laws, translated into Latin in the twelfth century,[6] of which Bromton

---

[1] Gale, *Script. XX.*, pp. 759, 819 *et seq.*, 835, 839, 847-851, 858-860, 893-901, 914.　　[2] Thorpe's *Ancient Laws*, vol. i. p. 280.
[3] *Ibid.*, p. 293.　　[4] *Ibid.*, p. 285.　　[5] *Ibid.*, p. 336.
[6] *Ibid.*, vol. ii. pp. 447-545, and see vol. i., preface, p. xvi. They are printed by Mr. Thorpe from the Cottonian manuscript 'Tiberius, A. 27,' which he describes (*ibid.*, p. xxvi.) as 'of the thirteenth century, containing perhaps the best text extant of the old Latin version of the Saxon laws.'

may be presumed to have made use (though by giving the Habam Ordinances he has shown that he had also access to òther materials), contains (with that exception) the same laws which are in Bromton.

The Latin translators, therefore, if they were acquainted (as is probable) with the documents omitted in both collections, but classed by more modern compilers among the public acts of King Ethelred's reign, did not regard them as possessing that character in any such sense as to make it fit that they should find a place in a code of Anglo-Saxon laws; and it may be inferred, that they found no such place in any records of a public nature to which those translators had access.

§ 2. *Ordinances of Habam.*

The date of the 'Habam' Ordinances[1] is uncertain, but they belong to a time of distress from the invasions of the pagan Danes; for remedy of which they enjoin special religious observances, as long as the necessity should continue (*quamdiu necessitas ista nobis est in manibus*).[2] The only provision in them which requires notice is one as to tithes and other church dues,[3] which, disregarding the rights conceded by King Edgar's laws to manorial churches with burial-grounds, directed them all to be paid to the 'nearest mother-churches.'

'And we enjoin that every man, for the love of God and all the saints, give church-scot and his rightful tithe (*rectam decimam suam*) as it stood in the days of our ancestors when it stood best: that is, as the plough shall traverse the tenth acre. And let everything customarily due (*omnis consuetudo*) be rendered, for God's sake (*propter amicitiam Dei*), to our

---

[1] Thorpe's *Ancient Laws*, vol. i. p. 336.
[2] *Ibid.*, p. 338 (art. 3). [3] *Ibid.* (art. 4).

nearest mother-church (*ad matrem nostram ecclesiam cui adjacet*). And let no one take away from God what belongs to God, and by our predecessors has been granted.'

§ 3. *Council of Enham, and Ordinance of* A.D. 1008.

It now becomes necessary to speak of the two first of four documents, classified by Mr. Thorpe among 'the laws of King Ethelred,' which are not found in the Latin translations. Of these, one contains the Acts or decrees of an ecclesiastical council held at Enham (or Eanham),[1] and the other an ordinance[2] of the king and his witenagemot, evidently founded on those Acts. Both are in the main ecclesiastical, though they contain some provisions relative to the defence of the realm. They go into detailed regulations as to morals, discipline, and religious observances, etc., in a manner until then without example (even after the treaty between Edward the Elder and Guthrum the Dane), in Anglo-Saxon legislation.

Of the circumstances under which the Council of Enham was held[3] our only information is derived from a Latin preamble[4] to a manuscript copy of its 'synodical decrees' (as they are there called), which is in the Cottonian collection:[5]

'It came to pass at a certain time that, under an edict of King Ethelred, and by the advice of the two archbishops,

---

[1] Thorpe's *Ancient Laws*, vol. i. p. 314. (This place is supposed to be Ensham in Oxfordshire.) [2] *Ibid.*, p. 304.
[3] See Hook, *Lives of Archbishops*, vol. i. p. 465.
[4] Mr. Thorpe (*Ancient Laws*, vol. i. p. 315), printing the Acts of the council from the Cambridge MS. (No. 201 of Nasmith; S. 18 of Wanley), omits this preamble.
[5] 'Claudius, A. 3,' a MS., according to Mr. Thorpe, of about the period of the Conquest. Selden quotes the preamble, describing the assembly as 'a council, or kind of parliament, held under King Ethelred' (*Hist. of Tithes*, ch. 8, § 10, ed. 1618, p. 220).

T

Alphege and Wulfstan, all the great men of the English (*universi Anglorum optimates*) were called together to meet on the holy day of Pentecost, at a place called by its inhabitants Eanham. An assembly of very many reverend servants of Christ being there collected, they reasoned and held discourse, as if divinely inspired, of many things concerning the recovery of the worship of the Catholic religion, and also for the amendment and furtherance of the state of the commonwealth' (*de Catholicæ cultu religionis recuperando deque etiam rei statu publicæ reparando vel consulendo*).

The 'synodical decrees' of this council do not purport to be enactments of a civil legislature; and, it is clear, as a matter of fact, that they were not. Their title, in the Parker manuscript, from which Mr. Thorpe's text is taken, is 'Ordinances of the Witan'; but even that title (not mentioning the king) repels, as far as it goes, the idea of a proper legislative enactment: and the word 'witan' might be used of the wise men of the church alone. That it was so used in this place, is clear from the introductory words of the first article[1]:—'These are the ordinances which *the councillors* of the English selected and decreed, and strictly enjoined that they should be observed,' after which the article proceeds:

'And this then is first, the primary ordinance *of the bishops*: that we all diligently turn from sins, as far as we can do so, and diligently confess our misdeeds, and strictly make *bot* (amends), and rightly love and worship one God, and unanimously hold one Christianity, and diligently eschew every heathenism, diligently promote prayer among us, and diligently love peace and concord, and faithfully obey one royal lord, and diligently support him with right fidelity.'

The Council of Enham, being held under Alphege as primate (whose predecessor in the see of Canterbury died

[1] Thorpe's *Ancient Laws*, vol. i. p. 315.

on the 16th November A.D. 1006,[1] and who went in the next year to Rome for his pall,[2] and returned), could not be earlier than A.D. 1008; which is the Latin date (in the same volume[3] of the Parker manuscripts which contains the Acts of the council, and also in a volume[4] of the Cottonian collection, different from that which contains the 'synodical decrees') of the civil ordinance, by which some of those synodical decrees (altogether fifty-three in number) were adopted and ratified; others being amended, and some disallowed, or omitted as unnecessary. The Anglo-Saxon title of the civil 'ordinance'[5] is:

'This is the ordinance that the king of the English and both the ecclesiastical and lay witan have chosen and advised.'

The points of agreement prove the relation of the Acts of the two assemblies to each other. The points of difference, as well as the fact that the Acts of both assemblies are preserved as distinct from each other in the same volume of the Parker manuscripts, prove that neither document is a corrupted or imperfect copy of the other. It is probable, that both assemblies may have been held about the same time (perhaps at the same place), the royal witenagemot succeeding the ecclesiastical synod.

On comparing the civil ordinance with the 'synodical decrees,' we find that, of the latter, twenty-six[6] were adopted and enacted, not in substance only, but for the most part

---

[1] Hook, *Lives of Archbishops*, vol. i. p. 454. (Archbishop Alphege fell into the hands of the Danes at Canterbury, A.D. 1011, and was murdered by them in the following year.)
[2] *Ibid.*, p. 463.   [3] No. 201 of Nasmith; S. 18 of Wanley.
[4] 'Nero, A. 1.' (Mr. Thorpe's print is from this MS.)
[5] Thorpe, *Ancient Laws*, vol. i. p. 304.
[6] Those numbered (by Mr. Thorpe) 1 to 4 inclusive, 6, 8 to 11 inclusive, 13, 15 to 21 inclusive, 24, 26, 30, 31, 33, 35, 37, 38, 40.

literally, and with little change of order, by the king and his witenagemot; that seven[1] more were adopted, with omissions or variations in the nature of amendments; that fifteen[2] were retrenched (probably as being didactic or superfluous), four articles in general terms of a like nature being substituted for them at the end of the civil ordinance; and that five[3] were disallowed, one of which had ordered the observance of ember-days and fasts, 'so as St. Gregory himself prescribed to the English nation.'[4] For this, the national witenagemot (either to do honour to the memory of Ethelred's murdered brother and predecessor, or perhaps from some apprehension[5] that judgments might have fallen upon the realm on account of that murder), substituted an article in these words[6]:—

'And the *witan* have chosen that St. Edward's massday shall be celebrated over all England on the XV Kal. April.'

---

[1] Arts. 5, 22, 25, 27, 28, 32, 36.

[2] Arts. 14, 29, 41 to 53 inclusive.

[3] Arts. 7, 12, 23, 34, 39. (They relate to the banishment of witches, etc., to prohibited marriages, to St. Gregory's rule as to fasts and festivals, to penalties for injuring ships of war, and to outrages against nuns and widows. Some of them were afterwards enacted by Canute.)

[4] Art. 23 (Thorpe, *Ancient Laws*, vol. i. p. 321).

[5] Stow (A.D. 978), following older chroniclers, says of Ethelred: 'Because he came to the kingdom by wicked means, and by killing his brother, he could never get the good-will of the people.' Gervase of Canterbury (Stubbs' ed., vol. ii. p. 52) says: 'He besieged rather than governed the kingdom for thirty-seven years. The course of his life began with cruelty, continued in misery, ended in disgrace. St. Dunstan, when unwillingly he put the crown upon his head, had foretold the evils which would come upon him and upon the whole kingdom.' Other chroniclers fill up the tradition with the words of Dunstan, predicting judgments upon him because he had profited by his brother's murder; though guilty of it he certainly was not.

[6] Thorpe, *Ancient Laws*, vol. i. p. 309 (art. 16).

The only parts of these documents which (with reference to my general subject) I think it necessary to mention, are two articles[1] of the civil ordinance, as to church dues and tithes, corresponding exactly with six[2] of the 'synodical decrees.' As to tithes, they merely provided that 'a tithe of young by Pentecost, and of earth-fruits by All-Hallows mass,' should be 'willingly paid every year.' As to the other dues, the only thing worthy of note is, that burial-fees (*soul-scot*) were ordered[3] to be paid 'to the minster' to which the corpse belonged, when an interment might take place out of 'its proper shrift-district.'

The monastic mind[4] is apparent in these 'decrees,' and in the provisions of the 'ordinance' which followed them. Whether from the disorders of the time, or from some constitutional objection to the manner in which the proceedings had been conducted, the fact appears to be, that they failed to take effect as laws. The party in whose interest they had been conceived considered their ratification, by re-enactment,[5] necessary within a very few years afterwards; and in one of the documents[6] which had that object in view there is an imputation of irregularity cast upon King Ethelred's

[1] Arts. 11, 12 (*ibid.*, pp. 307-309).
[2] Arts. 16-21 inclusive (*ibid.*, pp. 319-321).
[3] 'Ordinance,' art. 12 (*ibid.*, p. 309).
[4] See arts. 4 to 9 inclusive, of the civil ordinance (Thorpe, *Ancient Laws*, vol. i. pp. 304-307) corresponding with arts. 2 to 5 inclusive, of the synodical decrees (*ibid.*, pp. 314-317).
[5] See *Of Grith and of Mund* (*ibid.*, pp. 331-337), and *Of Church-Grith* (*ibid.*, 341-351), particularly articles 1, 9 to 13 inclusive, 17, 28, 30, 31, and 44 of *Church-Grith*. The greater number of them were afterwards incorporated into Canute's laws (see his Ecclesiastical Laws, arts. 1, 2, 5, 6, 8, 9, 12 to 17 inclusive, 19, 21, 24; Secular Laws, arts. 3, 5, 10, 36, 37, 51, 66, 74—Thorpe, *Ancient Laws*, vol. i. pp. 358-425).
[6] *Of Church-Grith*, arts. 37, 38 (*ibid.*, p. 349).

witenagemots, which does not seem applicable to the laws of Woodstock or Wantage, but may, perhaps, have reference to the separation, in A.D. 1008, of the national witenagemot from the ecclesiastical synod. 'In those gemots' (it is said), 'though deliberately held in places of note after Edgar's lifetime, the laws of Christ waned, and the king's laws were impaired; and then was separated what was before in common to Christ and the king in secular government; and it has ever been the worse, before God and before the world.'

§ 4. *Ethelred's supposed law for Partition of Tithes.*

Mr. Thorpe has classified, among 'the laws of King Ethelred,' two other documents, of which he has given (I cannot say translated) the titles as found in the Anglo-Saxon texts:— *Of Grith and of Mund*,[1] and *Of Church-Grith.*'[2] '*Grith*' means *peace* or *privilege;* such as that of a sanctuary or other privileged place or person. '*Mund*' is explained as *protection, guardianship*, and also as the price or penalty for the violation of a privileged person or thing.

The former of these documents[3] contains nothing about tithes or ecclesiastical organisation; it is a short collection of English, Kentish, South-Anglian, North-Anglian, and other laws, relative to the privileges of churches, etc.; which, in the thirteen last articles,[4] is followed by a wail of lamentation over the prevailing neglect of bishops and their precepts, and the hypocrisy of those who, making a formal profession of religion, and of reverence for priests,

---

[1] Thorpe, *Ancient Laws*, vol. i. p. 330.
[2] *Ibid.*, p. 340.   [3] *Ibid.*, p. 330.
[4] Arts. 19-31 (*ibid.*, pp. 333-339).

'plunder the Church, and corrupt or impair that which to the Church belongs,' and 'injure or revile (the clergy) by word or deed.' There is in it no pretension to, or indication of, legislative form or matter; and it is difficult to understand on what ground it could have been supposed by any one to be a law. I mention it only because its matter and character, its juxtaposition in the manuscripts [1] with the succeeding document entitled *Church-Grith*, and a remarkable sentence [2] which is found in both, suggest that those two documents may have had the same origin and a common purpose.

The document called *Of Church-Grith* was either a collection (as the late Mr. Price,[3] an eminent Anglo-Saxon scholar, thought it) of the same character with *Of Grith and of Mund*, or it was a draft or project of laws, which the framer—evidently an ecclesiastic of Aelfric's school—wished to have enacted. If the former was its true character, some things contained in it, especially the article as to a tripartite division of tithes, must have been of the same spurious quality with other monastic fabrications, of which, from the time of the false Isidore, there had been too many. If the latter (as I should myself rather conclude, from the relation which the contents of this document bear to the legislation of Canute), then the question is, when,

[1] The Cottonian MS., 'Nero A. 1'; and the Parker MS., No. 201, Nasmith; S. 18, Wanley.
[2] Opening of art. 24 in *Grith and Mund*: 'And wise were also in former days those secular witan, who first added secular laws to the just divine laws, for bishops and consecrated bodies;' and of art. 36 in *Church-Grith*: 'And wise were those secular witan, who to the divine laws of right added secular laws for the people's government."
[3] See Mr. Price's letter (26th June 1832) to Archdeacon Hale, in Hale's *Essay on Church-rates*, App., pp. 49-51. (As to Mr. Price, see preface to Thorpe's *Ancient Laws*, vol. i. p. xvii.)

and how far, and by what authority (if at all), the matter embodied in that project, or any part of it, became law?

In its first and sixth articles (the latter being that which was intended to enjoin a tripartite division of tithes) it speaks, beyond doubt, the language, either of past or of present national legislation. The first [1] article (which relates to the privileges of churches) is introduced with the words:

'This is *one* [2] *of* the ordinances which the king of the English composed with the counsel of his witan.'

The sixth article I give, with three more which succeed it; all relating to tithes.[3]

§ 6. 'And respecting tithe—the king and his witan have chosen and decreed, as is just, that one third part of the tithe which belongs to the church go to the reparation of the church, and a second part to the servants of God, the third to God's poor and to needy ones in thraldom.

§ 7. 'And be it known to every Christian man that he pay to his Lord his tithe justly, always as the plough traverses the tenth field, on peril of God's mercy, and of the full *wite* which King Edgar decreed—that is:

§ 8. If any one will not justly pay the tithe, then let the king's reeve go, and the mass-priest of the minster, or of the *land-rica*,[4] and the bishop's reeve, and take forcibly the tenth part for the minster to which it is due, and assign to him the ninth part; and let the eight parts be divided into two, and let the landlord take possession of half, half the bishop; be it a king's man, be it a thane's.

§ 9. 'And let every tithe of young be paid by Pentecost on pain of the *wite*, and of earth-fruits by the equinox, or at all events by All-Hallows mass.'

---

[1] Thorpe, *Ancient Laws*, vol. i. p. 341.
[2] This form of expression is singular. I do not think that anything exactly like it is to be found elsewhere. [3] *Ibid.*, 343.
[4] Mr. Thorpe explains '*land-rica*' as *the proprietor of the land, lord of the soil*.

On comparing these articles with King Edgar's laws,[1] it will be seen that, if enacted, they would have omitted the clause in those laws which authorised the payment of one-third of the local tithes to a manorial church having a burial-ground; and would have substituted for it a provision (new in Anglo-Saxon legislation) for a tripartite division of tithes, substantially the same with that of the *Capitulare Episcoporum*, though not expressed in exactly the same terms; the chief difference being that, as to one-third, we have here '*the servants of God*,' instead of '*the priests alone*'; a variation which (if it did not indicate), certainly included monks. And the tithes, to be so divided, would have been treated as wholly due to '*the minster*,' which (if this were read with the 'Habam Ordinances') would appear to mean the nearest *Mother-Church*.

That the framer of any project of law should express it in those terms in which it might stand, if adopted and passed by the legislature, is not extraordinary. That form cannot determine the question, whether it was so adopted and passed or not.

The internal evidence of the latter part of the document is strong against the supposition that, in the form in which it there appears, it was, or could have been, enacted as law. Five of its nine last articles are historical, rhetorical, expostulatory, didactic; such as might have been appended, by ecclesiastics dissatisfied with the actual state of things, to proposals of a practical character cast into the shape of laws which they wished to have passed; but such as, if their proposals were wholly or in part adopted, would certainly not be repeated in the law itself. Mr. Freeman, who seems to have accepted[2] the date A.D.

[1] *Ante*, p. 220.   [2] *Norman Conquest*, vol. i. p. 366.

1014 (found, as will presently be stated, in a Latin rubric to one of the manuscripts) as evidence that the document represents some public act of that year, was also led (I presume, by those latter clauses) to the conclusion,[1] that these were 'hardly laws at all,' but mere 'advice,' and 'an expression of pious and patriotic feeling, a promise of national amendment, rather than legislation, strictly so called.'

. The document is found in two (I believe only two) manuscripts, one of them imperfect:—in 'Nero A. 1' of the Cottonian collection, and in the volume of the Parker collection in the library of Corpus Christi College, Cambridge, numbered 201 by Nasmith, and by Wanley S. 18.

The contents of both those volumes (of the former especially) are miscellaneous in their character. The Saxon portion of the former (of which the Latin part includes some things belonging to the latter half of the twelfth century) is said by Mr. Thorpe to have been 'written apparently in the beginning and middle of the eleventh century'; the Parker volume he describes as 'apparently of the middle of the eleventh century.' If the present order of their contents can be relied on, *no part* of either volume was written before the end of Canute's reign, who died in November A.D. 1035; for the Worcester book *begins* with Canute's laws, which are followed by those of Edgar, Alfred, Athelstan, Edmund, Ethelred; and after them *Grith and Mund,* and *Church-Grith;*—all in Anglo-Saxon; not laws only, but in that order. In the other manuscript, Canute's laws do not come first; but they follow *Church-Grith.*

Selden knew and used the Worcester (Cottonian), and Spelman the Parker manuscript; and, as neither of them

---

[1] See his paper quoted by Rev. Morris Fuller, *Alleged Tripartite Division,* etc., p. 34.

made mention of this *Church-Grith* document, it may be inferred that they did not regard it as having the character or the authority of a law. If Lambarde, Whelock, and John Johnson were acquainted with either manuscript (the contrary supposition is improbable), the inference as to them also, from their silence about it, must be the same. David Wilkins was the first to publish it, in his *Leges Anglo-Saxonicæ*,[1] where he combined it, in a manner for which the manuscripts afforded no warrant, with the ordinances of Wantage. If he had regarded it as an authentic ecclesiastical law when he afterwards (in A.D. 1737) published his great collection of Acts of councils and other English ecclesiastical documents, it must[2] have found a place there; which it does not.

Mr. Thorpe professes to follow the (imperfect) Cottonian manuscript; which, however, does *not* contain his Latin heading, with the date A.D. 1014 (*'Anno MXIIII ab Incarnatione Domini nostri Jesu Christi'*). There is, indeed, now written in the margin of that manuscript, in a small modern hand (which I believe to be that of Josceline, Archbishop Parker's secretary), the date '*A$^{no.}$ dni.* 1014'; and this, no doubt, was done upon the authority of the other manuscript, then (if Josceline was the annotator) in Archbishop Parker's possession. The Parker manuscript is, therefore, the only authority for that date. It occurs there (with the figures, as given by Mr. Thorpe, but in other respects with contractions[3] which he has expanded) in a rubric, crowded into the right side of the first lines of

---

[1] *Leges Anglo-Saxonicæ* (1721), pp. 106, 113.

[2] Canute's Ecclesiastical Laws are in Wilkins's *Concilia*, vol. i., pp. 299-309.

[3] The rubric is in two lines of unequal length, thus:
        AN. MXIIII AB. INCARN
        DNI NRI IHV XPI.

the text, and therefore written at the same time with those lines—that is, not earlier than the middle of the eleventh century. In transcripts or copies of ancient documents, nothing is more liable to corruption than numerals: and, in this case, an error in a single figure might have made MXVIII pass into MXIIII. I have spoken of the marginal note (which I suppose to be Josceline's) to the Worcester manuscript. There are also two notes, in different hands of the sixteenth or seventeenth century, to the Parker manuscript: one, at the top of the page, '*Leges Aetheldredi*' (*Ethelred's Laws*); the other, in the margin, '*Fragmen. Legis Canuti*' (*A Fragment of Canute's Law*). The former gloss (for Ethelred's name occurs nowhere in the manuscript) was evidently founded on the rubrical date; the latter upon a suspicion of error in the date, not unreasonable (although the idea of the document being a 'fragment' seems to be incorrect) when its relation to the laws of Canute is perceived and considered.

Mr. Price[1] thought, that the date A.D. 1014 was confirmed by the internal evidence of a clause in the document itself; although he did not regard it as a law. The clause[2] is this:

'But let us do as is needful for us; let us take to us for an example that which former secular witan deliberately instituted, —Aethelstan, and Edmund, and Edgar who was last; how they worshipped God, and observed God's law, and rendered God's tribute, the while that they lived. And let us love God with inward heart, and heed God's laws, as well as we best can.'

I fail to see why the words, '*Edgar who was last*,' should be more appropriate to the end of Ethelred's than to the

[1] Letter to Archdeacon Hale (26th June 1832), Hale's *Essay on Church-rates*, App., pp. 49-51.
[2] Art. 43 (Thorpe's *Ancient Laws*, vol. i. p. 351).

beginning of Canute's reign. They could not, in either case, mean that Edgar was the immediate predecessor of the reigning king; for Edgar was not the immediate predecessor of Ethelred; Edward, 'the Martyr,' came between. If (as I think) they mean that Edgar was the last of those kings who were held up by the framer of the document as examples for imitation, that would be no less true at any time before a reform, after the model of those better times, had taken place, than in A.D. 1014. It would be true till Canute had satisfied the desires of those who looked back with regret to the days of Athelstan, and Edmund, and Edgar. That this is the real sense of the words, I think manifest from another clause[1] in the same document, already (for another purpose) referred to. 'But in those gemots, though deliberately held in places of note, after Edgar's lifetime, the laws of Christ waned, and the king's laws were impaired.' And it is further illustrated by a passage in the *Institutes of Polity*,[2] where it is said: 'It has been altogether too much the case, since Edgar ended, that there are more robbers than righteous.'

What, as bearing upon the question whether *Church-Grith* was an enactment of Ethelred in A.D. 1014, which had force and effect as law in England, is the evidence of history? Ethelred had before that year fled the country, and Sweyn, the father of Canute, reigned for a short time in his stead. It is true that at Easter, A.D. 1014, after Sweyn's unexpected death, Ethelred was recalled by his subjects, and returned, promising (a condition on which they insisted) that his government should be reformed. So say all the chroniclers; but not one of them says that the promise was fulfilled. On the contrary, his last days

[1] Art. 37 (Thorpe, *Ancient Laws*, vol. i. p. 349).
[2] *Ibid.*, vol. ii. p. 321.

seem to have been (if possible) worse than the first. He was in circumstances which left him practically without power. Canute never renounced, and never thought of renouncing, the crown which had been his father's. In the war which followed Ethelred's return he found his strength insufficient, without reinforcements; to obtain which he sailed to Denmark; but after a short interval he came back, stronger than ever. When the war was resumed Ethelred was in failing health. In 1016 he died. On his death Canute was accepted as king by the national witenagemot at Southampton, and he carried on the war with varying fortunes during the spring and summer of that year against Edmund Ironside. That war was terminated by an agreement for partition of the kingdom; but on the 30th of November in the same year Edmund died; and from that day Canute reigned throughout England without a competitor.

I find it difficult to suppose that if, during the year after Ethelred's return from Normandy, a national witenagemot had been assembled for the work of legislative reform, it would have been contented with a series of purely ecclesiastical laws and precepts, such as those contained in the document under consideration; or that, if Ethelred had in that way redeemed his promise to govern better than before, every chronicler who mentions that promise would have been silent about it; or that the laws of Edgar, the restoration of which in A.D. 1018 was one of Canute's first acts,[1] should have been still disregarded until that time. But if the mention of the 'king and witan' in *Church-Grith*, together with the rubrical date of the Parker manuscript, should seem to any one sufficient to outweigh those improbabilities,

[1] Saxon Chronicle, and Florence (following it), under A.D. 1018.

what was done by Ethelred in A.D. 1014 could not after his death in A.D. 1016 take any practical effect, except so far as it might be recognised as valid or confirmed by Canute; nor under the circumstances of those two miserable years[1] while Ethelred still lived, is it possible that anything so done could have effected a practical change (even during that interval) in the prior usages of the Anglo-Saxon Church. What Canute did,—whether *Church-Grith* represents anything done or proposed to be done in A.D. 1014, or whether it was (as I think more likely) a project of law which the ecclesiastics who called Canute to the throne in 1016 submitted to him, then or afterwards, and desired to have enacted by him,—what he did, proves unequivocally, that, although he conciliated the monastic party by accepting and enacting almost everything which was contained in that document, he did *not* accept, and did *not* enact or confirm, but, on the contrary, set aside and disallowed the article of that document as to a tripartite division of tithes.

§ 5. *Canute's Laws.*

Of all the kings who held sway in England before the Norman Conquest, Alfred and Canute were the most distinguished as legislators: Canute stands even before Alfred, as the author of the more complete, copious, and elaborate code.[2] That work must have been the result of careful deliberation; it was a well-considered endeavour to provide for the good government of his English subjects, and to meet, as far as possible, the reason-

---

[1] In the same Worcester (Cottonian) manuscript volume which contains *Church-Grith* is a sermon thus described in the table of contents at the beginning of the book: '*Sermo Lupi ad Anglos, quando Dani maxime persecuti sunt eos; quod fuit anno* 1014 *ab Incarnatione Domini nostri Jesu Christi.*'   [2] Thorpe's *Ancient Laws*, vol. i. pp. 358-430.

able wants and wishes of all orders and degrees of men among them. It contains twenty-six ecclesiastical laws, and eighty-four secular (including several on mixed subjects); in addition to which, there were thirty-four forest laws.

There is nothing in Canute's code material to my purpose, except the laws which show its relation to the documents called *Of Grith and of Mund*, and *Of Church-Grith*, and those relating to tithes and repairs of churches. Of the classification of 'minsters,' and 'field-churches,' contained in one of its articles, I have already[1] spoken.

That the document called *Of Grith and of Mund*, was made use of in the preparation of Canute's laws seems evident, from some of the provisions in the second[2] article of the ecclesiastical, and the sixtieth[3] of the secular laws; and also from the opening words of the twenty-sixth[4] article of the ecclesiastical laws, '*Bishops are heralds, and teachers of God's laws*,' which are found in the nineteenth article of *Grith and Mund*.

As to the other document, the state of the case is this. It contains, altogether,[5] forty-four clauses or articles; of which five[6] are of that historical, rhetorical, expostulatory, and didactic character of which I have spoken as not proper for laws which could, in that or any similar form, be enacted by any legislature. These do not appear in Canute's legislation; and one other was omitted,

---

[1] *Ante*, pp. 222, 223.
[2] 'Then is it very right, that God's *church-grith* within walls, and a Christian king's hand-grith, stand equally inviolate,' *ibid.*, p. 359; compare *Of Grith and of Mund*, art. 2, *ibid.*, p. 331.
[3] *Ibid.*, p. 409; compare *Of Grith and of Mund*, art. 9; *ibid.*, p. 331.
[4] *Ibid.*, p. 375; *G. and M.*, *ibid.*, p. 333.
[5] *Ibid.*, pp. 340-351.   [6] Arts. 36 to 39 inclusive, and 43.

apparently as superfluous. There remain thirty-eight of a more positive kind; and of these, thirty-two are found, without alteration, in Canute's laws (twenty-five in the ecclesiastical, seven in the secular), and four more, if not repeated in exactly the same terms, are covered in substance and by necessary implication.[1] Two [2] remain, which were evidently, on consideration, disallowed; one of these is the article for the tripartite division of tithes—of which (I may here add) there is no trace in any later collection or compilation of Anglo-Saxon laws,—not in those which go by the name of Edward the Confessor[3]; not in those ascribed to the Conqueror[4]; not in those called the laws of Henry I.,[5] The other rejected article[6] proposed to give extraordinary aid and protection to abbots and their stewards:

'And the king commands all his reeves, in every place, that ye protect the abbots on all secular occasions, as ye best may; and, as ye desire to have God's or my friendship, that ye aid their stewards everywhere to right; that they themselves may the more uninterruptedly dwell closely in their minsters, and live according to rule.'

Canute did more than *omit* the clause for the tripartite division of tithes. Instead of it, he restored[7] to its proper place in the ecclesiastical part of his code, Edgar's law[8] in favour of manorial churches with burial-grounds, (which the framers of *Church-Grith* had omitted). And by one of his secular laws,[9] 'all men' were required to 'give assistance to *church-bot*,'—that is, to the repair of churches.

[1] See Appendix E.
[2] Arts. 6 and 32. (That as to the partition of tithes is art. 6.)
[3] Thorpe's *Ancient Laws*, vol. i. pp. 442-464. [4] *Ibid.*, pp. 466-496.
[5] *Ibid.*, pp. 497-631.   [6] Art. 32 (*ibid.*, p. 347).
[7] Canute's Ecclesiastical Laws, art. 11 (Thorpe's *Ancient Laws*, vol. i. pp. 366, 367).
[8] *Ibid.*, p. 263 (and see *ante*, p. 320).   [9] *Ibid.* (p. 411, art. 66).

If we inquire how it happened that, on points such as these, the monastic party failed to obtain the legislation which they desired, the explanation may probably be found in the influence of Ethelnoth, who succeeded to the see of Canterbury in A.D. 1020. He was Canute's intimate friend, 'encouraging him' (in the words of Dean Hook's [1] quotation from William of Malmesbury) 'in his good actions by the authority of his sanctity, and restraining him in his excesses.'

'Although educated at Glastonbury, he was himself a secular, and the predilections of Canute for the party of the seculars were evinced by his placing the church he erected at Assingdon under the control of a secular priest ; but, wherever people desired it, Benedictine monasteries were established, and every facility was afforded to the chapters of cathedrals and larger churches to adopt the Benedictine rule when such was their pleasure. The consequence was that the seculars ceased to be persecuted ; and although, in deference to public opinion, the married clergy were not encouraged, they were permitted without molestation to cultivate the domestic virtues until the triumph of celibacy under the Normans.'[2]

I will state, before leaving this subject, my reasons for agreeing with the opinion of Mr. Kemble[3] and Schmid,[4] that Canute's laws ought to be referred, not (as Lappenberg[5] and some others have thought) to the latter, but to the earlier part of his reign. If they belong to the earlier time, the 'Mid-winter' witenagemot of Winchester, at which, according to the Anglo-Saxon title[6] in the Wor-

[1] *Lives of Archbishops*, vol. i. p. 479.   [2] *Ibid.*, pp. 480, 481.
[3] *Saxons in England*, vol. ii. p. 259.
[4] *Die Gesetze der Angelsachsen* (Leipsic 1882), preface, p. lv.
[5] *Hist. of England* (Thorpe's transl.), vol. ii. p. 202.
[6] See Thorpe, *Ancient Laws*, vol. i. pp. 358, 359.

cester manuscript, they were passed, may probably have been held between A.D. 1018 and 1021. Those who lean to the contrary opinion suppose them to have been passed after Canute's return from his pilgrimage to Rome; the true date of which (though assigned by the chroniclers to A.D. 1031) cannot be later than 1026.[1]

It is not likely that Canute, whose affairs in the north of Europe required him to be for long intervals absent from England, should have delayed for more than ten years from his accession to the throne a work of legislation, indispensably necessary for the pacification and settlement of his newly-acquired kingdom. It was expected from him by those who, upon the death of Ethelred, chose him for their king. The provisions of his laws generally, and especially the ecclesiastical laws, were founded upon materials ready to his hand. His policy must have been to conciliate, as much and as soon as possible, the goodwill of his new subjects, and to establish a contrast between his firm government and the preceding times of disorder. All these considerations were against unnecessary delay.

Lappenberg[2] gives no reasons for his opinion, that Canute's laws 'do not appear to have been composed in the first years of his reign,' beyond these—(1) that their preamble 'shows them to be posterior to the re-conquest of Norway in 1028;' and (2) that they contain a 'reintroduction of St. Peter's Penny.'

Of the latter reason it is sufficient to say, that the clause in Canute's ecclesiastical laws, which Lappenberg describes as 're-introducing' the *Rom-feoh*, or Peter's

---

[1] See Lappenberg, *History of England* (Thorpe's transl.), vol. ii. p. 211, note.   [2] *Ibid.*, p. 202.

penny, is taken directly from *Church-Grith*,[1] and could not be due to any special effect on Canute's mind of his visit to Rome. That impost had been recognised, as legally due, in the synodical decrees of Enham,[2] and in the ordinance of A.D. 1008.[3] And Canute's own letter[4] from Rome to the English archbishops and bishops (which, in Lappenberg's view, preceded his legislation) contains, to my mind, evidence to the contrary. He referred in that letter to plough-alms, tithes, Peter's pence, and church-scot (the payment of all which was enjoined by clauses of his code, repeating and confirming older laws), as 'due according to the ancient law to God'; he expressed his desire that none of them should be in arrear when he returned; and he gave notice that if they were not duly paid, the laws concerning them would be strictly enforced by him against defaulters ('*Hæc et his similia, si non erunt persoluta, regia exactio secundum leges, in quem culpa cadit, districte absque venia comparabit.*')

As for the description of Canute, in the Anglo-Saxon title of the Worcester manuscript, as 'king of all England, and king of the Danes and Norwegians,' it is not to be assumed that, because a later scribe gave him that style, it was found in the original record of his laws. It is not in the Rochester[5] text. Schmid[6] regarded it as an interpolation, on the ground that Canute never used his Danish or Norwegian titles in England. And Lappenberg,[7] when

[1] Art. 10. See Thorpe, *Ancient Laws*, vol. i. p. 343.
[2] *Ibid.*, p. 321.   [3] *Ibid.*, p. 309.
[4] See Florence of Worcester, *sub* A.D. 1031, and *post*, pp. 296, 297, note.
[5] *Textus Roffensis* (belonging to the Dean and Chapter of Rochester Cathedral, published by Hearne in A.D. 1720); see fol. 58.
[6] *Die Gesetze der Angelsachsen*, preface, p. lv.
[7] *Hist. of England* (Thorpe's transl.), vol. ii. p. 211, note.

investigating the question of the true date of Canute's letter from Rome,[1] was not embarrassed by a similar difficulty. 'The title assumed by Canute, in his letter, of *Rex Norveganorum et partis Suevorum* may' (he said) 'be a later interpolation.'

[1] The letter in Florence of Worcester (under A.D. 1031) is thus addressed: '*Canutus rex totius Angliæ, et Denemarciæ et Norreganorum, et partis Suavorum, Aethelnotho Metropolitano et Alfrico Eboracensi Archiepiscopo.*'

CHAPTER X

FOURTH PERIOD—FINAL SETTLEMENT OF THE PAROCHIAL SYSTEM

§ 1. *Summary of laws as to Tithes, down to Canute*

THE general effect of the Anglo-Saxon laws as to tithes, down to and including those of Canute, may be thus shortly summed up. The obligation of paying prædial tithes was recognised; they were to be paid at certain seasons, according to the nature of the different titheable subjects. Those who did not pay them were liable to penalties; and under Edgar's laws (confirmed and repeated by Canute), they might be taken forcibly, under process of law, from those who withheld them. Until Edgar's time, no law either enjoined, or expressly recognised, any special appropriation of tithes. That appears to have been determined by practice. There was not so much as a canon of the Church which laid down a rule on that subject. If we go so far back as to the precepts of Archbishop Theodore, it seems that, in his view, the ecclesiastical duty would have been satisfied by a gift, either directly to the poor or strangers, or (by laymen) to the giver's 'own church.'

From Edgar's laws, however, it may with reasonable certainty be inferred, that there was a general presumption in favour of the payment of tithes to the 'older minsters,' or 'mother-churches' (monastic, generally, or conventual)—

similar to the public baptismal churches of the Continent. Those laws were the first to introduce an innovation upon that general custom, in favour of churches in private patronage, with burial-grounds belonging to them, within the manors or estates of private landowners. But that concession extended only to one-third of the local tithes. The other two-thirds were still treated as payable to the 'older minster,' or 'mother-church.' Those laws were repeated[1] in Canute's code.

§ 2. *Course of transition to modern Parishes.*

There can be no doubt that, in the churches to which, under Edgar's laws, one-third of the local tithes was allowed to be given, we have the original type of modern parish churches. Of their multiplication, and gradual extension over the whole country, Selden's account [2] must be true. 'Most laymen of fair estate' (he says) 'desired the country residence of some chaplains that might be always ready for Christian instruction among them, their families, and adjoining tenants.' They built and endowed churches; and the endowment of every such church, on its consecration, 'was restrained from the common treasure of the diocese, and made the only revenue which became perpetually annexed to the church of that clerk who received it.' A district was attached to the church, determined generally by the extent of those neighbouring lands of the lay founder, which were intended to receive benefit from the foundation. This became the 'parish' of the priest in charge; and the inhabitants of that district were his parish-

[1] Thorpe's *Ancient Laws*, vol. i. p. 367 (arts. 8, 11).
[2] *Hist. of Tithes*, ch. 9, § 4, p. 259 (ed. 1618).

ioners. The older sense of the word 'parish' naturally lent itself to that application. The priest was nominated by the lord, or patron, and until the latter part of the twelfth century received investiture from him, without episcopal institution. This we know on the testimony of Pope Alexander III.,[1] who condemned the practice as wrong in principle, and against 'the constitutions of the Holy Fathers.' 'We have been certainly informed' (he wrote to Archbishop Becket, and his suffragans of the province of Canterbury) 'by many complaints which have reached us, that in your parts a very bad and irregular custom has obtained prevalence for a very long time past (*a multis retro temporibus invaluisse*); namely, that clerks, influenced by blind covetousness, accept churches and ecclesiastical benefices without consent of the bishop of the diocese, or his officials, to whom that duty belongs.' An earlier attempt to establish, in such cases, the episcopal power had been made by Paschal II., but had met with resistance in England. Archbishop Anselm [2] wrote to that Pope:

'After my return to England, on being recalled to my see, I produced the apostolical decrees which I heard when present in the council at Rome, forbidding any one to receive investitures of churches from the hand of the king or of any layman, doing homage for them (*ut pro his ejus homo fieret*); forbidding also the ordination of any one who might transgress this rule. It was, however, so ill taken by the king and his chief lords, and even by the bishops themselves, and by others of less degree, that they declared they would in no wise consent to it; and that they would rather expel me from the realm, and separate themselves from the Roman Church (*et a Romana ecclesia se discessuros*).'

---

[1] *Decret. Greg. IX.*, lib. iii., tit. vii., cap. 3.
[2] See Selden, *Hist. of Tithes*, ch. 12, § 2 (ed. 1618), p. 377.

The abolition of this practice, and also the establishment of the principle of lapse as to churches in lay patronage, were among the reforms accomplished by the third Lateran Council[1] (A.D. 1179-80); the decrees of which, notwithstanding the difficulty which Anselm had encountered, were not long afterwards received[2] in England, as in other parts of Western Christendom. Until then, if upon a vacancy taking place in any manorial parish church, upon the estate and in the patronage of a private landowner, it was not filled up, the bishop could neither make nor compel an appointment, and the parish might remain indefinitely without a minister. As long as that state of things continued, the patron had, in practice, upon every vacancy, large powers (whether recognised as canonically legitimate or not) over the church and its endowments; and it was not until the necessity for episcopal institution, and the right of the bishop to supply a vacancy in such a church after a certain delay, had become settled, that the modern parochial system was fully established.

From the first, however, bishops, when requested to consecrate churches upon private landowners' estates, were able to require, and according to general canonical usage did in practice require, such conditions as were usual and reasonable. The compliance of the founder with those conditions was, of course, voluntary; the whole operation originated in his will to erect the church, and to seek its consecration: he doubtless knew beforehand, according to the practice of each age, what the bishop would be likely to require, and determined to meet those requirements, by endowment and otherwise, as far as his means would allow. Two minds, therefore, that of the founder and that of the

[1] See Selden, *Hist. of Tithes*, ch. 12, § 5, pp. 388, 389.   [2] *Ibid.*

bishop, had to concur; there was no external compulsion operating upon either of them.

In ecclesiastical, as in other affairs, every innovation upon customary rights or interests is regarded with jealousy by those whose power it tends to diminish. The displacement, therefore, of the rights or claims of monastic and other public churches, by admitting other churches to participation in the like status and privileges, in a greater or less degree, was not likely to be regarded with favour by ecclesiastical authority, when in monastic hands. But, as the benefits which it was capable of conferring upon the common people, in country districts especially, made themselves more and more felt, bishops who understood their duty became more favourably disposed towards it; and, after it had reached a certain point of development, they, and other ecclesiastical corporations, themselves built and endowed churches, and constituted parishes of the new sort, upon their own ecclesiastical estates,[1] retaining in their hands the appointment of the priests of those churches. By these natural steps the system, after it had once been set on foot and recognised by law, had a tendency to become, and did by degrees become, universal.

This process, which (in England) probably began in the tenth, was an accomplished fact by the end of the twelfth century; but to trace its progress during that interval, from historical records, is not easy.

§ 3. *Canute's Letter, and 'Ecclesiastical Institutes.'*

The use of the word '*parochia*' in the letter,[2] already mentioned, which Canute wrote from Rome to his arch-

[1] Selden, *Hist. of Tithes*, ch. 9, § 4 (ed. 1618), pp. 260, 261.

[2] Florence, *sub anno* 1031: '*Nunc igitur præcipio, et obtestor omnes meos Episcopos et regni præpositos, per fidem quam Deo et mihi debetis,*

bishops and bishops, has by some been understood of modern parishes. It is used, however, only as to '*church-scot*,' which was to be paid 'to the church in whose parish each man lives' (*ad ecclesiam, sub cujus parochia quisque deget*). But neither in any older laws, nor in Canute's own, is there any provision which authorised or contemplated the payment of *church-scot* to any but the 'older minsters,' or mother-churches. I conclude, that in this letter '*parochia*' meant the ecclesiastical district of the old minster or mother-church, and not a parish of the modern kind.

Bishop Kennett,[1] following Spelman,[2] supposed the document, to which Mr. Thorpe has given the title of 'Ecclesiastical Institutes,' to be a collection of 'Saxon canons;' and he quoted from it this passage, as bearing upon the history of the parochial system in England:

'Let no mass-priest entice any man from the parish of another church to his church, nor instruct any one from another priest's district to attend his church and give him their tithe and the offerings which they ought to give to the other; but let every one be content with that which comes to him from his church, and thank God for it.'[3]

There are other articles,[4] following this in the same document, which it would be material to consider, if the *quatenus faciatis, ut antequam ego Angliam veniam omnia debita quæ Deo secundum legem antiquam debemus sint persoluta; scilicet eleemosynæ pro aratris, et decimæ animalium ipsius anni procreatorum, et denarii quos Romæ ad sanctum Petrum debemus, sive ex urbibus, sive ex villis; et mediante Augusto decimæ frugum; et in festivitate Sancti Martini primitiæ seminum ad ecclesiam sub cujus parochia quisque deget, quæ Anglice ciricsceat nominantur.'*

[1] *Case of Impropriations*, etc. (1704), p. 12, and note, *ibid.*
[2] *Concil. Anglic.*, vol. i. p. 593.
[3] See Thorpe, *Ancient Laws*, vol. ii. p. 411 (art. 14), and Johnson's *Laws and Canons* (ed. 1850), vol. i. p. 459.
[4] Arts. 15, 16, 17 (Thorpe, *Ancient Laws*, vol. ii. p. 413); Johnson, *ubi supra*, p. 460.

document had been of the nature which Bishop Kennett supposed. Mr. Johnson, who better understood its nature, and who in his translation did not use (as Mr. Thorpe does) the words '*parish*,' or '*parishioners*,'[1] drew from the article itself a different inference. The word for 'priest's *district*' in the Anglo-Saxon text is '*preost-scyre*'—(*priest's shire*)—on which Mr. Johnson[2] observed :

'By this it is evident, that bounds of parishes were not yet settled by law or established by custom ; and, as the diocese was then called the bishop's *shire*, so the houses and vills next adjacent to a little church were called the priest's *shire*. Just before, this *shire* is called *hyrnysse*.'

Whatever interest the proper interpretation of that document may have, it belongs really to the history of the Gallican Church in the ninth, and not of the English Church in the tenth or eleventh century. So far from being a collection of 'Saxon canons,' it is in fact (as has been elsewhere stated) an Anglo-Saxon translation—supposed to be by Aelfric—from a work written for the diocese of Orleans by its bishop, Theodulph,[3] in the first half of the ninth century ; and there is no evidence whatever, nor any ground for believing, that it ever had any authority in England greater than might belong to any other work of an eminent Frank divine of that period.

§ 4. *Laws of Edward the Confessor.*

In the preface to all the manuscripts which contain the compilation called the Laws of Edward the Confessor,[4] it is

---

[1] The word '*parishioners*' occurs frequently in Mr. Thorpe's translation (see articles 25-29), *Ancient Laws*, vol. ii. pp. 423-425.
[2] Johnson's *Laws and Canons*, vol. i. (ed. 1850), p. 460.
[3] *Ibid.*, pp. 450, 452, note.
[4] Thorpe, *Ancient Laws*, vol. i. p. 442.

represented as a report made to William the Conqueror by a sworn jury of twelve, chosen out of a body of English noblemen and men learned in Anglo-Saxon law, returned from all the counties of England, under a commission issued by William in the fourth year of his reign, that he might 'hear from themselves what their customs were, without omission, addition, or change.'

This, if authentic, and if its contents had corresponded to the supposed commission, would be a document of great interest. But nothing can be more remote than it is from the character which the preface claims for it.

It contains altogether thirty-three articles, some of them statements of laws or customs; some historical, and of later date than the Conqueror's time; which are interjected in a very extraordinary manner.

The first place is given to ecclesiastical subjects; and among these it is noticeable, that the joint jurisdiction of civil and ecclesiastical judges, sitting together in one court (as provided by the laws of Edgar[1] and Canute),[2] is affirmed.[3] Two articles relate to tithes;[4] of which (not prædial only, but personal), the payment to 'Holy Church' is in general terms prescribed, with an enumeration in detail of titheable matters; but without mention or indication of the churches entitled to receive them :

'Let any one' (it is said) 'who shall have kept them back be compelled to payment, if necessary, by the justice of the Church and the king. These things St. Augustin preached, and these were granted by the king, and confirmed by the

---

[1] Art. 5 of Edgar's Secular Ordinance (Thorpe, *Ancient Laws*, vol. i. p. 269).
[2] Art. 18 of Canute's Secular Ordinances (*ibid.*, p. 387).
[3] Arts. 3 and 9 of *Leges Regis Edwardi Confessoris* (*ibid.*, pp. 443 445).   [4] Arts. 7, 8 (*ibid.*, p. 445).

barons and people. But afterwards, by the instigation of the devil, many kept them back; and those priests who were rich were not very careful in looking after them (*non multum curiosi erant ad perquirendas cas*), because in many places there are now four or three churches, where there was then but one, and so they began to suffer diminution' (*quia in multis locis sunt modo* iiii *vel* iii *ecclesiæ, ubi tunc temporis non erat nisi una; et sic inceperunt minui*).

This passage might, by implication, afford light as to the progress of the parochial system, if the time of which it speaks were ascertained. But the clause as to Danegeld,[1] which follows soon afterwards, speaks of a time later than the Conqueror, and was probably not written earlier than the reign of Henry I., if so soon.

'From this Danegeld' (it says) 'all land was free, which was the property, or held under the lordship of churches (*quæ de ecclesiis propria et dominica erat*) ; also that held of parish churches thereto (?) belonging (*etiam de ecclesiis parochiarum ad idem pertinentibus*) ; and they paid nothing for its redemption, because they placed more trust in the prayers of the Church than in the defence of arms. *And this liberty had Holy Church even to the time of William the younger, who sought aid from the barons of the whole country for keeping Normandy from his brother Robert when he went to Jerusalem, and they granted him four shillings* (solidos) *from every ploughlana, not excepting Holy Church; which collection being made, the Church cried out, demanding back her liberty, but without success.*'

Among the secular articles (twenty-two of which follow the ecclesiastical) is one as to the royal power,[2] which no one can believe to have been delivered as law by any representatives of his Anglo-Saxon subjects to William the Conqueror. As characteristic of the compilation, though not directly germane to my subject, I extract it :

[1] Art. 11 (Thorpe, *Ancient Laws*, vol. i. p. 446).
[2] Art. 17 (*ibid.*, p. 449).

'The king, who is the vicar of the Supreme King, is appointed to this end, that he may govern and defend from wrong-doers the kingdom and people of the Lord, and, above all, Holy Church, and may destroy and root out criminals. If he do not this, he loses the name of king, as was declared by Pope John,[1] to whom Pepin and his son Charles, when they were not yet kings or princes, but under a foolish Frank king, wrote inquiring, "Whether the kings of the Franks ought so to remain content with the mere name of king?" Who answered, "It is fit that those should be called kings who vigilantly defend and govern the Church of God and His people after the example of the Psalmist King, who said, 'He who doeth proud things shall not dwell in my house,'" etc.'

After the thirty-third article (and before the last four, which are criminal and mercantile laws), comes the interjected historical matter.[2] This begins with a statement that King William, on hearing the preceding 'and other laws concerning the realm,' 'highly appreciated' it (*maxime appreciatus est eam*), and wished it to be observed throughout the kingdom; first, however, expressing a preference for the Norman law 'as deeper and more excellent' (*profundior et honestior*) 'than all others—that is, than all the laws of the Britons, English, and Picts.' But he yielded to the entreaties of the natives of the land who declared to him these laws (*omnes compatriotæ qui leges narraverunt*), and who prayed him to allow them to be observed, 'for the sake of the soul of King Edward, who had granted him the kingdom, and whose laws these were, and not of any strangers. At last he acquiesced in the counsel and prayer of the barons, and so were authorised (*auctorizatæ*) the laws of King Edward, which were devised and ordained

---

[1] The Pope of whom this is related by historians is Zacharias, not John.
[2] Arts. 34, 35 (Thorpe, *Ancient Laws*, vol. i. pp. 458-460).

previously in the time of King Edgar his grandfather, but after his death were set aside for sixty-eight years.'[1]

Then follows an account of the succession of kings and the duration of their reigns, from Edward the Martyr to the death of Hardiknute; 'so completing the sixty-eight years during which the laws were set aside.'

'But after King Edward came to the kingdom he, by the counsel of the barons of the realm, made them restore and confirm the law so disused, because it seemed to them good, and because his grandfather had ordained it; and so it was called the law of King Edward, which had been before set aside from the death of Edgar his grandfather till his own time.'

Then comes another historical chapter; explaining why the Confessor had not chosen Edgar Atheling for his successor, but had 'adopted William, Duke of the Normans, son of his uncle Robert, who afterwards, by God's help, conquered his right in war against Harold.'

The whole ends (in two of the three extant manuscript copies) with this note:[2]

'Here end the laws of Edward, first devised by Edgar his grandfather, and confirmed by William the Conqueror of England, and previously approved in King Cnuto's time.'

It must be added, that very little of the matter included in this compilation is contained in the laws of Edgar, nor is much of it in those of Canute. In the form in which it stands it is apocryphal, and not to be relied on for any historical purpose.

§ 5. *Laws of the Conqueror.*

The laws of William the Conqueror himself[3] have a

---

[1] Including in those sixty-eight years the reign of Canute.
[2] Thorpe, *Ancient Laws*, vol. i. p. 462.   [3] *Ibid.*, p. 467.

title prefixed to them, which, if properly so applied, tends still further to stamp the collection just mentioned as spurious, viz.—

'These are the laws and customs which King William, after his conquest of England, granted to be observed by all the people of the English, being the same which his predecessor and kinsman, King Edward, observed in the realm of the English.'

These laws, of which there seems no reason to doubt the authenticity (most of them taken from those of Canute and earlier kings), are different from the preceding. They contain no ecclesiastical matter, except one article,[1] repeating with some variation that law of Canute which imposed graduated penalties for the violation of the privileges of churches, according to their rank; and another,[2] for the payment of Peter's pence. The former makes the forfeiture, if the church violated is a cathedral, or a monastery, or other religious house (*cenobium vel quæcunque religiosorum ecclesia*), 100 shillings (*solidos*); if 'a mother parish church' (*matrix ecclesia parochialis*), 20 shillings; if a chapel, 10 shillings. The 'mother parish church' must here be one of lower degree than cathedrals and monastic or conventual churches. It can only be the church, with a burial-ground, of Edgar's laws; and the title assigned to it (from its relation, presumably, to chapels which might be dependent upon it) marks the progress of the parochial system.

That we have here really those 'laws of the Confessor,' which William confirmed (as the title says), is rendered probable by a later statute[3] of his own, containing this clause:[4]

[1] Art. 1 (Thorpe, *Ancient Laws*, vol. 1. p. 467).
[2] Art. 17 (*ibid.*, p. 475). [3] *Ibid.*, pp. 491-494. [4] *Ibid.*, p. 493.

'This also we enjoin, that all men hold and observe in all things the laws of King Edward, with these additions which we have ordained for the benefit of the English.'

In addition to these laws, William, by his well-known charter of jurisdiction [1] (probably in the year A.D. 1072), separated the ecclesiastical from the civil courts; and required all spiritual causes to be thenceforth brought before the bishop or his officials only.

§ 6. *Laws ascribed to Henry I.*

Into a criticism of the compilation called 'The Laws of Henry the First,'[2] or into the proof that it does not, and cannot, represent any body of Anglo-Saxon laws enacted or confirmed by Henry I., it would be superfluous to enter; as this has been adequately done by the late learned Dr. Allen, in his 'Notes,'[3] appended to it in Mr. Thorpe's *Ancient Laws*. The clauses[4] of its seventh chapter, providing that in the county courts '*the causes Christian*' should be first heard, then the pleas of the Crown, and last, civil actions; and of the thirty-first chapter, that 'there ought to be present in the county court, the bishops, counts, and other high officers, who should after just consideration determine God's laws and secular affairs' (*interesse comitatui debent episcopi, comites, et ceteræ potestates, quæ Dei leges et sæculi negotia justa consideratione diffiniant*),—are evident anachronisms, bringing back the mixed ecclesiastical and civil jurisdiction of Edgar and Canute, and ignoring the Conqueror's charter.

---

[1] Thorpe, *Ancient Laws*, vol. i. p. 495 (see *Defence of the Church*, etc., 3d ed., p. 11, and note, *ibid.*)   [2] *Ibid.*, pp. 497-608.
[3] *Ibid.*, pp. 609-631 (and see Mr. Thorpe's preface, p. xviii.)
[4] Ch. 7, § 3, and ch. 31, § 3 (*ibid.*, pp. 514, 534).

In the eleventh[1] chapter of this digest of laws and rules of procedure and forensic practice (for that is its real character), the compulsory provisions of the laws of Edgar and Canute, for taking tithes by civil process, and forfeiting eight-tenths of the gross produce of the land against which that remedy might be put in force, half to the lord, and half to the bishop, are exactly repeated.

In its clauses which relate to offences[2] by the clergy, and their privileges[3] (of which there are several), I find nothing which throws any light upon the development of the parochial system.

§ 7. *Endowments of parish churches with Tithes.*

The course of our inquiry has brought us down to the twelfth century without elucidating, any further than was done by the laws of Edgar and Canute, the origin of those endowments of modern parish churches (not appropriated to monasteries) with tithes, which by the end of that century had become so general, as to establish in church law—followed and allowed by the temporal law—a general presumption, that every parish church, in the absence of proof to the contrary, was endowed with its own tithes. There was certainly no such general appropriation of tithes to parish churches made by any law ever enacted in England: for the laws of Edgar and Canute, which made the nearest approach to such an enactment, gave to certain churches on private estates, and in private patronage, one-third only of the local tithes. The question is, how did that third pass into the whole? There is not, as far as I know, so much even as a canon of any council, or a decree

---

[1] Ch. 11, § 2 (Thorpe, *Ancient Laws*, vol. i. p. 520).
[2] Ch. 64, 73 (*ibid.*, pp. 566, 567, 578).   [3] Ch. 66 (*ibid.*, p. 569).

of any Pope, in the nature of a legislative act, enlarging the right, or appropriating tithes generally to parish churches, in England or elsewhere.

The explanation of Selden,[1] and of most English common lawyers,[2] has been, that until the third Council of Lateran (A.D. 1179-80), the lords or owners of the lands from which prædial tithes arose might dispose of them as they pleased, provided that they did so, in one way or other, for ecclesiastical purposes; and that, out of this power, all the endowments, both of monasteries and of parish churches, with tithes, which took place between the tenth and the thirteenth centuries, arose. Selden styled those endowments '*arbitrary consecrations.*' Ecclesiastical controversialists of his day, and for some time afterwards, to whom such a view of the facts seemed repugnant to that doctrine of the divine right of tithes, which (with or without modification) they generally maintained, assailed it with vehemence. Dean Comber[3] called it Mr. Selden's 'new device of arbitrary consecrations.' Dean Prideaux[4] (who arrived at the same point by reliance on divine precedent, rather than divine commandment) called it Mr. Selden's 'wild chimera,' 'wild conceit,' and by other hard names. Bishop Kennett's language was at least equally strong.[5] As, however, the institution of parishes and parish priests was not coeval either with the foundation of the Church, in England or elsewhere, or with the practice of paying tithes to the Church, the general parochial right is a thing

[1] *Hist. of Tithes*, ch. 7, § 1, and ch. 11, § 1 (ed. 1618, pp. 142, 297).
[2] Blackstone's *Commentaries*, vol. i. p. 112; Cruise's *Digest*, tit. xxii.; *Tithes*, § 53; and see Coke, *2nd Institute*, p. 641.
[3] *An Historical Vindication of the Divine Right of Tithes*, by Thos. Comber, D.D. (1682), p. 104.
[4] *Original and Right of Tithes*, published A.D. 1707 (2nd ed. 1736, pp. 138-192).   [5] See Appendix J.

to be historically accounted for; no theory of divine right, or inference from divine precedent, could be sufficient to account for it.

Selden may have been the author of the phrase '*arbitrary consecration*'; but the view of historical facts which he used it to describe was no 'new device,' no 'chimera,' or 'conceit' of his. That laymen did in fact, upon the continent of Europe, make many 'arbitrary' appropriations of tithes, some to religious houses, some to themselves and other laymen, is proved by the protests and denunciations of Popes and other ecclesiastical authorities who disapproved of it; and that, until the third Lateran Council, those protests and denunciations were ineffectual to set aside or nullify what was so done, is equally clear; because Pope Urban II.,[1] while making a decree against the future creation of new titles of the same kind without the bishop's consent, found it necessary, 'for the sake of peace, and to avoid scandal,' to confirm all such titles previously acquired, whether from clerks or monks, or from other persons. If the Church of Rome said of those 'arbitrary' appropriations, '*fieri non debent*,' she found herself compelled also to say of them, '*facta valent*.'

The authorities, in this country, for the proposition of fact (as to the period before the third Lateran Council), on which the views of Selden and those who followed him rest, are too ancient, and of too much weight, to be set aside by merely imputing ignorance of ecclesiastical matters to common lawyers. I may mention some of them.

1. In the *Chronicle of Battel Abbey*,[2] which extends from the foundation of that abbey in A.D. 1066 to A.D.

[1] *Ante*, p. 67.
[2] *Chronicle of Battel Abbey from 1066 to 1176* (transl. by M. A. Lower, London 1851), p. 21.

1176, and was written by an abbot or monk of that house about the time of the latest entries in it, there is this statement :

'*As it was permitted up to that time* (*i.e.* the time of the Conquest, when the abbey was founded), *for every one to pay his tithes where, or to whomsoever he would*, many of those who resided in the neighbourhood assigned theirs to the abbey in perpetuity; and these, being confirmed by episcopal authority, remain payable to the abbey until this day.'

2. Two writs of prohibition from the king's court to ecclesiastical courts (in cases involving, not the subtraction of tithes, but the title to them), are cited by Selden, one of the reign of King John, or Henry III.,[1] the other of A.D. 1279, the seventh year of King Edward I.[2] In both these (judicial forms of that time) it is averred, that, 'in certain of our demesnes, we' (the king) 'have power to grant such tithes, *and in like manner many of the great men of our kingdom in their demesnes.*' It is no objection to the authority of those writs, as evidence of early practice, that they were issued after the third Lateran Council. The old forms continued to be used, though new grants of the same kind might be no longer possible.

3. Sir Robert Parnynge,[3] Chief Justice in A.D. 1340 (afterwards Lord Treasurer and Chancellor), said from the bench in A.D. 1333 or 1334, that 'anciently, before a new constitution made by the Pope, a patron of a church might grant the tithes within that parish to another parish.'

---

[1] *Hist. of Tithes*, ch. 11, § 2 (ed. 1618), pp. 353-356. Cited from Fitzherbert's *Natura Brevium*, 40 N.
[2] *Ibid.*, p. 357. Cited from a Cottonian manuscript.
[3] *Year Book*, 7 Edw. III., fol. 5, pl. 8. (See Selden, *Ibid.*, p. 292.)

4. In A.D. 1371, Ludlow,[1] one of King Edward III.'s Judges of Assize, also said, 'Anciently every man might grant the tithes of his land to any church that he pleased.'

5. Lyndwode, the famous English Canonist, who was Official Principal of the Provincial Court of Canterbury under Henry VI., and afterwards Bishop of St. David's, said in his '*Provinciale*,'[2] that before the Lateran Council of A.D. 1179, a layman might obtain from a church entitled to tithes a grant of them, to be held by himself feudally, and might either retain them or grant them, with the consent of the bishop, to any other monastery or church. I raise no question as to the qualifications expressed in this passage: I refer to it only for the light which it throws on some of the ways in which parish churches might come to be endowed with tithes.

One entire chapter[3] of Selden's *History of Tithes* is occupied with a series of extracts from the chartularies of Abingdon, Osney, Guisborough, Rochester, Reading, Canterbury (St. Augustin's), Crowland, Tynemouth, Boxgrove, St. Neot's, St. Leonard's (Yorkshire), Battle, Lewes, Eye, Pershore, and other abbeys and priories, which prove conclusively that lay benefactors often granted the prædial tithes of their lands (apart from and without any appropriation of churches), in the eleventh and twelfth centuries, to those religious houses. If they could do that, they might with equal right and reason endow parish churches on their own estates with the prædial tithes of their lands within the parishes; and the probability was that they would do so. No more likely explanation of the general prevalence of

[1] *Year Book*, 44 Edw. III., fol. 5, pl. 22. (See Selden, *Hist. of Tithes*, p. 292, ed. 1618.)
[2] Title, '*De locato et conducto*.' (*Ibid.*, ch. 13, § 1, ed. 1618, p. 403.)
[3] Ch. 11.

such parochial endowments (where churches were not appropriated to monasteries) has yet been suggested.

Dean Comber[1] and others, who disputed Selden's views, suggested that all those lay grants of tithes to monasteries had episcopal confirmation. This (if subsequent ratification and confirmation only were meant) may generally—perhaps in all cases—have been true;[2] although there is no proof that the confirmation was always simultaneous with the grant; on the contrary, it may be inferred, both from the terms of the confirmatory charters, and from what is known of the history of monastic titles to tithes upon the continent of Europe, that it was often otherwise. But, so far as parochial endowments with tithes are concerned, it is not necessary for their explanation to suppose them to have been 'arbitrary,' in such a sense as to exclude the consent of the bishop, or (if the effect was to transfer the title to all, or to two-thirds, of the tithes from a religious house to a parish church) the consent of the religious corporation which ought, otherwise, to have received the tithes. Whenever the endowment with tithes took place (as in by far the greater number of parish churches erected after King Edgar's time it probably did), at the time, and as part of the solemnities, of consecration, the bishop's consent must necessarily have been given. And it is not too much to presume that, whenever a powerful landowner desired to enlarge the right of a manorial parish church on his land from the one-third of tithes conceded to it by King Edgar's laws to the whole, and to change it (in effect) from a vicarage into a rectory,

---

[1] Comber's *Divine Right of Tithes* (1682), ch. 11, p. 200.

[2] It was the habit of the religious houses to obtain, whenever they could, and from the heirs of lay founders or benefactors as well as from ecclesiastical authorities, charters of confirmation, not as to tithes only, but also as to lands.

he might be able, by influence or by gifts, to obtain from the 'older minster'—the bishop concurring—a relinquishment of its claim. It must be remembered, as to new churches, that the erection, consecration, and endowment of every one of them (the endowment being, as a rule, simultaneous with the consecration) was a distinct and separate act in each particular case.

Dean Prideaux[1] asked:

'Had the right of tithes here grown up from such arbitrary consecrations as Mr. Selden asserts, why among all his instances doth he not bring so much as one, of such a consecration of tithes in a parish made to the parish church? Is it likely that those who had such tithes in their power arbitrarily to consecrate should give them all from their parish church, and none to it?' And he added, 'It seems most likely that their first inclination should be to their own church, where they attended divine service, and received the sacraments. And therefore, had the civil right of tithes come this way into the church, there must have been some instances of the consecration of them to the parish church, where they arose, as well as to other churches out of the parish; and would Mr. Selden have brought but one such instance, it would have made more for his purpose than all the rest put together. And certainly such he would have brought, were there any such to be found; and since there can none such be found, it is a sufficient proof that there were never any such, but that all parochial tithes were from the time of King Ethelwulf due of common right to the parish church.'

Of King Ethelwulf, and his supposed grant of tithes, enough has been said elsewhere. Upon Selden's word '*arbitrary*' (if it is assumed to mean that all grants of tithes made by laymen were against or without the bishop's consent), I lay no stress for the present purpose. But Dean Prideaux was under the impression that the local tithes

[1] *Original and Right of Tithes* (ed. 1736), p. 195.

were appropriated to parish churches by some general law, and not by express and particular endowments, at the times of their consecration, or otherwise. In this he was certainly mistaken. The deeds of consecration and endowment of ancient parish churches have not often been preserved; but instances enough remain to prove what the course of practice was, although Selden may not have cited them.

The practice of the Gallican Churches in this respect is likely (at least after the middle of the tenth century) to have been known and followed here. Among the 'Forms' of Marculfus, there is one [1] which exemplifies the practice of the Gallican Church, at the beginning of the ninth century, as to churches founded and endowed by bishops. It is a deed of consecration and endowment of a church at Cadillac, in the south of France, made with the consent of the episcopal chapter. It recites that the Bishop had built the church, and had appointed it to be the church of certain specified townships, to which the inhabitants of those townships were to go for masses, baptism, and preaching, *and that they should pay their tithes to that church;* and he at the same time endowed it with a manse, and with part of a vineyard, and certain arable land.

Of consecration deeds in this country, in which the endowment of the churches consecrated by lay founders is recorded, one example was made public in Sir William Dugdale's *History of Warwickshire*,[2] and another by Bishop Kennett, in the Appendix to his *Case of Impropriations*.[3]

---

[1] Form 11 (Baluze, *Capit. Reg. Franc.*, vol. ii. p. 442).

[2] *Hist. of Warwickshire* (1656), p. 630.

[3] *Case of Impropriations*, etc. (1704), Appendix, p. 34; also in *Cartularium Prioratus S. Johannis Evangelistæ de Brecon* (London 1884). Both these charters are translated in an Appendix to *Defence of the Church*, etc. (3rd ed.) pp. 357-360; where the later history of the Church of Hay is also stated.

CHAP. X   SETTLEMENT OF PAROCHIAL SYSTEM   315

Both instances belong to the first half of the twelfth century; one to the diocese of Worcester, the other to that of St. David's. The consecrating bishop in the one case was Simon, Bishop of Worcester from A.D. 1125 to 1151; the church was that of Exhall in Warwickshire. By that deed, the bishop confirmed the endowment (*donationem*) made to the church on the day of its consecration, by lay benefactors, there named: the endowments being certain quantities of land, *with all the donors' tithes of every kind* (*cum decimis suis plenariis*), freed and acquitted from all secular service. In the other case, the consecration was by Bernard, the first Norman Bishop of St. David's; and the deed, being attested by a witness described as 'clerk of King Henry,' must have been executed before the death of Henry I., in A.D. 1135. The church consecrated in that case was for the parish of Hay, in Brecknockshire; and the deed witnesses, that at the time of its consecration the lay founder (who is named), with the permission of his superior lord (also named, and then present) 'gave and granted in perpetual alms, for the endowment (*dotem*) of the said church,' certain lands therein particularly described:

'Also, he gave to the said church all the tithes of all his land of Hay, in all things, and of all his tenants of the fee of Hay; and, to prevent question, he expressly gave and granted the tithes, to wit, of corn and hay, of colts and calves, of lambs and pigs, of wool and cheese, of coppice-wood, and of Welsh revenue, and of passage and pleas.'

There cannot be any reason to suppose that these[1] were exceptional cases: the forms are strong evidence that they were examples of a practice general on consecrations of new

[1] See *post*, Appendix H, for the Latin text of the three charters here referred to.

parish churches after the parochial system had begun to be established. How many more such deeds may have been preserved, I do not know; the preservation of these was due to the accident, that they passed into monastic hands. If they stood alone, they would give, as it seems to me, a sufficient and satisfactory answer to Dean Prideaux's challenge; justifying the conclusion, otherwise reasonable and probable, that it was by means of express and particular grants of this kind, that each parish church, as it was founded and consecrated (after King Edgar's time), obtained a title to the parochial tithes, when the landowner (whether lay or ecclesiastical) and the bishop were agreed in desiring that such an endowment should be made.

The inferences derived from these documents receive confirmation from other extant deeds of various kinds; such as endowments of Collegiate Churches with tithes by their Founders at the time of their Foundation;[1] endowments of canonries in Cathedral Churches with tithes, by landowners claiming the right to appropriate them as they pleased;[2] and grants of tithes to existing parish churches or chapelries,—sometimes original and independent,[3] sometimes by way of settlement of controversies.[4] Recent research has brought some of these to light; and I entertain no doubt, that more evidence, direct and indirect, to the same effect, may be found, by those who will take the trouble of carefully examining them, in public, cathedral, and college libraries, and private collections, in which chartularies, title-deeds, and other manuscripts of ancient ecclesiastical foundations are preserved.

[1] See Appendix J.
[2] Appendix I, No. 4.
[3] *Ibid.*, No. 3.
[4] *Ibid.*, Nos. 1, 2.

APPENDIX A (see pp. 37-40)

'CAPITULARE EPISCOPORUM'

N.B.—The first column exhibits the Andain text, as printed by Martene and Durand; some printer's errors (*e.g.* nominative forms instead of the contracted accusative) being corrected. The second column exhibits the Metz text, as printed by Sirmondi and Baluze.

At the foot is a collation of the Metz text, with the Vatican MS. (*Codd. Palatini Latini*, No. 182), and of the Andain text, with three 'Egbertine' compilations, viz. (B) the Bodleian 'Penitential'; (C) the Worcester 'Excerptions,' in the library of Corpus Christi College, Cambridge; and (N) the later Worcester 'Excerptions,' *Nero A.* 1 of the Cottonian collection in the British Museum.

ANDAIN TEXT.

Hæc sunt Capitula ex divinarum Scripturarum scripta, quæ electi Sacerdotes custodienda atque adimplenda censuerunt.

1. Ut unusquisque sacerdos ecclesiam suam cum omni diligentia ædificet et relliquias sanctorum cum summo studio vigiliarum noctis et divinis[1] officiis conservet.

METZ TEXT.

'CAPITULARE EPISCOPORUM.'[2]

Hæc sunt Capitula ex divinarum Scripturarum scriptis, quæ electi Sacerdotes custodienda atque adimplenda censuerunt.

INCIPIUNT CAPITULA.

1. *Ut sacerdotes assidue orent pro Domno Imperatore.*[3]

Ut cuncti sacerdotes precibus assiduis pro vita et imperio domni Imperatoris et filiorum ac filiarum salute orent.

---

[1] *Diurnis*, C. and N.   [2] Not in Vat. 582.
[3] This, and all the following sub-titles, are omitted in Vat. 582; which has rubrical numbers only.

ANDAIN TEXT.	METZ TEXT.
2. Ut omnes sacerdotes horis competentibus diei et noctis suarum sonent ecclesiarum signa et sacra tunc Deo[1] celebrent officia, et populos erudiant quomodo aut quibus Deus adorandus est horis.	2. *Ut orent pro episcopo suo.* Ut unusquisque sacerdos quotidianis[13] adsistat orationibus pro pontifice cujus gubernatur regimine.
3. Ut omnibus festis diebus et[2] dominicis unusquisque sacerdos evangelium Christi populo prædicet.[3]	3. *De cura ecclesiæ et sacrarum relliquiarum.* Ut unusquisque sacerdos ecclesiam suam cum omni diligentia ædificet et relliquias sanctorum cum summo studio vigiliarum noctis et diurnis officiis conservet.
4. Ut unusquisque sacerdos cunctos sibi pertinentes erudiat ut sciant qualiter decimas totius facultatis ecclesiis divinis debite offerant.	4. *Ut evangelium Christi populo prædicent.* Ut omnibus festis et dicbus dominicis unusquisque sacerdos evangelium Christi populo prædicet.
5. Ut ipsi sacerdotes populi[4] suscipiant decimas et nomina eorum et[5] quæcunque[6] dederint scripta habeant et secundum autoritatem canonicam coram testibus[7] dividant et ad ornamentum ecclesiæ primam eligant partem secundam autem ad usum pauperum adque peregrinorum per eorum manus misericorditer cum omni humilitate dispensant[8] tertiam vero partem sibimetipsis soli[9] sacerdotes reservant.[10]	5. *Quænam populo præcipue insinuanda sint.* Ut unusquisque sacerdos orationem dominicam et symbolum populo sibi commisso curiose insinuet ac totius religionis studium et Christianitatis cultum eorum mentibus ostendat.
6. Ut unusquisque sacerdos orationem dominicam et symbolum populo sibi commisso curiose insinuent[11] ac totius religionis studium et Christianitatis cultum eorum mentibus ostendant.[12]	6. *De decimis a populo dandis.* Ut unusquisque sacerdos cunctos sibi pertinentes erudiat ut sciant qualiter decimas totius facultatis ecclesiis divinis debite offerant.

[1] *Domino*, C. and N.   [2] *Festis et diebus*, B. C. N.
[3] *Prædicet populo*, B. C. N.   [4] *A populis*, B. C. N.
[5] *Et* omitted, B. C. N.   [6] *Quicunque*, B. C. N.
[7] *Timentibus*, B.; TIMTIB, C.; TIMTIBS, N.   [8] *Dispensent*, B. C. N.
[9] *Soli* omitted, B. C. N.   [10] *Reservent*, B. C. N.
[11] *Insinuet*, B. C. N.   [12] *Ostendat*, B. C. N.
[13] *Cotidianis*, Vat. 582.

APPENDIX A

ANDAIN TEXT.

7. Ut cuncti sacerdotes precibus assiduis pro vita et imperio domni Imperatoris et filiorum ac filiarum salute orent.

8. Ut unusquisque sacerdos quotidianis adsistat orationibus pro pontifice cujus gubernatur regimine.

9. Ut nullus sacerdos in domibus vel aliis locis nisi in ecclesiis Deo[1] dicatis[2] celebrare missas audeat.

10. Ut cunctis[3] sacerdotibus jus et tempus baptismatis temporibus congruis secundum canonicam institutionem cautissime observetur.

11. Ut omnes sacerdotes quibuscunque horis omnibus indigentibus baptismum infirmitatis causa diligentissime tribuant.

METZ TEXT.

7. *Quomodo dividendæ sint decimæ.*

Ut[4] ipsi sacerdotes populi suscipiant decimas et nomina eorum quicunque dederint scripta habeant et secundum autoritatem[5] canonicam coram testibus dividant et ad ornamentum ecclesiæ primam eligant partem secundam autem ad usum pauperum vel[6] peregrinorum per eorum manus misericorditer cum omni humilitate dispensent tertiam vero partem semetipsis soli sacerdotes reservent.

8. *Ut officia divina competentibus horis non prætermittant.*

Ut omnes sacerdotes horis competentibus diei et noctis[7] sonent signa ecclesiarum[8] et sacrata Deo celebrent officia et populos erudiant quomodo aut quibus Deus adorandus est horis.

9. *Ut missas extra ecclesiam non celebrent.*

Ut nullus sacerdos in domibus vel[9] aliis locis nisi in ecclesiis dedicatis celebrare missas audeat.

10. *Ut congrua tempora baptismi serventur.*

Ut a cunctis sacerdotibus jus et tempus baptismatis temporibus congruis secundum canonicam institutionem cautissime observetur.

11. *Ut infirmi quolibet tempore baptizentur.*

Ut omnes sacerdotes quibuscunque horis omnibus indigentibus baptismum infirmitatis causa diligentissime tribuant.

---

[1] *Deo* omitted in B. C. N.   [2] *Dedicatis*, B. C. N.   [3] *A cunctis*, B. C.
[4] *Ut et ipsi*, Vat. 582.   [5] *Auctoritatem*, Vat. 582.
[6] *Atque* (not *vel*), Vat. 582.   [7] *Suarum* (after *noctis*), Vat. 582.
[8] *Ecclesiarum signa*, Vat. 582.   [9] *In* (after *vel*), Vat. 582.

Andain Text.

12. Ut nullus presbyter sacrum officium sive baptismale sacramentum aut aliquid bonorum [1] spiritalium pro aliquo precio vendere præsumat ne vendentes et ementes in templo columbas imitentur ut pro [2] his quæ [3] adepti sunt gratia divina [4] non pretia concupiscant terrena sed solum [5] regni coelestis gloriam promereantur accipere.

13. Ut nullus presbyter a sede propria [6] sanctæ ecclesiæ sub cujus titulo ordinatus fuit ammonitionis causa ad alienam pergat ecclesiam sed in [7] eadem [8] devotus usque ad vitæ permaneat exitum.

14. Ut nullus ex sacerdotum numero ebrietatis vitium nutriet [9] nec alios cogat per suam jussionem inebriari.

15. Ut nullus sacerdos extranearum mulierum habeat familiaritatem nec in sua domu in qua ipse habitat nullam [10] mulierem nunquam [11] permittat habitare.

Metz Text.

12. *Ut pro baptismo et aliis spiritualibus pretium non exigant.*

Ut nullus presbyter sacrum officium sive baptismale [12] sacramentum aut aliquid bonorum [13] spiritualium [14] pro aliquo pretio vendere præsumat ne vendentes et ementes in templo columbas imitentur ut pro his qui adepti sunt gratiam divinam non pretia concupiscant terrena sed solum regni cælestis [15] gloriam promereantur accipere.

13. *Ut in qua ordinati sunt ecclesia permaneant.*

Ut nullus presbyter a sede propria sanctæ ecclesiæ sub cujus titulo ordinatus fuit ambitionis causa ad alienam pergat ecclesiam sed in eadem devotus usque ad vitæ permaneat exitum.

14. *Ut ebrietatem in se et in aliis caveant.*

Ut nullus ex sacerdotum numero ebrietatis vitium nutriat nec alios cogat per suam jussionem inebriari.

15. *Ut cum extraneis mulieribus non habitent.*

Ut nullus sacerdos extranearum mulierum habeat familiaritatem nec in sua domo in qua ipse habitat ullam mulierem unquam permittat habitare.

---

[1] *Donorum*, B. C. N.   [2] *Plus* (omitting *his*), C.   [3] *Qui*, C.
[4] *Gratiam divinam*, C. ; *per gratiam divinam*, B. N.
[5] *Solam*, B. C. N.   [6] *Propria* is omitted in N.
[7] For *in eadem*, C. and N. have *ibidem*.
[8] *Ea*, B.   [9] *Nutriat*, C. N.
[10] *Ullam*, B. C. N.   [11] *Unquam*, B. C. N.
[12] *Baptismatis*, Vat. 582.   [13] *Donorum*, Vat. 582.
[14] *Spiritalium*, Vat. 582.   [15] *Celestis*, Vat. 582.

Andain Text.

16. Nulli[1] sacerdotum liceat fide-jussorem esse neque derelicta propria lege ad sæcularia judicia accedere presumat.[2]

17. Nemo[3] ex sacerdotum numero[4] arma pugnantium unquam portet nec litem contra proximum ullam excitet.

18. Ut nullus presbyter edendi aut bibendi causa ingrediatur[5] in tabernis.

19. Ut nullus sacerdos quicquam cum juramento juret sed simpliciter cum puritate et veritate omnia dicat.

20. Ut cuncti sacerdotes omnibus illis confitentibus eorum crimina dignam pænitentiam cum summa vigilantia ipsis indicant[6] et omnibus infirmis ante exitum vitæ viaticum et communionem Corporis Christi misericorditer tribuant.

Metz Text.

16. *Ut fidejussores non sint et sæcularia judicia non adeant.*

Nulli sacerdotum liceat fidejussorem esse neque derelicta propria lege ad secularia judicia accedere præsumat.

17. *De possessione triginta annorum.*

Ut qui possessionem ecclesiæ vel parrochiam per triginta[7] annos sine alicujus interpellatione tenuerit jure perpetuo possideat Si vero inde crebro repetitum fuerit fiat diligens inquisitio Et si eam[8] qui repetit juste quærere potuisset[9] adhibitis veracibus et nobilibus testibus quod repetit confirmando vindicet.

18. *Ut arma non gerant nec lites moverint.*

Nemo ex sacerdotum numero arma pugnantium umquam portet nec litem contra proximum ullam excitet.

19. *Ut tabernas non ingrediantur.*

Ut nullus presbyterorum edendi aut bibendi causa ingrediatur in tabernas.

20. *Ut a juramento abstineant.*

Ut nullus sacerdos quicquam cum juramento juret sed simpliciter cum puritate et veritate omnia dicat.

---

[1] *Ut nulli*, N.   [2] *Præsumat* omitted in B. N.
[3] *Ut nemo*, N.   [4] *Sacerdotum ex numero*, B. C. N.
[5] *Gradiatur*, B. C. N.   [6] *Indicent*, B. N.; *judicent*, C.
[7] *xxx^{ta}*, Vat. 582.   [8] *Eum*, Vat. 582.   [9] *Patuerit*, Vat. 582.

Andain Text.

21. Ut secundum diffinitionem sanctorum patrum siquis infirmatur a sacerdotibus oleo sanctificato cum orationibus diligenter unguatur.

22. De nonis et decimis.[1]

Volumus atque jubemus ut de omni conlaboratu et de vino et feno fideliter et pleniter ab omnibus nona et decima persolvatur De nutrimine vero pro decima sicut hactenus consuetudo fuit ab omnibus observetur Siquis tamen episcoporum fuerit qui argentum pro hoc accipere velit in sua maneat potestate.

23. De antiquis ecclesiis ut non rem suam habeant.[2]

Ut nec decimis nec aliis possessionibus priventur ita ut oratoriis tribuatur.

24. De spiritalibus filiolis.[3]

Deinde præcipimus ut unusquisque compater vel proximi spiritales filios suos catholice instruant.

25. De sacerdotibus.[3]

Ut juxta Apostolicam vocem irreprehensibiles sint et moribus ornati et nequaquam turpibus

Metz Text.

21. *Ut pænitentiam confitentibus et viaticum infirmis tribuant.*

Ut cuncti sacerdotes omnibus illis confitentibus eorum crimina dignam pænitentiam cum summa vigilantia ipsis indicent[4] et omnibus infirmis ante exitum vitæ viaticum et communionem Corporis Christi misericorditer tribuant.

22. De unctione infirmorum.

Ut secundum diffinitionem[5] sanctorum patrum siquis infirmatur a sacerdotibus oleo sanctificato cum orationibus diligenter unguatur.

[*The Metz text ends here.*]

---

[1] Not in B, C, or N.
[2] Not in B, or C. Article 24 of N. is, '*Ut ecclesiæ antiquitus constitutæ nec decimis nec alia ulla possessione priventur, ita ut novis oratoriis tribuantur.*' [3] None of these are in B, C, or N.
[4] *Judicent*, Vat. 582. [5] *Definitionem*, Vat. 582.

ANDAIN LAWS.

lucris deserviant juxta illud quod est scriptum, *Nemo militans Deo implicet se negotiis sæcularibus ut ei placeat cui se probavit:* Et a turpibus lucris et usuris non solum ipsi abstineant verum etiam plebes sibi subditas abstinere instruant.

26. *De incestuosis.*[1]

Ut incestuosi juxta canonicam sententiam pænitentia multentur Qui vero decimas post crebras admonitiones et prædicationes sacerdotum dare neglexerint excommunicentur Juramento vero eos constringi nolumus.

27. *De discretione in Corporis et Sanguinis Domini perceptione.*[1]

Cavendum est enim ne si nimium in longum differatur ad

ANDAIN LAWS.

perniciem animæ pertineat; dicente Domino, *Nisi manducaveritis carnem filii hominis et biberitis ejus sanguinem non habebitis vitam in vobis.* Si vero indiscrete accipiatur timendum est illud quod ait Apostolus ; *Qui manducat et bibit indigne judicium sibi manducat et bibit.* Juxta ergo Apostoli documentum probare se debet homo et sic de pane illo manducare et de calice bibere, ut videlicet abstinens se aliquot diebus ab operibus carnis, et purificans corpus animamque suam, præparet se ad percipiendum tantum sacramentum ; exemplo David, qui nisi se confessus fuisset abstinuisse se ab opere conjugali ab heri et nudius tertius nequaquam panes propositionis a sacerdote accepisset.

---

[1] Not in B., C., or N.

APPENDIX B (see pp. 154, 155)

COMPARISON of corresponding passages in Archbishop Odo's Injunctions and the Legatine Injunctions of A.D. 785-787.

[*N.B.*—The text of Odo's Injunctions is from Spelman's *Concilia*, vol. i. p. 415; that of the Legatine Injunctions from the 'Magdeburg Centuries.']

ODO'S INJUNCTIONS.

Article 2.

Ammonemus Regem et Principes et omnes qui in potestate sunt, ut cum magna humilitate suis Archiepiscopis omnibus que aliis Episcopis obediant; quia illis claves regni cælorum datæ sunt, et habent potestatem ligandi atque solvendi. . . .

Habeatque Rex prudentes consiliarios Deum timentes super regni negotia; ut populus, bonis exemplis Regis et Principum eruditus, proficiat in laudem et gloriam Dei.

Article 3.

Ammonendi sunt Episcopi, . . . ut suas parrochias omni anno cum summa diligentia prædicantes verbum Dei circumeant, ne aliquis per incuriam pastoris per devia cujuslibet ignorantiæ errans lupinis pateat morsibus lacerandus. Ne quis turpis lucri gratia, sed spe

LEGATINE INJUNCTIONS.

Article 11.

Ita quoque Reges et Principes admonuimus, ut obediant ex corde cum magna humilitate suis Episcopis; quia illis claves cæli datæ sunt, et habent potestatem ligandi atque solvendi. . . .

Habeantque Reges consiliarios prudentes, Dominum timentes, moribus honestos, ut populus, bonis exemplis Regum et Principum eruditus et confortatus, proficiat in laudem et gloriam Omnipotentis Dei.

Article 3.

Unusquisque Episcopus parochiam suam omni anno circumeat; diligenter conventicula per loca congrua constituendo, quo cuncti convenire possint ad audiendum Verbum Dei; ne aliquis per incuriam pastoris per devia cujuslibet ignorantiæ errans, rugientis

Odo's Injunctions.

mercedis æternæ, gregem sibi commissum pascere studeat. Quod enim gratis excepimus, gratis impendere non differamus; absque ullo timore vel adulatione cum omni fiducia verbum veritatis prædicare Regi, Principibus populi sui, omnibus dignitatibus; et nunquam veritatem subterfugere, neminem injuste damnare, neminem nisi juste communicare, omnibus viam salutis demonstrare.

Article 7.

Interdicimus omnibus Christianis injusta connubia et incæstuosa, tam cum monialibus vel cognatis, vel cum aliis illicitis personis. Nos quippe eandem Apostolicam auctoritatem sequentes, simili modo jaculum maledictionis talibus imponimus, nisi correptus a tam nefanda præsumptione ad satisfactionem perveniat.

Article 8.

... Sit concordia ubique et unanimitas inter Episcopos et Principes omnemque populum Christianum; ut sit unitas ubique Ecclesiarum Dei et pax; immo una sit Ecclesia fide, spe, et charitate; unum habens Caput quod est Christus; cujus membra se invicem adjuvare, mutuaque

Legatine Injunctions.

leonis morsibus invadatur. ... Et ne quis turpis lucri gratia, sed spe mercedis æternæ, gregem sibi commissum pascere quærat; et quod gratis accepit, omnibus gratis præstare studeat. ...

Article 11.

... Autoritate Divina fiducialiter et veraciter, absque ullo timore vel adulatione loqui verbum Dei Regibus, Principibus, omnibusque dignitatibus; nunquam veritatem subterfugere; nulli parcere; neminem injuste damnare; neminem sine causa excommunicare; omnibus viam salutis, tam verbis quam exemplis, demonstrare.

Article 15.

Interdicuntur omnibus injusta connubia et incæstuosa, tam cum ancillis Dei vel aliis illicitis personis, quam cum propinquis et consanguineis, vel alienigenis uxoribus: et omnino anathematis mucrone perfoditur qui talia agit, nisi correctus resipiscat a tam nefanda præsumptione, et suo Episcopo obtemperans seipsum ad æquitatis normam corrigat et revocet.

Article 14.

Sit concordia ubique, et unanimitas inter Reges et Episcopos, ecclesiasticos et laicos, omnemque populum Christianum; ut sit unitas ubique Ecclesiarum Dei, et pax in una Ecclesia, in una fide, spe, et charitate permanens, unum Caput habens, quod est Christus; cujus membra se invicem

Odo's Injunctions.

charitate diligere debeant; ut Ipse ait: '*In hoc cognoscant omnes,*' et reliqua.

Article 10.

Decimo capitulo mandamus, et fideliter obsecramus, de decimis dandis, sicut in lege scriptum est: '*Decimam partem ex omnibus frugibus tuis seu primitiis deferas in domum Domini Dei tui.*' Rursum per Prophetam: '*Adferte,*' inquit, '*omnem decimam in horreum Meum, ut sit cibus in domo Mea; et probate Me super hoc, si non aperuero vobis cataractas coeli, et effudero benedictionem usque ad abundantiam; et increpabo pro vobis qui comedit et corrumpit fructum terræ vestræ; et non erit ultra in ea sterilis.*' Unde et cum obtestatione præcipimus, ut omnes studeant de omnibus quæ possident dare decimas; quia speciale Domini Dei est; et de novem partibus sibi vivant, et eleemosynas tribuant.

Legatine Injunctions.

adjuvare, mutuaque charitate diligere debeant; sicut Ipse dixit; '*In hoc cognoscent omnes quia Mei discipuli estis, si dilectionem habueritis ad invicem.*'

Article 17.

... De decimis dandis, sicut in Lege scriptum est: '*Decimam partem ex omnibus frugibus tuis seu primitiis deferas in domum Domini Dei tui.*' Rursum per Prophetam: '*Adferte,*' inquit, '*omnem decimam in horreum Meum ut sit cibus in domo Mea; et probate Me super hoc, si non aperuero vobis cataractas coeli, et effudero benedictionem usque ad abundantiam; et increpabo pro vobis devorantem, qui comedit et corrumpit fructum terræ vestræ; et non erit ultra vinea sterilis in agro*'; dicit Dominus.... Unde etiam cum obtestatione præcipimus, ut omnes studeant de omnibus quæ possident decimas dare; quia speciale Domini Dei est: et de novem partibus sibi vivat, et eleemosynas tribuat....

APPENDIX C (see pp. 235, 236)

COMPARISON OF THE EXETER 'PENITENTIAL' VOLUME IN THE BODLEIAN LIBRARY, NO. 718, WITH THE VATICAN (PALATINE) MANUSCRIPT, NO. 1352.

The Vatican MS. begins with an address, to a bishop or 'rector' not named, in these words:—

'Hæc pauca Beatitudo vestra gratifice excipiat, deflorata quæ non ex uno uniusque doctoris prato divinæ auctoritatis studui decerpere, sed per multorum Patrum florigera rura, mentis et corporis cervice summissa, studiose, succinctim, celeriterque, ut jussio sanctitatis extitit vestræ, curavi, et ex his hos odoriferos, Domino largiente, prout potui flores excerpsi, hancque quadriformem hujus voluminis intexui coronolam. Sic in hac præfatiuncula subsequente vestra sancta dinoscere poterit industria. Ex quibus vero auctoribus aut opusculis ac institutis ista sint excerpta, in margine aut titulis hujus opusculi nomina eorum retinentur adscripta. Obsecro ut, si cui transcribere placet eandem, Patrum omnium si in hac pauperrima excerptione apposita invenerit suis opusculis similiter affigat. Nemo autem in sanctorum Patrum eloquia præsumptiose reprehendat; sed potius consideret quæ prædicta, et studiose relegat, et opere sicut Dominus dederit studiosius adimpleat. Idcirco ex innumeris divinis constitutionibus ad corrigendos vel instruendos mores humanos, tam exigua in hoc corpusculo collegi dicta, quoniam vestra pia paternitas, in parvi spatii temporis curriculo, cursu hæc jussit explere velocissimo. Necnon et maxime obstitit mihi, quod codices huic operi necessarios, ubi aliquando ad hoc opus pertinentia repperi testimonia, minime habere potui. Opto paternitatem tuam bene semper valere in Domino.'

Then follows the preface to the whole work:—

'In nomine Dei summi, Incipit prœfatio operis subsequentis. Ex diversis sanctorum Patrum opusculis et institutis, largiente Domino nostro Jesu Christo, quatuor in hujus voluminis corpusculo excerpti continentur libelli. Prior denique de vita, prædicatione, ac discretione, necnon et sollicitudine sacerdotis enarrando, brevitatis studio, percurrit. Secundus de modis pænitentiæ, levioribus delictis, ac satisfactione eorum. Tertius de mortalibus peccatis, eorumque penitudine ac satisfactione, necnon et de octo principalium viciorum origine et vexatione ac curatione eorum elocutus. Quartus de diversis peccatis ac criminibus, eorumque judiciis ac satisfactionibus, ex sacrorum canonum orthodoxorumque Patrum institutis terminatus. Quisquis igitur indocti Excerptoris hujus percurrens excerpta reppererit deflorata, dignas Domino qui hæc dedit referat gratias. Siqua vero minus caute fortasse invenerit excerpta, compassus humana fragilitate Excerptori indulgeat; et pro cunctis illius commissis apud Piissimum Æternumque Judicem assiduus piissimusque intercessor existat.'

(Then) :—' Explicit Præfatio, Incipiunt capitula libri primi.'

1. De vita sacerdotum, qualis est.
2. De doctrina et exemplis sacerdotum.
3. De exemplis pravorum sacerdotum.
4. De sacerdotibus qui verbo et exemplo subjectos destruunt.
5. De sacerdotibus qui bene docent et male vivunt.
6. Quod nulli prosit sacerdotium, etiam si bene vivat, si male viventes tacendo non contradicat.
7. Qualis debet esse discretio in prædicatione doctoris.
8. Qualis debet esse ordo atque consideratio prædicationis in ore doctoris.
9. De doctrina et eruditione sacerdotis.
10. Qualiter sacerdos aliqua mala proximi taceat ut dicat.
11. Quanta esse debet diversitas in sermone prædicatoris.
12. Quanta esse debet discretio in confessione peccatorum.
13. Qui vult confiteri peccata sua, si omnibus debet confiteri et quibuslibet, aut certis, quibusque.
14. Si oportet gesta turpia aut obscena confitentem inverecunde nunciare omnibus, aut certis quibusque, et quibus illis.
15. Ut nullus sacerdoti ac confessori suo malas cogitationes suas occultet sed mox ut ortæ fuerint confiteatur.
16. Qualem debet habere sacerdos discretionem in judicio pænitentiæ.
17. Qualis debet esse sollicitudo circa pœnitentes.
18. Pœnitentem ex corde quomodo oportet suscipi.
19. Erga eum qui pro peccatis non pœnitet quales esse debemus.

(Then) :—' Explic. cap. ; Incip. lib. i. de vita sacerdotum.'
[The several articles, of which the titles are prefixed as

APPENDIX C

above, follow. But in the Vatican MS. one sheet, viz., that containing articles 8 to 13 inclusive, is wanting.]
(Then) :—' Explic. lib. i., Incip. pfatio lib. ii.'

' Post primum namque libellum, qui de sacerdotis rectorisque omni vita et sermone, necnon et sollicitudine, est utcunque breviter ex variis sanctorum paginis excerptus, secundus hic, opitulante Domino, ex eorundem libris defloratus incipit libellus. De modis videlicet pœnitentiæ, levioribusque excessibus, ac eorum satisfactione. Coepto igitur hujus excerptionis ordine cursim breviterque, ut Auctor lucis æternæ monstrare dignabitur, reliqua prosequamur.'

(Then) :—' Explic. præfatio. Incipiunt capp.'
Then follow the titles of the fifty-five articles or chapters of the Second Book.

Down to this point the Bodleian does not follow the Vatican MS. It substitutes Egbert's Penitential, with the interpolations and additions mentioned *ante* (pp. 226-240); of which no part is in the Vatican manuscript. From this point, however, the Bodleian MS. follows throughout (with slight variations,[1] the chief of which is the omission of the Vatican lists of titles, preceding the text of the articles or chapters of each book) the text of the Vatican MS., which I proceed to describe.

First comes this Rubric[2]:—' Incipit. libellus[3] secundus, ex opusculis et insitutis Catholicorum Patrum breviter excerptus, quibus modis cuncta per Christum[4] remittantur peccata,' which is followed by this Preamble :—

' Ut enim[5] in expositione sexti psalmi Cassiodorus ait, septem modis peccata nobis dimitti posse Patres sancti dixerunt. Primo, per baptismum. Secundum,[6] per passionem martirii. Tertio, per eleemosinam. Quarto, per hoc quod remittimus peccata fratribus nostris. Quinto, cum convertit quis peccatorem ab errore viæ suæ. Sexto, per abundantiam caritatis. Septimo, per pœnitentiam. Addenda quoque ex communicatione[7] corporis et sanguinis Domini nostri Jesu Christi, cum tamen suscipitur :—inveniantur[8] et alii fortasse modi remissionum ;

---

[1] In the notes of variations (B) denotes the Bodleian text ; the Vatican text being followed throughout in the body of this Appendix.
[2] B. prefixes ' *In nomine sanctæ Trinitatis.*' [3] *liber*, B.
[4] B. has '*per Christi gratiam, humano generi.*' [5] *Etenim*, B.
[6] *Secundo*, B. [7] *est communicatio*, B. [8] *inveniuntur*, B.

congruit enim, ut numerum supplicationis nostræ indulgentia divina transcendat. Abhinc latius de eadem re ex opusculis quorundam Patrum.'¹

After this the text of the fifty-five chapters or articles of the Second Book is given (with their titles) in full; agreeing (with clerical variations of no importance) in both manuscripts.
Then the Rubric :—' Explic. lib. ii. Incipit. pfatio, lib. iii.'

'De mortalibus peccatis ac criminibus eorumque penitudine et satisfactione seu de octo principalium viciorum origine, vexatione, indiciis, oblectationibus,² remediisque, necnon et de pugna virtutum contra viciorum impugnationem, et quibus modis, cogitatione, locutione, opere,³ perpetrantur peccata, tertius hic, largiente Domino, ex edictis sanctorum Patrum defloratus,⁴ ut in prologo hujus opusculi præfati sumus, inchoat libellus. Tuis igitur meritis precibusque animatus studiosissime, Pater, et si non ut debeo tamen prout potero, Deo favente, præceptis tuis satisfacere humiliter studebo.'

Then Rubric :—' Explicit præfatio, Incip., lib. iii. capp.'
Then follow the titles ⁵ of eighty-two chapters or articles.
Then Rubric :—' Explicit cap. Incipit textus libri tertii.'
The text of the eighty-five chapters or articles (with their titles) follows; agreeing (except clerical variations) in both manuscripts.
Then Rubric :—' Explic. lib. iii. Incip. plogus libri iiii.'

'Magnopere poposcisti ac precepisti, carissime rector, ut ad corrigendos vel ⁶ instruendos tuorum mores subditorum quædam ex divinis constitutionibus breviter et succinctim excerperem capitula, ut mens in cunctis Deo familiariter dedita non per simplices et densissimas librorum fatigetur silvas, sed potius compendio breviante, divinis uno in sancto divinarum scripturarum prato circumvallata auctoritatibus, facili⁷ Deo donante, odoriferos quos cupit, etsi non omnes, saltem vel paucos possit decerpere flores. Et quia sanctæ caritati tuæ summum dilectionis et benevolentiæ obsequium debeo, ut potui, Domino miserante, juxta exiguitatem sensus mei, feci quod jussisti, et quod per te mihi imperavit qui in sancto tuo jugiter residet pectore Deus. Quartus igitur pauperrimæ Excerptionis nostræ ex sanctorum opusculis, *sicut et tres anteriores*, excerptus hic incipit libellus. Quos omnes, auctore ⁸

---

¹ B. adds : '*Item quibus modis cuncta per Christi gratiam remittantur peccata.*' ² *objectionibus*, B. ³ B. has *et* before *opere*.
⁴ *defloratis*, B. ⁵ Not in B. ⁶ *et*, B.
⁷ *facilius*, B. ⁸ *ductore*, B.

Deo, tuo sancto nomine [1] dicatos esse cupio. Iste enim [2] libellus hujus opusculi quartus [3] constat esse, studio brevitatis ut jam dictum est excerptus, de diversis peccatis ac criminibus eorumque indiciis ac satisfactionibus, ex sacrorum canonum orthodoxorumque Patrum libris vel [4] institutis.

Then Rubric :—' Explicit prologus. Incip. capp. lib. iiii.'
Then follow the titles [5] of 381 chapters or articles.
Then the text of these chapters or articles (the same, except clerical variations, in both MSS.).
Then this Postscript to the Fourth Book :—

'Ecce hæc sunt pauca ex multis sanctarum Scripturarum edictis, Deo favente, succinctim breviterque [6] excerpta. Dum enim sanctæ jussioni vestræ parere volui, præsumsi [7] ultra vires meas facere quod optime non novi. Parcat hoc, cum ceteris secus [8] commissis michi, [9] meritis precibusque vestris, Omnipotens Deus. Sed quia, ut potui, Deo donante [10] feci quod jussisti, obsecro Beatitudinem vestram facere [11] ut mercedem orationum vestrarum mihi reddere procuretis.'

---

[1] *nomini*, B. [2] *etenim*, B. [3] *quantus*, B.
[4] *et*, B. [5] Not in B. [6] B. omits *breviterque*.
[7] B. has *si* before *ultra*. [8] B. omits *secus*. [9] *mihi*, B.
[10] *donum*, B. [11] B. omits *facere*.

APPENDIX D (see p. 244)

COMPARISON of the Extracts of Canons, etc., in the Worcester Manuscript belonging to Corpus Christi College, Cambridge (No. 265 of Nasmith), with those in the Cottonian Manuscript (Nero A. 1).

Parker MS. In Library of C.C.C. Cambridge.	*Cottonian MS.* Printed in Thorpe's *Ancient Laws*, vol. ii. pp. 97-127.	*Parker MS.* In Library of C.C.C. Cambridge.	*Cottonian MS.* Printed in Thorpe's *Ancient Laws*, vol. ii. pp. 97-127.
{ 'Sacerdotal Laws.' Nos. 1-21	Nos. 1-21.		
22	(In the Introduction: '*Augustinus*,' etc.)	No. 44	No. 53
		45	56
23	49	46	—
24	—	47	—
25	29	48	57
26	34	49	58
27	—	50	59
28	37	51	61
29	40	52	63
30	44	53	64
31 } 32 }	98	54	65
		55	66
33	99	56	67
34	97	57	68
35	—	58	69
36	—	59	70
37	45	60	71
38	46	61	72
39	47	62	73
40	48	63	75
41	50	64	76
42	51	65	78
43	52	66	—

APPENDIX D

Parker MS. In Library of C.C.C. Cambridge.	Cottonian MS. Printed in Thorpe's *Ancient Laws*, vol. ii. pp. 97-127.	Parker MS. In Library of C.C.C. Cambridge.	Cottonian MS. Printed in Thorpe's *Ancient Laws*, vol. ii. pp. 97-127.
No. 67	No. —	No. 96	No. —
68	—	97	157
69	80	98	—
70	81	99	—
71	83	100	—
72	84	101	33
73	85	102	31
74	86	103	129
75	87	104	32
76	88	105	118
77	89	106	—
78	90	107	38
79	91	108	122
80	112	109	—
81	92	110	—
82	93	111	—
83	94	112	120
84	95	113	—
85	106	114	39
86	107	115	—
87	101	116	—
88	104	117	—
89	105	118	115
90	149	119	—
91	—	120	—
92	152	121	—
93	155	122	—
94	—	123	—
95	—		

APPENDIX E (see pp. 287-289)

COMPARISON of *Church-Grith* with the corresponding provisions of Canute's Laws, Ecclesiastical (C. E.), and Secular (C. S.) [The passages which differ more than verbally, or (in Canute's Laws) more than by enlargement of details, are printed in italics.]

'CHURCH-GRITH.'   CANUTE'S LAWS.

Article 1.   *C. E. Article 2.*

'Church-Grith.' Article 1.	Canute's Laws. C. E. Article 2.
This is one of the ordinances which the king of the English composed with the counsel of his witan:—That is, first, that he will that all God's churches be entitled to full 'grith,' and if ever any man henceforth so violate God's church-grith that he be a homicide within church-walls, then be that 'bot-less'; and let every one of those who are friends to God pursue him, unless it happen that he escape thence, and seek so awful a sanctuary, that the king through that grant him life against full 'bot,' both to God and to men.	Every church is by right in Christ's own 'grith' (protection), and every Christian man has great need that he show great reverence for that 'grith,' because God's 'grith' is of all griths the most excellent in merit, and the best to preserve. . . . And if ever any man henceforth so break God's 'church-grith,' that he be a homicide within church-walls, then be that 'bot-less'; and let every one of them who is a friend to God pursue him: unless it happen that he escape thence, and seek so awful a sanctuary, that the king through that grant him life against full 'bot,'[1] both to God and to men.

[1] Amends by compensation.

'CHURCH-GRITH.'

Article 2.

And that then is first; that he pay his own 'wer' to the king and to Christ, and thereby inlaw himself to 'bot'; *because a Christian king is accounted Christ's vice-gerent among Christian people, and his duty it is to avenge offence to Christ very severely.*

Article 3.

And if it then come to 'bot,' and the king allow it, then let 'bot' be made for the 'church-grith' to that church, according to the king's full 'mund-bryce;' and let purification of the minster be gotten, as is thereto befitting; and especially let intercession be fervently made with God.

Article 4.

And if else, no man being slain, 'church-grith' be broken, let 'bot' be strictly made, as the deed may be: be it through fighting, be it through robbery, be it through fornication, be it through what it may; first, let 'bot' be made for the 'grith-bryce' to the church, as the deed may be, and as the rank of the church may be.

Article 5.

All churches are not secularly entitled to equal rank, although divinely they have like consecration.

CANUTE'S LAWS.

C. E. Article 2 (continued).

And that is then first; that he pay his own 'wer'[1] to Christ and to the king; and thereby inlaw himself to 'bot.'

C. E. Article 2 (continued).

And if it then come to 'bot,' and the king allow it, then let 'bot' be made for the 'church-grith' to that church, according to the king's full 'mund-bryce,'[2] and the purification of the minster be gotten as is thereto befitting; and let 'bot' be fully made, both with 'maeg-bot' and 'man-bot';[3] and especially let intercession be fervently made with God.

C. E. Article 3.

And if else, no man being slain, 'church-grith' be broken, let 'bot' be strictly made, according as the deed may be; be it through fighting, be it through robbery, be it through what it may be. First, let 'bot' be made for the 'grith-bryce' to the church, according as the deed may be, and as the rank of the church may be.

C.E. Article 3 (continued).

All churches are not secularly entitled to a like degree of reverence, although divinely they

---

[1] The price at which a man's life was valued, according to his degree.
[2] Compensation for breach of protection.
[3] Compensations paid for homicide to kinsmen, and to the lord.

'CHURCH-GRITH.'

For the 'grith-bryce' of a chief minster, in cases entitled to 'bot,' let 'bot' be made according to the king's 'mund'; that is, with five pounds by English law; and of a minster of the middle class with a hundred and twenty shillings, that is, according to the king's 'wite'; but of a yet less, with sixty shillings; and for a field-church, with thirty shillings. *Judgment shall ever be with justice, according to the deed, and mitigation according to its degree.*

Article 6.

And respecting tithes, the king and his 'witan' have chosen and decreed, as is just, that one-third part of the tithe which belongs to the church go to the reparation of the church, and a second part to the servants of God; the third to God's poor, and to needy ones in thraldom.

Articles 7, 8.

And be it known to every Christian man that he pay to his Lord his tithe justly, always as the plough traverses the tenth field, on peril of God's mercy, and of

CANUTE'S LAWS.

have like consecration. The 'grith-bryce' of a chief minster, in cases entitled to 'bot,' is according to the king's 'mund,' that is, five pounds by English law; *and in Kent, for the 'mund-bryce,' five pounds to the king, and three to the archbishop;* and of a minster of the middle class, a hundred and twenty shillings, that is, according to the king's 'wite';[1] and of one yet less, *where there is little service, provided there be a burial-place,* sixty shillings; and of a field-church, *where is no burial-place,* thirty shillings.

[*Omitted in Canute's Laws, which restored, in C. E. Article* 11, *the law of Edgar as to manorial churches,* which 'Church-Grith' had omitted, thus:

C. E. Article 14.

'But if there be any thane who has a church on his boc-land, at which there is a burial-place, let him give the third part of his own tithe to his church. And if any one have a church at which there is no burial-place, let him do for his priest what he will from the nine parts. And let every church-scot go to the old minster, according to every free hearth.']

C. E. Article 8.

And if then any one will not pay the tithe as we have decreed, that is, the tenth acre, so as the plough traverses it; then let the king's reeve go, and the bishop's,

---

[1] Fine or mulct.

'CHURCH-GRITH.'

the full 'wite' which King Edgar decreed; that is (8), if any one will not justly pay the tithe, then let the king's reeve go, and the mass-priest of the minster, or of the 'land-rica,' and the bishop's reeve, and take forcibly the tenth part for the minster to which it is due, and assign to him the ninth part, and let the eight parts be divided into two, and let the landlord take possession of half, half the bishop; be it a king's man, be it a thane's.

Article 9.

And let every tithe of young be paid by Pentecost, on pain of the 'wite,' and of earth-fruits by the equinox, or, at all events, by All Hallows mass.

Article 10.

And let 'Rome-feoh' be paid every year by St. Peter's mass; and let him who will not pay it give in addition thirty pence, and to the king pay a hundred and twenty shillings.

Article 11.

And let church-scot be paid by Martinmas; and let him who does not pay it indemnify it with twelve-fold, and a hundred and twenty shillings to the king.

Article 12.

Plough-alms, it is fitting that they be paid, on pain of the 'wite,'

CANUTE'S LAWS.

and the 'land-rica's,'[1] and the mass-priest of the minster, and take forcibly the tenth part for the minster to which it is due, and assign to him the ninth part; and let the eight parts be divided into two, and let the landlord take possession of half, half the bishop; be it a king's man, be it a thane's.

C. E. Article 8 (*first part*).

And let God's dues be lawfully and willingly paid every year, that is . . . a tithe of young by Pentecost, and of earth-fruits by All-Hallows mass.

C. E. Article 9.

And 'Rome-feoh' by St. Peter's mass; and whoever withholds it over that day, let him pay the penny to the bishop, and thirty pence thereto, and to the king a hundred and twenty shillings.

C. E. Article 10.

And church-scot at Martinmas; and whoever withholds it over that day let him pay it to the bishop, and indemnify him eleven-fold, and to the king a hundred and twenty shillings.

C. E. Article 8.

Plough-alms at least by fifteen days after Easter.

---

[1] *Land-rica* means lord of the soil.

'CHURCH-GRITH.'	CANUTE'S LAWS.
every year, when fifteen days are passed after Easter-tide: and let light-scot be paid at Candlemass; let him do it oftener who will.	C. E. Article 12. And light-scot *thrice in the year*: first on *Easter-eve*, a half-penny worth of wax for every hide; and again on All-Hallows mass, as much; and again on the Purification of St. Mary, the like.
Article 13.	C. E. Article 13 (*first part*).
And it is most proper that soul-scot be always paid at the open grave.	And it is most proper that soul-scot be always paid at the open grave.
Article 14.	C. E. Article 14 (*first part*).
And let all God's dues be furthered diligently, as is needful.	And let all God's dues be diligently furthered, as it is needful.
Article 15.	C. S. Article 49 (*first part*).
And if any one refuse that, let him be compelled to what is right by secular correction; and let that be in common to Christ and to the king, as it formerly was.	If any one with violence refuse divine dues, let him pay 'lah-slit' among the Danes, and full 'wite' among the English, or let him clear himself; let him take eleven [parts] and he himself the twelfth.
	C. S. Article 38 (*last part*). Let divine 'bot' be earnestly and constantly sought, according as the books prescribe; and let secular 'bot' be sought according to secular laws.
Article 16.	C. E. Article 14 (*last part*).
And let festivals and fasts be rightly held, on peril of the 'wite.'	And let festivals and fasts be rightly held, and let every Sunday's festival be held from the noon of Saturday till the dawn of Monday, and every other mass-day as it is commanded.

'Church-Grith.'	Canute's Laws.
Article 17.	*C. E. Article* 15.
And let Sunday marketings be strictly forbidden, on peril of full secular 'wite.'	And Sunday marketings are also strictly forbid; and every folkmote, unless it be for great necessity; and let huntings and all other worldly works be strictly abstained from on that holy day.
Article 18.	*C. E. Article* 4 (*first and last clauses*).
And let the rank of the servants of the altar be respected for fear of God.	It is very justly incumbent on all Christian men that . . . they reverence every holy order, according to its rank. . . . Therefore, for fear of God, rank is discreetly to be acknowledged in holy orders.
Article 19.	*C. E. Article* 5.
If a mass-priest, living according to rule, be accused in a simple suit, let him celebrate mass, if he dare, and clear himself on the housel, himself alone; and in a triple suit, let him clear himself, if he dare, likewise on the housel, with two of his fellow-ecclesiastics.	And if it happen that a priest who lives according to rule be charged with an accusation and with evil practices, and he know himself innocent thereof, let him celebrate mass if he dare, and himself clear himself on the housel in a simple suit; and in a threefold suit let him also, if he dare, clear himself on the housel, with two of his fellow-ecclesiastics.
Article 20.	*C. E. Article* 5 (*continued*).
If a deacon, living according to rule, be accused in a simple suit, let him take two of his fellow ecclesiastics, and clear himself with them: and if he be accused in a triple suit, let him take six of his fellow ecclesiastics, and clear himself with them, and be himself the seventh.	If a deacon, living according to rule, be accused in a simple suit, let him take two of his fellow ecclesiastics, and with them clear himself: and if he be accused in a threefold suit, let him take six of his fellow ecclesiastics, and with them clear himself, and be himself the seventh.

'CHURCH-GRITH.'	CANUTE'S LAWS.
Article 21.	*C. E. Article 5 (continued).*
And if a secular mass-priest be charged with an accusation, who follows no life of rule, let him clear himself so as a deacon who lives a life of rule.	If a secular mass-priest be charged with an accusation, who has no regular life, let him clear himself as a deacon who lives a life of rule.
Article 22.	*C. E. Article 5 (continued).*
If a friendless servant of the altar be charged with an accusation, who has no supporters to his oath; let him go to the 'corsnæd,'[1] and then fare thereat as God will, unless he may clear himself on the housel.	And if a friendless servant of the altar be charged with an accusation, who has no support to his oath, let him go to the 'corsnæd,' and then thereat fare as God will, unless he may clear himself on the housel.
Article 23.	*C. E. Article 5 (continued).*
And if any one charge one in in holy orders with 'fæhthe,'[2] and say that he was a perpetrator or adviser of homicide, let him clear himself with his kinsmen, who must bear the 'fæhthe' with him, or make 'bot' for it.	And if a man in orders be charged with 'fæhthe,' and it be said, that he was perpetrator or adviser of homicide, let him clear himself with his kinsmen, who must bear the 'fæhthe' with him, or make 'bot' for it.
Article 24.	*C. E. Article 5 (continued).*
And if he be kinless, let him clear himself with his associates, or fast for 'corsnæd'; and thereat fare as God may ordain.	And if he be kinless, let him clear himself with his associates, or betake himself to fasting, if that be necessary, and go to the 'corsnæd,' and thereat fare as God may ordain.
Article 25.	*C. E. Article 5 (continued).*
And no minster-monk may anywhere lawfully demand 'fæhthe-bot' nor pay 'fæhthe-bot'; he forsakes his law of kin when he submits to monastic law.	And no minster-monk may lawfully anywhere demand 'fæhthe bot,' nor pay 'fæhthe-bot'; he forsakes his kin when he submits to monastic law.

---

[1] Ordeal.   [2] A deadly feud.

APPENDIX E

'CHURCH-GRITH.'	CANUTE'S LAWS.
Article 26.	*C. S. Article* 41.
If a mass-priest become a homicide, or otherwise flagrantly commit crime, let him then forfeit both his order and his country, and be an exile as far as the Pope may prescribe to him, and strictly do penance.	If a servant of the altar be a homicide, or else work iniquity very enormously; let him then forfeit both degree and country, and go in exile as far as the Pope shall prescribe to him, and earnestly do penance.
Article 27.	*C. E. Article* 5 (*continued*).
If a mass-priest stand anywhere in false witness or in perjury, or be cognisant and perpetrator of thefts; let him then be cast out from the community of ecclesiastics, and forfeit both their society and friendship, and every dignity; unless he the more deeply make 'bot' to God and men, entirely as the bishop may direct him, and find himself 'borh,'[1] that henceforth he will ever abstain from the like; and if he desire to clear himself, let him clear himself according to the degree of the deed, either with a threefold or with a simple 'lad,'[2] according as the deed may be.	And if ever a mass-priest stand anywhere in false witness or in perjury, or be cognisant of and perpetrator of thefts, then let him be cast out from the community of ecclesiastics, and forfeit both their society and friendship, and every dignity; unless he the more deeply make 'bot' to God and men, as the bishop may direct him, and find himself 'borh' that henceforth he will ever abstain from the like. And if he desire to clear himself, then let him clear himself according to the degree of the deed, either with a threefold or with a simple 'lad,' according as the deed may be.
Articles 28, 29.	*C. E. Article* 9.
If a servant of the altar, by the instruction of books, his own life rightly order, then let him be entitled to the full 'wer' and dignity of a thane, both in life and in the grave. (29) *And if he misorder his life, let his honour wane, according as the deed may be.*	We beseech and instruct all God's servants, and especially priests, that they obey God and love chastity. . . . And let him who will abstain from this (intercourse with women) and preserve his chastity, have God's mercy, and, for worldly honour, be he worthy of thane-law.

[1] Security. [2] Purgation.

'Church-Grith.'

Article 30.

Let him know, if he will, that it befits him not to have any concern either with women, *or with temporal war;* if he desire uprightly to obey God, and observe God's laws, as is properly becoming to his order.

Article 31.

And we earnestly instruct, and affectionately beseech, that men of every order live that life which is becoming to them: and we will that henceforth abbots and monks live more according to rule than before this they had in custom.

Article 32.

And the king commands all his reeves, in every place, that ye protect the abbots on all secular occasions, as ye best may; and, as ye desire to have God's or my friendship, that ye aid their stewards everywhere to right; that they themselves may the more uninterruptedly dwell closely in their minsters, and live according to rule.

Articles 33, 34.

And if any one wrong an ecclesiastic or a foreigner, through any means, as to money or as to life; or bind, or beat, or insult him in

Canute's Laws.

C. E. Article 6 (*middle part*).

And we beseech and instruct all God's servants, and especially priests, that they obey God and love chastity, and secure themselves against God's ire, and against the fierce burning which rageth in hell. Full well they know that they have not lawfully through concubinage intercourse with women.

C. E. Article 6 (*first part*).

And we will, that men of every order readily submit, each to that law which is becoming to him; and above all, let the servants of God, bishops and abbots, monks and mynchens,[1] submit to law, and live according to rule.

[*Omitted in Canute's Laws.*]

C. S. Article 40.

And if any one wrong a man in holy orders, or a foreigner, through any means, as to money or as to life, then shall the king

---

[1] Nuns.

'Church-Grith.'

any way, then shall the king be unto him in the place of a kinsman and of a protector, unless he else have another. (34) And let 'bot' be made both to him and the king, as is fitting, according as the deed may be, or let him avenge the deed very deeply.

Canute's Laws.

be unto him in the place of a kinsman and of a protector, unless he have another lord besides; and let 'bot' be made to the king as it may be fitting, or let him avenge the deed very deeply.

C. S. Article 42.

If any one bind or beat or grossly insult a man in holy orders, let him make 'bot' to him as may be right, and to the bishop, with an 'altar-bot,' according to the degree of his order; and to the lord or the king, according to the full 'mund-bryce,' or clear himself with a full 'lad.'

Article 35.

It is very justly incumbent on Christian men that they very diligently avenge any offence against God.

C. S. Article 40 (end).

It belongs very rightly to a Christian king, that he avenge God's anger very deeply, according as the deed may be.

Articles 36, 37, 38, 39.
(*See below.*)

Article 40.

And if any one will properly cleanse the land, then must he inquire and diligently trace where the criminals have their dwelling, who will not desist, nor make 'bot' before God; but wherever they may be found, let them be compelled to right, willingly or unwillingly; or let them altogether

C. S. Article 4.

And we command that ye undertake diligently to cleanse the country on every side, and everywhere to desist from evil deeds; and if witches or diviners, 'morth'-workers[1] or adulterers be anywhere found in the land, let them be diligently driven out of this country; or let them

---
[1] Assassins.

'CHURCH-GRITH.'

withdraw from the country unless they submit and turn to right.

CANUTE'S LAWS.

totally perish in the country, except they desist and the more thoroughly amend. And we command that adversaries and outlaws of God and men retire from the country, unless they submit and the more earnestly amend; and let thieves and public robbers forthwith perish unless they desist.

C. S. Article 6.

Let manslayers and perjurers, violators of holy orders and adulterers, submit and make 'bot,' or with their sins retire from the country.

C. S. Article 7.

Let cheats and liars, robbers and reavers, have God's anger, unless they desist, and the more thoroughly amend: and whoever will lawfully cleanse the country, and suppress injustice, and love righteousness, then must he diligently correct such things, and shun the like.

Article 41.

If a monk or a mass-priest become altogether an apostate, let him be for ever excommunicated, unless he the more readily submit to his duty.

[Omitted in Canute's Laws—probably as superfluous.]

Article 42.

And he who holds an outlaw of God in his power over the term that the king may have appointed, he acts, at peril of himself and all

C. S. Article 67.

If any one unlawfully have a God-'flyma,'[1] let him give him up to justice, and compensate to him to whom it is due, and pay

---

[1] A fugitive from ecclesiastical justice.

'CHURCH-GRITH.'

his property, *against Christ's vicegerent, who preserves and sways over Christianity and kingdom as long as God grants it.*

Article 43. (See below.)

Article 44.

And let us zealously venerate right Christianity, and totally despise every heathenism; and let us faithfully cherish our royal lord; and let every friend love his fellow with right fidelity, and cherish him with justice.

CANUTE'S LAWS.

to the king according to his 'wergild.'[1] If any one have and hold an excommunicated person or an outlaw, let him peril himself and all his property.

C. E. Article 19.

And let every Christian man do as is needful to him; let him strictly keep his Christianity. . . . And let every friend guide his words and works aright, and carefully keep oath and 'wed' (pledge): and let every injustice be strictly cast out of the country, as far as it can be done: and let God's law be henceforth earnestly loved by word and by works; then will God's mercy be the more ready for us all.

C. E. Article 20.

Let us also earnestly do, as we will yet teach; let us all be always faithful and true to our lord, and ever exalt his dignity with all our powers, and execute his will; because all that we ever do as just fidelity to our lord, we do it all to our own great behoof; because God verily is faithful to him who is rightly faithful to his lord. . .

C. S. Article 5.

And we earnestly forbid every heathenism, etc.

---

[1] A fine, for which the relatives or guild-brethren of an offender were answerable.

THE following five articles, which are in *Church-Grith* only, are historical and didactic.

Article 36.

And wise were those secular witan, who to the divine laws of right added secular laws, for the people's government; and directed the ' bot ' to Christ and the king, that many should thus of necessity be compelled to do right.

Article 37.

But in those ' gemots,' though deliberately held in places of note, after Edgar's lifetime, the laws of Christ waned, and the king's laws were impaired.

Article 38.

And then was separated what was before in common to Christ and the king in secular government; and it has ever been the worse before God and before the world: let it now come to an amendment, if God will it.

Article 39.

And an amendment, however, may yet come, if it be diligently and earnestly undertaken.

Article 43.

But let us do as is needful to us; let us take to us for an example that which former secular ' witan ' deliberately instituted; Aethelstan, and Edmund, and Edgar who was last; how they worshipped God, and observed God's law, and rendered Christ's tribute, the while that they lived. And let us love God with inward heart, and heed God's laws, as well as we best can.

APPENDIX F (see pp. 235, 269)

LETTER of Pope Leo IX. to King Edward the Confessor, urging the removal of the see of Crediton, and its bishop, Leofric, to Exeter: written on the last page of the 'Penitential' manuscript volume, presented by Bishop Leofric to the Church of Exeter, and now in the Bodleian Library (No. 718):

Leo episcopus, servus servorum Dei, Eadwardo Anglorum Regi, salutem carissimam, cum benedictione Apostolica. Si bene habes, et bene vales, inde non modicas Domino Jesu Christo referimus gratias; et hoc optamus, ut ita luculenter possideas regni gubernacula, ut in æterna maneas tabernacula. Et quia audivimus te circa Dei æcclesias et æcclesiasticos viros studiosum et religiosum esse, inde multum gaudemus, et hoc ammonemus, atque benigne rogamus, ut ita in Dei opere perseverare studeas, quatinus Regi regum Deo placere valeas, atque cum Illo in caelesti regno permaneas.

Notum itaque est nostræ pietati, qualiter Leowricus Episcopus sine Civitate sedem pontificalem tenet; unde multum miramur, non de illo solo, sed de omnibus illis Episcopis qui talia agunt. Cum vero ad vos nostrum miserimus Legatum, de aliis dicemus. Nunc hoc de nostro fratre jam dicto Leowrico præcipimus atque rogamus; ut propter Deum, et nostri amoris causa, adjutorium praebeas, ut a Credionensi villula ad civitatem Exonia (? Exoniæ) sedem Episcopalem possit mutare. Hæc et alia bona opera ita agere studeas, ut a Christo Domino æternum regnum adquirere valeas.

Vale Karissime semper in Domino.

APPENDIX G (see pp. 264-269)

CLAUSES in the Exeter Rule of Life for Canons, which relate to meals and the dormitory. (From the manuscript in the Library of Corpus Christi College, Cambridge: Nasmith's No. 191.)

Article 5. De eo quod in congregatione canonica equaliter cibus et potus accipiatur.

Solet in plerisque canonicorum congregationibus inrationabiliter atque indiscrete fieri, ut non nulli clerici qui divitiis affluant aut parvum aut nihil utilitatis ecclesie conferant, majorem ceteris divinum strenue peragentibus officium annonam accipiant; cum hoc ita fieri debere nunquam in auctoritate scripturarum, nec in traditionibus sanctorum patrum, possit inveniri. Est nempe rationabile, justumque coram Deo et hominibus, ut in unaquaque canonica congregatione, a minimo usque ad maximum, cibum et potum æqualiter accipiant. Hi videlicet, qui propter aliquam utilitatem in numero canonicorum fuerint admissi, quanquam enim plerique subditorum a prælatis rebus quibuslibet aliis plus ceteris merito solent honorari, in hac tamen societate, reclusa personarum acceptione, una (? usus) debet cibi et potus equalis esse.

Article 6. De mensura cibi et potus.

Quando clerus una aut bina vice in die reficit, accipiat a minore usque ad maximum iiii libras panis; et quando bis in die reficit, pulmentum vero ad sextam, unam ministrationem de carne inter duos, et cibaria alia, una accipiant; et, si cibaria non habent, tunc duas ministrationes de carne habeant. Illo tempore quando quadragesimalem vitam debent ducere, tunc ad sextam inter duos clericos portionem de formatico, et cibaria alia, accipiant. Et si pisces habuerint aut legumen aut aliud aliquid, addatur et tertium; et ad cenam cibaria alia inter duos, et portionem de formatico accipiant; et si Deus amplius dederit, cum gratiarum actione accipiant. Quando autem in die una refectio fuerit, tunc cibaria una inter duos, et portionem de formatico et ministrationem de legumine aut aliud pulmentum accipiant. Et si contigerit quod illo anno glandes vel fagina non sint, et non habent unde hanc mensuram de carne impleant, prevideat Episcopus, vel qui sub eo est, juxta quod Deus possibilitatem dederit, aut de quadragesimali alimento, aut alio, unde consolationem habeant. Et si eadem regio vinifera fuerit, accipiant per singulos dies quinque libras vini, si tamen sterilitas impedimentum non fecerit temporis. Si vero vinifera plena non fuerit, tres libras vini, et tres cervise, et caveant ebrietatem. Si vero contigerit quod vinum minus fuerit, et istam mensuram Episcopus, vel qui sub eo est, implere non potest, juxta quod prevalet impleat de cervisa, et eis consolationem faciat ; et illis qui se a vino abstinent prævideat Episcopus, vel qui sub eo est, ut tantum habeant de cervisa quantum de vino habere debuerant. Quando vero facultas ecclesie non supetit, aut sterilitas terre extiterit, sicut crebro, peccatis nostris prepedientibus, evenire solet, et prelati quantum debent dare vinum aut siceram seu cervisam canonicis nequiverint, provideant eis potum ex diversis materiis confectum ; non ei autem murmurent, sed magis cum gratiarum actione quod dari sibi potest accipiant, animadvertentes Johannem Baptistam, qui nec vinum, nec siceram, nec aliquid quod potest inebriare bibit ; quia ubi ebrietas fit, ibi flagitium atque peccatum est. Et hoc admonemus, ut clerus sobriam semper ducat vitam ; et, quia persuadere non possumus ut vinum non bibant, vel consentiamus hoc, ut saltem in illis ebrietas non dominetur ; quia omnes ebriosos Apostolus a regno Dei extraneos esse denuntiat, nisi per dignam pænitentiam emendaverint. Habeant igitur canonici ortos olerum, ut cum ceteris additamentis aliquod pulmentum cotidie sibi vicissim ministrent.

Article 7. De sephalanaxiis coquini.

Clerici canonici sic sibi invicem serviant, ut nullus excussetur a coquine officio, nisi egritudine aut causa gravis utilitatis quis preoccupatus fuerit ; quia exinde major merces et caritas adquiritur, imbecillibus autem fratribus procurrentur solacia, ut non cum tristitia hoc faciant, sed habeant solacia omnes secundum modum congregationis aut positionem loci. Archidiaconus, aut prepositus, vel cellerarius, et qui in majoribus utilitatibus occupati sunt, isti excusentur a coquina ; ceteri autem sub caritate invicem serviant. Egressurus de septimana sabbato munditias vasorum faciat, et vasa ministerii sui que ad ministrandum accepit sana et munda cellerario reconsignet ; et si aliquid ex illis minuatum fuerit, ad capitulum die sabbato veniam petat, et vasa vel quod minuatum est in loco restituat.

Article 11. *De eo quod diligenter munienda sunt claustra canonicorum in quibus dormiunt canonici.*

Prepositorum cura sit, ut subditorum mentes sacrarum scripturarum lectionibus assidue muniant, ne lupus invisibilis aditum inveniat, quo ovile Domini ingredi et aliquam ovium subripere valeat. Et præterea necesse est, ut claustra que clero sibi commisso canonice servandum est firmis undique circumdent munitionibus, ut nulli omnino intrandi aut exeundi nisi per portam pateat aditus. Sint etiam interius dormitoria, refectoria, cellaria, et cetere habitationes usibus fratrum in una societate viventium necessaria. Omnes enim in uno dormiant dormitorio, præter illos quibus Episcopus licentiam dederit secundum quod ei rationabiliter visum fuerit. Et in ipsis claustris per dispositas mansiones dormiant separatim per singulos singuli lectulos, mixti cum senioribus propter prudentiam bonam ; ut seniores provideant quod juniores secundum Deum agant ; et in ipsa claustra nulla femina introeat, nec laicus homo, præter tantum, si Episcopus aut archidiaconus vel præpositus jusserint ut in refectorio pro refectionis causa veniant, relictis armis suis ante refectorium. Et, si necesse fuerit ad opera facienda, intrent ibi laici homines ; ut, ubi perfectum habuerint opus suum, cum summa festinatione egrediantur foras. Et si coci clerici desunt, et opus fuerit ut laici coci ad coquinandum tantum ingrediantur, ut expleto ministerio suo cum celeritate exeant foras.

APPENDIX H (see pp. 313-316).

CONSECRATION Charters of Churches, endowed by their Founders at the time of consecration with tithes.

1. *Cadillac in France:* (from 'Forms of Marculfus,' Baluze, Capitularia Regum Francorum; vol. ii. p. 442.)

'Regnante Domino Jesu Christo in perpetuum; Ego ille Episcopus: Omnibus non habetur incognitum, qualiter ego, ampliante Domino, in pago in villa cujus vocabulo est ibi Sancti . . . atque Sancti Stephani, vel in honore ceterorum sanctorum quorum ibidem reliquiæ quiescunt, construxi, atque Kalendas Junii dedicare certavi, consentientibus etiam confratribus, tam canonicis quam et monachis, vel ceteris hominibus qui ad præsentes fuerunt, ut villæ quarum vocabula sunt Cadiliaco, etc. etc. etc., ut ibidem aspicere deberent, ad missas veniendi et ad baptismum vel prædicationem, *et ut decimas suas ad memoratam basilicam dare deberent.* Propterea, pro firmitatis studium hanc consensionem scribere rogavimus, ut temporibus nostris atque successoribus nostris hæc nostra consensio firma et stabilis valeat permanere, et sciant omnes, tam præsentes quam et absentes, seu successores nostri, quia dedimus in memoratum illum Cadiliaco duos mansos ad ipsam luminariam providendam, vel unde presbyter qui ibidem officium fungere videtur vivere debeat. Et addimus ad hoc insuper de terra arabile . . ., et de vinea aripenne uno et dimidio, ut ævo tempore in elimosinam nostram seu successorum nostrorum ita valeat perdurare. Actum fuit hoc ab die memorato KL. Junii, in anno VIII Christo propitio Imperii Domni Karoli Serenissimi Augusti, et anno [xliii] regni ejus in Francia, atque xxxv in Italia, Indictione prima; in Dei nomine feliciter: Amen. His præsentibus qui adfuerunt illuc his præsentibus.'

2. *Exhall, in Warwickshire* (from Dugdale's *History of Warwickshire,* 1656; p. 630).

'Universis etc. Simon, Dei Gratia Wigorniensis Ecclesiæ minister humilis, in Domino salutem. Confirmo præsenti pagina donationem quam probi homines de Eccleshala donaverunt ecclesiæ prædicti manerii, in die qua eam dedicavi. Sciendum est autem, quod Robertus Corbusceon et ejus uxor donaverunt eidem ecclesiæ in perpetuum unam virgatam terræ, cum prato ad tantum terræ pertinente, et totam suam partem ejusdem crofti, exceptis duabus acris, quas Wido erga eum excambiavit ad opus ejusdem ecclesiæ, et cum moro sub crofto. Wido vero ex sua parte quatuor acras in campo, et dimidium in prato; et Robertus similiter duas acras. Hanc donationem similiter omnes fecerunt, *cum decimis suis plenariis*, eidem ecclesiæ, liberam et quietam ab omni seculari servitio. Et ego ex mea parte volo et præcipio, ut libera sit et quieta ab omni Episcopali consuetudine. Qui autem aliquid inde subtraxerit, sive minuere vel perturbare præsumpserit, anathematis gladio feriatur. Testibus, Gervasio Archidiacono, Radulpho Priore de Stanes, Pagano Capellano, etc.'

3, *Hay, in Brecknockshire* (from Kennett's *Case of Impropriations*, 1704; Appendix 3, p. 4).

' Bernardus, Dei gratia Episcopus de Sancto David, omnibus sanctæ Dei Ecclesiæ fidelibus salutem, Deique benedictionem et suam. Sciant tam presentes quam futuri, quod quando dedicavimus ecclesiam beatæ Mariæ de Haya, Willielmus Revel, concessu Bernardi de Novo Mercato qui interfuit dedicationi, dedit et concessit in perpetuam elemosinam et dotem ipsius ecclesiæ xv acras terræ, et duas mansuras terræ, videlicet, Lavenochi prepositi et Alverici bubulci, et totam illam terram quæ est ab illis mansuris sursum in nemore usque ad divisas de Ewias, et in bosco et in plano; *dedit etiam eidem ecclesiæ totam decimam totius terræ suæ de Haia, in omnibus rebus, et de terra Ivonis et de Meleniauc, et de omnibus istis qui de feudo Haiæ tenebant. Et ne in posterum inde fiat dubitatio, has determinate dedit et concessit decimas; videlicet, de blado et foeno, et de pullanis et vitulis, de agnis et porcellis, de lana et caseo, et virgulto, et de reditu Walensium, et pasnagio, et placitis.* Quicunque vero aliquid inde subtraxerint vel diminuerint, excommunicentur, et a consortio Dei omniumque Sanctorum ejus sequestrentur, donee ad emendationem veniant. Hujus autem donationis testes sunt clerici nostri; videlicet, Willelmus archidiaconus de Kermerdin, et Elias Archidiaconus de Brechon, et Brientius clericus Regis Henrici, et Bernardus de Novo Mercato, et Ricardus Filius Puncii, Valete.

[*Ex Cartulario Prioratus S. Johannis Evang. de Brechon.* MS. f. 47.]

APPENDIX I (see p. 316)

ANCIENT GRANTS OF, OR COMPOSITIONS AS TO, TITHES

1. A.D. 1100. [Between the new parish church of Chale, on its consecration, and the old parish church of Carisbrook, in the Isle of Wight.—From *Archæological Journal*, vol. i. p. 392 : London, 1845.]

Carta Willielmi Wint. Episcopi de Ecclesia de Chale. Anno ab incarnatione Domini MC. xiiii. Kal. Decembr. facta est Conventio in Insula Vecta inter Ecclesiam Sanctae Mariae de Caresbroc et Almetum eiusdem Ecclesiae presbiterum, et ecclesiam S. Andreae de Chale et Hugonem Gernun qui eandem Ecclesiam fundavit, in presentia Willielmi Giffard Wintoniensis, qui eadem die praedictam Ecclesiam de Chale dedicavit; apud quam dedicationem exclamata et confirmata est haec Conventio multorum testimonio. Almetus presbiter calumpniabatur quod Ecclesia de Chale erat de parochia Ecclesiæ Sanctae Mariae de Caresbroc, et Hugo Gernun dicebat quod homines de feodo suo non erant de Ecclesia de Caresbroc vel alibi attitulati, set vivi potuerant ire antiqua consuetudine ad quam vellent Ecclesiam, et mortuorum corpora ubicunque vellent sepelire. Hoc dicebat eos potuisse et fecisse. Almetus autem hoc negabat, et per considerationem calumpniae suae probationem offerebat. Sed ne dampnum super utramlibet Ecclesiam verteretur et ut pax et amor inter eos et ipsorum amicos confirmaretur, per considerationem communium amicorum et per concessionem et confirmationem Episcopi facta est haec Concordia. Hug. Gernon concessit Ecclesiae S. M. de Caresbroc totam medictatem terrae et decimarum et sepulturae et oblationum, eccepta propria domo sua, quas miserunt vel mittent ad Ecclesiam de Chale sive homines in ipsius Hugonis feodo manentes, sive quicunque alii. Et ad servicium et sustentationem et defensionem et reparationem Ecclesiae remanet sine participatione terra qua Hugo dotavit Ecclesiam et decima propriarum carucarum, et ut supradictum est oblationes propriae domus. Et presbiter de Chale faciet totum servicium Ecclesiae in vivis et defunctis, in libris et vestimentis, in defensione et reparatione, eciam si funditus corruerit. Et hoc totum faciet sine auxilio et erogatione presbiteri de Caresbroc. Et per hanc Concordiam concessit Almetus presbiter fieri atrium apud Ecclesiam de Chale. Hanc Conventionem Episcopus sigilli sui testimonio approbavit, et sub perpetuo Anathemate confirmavit ut quicunque hanc Conventionem scienter violaverit anathema sit. Testibus hiis Richerio Capellano Episcopi et decano, Stephano clerico, Rogero de Melafold, Radulfo Mansello.

2. Translation of a composition, dated A.D. 1181, in the Register of Llanthony Abbey, between the Prior of Llanthony, claiming in right of the parish church of Hasfield in Gloucestershire (appropriated to his Abbey), and Roger Fitz-Alan, on behalf of the chapel of Harescombe in the same county.

Be it known, that the contention which had sprung up between Roger Prior of Lanthony and Roger Fitz-Alan concerning the Chapel of Hassefeld which appertains to the Mother Church of Hassefeld, has been settled in the manner following :—The Church of Hassefeld is to receive in full everything which appertains to parochial rights in the vill of Harsecumbe, *i.e.* all tithes, as well of the Curia as of the Villeins, Oblations, Baptisms, Confessions, and Devises of the dying, with Burials, and in fact all things pertaining to parochial rights, so that of all these let the Chaplain of the said Chapel usurp nothing. The said Chaplain shall be sustained by those things which Alan Fitzmayer granted him at the constitution of the said Chapel, *i.e.* the second tithing of the wheat of his demesne of Harsecumbe; the first, together with all the lesser tythes, pertaining to the Mother Church of Hassefeld. The said Alan also granted for the sustentation of the Chaplain ten acres of land (saving the Tythe of the same to the Mother Church). He also gave to the Mother Church of Hassefeld one acre of land for a Cemetery; which things Roger his son confirmed and ratified.

But the Prior and Canons, at the petition of Roger Fitz-Alan, have granted to the said Chaplain the tythes of five virgates of land which the villeins of Brockthrop hold (the tythe of which pertains to the Church of St. Owen), and the small tythes of the said villeins, with their burial, to be held of them [*i.e.* the Prior and Canons] by the yearly payment of five shillings at the Feast of St. Michael. All the tythes of the demesne of Brockthrop, as from the time of Walter the Constable, as also now, pertain to the Church of St. Owen.

The Canons have also granted that if the wife of the said Roger, or any other free woman in his house, bring forth children, they may go whither they will for their Purification, and that the said Roger and his wife and the free men of his house at their departing (*fine suo*) may transfer their bodies to whatsoever church they will; but if they decease without desire, let them remain for their burial to their mother church. The tythes of one mill the Canons have also granted for the sustentation of the Chaplain of the said Chapel. They have also granted to the said Roger and his heirs that, on the decease of the said Chaplain of the said Chapel, they themselves shall present a Chaplain to the said Canons, whom (if he shall appear to them to be meet for the Ministry) they shall cause to be instituted to the said Chapel by the Bishop or by his official, the usual chaplain's oath being first taken for the faithful observance of all the ordinances [of the said Chapel] in our Chapter House.

All these things were settled in the year of our Lord MCLXXXI, in the presence of the Illustrious Lady and Patroness of the Church of Lanthony, Margaret de Bohun [Countess of Hereford], and of William Fitz-Stephen, then Sheriff of Gloucester, whose seals are affixed to this present writing in two portions for a perpetual testimony, so that either being possessed of a writing duly sealed with their seals, this agreement and concord may perpetually exist.

3. A.D. 1239. [Between Almeric de Soleham and William, Rector of Chinnor.—From a copy on parchment, written in the early part of the fourteenth century, and now preserved among the muniments of Magdalen College, Oxford.[1]]

Notum sit omnibus ad quos præsens scriptum pervenerit, quod ita convenit inter Aumaricum de Soleham et Willelmum Rectorem ecclesiae de Chynnore, videlicet quod dictus Aumericus concessit quantum in eo est pro se et heredibus suis imperpetuum matrice ecclesie de Chynnore omnes decimas tam majores quam minores provenientes de dominicis suis in Hentone, Habendas et possidendas eidem ecclesie integre et pacifice, et dictus Willelmus quantum in eo est concessit dicto Aumarico de Soleham, quod habeat cum sibi placuerit capellanum sumptibus suis in dicta capella ministrantem ei divina, Ita quidem quod dictus capellanus qui in ea celebrabit omnes oblaciones pro persona dicti militis et libere familie sue et hospitum suorum in dicta capella factas habebit. Dictus vero Aumaricus ad sustentationem cantarie in dicta capella habebit terram ad eandem capellam pertinentem, salvis inde decimis matrice ecclesie. De non vero libere familie et cottariis et aliis servis dicti militis percipiet dicta matrix ecclesia oblaciones decimas et omnes

---

[1] For this transcript I am indebted to the Rev. W. D. Macray, Rector of Ducklington, Oxon, in whose *Notes from the Muniments of St. Mary Magdalen College* (Oxford, 1882) the agreement is mentioned, p. 135.

obvenciones, et venient ad matricem ecclesiam audituri divina et recepturi ibidem sacramenta ecclesiastica. Capellanus vero qui in dicta capella celebrabit prestabit fidelitatem Rectori dicte matricis ecclesie antequam celebret in ea divina quod non admittet aliquem parochienorum matricis ecclesie ad sacramenta ecclesiastica, et quod non recipiet aliquid vel faciet unde dampnum vel prejudicium dicte matrici ecclesie generetur. Hanc autem convencionem fideliter observand. juravit dictus Aumaricus desuper sacrament. pro se et heredibus suis, et dictus Willelmus similiter quantum in eo est pro se fideliter observand. imperpetuum. In cujus rei testimonium dictus Aumaricus sigillum suum parti istius cirographi apposuit residenti penes dictam matricem ecclesiam. Et dictus Willelmus sigillum suum apposuit parti hujus cirographi residenti penes Aumaricum. Et Magister Rogerus de Wescham,[1] archidiaconus Oxon, ad instantiam eorum sigillum suum utrique parti ejusdem cirographi fecit apponi. Actum anno gratia M°CC°. tricesimo IX°. Mense Februarii, in vigilia sancti Mathei Apostoli.

4. A.D. 1242. [Endowment of a Canonry in Salisbury Cathedral by Bartholomew Turberville.—Confirmed by the Bishop, 16th August 1242.[2]]

Noverit universitas vestra me, divino intuitu, dedisse et concessisse Deo et beatae Mariae, et domino Roberto de Lexinton, canonico Sarum de Cerminstre et de Bere, ac successoribus suis, omnes decimas majores et minores, quocunque nomine censentur, de toto dominico meo de Vinterburne et Turberville, plenarie integre et pacifice in perpetuum possidendas, *quas semper antea predecessores mei cui volebant pro voluntate sua contulerunt.*

Of the four preceding documents, it will be observed that Nos. 1 and 4 had Episcopal confirmation—the other two, so far as appears, had not. It will also be observed that Nos. 3 and 4 were later, by more than half a century, than the Third Council of Lateran; showing (as is rendered emphatic by the words at the end of No. 4, which I have printed in italics) that in other parts of England, as well as the archdiocese of Canterbury, the custom reproved by Pope Innocent

[1] Roger de Weseham became Bishop of Coventry and Lichfield, A.D. 1245.
[2] I am indebted also to the Rev. W. D. Macray for this extract from Register C of the Dean and Chapter of Salisbury, in which it is numbered 328, p. 230.

III., in his letter of A.D. 1200 to Archbishop Walter of Canterbury,[1] continued for some years after that Council.

I add a fifth document (without date), for which I am also indebted to the Rev. W. D. Macray, although it is a grant (like those collected by Selden) to a religious house, because of the solemnities which accompanied it, in the church of the parish within which the tithes granted arose.

5. [From the Rawlinson MSS. in the Bodleian Library.— B. 102, Collections of John Gwillim the herald, fol. 21.]

Notum sit omnibus hominibus, tam laicis quam clericis, quod in die dominica Quadragesimae Wiscardus Laident, cum uxore sua Berta et filiis suis, super altare S. Mariae Virginis ecclesiae Kanefend coram omnibus parochianis illius ecclesiae, decimam suam et elemosinam ibi dedisse et concessisse Deo et Beatae Mariae et Sancto Pancratio et monachis de Leves. . . . Et qui istam decimam praesumperit male extra ecclesiam S. Mariae Kanefend (*sic*) cum Belzebub principe demoniorum novissimum locam in inferno teneat. Amen. Fiat.

---

[1] See *Defence of Church of England against Disestablishment* (4th ed.), p. 144.

APPENDIX J (see p. 308)

BISHOP KENNETT AND SELDEN

AMONG other notices of donations of tithes to religious houses by laymen, Mr. Selden mentioned one, on which, if he had known all the facts, he might have laid more stress than he did, for it was notably to his purpose; the case of certain tithes in Oxfordshire and elsewhere, which, having originally formed part of the endowment of the Church of St. George in the Castle at Oxford, afterwards became vested, together with that church itself, in Oseney Abbey. Dean Comber and Bishop Kennett attacked Selden as having misrepresented that case; of which, before quoting their comments on it, I will shortly state the material facts, as they are related in Bishop Kennett's own 'Parochial Antiquities.'

The Collegiate Church of St. George in the Castle of Oxford was built, with the castle, by one of William the Conqueror's followers, Robert de Oily, in 1073, and the founder then established in it a body of secular canons, and, with the consent of his wife and brothers, granted for its endowment two parts of the tithe of his demesne in eight places, and the whole tithes of three other places in Oxfordshire. In the extract from the original grant [1] preserved in the Oseney Register (in the archives of Christ Church, Oxford) tithes are mentioned; and the particular places within which those tithes arose are known from later charters of confirmation by Robert de Oily's heirs. Of Episcopal, or other Ecclesiastical, confirmation of that grant there is no trace till A.D. 1149, in King Stephen's

[1] Kennett's *Parochial Antiquities*, vol. i. p. 81 (Oxford, ed. 1818) *sub anno* 1073.

reign, when the church or chapel of St. George (which had in the meantime been made a parish church, and afterwards lost that character) was, with its tithes and all other endowments, given to Oseney Abbey by another Robert de Oily, the founder's nephew and heir, with the consent of Theobald Archbishop of Canterbury and Robert [de Chesney] Bishop of Lincoln.[1]

Dean Comber[2] accused Selden of 'basely concealing old testimonies of the Bishop's consent to and confirmation of the founder's grant.' Bishop Kennett took pains to show that the Dean was not himself acquainted with the ancient records on the subject, of which he states the effect, as I have done; not alleging that there was evidence of any consent or confirmation by any bishop earlier than A.D. 1149. But he adds, that if Dean Comber had been better acquainted with the facts, 'he would have drawn better conclusions, and more effectually exposed the partiality and falseness of Mr. Selden in that tract which least deserves his name.'[3] The only error, however, with which Kennett reproaches Selden is one into which Selden did *not* fall. Dr. Comber, he says, would have found that the charter of Robert de Oily the younger to Oseney Abbey of A.D. 1149 'conveyed no new charity of his own, but only confirmed the antecedent donations of his uncle Robert de Oily, senior; who, after he had built the castle of Oxford, placed secular canons in the church of St. George's, and endowed them with the several tithes here again recited.' He continued:—

'So as the application of this story by Mr. Selden stands wholly on a false bottom; he supposes this an original grant by Robert de Oily, junior, when it was really made by a predecessor. This fundamental error the Doctor [Comber] would have more gladly discovered, because he had observed the same disingenuous shuffling in other cases, and had charged Mr. Selden for often citing later confirmations of the lay granter's heirs as if they were original grants. He gives other instances of it, to which he might justly have added this.'

Kennett concludes:[4]—'How strangely would Mr. Selden impose upon his readers, to advance an odd notion, prejudi-

---
[1] Kennett, *Par. Antiq.*, vol. i. p. 141, *sub anno* 1149.
[2] *Hist. Vindication of the Divine Right of Tithes* (1682), p. 209.
[3] Kennett (*ubi supra*, A.D. 1149).   [4] *Ibid.*, p. 147.

cial to the church, and only serviceable to sacrilege and atheism, namely, that parochial tithes were of old purely arbitrary, and left to the absolute pleasure of the lay patron; and, citing but one testimony relating to this county [Oxfordshire], should represent it palpably false, when he consulted the original records, and must needs have failed in his eyes or in his conscience.'

It is not very wonderful that a writer who could thus talk of 'partiality and falseness,' 'disingenuous shuffling,' 'sacrilege,' and 'atheism,' should have found in Selden what Selden did not say, and missed what he did. Selden did *not* represent the Charter of Robert de Oily the younger to Oseney Abbey as the original grant of the tithes in question; nor did he overlook the earlier title to them of the Church of St. George in the Castle. He expressly said in the place referred to,[1] that Oseney Abbey enjoyed those tithes 'through their having St. George's Church in the castle, by d'Oily's gift,' and asked, 'Which way is it likely, that *the Church of St. George* came to two parts of the tithes of so many manors if not -by consecration of the owners?' The 'fundamental error,' therefore, was really Kennett's, not Selden's. Kennett's own account[2] of the endowment of the Church of St. George by d'Oily the elder shows that the fact was exactly as Selden supposed: that those tithes of manors *did* come to the Church of St. George 'by consecration of the owners;' without (so far as appears) Episcopal authority or confirmation, either at the time of the endowment, or at any time afterwards before the appropriation of that church to Oseney Abbey in A.D. 1149.

This is a specimen of the way in which Selden's arguments and facts were dealt with by the champions of Divine Right in the seventeenth and eighteenth centuries. Of these champions Kennett was perhaps the most learned; but his learning, so far as relates to the history of tithes in this country, was much over-estimated by the respectable modern writers who have treated him as an authority upon the subject, particularly Southey, and the late Dr. Brewer.[3] He confounded Continen-

[1] *History of Tithes* (1618), p. 307.
[2] *Parochial Antiquities*, (ed. 1818), vol. i. p. 81.
[3] Brewer's *Endowments*, etc., of the Church of England (1885), pp. 77, 94, 108, 110, 120, 123, etc., etc.

tal with English laws and customs; he believed [1] the Cottonian 'Excerptions' to be Archbishop Egbert's work; he mistook [2] the Pastoral Injunctions of Theodulph Bishop of Orleans for Saxon canons; he represented [3] the quadripartite division of church-revenues as 'prescribed by Pope Gregory to his missionary, Augustin Archbishop of Canterbury,' and the tripartite division of tithes, 'one part to the reparation of churches, one for distributing to the poor, a third to the ministers of God who have care of the Church,' as '*at last settled by a law of King Alfred*,' for which he refers, in a note, to '*Leges Alfredi, num.* 24.' [4] This last error, confounding Alfred's laws with the (so-called) 'canons of Aelfric the Grammarian,[5] must have been borrowed, without verifying the reference, from Sir Simon Degge's 'Parson's Counsellor.' [6] It was peculiar, so far as I know, to Degge and Kennett.

[1] Kennett's *Case of Impropriations*, p. 10, *note*.
[2] *Ibid.*, p. 12. (*Ante*, pp. 299, 300.)
[3] *Parochial Antiquities* (ed. 1818), vol. i. p. 107. (See *ante*, p. 103, 104.) [4] *Ibid.*, vol. i. p. 108.   [5] See *ante*, p. 260.
[6] *Parson's Counsellor* (7th ed. 1820) p. 80. (See *Defence against Disestablishment*, 4th ed., pp. 153, 154.)

SUPPLEMENT

REMARKS UPON A RECENT 'HISTORY OF TITHES'[1]

AFTER the proofs of this edition had received my final corrections, and had gone to press, a work appeared under the title of *A History of Tithes*, by the Rev. Henry J. Clarke, who had previously (in 1887) published another book on the same subject, entitled *The History of Tithes from Abraham to Queen Victoria*. He was good enough to direct my attention to it, and to inform me that I should find myself and my writings frequently referred to in it, and some of the positions which I had taken up controverted. I read it, I hope, with an open mind; but found in it nothing which, if seen earlier, would have led me to do more than alter a few words in one or two pages, as I have now done.[2] Fortunately, it was not too late for me to add, by way of Supplement, some remarks upon those among the points of difference between the Author and myself which seemed to call for notice. In these remarks I shall speak of Mr. Clarke as 'the Author,' and of his latest work as the new 'History.'

In the preface to the former as well as this edition of *Ancient Facts and Fictions*, I have stated my opinion, that the questions of which I have treated in that work have not any real bearing upon controversies of the present day, though they are sometimes represented as if they had. I endeavoured

---

[1] In the notes to this *Supplement*, C stands for Mr. Clarke's new *History*: C 1887 for his former *History*; and AF for *Ancient Facts and Fictions*.

[2] See *post*, pp. 382, 383, 385-388.

to examine them critically (thinking that this had not been already done in a satisfactory manner), without any other controversial intention. In that respect, I may perhaps have had some advantage over the Author of the new History; whose motive for writing it, and his former work, of which this is an enlargement with variations, seems to have been an ardent zeal against all church endowments, particularly tithes. Of the tone and spirit of his work I will only say, that it is not that of historical criticism.

§ 1. *Modern writers as to the division of tithes.*

He has cited and adopted, from Professor Freeman, some words 'as to modern writers on the subject of the division of tithes,' in which 'the opinion of mere lawyers, Blackstone or any other,' upon historical questions, is spoken of as 'worse than useless.'[1] I am of much the same way of thinking, if Professor Freeman's meaning is what I suppose it to be; and I should extend the observation to others, even historians, when they do no more than repeat the statements of writers of no authority, on points which they have not themselves investigated. But lawyers, upon historical subjects which they have investigated, are perhaps not less qualified than other men to discern the false from the true;—Selden, for example, whom the Author of the new History estimates as highly as I do. Nor is the authority of lawyers within their own province restricted to the law in force in their own time. They can know little of that, if they do not know a good deal also about the law of their own country from the time (going back in England to the Norman Conquest) since which there has been no disturbance of its continuity by the introduction of any foreign element. They are better judges of such matters than an author who does not seem to know the legal import of the words '*in liberam eleemosynam*'[2] (the Latin equivalent of '*in frank-almoigne*'), in charters and grants of land to ecclesiastics; or than the mendicant friars or Wycliffe,[3] if, instead of denouncing (as they did) a state of law and practice as to

---

[1] C, p. 25. [2] *Ibid.*, pp. 174-176. [3] *Ibid.*, p. 175.

church-endowments of which they disapproved, they had taken upon themselves (which as far as I know they did not) the office of expositors of the law of England.

I cannot but wonder, (considering his agreement with Professor Freeman as to lawyers, and his severity against the clergy, both of his own and of former times), at the way in which the Author impresses into his service the statements, when they suit his purpose, of all sorts of 'modern writers on the subject of the division of tithes,'—lawyers or not lawyers; Blackstone,[1] Degge,[2] Prideaux,[3] Kennett,[4] even Henry Wharton,[5] and many more. And, what is singular, he acknowledges his own opinion as to some documents, on a particular view of which he relied in his first History (published only four years ago), to have since undergone a change; yet disallows with warmth the right of Bishop Stubbs and Professor Freeman to be heard, when they seem to modify, in a direction opposed to his own, statements made by them in works of large scope, upon topics a very close investigation of which may perhaps not have been necessary for the purposes of those works. He calls letters of those eminent scholars, written for publication and published with their authority, 'private';[6] and says:

'Dr. Stubbs cannot go behind what he states in his published history. . . . Bishop Stubbs and Mr. Freeman must be kept strictly to what they have published in their well-known histories until they publicly repudiate what they have written. Private letters which contradict historical statements must be ignored.'[7] And of Professor Freeman: 'Contradictory statements, coupled with an immense display of pedantry and egotism, characterise the recent writings of this author.'[8]

It is not for me to vindicate Professor Freeman or Bishop Stubbs. I have sometimes found reason to differ from them, notwithstanding their great learning; and, though I have a high and well-founded respect for them both, I have not relied for my conclusions, as to any disputable question, upon their or any other modern writer's authority. But why, upon this particular subject of the division of tithes, they should not

[1] C, p. 18. [2] *Ibid.*, pp. 128, 129. [3] *Ibid.*, p. 72.
[4] *Ibid.*, pp. 24, 85. [5] *Ibid.*, p. 18 (see *post*, p. 368).
[6] *Ibid.*, pp. 98, 109. [7] *Ibid.*, pp. 97, 98. [8] *Ibid.* p. 111.

be as much at liberty as other men to reconsider anything which they may at any time have written, is a thing which I do not understand.

§ 2. '*Lord Selborne's favourite argument.*'

For my own part, I am not extremely sensitive: but there are, in the new History, some rash statements concerning myself, on points unconnected with any antiquarian question, which the Author, if he has the opportunity, may perhaps wish to correct. I will mention here two of them, which are not only put forward with confidence in the body of the work, but are thought worthy of a place in the table of contents prefixed to it, as if to direct special attention to them. One is of minor importance, but characteristic. 'It is' (we are told [1]) 'a favourite argument with Lord Selborne, and others who follow him, that the part allotted out of the tithes for the poor would be insufficient for their support. But he omits the important fact, that in one of Edgar's Canons it was enacted, that the people should also distribute alms to the poor; so that the part allotted out of the tithes was not intended to be the whole maintenance which the poor should receive.' I have never used that argument, or anything like it; and the Canon to which the Author refers (inaccurately, though in a footnote he directs his readers to another page in which it is correctly given) is quoted by me *verbatim*, in more than one page [2] of *Ancient Facts and Fictions*. I may add that, if any one else has used the argument which the Author erroneously attributes to myself, he will hardly be likely to perceive the relevancy to it of that Canon, which the Author calls Edgar's, but which I call Dunstan's.[3]

§ 3. *Degge's* '*Parson's Counsellor.*'

The other instance of the Author's rashness which I think it right here to notice is less inoffensive.

[1] C, p. 127. (And see Contents, xii. ch. ii.)   [2] AF, pp. 216, 265.
[3] Those Canons are merely ecclesiastical; and the only connection of King Edgar with them is that they were made in his reign.

In my *Defence of the Church of England against Disestablishment*,[1] I had occasion to comment upon a tract circulated by the 'Liberation' Society, entitled *The Church and the Poor*: most of the ideas of which I find reproduced and expanded in this new History. One of the authorities to which it appealed was a book of the seventeenth century, by Sir Simon Degge, called the *Parson's Counsellor*. Upon this I made some observations, to show the value of that authority, and its probable meaning. I spoke[2] of Degge as 'a (not particularly distinguished) lawyer of Charles the Second's time;' and showed, that he had quoted (in support of 'the sentiment which made him an oracle with the tract-writer, that the poor had a share in the tithes with the clergyman') a supposed decree of Pope Sylvester; one of Aelfric's (so-called) Canons, which he called 'a Canon of our own, made in the time of King Alfred;' and a provincial constitution of Archbishop Stratford, which he seemed to have misunderstood. After which references (I said), 'the Parson's Counsellor thus closed his admonition: "*By all which it appears, that originally the poor had a share of the tithe.*" His object was to impress upon his clerical readers (by authorities not greatly to the purpose) the moral obligation of beneficence towards the poor, as one of the things contemplated and intended in the parochial system and its endowments. He could not have meant to assert that in his own time, as well as "originally," the poor "had a share in the tithes" by law: every lawyer's apprentice, and every clergyman, must have known that not to be true. For his citation of Pope Sylvester, etc., he was called to account in his own day: and in a later edition he defended it, lamely enough; maintaining, on the authority of some Roman canonists, the genuineness of the extracts from the Synodical Acts of Pope Sylvester published by Isidore, and it must therefore be supposed of the other forgeries in the same collection also.'

The Author of the new History[3] refers to this passage in my *Defence*, etc., of which he quotes two sentences which do not stand together in it, as if they did: but that is of no

---

[1] *Defence*, etc., pp. 147-159 (4th ed.)   [2] *Ibid.*, pp. 153, 154.
[3] C, pp. 129, 130.

importance. But he seems to think, that I ought not to have spoken of Degge as being criticised in his lifetime, without saying that the critic was Henry Wharton, author of *Anglia Sacra*; a 'boy-pluralist'; of whom Bishop Burnet and some others had a bad opinion; and who had been accused of falling into a 'legion of blunders' in his own works. He charges me with '*traducing the character*' of Sir Simon Degge, because I said that he was a 'not particularly distinguished' lawyer; and with '*carefully avoiding*' any mention of Wharton's name. These specimens of a peculiar style might not have been worthy of notice, but for what follows; they may be quickly disposed of. Why I should have entered into a digression about Wharton, unless it would have had something to do with the matter in hand, is not apparent. It could not have anything to do with the matter in hand, unless Wharton's demerits (supposing them to be as great as Burnet or any one else thought, though learned men[1] were not all agreed in that opinion), would have had some tendency to establish the genuineness of the pretended Acts of Pope Sylvester. As to Degge's 'character,' which I am supposed to have 'traduced,' I have yet to learn that none but a very distinguished lawyer could in the reign of Charles the Second be 'a Judge of West Wales; Recorder of Derby; knighted; a Bencher of the Inner Temple; and High Sheriff of Derbyshire'; and also writer of a book 'dedicated to a bishop,' and sufficiently useful to the clergy (I believe it was the first of its kind) to pass through six editions in his lifetime: on all which facts the Author relies,[2] to show that I did Sir Simon Degge some injustice.

The sequel I must give in the Author's exact words. Having just before mentioned Degge's sixth and last edition, published in 1703, he proceeds[3]:—

'In this edition he says, "*Nor is there any doubt but that by the Canon Law the poor ought to have a share in the*

---

[1] Hearne, the Antiquary, called him '*auctorem omni exceptione majorem, quicquid obganniant invidi obtrectatores.*' (Preface to his edition of *Robert de Avesbury's History of the Wonderful Acts of Edward III.* Oxford, 1720.)

[2] C, p. 130.

[3] *Ibid.*, p. 130. (And see Contents, xii. ch. ii.)

revenues of the Church, which was all I endeavoured to prove." Lord Selborne quotes his closing admonition from the seventh revised edition of 1820, *i.e.* 116 years after Degge's death: "*By which it appears, that originally the poor had a share of the tithe.*" Degge never wrote these words; and it is not fair or just to a dead author to publish a garbled edition of his work, and to quote against him from this garbled edition. I have given above his own words from his last edition published in 1703.'

How stand the facts? I had quoted from pages 80, 81 of Mr. Ellis's edition [1] of 1820, giving the reference to those pages in a footnote; [2] and in the text describing the words (which the Author says 'Degge never wrote'), as immediately following his references to Pope Sylvester, etc. As it happens, Mr. Ellis preserved, so far, the paging of the edition of 1703: and, if the Author had looked at page 80 of the edition of 1703, which he had before him, he would have found in it those words, immediately following the references to Pope Sylvester, etc. And he might also have found them, in the same place, in every earlier edition except the first; the references to Pope Sylvester, etc., having been first made by Degge in his second edition of 1677.[3] The words, for which the Author imagines them to have been substituted in Mr. Ellis's edition, which he calls 'garbled,' occur (in a different place, winding up Degge's reply to his critic) in the two editions published after 1692, in which year Wharton's *Defence of Pluralities* appeared; being part of the reply to that book, they did not, and they could not, appear earlier.

---

[1] It is in the Library of Lincoln's Inn, and the only edition there. I quoted from it, as likely to be more easily accessible than the earlier editions to others, as well as to myself.

[2] *Defence*, etc. (4th ed.), p. 154.

[3] The first edition (1676) is in the British Museum and the Bodleian Library; the second (1677) in the Library of Queen's and All Souls' Colleges, Oxford; the third (1681) in the British Museum and the Library of Corpus Christi College, Oxford; the fifth (1695) in the Library of Christ Church, Oxford; the sixth (1703) in the British Museum and the Library of New College, Oxford. I have not seen the fourth, but there can be no doubt of its agreement, as to the words quoted, with the third and fifth.

§ 4. *The Author and 'Ancient Facts and Fictions.'*

I pass to the Author's criticisms on *Ancient Facts and Fictions*. I am happy to think that, by giving references throughout that work to the sources of my information, I have enabled others to verify the evidence on which my statements rest. That the Author of the new History has closely followed up my references, I know from himself: when, therefore, he expresses no dissent as to any important question of fact, it may be presumed that he has found no reason to do so; it is even possible that I may have assisted to remove from his mind some erroneous impressions. He maintained in 1887 opinions, as to the bearing of the (so-called) 'Excerptions of Archbishop Egbert' upon the question of a tripartite division of tithes in England, and as to the charters of King Ethelwulf, which he has now relinquished; ascribing his change of mind to a fuller consideration of authorities, which were as accessible in 1887 as in 1891.[1] During the interval between those years, *Ancient Facts and Fictions* had been published. In his present chapter[2] on the 'Excerptions,' he takes notice of the fact, that the twenty-one first articles (he calls them 'Canons') in that collection are taken from the Andain manuscript in the monastery of St. Hubert (he prints the name *Herbert*) in the Ardennes. It was by myself, in *Ancient Facts and Fictions*, that attention was first directed to that fact, and the evidence of it brought forward.[3] I may therefore fairly claim to have conveyed the knowledge of it to the Author's mind; and in it may doubtless be found the explanation of his now ceasing to insist that, 'although this collection bears internal evidence of having been compiled some centuries after the Archbishop's death, yet it shows that a tripartite division of the tithes must have been made in England at the time the collection was formed, otherwise the compiler or compilers would not have mentioned the division as having existed in Egbert's time, meaning his or their own time.'[4] As to the

---

[1] C, Preface, v. [2] *Ibid.*, p. 32. [3] AF, pp. 37-45.
[4] C 1887, p. 27. (The compilers of the 'Excerptions' do *not* anywhere mention the division as having existed in England, either in Egbert's, or in their own time.)

charters of Ethelwulf, the Author in 1887 strenuously maintained the opinion that the charter of A.D. 855 was a law, 'granting tithes to the Church from all England.'[1] But now he has a chapter[2] proving the contrary; in which I recognise seven of my own quotations from Chroniclers, and other arguments, the same in substance with my own.

The Author thinks[3] that in *Ancient Facts and Fictions* I have relied too much upon negative evidence. I am not conscious of having done so. I have not in any instance founded conclusions upon it, or referred to it at all, except in confirmation of positive reasons for my own conclusions. And though on many points I have thought it right to mention other men's opinions, whether in accordance with or contrary to my own, I have never, that I am aware of, confounded those opinions with evidence.

§ 5. *The document entitled, 'Of Church-Grith.'*

I now come to historical questions; and I will take first those criticisms on which the Author seems to have bestowed the greatest pains, and which I suppose him to have had most in view when he directed my attention to his work. They relate to my chapter on the legislation of Ethelred and Canute, and more particularly to the question there discussed[4] as to the character and effect of the document entitled (as Mr. Thorpe renders the Anglo-Saxon *Be Cyric Grithe*) '*Of Church-Grith.*'

I have stated in another chapter,[5] that the uncritical acceptance of the 'Excerptions' as the genuine work of Archbishop Egbert had more influence than anything else in establishing the notion that a tripartite division of tithes or other church revenues was anciently customary in England, in the minds of those writers who entertained it down to the present century. Next to the 'Excerptions,' their reliance was on the (so-called) 'Canons' of Aelfric. I do not know that any one appealed for that purpose to the document entitled '*Of Church-Grith,*'

[1] C 1887, pp. 35-39.
[2] C, pp. 53-66. Compare AF, pp. 186-206.
[3] C., Preface. vi. [4] AF, pp. 278-285. [5] *Ibid.*, p. 227.

until after the first quarter of the present century; but now it seems to be relied on more than anything else by those who still hold to that opinion. The Author says:[1]

'King Ethelred's law on the three-fold division of tithe has been found so important in the discussion on the tripartite division, that Lord Selborne has devoted all his eminent legal powers, though unsuccessfully, to upset this Anglo-Saxon law.'

I disclaim the motive suggested. I have dealt with the questions arising on *Church-Grith* exactly in the same way as with the other historical questions examined by me; that is, with a desire, not to 'upset' anything, or to establish any foregone conclusion, but correctly to understand and present to my readers the real facts and their practical import. That there should be some who cling to this supposed law of King Ethelred as a *tabula in naufragio* for a theory of which the original grounds have been displaced is intelligible enough; I must take the liberty of saying that the zeal is on their side, rather than on my own.

I prefer as to this matter to meet the Author, first by showing how the case stands upon the main question, apart from all inferences from anything said or not said by any writer, ancient or modern. The Author thinks, and has taken some trouble to prove,[2] (with what success will be hereafter seen), that I have attached undue importance to the silence of some writers, whom he calls my 'witnesses.' If that had been so, I should so far stand corrected; but my facts and arguments upon the principal question would remain the same.

Whatever else may have been done in *Ancient Facts and Fictions*, I may fairly claim to have established these propositions:—

1. That there is no ground for believing any part of the Anglo-Saxon literature, which has been or can be cited as evidence of the existence in this country of any law or custom for the partition of tithes, to be earlier than the reign of Ethelred the Unready.[3]

[1] C, p. 102. (In Contents, xii. ch. x.; also, 'Lord Selborne's *object* is to upset the Act of A.D. 1014.')
[2] *Ibid.*, pp. 102-106.
[3] AF, pp. 227-269.

2. That all the passages in that literature which appear to favour the notion of any such law or custom are traceable to a definite foreign source, the Andain text (printed by Martene and Durand) of the document, bearing in another text (from which it was printed by Sirmondi) the title '*Capitulare Episcoporum.*'[1]

3. That there is no evidence of the prevalence of the tripartite division of tithes enjoined by the *Capitulare Episcoporum*, even upon the continent of Europe, except in some parts of the Low countries and the northern provinces of France.[2]

4. That the intercourse which took place between English and French ecclesiastics and religious houses in the tenth century explains the introduction into this country of copies of the *Capitulare Episcoporum*, such as are found in the manuscripts of which an account is given in my chapter on the Egbertine Compilations, and the desire of some learned men and persons of influence among the English Benedictines of King Ethelred's time to procure the adoption in England (among other things derived from foreign sources) of the tripartite division of tithes, enjoined by one of the articles in that Capitular.[3]

5. That there is no trace of any such tripartite division, or of any other apportionment of tithes, having been enjoined by any law or established by any custom in England before the reign of Ethelred the Unready; nor in his time, unless it was done by the disputed document entitled '*Of Church-Grith*' in the last year but one of his reign.[4]

6. That if the document entitled '*Of Church-Grith*' ought to be regarded as agreed to by a Witenagemot in the last year but one of King Ethelred's reign, on account of the date which it bears in one of the two manuscripts which (wholly or in part) contain it, and of what it says as to 'the king of the English with the counsel of his *witan*,'[5] the circumstances of

---

[1] AF, pp. 37-45, 229, 231, 237, 242, 248, 258.
[2] *Ibid.*, pp. 29-37.   [3] *Ibid.*, pp. 207-218, 233.
[4] *Ibid.*, pp. 179-185, 213-225.
[5] In *Ancient Facts*, etc. (p. 280, note), I noticed, but did not lay stress on, the peculiar form of the sentence in which those words first occur, which I thought 'not exactly like' anything to be found elsewhere; and in the

the time nevertheless preclude the supposition that anything contained in it, which was not afterwards confirmed by Canute, was ever practically law in England; and that, while every other article in it capable of having any practical operation (with at most two exceptions) was confirmed by Canute, that as to a tripartite division was not.[1]

7. That from the accession of Canute in A.D. 1016 downwards there is again no trace of any law or custom of tripartite or any other division of tithes in England.[2]

These propositions, firmly established as I believe them to be, are enough; they show that the document in question (which I have never treated as spurious) was inoperative, even upon the hypothesis most favourable to its authority. But I added, that there was no sufficient proof or presumption in favour of that hypothesis. The document did, in two of its articles, 'speak the language either of past or of present national legislation.'[3] But this it might do, though it was no more than the draft or project of a law.[4] That this was the true character of '*Church-Grith*,' seemed to me, from the internal evidence, most probable; because it contained towards its close five articles, didactic, expostulatory, casting censure upon the whole course of legislation and government after the death of King Edgar,[5]—articles which, in a draft or project of law, might perhaps have the effect of

---

Appendix to my *Defence*, etc. (4th ed., p. 362), I also noticed the difference between the title '*Church-Grith*' (both in the MSS. and in Mr. Thorpe's *Ancient Laws*, etc., vol. i. pp. 340-341), and the usual general titles of other undoubted laws of Ethelred's reign. The Author (C, pp. 113, 114) dissents. I am content that, on this point, any one who will look at pp. 281-282, 284-285, 292-293, 304-305, 306 of Mr. Thorpe's first volume shall judge for himself whether my observations were warranted or not.   [1] AF, 285-290.

[2] *Ibid.*, pp. 289, 294-307.   [3] *Ibid.*, p. 280.

[4] Every Bill introduced into the British Parliament, or drawn up with that view, is in the form of an enactment by the proper authority; though until actually passed by that authority it is no more than a draft or project of law. The mere style and form need not be conclusive in the case of an Anglo-Saxon manuscript standing by itself, of which the history is unknown, more than in any other case of an instrument prepared with a view to its becoming law.

[5] AF, p. 281; and Appendix E.

setting before the legislature motives for the proposed enactment; but which in the law itself, if enacted, would be nugatory and out of place. Those articles were all (as might have been expected) omitted from Canute's legislation.

I suggested also [1] (though without laying stress upon the suggestion) that in such a case it might not be safe to rely upon a date such as appears on the face of the Parker manuscript, assigned by Mr. Thorpe to the middle of the eleventh century. The name of the reigning king is not mentioned in either of the two manuscripts; and, as I showed, the words '*Edgar who was last*' (after 'Athelstan' and 'Edmund') could not mean that Edgar was the immediate predecessor of the king in whose reign the document was drawn up, whether that king was Ethelred or Canute. If they meant (as I thought they did) the last lawgiver who ruled and made ecclesiastical laws in a proper constitutional way, they would be as appropriate, if the document was drawn up early in the reign of Canute (in which case it would be clear that nothing in it which is not found in Canute's code was enacted as law) as they would have been in the last year but one of King Ethelred.[2] I observed, that it would make all the difference if the scribe had written MXIIII. instead of MXVIII., and that such a clerical error in numerals might easily occur. Of the reasonableness of that observation the same manuscript volumes which contain (wholly or partially) the text of '*Church-Grith*' supply a remarkable confirmation, of which, when I made it, I had not taken notice. They both contain a document, entitled in both, '*Sermo Lupi ad Anglos, quando Dani maxime persecuti sunt eos;*' to which (in both) are added the words, '*quod fuit anno*'—the date following, but differing in the two manuscripts, by a manifest clerical error in one of them, probably in the Cottonian *Nero A.* 1; where it is, '*Anno* $M^{Lo}XIIII$ *ab incarnatione* D^{ni} N^{ri} IHV XPI. In the Parker manuscript it is, 'AN $M^{LO}VIIII$· *ab in-*

---

[1] AF, pp. 283, 284.
[2] *Ibid.*, p. 285. The Author's reference to Edred and Edwy, (C, p. 102), in connection with the question about the words, 'Edgar, who was *last*,' is unintelligible to me. In A.D. 1014 Edgar could not be named simply as the last lawgiver, without passing by Ethelred himself, which might as well be done in Canute's as in Ethelred's time.

carnatione Dⁿⁱ N^{ri} IHV XPI.' This date (A.D. 1009) agrees better with the facts of history than the other (A.D. 1014). Wanley has made that document the subject of a note in his catalogue of the Parker manuscripts.[1]

I cannot perceive that the Author has attempted any real answer to anything which I have thus said, upon the main question. Of the little which may have an indirect bearing upon it, I find in his History only three things worthy of remark; on two of which (as to Archbishop Odo borrowing from 'Egbert's Excerptions,' and as to the gloss on one of Dunstan's canons, commented on in my chapter on '*Aelfric and his school*') I shall hereafter observe. The other is this sentence:[2]

'It has escaped Lord Selborne's notice that Canute's confirmation of Edgar's law, which grants one-third of the tithes to the manorial priests, comes to the same thing as the threefold division of tithes in the '*Church-Grith*' law. The principle is the same in both, namely, that the manorial priest, or the priest of the mother Church, *was legally entitled* to no more than one-third part of the tithes, and that the modern use of taking all the tithes was *contrary to all rules, laws, and customs.*'

A characteristic sentence, which, with infinite coolness, begs the whole question! It had by no means 'escaped my notice' that the argument as to Edgar's law, here advanced, might be, and had been, suggested by writers whose minds were preoccupied with the notion of a tripartite division of tithes. I gave what I thought a sufficient answer to it, at the end of that section of my chapter on '*The Primacies of Odo and Dunstan*,' which relates to King Edgar's laws.[3] For what conceivable reason should the framers of *Church-Grith*, leaving out that particular law of Edgar while they repeated other tithe-laws of that king found in the same ordinance, have put (as it were) into its place their own clause for a tripartite division,—for what conceivable reason should Canute, while

---

[1] *Antiq. Literat. Septen:r. lib.*, p. 137 (under No. XXXIX. of the catalogue). I had not observed the date in the Parker MS. when the note at page 287 of *Ancient Facts*, etc., was written.

[2] C, p. 122.
[3] AF, pp. 225, 226.

re-enacting Edgar's law, have omitted from his code that article of '*Church-Grith*' as to the tripartite division,—if the one 'comes to the same thing' with the other? In that case they would at least have been found standing together in Canute's code. If the assignment of one-third of the local tithes to the local priest had been founded on some legal or customary partition of tithes between clergy, poor, and church-repairs, then the other two-thirds ought, upon the same 'principle,' to have been assigned to the local poor and the repair of the manorial church. But they were left to 'the old minster.' The suggestion that the lawgiver, without saying so, intended the clergy of 'the old minster' to divide those two-thirds between the poor (I suppose, the *matricularii*[1] of their own church) and the repairs (I suppose of that church also), without carrying them into the common fund of the monastery, or drawing anything from them for their own maintenance, is purely arbitrary. And to suppose that the clergy of 'the old minster' would have so understood or acted upon Edgar's law, in the absence of words requiring them to do so, is a hypothesis at variance with all that is known as to the rule and practice of the English Benedictine monasteries in that king's time.

§ 6. *My 'Witnesses.'*

So much with respect to the state of the issue between the Author and myself upon the main question. He expends his ammunition in an attack upon outworks, the demolition of which, if accomplished, would not bring him nearer to the mark. But how stands the case as to those outworks?

I have said in my chapter on the legislation of Ethelred and Canute, (and it is true):—

1. That if the ancient collectors and translators into Latin of Anglo-Saxon laws knew of the existence of the document entitled '*Of Church-Grith*,'—which I thought probable,—they cannot have regarded it as an Anglo-Saxon law; for it has no place in their translations.[2]

2. That the English antiquaries and Anglo-Saxon scholars

[1] AF, pp. 77-79, 215.   [2] *Ibid.*, pp. 271, 272.

of the sixteenth and seventeenth century, whose attention was given to the same class of documents,—Lambarde, Selden, Spelman, Whelock, and John Johnson,—(if, again, they knew of the existence of '*Church-Grith*,' which also I thought probable),—did not so regard it; for no mention of it is found in the collections or writings of any of them.[1]

3. That David Wilkins, who first published '*Church-Grith*' in his *Leges Anglo-Saxonicæ*, did not include it in his *Concilia*, where it would have been entitled to a place, if he had taken the Author's view of it.[2]

The Author calls these my '*witnesses*,' though I have built nothing upon their silence, or (if they had the necessary knowledge) on their presumable opinions. The Author arrays them, one after another, as witnesses for cross-examination, disparaging the authority of some; and, as to all, taking issue with me as to the probability of their having known anything of the document in question. This is all that he does; and, except as to certain discoveries which he thinks he has made (as to a supposed difference between the present contents of the Cottonian volume, *Nero A.* 1, and its condition in the time of Selden and Spelman), it will be enough for me to show that, in the little which I said in that chapter about those writers, I did not speak unadvisedly.

First, as to the ancient translators of Anglo-Saxon laws, I think it cannot reasonably be doubted (though the Author has taken exception to my saying so[3]) that they *intended* their collections to be complete—by which I mean, complete so far as relates to the general laws of Wessex, and of England under the supremacy of Wessex, in Anglo-Saxon times. There is no indication of a design on their part to do either less or more than this:—it is nothing, therefore, to the purpose that their collections did not include the laws of the Kentish kings, enumerated among their omissions by the Author.[4]

If they knew nothing of '*Church-Grith*,' their ignorance might perhaps be of more importance (as negative evidence) than their opinion of its character, if they did know it.

---

[1] AF, pp. 282, 283.   [2] *Ibid.*, p. 283.
[3] In the Appendix to my *Defence of the Church of England*, etc. (4th ed., p. 361). See C, p. 113.   [4] C, p. 112.

The Latin translations printed by Mr. Thorpe[1] are ascribed by him to the twelfth century—a time sufficiently near to the Anglo-Saxon monarchy to make it improbable that any Anglo-Saxon enactments of general (especially ecclesiastical) importance, which had in the preceding century been acknowledged and acted upon as laws, would have been beyond the knowledge of the translators, or have escaped their research. If the document entitled '*Of Church-Grith*' was not found in any of the repositories to which they had access, the inference would not, I think, be favourable to that view of its character and operation which the Author maintains. I thought it, however, probable that copies of a document of that nature, of which manuscripts have come down to our own times, might have been found in those repositories in the twelfth century, and even so late as Bromton's time; and, giving credit to the translators for knowledge of the places where the materials for their work were most likely to be found, and for a reasonable amount of diligence and research, I thought they were likely to have been acquainted with it, if it were there. I leave it to others to judge of the degree of probability, one way or the other. It is a perfectly fair observation of the Author,[2] that some undoubted secular laws,—those of Thundersfield (the *Decretum Sapientum Angliæ*) under Athelstan, and of the Council of Colinton under Edmund (both which are in Bromton), and Canute's Forest Laws, are not in those old Latin translations; and I cannot doubt that the two earlier would have been there, if the translators had found them in the places to which they had access. All that it occurs to me to suggest is, that there was nothing in them of special interest to ecclesiastics, and so that they might be preserved in fewer places. Canute's Forest Laws are less likely to have been unknown: their limited application to the Royal Forests may perhaps have been the reason for their omission; but that, of course, is no more than conjecture.

The other omissions which the Author mentions are of

[1] *Ancient Laws*, etc., vol. ii. pp. 447-551. (See Mr. Thorpe's Preface to vol. i. p. xvi.)
[2] C, pp. 112, 113.

little weight. Some of them are irrelevant, if my view of the translators' design is correct;—the laws of the Kentish kings; Alfred's summary of Mosaical precepts, which (though the Author calls it 'King Alfred's Scriptural Laws'), was no law at all; the '*Decretum Cantianum*,' which also was no law at all; and *Grith and Mund*. And, with respect to the omitted Acts of that latter part of King Ethelred's reign during which the Danes were ravaging England, there seems good reason to believe, from what appears in '*Church-Grith*' itself, that constitutional objections were taken in that king's time to the way in which they were passed, and that they never had practical operation, except so far as they were confirmed and re-enacted by Canute.[1] The 'Supplement to Edgar's Laws' raises by that title, as well as by the form of its contents, a question as to its character.[2]

Next, as to the learned men of the sixteenth and seventeenth centuries;—I will take the less considerable of them first.

1. My reason for thinking it probable that Lambarde knew of the existence of '*Church-Grith*' is, that he tells us in the preface to his *Archaionomia*[3] that he had access to and made use of the Anglo-Saxon manuscripts in Archbishop Parker's library; of which not the least interesting and important were those contained in the same volume with '*Church-Grith*.' It is nothing to the purpose that he did not print the laws of the Kentish Kings (of which there is only one original manuscript, the *Textus Roffensis*, forming no part of the Parker collection), or the laws of William the Conqueror, or the Latin compilation, falsely called 'Laws of Henry the First.'

2. My reason for thinking the same of Whelock is, that he lived in Cambridge, and appears, on the face of his editions of Lambarde's *Archaionomia* and Bede's *History*, to have made full use of the opportunities which he had of becoming

---

[1] See AF, pp. 277, 278.
[2] Thorpe, *Anc. Laws*, vol. i. pp. 274-279. None of the MSS., which contain the 'Laws,' also contain the 'Supplement'; and I infer, from the collation of texts in Mr. Thorpe's notes, that neither of the two MSS. from which he prints the 'Supplement' contains the laws.
[3] Published by Day in 1568.

acquainted with the Anglo-Saxon manuscripts bequeathed by Archbishop Parker to Corpus Christi College. That he should have overlooked, or (if he did not overlook) that he should have failed to make himself acquainted with the contents of, the volume which contains '*Church-Grith*,' seemed to me improbable.

3. My reason for thinking the same of John Johnson is, that he refers to that volume itself, in his preface to the *Laws of the Northumbrian Priests;* saying:[1] 'These laws stand before those of Edgar, in the MS. of C.C.C.C., S. 18, though Sir H. Spelman placed them after.' Knowing thus from himself that he was acquainted with and made use of the volume, I must be excused for disregarding Mr. Baron's *dictum* in 1850 (which the Author quotes[2] as if it were evidence), that '*Church-Grith*' was 'altogether unknown to him.'

4. As to Selden, the Author[3] agrees with me, that he was well acquainted with the Cottonian volume, now known as *Nero A.* 1, in the state in which it was when he published his *History of Tithes* in 1618; but he rejects my inference; because (he says) 'that law was not in the volume for him to see or read, nor was it in the [Cottonian] Library.' This is the Author's discovery, which he undertakes to prove; it will be seen whether he proves it or not. Meanwhile, I shall take the liberty to assume that, when Selden wrote, so much of ·'*Church-Grith*' as is now in *Nero A.* 1 was in Sir Robert Cotton's Library, and in that volume. Selden not only referred to the Cottonian manuscript of 'Egbert's Excerptions' (as the Author acknowledges), but he made use of the texts of Athelstan's tithe-ordinance and Edgar's tithe law contained in the same volume, for the purpose of collating them with Lambarde.[4] The copy of Athelstan's tithe-ordinance,

---

[1] Johnson's *Laws and Canons* (Baron's ed. 1850), vol. i. p. 372. (Compare Spelman, *Concil,* p. 502; and Wanley, p. 137, Nos. xxi. xxii.)
[2] C, p. 105. (Mr. Baron's words, '*in the face of which*' I have presumed to form an opinion for myself, are at p. vii. of his Preface.)
[3] *Ibid.*, p. 103. (Selden's *History of Tithes* was dedicated to Sir Robert Cotton, with an acknowledgment of the use made of his Library.)
[4] See the list of '*The ancient Records and other Manuscripts*' used by Selden for his *Historie of Tithes*, at the end of the original edition of 1618. Those '*in Sir Robert Cotton's Librarie*' exceed all the rest in number.

of which Selden so made use, is part of the same manuscript (among the different pieces brought together in *Nero A.* 1) which contains '*Church-Grith*,' so far as *Church-Grith* is there.

5. The Author concedes, as to Spelman, what he does as to Selden. He 'had access to every book and manuscript in Sir Robert Cotton's Library.'[1] In the margin of the manuscript of 'Egbert's Excerptions' in *Nero A.* 1, there is a note (in writing, I think, of the latter part of the seventeenth century), saying that Spelman printed the 'Excerptions' from it. But, on looking to what Spelman himself says,[2] I feel more doubtful of this, than I did when *Ancient Facts and Fictions* was published; and I have, for that reason, modified what I said as to his knowledge of *Nero A.* 1. Spelman had not only some knowledge, greater or less, of Sir Robert Cotton's manuscripts; he was also very familiar with the Parker manuscripts in the library of Corpus Christi College, Cambridge; and he printed the *Laws of the Northumbrian Priests* from the volume in that library which contains '*Church-Grith*,' where only the Anglo-Saxon text of the *Laws of the Northumbrian Priests* is found.[3]

6. As to Wilkins, I said,[4] that he was the first to publish '*Church-Grith*' in his *Leges Anglo-Saxonicæ*, 'where he combined it, in a manner for which the manuscripts afforded no warrant, with the ordinances of Habam, etc. If he had regarded it as an authentic ecclesiastical law when he afterwards (in A.D. 1737) published his great collection of Acts of Councils and other English ecclesiastical documents, it must have found a place there, which it does not.'

In this passage, the word *Habam* has been rightly pointed

Among them are '*Saxon Laws in Saxon*,' with references to pp. 213, 219, 222. Page 213 contains in the margin a reading of part of King Athelstan's Tithe Ordinance, from the Cottonian MS. (*In MS. Cottoniano*); and p. 219 has another, of two words in Edgar's Tithe-Law. [Compare Mr. Thorpe's collation of the same places, from his MS. G, *i.e. Nero A.* 1, in *Anc. Laws*, vol. i. pp. 194 (note 11), 195 (note *b*), 264 (note 5).]

[1] C, p. 104.
[2] Spelman's *Concilia* (ed. 1639), p. 275.
[3] *Ibid.*, p. 502; and see Wanley's *Antiq. Literat. Septentr. lib.*, p. 137, Nos. xxi., xxii.   [4] AF, p. 281 (first ed.)

out by the Author[1] as a mistake; it is a clerical error, not perceived before, because absolutely unimportant, except as showing that I may be guilty of a slip through *incuria*, like other men. I have corrected it to *Wantage* (the right word). I suppose it was that slip which led the Author to say[2] that I confounded the Ordinances of Habam with another document, the ordinance of A.D. 1008, which he calls (after Mr. Thorpe) '*Liber Constitutionum*.' If he had read the earlier sections of the same chapter of *Ancient Facts and Fictions* in which the slip occurs, he would have seen that I did not confound those two documents, and could not possibly have done so. Nevertheless, I thank him for enabling me to set right the mistake.

What Wilkins did, 'in a manner for which the manuscripts afforded no warrant,' was to combine four documents (of which the Ordinance of 1008 was the first, *Grith and Mund* the second, *Church-Grith* the third, and the laws of Wantage the fourth), under the title '*Liber Constitutionum tempore Aethelredi Regis*'; which he placed after his next preceding title, '*Leges Aethelredi Regis*,' and before the next following, '*Concilium Aenhamense*.'[3] That combination was not found in any manuscript (though the three first of the four documents did follow each other in the same order in *Nero A.* 1); and the title under which he placed them (which Mr. Thorpe,[4] in the table of contents of his first volume, though not in the body of that work, has borrowed from him, applying it only to the first document of the four) was one of his own invention; there being no such 'book,' and no manuscript in which that title, or anything like it, is applied to all or any of those documents. I cannot but think that, by placing them under such a title, Wilkins showed that (rightly or wrongly) he did not consider them as well-authenticated laws of King Ethelred. And I adhere to the opinion that *Church-Grith* (of which all the articles are ecclesiastical), must have found a place in his *Concilia*, if he had in 1737 regarded it as a document of

---

[1] C, p. 106.   [2] *Ibid.*, p. 94.
[3] Wilkins, *Leges Anglo-Saxonicæ* (1721), pp. 106, 110, 113, 117, 119.
[4] Thorpe, *Ancient Laws*, vol. i. Table of Contents, xxviii. (Compare *ibid.*, pp. 304, 305.)

authority. The Author says, that he also omitted from his *Concilia* the Ordinance of 1008, which contained a considerable number of ecclesiastical articles. That is true; but he included in that collection the Acts of the Council of Enham; and he doubtless saw, that those Acts and the Ordinance of 1008 could not stand together, as having concurrent authority. I do not doubt that he took the same view of the Ordinance of 1008 that he did of *Church-Grith*. It is nothing to the purpose, that an eminent Anglo-Saxon scholar, with whom Archdeacon Hale conversed, thought no weight due to Wilkins's opinion, whatever it was.[1] I have said nothing about the weight of his opinion: I have only shown what it was, or may be presumed to have been. But, if the question with Wilkins was as to the character, and not as to the genuineness of the document, it is not clear to me that his judgment ought to be set aside as unworthy of consideration, because the Archdeacon's friend thought meanly of him as an Anglo-Saxon scholar, in comparison with Schmid, and may perhaps have been right in thinking so: which is all that the conversation amounts to.

§ 7. *The Cottonian Volume, Nero A.* 1.

I come now to the Author's supposed discovery,[2] that the documents, which he calls '*the Church Mund and Church-*

---

[1] C, p. 107. See Archdeacon Hale's tract on *The Antiquity of the Church-Rate considered, etc.* (Rivingtons, 1837), p. 31. The Author says, that I (and others), 'while quoting Price's opinion, *carefully avoided any reference whatever* to the second or favourable opinion, though it is printed in a footnote to the page in which Price's letter appears' (the *italics* here are his). And in his preface, p. vii, he speaks of this as · '*most unfair*' (his own *italics* also), and as a 'careful omission' of '*material evidence* furnished by Archdeacon Hale, which is dead against their opinions.' It is as little against my opinion, as it is '*evidence*.' If I had called in question the *genuineness* of the document, there might have been some reason for my mentioning that anonymous opinion in its favour, though resting on the mere fact that Schmid had published it in his collection of Anglo-Saxon laws. But I did not adopt Mr. Price's opinion ; I stated my own opinion to be, that the document was genuine; but was 'a draft or project of laws, which the framer, evidently an ecclesiastic of Aelfric's school, wished to have enacted.'—AF, p. 279.

[2] C, pp. 98-101 ; and preface, p. vii.

Grith laws,' were not in the volume now called *Nero A.* 1, nor in the Cottonian Library, in Selden's time, nor during the life of Sir Robert Cotton (who died in 1631), or of his son; but that they were added to the Library, and put into *Nero A.* 1, by his grandson, Sir John Cotton (who died in 1702), towards the end of his life. For proof of which, the Author relies upon the absence of any titles descriptive of those particular documents, in certain lists or catalogues, of which I shall in due course speak—upon that, and nothing else. Those lists or catalogues are silent, not as to *Grith and Mund* and *Church-Grith* only, but also as to the Ordinance of A.D. 1008, which immediately precedes them, and several other documents now in *Nero A.* 1, which I shall hereafter describe. If the Author's inference were good as to any of those documents, it would be equally good as to them all.

Before addressing myself to that issue (relevant only, of all the matters discussed in *Ancient Facts and Fictions*, to the question of the accessibility of those documents, as found in *Nero A.* 1, to Selden and Spelman), I have to make my acknowledgments to the Author for taking notice of one or two points in my description of the manuscript volume *Nero A.* 1 itself, which were either incorrect, or too confidently put forward. They are of no importance to any historical question; but I am glad to set them right; and they have led me, in my further examination of the same volume for the purposes of this supplement, to observe exactly every part of it, in a way which was not necessary for any purpose which I formerly had in view.

I acknowledge, that my eyes were at fault in deciphering the very minute and faded writing of the date added by John Josceline,[1] at the head of the undated rubric of *Church-Grith* in *Nero A.* 1. I read it, 'A^o *dom* 1014': the Author truly says, that it is 'A^{no} *dni* 1014.' It is now corrected in my text.

My next slip has been, while making use of some short memoranda taken down when I first looked at *Nero A.* 1, to give an unduly wide application to the words, '*without break,*' which ought to have been restricted to one portion of the first

---

[1] C, p. 101.

half of the volume; that contained in folios 71 to 97; the most material, and as to which they would have been correct. I wrote:[1] 'The Worcester book begins with Canute's laws, which are followed by those of Edgar, Alfred, Athelstan, Edmund, Ethelred;[2] and after them *Grith and Mund* and *Church-Grith;* all in Anglo-Saxon, without break, and in that order.' It was not necessary for me to take notice of any other original matters found in, and forming integral parts of, the identical manuscripts which contained those laws; and, so far, I might have had nothing to change. But it was not correct to describe the volume as if it had been, from the laws of Canute down to *Church-Grith,* one continuous manuscript. The Author's division of it,[3] down to that point, into four 'tracts,' is not far from the mark; though I should not, like him, call Josceline's modern supplement to Alfred's laws one of those 'tracts,' or take it into account at all. The laws of Canute, which are in one handwriting, and have at their end two blank pages, may without impropriety be called one 'tract': the laws of Edgar, and the chapter-titles and part of the preamble of Alfred's laws (with other matters interposed in the same manuscript), are in another handwriting, and may be called a second 'tract'; part of which has been lost, for it comes abruptly to an end, at the bottom of the second page of folio 56, with an imperfect sentence, which Josceline has completed by adding the words '*odnum mannum,*'[4] followed by his own Supplement, in fourteen folios. And the part of the volume which for the present purpose is most material—that which contains certain clauses of *Church-Grith*—beginning at folio 71 and ending with folio 97, is in a third handwriting, and may be called another 'tract.' I am well inclined to adopt that phraseology; especially as the list at the beginning of *Nero A.* 1, on which

[1] AF, p. 280 (first ed.)
[2] Here, and in another place where the same enumeration is made (AF, p. 242), I have named Ethelred; who, however, is not named in the manuscript. I did so, because the Ordinance of 1008 (whatever question there might be as to its authority) purports on its face to have been made by king and witenagemot; and Ethelred was then king.
[3] C. pp. 117, 118.
[4] See Thorpe, *Ancient Laws*, vol. i. p. 56 (sixth line from foot of the Anglo-Saxon text).

the Author's supposed discovery depends, is headed, '*Catalogus Tractatuum in isto volumine.*'

But when the Author says :[1]

'There are several breaks in the volume between the laws of the five kings. . . . The first break is of six folios, between the first and second parts of Alfred's laws. Then a second break of no less than twenty-eight folios between the last part of Alfred's and the beginning of Athelstan's. Here there are two breaks of thirty-four folios; and there are seven heads of *other manuscripts which are bound up in those breaks of thirty-four folios*':—

I must confess my inability to understand him. It is *not* the fact, that there is *any* 'other manuscript bound up,' either (1) between (what he calls) the first and second parts of Alfred's laws, or (2) between the last part of Alfred's and the beginning of Athelstan's, except Josceline's modern supplement of the laws of Alfred and Ina ; which contains not twenty-eight but only fourteen folios, and has interposed between it and the beginning of Athelstan's laws seventeen folios, of another and an entirely different manuscript. The pieces which occupy those seventeen folios, before Athelstan's laws, and those interposed between the chapter titles and the preamble of Alfred's laws, are not '*other manuscripts bound up*' with the laws ; they are as much original and integral parts of the two 'tracts,' or manuscripts containing the laws, as the laws themselves. What the Author means by a 'break,' I do not know; what I mean is a breach in, or interruption of, the continuity of a manuscript.

I have corrected the inaccuracies which I have acknowledged. Nothing turns, in the question as to the character and authority of *Church-Grith*, upon the precise date of the 'tract,' or manuscript, containing it (so far as it is contained) in *Nero A.* 1. As to that, it is possible that both the Author and myself may have been too confident. He is certain [2] that the handwriting is earlier than A.D. 1035, the year of Canute's death. I thought it might 'be asserted, without risk of error,'[3] that nothing in the volume was written before the end of

---

[1] C, p. 118.   [2] *Ibid.*   [3] AF, p. 280 (first edition).

Canute's reign. In so saying, I founded more than I now think I ought to have done upon the priority of place which Canute's laws have in the volume. I did not doubt then, nor do I now, that the contents of all the ancient manuscripts in *Nero A.* 1 were the same, and arranged in the same order, as they are now, when that volume first came into Sir Robert Cotton's possession, and also when the book was in the monastic library of Worcester. But it is certainly possible, that, when the several 'tracts' contained in the volume were first put together, they may have been arranged in a different order from that in which they were written. The Author has persuaded himself,[1] by a comparison of the handwriting with some ancient charters, that all the earlier portions of the volume down to folio 56 (*i.e.* the two first 'tracts') were written in, or not before, the reign of William the Conqueror; differing, in that respect, from Mr. Thorpe.[2] My own judgment, from a similar comparison with charters which I also have seen, might not be the same; but I make no claim to be an expert in palæography, and I am therefore content, on this point, to qualify what I originally wrote.

The ground being thus cleared for an examination of the Author's supposed discovery, I will lay before my readers the evidence of the volume itself.

I do not know when the manuscripts of the Cottonian Library were first classified under the names of the Roman emperors, etc., derived from their busts which stood above the several compartments of the library. It was certainly before 1695, when Dr. Smith's catalogue[3] was made—I believe long before. Whenever that classification was made, the volume in question must have been placed under its present title, *Nero A.* 1, which is the first of a series; being followed by sixteen other numbers of Nero A., and then by Nero B. and Nero C., etc. That it should have received that place, may be presumed

[1] C, p. 118.
[2] Mr. Thorpe says of *Nero A.* 1 (List of Manuscripts, etc., following Preface to vol. i. p. xxv), '*Octavo, formerly belonging to Worcester; written at various times; the Anglo-Saxon portion apparently in the beginning and middle of the* 11*th century.*'
[3] It is the classification of that catalogue.

to have been due to its antiquity and importance; and the owner of the library would hardly have been likely to tamper with it afterwards. The name of Sir Robert Cotton, '*Ro: Cotton Bruceus,*' written in a fair hand,—doubtless Sir Robert's own,—is at the foot of its first page.

Of this volume, *Nero A.* 1, we know for certain, that it belonged, as early as A.D. 1580, to John Josceline,[1] Archbishop Parker's celebrated librarian and secretary, and afterwards came into the hands of Sir Robert Cotton. There is another manuscript volume in the Cottonian collection (*Julius C.* 2) which contains some extracts from the *Textus Roffensis,*[2] and others from *Nero A.* 1, by Francis Tate,[3] an Anglo-Saxon scholar of some note in his day, a friend of Josceline and of Sir Robert Cotton, who was born in A.D. 1560, and died in 1616. Prefixed to the extracts from *Nero A.* 1, is the heading: '*Ex libro admodum antiquo quem habet dominus Joannes Jocelinus* 1580 *Novemb.;*'—with the postscript added,[4] '*Remanet apud Rob. Cotton, militem et baronettum,* 27 *Maii* 1613, *F. Tate.*' There is ample proof that the state of *Nero A.* 1, when Tate made his extracts and wrote in those terms of the book, was the same that it is now.

It contains, besides the interpolated laws of Alfred and Ina, much of Josceline's writing scattered through its different component parts,—sometimes interlineations, sometimes marginal notes, sometimes short pieces crowded into vacant spaces in the lower part of leaves partially filled in the old manuscript. The laws of Canute, Edgar, and Alfred are interlined

---

[1] In so spelling the name, I follow Selden (except as to the final *e*), and Hearne (Seld. *Hist. of Tithes,* ch. ix. p. 286, ed. 1618. Hearne, Preface to Avesbury's *Hist. of Edw. III.* § 9). In *Athenæ Cantabrigienses* (vol. ii. p. 366) it is written *Joscelyn*; and in the inscription on his monument, *Joceline.* Wanley calls him *Josselinus.*

[2] 'H,' in Mr. Thorpe's list of MSS. etc. (Preface to vol. i. of *Ancient Laws,* p. 25).

[3] See Smith's Catalogue of 1695, under *Julius C.* 2; and Tate's own signature in *Julius C.* 2 before the extracts from the Rochester book, and also at fol. 99b. Some of the side-notes, etc., in *Julius C.* 2, are in Sir Robert Cotton's writing. (As to Tate himself, see Wood's *Athenæ Oxonienses* (Bliss' ed.), vol. ii. 179).

[4] Crowded in, between the original heading, and the beginning of the extracts.

by him; at folio 49b (after the end of the piece entitled by Wanley '*Officium justi Judicis*'), he has filled a vacant space with an extract from Bromton. In the 'fourth tract' (as the Author numbers them), he has made a note after the *exordium* of Edmund's laws; and in the very part of it which the Author supposes not to have been in the Cottonian Library till more than ninety years after Josceline's death, he has noted on folio 90a, before the Ordinance of A.D. 1008, '*This is not in print*'; and on folio 96b, before *Church-Grith*, he has added the date already mentioned, evidently taken from the manuscript, now at Cambridge, which had belonged to Archbishop Parker. At the foot of folio 118a, after the closing lines of the '*Sermo Lupi ad Anglos*,' he has put in a hymn on St. Dunstan. At folio 119b he has written '*Parliament holden A⁰ 1008*' in the margin of (what seems to have been a first draft of)[1] the Ordinance of A.D. 1008, which there occurs as a separate undated piece, under the rubrical title, '*Be Angol witena Gerædnesse*.'

It was after the date 1014 had been added by Josceline to the Rubric of *Church-Grith*, in *Nero A.* 1, that Tate's extracts from that volume, in *Julius C.* 2, were made; he has copied that date, within lines distinguishing it as no part of the manuscript. His extracts consist: (1) of the complete text of the Ordinance of 1008; (2) of the complete text of *Grith* and *Mund;* (3) of the Rubric and first sentence of *Church-Grith*, down to the Saxon word '*heonanforth*'; which is followed by '&c.', and by a scrawl in shorthand,[2] which has been thus deciphered for me:—'*Sed nihil habet quod non in aliis reperatur*' (sic), '*atque quod habet mancum et mutilum est*': and (4) of some parts of the 'Institutes,' with which (what the Author reckons as) the 'fourth tract' in *Nero A.* 1 opens.

[1] Its first clause (except as to bishops) is the same as that of the Council of Enham. From clause 2 to the end, it corresponds, except in a few words, with the Ordinance of 1008; although the contrary might be supposed from Wanley's account of its ending. (See Schmid, *Gesetze der Angel-Sachsen*, ed. 1858; Preface, p. xxii:—where there is more than one misprint in the references.)

[2] This has been deciphered for me, by the kindness of Mr. Warner of the British Museum.

These facts make it certain, that those folios of (what the Author calls) the 'fourth tract,' which contain *Grith and Mund* and *Church-Grith*, were in their proper and present place in the volume when it was in Josceline's possession, and when Tate described it as 'remaining' with Sir Robert Cotton.

But the case against the Author's supposed discovery does not rest there. That 'fourth tract'—one manuscript in one handwriting, earlier (in the Author's opinion) than A.D. 1035 —consists, as I reckon them, of eight pieces, of which, and of the way in which they succeed each other in it, I will now give an account.

The three first pieces are ecclesiastical compositions, not national laws: (1) Fourteen chapters[1] of the treatise which Mr. Thorpe[2] has printed under the title '*Institutes of Polity, Civil and Ecclesiastical*,' to which I refer by the word '*Institutes*'; (2) a piece with the rubric '*Be Cristendome*'; and (3) another with the rubric '*Be Godcundre Warnunge*.' The second of these begins on the same page (folio 77b) on which the first ends, and finishes on the eighth line of folio 84b, on which page the space which originally remained blank is filled up in an ancient, clear, and large hand (later than that of the principal manuscript), with an extract from a book of St. Augustine on certain heretics. The third begins at the top of folio 85a, and ends on the fourteenth line of folio 87b. On the same folio where it ends (87b) the rubric of Athelstan's Tithe Ordinance, *Aethelstanes Gerædnes*, immediately follows; and the text of that Ordinance ends on the sixteenth line of folio 88b. Then comes the rubric (immediately following on the same page) of Edmund's laws, '*Eadmundes Gerædnes*,' appearing (on the face of the manuscript apart from modern marginal notes) to cover the succeeding context down to and including the second line of folio 90a. Then, on the same page, follows the Ordinance of A.D. 1008 under the rubric '*In Nomine Dni An Dnic Incarn*

---

[1] The chapters not included in those fourteen are also in *Nero A.* 1, but in distinct manuscripts, later in the volume. They are numbered in Plaxta's catalogue of the contents of that volume, 19, 20, 21, 26, 31, 32, 33.

[2] Thorpe, *Ancient Laws*, etc., vol. ii. pp. 304-341. (See AF, pp. 252, 285.)

MVIII,' continuing to the sixteenth line of folio 93b,' where it is succeeded by the rubric of *Grith and Mund* (closely crowded within the lines), '*Be Grithe⸏Be Munde*,' and by the text of that document, continuing to the nineteenth line of folio 96b. Then comes, on the same page, the rubric '*Be Cyric Grithe*,' and the beginning of the text of *Church-Grith*, with the sixth clause of which document (not the same with the sixth clause of the Parker manuscript) the whole 'tract' or manuscript ends at folio 97b.

Mr. Thorpe[1] published his text of *Church-Grith* as from *Nero A.* 1, with collations from the Parker manuscript; and in the first edition of *Ancient Facts and Fictions*, I took it on his authority, that the whole of that document was really in *Nero A.* 1. Wanley, however, and after him Wilkins[2] and Planta (as well as Tate in 1580), had all described the text which follows the rubric '*Be Cyric Grithe*,' at folios 96b to 97b of *Nero A.* 1, as 'mutilated':—Wanley's words being: '*Calce mutila est hæc Constitutio; sed eandem habes paginam integram.*' Schmid[3] perceived the difficulty of reconciling the mutilation so spoken of with Mr. Thorpe's account of the text which he followed. He thought, that by the words, '*eandem habes paginam integram*' (which I understand to mean that page 97b of *Nero A.* 1 is perfect) Wanley meant, that what was missing there was found in some other part of the same volume:—which (though it does not appear that he had seen the book) he judged to be a mistake. The fact is, that no more than the five first, out of the forty-four clauses contained in the Parker text of *Church-Grith*, are found in pages 96b to 97b of *Nero A.* 1; and I have myself searched in vain for anything like the other thirty-nine clauses in the rest of the volume. I took notice, in my first edition, of the fact that Mr. Thorpe had prefixed to his text of *Church-Grith* the title found in the Parker manuscript, but not in *Nero A.* 1;— I might have added, that he has omitted the opening words,

---

[1] The real source of Mr. Thorpe's text is unknown to me. His collation of it with the Parker manuscript exhibits no more than twelve verbal variations; all slight, and merely clerical.

[2] *Leges Anglo-Saxonicæ*, p. 106.

[3] *Gesetze der Angel-Sachsen*, ed. 1858; Preface, p. xxii.

'*In nomine Domini*,' which are found in *Nero A.* 1, but not in the Parker manuscript. And, if I had then known what I know now, I might have further added (what is of much greater importance) that, although the five first clauses of *Church-Grith*, in folios 96b-97b of *Nero A.* 1, are the same with the five first of the Parker manuscript, the sixth is *not* found there, nor anywhere else that I can discover. That part of folio 97b is not in all parts easy to decipher, being worn and discoloured; but the sense of its sixth clause,[1] (evidently in *pari materia* with the preceding clauses, as to penalties for different kinds and degrees of sacrilege), appears to be, that by the Northumbrian law some churches dedicated to St. Peter, St. Wilfrid, and two other saints whose names are not clear, had greater, and others less, privileges of sanctuary, under certain rules and conditions. Such a difference from the Parker manuscript can hardly, I think, be explained on any other view than that taken in *Ancient Facts and Fictions*; viz., that we have not, in *Church-Grith*, the text of any legislative enactment, by any king and witenagemot; but only a draft or project of a proposed law, which might well vary (as these two texts do) in different editions or stages.

It is of no importance, with respect to the question with which we have to do, that in *Nero A.* 1 the *exordium*[2] of Edmund's laws, after the rubric near the foot of folio 88b, is followed by a text which really contains not Edmund's, but part of Edgar's laws.[3] Folio 89a begins with words[4] which belong to the third clause of Edgar's secular Ordinance; which Ordinance is continued to the end, on the second line

---

[1] I am indebted to Mr. Warner for a transcript, of so much of it as is legible in an ordinary light; and to Professor Earle, of Oxford, for a translation. The Northumbrian churches which had great privileges of sanctuary were York (St. Peter), Ripon (St. Wilfrid), Durham (St. Cuthbert), Hexham (St. Andrew), and Beverley (St. John).

[2] See Wanley's Catalogue (*Antiq. Literat. Septentr. lib.*, p. 212):— No. xiii. 'Fol. 88b. EADMUNDES GERŒDNES (*quod est tantum Exordium legun Edmundi*'). This 'exordium,' or preamble, consists of less than five lines; agreeing (down to the word which Mr. Thorpe translates '*souls*') with the text in *Ancient Laws*, vol. i. p. 244.

[3] See C, p. 118.

[4] The Saxon equivalent of ' 120 *shillings as bot*.'—See Thorpe, *Ancient Laws*, vol. i. p. 267.

of folio 90a. This may have happened in one of two ways; one fold or sheet of parchment, containing the ecclesiastical laws of Edmund and Edgar, and the earlier part of Edgar's secular Ordinance (the uppermost of the folds in that part of the volume),[1] may have fallen out and been lost; or the scribe may have turned over, inadvertently, more pages than one at a time. Whichever may be the true explanation, the volume was, in that respect, in the same state, when it came into Josceline's hands; for there is a note of his at the foot of folio 88b (so faint, and in such minute letters, that it might easily escape notice) which was originally in two lines; but the lower line has been cut off,[2] probably when the volume was bound in Sir Robert Cotton's time. The upper line, which now remains, is: '*The rest of Edmund's laws and all*': —the sequel having doubtless been, '*the earlier part of Edgar's, are wanting.*' The note, thus mutilated, did not bring to the notice of casual observers the fact, that Edmund's laws, beyond their mere *exordium*, did not follow their proper rubric. This does not appear to have been observed until after Dr. Smith's catalogue of 1695 was made; for he takes no notice of it; nor did the framers of the Privy Council list of Sir Robert Cotton's library in 1632; nor did the original catalogue at the beginning of *Nero A.* 1, in which a later hand has suggested the correction of *Edmund* to Edgar. And a later hand (probably the same) has also written, at the top of folio 89a, the words, '*Edgari legû pars.*' This was, no doubt, done after Spelman's time; for there are elsewhere, in the same hand, one or two marginal notes referring to Spelman's *Concilia*.

It is significant—especially if this manuscript was written (as the Author believes) before the end of Canute's reign— that, while the laws of Athelstan and Edmund have rubrics with those kings' names, there is no corresponding rubric, such as *Aethelredě's Gerædnes*, before the ordinance of A.D. 1008, or either of the succeeding documents. The name of Ethelred is not mentioned.

[1] Folios 88, 89, are now the uppermost fold. Two folios would allow sufficient space.

[2] Many of the marginal notes, etc., have been so clipped, throughout the volume.

From the foregoing account it will be seen, that (with the exception of *Be Godcundre Warnunge*) there is not in this manuscript any single document which is not inseparably connected with that immediately preceding it, by being written partly on the same page. But the unity of the whole 'tract,' and the inseparableness from the rest of those parts which the Author supposes to have been missing from it when in Sir Robert Cotton's hands, may be still further demonstrated. For this purpose the catalogues on which the Author's reliance is placed become evidence against him; for they all mention among the contents of the volume the '*Institutes*,' and the laws of Athelstan and Edmund; and it is demonstrable, from the structure of the volume, that, if these pieces were in it others belonging to the same 'tract,'—'*Be Cristendome*,' '*Be Godcundre Warnunge*,' the ordinance of A.D. 1008, and *Grith and Mund* (although not mentioned in the catalogues)— must have been there; and, if so, there is nothing to support the notion, that *Church-Grith* (as far as it is now in the volume) was not there also.

The whole of this manuscript volume is written on parchment, folded (generally)[1] as the leaves of modern printed books are; and in some parts of it the physical continuity of the pair of folios belonging to the same fold is patent to sight and touch. Several such pairs of folios are folded one within another; the folios formed by the lowest pair of the same bundle being necessarily divided from each other by all those lying above and within it, so that the same piece of parchment constitutes the first and the last folios of that bundle, and so on (the distance diminishing) till the highest fold of the bundle is reached. I have verified in this way the continuity of several pairs of folios, and might doubtless have verified more; but the following are enough. Folio 74 contains part of the '*Institutes*,' which are mentioned in all the catalogues. The other side of the same fold of parchment comes out at folio 79 in the middle of '*Be Cristendome*,' which the catalogues relied on by the Author do not mention. Folio 84 contains the last page of *Be Cristendome*. The other side of the same fold of parchment

[1] Not invariably: the pair of leaves containing the end of *Grith and Mund*, and all that is in the book of *Church-Grith*, are an exception.

comes out at folio 93, on the second page of which are the rubric and the commencement of *Grith and Mund.* Above and within that fold of parchment are all the leaves on which '*Be Godcundre Warnunge,*' Athelstan's laws, the rubric of Edmund's laws, the extract from Edgar's laws, and the ordinance of A.D. 1008 (down to folio 93) are written. To take the first of those inner folds. Folio 85 contains the two first pages of '*Be Godcundre Warnunge.*' The other side of the same fold comes out at folio 92, which (as well as the greater part of folio 93) belongs to the copy (not mentioned in the catalogues on which the Author relies) of the ordinance of A.D. 1008.

I have thus made the Cottonian volume *Nero A.* 1 tell its own tale, which conclusively settles the question; and, after it, not much need be said of the catalogues. That prefixed to the volume itself[1] enumerates twenty-one pieces: a number which, in Smith's Catalogue of 1695, rose to twenty-nine; in Wanley's to 36, and in Plaxta's to 49.

The contents of the first half of the volume, specified in that original list, are (1) Canute's Laws; (2) Edgar's Laws; (3) Alfred's Laws (no notice being taken of their imperfect state in the manuscript, or of Josceline's supplement); (4) the *Institutes;* (5) Athelstan's Laws; and (6) Edmund's Laws (no notice being taken of the fragment of Edgar's laws). Not only were (1) *Be Cristendome*, (2) *Be Godcundre Warnunge*, (3) the copy contained in the same 'tract' of the Ordinance of A.D. 1008, (4) *Grith and Mund*, and (5) *Church-Grith,* left unnoticed; but the same was the case as to the two pieces (6) *Romescot,* and (7) *Officium justi Judicis,* which in the second 'tract' of the volume came between the chapter-titles and the preamble of Alfred's laws; beginning (as they both do)[2] on the same page on which the

[1] The Author says (C, p. 104): 'If Lord Selborne *had only taken the trouble of reading* the original list of manuscripts on the first page of the volume, he would see at once that the Church Mund and Church Grith are not in the list of manuscripts contained then in that volume.' It would not do to take too seriously the Author's fashions of speech. If he will look at pp. 242 and 287 (note) of *Ancient Facts,* etc. (pp. 242 and 285 of the first edition), he will see whether I had 'taken the trouble to read' that list, or not.

[2] *Romescot* is a very short piece, beginning on folio 47 after the concluding chapter-title of Alfred's laws, but not filling the whole page.

chapter-titles end, and forming (as they do beyond question) original and integral parts of the same manuscript. The ancient addition, at folio 84b, of the Latin extract from St. Augustine, is also omitted: which Dr. Smith's catalogue inserts, while in the other omissions it follows the original list.

If it were more difficult than it is to suggest an explanation of the absence of any specification in this catalogue of those pieces included in the second and 'fourth' tracts which it omits, those omissions could not be set against the evidence of the book itself. But it is to be observed, that it purports to be a catalogue '*Tractatuum*,' and not of all the pieces included in every '*Tractatus*.' Its framer (some amanuensis doubtless of Sir Robert Cotton, if not himself) appears to have thought it sufficient to note, as to each 'tract' which had no general title of its own, those things in it which he regarded as of special importance, without multiplying the entries by giving a place to what may have seemed to him secondary matters, occurring in the same 'tract' under rubrics more or less obscure. Be this as it might, his mention of pieces, inseparable from others as to which he was silent, really proves that those others were there at the same time, although he did not mention them.

The Author appears[1] to attach importance to the general list of the Cottonian Library drawn up by order of the Privy Council in 1632. But it adds nothing, so far as *Nero A*. 1 is concerned, to the original catalogue in the volume itself.

The purpose for which that list was made out was to discover whether the Library contained anything which could be claimed as public property, or might be dangerous to the State. For this it could not be necessary to look, in *Nero A*. 1, beyond the Table of Contents prefixed to it; and it is manifest that the framers of that general list did this, and no

Then, on the same page, follows the longer piece, Wanley's *Officium justi Judicis*, continued to folio 49b, which Josceline has filled up, after its last lines, with his extract from Bromton. All this (except what Josceline wrote) is in the same ancient writing with the chapter-titles, and with the preamble (which follows at folio 50a), of Alfred's laws.

[1] C, pp. 99, 100. At p. 104 the Author says: 'The original list, and no more, is in the Catalogue of 1632.' In point of fact, it is less, rather than more.

more. This is their enumeration: (1) *Canuti Edgari et Aluredi Regum Leges;* (2) *Institutio Regum,* etc. (in the words of the Nero catalogue, with the omission only of one superfluity [1]); (3) *Athelstani et Edmundi Regum Leges;* (4) *Officium episcopi, etc., breviter* (abridged from the seventh item, and probably meant to include the twelfth, of the Nero catalogue); (5) *Sermo Lupi,* etc. (in the words of the Nero catalogue, except that it gives the date in a shorter form, *anno stil.* 1014); (6) *Sermo brevis pareneticus ad Dei cultum;* (7) '*Anglo-witena gerednesse, i.e. Sapientum et optimatum regni Angliæ consilium Adnotatur recenti charactere Parliamentum fuisse anno* 1008.' The two last items are in the exact words of the 14th and 15th entries in the *Nero* list. A stream cannot rise higher than its source; this Privy Council list cannot prove more than the other from which it was taken.

I have said enough upon this side-issue of the Author. There remain two points, which I reserved as having some indirect bearing upon the principal question:—(1) as to the (so-called) Excerptions of Egbert, and (2), as to the gloss on one of Dunstan's canons.

§ 8. *Odo's Injunctions and 'Egbert's Excerptions.'*

The Author says:[2] 'Odo's Canons' (they are *not* Canons) 'were compiled from Egbert's Excerptions and [the] Legatine Injunctions.' As to the Legatine Injunctions, I have shown, in parallel columns,[3] what passages in them were repeated by Archbishop Odo. But for the statement, that anything in Odo's Injunctions was taken from 'Egbert's Excerptions,' there is no foundation in fact. Those Injunctions and the 'Excerptions' have nothing in common, except a quotation by Odo (as to nuns only) from a sentence of anathema against incestuous marriages by a Roman Council under Pope Gregory II., which is extracted, more at large, in the 'Excerptions.'[4]

[1] *i.e. seu officia,* after '*Institutis.*'
[2] C, p. 88.   [3] AF, Appendix B, p. 325.
[4] See for Odo's Injunctions, Spelman's *Concil.,* vol. i. p. 415. The quotation from Pope Gregory is in the 7th Injunction; the '*Excerption*' here referred to is the 131st (Thorpe, *Ancient Laws,* etc., vol. ii. p. 117).

There is, beyond this, some correspondence (not verbal, but of matter) between the rule of monastic duty laid down by Odo in his sixth Injunction, and a Canon of Orleans of A.D. 501, and a precept of Archbishop Theodore, both extracted in the 'Excerptions.'[1] But that matter was *communis juris* in the Church, as may be seen (*e.g.*) from the 29th Canon of the Council of Cloveshoo, held under Archbishop Cuthbert in A.D. 747.[2] If Odo (educated at Fleury[3]) had quoted directly from the Canon of Orleans, or from the precepts of his famous predecessor in the Primacy—as he did from Gregory the Second's sentence of anathema—there would be no ground for supposing that he obtained his knowledge of those authorities at second-hand; much less, that there was no compilation or treatise, other and earlier than the 'Excerptions,'[4] from which it might have been derived.

§ 9. *The gloss on Dunstan's 55th Canon.*

I have commented, in *Ancient Facts and Fictions*,[5] upon a gloss on one (the 55th) of Dunstan's Canons, found in a manuscript copy of those Canons now in the Bodleian Library, which Mr. Thorpe considered to be of the tenth century, but which (as to the gloss) I proved to be not earlier than *Church-Grith*. That Canon relates to the distribution of the people's alms by the priests; the gloss appended to it is: '*It is right, that one part be delivered to the priests, a second part for the need of the Church, a third part for the poor.*' I proved the commentator to have copied verbatim from three articles[6] of *Church-Grith*, in another of his glosses on another of Dunstan's Canons (the 60th, relating, not to alms or tithes, but to the chastity of priests), in the same manuscript. The proof was complete: if it had been necessary to go beyond

---

[1] '*Excerptions,*' Arts. 63 and 67 (Thorpe, vol. ii. pp. 106, 107).
[2] Johnson's *Laws and Canons*, vol. i. p. 261.
[3] See AF, p. 208.
[4] Such, *e.g.*, as the *Statuta Synodorum* of Odo's own time, which was in the Conventual Library of St. Augustin's Abbey, Canterbury (AF, p. 248). [5] AF, pp. 263, 264.
[6] Arts. 28, 29, 30 (AF, pp. 264, 341, 342).

the *evidentia rei*, exhibited in my notes by giving Mr. Thorpe's translation of the text of both documents, I might have strengthened it by adding the Anglo-Saxon text,[1] and by referring to the fifth article of the Council of Enham,[2] and the ninth article of the Ordinance of A.D. 1008,[3] both *in pari materia*; but in which some particular phrases, and some additional matter, which are found both in the gloss and in *Church-Grith*, do not occur.

Of this argument the Author takes no notice. He seems to think[4] that the difference between *alms* and *tithe* (though in the same breath he asserts that 'alms' in the Canon included tithe) is sufficient proof that *Church-Grith* was not the source of the gloss on the 55th Canon. He propounds as 'probable' a strange conjecture of his own, 'that the Bodleian manuscript was a gloss made in the tenth century *on the original copy of the Canon*;' and he insists on 'Mr. Thorpe's commanding position as an Anglo-Saxon scholar;' saying that I date the manuscript '*a century later than Mr. Thorpe.*' Instead of a century, the difference on that point between Mr. Thorpe and myself need not be more than some fifteen or sixteen years; for anything earlier than A.D. 1000 was in the tenth century. When the question is of the date, within less than twenty years, of an Anglo-Saxon manuscript, I cannot be persuaded that the opinion of any archæologist, however 'commanding' his position, ought to be preferred to the internal evidence of the document itself, when it is (as in this case) strong and clear.

§ 10. *Legatine Injunctions and Athelstan's Tithe Ordinance.*

There are many other things on which I might have been tempted to observe if I could afford space for them; such (*e.g.*) as the notions advanced by the Author in opposition to my criticisms of the Legatine Injunctions of A.D. 785-7,[5] and of King Athelstan's Tithe Ordinance.[6] If I understand him

[1] Thorpe, *Anc. Laws*, vol. i. p. 346.
[2] *Ibid.*, p. 317.
[3] *Ibid.*, pp. 306, 307.
[4] C, pp., 86, 87.
[5] AF, pp. 144-167.
[6] *Ibid.*, pp. 183-185. In a note at p. 184 I had spoken as if the same Anglo-Saxon MS. which contains Athelstan's Tithe Ordinance also con-

rightly, his opinion is,[1] that everything done by an Anglo-Saxon king, with the consent of any of his councillors selected by himself who would have voice and vote in a Witenagemot, although bishops only,[2] and whether the matter was ecclesiastical or civil, had the force which an Act of Parliament would have in modern times; and that, although upon the face of the record something different from legislation might appear to be intended, and though the thing might be done in an assembly presided over by an Italian Legate delivering a Pope's spiritual injunctions for the submissive acceptance of all present, and though strangers, who could not have a place in a national Witenagemot, might be present and taking part in those proceedings. He seems to think that the classification of any document by Mr. Thorpe as a 'law' is enough to prove that it was an enactment by a king with the consent of a regularly-constituted Witenagemot. But Mr. Thorpe, notwithstanding the note in his preface[3] to which the Author refers, has certainly included in his first volume a considerable number of documents, on the face of which there is not a word either claiming that character, or making it probable that they could have possessed it; of which *Grith* and *Mund* is one notable example. And Mr. Thorpe's ideas of the constitution of a National Witenagemot in Anglo-Saxon times were not so loose as those of the Author.[4] It is difficult

tained that king's secular Ordinances of Greatanlea. But, in point of fact, there is no MS. which contains both; as there are, in other cases, under Edmund, Edgar, and Canute, when civil and ecclesiastical laws, distinguished from each other, were enacted at the same time. (See Thorpe, *Ancient Laws*, vol. i. pp. 194-215; and pp. 244-5, 246-7, 262-3, 266-7, 358-9.)   [1] C, pp. 71-74.

[2] The Author (p. 72) places on some words of Bishop Stubbs the construction, that King Athelstan's letter to his reeves, 'with the counsel of the bishops,' was in a formula proper to signify the concurrence of a regular witenagemot with the king. It is impossible that the bishop could have meant to deduce a general conclusion to that effect from a single example, about the import and effect of which there was controversy; and this is a case which stands alone, among the documents which Mr. Thorpe has collected. If he did, I must respectfully demur to such an induction.

[3] Thorpe, vol. i. Preface, p. xiv.

[4] *Ibid.*, vol. i. pp. 190, 191 (note). And see Glossary at the end of Mr. Thorpe's second volume, in *voce* 'Witenagemot.'

to suppose that Mr. Thorpe intended to pledge his reputation to the accuracy of all the titles under which he has classified or described particular documents; such (*e.g.*) as '*Leges Regis Edwardi Confessoris*,'[1] and '*Excerptiones Ecgberti Eboracensis Archiepiscopi*.'[2] As to the '*Leges Regis Henrici Primi*,'[3] we know that he did not. It is but justice to him to add, that (although he prints some documents which are extant in Latin only) he gives no place in his collection of laws of the Anglo-Saxon kingdoms to the Legatine Injunctions of A.D. 795-797.

[1] Thorpe, vol. i. p. 442. [2] *Ibid.*, vol. ii. p. 97.
[3] *Ibid.*, vol. i. p. 497; and Preface, p. xiv.

INDEX

ABBO, 36, 37, 65, 209 note, 210, 217
Abingdon Monastery, 124, 171, 199, 203, 211, 311
Adrian I., Pope, 3, 5, 7, 9, 49, 144, 146, 148; Abbot of St. Augustine's, Canterbury, 124
Aelfric, Archbishop of Canterbury, 249, 250, 254; Archbishop of York, 249-252; 'the Grammarian,' 212, 231, 249-254, 264, 265; his 'Canons,' 255-262; other Aelfrics, 250 note
Aelfwald, King of Northumbria, 157, 159
Ahlstan, Bishop of Sherborne, 201, 202, 206
Ahyto, Bishop of Basle, 30
Ailred, Abbot of Rievaulx, 108, 213
Aimonius, biographer of Abbo, 65
Aix-la-Chapelle, capitulars of (A.D. 816), 62, 63, 84-86, 112
Alcuin, 5 note, 77, 125, 138, 142, 148 note, 169, 170, 231, 233, 234
Aldhelm, Bishop of Sherborne, 125, 251
Alexander the Great, Edgar compared to, 212
Alfred, King, 172, 179, 180, 207, 271, 287; his Laws, 179-181, 271, 282, 287
Allen, John, 196, 197, 198, 306
Altsig, Abbot of York, 59 note
Amulo, Archbishop of Lyons, 60

Andain, St. Hubert's monastery, 38-42, 229 note, 231, 232, 240, 242
Andover, laws made at, 219
Angilram, Archbishop of Metz, 11
Anglo-Saxon Chronicle, 141, 151, 187, 195
Anglo-Saxon Church (first period), 99-123; (second period), 124-168; (third period), 169-206; (fourth period), 207-316
Anlaf, King of Norway, 271
Ansegisus, Abbot of Fontenelle, 10, 31
Apostolical canons, 14, 24
Appropriations of churches, 224; of tithes, 63-68, 224, 307-316
Archbishops of Canterbury—Augustin, 99-103, 151; Mellitus, 109; Justus, 109; Honorius, 109, 112-116, 219; Theodore, 99, 110-112, 173, 219, 264, 265; Brihtwald, 99, 126; Tatwine, 126; Nothelm, 126; Cuthbert, 126, 128, 129; Jaenberht, 147, 151, 156; Ethelhard, 231; Wulfred, 174-177, 219; Plegmund, 171, 172 note, 207; Wulfhelm, 184; Odo, 99, 154, 208, 209, 218; Dunstan, 208-218, 241, 250, 253, 264; Aelfric, 249, 250; Alphege, 274, 275 note; Ethelnoth, 290; Anselm, 296, 297; Becket, 296; Baldwin, 270; Peccham, 226; note

INDEX

Archbishops of York—Paulinus, 109; Egbert, 125, 129-131, 173, 227-245; Eanbald, 148 note, 157, 231; Wigmund, 59 note; Oswald, 79, 208-210, 213, 217, 233, 249; Wulstan, 230, 233, 251, 262; Aelfric Putta, 249, 250 note, 251, 252
Ardennes, 37, 44
Arnulph, Bishop of Orleans, 65, 210, 218
Arsaces, Edgar compared to, 212
Arthur, King, Edgar compared to, 212
Artois, 37
Asser, 141, 172 note, 190, 195, 207
Athelstan, King, 183, 212, 248, 249, 271, 282, 284, 285; his Laws, 183-185, 271, 282, 400
Auerbach, 53 note
Augustin of Canterbury, 99-103, 151; Bishop of Orleans, 244
Augustine, St., 41, 248
Austrasia, 42

BALE, John, 245 note
Balsamon, 75 note
Baluze, 11, 40, 60, 229; and many references in notes
Baptismal churches, 57-60, 71-73, 91, 92, 101, 122, 126, 173, 220, 223, 226
Bardney Monastery, 171
Baron, Mr., 250 note, 381
Bath Abbey, 140
Battle Abbey, 309, 311; Chronicle of, 309, 310
Beauvais, diocese, question as to tithes, 93
Bede, 107, 117, 120, 121, 124, 129-133, 137, 172, 232, 233
Benedict, Biscop, 124 note
Benedict, Levite, 10, 33, 83
Benedict, St., 103, 257
Benedictine Order, 102, 103, 208-216
Benefices, ecclesiastical, 94, 95; lay, 72

Beohrtric, King of Wessex, 151
Bernard, first Norman Bishop of St. David's, 315
Bertin, St., monastery of, 211 note, 233
Birch, *Cartularium Saxonicum*, 196 and references in notes
Bishoprics, Anglo-Saxon, 108-112, 214
Bishops, their power over church revenues, 24-26, 70-74, 137; their share of church revenues, 27, 30, 32-36, 69, 70, 95, 96
Blackstone, Sir William, 32, 197, 219
Bocland, 196, 198, 220, 223, 224
Boniface, St., Archbishop of Mentz, 125, 128, 137, 172
Boxgrove Abbey, 311
Brabant, 37
Brewer, J. S., 228 note, 360
British Church, ancient, 100-102
Bromton, Abbot of Jorvaulx, 138, 139, 271
Burchard, Bishop of Worms, 19, 81 note, 83
Burial-grounds, 61, 173, 220, 222, 223

CADILLAC, 314, 351
Cæsarius, Archbishop of Arles, 47
Camden, William, 113
Canon Law, ancient Roman, 9, 24, 49; modern Roman, 20, 91
Canons, Anglo-Saxon, of Hertford, 127, 128; Archbishop Cuthbert's, 133-136; of Legatine Councils (A.D. 785-787), 160-167; of Archbishop Wulfred, 174-177; of Archbishop Dunstan, 216, 217; of Enham, 274-277; pseudo-Nicene, 76; so-called, of Aelfric, 255-262
Canterbury, Primacy of, 108, 109, 147-149, 151, 152; Cathedral, 128, 198; Monastery, 124, 247, 311
Canute, King, 177, 193, 271, 277 note, 279, 282, 287, 298, 299;

his laws, 287-292, and Appendix E
Capitulare Episcoporum, 36-45, 57, 217, 218, 225, 227, 232, 258, 262, 268, 269, 281; Metz MS. of, 38-40, 57, 232, 243, 258; Andain MS. of, 39-41, 227, 229, 231, 232, 236, 237, 243, 258-262; both texts collated, Appendix A, Suppl. 373
Capitulars of Frank princes, 3, 4, 25, 27, 41, 50, 51, 57, 61, 64, 71, 72, 73, 81, 84 note, 87, 88, 242
Carisbrooke, tithes of, 353, 354
Caroline Books, 5
Cartularium Saxonicum, Birch, 196
Cassian, 59
Centenarions, 59
Chalchyth, Legatine Council of, 144-167, Suppl. 400
Chale, tithes of, 353, 354
Chapels, 56, 81, 89, 173
Charlemagne, 3, 4, 5, 6, 7, 8, 42-44, 61, 146-148
Charles the Bald, Emperor, 64, 73, 88
Chester-le-Street, Bishopric of, 171
Chinnor, tithes of, 355, 356
Chrodegang, Bishop of Metz, 269
Church appointments, under Frank princes, 6, 7; in Spain, 6
Church-Grith, Of, document entitled, 222 note, 263, 278-289, 292, Append. E, Suppl. 371-395
Church-scot, 181 note, 218, 220
Clement of Rome, his pretended epistle to St. James, 14, 15, 19
Clergy, their share of church revenues, 27, 70, 71
Clovis I., 3, 35, 42; II., 65
Codex Diplomaticus, Kemble, 196, and references in notes
Co-heirs of churches, 83, 84
Comber, Thomas, Dean of Carlisle, 186, 308, 312, 358, 359
Condros, 43
'Congrua portio,' 224
Consecration of churches, 81, 120, 297; of tithes, 90, 308-316; charters, 313-316, and Appendix H
Constantine the Great, his pretended Donation, 14-18
Constantine, monk of Fleury, 233
Corbey Abbey, 77, 79, 211, 233
Cornwall, Bishopric of, 171
Councils, English—Chalchyth (A.D. 785-787), 143-151; (A.D. 816), 174-177; Cloveshoo (A.D. 747), 126, 133-136; (A.D. 803), 99, 147; Enham (or Eanham), 273-278; Geddington (A.D. 1188), 194; Hatfield, 117; Hertford, 9, 117; Winchester (A.D. 975), 213, 217
Councils, Foreign—Antioch, 24; Aix-la-Chapelle, V., 62, 84-86, 112, 243; VIII., 7; Arles, VI., 5 note, 25 note, 42, 62, 242; Braga, I., 34; II., 34, 55 note, 218; Chalcedon, 55, 59, 75 note; Chalons, II., 25; III., 5 note, 83; Clermont, IV., 67; Frankfort, 25 note, 72 note, 73, 81; Lateran (A.D. 1078), 66; III., 68, 297, 308, 309-311; Macon, II., 47, 48; Martzen, 31; Mentz, I., 5 note, 25 note, 42, 62, 72 note, 242, 243; III., 25 note, 31, 62; Merida, 34, 55 note; Metz, V., 90; Neo-Cæsarea, 257 note; Nicæa, I., 256, 265; II., 5; Orleans, I., 24, 35, 75, 81, 218; III., 26; Paris, V., 6 note; VI., 30, 32; Pavia, I., 25 note, 64 note; II., 25 note, 63, 64 note; Poictiers, 67; Ravenna, 89; Rheims, II., 5 note; Rome (A.D. 848-854), 82; Rouen, 49; St. Denis, 65; Salzburg, 30; Seville, I., 49; II., 55; Tarragona, 33; Thionville, 30 note; Toledo, III., 25; IV., 32, 33; IX., 33, 81, 82; XII., 6; XVI., 32, 33, 218; Toul, I., 73; Tours, II., 4, 7, 8; III., 5 note, 41, 51, 52;

(A.D. 1163), 67 ; Tribur, 31, 61, 88 ; Verneuil, I., 57, 58 ; II., 59 note ; Worms, I., 31, 71 note, 75, 88.
Crediton, Bishopric of, 171, 235, 241, 252, and Appendix F
Crowland Abbey, 124, 171, 311 ; charters, 178
Customs of churches, 26
Cuthbert, St., 107, 121, 129, 130 ; Archbishop, 126, 128, 129, 130-136
Cynethryth, Queen of Offa, 142 note

D'AGNESSEAU, Chancellor, 95
Danegeld, 302
Danes, their ravages, 168-171 ; their government in East Anglia under Alfred and his son, 180 ; in Ethelred's time, 272, 287, 375
Dauphiné, modern custom of, as to division of tithes, 91 note
Decimation, principle of, 194
Decretals, forged, of Isidore 'Mercator,' 1, 2, 13-19, 244 ; of Pope Gregory IX., 64 note, 67 note, 68 note, 82 note, 93 note
'Decuriones,' 59
Denis, St., Abbey of, 211 note, 233
Diceto, Ralph de, Dean of St. Paul's, 141, 147 note, 150, 190, 191
'Dioecesis,' of a baptismal church, 55, 56 note, 61
Dionysius 'Exiguus,' 9, 24 note, 47, 49 note
Dominicans, 80 note
'Dominium,' of parochial endowments, 95
Dorchester, Bishopric of, 110, 111, 171
Ducange, 36 note, 56 note, 73 note, 77 note, 79 note
Dugdale, Sir William, 314
Dunne, officer of King Ethelwulf, 205
Dunstan, Archbishop, 208-218, 241, 250, 253, 264 ; his Canons,

216, 217 ; glosses on them, 263, 264, Suppl. 399, 400
Dunwich, Bishopric of, 110
Durham, Bishopric of, 171

EADBERT, British Bishop of Lindisfarne, 107
Ecclesiastical Institutes, translated from Theodulph, 262, 299, 361
Echard, *History of England*, 186
Edgar, King, 173, 177, 178, 193, 212-216, 219-226, 253, 271, 272, 278, 284, 285, 286 ; his laws, 219-226, 271, 272, 282, 286, 289, 294, 295, 301, 304, 305, 307, 376-7
Edgar Atheling, 304
Edmund, King of England, 155, 212, 218, 271, 284, 285 ; his laws, 218, 271, 282
Edmund Ironside, 286
Edmund, St., King of East Anglia, 210
Edred, King, 178, 209, 212
Edward, King, the Elder, 172, 180, 182, 207, 271 ; his treaty with Guthrum II., 180-183, 271
Edward, King, the Martyr, 276, 285, 304
Edward the Confessor, King, 235 note, 289, 300-309 ; laws ascribed to him, 300-306
Edward III., King, 310, 311
Edwy, King, 212
Egbert, Archbishop of York, 125, 129-131, 173 ; his 'Penitential,' 136, 229, 231, 232, 233, 236, 237, 241 ; his 'Dialogue,' 136 ; 'Excerptions' attributed to him, 40, 177, 241-245
Egbert, King, 147, 170
'Egbertine' compilations of tenth or eleventh centuries, 227-245 ; Bodleian 'Penitential,' 229, 235-241, and Appendix C ; Cottonian 'Excerptions,' 229, 241-245 ; Parker manuscript in Corpus Christi College, Cambridge ; 229-235 ; fragment in National Lib-

rary at Paris, 229, 236; collation and comparison, Appendices A and D, Suppl. 370, 398
Egferth or Egfrid, son of Offa, 151
Elmham, Bishopric of, 111
Elmham, Thomas of, 116, 117, 120-122
Ely Monastery, 171
Enham or Eanham, Council of, 273-277
Ercombert, King of Kent, 113
Ethelbald, King of Mercia, 198
Ethelbert, King of East Anglia, 141
Ethelbert, King of Kent, 181
Ethelbert, King of Wessex, 170
Ethelred I., King of Wessex, 170.
Ethelred the Unready, King, 193, 217, 250, 252, 253, 271-287; his Laws, 271-278; his supposed law for partition of tithes, 278-287, Suppl. 386, 394
Ethelric, Bishop of Sherborne, 250 note
Ethelward, Chronicle, 141, 188
Ethelwold, St., Bishop of Winchester, 208, 209, 211, 213, 217, 249
Ethelwulf, King, 59 note, 170, 179; his charters, 186-206, 313, 371
Eucharist, Holy, Aelfric's doctrine concerning, 231, 258
Evesham Abbey, 124, 171
Exeter, Bishopric of, 235, and Appendix F
Exeter 'Penitential,' in Bodleian Library, 229, 235-241, and Appendix C
Exeter Rule for Secular Canons, 264-270, and Appendix G
Exhall parish church, its charter of consecration and endowment, 315, and Appendix H
Eye Monastery, 311

FABRIC-FUNDS OF CHURCHES, 71
'Familia,' 44, 66, 73
Ferrieres, Abbey of, 138
Feudalised tithes, 63, 224
Field-churches, 223

Finan, St., of Lindisfarne, 110
Flamens of ancient Rome, 2
Flanders, Dunstan's flight to, 212
Fleury, Abbey of, 36, 79, 209-212, 214, 217, 233, 234
Florence of Worcester, 140, 151, 190
Folcland, 196, 197, 202, 204, 206
Forged decretals of early Popes, 1, 2, 13, 14-19
Franciscans, 80 note
Freeman, E. A., 250 note, 281
French Annalist, quoted by Selden, 189

GELASIUS, Pope, 27, 81
George, Bishop of Ostia (A.D. 785-787), 146, 148 note, 131-153, 156
Gerald, monk of Fleury, 66
'Gerocomia,' of Eastern Church, 75
Gervase of Canterbury, 141, 207 note, 276 note
Ghaerbald, Bishop of Liege, 42, 45, 57, 58
Ghent, St. Peter's Monastery at, 212, 214, 217
Gildas, 247
Giraldus Cambrensis, 101, 194
Glastonbury Abbey, 124, 181 note, 211, 212
Gloucester, Robert of, 189
Godwin, *De Præsulibus*, 114
Gratian's *Decretum*, 2, 7, 8, 19, 25 note, 26 note, 46, 49, 55 note, 56 note, 58, 60, 61, 63, 64 note, 66 note, 67 note, 79, 81 note, 82, 83, 91, 92
Gregory the Great, Pope, 26, 28, 66, 69, 70, 74, 103, 108, 151, 216, 248
Gregory VII., Pope, 7, 25, 66
Grimbald, 172 note
Grith and Mund, Of, document entitled, 278, 279, 282, 288, 390
Guisborough Abbey, 311
Guthmund of Norway, 271
Guthrum I., his treaty with Alfred, 180

Guthrum II., his treaty with Edward the Elder, 180-183

HABAM, King Ethelred's Laws of, 193, 271-273, 281
Haddan and Stubbs, *Councils*, 106, 121, 122, 152, 178, 196, 200, 206, 229, 231, 232, and Appendix C, references in notes very frequent
Hardiknute, King, 304
Hardyng, rhyming Chronicler, 192
Harescombe, tithes of, 354, 355
Harold I., King, 245
Harold II., King, 304
Hasbain, 44
Hasfield, tithes of, 354, 355
Hay, parish church, charter of consecration and endowment, 314, 315, and Appendix H
Helmstan, Bishop of Winchester, 201, 202, 204
Henry the Fowler, Emperor, 8
Henry I., King of England, 242, 289, 306, 315; laws ascribed to, 306, 307
Henry III., King of England, 310
Herard, Archbishop of Tours, 63
Hereford, Bishopric of, 111
Hexham, Bishopric of, 111, 170
Higbert, Archbishop of Lichfield, 151, 152
Higden, Ralph, 150
Hincmar, Archbishop of Rheims, 11, 13, 30, 52, 73, 74, 77, 78, 86, 88
Hinschius, *Decretales Pseudo-Isidorianæ*, 10 note, 13
Holinshed, 139, 191, 192
Honorius, Archbishop of Canterbury, 109, 112-116, 219
Hook, W. F., Dean of Chichester, 119, 147, 168, 249, 250 note, 273 note, 275 note, 290
Hospitality, ecclesiastical duty of, 23, 69, 74, 75, 225, 226
Hoveden, Roger, 141, 150, 187, 188

Howel Dha, Prince of Wales, his Laws, 101 note, 102
Hucarius, 245
Hume, *History of England*, 115, 186
Hunsige, thane of King Ethelwulf, 205
Huntingdon, Henry of, 141, 150, 151, 188

IMAGE-WORSHIP, 5
Ina, King of Wessex, 126, 127, 150, 181; his Laws, 127, 271
Ingilram or Angilram, Archbishop of Metz, 11
Ingulph, 140, 178, 191, 193, 195, 199
Institutes of Polity, 222 note, 252, 285, Suppl. 391
Investiture, of bishops, 7; of parish priests, 296
Irish Church, ancient, 101, 103, 157, 248
Isidore, Archbishop of Seville, 13, 247; the forger, 1, 13-19, 244, 279
Ivo, Bishop of Chartres, 19, 49, 83

JARROW MONASTERY, 124, 170
Jerome, St., 46
John, deacon, biographer of Gregory the Great, 244
John, King of England, 310
John, King of the Franks, 65
John, 'Scotus Erigena,' 172 note, 207
Johnson, John, 158 note, 228, 245 note; 283, 300, and other references in notes, Suppl. 381
Josceline, secretary to Archbishop Parker, 112, 113, 115, 122, 123, 283, Suppl. 389, 390
Jouy, Louis François, his work on tithes in France, 68 note, 89 note, 91 note, 224 note, 225 note
Justin, Prince of Norway, 271

KANEFIELD, tithes of, 357

Kemble, *Codex Diplomaticus*, 196 note, 200, 205; *Saxons in England*, 76 note, 180, 201 note, 206, 228, 290
Kennett, Bishop, 32, 114 note, 225, 226, 299, 300, 308, 314, and Appendix J
Kenwulf, King of Mercia, 147 note, 151
Kenwulf, King of Wessex, 151, 156

LAMBARDE, William, 197, 283, 380
Langtoft, rhyming Chronicler, 192
Lappenberg, Dr. J. M., his *History*, 121, 129, 130, 290, 291, 292
Lapse of private patronage to Bishops, 297
Latin translations of Anglo-Saxon laws, 271, 378-380
Laws of Ina, 127, 197 note, 271; of Wihtraed, 127, 128, 198; of Alfred, 179-181, 271, 282, 287; of Athelstan, 183-185, 271, 282; of Edmund, 218, 271, 282; of Edgar, 216-226, 281, 282, 286, 289, 294, 295, 307; of Ethelred the Unready, 271-287; of Canute, 279, 282, 287-295, 299, 301, 305, 307; of Edward the Confessor, 300-306; of William the Conqueror, 304-306; of Henry I., 306, 307
Lay grants of tithes, 63-68, 307-316, and Appendices H, I, J
Legatine Injunctions of Chalchyth (A.D. 785-787), 144, 145, 160-167
Leicester, Bishopric of, 111 171
Leland, John, 245 note
Le Mans, early grant of tithes to nuns, 65; Ordinance of Henry II., King of England, 194
Leofric, first Bishop of Exeter, 235, 241, and Appendix F; his Rule for Secular Canons, 264-270, and Appendix G
Lewes, Abbey, 311
Lichfield, Bishopric of, 111 note, 112, 147, 149, 151, 152

Liege, Bishopric, in Charlemagne's time, 43, 57, 58
Light-scot, 180
Lindisfarne Monastery, 169, 170; Bishopric, 111, 170
Lindsey, Bishopric of, 111, 171
Lingard, Dr., 155, 177, 206, 228
Livingus, Bishop of Crediton, translated to Worcester, 241
Lombard Laws, 51, 72 note, 87
London, Bishopric of, 108, 109, 212
Loortz, 43
Lorraine, 37, 42, 235, 268
Lothair I., Emperor, 4, 8, 53, 87
Louis the Pious, Emperor, 7, 8, 49, 53, 84-86, 112, 177, 233, 243
Louis II., Emperor, 54, 60, 64, 87
Ludlow, Judge, *temp*. Edward III., 311
'Luminaria,' 71
Lupus, Abbot of Ferrieres, 59, 61 note
Lupus, author of discourse to the English (A.D. 1014), 287, 375
Luxemburg, 37
Lyndewode's *Provinciale*, 226 note, 311

MABILLON, *Analecta Vetera*, 65 note
Magdeburg Centuries, 153, 154, 155, 156
Malmesbury Abbey, 124, 171, 200, 251
Malmesbury, William of, 141, 148 note, 189, 195, 196, 199, 250 note, 251, 268, 269
Manorial churches, 219, 220, 221, 222, 223, 224, 225, 295-298
Mansi, *Concilia*, 38 note, 40 note, 53 note, 229, 244, 245 note, and frequent references
Marculfus, his Forms, 86 note, 314, and Appendix H
Martene and Durand, 38, 53 note, 233, and references in notes
'Matrices ecclesiæ,' 56, 61 note, 76, 303

'Matricula,' 77
'Matricularii,' 77, 78
Matthew Paris, 142, 147 note
Mayo, Bishop of (A.D. 785-787), 157
Melrose Chronicle, 141
Metz, Monastery of St. Vincent, 37, 38, 40, 43
Milman, H. H., Dean of St. Paul's, 54 note, 55 note, 186
Milton, 195
Minsters, 56, 127, 220, 221, 222, 223, 224
'Missi Dominici,' 4
Monastic tithes, 64-68, 79, 80; exemptions, 64
Monks, before Benedict, 102, 103; their participation in alms of the Church, 79, 80
Montreuil Abbey, 67
Mores, E. R., his work on Aelfric, 249
Muratori, 53 note, 54 note

NASMITH, his catalogue of manuscripts in Library of Corpus Christi College, Cambridge, 230 note, 265, and other references
'Ninths and Tenths,' 72
Northumbria, kingdom of, 170, 179, 393
Northumbrian schools, 106
Noy, Attorney-General to Charles I., 225 note

ODO, Archbishop of Canterbury, 154, 155, 208, 209, and Appendix B, Suppl. 398, 399
'Oeconomi' of churches, 55
Offa, King of Mercia, 99, 138-143, 146-148, 151, 156, 159, 170-181; *Lives of two Offas*, 141, 149
Oratories, private, 25, 56, 72, 81-84, 173
Orleans diocese, customs of, 36, 37, 217, 300
'Orphanotrophia' in Eastern Church, 75
Osgar, Abbot of Abingdon, 211
Osney Abbey, 311, Appendix J

Oswald, St., Bishop of Worcester, 79, 208, 209, 210, 213, 217, 249
Oswald the younger, monk of Worcester, 210, 211 note, 234
Otgar, Archbishop of Mentz, 10
Othelon, biographer of St. Boniface, 76
Otho I., Emperor, 7, 8
Otho III., Emperor, 8
Oxford University, complaints of, under Henry V., 226 note

'PAGENSES PRESBYTERI,' 59
Palatine MSS. in Vatican Library, 38, 230
Papacy, 1, 2, 8
Paphnutius, 239, 256 note
Paris diocese, custom of, 30, 37, 217
Parker, Matthew, Archbishop of Canterbury, 112-114, 122, 229, 283
Parnynge, Chief Justice Sir Robert, 310
'Parochia,' its different senses, 56 note, 62, 115, 117, 127, 129, 299
'Parochiæ rusticanæ,' in France (A.D. 874), 86, 88, 89
Parochial system, modern, 83-95, 173, 219, 224, 295-298, 307-316
'Parochiales ecclesiæ,' in Portugal (A.D. 610), 34
'Parochitanæ ecclesiæ,' in Portugal (A.D. 666), 34 note
Pastoral Epistle of Aelfric, 252
Patrick, St., 248
Patrons of churches, 295-297
Paul, deacon of Aquileia, 5
Paulinus, first Archbishop of York, 109
'Pauperes Christi,' 75, 79, 80
'Peculium,' its ecclesiastical sense, 94, 95
'Penitentials' of Archbishop Theodore, 106, 118, 119; of Bede, 232; of Archbishop Egbert, 136, 229, 231, 232, 233, 236, 237, 241; in Bodleian Library, 229, 235-241
Pepin I. (or Pippin), King, his law of A.D. 794, 40 note, 72 note, 269

INDEX

Pershore, Abbey, 181 note, 311
Peterborough Abbey, 124, 171
Peterborough, John, Abbot of, 7 note, 141, 191
Peter's-pence, 138, 150, 180, 218, 221, 291, 292, 307
Picardy, 37
Pithou, *Codex Canonum Vetus*, 65 note, 66 note
Pitseus, 211 note
'Plebes,' public churches, 56, 60, 73
Plough-alms, 180, 218
Polydore Vergil, 139
Ponthieu, 234
Poor, their interest in church revenues, 23, 24; how relieved, 74-80, 215, 216, 267
Popes—Adrian I., 3, 5, 7, 9, 49, 144, 146, 152, 168; Alexander III., 67, 296; Anastasius, 9; Boniface VIII., 194; Calixtus II., 68; Eugenius III., 19; Formosus, 171; Gelasius, 27, 28, 70, 81; Gregory I., 26, 28, 69, 70, 74, 103, 108, 214; Gregory VII., 7, 25, 66; Gregory IX., 80; Innocent III., 20, 68 note, 79 note, 82, 93; John VIII., 244; John IX., 8; Leo I., 2; Leo III., 151, 152; Leo IV., 4, 7, 60, 82, 179; Leo VIII., 7, 8; Leo IX., 235 note, and Appendix F; Paschal II., 64, 296; Siricius, 9; Stephen IV., 8; Stephen V., 7; Sylvester, 10, 28 note, 244; Urban II., 67, 309; Urban III., 269; Zacharias, 134, 136, 168, 303 note
Portugal, 34
Preaching friars, 80, 364
Price, Richard, 279, 284
Prideaux, Humphrey, Dean of Norwich, 138, 186, 308, 313, 316
'Priest's-shire,' 300
'Procurator pauperum,' 76
Prohibition, writs of, as to tithes, 310

'Ptochodochia,' in Eastern Church, 75
Public Churches, 56, 60, 72, 73, 75

QUADRIPARTITE division of church revenues, 27, 28, 29-32; of offerings at shrine of Thomas à Becket, 269

RABANUS MAURUS, Archbishop of Mentz, 31, 62
Ramsbury, Bishopric of, 171
Ramsey Abbey, 210
Rapin, *History of England*, 186
Reading Monastery, 311
Regino, Abbot of Prum, 19, 83
Regularis Concordia, 213-216
Repairs of churches, 71-74, 89 note, 91, 219, 289
Report of Papal Legates (A.D. 785-787), 153-158, Suppl. 400
Repton Bishopric, 41 note; monastery, 171
Rheims diocese, custom of, 30, 37, 217
Richter, A. L., notes to Roman Canon Law, 67 note, 68 note
Riculf, Archbishop of Mentz, 13; Bishop of Soissons, 30, 32 note, 74
Robert, King of Franks, 65
Robert I., Duke of Normandy, 304
Robert II., Duke of Normandy, 302
Rochester, Bishopric of, 109; Cathedral chapter, 128, 198, 311
Rodolph, Archbishop of Bourges, 87
Romulus, King Edgar compared to, 212
'Rusticanæ parochiæ,' 86.

SACERDOTAL Laws of Egbertine compilations, 227, 232, 235, 236-240, 243, 245, 249, 259
St. Alban's Abbey, 139, 150 note
St. Josse Monastery, in Ponthieu, 234
St. Leonard's Monastery, Yorkshire, 311

St. Neot's Monastery, 311
Saladin tithe, 194
Salisbury, endowment of a Canonry with tithes, 356
Schmid, Reinhold, 290, 292, 392
Schools of learning, Anglo-Saxon, 124
Scottish Church, ancient, 101, 103
Selden, John, 41, 52, 59, 68 note, 72 note, 79 note, 80 note, 112, 114, 118, 140, 177, 178, 186, 187, 192-195, 199, 202 note, 219, 222, 223, 224, 228, 247, 248, 282, 295, 308-314, and Appendix J
Selsey, Bishopric of, 112
Sexti Decretales, 64 note, 80 note
Sherborne, Bishopric of, 111, 125, 250; chapter of, 250
'Shrift-district,' 223, 224
Sigebert II., King of Franks, 3
Sigebert of Gembloux, 7
Sirmondi, 6 note, 7 note, 38, 40, 50 note
Soames, *History of Anglo-Saxon Church*, 119
Soissons diocese, custom of, 30, 37
Somner, William, 197
Suol-scot, 221
Southey, Robert, 228 note, 360
Spain, 3, 33, 69
Spelman, Sir Henry, 115, 197, 228, 241, 282, 299, Suppl. 382
Statuta Synodorum, MS. formerly belonging to St. Augustine's Abbey, Canterbury, 247, 248
Stow's *Annals*, 113, 122, 123, 213 note, 277 note
Stubbs, Right Rev. William, Bishop of Chester, 208, 209, and frequent references
Supplement to King Edgar's Laws, 221, 380
Surtees Society, 229, 236
Sweyn, King of Denmark, 285
Swithun, St., Bishop of Winchester, 204, 206
Symeon of Durham, 5 note, 141, 151, 170, 171, 188

THEOBALD, Bishop of Langres, 60
Theodore, Archbishop of Canterbury, 9, 106, 110, 111, 116-123, 124-126, 173, 219, 234, 264, 265, 294
Theodoric, or Thierry, King of Austrasia, 42
Theodulph, Bishop of Orleans, 231, 233, 234, 262, 300
Theophylact, Bishop of Todi, 146, 152, 156
Thomassinus, *De Beneficiis*, 47 note, 72 note
Thorpe, Benjamin, 178, 201 note, 222, 228, 241, 250 note, and frequent references, Suppl. 392
Tithes, 23, 24, 27, 30 note, 31 note, 46-68, 73, 76, 78, 80, 86, 87, 88, 90, 91, 93, 95, 96, 106-108, 137, 144, 179, 180, 183-185, 187-206, 218, 220, 224-226, 267, 268, 277, 279, 294, 297, 301, 307-316, and Appendices A, B, G, H, I, J
Titles to benefices, 94, 95
Tripartite division of church revenues and tithes, 32-37, 91 note, 101, 102, 225-264, 267, 268, 279-287, 289, and Appendices A, E
Turner, Sharon, 176 note, 206
Turrianus, Francis, 76 note

VAN ESPEN, 20, 23 note, 26, 29, 59, 64, 74, 75 note, 82 note, 91 note, 93-95
Vatican MS. (compared with Egbertine MS. in the Bodleian), 230, and Appendix C
Vedast, St., monastery of, 211 note, 233
Vicars, 224, 226 note
'Vici publici,' 56

WALAFRID STRABO, 31, 37 note, 58, 59, 179
Wallingford, John of, 141
Walter, Bishop of Orleans, 88
Wanley, 230 note, 265, and other references, Suppl. 392, 393

INDEX

Wantage, King Ethelred's Laws of, 271, 278, 383
Wasserschleben, 106, 173, 229, 230 note, 231, 232, 245 note
Wearmouth Monastery, 124, 170
Wells, Bishopric of, 171
Welsh Church, ancient, 100 note, 101, 102, 103, 158
Wendover, Roger of, 141, 147 note, 190, 199, 200
Wenefrid, Bishop of Worcester, 207 note
Westminster, Matthew of, 143, 147 note, 189, 190, 199
Wharton, *Anglia Sacra*, 249, and references in notes
Whelock, Abraham, 116, 264, 283, 380
Whitby Abbey, 171
Wiferth, thane of King Ethelwulf, 205
Wigbod, Abbot, 148 note, 156
Wihtraed, King of Kent, 126-128, 198
Wilkins, David, 228, 241, 283, 383
William the Conqueror, 301, 302-303; Rufus, 302

Winchester, Bishopric of, 110, 111, 209-213; Cathedral, 205
'Wite-ræden,' 197, 201
Witnesses as to tithes, 41, 51-54, 240, 260
Woodstock, King Ethelred's Laws of, 271, 278
Worcester, Bishopric of, 111, 209, 212; monastery, 181 note, 241; manuscripts formerly belonging to, 229-234, 241-245, 282-284
Wulfred, Archbishop, his canons, 174-177; 219
Wulfsin, Bishop of Sherborne, 249, 250
Wulstan, Bishop of Worcester and Archbishop of York, 230, 233, 251-254

'XENODOCHIA,' 75, 76, 136

YORK, Archbishopric of, 108; school of learning, 125, 171

ZACHARIAS, Pope, 134, 136, 168, 303 note
Zonaras, 75 note

ADDENDA TO INDEX

Anglo-Saxon books in Sir Robert Cotton's Library, list of, in 1632, Suppl. 397.
Degge's *Parson's Counsellor*, Suppl. 366-369.
Clarke, Rev. H. J., Suppl. 363.
Nero A. 1 (Cottonian MS. volume), 241-242, 282-284; its state in 1580 and 1613, Suppl. 389-391; its present state, 386, 387, 391-396; catalogue prefixed to, 396, 397.
Smith, Dr. Thomas, his catalogue of the Cottonian Library in 1698, Suppl. 389 note, 397.
Tate, Francis, Suppl. 389-391, 392.

Printed by R. & R. CLARK, *Edinburgh*

MESSRS. MACMILLAN & CO.'S PUBLICATIONS.

BOOKS BY THE SAME AUTHOR.

A DEFENCE OF THE CHURCH OF ENGLAND AGAINST DISESTABLISHMENT. By ROUNDELL, Earl of Selborne. Crown 8vo. 2s. 6d.

TIMES—"Friends and foes of the Church of England will alike turn with attentive interest to the Earl of Selborne's new book. To say that the argument advanced in this important treatise is weighty, judicious, temperate, learned, and cogent, is only to say that it is the work of Lord Selborne.... It will fortify the friends of the Church in the convictions they entertain, and it will also compel its adversaries to revise many of their arguments and to reconsider their whole position. For this reason the publication of this volume at the present juncture is singularly opportune."

GUARDIAN—"Upon his *Defence* Lord Selborne has concentrated the acumen of the distinguished lawyer, the practical sagacity of the experienced statesman, the laborious research of the careful historian. The combined result of these varied qualifications is the valuable volume before us, a volume which forms a well-furnished armoury of weapons both of offence and defence, arranged and set in order for immediate service, a volume which, if thoroughly mastered and rightly understood, places a winning brief in the hands of every Churchman who pleads the cause of the Establishment at the bar of an intelligent public opinion."

THE BOOK OF PRAISE. From the best English Hymn Writers. Selected by ROUNDELL, Earl of Selborne. 18mo. 2s. 6d. net.
[*Golden Treasury Series.*

A HYMNAL. Chiefly from *The Book of Praise.* In various sizes. —A. In Royal 32mo, cloth limp. 6d.—B. Small 18mo, larger type, cloth limp. 1s.—C. Same Edition, fine paper, cloth. 1s. 6d.—An Edition with Music, Selected, Harmonised, and Composed by JOHN HULLAH. Square 18mo. 3s. 6d.

BOOKS ON THE CHURCH OF ENGLAND

DISESTABLISHMENT AND DISENDOWMENT. What are they? By Prof. E. A. FREEMAN. Fourth Edition. Crown 8vo. 1s.

DISESTABLISHMENT: or, A Defence of the Principle of a National Church. By GEORGE HARWOOD. 8vo. 12s.

DISSENT IN ITS RELATION TO THE CHURCH OF ENGLAND. By Rev. G. H. CURTEIS. Bampton Lectures for 1871. Crown 8vo. 7s. 6d.

JUDGMENT IN THE CASE OF READ AND OTHERS *v.* THE LORD BISHOP OF LINCOLN. Nov. 21, 1890. By His Grace the ARCHBISHOP OF CANTERBURY. 8vo. 1s. 6d. net.

MACMILLAN AND CO., LONDON.

MESSRS. MACMILLAN & CO.'S PUBLICATIONS.

NEW AND CHEAPER EDITION.

LIFE OF ARCHIBALD CAMPBELL TAIT, Archbishop of Canterbury. By RANDALL THOMAS DAVIDSON, D.D., Bishop of Rochester, late Dean of Windsor, and WILLIAM BENHAM, B.D., Hon. Canon of Canterbury. Third Edition. 2 vols. Crown 8vo, cloth. 10s. net.

By the late DEAN CHURCH.

THE OXFORD MOVEMENT. TWELVE YEARS, 1833-1845. New and Cheaper Edition. Globe 8vo. 5s.

* *A new volume of the uniform edition of Dean Church's Miscellaneous Works.*

VILLAGE SERMONS. Crown 8vo. 6s.

HUMAN LIFE AND ITS CONDITIONS. Sermons at Oxford, 1876-78, etc. Crown 8vo. 6s.

THE GIFTS OF CIVILISATION, and other Sermons and Lectures delivered at Oxford and in St. Paul's Cathedral. Crown 8vo. 7s. 6d.

THE DISCIPLINE OF THE CHRISTIAN CHARACTER. Crown 8vo. 4s. 6d.

ADVENT SERMONS, 1885. Crown 8vo. 4s. 6d.

By Ven. Archdeacon WILSON, M.A.

SERMONS PREACHED IN CLIFTON COLLEGE CHAPEL, 1879-83. Crown 8vo. 6s. Second Series. 1888-90. 6s.

ESSAYS AND ADDRESSES. An Attempt to treat some Religious Questions in a Scientific Spirit. Crown 8vo. 4s. 6d.

SOME CONTRIBUTIONS TO THE RELIGIOUS THOUGHT OF OUR TIME. 6s.

By Rev. Professor SALMON, D.D.

NON-MIRACULOUS CHRISTIANITY, AND OTHER SERMONS. 8vo. 6s.

GNOSTICISM AND AGNOSTICISM, AND OTHER SERMONS. Crown 8vo. 7s. 6d.

By Various Authors.

SERMONS. By the Right Rev. JAMES FRASER, D.D., Second Bishop of Manchester. In 2 vols. I. University Sermons. II. Parochial Sermons. Edited by Rev. JOHN W. DIGGLE. 6s. each.

THE LIGHT THAT LIGHTETH EVERY MAN: Sermons. By ALEXANDER RUSSELL, B.D., late Dean of Adelaide. With an Introduction by the Very Rev. E. H. PLUMPTRE, D.D. Crown 8vo. 6s.

WELLINGTON COLLEGE SERMONS. By the Rev. E. C. WICKHAM, M.A., Master of Wellington College, late Fellow of New College, Oxford. Crown 8vo. 6s.

LESSONS OF HOPE: Readings from the Works of FREDERICK DENISON MAURICE. Selected by the Rev. J. LLEWELYN DAVIES, M.A. Crown 8vo. 5s.

SERMONS. By MARK PATTISON, late Rector of Lincoln College, Oxford. Crown 8vo. 6s.

THE COUNTRY CLERGYMAN AND HIS WORK. By Rev. HERBERT JAMES, M.A. Crown 8vo. 6s.

THE SPIRITUAL LIFE, AND OTHER SERMONS. By the Rev. J. E. C. WELLDON, M.A. Crown 8vo. 6s.

MACMILLAN AND CO., LONDON.

September, 1891.

A CLASSIFIED

CATALOGUE OF BOOKS
IN GENERAL LITERATURE
PUBLISHED BY

MACMILLAN AND CO.
BEDFORD STREET, COVENT GARDEN, LONDON, W.C.

For purely Educational Works see MACMILLAN AND CO.'s *Educational Catalogue.*

AGRICULTURE.
(*See also* BOTANY; GARDENING.)
FRANKLAND (Prof. P. F.).—A HANDBOOK OF AGRICULTURAL CHEMICAL ANALYSIS. Cr. 8vo. 7s. 6d.
TANNER (Henry).—ELEMENTARY LESSONS IN THE SCIENCE OF AGRICULTURAL PRACTICE. Fcp. 8vo. 3s. 6d.
—— FIRST PRINCIPLES OF AGRICULTURE. 18mo. 1s.
—— THE PRINCIPLES OF AGRICULTURE. For Use in Elementary Schools. Ext. fcp. 8vo.—THE ALPHABET OF THE PRINCIPLES OF AGRICULTURE. 6d.—FURTHER STEPS IN THE PRINCIPLES OF AGRICULTURE. 1s.—ELEMENTARY SCHOOL READINGS ON THE PRINCIPLES OF AGRICULTURE FOR THE THIRD STAGE. 1s.

—— THE ABBOT'S FARM; or, Practice with Science. Cr. 8vo. 3s. 6d.

ANATOMY, Human. (*See* PHYSIOLOGY.)
ANTHROPOLOGY.
BROWN (J. Allen).—PALÆOLITHIC MAN IN NORTH-WEST MIDDLESEX. 8vo. 7s. 6d.
DAWKINS (Prof. W. Boyd).—EARLY MAN IN BRITAIN AND HIS PLACE IN THE TERTIARY PERIOD. Med. 8vo. 25s.
DAWSON (James). — AUSTRALIAN ABORIGINES. Small 4to. 14s.
FINCK (Henry T.).—ROMANTIC LOVE AND PERSONAL BEAUTY. 2 vols. Cr. 8vo. 18s.
FISON (L.) and HOWITT (A. W.).—KAMILAROI AND KURNAI GROUP. Group-Marriage and Relationship, and Marriage by Elopement. 8vo. 15s.
FRAZER (J. G.).—THE GOLDEN BOUGH: A Study in Comparative Religion. 2 vols. 8vo. 28s.
GALTON (Francis).—ENGLISH MEN OF SCIENCE: THEIR NATURE AND NURTURE. 8vo. 8s. 6d.
—— INQUIRIES INTO HUMAN FACULTY AND ITS DEVELOPMENT. 8vo. 16s.
—— RECORD OF FAMILY FACULTIES. Consisting of Tabular Forms and Directions for Entering Data. 4to. 2s. 6d.
—— LIFE-HISTORY ALBUM : Being a Personal Note-book, combining Diary, Photograph Album, a Register of Height, Weight, and other Anthropometrical Observations, and a Record of Illnesses. 4to. 3s. 6d.—Or with Cards of Wool for Testing Colour Vision. 4s. 6d.
—— NATURAL INHERITANCE. 8vo. 9s.

M'LENNAN (J. F.).—THE PATRIARCHAL THEORY. Edited and completed by DONALD M'LENNAN, M.A. 8vo. 14s.
—— STUDIES IN ANCIENT HISTORY. Comprising "Primitive Marriage." 8vo. 16s.
MONTELIUS—WOODS. — THE CIVILISATION OF SWEDEN IN HEATHEN TIMES. By Prof. OSCAR MONTELIUS. Translated by Rev. F. H. WOODS. Illustr. 8vo. 14s.
TURNER (Rev. Geo.).—SAMOA, A HUNDRED YEARS AGO AND LONG BEFORE. Cr. 8vo. 9s.
TYLOR (E. B.).—ANTHROPOLOGY. With Illustrations. Cr. 8vo. 7s. 6d.
WESTERMARCK (Dr. Edward).—THE HISTORY OF HUMAN MARRIAGE. With Preface by Dr. A. R. WALLACE. 8vo. 14s. net.
WILSON (Sir Daniel).—PREHISTORIC ANNALS OF SCOTLAND. Illustrated. 2 vols. 8vo. 36s.
—— PREHISTORIC MAN : Researches into the Origin of Civilisation in the Old and New World. Illustrated. 2 vols. 8vo. 36s.
—— THE RIGHT HAND ; LEFT HANDEDNESS. Cr. 8vo. 4s. 6d.

ANTIQUITIES.
(*See also* ANTHROPOLOGY.)
ATKINSON (Rev. J. C.).—FORTY YEARS IN A MOORLAND PARISH. Ext. cr. 8vo. 8s. 6d. net.—*Illustrated Edition.* 12s. net.
BURN (Robert).—ROMAN LITERATURE IN RELATION TO ROMAN ART. With Illustrations. Ext. cr. 8vo. 14s.
DILETTANTI SOCIETY'S PUBLICATIONS.
ANTIQUITIES OF IONIA. Vols. I.—III. 2l. 2s. each, or 5l. 5s. the set, net.—Vol. IV. Folio, half morocco, 3l. 13s. 6d. net.
AN INVESTIGATION OF THE PRINCIPLES OF ATHENIAN ARCHITECTURE. By F. C. PENROSE. Illustrated. Folio. 7l. 7s. net.
SPECIMENS OF ANCIENT SCULPTURE : EGYPTIAN, ETRUSCAN, GREEK, AND ROMAN. Vol. II. Folio. 5l. 5s. net.
DYER (Louis).—STUDIES OF THE GODS IN GREECE AT CERTAIN SANCTUARIES RECENTLY EXCAVATED. Ext. cr. 8vo. 8s. 6d. net.
GARDNER (Percy).—SAMOS AND SAMIAN COINS : An Essay. 8vo. 7s. 6d.
GOW (J., Litt.D.).—A COMPANION TO SCHOOL CLASSICS. Illustrated. 3rd Ed. Cr. 8vo. 6s.
HARRISON (Miss Jane) and VERRALL (Mrs.).—MYTHOLOGY AND MONUMENTS OF ANCIENT ATHENS. Illustrated. Cr. 8vo. 16s.

ANTIQUITIES—ASTRONOMY.

ANTIQUITIES—continued.

LANCIANI (Prof. R.).—ANCIENT ROME IN THE LIGHT OF RECENT DISCOVERIES. 4to. 24s.

MAHAFFY (Prof. J. P.).—A PRIMER OF GREEK ANTIQUITIES. 18mo. 1s.
— SOCIAL LIFE IN GREECE FROM HOMER TO MENANDER. 6th Edit. Cr. 8vo. 9s.
— RAMBLES AND STUDIES IN GREECE. Illustrated. 3rd Edit. Cr. 8vo. 10s. 6d.
(See also HISTORY, p. 11.)

NEWTON (Sir C. T.).—ESSAYS ON ART AND ARCHÆOLOGY. 8vo. 12s. 6d.

SHUCHHARDT (Carl).—DR. SCHLIEMANN'S EXCAVATIONS AT TROY, TIRYNS, MYCENAE, ORCHOMENOS, ITHACA, IN THE LIGHT OF RECENT KNOWLEDGE. Trans. by EUGENIE SELLERS. Preface by WALTER LEAF, Litt.D. Illustrated. 8vo. 18s. net.

STRANGFORD. (See VOYAGES AND TRAVELS.)

WALDSTEIN (C.).—CATALOGUE OF CASTS IN THE MUSEUM OF CLASSICAL ARCHÆOLOGY, CAMBRIDGE. Crown 8vo. 1s. 6d.—Large Paper Edition. Small 4to. 5s.

WHITE (Gilbert). (See NATURAL HISTORY.)

WILKINS (Prof. A. S.).—A PRIMER OF ROMAN ANTIQUITIES. 18mo. 1s.

ARCHÆOLOGY. (See ANTIQUITIES.)

ARCHITECTURE.

FREEMAN (Prof. E. A.).—HISTORY OF THE CATHEDRAL CHURCH OF WELLS. Cr. 8vo. 3s. 6d.
— HISTORICAL AND ARCHITECTURAL SKETCHES, CHIEFLY ITALIAN. Illustrated by the Author. Cr. 8vo. 10s. 6d.

HULL (E.).—A TREATISE ON ORNAMENTAL AND BUILDING STONES OF GREAT BRITAIN AND FOREIGN COUNTRIES. 8vo. 12s.

MOORE (Prof. C. H.).—THE DEVELOPMENT AND CHARACTER OF GOTHIC ARCHITECTURE. Illustrated. Med. 8vo. 18s.

PENROSE (F. C.). (See ANTIQUITIES.)

STEVENSON (J. J.).—HOUSE ARCHITECTURE. With Illustrations. 2 vols. Roy. 8vo. 18s. each.—Vol. I. ARCHITECTURE; Vol. II. HOUSE PLANNING.

ART.
(See also MUSIC.)

ART AT HOME SERIES. Edited by W. J. LOFTIE, B.A. Cr. 8vo.
THE BEDROOM AND BOUDOIR. By Lady BARKER. 2s. 6d.
NEEDLEWORK. By ELIZABETH GLAISTER. Illustrated. 2s. 6d.
MUSIC IN THE HOUSE. By JOHN HULLAH. 4th edit. 2s. 6d.
THE LIBRARY. By ANDREW LANG, with a Chapter on English Illustrated Books, by AUSTIN DOBSON. 3s. 6d.
THE DINING-ROOM. By Mrs. LOFTIE. With Illustrations. 2nd Edit. 2s. 6d.
AMATEUR THEATRICALS. By WALTER H. POLLOCK and LADY POLLOCK. Illustrated by KATE GREENAWAY. 2s. 6d.

ATKINSON (J. B.).—AN ART TOUR TO NORTHERN CAPITALS OF EUROPE. 8vo. 12s.

BURN (Robert). (See ANTIQUITIES.)

CARR (J. Comyns).—PAPERS ON ART. Cr. 8vo. 8s. 6d.

COLLIER (Hon. John).—A PRIMER OF ART. 18mo. 1s.

COOK (E. T.).—A POPULAR HANDBOOK TO THE NATIONAL GALLERY. Including Notes collected from the Works of Mr. RUSKIN. 3rd Edit. Cr. 8vo, half morocco. 14s.—Large paper Edition, 250 copies. 2 vols. 8vo.

CRANE (Lucy).—LECTURES ON ART AND THE FORMATION OF TASTE. Cr. 8vo. 6s.

DELAMOTTE (Prof. P. H.).—A BEGINNER'S DRAWING-BOOK. Cr. 8vo. 3s. 6d.

ELLIS (Tristram).—SKETCHING FROM NATURE. Illustr. by H. STACY MARKS, R.A., and the Author. 2nd Edit. Cr. 8vo. 3s. 6d.

HAMERTON (P. G.).—THOUGHTS ABOUT ART. New Edit. Cr. 8vo. 8s. 6d.
— ETCHING AND ETCHERS. 3rd Edit., revised. With 48 Plates. Colombier 8vo.

HOOPER (W. H.) and PHILLIPS (W. C.).—A MANUAL OF MARKS ON POTTERY AND PORCELAIN. 16mo. 4s. 6d.

HUNT (W.).—TALKS ABOUT ART. With a Letter from Sir J. E. MILLAIS, Bart., R.A. Cr. 8vo. 3s. 6d.

LECTURES ON ART. By REGD. STUART POOLE, Professor W. B. RICHMOND, E. J. POYNTER, R.A., J. T. MICKLETHWAITE, and WILLIAM MORRIS. Cr. 8vo. 4s. 6d.

NEWTON (Sir C. T.).—(See ANTIQUITIES.)

PALGRAVE (Prof. F. T.).—ESSAYS ON ART. Ext. fcp. 8vo. 6s.

PATER (W.).—THE RENAISSANCE: Studies in Art and Poetry. 4th Edit. Cr. 8vo. 10s. 6d.

PENNELL (Joseph).—PEN DRAWING AND PEN DRAUGHTSMEN. With 158 Illustrations. 4to. 3l. 13s. 6d. net.

PROPERT (J. Lumsden).—A HISTORY OF MINIATURE ART. Illustrated. Super roy. 4to. 3l. 13s. 6d.—Bound in vellum. 4l. 14s. 6d.

TURNER'S LIBER STUDIORUM: A DESCRIPTION AND A CATALOGUE. By W. G. RAWLINSON. Med. 8vo. 12s. 6d.

TYRWHITT (Rev. R. St. John).—OUR SKETCHING CLUB. 5th Edit. Cr. 8vo. 7s. 6d.

WYATT (Sir M. Digby).—FINE ART: A Sketch of its History, Theory, Practice, and Application to Industry. 8vo. 5s.

ASTRONOMY.

AIRY (Sir G. B.).—POPULAR ASTRONOMY. Illustrated. 7th Edit. Fcp. 8vo. 4s. 6d.
— GRAVITATION. An Elementary Explanation of the Principal Perturbations in the Solar System. 2nd Edit. Cr. 8vo. 7s. 6d.

BLAKE (J. F.).—ASTRONOMICAL MYTHS. With Illustrations. Cr. 8vo. 9s.

CHEYNE (C. H. H.).—AN ELEMENTARY TREATISE ON THE PLANETARY THEORY. Cr. 8vo. 7s. 6d.

CLARK (L.) and SADLER (H.).—THE STAR GUIDE. Roy. 8vo. 5s.

CROSSLEY (E.), GLEDHILL (J.), and WILSON (J. M.).—A HANDBOOK OF DOUBLE STARS. 8vo. 21s.
— CORRECTIONS TO THE HANDBOOK OF DOUBLE STARS. 8vo. 1s.

ATLASES—BIOGRAPHY. 3

FORBES (Prof. George).—THE TRANSIT OF VENUS. Illustrated. Cr. 8vo. 3s. 6d.
GODFRAY (Hugh).—AN ELEMENTARY TREATISE ON THE LUNAR THEORY. 2nd Edit. Cr. 8vo. 5s. 6d.
—— A TREATISE ON ASTRONOMY, FOR THE USE OF COLLEGES AND SCHOOLS. 8vo. 12s. 6d.
LOCKYER (J. Norman, F.R.S.).—A PRIMER OF ASTRONOMY. Illustrated. 18mo. 1s.
—— ELEMENTARY LESSONS IN ASTRONOMY. Illustr. New Edition. Fcp. 8vo. 5s. 6d.
—— QUESTIONS ON THE SAME. By J. FORBES ROBERTSON. Fcp. 8vo. 1s. 6d.
—— THE CHEMISTRY OF THE SUN. Illustrated. 8vo. 14s.
—— THE METEORITIC HYPOTHESIS OF THE ORIGIN OF COSMICAL SYSTEMS. Illustrated. 8vo. 17s. net.
—— THE EVOLUTION OF THE HEAVENS AND THE EARTH. Illustrated. Cr. 8vo.
—— STAR-GAZING PAST AND PRESENT. Expanded from Notes with the assistance of G. M. SEABROKE. Roy. 8vo. 21s.
MILLER (R. Kalley).—THE ROMANCE OF ASTRONOMY. 2nd Edit. Cr. 8vo. 4s. 6d.
NEWCOMB (Prof. Simon).—POPULAR ASTRONOMY. Engravings and Maps. 8vo. 18s.
PENROSE (Francis).—ON A METHOD OF PREDICTING, BY GRAPHICAL CONSTRUCTION, OCCULTATIONS OF STARS BY THE MOON AND SOLAR ECLIPSES FOR ANY GIVEN PLACE. 4to. 12s.
RADCLIFFE (Charles B.).—BEHIND THE TIDES. 8vo. 4s. 6d.
ROSCOE—SCHUSTER. (See CHEMISTRY.)

ATLASES.
(See also GEOGRAPHY.)
BARTHOLOMEW (J. G.).—ELEMENTARY SCHOOL ATLAS. 4to. 1s.
—— PHYSICAL AND POLITICAL SCHOOL ATLAS. 80 maps. 4to. 8s. 6d.; half mor. 10s. 6d.
—— LIBRARY REFERENCE ATLAS OF THE WORLD. With Index to 100,000 places. Folio. 52s. 6d. net.—Also in 7 monthly parts, Part I. March, 1891. 5s. net; Geographical Index, 7s. 6d. net.
LABBERTON (R. H.).—NEW HISTORICAL ATLAS AND GENERAL HISTORY. 4to. 15s.

BIBLE. (See under THEOLOGY, p. 30.)

BIBLIOGRAPHY.
A BIBLIOGRAPHICAL CATALOGUE OF MACMILLAN AND CO.'S PUBLICATIONS, 1843—89. Med. 8vo. 10s. net.
MAYOR (Prof. John E. B.).—A BIBLIOGRAPHICAL CLUE TO LATIN LITERATURE. Cr. 8vo. 10s. 6d.
RYLAND (F.).—CHRONOLOGICAL OUTLINES OF ENGLISH LITERATURE. Cr. 8vo. 6s.

BIOGRAPHY.
(See also HISTORY.)
For other subjects of BIOGRAPHY, see ENGLISH MEN OF LETTERS, ENGLISH MEN OF ACTION, TWELVE ENGLISH STATESMEN.
AGASSIZ (Louis): HIS LIFE AND CORRESPONDENCE. Edited by ELIZABETH CARY AGASSIZ. 2 vols. Cr. 8vo. 18s.

ALBEMARLE (Earl of).—FIFTY YEARS OF MY LIFE. 3rd Edit., revised. Cr. 8vo. 7s. 6d.
ALFRED THE GREAT. By THOMAS HUGHES. Cr. 8vo. 6s.
AMIEL (Henri Fréderic).—THE JOURNAL INTIME. Translated by Mrs. HUMPHRY WARD. 2nd Edit. Cr. 8vo. 6s.
ANDREWS (Dr. Thomas). (See PHYSICS.)
ARNAULD, ANGELIQUE. By FRANCES MARTIN. Cr. 8vo. 4s. 6d.
ARTEVELDE. JAMES AND PHILIP VAN ARTEVELDE. By W. J. ASHLEY. Cr. 8vo. 6s.
BACON (Francis): AN ACCOUNT OF HIS LIFE AND WORKS. By E. A. ABBOTT. 8vo. 14s.
BARNES. LIFE OF WILLIAM BARNES, POET AND PHILOLOGIST. By his Daughter, LUCY BAXTER ("Leader Scott"). Cr. 8vo. 7s. 6d.
BERLIOZ (Hector): AUTOBIOGRAPHY OF. Trns. by R. & E. HOLMES. 2 vols. Cr. 8vo. 21s.
BERNARD (St.). THE LIFE AND TIMES OF ST. BERNARD, ABBOT OF CLAIRVAUX. By J. C. MORISON, M.A. Cr. 8vo. 6s.
BLACKBURNE. LIFE OF THE RIGHT HON. FRANCIS BLACKBURNE, late Lord Chancellor of Ireland, by his Son, EDWARD BLACKBURNE. With Portrait. 8vo. 12s.
BLAKE. LIFE OF WILLIAM BLAKE. With Selections from his Poems, etc. Illustr. from Blake's own Works. By ALEXANDER GILCHRIST. 2 vols. Med. 8vo. 42s.
BOLEYN (Anne): A CHAPTER OF ENGLISH HISTORY, 1527—36. By PAUL FRIEDMANN. 2 vols. 8vo. 28s.
BROOKE (Sir Jas.), THE RAJA OF SARAWAK (Life of). By GERTRUDE L. JACOB. 2 vols. 8vo. 25s.
BURKE. By JOHN MORLEY. Globe 8vo. 5s.
CALVIN. (See SELECT BIOGRAPHY, p. 5.)
CARLYLE (Thomas). Edited by CHARLES E. NORTON. Cr. 8vo.
—— REMINISCENCES. 2 vols. 12s.
—— EARLY LETTERS, 1814—26. 2 vols. 18s.
—— LETTERS, 1826—36. 2 vols. 18s.
—— CORRESPONDENCE BETWEEN GOETHE AND CARLYLE. 9s.
CARSTARES (Wm.): A CHARACTER AND CAREER OF THE REVOLUTIONARY EPOCH (1649—1715). By R. H. STORY. 8vo. 12s.
CAVOUR. (See SELECT BIOGRAPHY, p. 5.)
CHATTERTON: A STORY OF THE YEAR 1770. By Prof. DAVID MASSON. Cr. 8vo. 5s.
—— A BIOGRAPHICAL STUDY. By Sir DANIEL WILSON. Cr. 8vo. 6s. 6d.
CLARK. MEMORIALS FROM JOURNALS AND LETTERS OF SAMUEL CLARK, M.A. Edited by his Wife. Cr. 8vo. 7s. 6d.
CLOUGH (A. H.). (See LITERATURE, p. 19.)
COMBE. LIFE OF GEORGE COMBE. By CHARLES GIBBON. 2 vols. 8vo. 32s.
CROMWELL. (See SELECT BIOGRAPHY, p. 5.)
DAMIEN (Father): A JOURNEY FROM CASHMERE TO HIS HOME IN HAWAII. By EDWARD CLIFFORD. Portrait. Cr. 8vo. 2s. 6d.
DANTE: AND OTHER ESSAYS. By Dean CHURCH. Globe 8vo. 5s.

BIOGRAPHY.

BIOGRAPHY—*continued.*

DARWIN (Charles): MEMORIAL NOTICES, By T. H. HUXLEY, G. J. ROMANES, Sir ARCH. GEIKIE, and W. THISELTON DYER. With Portrait. Cr. 8vo. 2s. 6d.

DEÁK (Francis): HUNGARIAN STATESMAN. A Memoir. 8vo. 12s. 6d.

DRUMMOND OF HAWTHORNDEN. By Prof. D. MASSON. Cr. 8vo. 10s. 6d.

EADIE. LIFE OF JOHN EADIE, D.D. By JAMES BROWN, D.D. Cr. 8vo. 7s. 6d.

ELLIOTT. LIFE OF H. V. ELLIOTT, OF BRIGHTON. By J. BATEMAN. Cr. 8vo. 6s.

EMERSON. LIFE OF RALPH WALDO EMERSON. By J. L. CABOT. 2 vols. Cr. 8vo. 18s.

ENGLISH MEN OF ACTION. Cr. 8vo. With Portraits. 2s. 6d. each.
CLIVE. By Colonel Sir CHARLES WILSON.
COOK (CAPTAIN). By WALTER BESANT.
DAMPIER. By W. CLARK RUSSELL.
DRAKE. By JULIAN CORBETT.
GORDON (GENERAL). By Col. Sir W. BUTLER.
HASTINGS (WARREN). By Sir A. LYALL.
HAVELOCK (SIR HENRY). By A. FORBES.
HENRY V. By the Rev. A. J. CHURCH.
LAWRENCE (LORD). By Sir RICH. TEMPLE.
LIVINGSTONE. By THOMAS HUGHES.
MONK. By JULIAN CORBETT.
MONTROSE. By MOWBRAY MORRIS.
MOORE(SIR JOHN). By Col. MAURICE.[*In prep.*
NAPIER (SIR CHARLES). By Colonel Sir WM. BUTLER.
PETERBOROUGH. By W. STEBBING.
RODNEY. By DAVID HANNAY.
SIMON DE MONTFORT. By G. W. PROTHERO. [*In prep.*
STRAFFORD. By H. D. TRAILL.
WARWICK, THE KING-MAKER. By C. W. OMAN.
WELLINGTON. By GEORGE HOOPER.

ENGLISH MEN OF LETTERS. Edited by JOHN MORLEY. Cr. 8vo. 2s. 6d. each. Cheap Edition, 1s. 6d.; sewed, 1s.
ADDISON. By W. J. COURTHOPE.
BACON. By Dean CHURCH.
BENTLEY. By Prof. JEBB.
BUNYAN. By J. A. FROUDE.
BURKE. By JOHN MORLEY.
BURNS. By Principal SHAIRP.
BYRON. By Prof. NICHOL.
CHAUCER. By Prof. A. W. WARD.
COLERIDGE. By H. D. TRAILL.
COWPER. By GOLDWIN SMITH.
DEFOE. By W. MINTO.
DE QUINCEY. By Prof. MASSON.
DICKENS. By A. W. WARD.
DRYDEN. By G. SAINTSBURY.
FIELDING. By AUSTIN DOBSON.
GIBBON. By J. COTTER MORISON.
GOLDSMITH. By WILLIAM BLACK.
GRAY. By EDMUND GOSSE.
HAWTHORNE. By HENRY JAMES.
HUME. By T. H. HUXLEY.
JOHNSON. By LESLIE STEPHEN.
KEATS. By SIDNEY COLVIN.
LAMB. By Rev. ALFRED AINGER.
LANDOR. By SIDNEY COLVIN.
LOCKE. By Prof. FOWLER.
MACAULAY. By J. COTTER MORISON.
MILTON. By MARK PATTISON.
POPE. By LESLIE STEPHEN.
SCOTT. By R. H. HUTTON.

ENGLISH MEN OF LETTERS—*contd.*
SHELLEY. By J. A. SYMONDS.
SHERIDAN. By Mrs. OLIPHANT.
SIDNEY. By J. A. SYMONDS.
SOUTHEY. By Prof. DOWDEN.
SPENSER. By Dean CHURCH.
STERNE. By H. D. TRAILL.
SWIFT. By LESLIE STEPHEN.
THACKERAY. By ANTHONY TROLLOPE.
WORDSWORTH. By F. W. H. MYERS.

ENGLISH STATESMEN, TWELVE Cr. 8vo. 2s. 6d. each.
WILLIAM THE CONQUEROR. By EDWARD A. FREEMAN, D.C.L., LL.D.
HENRY II. By Mrs. J. R. GREEN.
EDWARD I. By F. Y. POWELL. [*In prep.*
HENRY VII. By JAMES GAIRDNER.
CARDINAL WOLSEY. By Bp. CREIGHTON.
ELIZABETH. By E. S. BEESLY.
OLIVER CROMWELL. By F. HARRISON.
WILLIAM III. By H. D. TRAILL.
WALPOLE. By JOHN MORLEY.
CHATHAM. By JOHN MORLEY.
PITT. By the EARL OF ROSEBERY.
PEEL. By J. R. THURSFIELD.

EPICTETUS. (*See* SELECT BIOGRAPHY, p. 5.)

FAIRFAX. LIFE OF ROBERT FAIRFAX OF STEETON, Vice-Admiral, Alderman, and Member for York, A.D. 1666-1725. By CLEMENTS R. MARKHAM, C.B. 8vo. 12s. 6d.

FITZGERALD (Edward). (*See* LITERATURE, p. 20.)

FORBES (Edward): MEMOIR OF. By GEORGE WILSON, M.P., and Sir ARCHIBALD GEIKIE, F.R.S., etc. Demy 8vo. 14s.

FRANCIS OF ASSISI. By Mrs. OLIPHANT. Cr. 8vo. 6s.

FRASER. JAMES FRASER, SECOND BISHOP OF MANCHESTER: A Memoir. By T. HUGHES. Cr. 8vo. 6s.

GARIBALDI. (*See* SELECT BIOGRAPHY, p. 5.)

GOETHE: LIFE OF. By Prof. HEINRICH DÜNTZER. Translated by T. W. LYSTER. 2 vols. Cr. 8vo. 21s.

GOETHE AND CARLYLE. (*See* CARLYLE.)

GORDON (General): A SKETCH. By REGINALD H. BARNES. Cr. 8vo. 1s.
—— LETTERS OF GENERAL C. G. GORDON TO HIS SISTER, M. A. GORDON. 4th Edit. Cr. 8vo. 3s. 6d.

HANDEL: LIFE OF. By W. S. ROCKSTRO. Cr. 8vo. 10s. 6d.

HOBART. (*See* COLLECTED WORKS, p. 21.)

HODGSON. MEMOIR OF REV. FRANCIS HODGSON, B.D. By his Son, Rev. JAMES T. HODGSON, M.A. 2 vols. Cr. 8vo. 18s.

JEVONS (W. Stanley).—LETTERS AND JOURNAL. Edited by HIS WIFE. 8vo. 14s.

KAVANAGH (Rt. Hon. A. McMurrough): A BIOGRAPHY. From papers chiefly unpublished, compiled by his Cousin, SARAH L. STEELE. With Portrait. 8vo. 14s. net.

KINGSLEY: HIS LETTERS, AND MEMORIES OF HIS LIFE. Edited by HIS WIFE. 2 vols. Cr. 8vo. 12s.—Cheap Edition. 1 vol. 6s.

LAMB. THE LIFE OF CHARLES LAMB. By Rev. ALFRED AINGER, M.A. Globe 8vo. 5s.

LOUIS (St.). (*See* SELECT BIOGRAPHY, p. 5.)

MACMILLAN (D.). MEMOIR OF DANIEL MACMILLAN. By THOMAS HUGHES, Q.C. With Portrait. Cr. 8vo. 4s. 6d.—Cheap Edition. Cr. 8vo, sewed. 1s.

MALTHUS AND HIS WORK. By JAMES BONAR. 8vo. 12s. 6d.

MARCUS AURELIUS. (*See* SELECT BIOGRAPHY, p. 5.)

MATHEWS. THE LIFE OF CHARLES J. MATHEWS. Edited by CHARLES DICKENS. With Portraits. 2 vols. 8vo. 25s.

MAURICE. LIFE OF FREDERICK DENISON MAURICE. By his Son, FREDERICK MAURICE, Two Portraits. 2 vols. 8vo. 36s.—Popular Edit. (4th Thousand). 2 vols. Cr. 8vo. 16s.

MAXWELL. PROFESSOR CLERK MAXWELL, A LIFE OF. By Prof. L. CAMPBELL, M.A., and W. GARNETT, M.A. Cr. 8vo. 7s. 6d.

MAZZINI. (*See* SELECT BIOGRAPHY, p. 5.)

MELBOURNE. MEMOIRS OF VISCOUNT MELBOURNE. By W. M. TORRENS. With Portrait. 2nd Edit. 2 vols. 8vo. 32s.

MIALL. LIFE OF EDWARD MIALL. By his Son, ARTHUR MIALL. 8vo. 10s. 6d.

MILTON. THE LIFE OF JOHN MILTON. By Prof. DAVID MASSON. Vol. I., 21s.; Vol. III., 18s.; Vols. IV. and V., 32s.; Vol. VI., with Portrait, 21s. (*See also* CLASSICAL WRITERS, p. 13.)

NAPOLEON I., HISTORY OF. By P. LANFREY. 4 vols. Cr. 8vo. 30s.

NELSON. SOUTHEY'S LIFE OF NELSON. With Introduction and Notes by MICHAEL MACMILLAN, B.A. Globe 8vo. 3s. 6d.

NORTH (M.).—RECOLLECTIONS OF A HAPPY LIFE. Being the Autobiography of MARIANNE NORTH. Edited by Mrs. J. A. SYMONDS.

OXFORD MOVEMENT, THE, 1833—45. By Dean CHURCH. 8vo. 12s. 6d. net.

PATTESON. LIFE AND LETTERS OF JOHN COLERIDGE PATTESON, D.D., MISSIONARY BISHOP. By C. M. YONGE. 2 vols. Cr. 8vo. 12s. (*See also* BOOKS FOR THE YOUNG.)

PATTISON (M.).—MEMOIRS. Cr. 8vo. 8s. 6d.

PITT. (*See* SELECT BIOGRAPHY, p. 5.)

POLLOCK (Sir Frdk., 2nd Bart.).—PERSONAL REMEMBRANCES. 2 vols. Cr. 8vo. 16s.

POOLE, THOS., AND HIS FRIENDS. By Mrs. SANDFORD. 2 vols. Cr. 8vo. 15s.

PYM. (*See* SELECT BIOGRAPHY, p. 5.)

ROBINSON (Matthew): AUTOBIOGRAPHY OF. Edited by J. E. B. MAYOR. Fcp. 8vo. 5s.

ROSSETTI (Dante Gabriel): A RECORD AND A STUDY. By W. SHARP. Cr. 8vo. 10s. 6d.

RUMFORD. (*See* COLLECTED WORKS, p. 22.)

SCHILLER, LIFE OF. By Prof. HEINRICH DÜNTZER. Translated by PERCY E. PINKERTON. Cr. 8vo. 10s. 6d.

SENECA. (*See* SELECT BIOGRAPHY, p. 5.)

SHELBURNE. LIFE OF WILLIAM, EARL OF SHELBURNE. By Lord EDMOND FITZMAURICE. In 3 vols.—Vol. I. 8vo. 12s.—Vol. II. 8vo. 12s.—Vol. III. 8vo. 16s.

SIBSON. (*See* MEDICINE.)

SMETHAM (Jas.).: THE CORRESPONDENCE OF. By W. DAVIES and SARAH SMETHAM. Cr. 8vo.

SPINOZA: A STUDY OF. By JAMES MARTINEAU. LL.D. 2nd Edit. Cr. 8vo. 6s.

TAIT. THE LIFE OF ARCHIBALD CAMPBELL TAIT, ARCHBISHOP OF CANTERBURY. By the BISHOP OF ROCHESTER and Rev. W. BENHAM, B.D. 2 vols. 8vo. 30s. net.

—— CATHARINE AND CRAWFURD TAIT, WIFE AND SON OF ARCHIBALD CAMPBELL, ARCHBISHOP OF CANTERBURY: A Memoir. Ed. by Rev. W. BENHAM, B.D. Cr. 8vo. 6s. —Popular Edit., abridged. Cr. 8vo. 2s. 6d.

THRING (Edward): A MEMORY OF. By J. H. SKRINE. Cr. 8vo. 6s.

VICTOR EMMANUEL II., FIRST KING OF ITALY. By G. S. GODKIN. Cr. 8vo. 6s.

WARD. WILLIAM GEORGE WARD AND THE OXFORD MOVEMENT. By his Son, WILFRID WARD. With Portrait. 8vo. 14s.

WATSON. A RECORD OF ELLEN WATSON. By ANNA BUCKLAND. Cr. 8vo. 6s.

WHEWELL. DR. WILLIAM WHEWELL, late Master of Trinity College, Cambridge. An Account of his Writings, with Selections from his Literary and Scientific Correspondence By I. TODHUNTER, M.A. 2 vols. 8vo. 25s.

WILLIAMS (Montagu).—LEAVES OF A LIFE. Cr. 8vo. 3s. 6d.; sewed., 2s. 6d.

—— LATER LEAVES. Being further Reminiscences. With Portrait. Cr. 8vo. 3s. 6d.

WILSON. MEMOIR OF PROF. GEORGE WILSON, M.D. By HIS SISTER. With Portrait. 2nd Edit. Cr. 8vo. 6s.

WORDSWORTH. DOVE COTTAGE, WORDSWORTH'S HOME, 1800—8. Gl. 8vo, swd. 1s.

Select Biography.

FARRAR (Archdeacon).—SEEKERS AFTER GOD. THE LIVES OF SENECA, EPICTETUS, AND MARCUS AURELIUS. Cr. 8vo. 6s.

FAWCETT (Mrs. H.). — SOME EMINENT WOMEN OF OUR TIMES. Cr. 8vo 2s. 6d.

GUIZOT.—GREAT CHRISTIANS OF FRANCE: ST. LOUIS AND CALVIN. Cr. 8vo. 6s.

HARRISON (Frederic).—THE NEW CALENDAR OF GREAT MEN. Ext. cr. 8vo.

MARRIOTT (J. A. R.).—THE MAKERS OF MODERN ITALY: MAZZINI, CAVOUR, GARIBALDI. Cr. 8vo. 1s. 6d.

MARTINEAU (Harriet). — BIOGRAPHICAL SKETCHES, 1852—75. Cr. 8vo. 6s.

SMITH (Goldwin).—THREE ENGLISH STATESMEN: CROMWELL, PYM, PITT. Cr. 8vo. 5s.

WINKWORTH (Catharine). — CHRISTIAN SINGERS OF GERMANY. Cr. 8vo. 4s. 6d.

YONGE (Charlotte M.).—THE PUPILS OF ST. JOHN. Illustrated. Cr. 8vo. 6s.

—— PIONEERS AND FOUNDERS; or, Recent Workers in the Mission Field. Cr. 8vo. 6s.

—— A BOOK OF WORTHIES, GATHERED FROM THE OLD HISTORIES AND WRITTEN ANEW. 18mo. 4s. 6d.

—— A BOOK OF GOLDEN DEEDS. 18mo. 4s. 6d. —*Abridged Edition.* 18mo. 1s.—*Globe Readings Edition.* Globe 8vo. 2s.

BIOLOGY.

(*See also* BOTANY; NATURAL HISTORY; PHYSIOLOGY; ZOOLOGY.)

BALFOUR (F. M.). — ELASMOBRANCH FISHES. With Plates. 8vo. 21s.

—— COMPARATIVE EMBRYOLOGY. Illustrated. 2 vols. 8vo. Vol. I. 18s. Vol. II. 21s.

BIOLOGY—BOTANY.

BIOLOGY—*continued.*

BALL (W. P.).—ARE THE EFFECTS OF USE AND DISUSE INHERITED? Cr. 8vo. 3s. 6d.

BASTIAN (H. Charlton).—THE BEGINNINGS OF LIFE. 2 vols. Crown 8vo. 28s.
—— EVOLUTION AND THE ORIGIN OF LIFE. Cr. 8vo. 6s. 6d.

BATESON (W.).—MATERIALS FOR THE STUDY OF VARIATION IN ANIMALS. Part I. DISCONTINUOUS VARIATION. Illustr. 8vo.

BIRKS (T. R.).—MODERN PHYSICAL FATALISM, AND THE DOCTRINE OF EVOLUTION. Including an Examination of Mr. Herbert Spencer's "First Principles." Cr. 8vo. 6s.

EIMER (G. H. T.).—ORGANIC EVOLUTION AS THE RESULT OF THE INHERITANCE OF ACQUIRED CHARACTERS ACCORDING TO THE LAWS OF ORGANIC GROWTH. Translated by J. T. CUNNINGHAM, M.A. 8vo. 12s. 6d.

FISKE (John).—OUTLINES OF COSMIC PHILOSOPHY, BASED ON THE DOCTRINE OF EVOLUTION. 2 vols. 8vo. 25s.
—— MAN'S DESTINY VIEWED IN THE LIGHT OF HIS ORIGIN. Cr. 8vo. 3s. 6d.

FOSTER (Prof. Michael) and BALFOUR (F. M.).—THE ELEMENTS OF EMBRYOLOGY. Edited by ADAM SEDGWICK, M.A., and WALTER HEAPE. Illustrated. 3rd Edit., revised and enlarged. Cr. 8vo. 10s. 6d.

HUXLEY (T. H.) and MARTIN (H. N.).—(*See under* ZOOLOGY, p. 40.)

KLEIN (Dr. E.).—MICRO-ORGANISMS AND DISEASE. An Introduction into the Study of Specific Micro-Organisms. With 121 Engravings. 3rd Edit. Cr. 8vo. 6s.

LANKESTER (Prof. E. Ray).—COMPARATIVE LONGEVITY IN MAN AND THE LOWER ANIMALS. Cr. 8vo. 4s. 6d.

LUBBOCK (Sir John, Bart.).—SCIENTIFIC LECTURES. Illustrated. 2nd Edit. 8vo. 8s. 6d.

PARKER (T. Jeffery).—LESSONS IN ELEMENTARY BIOLOGY. Illustr. Cr. 8vo. 10s. 6d.

ROMANES (G. J.).—SCIENTIFIC EVIDENCES OF ORGANIC EVOLUTION. Cr. 8vo. 2s. 6d.

WALLACE (Alfred R.).—DARWINISM: An Exposition of the Theory of Natural Selection, with some of its Applications. Illustrated. 3rd Edit. Cr. 8vo. 9s.
—— CONTRIBUTIONS TO THE THEORY OF NATURAL SELECTION, AND TROPICAL NATURE: and other Essays. New Ed. Cr. 8vo. 6s.
—— THE GEOGRAPHICAL DISTRIBUTION OF ANIMALS. Illustrated. 2 vols, 8vo. 42s.
—— ISLAND LIFE. Illustr. Ext. Cr. 8vo. 6s.

BIRDS. (*See* ZOOLOGY; ORNITHOLOGY.)

BOOK-KEEPING.

THORNTON (J.).—FIRST LESSONS IN BOOK-KEEPING. New Edition. Cr. 8vo. 2s. 6d.
—— KEY. Oblong 4to. 10s. 6d.
—— PRIMER OF BOOK-KEEPING. 18mo. 1s.
—— KEY. Demy 8vo. 2s. 6d.

BOTANY.

(*See also* AGRICULTURE; GARDENING.)

ALLEN (Grant).—ON THE COLOURS OF FLOWERS. Illustrated. Cr. 8vo. 3s. 6d.

BALFOUR (Prof. J. B.) and WARD (Prof. H. M.).—A GENERAL TEXT-BOOK OF BOTANY. 8vo. [*In preparation.*

BETTANY (G. T.).—FIRST LESSONS IN PRACTICAL BOTANY. 18mo. 1s.

BOWER (Prof. F. O.).—A COURSE OF PRACTICAL INSTRUCTION IN BOTANY. Cr. 8vo. 10s. 6d.—Abridged Edition. [*In preparation.*

CHURCH (Prof. A. H.) and SCOTT (D. H.).—MANUAL OF VEGETABLE PHYSIOLOGY. Illustrated. Crown 8vo. [*In preparation.*

GOODALE (Prof. G. L.).—PHYSIOLOGICAL BOTANY.—1. OUTLINES OF THE HISTOLOGY OF PHÆNOGAMOUS PLANTS; 2. VEGETABLE PHYSIOLOGY. 8vo. 10s. 6d.

GRAY (Prof. Asa).—STRUCTURAL BOTANY; or, Organography on the Basis of Morphology. 8vo. 10s. 6d.
—— THE SCIENTIFIC PAPERS OF ASA GRAY. Selected by C. S. SARGENT. 2 vols. 8vo. 21s.

HANBURY (Daniel). — SCIENCE PAPERS, CHIEFLY PHARMACOLOGICAL AND BOTANICAL. Med. 8vo. 14s.

HARTIG (Dr. Robert).—TEXT-BOOK OF THE DISEASES OF TREES. Transl. by Prof. WM. SOMERVILLE, B.Sc. With Introduction by Prof. H. MARSHALL WARD. 8vo.

HOOKER (Sir Joseph D.).—THE STUDENT'S FLORA OF THE BRITISH ISLANDS. 3rd Edit. Globe 8vo. 10s. 6d.
—— A PRIMER OF BOTANY. 18mo. 1s.

LASLETT (Thomas).—TIMBER AND TIMBER TREES, NATIVE AND FOREIGN. Cr. 8vo. 8s. 6d.

LUBBOCK (Sir John, Bart.).—ON BRITISH WILD FLOWERS CONSIDERED IN RELATION TO INSECTS. Illustrated. Cr. 8vo. 4s. 6d.
—— FLOWERS, FRUITS, AND LEAVES. With Illustrations. Cr. 8vo. 4s. 6d.

MÜLLER—THOMPSON.—THE FERTILISATION OF FLOWERS. By Prof. H. MÜLLER. Transl. by D'ARCY W. THOMPSON. Preface by CHARLES DARWIN, F.R.S. 8vo. 21s.

OLIVER (Prof. Daniel).—LESSONS IN ELEMENTARY BOTANY. Illustr. Fcp. 8vo. 4s. 6d.
—— FIRST BOOK OF INDIAN BOTANY. Illustrated. Ext. fcp. 8vo. 6s. 6d.

ORCHIDS: BEING THE REPORT ON THE ORCHID CONFERENCE HELD AT SOUTH KENSINGTON, 1885. 8vo. 2s. 6d. net.

PETTIGREW (J. Bell).—THE PHYSIOLOGY OF THE CIRCULATION IN PLANTS, IN THE LOWER ANIMALS, AND IN MAN. 8vo. 12s.

SMITH (J.).—ECONOMIC PLANTS, DICTIONARY OF POPULAR NAMES OF; THEIR HISTORY, PRODUCTS, AND USES. 8vo. 14s.

SMITH (W. G.).—DISEASES OF FIELD AND GARDEN CROPS, CHIEFLY SUCH AS ARE CAUSED BY FUNGI. Illust. Fcp. 8vo. 4s. 6d.

STEWART (S. A.) and CORRY (T. H.).—A FLORA OF THE NORTH-EAST OF IRELAND. Cr. 8vo. 5s. 6d.

WARD (Prof. H. M.).—TIMBER AND SOME OF ITS DISEASES. Illustrated. Cr. 8vo. 6s.

YONGE (C. M.).—THE HERB OF THE FIELD. New Edition, revised. Cr. 8vo. 5s.

BREWING AND WINE.

PASTEUR—FAULKNER. — STUDIES ON FERMENTATION : THE DISEASES OF BEER, THEIR CAUSES, AND THE MEANS OF PREVENTING THEM. By L. PASTEUR. Translated by FRANK FAULKNER. 8vo. 21*s*.

THUDICHUM (J. L. W.) and (DUPRÉ (A.). —TREATISE ON THE ORIGIN, NATURE, AND VARIETIES OF WINE. Med. 8vo. 25*s*.

CHEMISTRY.
(*See also* METALLURGY.)

BRODIE (Sir Benjamin).—IDEAL CHEMISTRY. Cr. 8vo. 2*s*.

COHEN (J. B.). — THE OWENS COLLEGE COURSE OF PRACTICAL ORGANIC CHEMISTRY. Fcp. 8vo. 2*s*. 6*d*.

COOKE (Prof. J. P., jun.).—ELEMENTS OF CHEMICAL PHYSICS. 4th Edit. 8vo. 21*s*.
—— PRINCIPLES OF CHEMICAL PHILOSOPHY. New Edition. 8vo. 16*s*.

FLEISCHER (Emil).—A SYSTEM OF VOLUMETRIC ANALYSIS. Transl. with Additions, by M. M. P. MUIR, F.R.S.E. Cr.8vo. 7*s*.6*d*.

FRANKLAND (Prof. P. F.). (*See* AGRICULTURE.)

GLADSTONE (J. H.) and TRIBE (A.).— THE CHEMISTRY OF THE SECONDARY BATTERIES OF PLANTÉ AND FAURE. Cr.8vo. 2*s*.6*d*.

HARTLEY (Prof. W. N.).—A COURSE OF QUANTITATIVE ANALYSIS FOR STUDENTS. Globe 8vo. 5*s*.

HEMPEL (Dr. W.). — METHODS OF GAS ANALYSIS. Translated by L. M. DENNIS. Cr. 8vo. [*In the Press.*

HOFMANN (Prof. A. W.).—THE LIFE WORK OF LIEBIG IN EXPERIMENTAL AND PHILOSOPHIC CHEMISTRY. 8vo. 5*s*.

JONES (Francis).—THE OWENS COLLEGE JUNIOR COURSE OF PRACTICAL CHEMISTRY. Illustrated. Fcp. 8vo. 2*s*. 6*d*.
—— QUESTIONS ON CHEMISTRY. Fcp.8vo. 3*s*.

LANDAUER (J.). — BLOWPIPE ANALYSIS. Translated by J. TAYLOR and W. E. KAY.

LOCKYER (J. Norman, F.R.S.). — THE CHEMISTRY OF THE SUN. Illustr. 8vo. 14*s*.

LUPTON (S.). — CHEMICAL ARITHMETIC. With 1200 Problems. Fcp. 8vo. 4*s*. 6*d*.

MANSFIELD (C. B.).—A THEORY OF SALTS. Cr. 8vo. 14*s*.

MELDOLA (Prof. R.).—THE CHEMISTRY OF PHOTOGRAPHY. Illustrated. Cr. 8vo. 6*s*.

MEYER (E. von).—HISTORY OF CHEMISTRY FROM THE EARLIEST TIMES TO THE PRESENT DAY. Translated by G. McGOWAN, Ph.D. 8vo. 14*s*. net.

MIXTER (Prof. W. G.).—AN ELEMENTARY TEXT-BOOK OF CHEMISTRY. Cr. 8vo. 7*s*. 6*d*.

MUIR (M. M. P.).—PRACTICAL CHEMISTRY FOR MEDICAL STUDENTS (First M. B. Course). Fcp. 8vo. 1*s*. 6*d*.

MUIR (M. M. P.) and WILSON (D. M.).— ELEMENTS OF THERMAL CHEMISTRY. 12*s*.6*d*.

OSTWALD (Prof.).—OUTLINES OF GENERAL CHEMISTRY. Trans. Dr. J. WALKER. 10*s*. net.

RAMSAY (Prof. William).—EXPERIMENTAL PROOFS OF CHEMICAL THEORY FOR BEGINNERS. 18mo. 2*s*. 6*d*.

REMSEN (Prof. Ira).—THE ELEMENTS OF CHEMISTRY. Fcp. 8vo. 2*s*. 6*d*.
—— AN INTRODUCTION TO THE STUDY OF CHEMISTRY (INORGANIC CHEMISTRY). Cr. 8vo. 6*s*. 6*d*.
—— A TEXT-BOOK OF INORGANIC CHEMISTRY. 8vo. 16*s*.
—— COMPOUNDS OF CARBON ; or, An Introduction to the Study of Organic Chemistry. Cr. 8vo. 6*s*. 6*d*.

ROSCOE (Sir Henry E., F.R.S.).—A PRIMER OF CHEMISTRY. Illustrated. 18mo. 1*s*.
—— LESSONS IN ELEMENTARY CHEMISTRY, INORGANIC AND ORGANIC. Fcp. 8vo. 4*s*. 6*d*.

ROSCOE (Sir H. E.) and SCHORLEMMER (Prof. C.).—A COMPLETE TREATISE ON INORGANIC AND ORGANIC CHEMISTRY. Illustr. 8vo.—Vols. I. and II. INORGANIC CHEMISTRY : Vol. I. THE NON-METALLIC ELEMENTS, 2nd Edit., 21*s*. Vol. II. Parts I. and II. METALS, 18*s*. each.—Vol. III. ORGANIC CHEMISTRY : THE CHEMISTRY OF THE HYDRO-CARBONS AND THEIR DERIVATIVES. Parts I. II. and IV. 21*s*. ; Parts III. and V. 18*s*. each. Part VI.

ROSCOE (Sir H. E.) and SCHUSTER (A.). —SPECTRUM ANALYSIS. By Sir HENRY E. ROSCOE. 4th Edit., revised by the Author and A. SCHUSTER, F.R.S. With Coloured Plates. 8vo. 21*s*.

THORPE (Prof. T. E.) and TATE (W.).— A SERIES OF CHEMICAL PROBLEMS. With KEY. Fcp. 8vo. 2*s*.

THORPE (Prof. T. E.) and RÜCKER (Prof. A. W.).—A TREATISE ON CHEMICAL PHYSICS. Illustrated. 8vo. [*In preparation.*

WURTZ (Ad.).—A HISTORY OF CHEMICAL THEORY. Transl. by H. WATTS. Cr. 8vo. 6*s*.

CHRISTIAN CHURCH, History of the.
(*See under* THEOLOGY, p. 31.)

CHURCH OF ENGLAND, The.
(*See under* THEOLOGY, p. 32.)

COLLECTED WORKS.
(*See under* LITERATURE, p. 19.)

COMPARATIVE ANATOMY.
(*See under* ZOOLOGY, p. 39.)

COOKERY.
(*See under* DOMESTIC ECONOMY, p. 8.)

DEVOTIONAL BOOKS.
(*See under* THEOLOGY, p. 32.)

DICTIONARIES AND GLOSSARIES.

AUTENRIETH (Dr. G.).—AN HOMERIC DICTIONARY. Translated from the German, by R. P. KEEP, Ph.D. Cr. 8vo. 6*s*.

BARTLETT (J.).—FAMILIAR QUOTATIONS.
—— A SHAKESPEARE GLOSSARY.

GROVE (Sir George).—A DICTIONARY OF MUSIC AND MUSICIANS. (*See* MUSIC.)

HOLE (Rev. C.).—A BRIEF BIOGRAPHICAL DICTIONARY. 2nd Edit. 18mo. 4*s*. 6*d*.

MASSON (Gustave).—A COMPENDIOUS DICTIONARY OF THE FRENCH LANGUAGE. Cr. 8vo. 3*s*. 6*d*.

PALGRAVE (R. H. I.).—A DICTIONARY OF POLITICAL ECONOMY. (*See* POLITICAL ECONOMY.)

DICTIONARIES—*continued.*
WHITNEY (Prof. W. D.).—A COMPENDIOUS GERMAN AND ENGLISH DICTIONARY. Cr. 8vo. 7s. 6d.—German-English Part separately. 5s.
WRIGHT (W. Aldis).—THE BIBLE WORD-BOOK. 2nd Edit. Cr. 8vo. 7s. 6d.
YONGE (Charlotte M.).—HISTORY OF CHRISTIAN NAMES. Cr. 8vo. 7s. 6d.

DOMESTIC ECONOMY.
Cookery—Nursing—Needlework.

Cookery.
BARKER (Lady).—FIRST LESSONS IN THE PRINCIPLES OF COOKING. 3rd Ed. 18mo. 1s.
FREDERICK (Mrs.).—HINTS TO HOUSEWIVES ON SEVERAL POINTS, PARTICULARLY ON THE PREPARATION OF ECONOMICAL AND TASTEFUL DISHES. Cr. 8vo. 1s.
MIDDLE-CLASS COOKERY BOOK, THE. Compiled for the Manchester School of Cookery. Fcp. 8vo. 1s. 6d.
TEGETMEIER (W. B.).—HOUSEHOLD MANAGEMENT AND COOKERY. 18mo. 1s.
WRIGHT (Miss Guthrie).—THE SCHOOL COOKERY-BOOK. 18mo. 1s.

Nursing.
CRAVEN (Mrs. Dacre).—A GUIDE TO DISTRICT NURSES. Cr. 8vo. 2s. 6d.
FOTHERGILL (Dr. J. M.).—FOOD FOR THE INVALID, THE CONVALESCENT, THE DYSPEPTIC, AND THE GOUTY. Cr. 8vo. 3s. 6d.
JEX-BLAKE (Dr. Sophia).—THE CARE OF INFANTS: A Manual for Mothers and Nurses. 18mo. 1s.
RATHBONE (Wm.).—THE HISTORY AND PROGRESS OF DISTRICT NURSING, FROM ITS COMMENCEMENT IN THE YEAR 1859 TO THE PRESENT DATE. Cr. 8vo. 2s. 6d.
RECOLLECTIONS OF A NURSE. By E. D. Cr. 8vo. 2s.
STEPHEN (Caroline E.).—THE SERVICE OF THE POOR. Cr. 8vo. 6s. 6d.

Needlework.
GLAISTER (Elizabeth).—NEEDLEWORK. Cr. 8vo. 2s. 6d.
GRAND'HOMME.—CUTTING OUT AND DRESSMAKING. From the French of Mdlle. E. GRAND'HOMME. 18mo. 1s.

DRAMA, The.
(*See under* LITERATURE, p. 14.)

ELECTRICITY.
(*See under* PHYSICS, p. 26.)

EDUCATION.
ARNOLD (Matthew).—HIGHER SCHOOLS AND UNIVERSITIES IN GERMANY. Cr. 8vo. 6s.
—— REPORTS ON ELEMENTARY SCHOOLS, 1852-82. Ed. by Lord SANDFORD. 8vo. 3s. 6d.
BLAKISTON (J. R.).—THE TEACHER: HINTS ON SCHOOL MANAGEMENT. Cr. 8vo. 2s. 6d.
CALDERWOOD (Prof. H.).—ON TEACHING. 4th Edit. Ext. fcp. 8vo. 2s. 6d.
COMBE (George).—EDUCATION: ITS PRINCIPLES AND PRACTICE AS DEVELOPED BY GEORGE COMBE. Ed. by W. JOLLY. 8vo. 15s.
CRAIK (Henry).—THE STATE IN ITS RELATION TO EDUCATION. Cr. 8vo. 3s. 6d.

FEARON (D. R.).—SCHOOL INSPECTION. 6th Edit. Cr. 8vo. 2s. 6d.
FITCH (J. G.).—NOTES ON AMERICAN SCHOOLS AND TRAINING COLLEGES. Reprinted by permission. Globe 8vo. 2s. 6d.
GLADSTONE (J. H.).—SPELLING REFORM FROM AN EDUCATIONAL POINT OF VIEW. 3rd Edit. Cr. 8vo. 1s. 6d.
HERTEL (Dr.).—OVERPRESSURE IN HIGH SCHOOLS IN DENMARK. With Introduction by Sir J. CRICHTON-BROWNE. Cr. 8vo. 3s. 6d.
KINGSLEY (Charles).—HEALTH AND EDUCATION. Cr. 8vo. 6s.
LUBBOCK (Sir John, Bart.).—POLITICAL AND EDUCATIONAL ADDRESSES. 8vo. 8s. 6d.
MAURICE (F. D.).—LEARNING AND WORKING. Cr. 8vo. 4s. 6d.
THRING (Rev. Edward).—EDUCATION AND SCHOOL. 2nd Edit. Cr. 8vo. 6s.
TODHUNTER (Isaac).—THE CONFLICT OF STUDIES. 8vo. 10s. 6d.

ENGINEERING.
ALEXANDER (T.) and THOMSON (A. W.) —ELEMENTARY APPLIED MECHANICS. Part II. TRANSVERSE STRESS. Cr. 8vo. 10s. 6d.
CHALMERS (J. B.).—GRAPHICAL DETERMINATION OF FORCES IN ENGINEERING STRUCTURES. Illustrated. 8vo. 24s.
COTTERILL (Prof. J. H.).—APPLIED MECHANICS: An Elementary General Introduction to the Theory of Structures and Machines. 2nd Edit. 8vo. 18s.
COTTERILL (Prof. J. H.) and SLADE (J. H.).—LESSONS IN APPLIED MECHANICS. Fcp. 8vo. 5s. 6d.
KENNEDY (Prof. A. B. W.).—THE MECHANICS OF MACHINERY. Cr. 8vo. 12s. 6d.
PEABODY (Prof. C. H.).—THERMODYNAMICS OF THE STEAM ENGINE AND OTHER HEAT-ENGINES. 8vo. 21s.
SHANN (G.).—AN ELEMENTARY TREATISE ON HEAT IN RELATION TO STEAM AND THE STEAM-ENGINE. Illustrated. Cr. 8vo. 4s. 6d.
WHITHAM (Prof. J. M.).—STEAM-ENGINE DESIGN. For the use of Mechanical Engineers, Students, and Draughtsmen. Illustrated. 8vo. 25s.
WOODWARD (C. M.).—A HISTORY OF THE ST. LOUIS BRIDGE. 4to. 2l. 2s. net.
YOUNG (E. W.).—SIMPLE PRACTICAL METHODS OF CALCULATING STRAINS ON GIRDERS, ARCHES, AND TRUSSES. 8vo. 7s. 6d.

ENGLISH CITIZEN SERIES.
(*See* POLITICS.)

ENGLISH MEN OF ACTION.
(*See* BIOGRAPHY.)

ENGLISH MEN OF LETTERS.
(*See* BIOGRAPHY.)

ENGLISH STATESMEN, Twelve.
(*See* BIOGRAPHY.)

ENGRAVING. (*See* ART.)

ESSAYS.
(*See under* LITERATURE, p. 19.)

ETCHING. (*See* ART.)

ETHICS.
(*See under* PHILOSOPHY, p. 25.)

FATHERS, The.
(*See under* THEOLOGY, p. 32.)

FICTION, Prose.
(*See under* LITERATURE, p. 17.)

GARDENING.
(*See also* AGRICULTURE; BOTANY.)

BLOMFIELD (Reginald).—THE FORMAL GARDEN. Illustrated.

BRIGHT (H. A.).—THE ENGLISH FLOWER GARDEN. Cr. 8vo. 3s. 6d.
— A YEAR IN A LANCASHIRE GARDEN. Cr. 8vo. 3s. 6d.

HOBDAY (E.).— VILLA GARDENING. A Handbook for Amateur and Practical Gardeners. Ext. cr. 8vo. 6s.

HOPE (Frances J.).—NOTES AND THOUGHTS ON GARDENS AND WOODLANDS. Cr. 8vo. 6s.

GEOGRAPHY.
(*See also* ATLASES.)

BLANFORD (H. F.).—ELEMENTARY GEOGRAPHY OF INDIA, BURMA, AND CEYLON. Globe 8vo. 2s. 6d.

CLARKE (C. B.).—A GEOGRAPHICAL READER AND COMPANION TO THE ATLAS. Cr. 8vo. 2s.
— A CLASS-BOOK OF GEOGRAPHY. With 18 Coloured Maps. Fcp. 8vo. 3s.; swd., 2s. 6d.

DAWSON (G. M.) and SUTHERLAND (A.). —GEOGRAPHY OF THE BRITISH COLONIES.

ELDERTON (W. A.).—MAPS AND MAP DRAWING. Pott 8vo. 1s.

GEIKIE (Sir Archibald).—THE TEACHING OF GEOGRAPHY. A Practical Handbook for the use of Teachers. Globe 8vo. 2s.
— GEOGRAPHY OF THE BRITISH ISLES. 18mo. 1s.

GREEN (J. R. and A. S.).—A SHORT GEOGRAPHY OF THE BRITISH ISLANDS. Fcp. 8vo. 3s. 6d.

GROVE (Sir George).—A PRIMER OF GEOGRAPHY. Maps. 18mo. 1s.

KIEPERT (H.).— MANUAL OF ANCIENT GEOGRAPHY. Cr. 8vo. 5s.

MILL (H. R.).—ELEMENTARY CLASS-BOOK OF GENERAL GEOGRAPHY. Cr. 8vo. 3s. 6d.

SIME (James).—GEOGRAPHY OF EUROPE. With Illustrations. Globe 8vo. 3s.

STRACHEY (Lieut.-Gen. R.).—LECTURES ON GEOGRAPHY. Cr. 8vo. 4s. 6d.

TOZER (H. F.).—A PRIMER OF CLASSICAL GEOGRAPHY. 18mo. 1s.

GEOLOGY AND MINERALOGY.

BLANFORD (W. T.). — GEOLOGY AND ZOOLOGY OF ABYSSINIA. 8vo. 21s.

COAL: ITS HISTORY AND ITS USES. By Profs. GREEN, MIALL, THORPE, RÜCKER, and MARSHALL. 8vo. 12s. 6d.

DAWSON (Sir J. W.).—THE GEOLOGY OF NOVA SCOTIA, NEW BRUNSWICK, AND PRINCE EDWARD ISLAND; or, Acadian Geology. 4th Edit. 8vo. 21s.

GEIKIE (Sir Archibald).—A PRIMER OF GEOLOGY. Illustrated. 18mo. 1s.
— CLASS-BOOK OF GEOLOGY. Illustrated. Cr. 8vo. 4s. 6d.
— OUTLINES OF FIELD GEOLOGY. With numerous Illustrations. Gl. 8vo. 3s. 6d.

GEIKIE (Sir A.).—GEOLOGICAL SKETCHES AT HOME AND ABROAD. With Illustrations. 8vo. 10s. 6d.
— TEXT-BOOK OF GEOLOGY. Illustrated. 2nd Edit. 7th Thousand. Med. 8vo. 28s.
— THE SCENERY OF SCOTLAND. Viewed in connection with its Physical Geology. 2nd Edit. Cr. 8vo. 12s. 6d.

HULL (E.).—A TREATISE ON ORNAMENTAL AND BUILDING STONES OF GREAT BRITAIN AND FOREIGN COUNTRIES. 8vo. 12s.

PENNINGTON (Rooke).—NOTES ON THE BARROWS AND BONE CAVES OF DERBYSHIRE. 8vo. 6s.

RENDU—WILLS.—THE THEORY OF THE GLACIERS OF SAVOY. By M. LE CHANOINE RENDU. Trans. by A. WILLS, Q.C. 8vo. 7s. 6d.

ROSENBUSCH—IDDINGS.— MICROSCOPICAL PHYSIOGRAPHY OF THE ROCK-MAKING MINERALS. By Prof. H. ROSENBUSCH. Transl. by J. P. IDDINGS. Illustr. 8vo. 24s.

WILLIAMS (G. H.).—ELEMENTS OF CRYSTALLOGRAPHY. Cr. 8vo. 6s.

GLOSSARIES. (*See* DICTIONARIES.)

GRAMMAR. (*See* PHILOLOGY.)

HEALTH. (*See* HYGIENE.)

HEAT. (*See under* PHYSICS, p. 27.)

HISTOLOGY. (*See* PHYSIOLOGY.)

HISTORY.
(*See also* BIOGRAPHY.)

ARNOLD (T.).—THE SECOND PUNIC WAR. By THOMAS ARNOLD, D.D. Ed. by W. T. ARNOLD, M.A. With 8 Maps. Cr. 8vo. 5s.

ARNOLD (W. T.).—A HISTORY OF THE EARLY ROMAN EMPIRE. Cr. 8vo. [*In prep.*

BEESLY (Mrs.).—STORIES FROM THE HISTORY OF ROME. Fcp. 8vo. 2s. 6d.

BLACKIE (Prof. John Stuart).—WHAT DOES HISTORY TEACH? Globe 8vo. 2s. 6d.

BRYCE (James, M.P.).—THE HOLY ROMAN EMPIRE. 8th Edit. Cr. 8vo. 7s. 6d.—*Library Edition.* 8vo. 14s.

BUCKLEY (Arabella).—HISTORY OF ENGLAND FOR BEGINNERS. Globe 8vo. 3s.

BURKE (Edmund). (*See* POLITICS.)

BURY (J. B.).—A HISTORY OF THE LATER ROMAN EMPIRE FROM ARCADIUS TO IRENE, A.D. 390—800. 2 vols. 8vo. 32s.

CASSEL (Dr. D.).— MANUAL OF JEWISH HISTORY AND LITERATURE. Translated by Mrs. HENRY LUCAS. Fcp. 8vo. 2s. 6d.

COX (G. V.).—RECOLLECTIONS OF OXFORD. 2nd Edit. Cr. 8vo. 6s.

ENGLISH STATESMEN, TWELVE. (*See* BIOGRAPHY.)

FISKE (John).—THE CRITICAL PERIOD IN AMERICAN HISTORY, 1783—89. Ext. cr. 8vo. 10s. 6d.
— THE BEGINNINGS OF NEW ENGLAND; or, The Puritan Theocracy in its Relations to Civil and Religious Liberty. Cr. 8vo. 7s. 6d.
— THE AMERICAN REVOLUTION. 2 vols. Cr. 8vo. 18s.

FRAMJI (Dosabhai). — HISTORY OF THE PARSIS, INCLUDING THEIR MANNERS, CUSTOMS, RELIGION, AND PRESENT POSITION. With Illustrations. 2 vols. Med. 8vo. 36s.

HISTORY

HISTORY—*continued.*

FREEMAN (Prof. E. A.).—HISTORY OF THE CATHEDRAL CHURCH OF WELLS. Cr. 8vo. 3s. 6d.
—— OLD ENGLISH HISTORY. With 3 Coloured Maps. 9th Edit., revised. Ext. fcp. 8vo. 6s.
—— HISTORICAL ESSAYS. First Series. 4th Edit. 8vo. 10s. 6d.
—— —— Second Series. 3rd Edit., with Additional Essays. 8vo. 10s. 6d.
—— —— Third Series. 8vo. 12s.
—— THE GROWTH OF THE ENGLISH CONSTITUTION FROM THE EARLIEST TIMES. 5th Edit. Cr. 8vo. 5s.
—— COMPARATIVE POLITICS. Lectures at the Royal Institution. To which is added "The Unity of History." 8vo. 14s.
—— HISTORICAL AND ARCHITECTURAL SKETCHES, CHIEFLY ITALIAN. Illustrated by the Author. Cr. 8vo. 10s. 6d.
—— SUBJECT AND NEIGHBOUR LANDS OF VENICE. Illustrated. Cr. 8vo. 10s. 6d.
—— ENGLISH TOWNS AND DISTRICTS. A Series of Addresses and Essays. 8vo. 14s.
—— THE OFFICE OF THE HISTORICAL PROFESSOR. Cr. 8vo. 2s.
—— DISESTABLISHMENT AND DISENDOWMENT; WHAT ARE THEY? Cr. 8vo. 1s.
—— GREATER GREECE AND GREATER BRITAIN; GEORGE WASHINGTON THE EXPANDER OF ENGLAND. With an Appendix on IMPERIAL FEDERATION. Cr. 8vo. 3s. 6d.
—— THE METHODS OF HISTORICAL STUDY. Eight Lectures at Oxford. 8vo. 10s. 6d.
—— THE CHIEF PERIODS OF EUROPEAN HISTORY. With Essay on "Greek Cities under Roman Rule." 8vo. 10s. 6d.
—— FOUR OXFORD LECTURES, 1887; FIFTY YEARS OF EUROPEAN HISTORY; TEUTONIC CONQUEST IN GAUL AND BRITAIN. 8vo. 5s.
—— ESSAYS. I. Historical. II. Miscellaneous.

FRIEDMANN (Paul). (*See* BIOGRAPHY.)

GIBBINS (H. de B.).—HISTORY OF COMMERCE IN EUROPE. Globe 8vo. 3s. 6d.

GREEN (John Richard).—A SHORT HISTORY OF THE ENGLISH PEOPLE. New Edit., revised. 159th Thousand. Cr. 8vo. 8s. 6d.—Also in Parts, with Analysis. 3s. each.—Part I. 607—1265; II. 1204—1553; III. 1540—1689; IV. 1660—1873.—*Illustrated Edition*, in Parts. Super roy. 8vo. 1s. each net.—Part I. Oct. 1891.
—— HISTORY OF THE ENGLISH PEOPLE. In 4 vols. 8vo. 16s. each.
—— THE MAKING OF ENGLAND. 8vo. 16s.
—— THE CONQUEST OF ENGLAND. With Maps and Portrait. 8vo. 18s.
—— READINGS IN ENGLISH HISTORY. In 3 Parts. Fcp. 8vo. 1s. 6d. each.

GREEN (Alice S.).—THE ENGLISH TOWN IN THE 15TH CENTURY. 2 vols. 8vo.

GUEST (Dr. E.).—ORIGINES CELTICÆ. Maps. 2 vols. 8vo. 32s.

GUEST (M. J.)—LECTURES ON THE HISTORY OF ENGLAND. Cr. 8vo. 6s.

HISTORY PRIMERS. Edited by JOHN RICHARD GREEN. 18mo. 1s. each.
EUROPE. By E. A. FREEMAN, M.A.
GREECE. By C. A. FYFFE, M.A.
ROME. By Bishop CREIGHTON.
FRANCE. By CHARLOTTE M. YONGE.

HISTORICAL COURSE FOR SCHOOLS. Ed. by EDW. A. FREEMAN, D.C.L. 18mo.
GENERAL SKETCH OF EUROPEAN HISTORY. By E. A. FREEMAN. Maps. 3s. 6d.
HISTORY OF ENGLAND. By EDITH THOMPSON. Coloured Maps. 2s. 6d.
HISTORY OF SCOTLAND. By MARGARET MACARTHUR. 2s.
HISTORY OF ITALY. By the Rev. W. HUNT, M.A. With Coloured Maps. 3s. 6d.
HISTORY OF GERMANY. By JAMES SIME, M.A. 3s.
HISTORY OF AMERICA. By J. A. DOYLE. With Maps. 4s. 6d.
HISTORY OF EUROPEAN COLONIES. By E. J. PAYNE, M.A. Maps. 4s. 6d.
HISTORY OF FRANCE. By CHARLOTTE M. YONGE. Maps. 3s. 6d.

HOLE (Rev. C.).—GENEALOGICAL STEMMA OF THE KINGS OF ENGLAND AND FRANCE. On a Sheet. 1s.

INGRAM (T. Dunbar).—A HISTORY OF THE LEGISLATIVE UNION OF GREAT BRITAIN AND IRELAND. 8vo. 10s. 6d.
—— TWO CHAPTERS OF IRISH HISTORY: 1. The Irish Parliament of James II.; 2. The Alleged Violation of the Treaty of Limerick. 8vo. 6s.

IRVING (Joseph).—ANNALS OF OUR TIME. A Diurnal of Events, Social and Political, Home and Foreign. 2 vols. 8vo. 18s. each.—Vol. I. June 20th, 1837, to Feb. 28th, 1871; Vol. II. Feb. 24th, 1871, to June 24th, 1887. Also Vol. II. in 3 parts: Part I. Feb. 24th, 1871, to March 19th, 1874, 4s. 6d.; Part II. March 20th, 1874, to July 22nd, 1878, 4s. 6d.; Part III. July 23rd, 1878, to June 24th, 1887, 9s.—SUPPLEMENT, June 25th, 1887, to Dec. 30th, 1890. By J. H. FYFE.

JAMES (Right Hon. Sir William Milbourne). —THE BRITISH IN INDIA. 8vo. 12s. 6d.

JEBB (Prof. R. C.).—MODERN GREECE. Two Lectures. Crown 8vo. 5s.

JENNINGS (A. C.).—CHRONOLOGICAL TABLES OF ANCIENT HISTORY. 8vo. 5s.

KEARY (Annie).—THE NATIONS AROUND. Cr. 8vo. 4s. 6d.

KINGSLEY (Charles).—THE ROMAN AND THE TEUTON. Cr. 8vo. 3s. 6d.
—— HISTORICAL LECTURES AND ESSAYS. Cr. 8vo. 3s. 6d.

LABBERTON (R. H.). (*See* ATLASES.)

LEGGE (Alfred O.).—THE GROWTH OF THE TEMPORAL POWER OF THE PAPACY. Cr. 8vo. 8s. 6d.

LETHBRIDGE (Sir Roper).—A SHORT MANUAL OF THE HISTORY OF INDIA. Cr. 8vo. 5s.
—— THE WORLD'S HISTORY. Cr. 8vo, swd. 1s.
—— EASY INTRODUCTION TO THE HISTORY OF INDIA. Cr. 8vo, sewed. 1s. 6d.
—— HISTORY OF ENGLAND. Cr. 8vo, swd. 1s. 6d.
—— EASY INTRODUCTION TO THE HISTORY AND GEOGRAPHY OF BENGAL. Cr. 8vo. 1s. 6d.

LYTE (H. C. Maxwell).—A HISTORY OF ETON COLLEGE, 1440—1884. Illustrated. 8vo. 21s.
—— A HISTORY OF THE UNIVERSITY OF OXFORD, FROM THE EARLIEST TIMES TO THE YEAR 1530. 8vo. 16s.

HISTORY—HYGIENE.

MAHAFFY (Prof. J. P.). — SOCIAL LIFE IN GREECE, FROM HOMER TO MENANDER. 6th Edit. Cr. 8vo. 9s.
—— GREEK LIFE AND THOUGHT, FROM THE AGE OF ALEXANDER TO THE ROMAN CONQUEST. Cr. 8vo. 12s. 6d.
—— THE GREEK WORLD UNDER ROMAN SWAY, FROM POLYBIUS TO PLUTARCH. Cr. 8vo. 10s. 6d.

MARRIOTT (J. A. R.). (*See* SELECT BIOGRAPHY, p. 5.)

MICHELET (M.).—A SUMMARY OF MODERN HISTORY. Translated by M. C. M. SIMPSON. Globe 8vo. 4s. 6d.

MULLINGER (J. B.).—CAMBRIDGE CHARACTERISTICS IN THE SEVENTEENTH CENTURY. Cr. 8vo. 4s. 6d.

NORGATE (Kate).—ENGLAND UNDER THE ANGEVIN KINGS. In 2 vols. 8vo. 32s.

OLIPHANT (Mrs. M. O. W.).—THE MAKERS OF FLORENCE: DANTE, GIOTTO, SAVONAROLA, AND THEIR CITY. Illustr. Cr. 8vo. 10s. 6d.—*Edition de Luxe.* 8vo. 21s. net.
—— THE MAKERS OF VENICE: DOGES, CONQUERORS, PAINTERS, AND MEN OF LETTERS. Illustrated. Cr. 8vo. 10s. 6d.
—— ROYAL EDINBURGH: HER SAINTS, KINGS, PROPHETS, AND POETS. Illustrated by G. REID, R.S.A. Cr. 8vo. 10s. 6d.
—— JERUSALEM. Illustrated. 8vo. 21s.

OTTÉ (E. C.).—SCANDINAVIAN HISTORY. With Maps. Globe 8vo. 6s.

PALGRAVE (Sir Francis). — HISTORY OF NORMANDY AND OF ENGLAND. 4 vols. 8vo. 4l. 4s.

PARKMAN (Francis). — MONTCALM AND WOLFE. Library Edition. Illustrated with Portraits and Maps. 2 vols. 8vo. 12s. 6d. each.
—— THE COLLECTED WORKS OF FRANCIS PARKMAN. Popular Edition. In 10 vols. Cr. 8vo. 7s. 6d. each; or complete, 3l. 13s. 6d.
—— PIONEERS OF FRANCE IN THE NEW WORLD, 1 vol.; THE JESUITS IN NORTH AMERICA, 1 vol.; LA SALLE AND THE DISCOVERY OF THE GREAT WEST, 1 vol.; THE OREGON TRAIL, 1 vol.; THE OLD RÉGIME IN CANADA UNDER LOUIS XIV., 1 vol.; COUNT FRONTENAC AND NEW FRANCE UNDER LOUIS XIV., 1 vol.; MONTCALM AND WOLFE, 2 vols.; THE CONSPIRACY OF PONTIAC, 2 vols.

POOLE (Reginald Lane).—A HISTORY OF THE HUGUENOTS OF THE DISPERSION AT THE RECALL OF THE EDICT OF NANTES. Cr. 8vo. 6s.

ROGERS (Prof. J. E. Thorold).—HISTORICAL GLEANINGS. Cr. 8vo.—1st Series. 4s. 6d.—2nd Series. 6s.

SAYCE (Prof. A. H.).—THE ANCIENT EMPIRES OF THE EAST. Cr. 8vo. 6s.

SEELEY (Prof. J. R.). — LECTURES AND ESSAYS. 8vo. 10s. 6d.
—— THE EXPANSION OF ENGLAND. Two Courses of Lectures. Cr. 8vo. 4s. 6d.
—— OUR COLONIAL EXPANSION. Extracts from the above. Cr. 8vo. 1s.

SEWELL (E. M.) and YONGE (C. M.).—EUROPEAN HISTORY, NARRATED IN A SERIES OF HISTORICAL SELECTIONS FROM THE BEST AUTHORITIES. 2 vols. 3rd Edit. Cr. 8vo. 6s. each.

SHUCKBURGH (E. S.).—A SCHOOL HISTORY OF ROME. Cr. 8vo. [*In preparation.*

STEPHEN (Sir J. Fitzjames, Bart.).—THE STORY OF NUNCOMAR AND THE IMPEACHMENT OF SIR ELIJAH IMPEY. 2 vols. Cr. 8vo. 15s.

TAIT (C. W. A.).—ANALYSIS OF ENGLISH HISTORY, BASED ON GREEN'S "SHORT HISTORY OF THE ENGLISH PEOPLE." Cr. 8vo. 4s. 6d.

TOUT (T. F.).—ANALYSIS OF ENGLISH HISTORY. 18mo. 1s.

TREVELYAN (Sir Geo. Otto).—CAWNPORE. Cr. 8vo. 6s.

WHEELER (J. Talboys).—PRIMER OF INDIAN HISTORY, ASIATIC AND EUROPEAN. 18mo. 1s.
—— COLLEGE HISTORY OF INDIA, ASIATIC AND EUROPEAN. Cr. 8vo. 3s.; swd. 2s. 6d.
—— A SHORT HISTORY OF INDIA. With Maps. Cr. 8vo. 12s.
—— INDIA UNDER BRITISH RULE. 8vo. 12s. 6d.

WOOD (Rev. E. G.).—THE REGAL POWER OF THE CHURCH. 8vo. 4s. 6d.

YONGE (Charlotte).—CAMEOS FROM ENGLISH HISTORY. Ext. fcp. 8vo. 5s. each.—Vol. 1. FROM ROLLO TO EDWARD II.; Vol. 2. THE WARS IN FRANCE; Vol. 3. THE WARS OF THE ROSES; Vol. 4. REFORMATION TIMES; Vol. 5. ENGLAND AND SPAIN; Vol. 6. FORTY YEARS OF STEWART RULE (1603—43); Vol. 7. THE REBELLION AND RESTORATION (1642—1678).
—— THE VICTORIAN HALF-CENTURY. Cr. 8vo. 1s. 6d.; sewed, 1s.
—— THE STORY OF THE CHRISTIANS AND MOORS IN SPAIN. 18mo. 4s. 6d.

HORTICULTURE. (*See* GARDENING.)

HYGIENE.

BERNERS (J.)—FIRST LESSONS ON HEALTH. 18mo. 1s.

BLYTH (A. Wynter).—A MANUAL OF PUBLIC HEALTH. 8vo. 17s. net.

BROWNE (J. H. Balfour).—WATER SUPPLY. Cr. 8vo. 2s. 6d.

CORFIELD (Dr. W. H.).—THE TREATMENT AND UTILISATION OF SEWAGE. 3rd Edit. Revised by the Author, and by LOUIS C. PARKES, M.D. 8vo. 16s.

GOODFELLOW (J.).—THE DIETETIC VALUE OF BREAD. Cr. 8vo.

KINGSLEY (Charles).—SANITARY AND SOCIAL LECTURES. Cr. 8vo. 3s. 6d.
—— HEALTH AND EDUCATION. Cr. 8vo. 6s.

REYNOLDS (Prof. Osborne).—SEWER GAS, AND HOW TO KEEP IT OUT OF HOUSES. 3rd Edit. Cr. 8vo. 1s. 6d.

RICHARDSON (Dr. B. W.).—HYGEIA: A CITY OF HEALTH. Cr. 8vo. 1s.
—— THE FUTURE OF SANITARY SCIENCE. Cr. 8vo. 1s.
—— ON ALCOHOL. Cr. 8vo. 1s.

HYMNOLOGY.

(*See under* THEOLOGY, p. 33.)

ILLUSTRATED BOOKS.

BALCH (Elizabeth). — GLIMPSES OF OLD ENGLISH HOMES. Gl. 4to. 14s.

BLAKE. (See BIOGRAPHY.)

BOUGHTON (G. H.) and ABBEY (E. A.). (See VOYAGES AND TRAVELS.)

CHRISTMAS CAROL (A). Printed in Colours, with Illuminated Borders from MSS. of the 14th and 15th Centuries. 4to. 21s.

CRANE (Walter).—THE SIRENS THREE. A Poem. Roy. 8vo. 10s. 6d.

DAYS WITH SIR ROGER DE COVERLEY. From the *Spectator*. Illustrated by HUGH THOMSON. Fcp. 4to. 6s.

DELL (E. C.).—PICTURES FROM SHELLEY. Engraved by J. D. COOPER. Folio. 21s. net.

ENGLISH ILLUSTRATED MAGAZINE, THE. (See PERIODICALS.)
— Proof Impressions of Engravings originally published in *The English Illustrated Magazine*. 1884. In Portfolio 4to. 21s.

GASKELL (Mrs.).—CRANFORD. Illustrated by HUGH THOMSON. Cr. 8vo. 6s.

GOLDSMITH (Oliver). — THE VICAR OF WAKEFIELD. New Edition, with 182 Illustrations by HUGH THOMSON. Preface by AUSTIN DOBSON. Cr. 8vo. 6s.—Also with Uncut Edges, paper label. 6s.

GREEN (John Richard). — ILLUSTRATED EDITION OF THE SHORT HISTORY OF THE ENGLISH PEOPLE. In Parts. Super roy. 8vo. 1s. each net. Part I. Oct. 1891.

GRIMM. (See BOOKS FOR THE YOUNG.)

HALLWARD (R. F.).—FLOWERS OF PARADISE. Music, Verse, Design, Illustration. 6s

IRVING (Washington).—OLD CHRISTMAS. From the Sketch Book. Illustr. by RANDOLPH CALDECOTT. Gilt edges. Cr. 8vo. 6s.—Also with uncut edges, paper label. 6s.
— BRACEBRIDGE HALL. Illustr. by RANDOLPH CALDECOTT. Gilt edges. Cr. 8vo. 6s.—Also with uncut edges, paper label. 6s.
— OLD CHRISTMAS AND BRACEBRIDGE HALL. *Edition de Luxe*. Roy. 8vo. 21s.

KINGSLEY (Charles).—THE WATER BABIES. (See BOOKS FOR THE YOUNG.)
— THE HEROES. (See BOOKS for the YOUNG.)
— GLAUCUS. (See NATURAL HISTORY.)
— SONG OF THE RIVER. 31s. 6d.

LANG (Andrew).—THE LIBRARY. With a Chapter on Modern Illustrated Books, by AUSTIN DOBSON. Cr. 8vo. 3s. 6d.

LYTE (H. C. Maxwell). (See HISTORY.)

MAHAFFY (Rev. Prof. J. P.) and ROGERS (J. E.). (See VOYAGES AND TRAVELS.)

MEREDITH (L. A.).—BUSH FRIENDS IN TASMANIA. Native Flowers, Fruits, and Insects, with Prose and Verse Descriptions. Folio. 52s. 6d. net.

OLD SONGS. With Drawings by E. A. ABBEY and A. PARSONS. 4to, mor. gilt. 31s. 6d.

PROPERT (J. L.). (See ART.)

STUART, RELICS OF THE ROYAL HOUSE OF. Illustrated by 40 Plates in Colours drawn from Relics of the Stuarts by WILLIAM GIBB. With an Introduction by JOHN SKELTON, C.B., LL.D., and Descriptive Notes by W. ST. JOHN HOPE. Folio, half morocco, gilt edges. 7l. 7s. net.

TENNYSON (Hon. Hallam).—JACK AND THE BEAN-STALK. English Hexameters. Illustrated by R. CALDECOTT. Fcp. 4to. 3s. 6d.

TRISTRAM (W. O.).—COACHING DAYS AND COACHING WAYS. Illustrated by HERBERT RAILTON and HUGH THOMSON. Ext. cr. 4to. 31s. 6d.

TURNER'S LIBER STUDIORUM : A DESCRIPTION AND A CATALOGUE. By W. G. RAWLINSON. Med. 8vo. 12s. 6d.

WALTON and COTTON—LOWELL.—THE COMPLETE ANGLER. With Introduction by JAS. RUSSELL LOWELL. 2 vols. Ext. cr. 8vo. 52s. 6d. net.—Large Paper Edition, Proofs on Japanese paper. 73s. 6d. net.

LANGUAGE. (See PHILOLOGY.)

LAW.

ANGLO-SAXON LAW : ESSAYS ON. Med. 8vo. 18s.

BERNARD (M.).—FOUR LECTURES ON SUBJECTS CONNECTED WITH DIPLOMACY. 8vo. 9s.

BIGELOW (M. M.).—HISTORY OF PROCEDURE IN ENGLAND FROM THE NORMAN CONQUEST, 1066-1204. 8vo. 16s.

BOUTMY (E.). — STUDIES IN CONSTITUTIONAL LAW. Transl. by Mrs. DICEY. Preface by Prof. A. V. DICEY. Cr. 8vo. 6s.
— THE ENGLISH CONSTITUTION. Transl. by Mrs. EADEN. Introduction by Sir F. POLLOCK, Bart. Cr. 8vo. 6s.

CHERRY (R. R.). — LECTURES ON THE GROWTH OF CRIMINAL LAW IN ANCIENT COMMUNITIES. 8vo. 5s. net.

DICEY (Prof. A. V.).—LECTURES INTRODUCTORY TO THE STUDY OF THE LAW OF THE CONSTITUTION. 3rd Edit. 8vo. 12s. 6d.

ENGLISH CITIZEN SERIES, THE. (See POLITICS.)

HOLLAND (Prof. T. E.).—THE TREATY RELATIONS OF RUSSIA AND TURKEY, FROM 1774 TO 1853. Cr. 8vo. 2s.

HOLMES (O. W., jun.). — THE COMMON LAW. 8vo. 12s.

LIGHTWOOD (J. M.).—THE NATURE OF POSITIVE LAW. 8vo. 12s. 6d.

MAITLAND (F. W.).—PLEAS OF THE CROWN : FOR THE COUNTY OF GLOUCESTER, A.D. 1221. 8vo. 7s. 6d.
— JUSTICE AND POLICH. Cr. 8vo. 3s. 6d.

MONAHAN (James H.).—THE METHOD OF LAW. Cr. 8vo. 6s.

PATERSON (James).—COMMENTARIES ON THE LIBERTY OF THE SUBJECT, AND THE LAWS OF ENGLAND RELATING TO THE SECURITY OF THE PERSON. 2 vols. Cr. 8vo. 21s.
— THE LIBERTY OF THE PRESS, SPEECH, AND PUBLIC WORSHIP. Cr. 8vo. 12s.

PHILLIMORE (John G.).—PRIVATE LAW AMONG THE ROMANS. 8vo. 6s.

POLLOCK (Sir F., Bart.).—ESSAYS IN JURISPRUDENCE AND ETHICS. 8vo. 10s. 6d.
— THE LAND LAWS. Cr. 8vo. 3s. 6d.

RICHEY (Alex. G.).—THE IRISH LAND LAWS. Cr. 8vo. 3s. 6d.

SELBORNE (Earl of).—JUDICIAL PROCEDURE IN THE PRIVY COUNCIL. 8vo. 1s. net.

STEPHEN (Sir J. Fitzjames, Bart.).—A Digest of the Law of Evidence. Cr. 8vo. 6s.
—— A Digest of the Criminal Law: Crimes and Punishments. 4th Ed. 8vo. 16s.
—— A Digest of the Law of Criminal Procedure in Indictable Offences. By Sir J. F., Bart., and Herbert Stephen, LL.M. 8vo. 12s. 6d.
—— A History of the Criminal Law of England. 3 vols. 8vo. 48s.
—— A General View of the Criminal Law of England. 2nd Edit. 8vo. 14s.
STEPHEN (J. K.).—International Law and International Relations. Cr. 8vo. 6s.
WILLIAMS (S. E.).—Forensic Facts and Fallacies. Globe 8vo. 4s. 6d.

LETTERS. (*See under* LITERATURE, p. 19.)

LIFE-BOAT.

GILMORE (Rev. John).—Storm Warriors; or, Life-Boat Work on the Goodwin Sands. Cr. 8vo. 3s. 6d.
LEWIS (Richard).—History of the Life-Boat and its Work. Cr. 8vo. 5s.

LIGHT. (*See under* Physics, p. 27.)

LITERATURE.

History and Criticism of—Commentaries, etc.—Poetry and the Drama—Poetical Collections and Selections—Prose Fiction—Collected Works, Essays, Lectures, Letters, Miscellaneous Works.

History and Criticism of.

(*See also* Essays, p. 19.)
ARNOLD (M.). (*See* Essays, p. 19.)
BROOKE (Stopford A.).—A Primer of English Literature. 18mo. 1s. — Large Paper Edition. 8vo. 7s. 6d.
—— A History of Early English Literature. 2 vols. 8vo.
CLASSICAL WRITERS. Edited by John Richard Green. Fcp. 8vo. 1s. 6d. each.
Demosthenes. By Prof. Butcher, M.A.
Euripides. By Prof. Mahaffy.
Livy. By the Rev. W. W. Capes, M.A.
Milton. By Stopford A. Brooke.
Sophocles. By Prof. L. Campbell, M.A.
Tacitus. By Messrs. Church and Brodribb.
Vergil. By Prof. Nettleship, M.A.
ENGLISH MEN OF LETTERS. (*See* Biography.)
HISTORY OF ENGLISH LITERATURE. In 4 vols. Cr. 8vo.
Early English Literature. By Stopford Brooke, M.A. [*In preparation.*
Elizabethan Literature (1560—1665). By George Saintsbury. 7s. 6d.
Eighteenth Century Literature (1660—1780). By Edmund Gosse, M.A. 7s. 6d.
The Modern Period. By Prof. Dowden. [*In preparation.*
JEBB (Prof. R. C.).—A Primer of Greek Literature. 18mo. 1s.
—— The Attic Orators, from Antiphon to Isaeos. 2 vols 8vo. 25s.
JOHNSON'S LIVES OF THE POETS. Milton, Dryden, Pope, Addison, Swift, and Gray. With Macaulay's "Life of Johnson." Ed. by M. Arnold. Cr.8vo. 4s.6d.

KINGSLEY (Charles). — Literary and General Lectures. Cr. 8vo. 3s. 6d.
MAHAFFY (Prof. J. P.).—A History of Classical Greek Literature. 2 vols. Cr. 8vo.—Vol. 1. The Poets. With an Appendix on Homer by Prof. Sayce. In 2 Parts.—Vol. 2. The Prose Writers. In 2 Parts. 4s. 6d. each.
MORLEY (John). (*See* Collected Works, p. 22.)
NICHOL (Prof. J.) and McCORMICK (Prof. W. S.).—A Short History of English Literature. Globe 8vo. [*In preparation.*
OLIPHANT (Mrs. M. O. W.).—The Literary History of England in the End of the 18th and Beginning of the 19th Century. 3 vols. 8vo. 21s.
RYLAND (F.).—Chronological Outlines of English Literature. Cr. 8vo. 6s.
WARD (Prof. A. W.).—A History of English Dramatic Literature, to the Death of Queen Anne. 2 vols. 8vo. 32s.
WILKINS (Prof. A. S.).—A Primer of Roman Literature. 18mo. 1s.

Commentaries, etc.

BROWNING.
A Primer of Browning. By Mary Wilson.
DANTE.
Readings on the Purgatorio of Dante. Chiefly based on the Commentary of Benvenuto da Imola. By the Hon. W. W. Vernon, M.A. With an Introduction by Dean Church. 2 vols. Cr. 8vo. 24s.
HOMER.
Homeric Dictionary. (*See* Dictionaries.)
The Problem of the Homeric Poems. By Prof. W. D. Geddes. 8vo. 14s.
Homeric Synchronism. An Inquiry into the Time and Place of Homer. By the Rt. Hon. W. E. Gladstone. Cr. 8vo. 6s.
Primer of Homer. By the same. 18mo. 1s.
Landmarks of Homeric Study, together with an Essay on the Points of Contact between the Assyrian Tablets and the Homeric Text. By the same. Cr. 8vo. 2s. 6d.
Companion to the Iliad for English Readers. By W. Leaf, Litt.D. [*In prep.*
HORACE.
Studies, Literary and Historical, in the Odes of Horace. By A. W. Verrall, Litt.D. 8vo. 8s. 6d.
SHAKESPEARE.
Shakespeare Glossary. *See* Dictionaries.
A Primer of Shakspere. By Prof. Dowden. 18mo. 1s.
A Shakespearian Grammar. By Rev. E. A. Abbott. Ext. fcp. 8vo. 6s.
A Shakespeare Manual. By Rev. F. G. Fleay. Ext. fcp. 8vo. 4s. 6d.
Shakespeareana Genealogica. By G. R. French. 8vo. 15s.
A Selection from the Lives in North's Plutarch which illustrate Shakespeare's Plays. Edited by Rev. W. W. Skeat, M.A. Cr. 8vo. 6s.
Short Studies of Shakespeare's Plots. By Prof. Cyril Ransome. Cr. 8vo. 3s. 6d.
CALIBAN: A Critique on "The Tempest" and "A Midsummer Night's Dream." By Sir Daniel Wilson. 8vo. 10s. 6d.

LITERATURE.

LITERATURE.
Commentaries, etc.—*continued.*

TENNYSON.
A COMPANION TO "IN MEMORIAM." By ELIZABETH R. CHAPMAN. Globe 8vo. 2s.

WORDSWORTH.
WORDSWORTHIANA: A Selection of Papers read to the Wordsworth Society. Edited by W. KNIGHT. Cr. 8vo. 7s. 6d.

Poetry and the Drama.

ALDRICH (T. Bailey).—THE SISTERS' TRAGEDY: with other Poems, Lyrical and Dramatic. Fcp. 8vo. 3s. 6d. net.
AN ANCIENT CITY: AND OTHER POEMS. Ext. fcp. 8vo. 6s.
ANDERSON (A.).—BALLADS AND SONNETS. Cr. 8vo. 5s.
ARNOLD (Matthew).—THE COMPLETE POETICAL WORKS. New Edition. 3 vols. Cr. 8vo. 7s. 6d. each.
  Vol. 1. EARLY POEMS, NARRATIVE POEMS AND SONNETS.
  Vol. 2. LYRIC AND ELEGIAC POEMS.
  Vol. 3. DRAMATIC AND LATER POEMS.
— COMPLETE POETICAL WORKS. 1 vol. Cr. 8vo. 7s. 6d.
— SELECTED POEMS. 18mo. 4s. 6d.
AUSTIN (Alfred).—POETICAL WORKS. New Collected Edition. 6 vols. Cr. 8vo. 5s. each.
  Vol. 1. THE TOWER OF BABEL.
  Vol. 2. SAVONAROLA, etc.
  Vol. 3. PRINCE LUCIFER.
  Vol. 4. THE HUMAN TRAGEDY.
  Vol. 5. LYRICAL POEMS.
  Vol. 6. NARRATIVE POEMS.
— SOLILOQUIES IN SONG. Cr. 8vo. 6s.
— AT THE GATE OF THE CONVENT: and other Poems. Cr. 8vo. 6s.
— MADONNA'S CHILD. Cr. 4to. 3s. 6d.
— ROME OR DEATH. Cr. 4to. 9s.
— THE GOLDEN AGE. Cr. 8vo. 5s.
— THE SEASON. Cr. 8vo. 5s.
— LOVE'S WIDOWHOOD: and other Poems. Cr. 8vo. 6s.
— ENGLISH LYRICS. Cr. 8vo. 3s. 6d.
BETSY LEE: A FO'C'S'LE YARN. Ext. fcp. 8vo. 3s. 6d.
BLACKIE (John Stuart).—MESSIS VITAE: Gleanings of Song from a Happy Life. Cr. 8vo. 4s. 6d.
— THE WISE MEN OF GREECE. In a Series of Dramatic Dialogues. Cr. 8vo. 9s.
— GOETHE'S FAUST. Translated into English Verse. 2nd Edit. Cr. 8vo. 9s.
BLAKE. (*See* BIOGRAPHY.)
BROOKE (Stopford A.).—RIQUET OF THE TUFT: A Love Drama. Ext. cr. 8vo. 6s.
— POEMS. Globe 8vo. 6s.
BROWN (T. E.).—THE MANX WITCH: and other Poems. Cr. 8vo. 7s. 6d.
BURGON (Dean).—POEMS. Ex.fcp.8vo. 4s.6d.
BURNS. THE POETICAL WORKS. With a Biographical Memoir by ALEXANDER SMITH. In 2 vols. Fcp. 8vo. 10s. (*See also* GLOBE LIBRARY, p. 20.)
BUTLER (Samuel).—HUDIBRAS. Edit. by ALFRED MILNES. Fcp. 8vo.—Part I. 3s. 6d.; Parts II. and III. 4s. 6d.

BYRON. (*See* GOLDEN TREASURY SERIES, p. 20.)
CALDERON.—SELECT PLAYS. Edited by NORMAN MACCOLL. Cr. 8vo. 14s.
CAUTLEY (G. S.).—A CENTURY OF EMBLEMS. With Illustrations by Lady MARION ALFORD. Small 4to. 10s. 6d.
CLOUGH (A. H.).—POEMS. Cr. 8vo. 7s. 6d.
COLERIDGE: POETICAL AND DRAMATIC WORKS. 4 vols. Fcp. 8vo. 31s. 6d.—Also an Edition on Large Paper, 2l. 12s. 6d.
COLQUHOUN.—RHYMES AND CHIMES. By F. S. COLQUHOUN (*née* F. S. FULLER MAITLAND). Ext. fcp. 8vo. 2s. 6d.
COWPER. (*See* GLOBE LIBRARY, p. 20; GOLDEN TREASURY SERIES, p. 20.)
CRAIK (Mrs.).—POEMS. Ext. fcp. 8vo. 6s.
CRANE (Walter).—THE SIRENS THREE. A Poem. Written and Illustrated by WALTER CRANE. Roy. 8vo. 10s. 6d.
DOYLE (Sir F. H.).—THE RETURN OF THE GUARDS: and other Poems. Cr. 8vo. 7s. 6d.
DRYDEN. (*See* GLOBE LIBRARY, p. 20.)
EMERSON. (*See* COLLECTED WORKS, p. 20.)
EVANS (Sebastian). — BROTHER FABIAN'S MANUSCRIPT: and other Poems. Fcp. 8vo. 6s.
— IN THE STUDIO: A Decade of Poems. Ext. fcp. 8vo. 5s.
FITZ GERALD (Caroline).—VENETIA VICTRIX; and other Poems. Ext.fcp.8vo. 3s.6d.
FITZGERALD (Edward).—THE RUBÁIYÁT OF OMAR KHÁYYÁM. Ext. cr. 8vo. 10s. 6d.
FO'C'SLE YARNS, including "Betsy Lee," and other Poems. Cr. 8vo. 7s. 6d.
FRASER-TYTLER. — SONGS IN MINOR KEYS. By C. C. FRASER-TYTLER (Mrs. EDWARD LIDDELL). 2nd Edit. 18mo. 6s.
FURNIVALL (F. J.).—LE MORTE ARTHUR. Edited from the Harleian MSS. 2252, in the British Museum. Fcp. 8vo. 7s. 6d.
GARNETT (R.).—IDYLLS AND EPIGRAMS. Chiefly from the Greek Anthology. Fcp. 8vo. 2s. 6d.
GOETHE.—FAUST. (*See* BLACKIE.)
— REYNARD THE FOX. Transl. into English Verse by A. D. AINSLIE. Cr. 8vo. 7s. 6d.
GOLDSMITH.—THE TRAVELLER AND THE DESERTED VILLAGE. With Introduction and Notes, by ARTHUR BARRETT, B.A. 1s. 9d.; sewed, 1s. 6d.—THE TRAVELLER (separately), sewed, 1s.—By J. W. HALES. Cr. 8vo. 6d. (*See also* GLOBE LIBRARY, p. 20.)
GRAHAM (David).—KING JAMES I. An Historical Tragedy. Globe 8vo. 7s.
GRAY.—POEMS. With Introduction and Notes, by J. BRADSHAW, LL.D. Gl. 8vo. 1s. 9d., sewed, 1s. 6d. (*See also* COLLECTED WORKS, p. 21.)
HALLWARD. (*See* ILLUSTRATED BOOKS.)
HAYES (A.).—THE MARCH OF MAN: and other Poems. Fcp. 8vo. 3s. 6d. net.
HERRICK. (*See* GOLDEN TREASURY SERIES, p. 20.)
HOPKINS (Ellice).—AUTUMN SWALLOWS: A Book of Lyrics. Ext. fcp. 8vo. 6s.

POETRY AND THE DRAMA. 15

JONES (H. A.).—SAINTS AND SINNERS. Ext. fcp. 8vo. 3s. 6d.
KEATS. (See GOLDEN TREASURY SERIES, p. 20.)
KINGSLEY (Charles).—POEMS. Cr. 8vo. 3s. 6d.—*Pocket Edition.* 18mo. 1s. 6d.—*Eversley Edition.* 2 vols. Cr. 8vo. 10s.
LAMB. (See COLLECTED WORKS, p. 21.)
LANDOR. (See GOLDEN TREASURY SERIES, p. 20.)
LONGFELLOW. (See GOLDEN TREASURY SERIES, p. 20.)
LOWELL (Jas. Russell).—COMPLETE POETICAL WORKS. 18mo. 4s. 6d.
—— With Introduction by THOMAS HUGHES. Cr. 8vo. 7s. 6d.
—— HEARTSEASE AND RUE. Cr. 8vo. 5s. (See also COLLECTED WORKS, p. 21.)
LUCAS (F.).—SKETCHES OF RURAL LIFE. Poems. Globe 8vo. 5s.
MEREDITH (George).— A READING OF EARTH. Ext. fcp. 8vo. 5s.
—— POEMS AND LYRICS OF THE JOY OF EARTH. Ext. fcp. 8vo. 6s.
—— BALLADS AND POEMS OF TRAGIC LIFE. Cr. 8vo. 6s.
MILTON.—POETICAL WORKS. Edited, with Introductions and Notes, by Prof. DAVID MASSON, M.A. 3 vols. 8vo. 2l. 2s.—[Uniform with the Cambridge Shakespeare.]
—— —— Edited by Prof. MASSON. 3 vols. Fcp. 8vo. 15s.
—— —— *Globe Edition.* Edited by Prof. MASSON. Globe 8vo. 3s. 6d.
—— PARADISE LOST, BOOKS 1 and 2. Edited by MICHAEL MACMILLAN, B.A. 1s. 9d.; sewed, 1s. 6d.—BOOKS 1 and 2 (separately), 1s. 3d. each; sewed, 1s. each.
—— L'ALLEGRO, IL PENSEROSO, LYCIDAS, ARCADES, SONNETS, ETC. Edited by WM. BELL, M.A. 1s. 9d.; sewed, 1s. 6d.
—— COMUS. By the same. 1s. 3d.; swd. 1s.
—— SAMSON AGONISTES. Edited by H. M. PERCIVAL, M.A. 2s.; sewed, 1s. 9d.
MINCHIN (Prof. G. M.).—NATURÆ VERITAS. Fcp. 8vo. 2s. 6d.
MORISON (Jeanie).—THE PURPOSE OF THE AGES. Cr. 8vo. 9s.
MOULTON (Louise Chandler). — IN THE GARDEN OF DREAMS; Lyrics and Sonnets. Cr. 8vo. 6s.
MUDIE (C. E.).—STRAY LEAVES: Poems. 4th Edit. Ext. fcp. 8vo. 3s. 6d.
MYERS (E.).—THE PURITANS: A Poem. Ext. fcp. 8vo. 2s. 6d.
—— POEMS. Ext. fcp. 8vo. 4s. 6d.
—— THE DEFENCE OF ROME: and other Poems. Ext. fcp. 8vo. 5s.
—— THE JUDGMENT OF PROMETHEUS: and other Poems. Ext. fcp. 8vo. 3s. 6d.
MYERS (F. W. H.).—THE RENEWAL OF YOUTH: and other Poems. Cr. 8vo. 7s. 6d.
—— ST. PAUL: A Poem. Ext. fcp. 8vo. 2s. 6d.
NORTON (Hon. Mrs.).—THE LADY OF LA GARAVE. 9th Edit. Fcp. 8vo. 4s. 6d.
PALGRAVE (Prof. F.T.).—ORIGINAL HYMNS. 3rd Edit. 18mo. 1s. 6d.
—— LYRICAL POEMS. Ext. fcp. 8vo. 6s.
—— VISIONS OF ENGLAND. Cr. 8vo. 7s. 6d.
PALGRAVE (W. G.).—A VISION OF LIFE: SEMBLANCE AND REALITY. Globe 8vo.

PEEL (Edmund).—ECHOES FROM HOREB: and other Poems. Cr. 8vo. 3s. 6d.
POPE. (See GLOBE LIBRARY, p. 20.)
RAWNSLEY (H. D.).—POEMS, BALLADS, AND BUCOLICS. Fcp. 8vo. 5s.
ROSSETTI (Christina).—POEMS. New Collected Edition. Globe 8vo. 7s. 6d.
—— A PAGEANT: and other Poems. Ext. fcp. 8vo. 6s.
SCOTT.—THE LAY OF THE LAST MINSTREL, and THE LADY OF THE LAKE. Edited by Prof. F. T. PALGRAVE. 1s.
—— THE LAY OF THE LAST MINSTREL. By G. H. STUART, M.A., and E. H. ELLIOT, B.A. Globe 8vo. 2s.; sewed, 1s. 9d.—Canto I. 9d.—Cantos I.—III. and IV.—VI. 1s. 3d. each; sewed, 1s. each.
—— MARMION. Edited by MICHAEL MACMILLAN, B.A. 3s.; sewed, 2s. 6d.
—— MARMION, and THE LORD OF THE ISLES. By Prof. F. T. PALGRAVE. 1s.
—— THE LADY OF THE LAKE. By G. H. STUART, M.A. Gl. 8vo. 2s. 6d.; swd. 2s.
—— ROKEBY. By MICHAEL MACMILLAN, B.A. 3s.; sewed, 2s. 6d.
(See also GLOBE LIBRARY, p. 20.)
SHAIRP (John Campbell).—GLEN DESSERAY: and other Poems, Lyrical and Elegiac. Ed. by F. T. PALGRAVE. Cr. 8vo. 6s.
SHAKESPEARE.—THE WORKS OF WILLIAM SHAKESPEARE. *Cambridge Edition.* New and Revised Edition, by W. ALDIS WRIGHT, M.A. 9 vols. 8vo. 10s. 6d. each.—Quarterly Vols. Vol. I. Jan. 1891.
—— —— *Victoria Edition.* In 3 vols.—COMEDIES; HISTORIES; TRAGEDIES. Cr. 8vo. 6s. each.
—— THE TEMPEST. With Introduction and Notes, by K. DEIGHTON.. Gl. 8vo. 1s. 9d.; sewed, 1s. 6d.
—— MUCH ADO ABOUT NOTHING. 2s.; sewed, 1s. 9d.
—— A MIDSUMMER NIGHT'S DREAM. 1s. 9d.; sewed, 1s. 6d.
—— THE MERCHANT OF VENICE. 1s. 9d.; sewed, 1s. 6d.
—— AS YOU LIKE IT. 1s. 9d.; sewed, 1s. 6d.
—— TWELFTH NIGHT. 1s. 9d.; sewed, 1s. 6d.
—— THE WINTER'S TALE. 2s.; sewed, 1s. 6d.
—— KING JOHN. 1s. 9d.; sewed, 1s. 6d.
—— RICHARD II. 1s. 9d.; sewed, 1s. 6d.
—— HENRY V. 1s. 9d.; sewed, 1s. 6d.
—— RICHARD III. By C. H. TAWNEY, M.A. 2s. 6d.; sewed, 2s.
—— CORIOLANUS. By K. DEIGHTON. 2s. 6d.; sewed, 2s.
—— JULIUS CÆSAR. 1s. 9d.; sewed, 1s. 6d.
—— MACBETH. 1s. 9d.; sewed, 1s. 6d.
—— HAMLET. 2s.; sewed, 1s. 6d.
—— KING LEAR. 1s. 9d.; sewed, 1s. 6d.
—— OTHELLO. 2s.; sewed, 1s. 9d.
—— ANTONY AND CLEOPATRA. 2s. 6d.; swd. 2s.
—— CYMBELINE. 2s. 6d.; sewed, 2s.
(See also GLOBE LIBRARY, p. 20; GOLDEN TREASURY SERIES, p. 20.)
SHELLEY.—COMPLETE POETICAL WORKS. Edited by Prof. DOWDEN. Portrait. Cr. 8vo. 7s. 6d. (See GOLDEN TREASURY SERIES, p. 20.)
SKRINE (J. H.).—UNDER TWO QUEENS. Cr. 8vo. 3s.

LITERATURE.
Poetry and the Drama—*continued.*

SMITH (C. Barnard).—POEMS. Fcp. 8vo. 5s.
SMITH (Horace).—POEMS. Globe 8vo. 5s.
SPENSER. (*See* GLOBE LIBRARY, p. 20.)
STEPHENS (J. B.).—CONVICT ONCE: and other Poems. Cr. 8vo. 7s. 6d.
STRETTELL (Alma).—SPANISH AND ITALIAN FOLK SONGS. Illustr. Roy.16mo. 12s.6d.
SYMONS (Arthur).— DAYS AND NIGHTS. Globe 8vo. 6s.
TENNYSON (Lord).— COMPLETE WORKS. New and Enlarged Edition, with Portrait. Cr. 8vo. 7s. 6d.—*School Edition.* In Four Parts. Cr. 8vo. 2s. 6d. each.
—— POETICAL WORKS. *Pocket Edition.* 18mo, morocco, gilt edges. 7s. 6d. net.
—— WORKS. *Library Edition.* In 8 vols. Globe 8vo. 5s. each. [Each volume may be had separately.]—POEMS, 2 vols.—IDYLLS OF THE KING.—THE PRINCESS, and MAUD.—ENOCH ARDEN, and IN MEMORIAM.—BALLADS, and other Poems.—QUEEN MARY, and HAROLD.—BECKET, and other Plays.
—— WORKS. *Ext.fcp. 8vo. Edition,* on Handmade Paper. In 7 vols. (supplied in sets only). 3l. 13s. 6d.—EARLY POEMS.—LUCRETIUS, and other Poems.—IDYLLS OF THE KING.—THE PRINCESS, and MAUD.—ENOCH ARDEN, and IN MEMORIAM.—QUEEN MARY, and HAROLD.—BALLADS, and other Poems.
—— WORKS. *Miniature Edition,* in 14 vols., viz. THE POETICAL WORKS, 10 vols. in a box. 25s.—THE DRAMATIC WORKS. 4 vols. in a box. 10s. 6d.
—— *The Original Editions.* Fcp. 8vo.
POEMS. 6s.
MAUD: and other Poems. 3s. 6d.
THE PRINCESS. 3s. 6d.
ENOCH ARDEN, etc. 3s. 6d.
THE HOLY GRAIL: and other Poems. 4s.6d.
BALLADS: and other Poems. 5s.
HAROLD: A Drama. 6s.
QUEEN MARY: A Drama. 6s.
THE CUP, and THE FALCON. 5s.
BECKET. 6s.
TIRESIAS: and other Poems. 6s.
LOCKSLEY HALL SIXTY YEARS AFTER, etc. 6s.
DEMETER: and other Poems. 6s.
—— *The Royal Edition.* 1 vol. 8vo. 16s.
—— THE TENNYSON BIRTHDAY BOOK. Edit. by EMILY SHAKESPEAR. 18mo. 2s. 6d.
—— THE BROOK. With 20 Illustrations by A. WOODRUFF. 32mo. 2s. 6d.
—— SELECTIONS FROM TENNYSON'S WORKS. Square 8vo. 3s. 6d.
—— SONGS FROM TENNYSON'S WRITINGS. Square 8vo. 2s. 6d.
—— SELECTIONS FROM TENNYSON. With Introduction and Notes, by F. J. ROWE, M.A. and W. T. WEBB, M.A. Globe 8vo. 3s. 6d.
—— ENOCH ARDEN. By W. T. WEBB, M.A. Globe 8vo. 2s.
—— AYLMER'S FIELD. By W. T. WEBB, M.A. Globe 8vo. 2s.
—— THE COMING OF ARTHUR, and THE PASSING OF ARTHUR. By F. J. ROWE. Gl. 8vo. 2s.
—— THE PRINCESS. By P. M. WALLACE, B.A.
TENNYSON (Frederick).—THE ISLES OF GREECE: SAPPHO AND ALCAEUS. Cr. 8vo. 7s. 6d.
—— DAPHNE: and other Poems. Cr.8vo. 7s.6d.

TENNYSON (Hon. Hallam). (*See* ILLUSTRATED BOOKS.)
TRUMAN (Jos.).—AFTER-THOUGHTS: Poems. Cr. 8vo. 3s. 6d.
TURNER (Charles Tennyson).—COLLECTED SONNETS, OLD AND NEW. Ext.fcp.8vo. 7s.6d.
TYRWHITT (R. St. John).—FREE FIELD. Lyrics, chiefly Descriptive. Gl. 8vo. 3s. 6d.
—— BATTLE AND AFTER, CONCERNING SERGEANT THOMAS ATKINS, GRENADIER GUARDS: and other Verses. Gl. 8vo. 3s.6d.
WARD (Samuel).—LYRICAL RECREATIONS. Fcp. 8vo. 6s.
WHITTIER.—COMPLETE POETICAL WORKS OF JOHN GREENLEAF WHITTIER. With Portrait. 18mo. 4s. 6d. (*See also* COLLECTED WORKS.)
WILLS (W. G.).—MELCHIOR. Cr. 8vo. 9s.
WOOD (Andrew Goldie).—THE ISLES OF THE BLEST: and other Poems. Globe 8vo. 5s.
WOOLNER (Thomas). — MY BEAUTIFUL LADY. 3rd Edit. Fcp. 8vo. 5s.
—— PYGMALION. Cr. 8vo. 7s. 6d.,
—— SILENUS. Cr. 8vo. 6s.
WORDSWORTH. — COMPLETE POETICAL WORKS. Copyright Edition. With an Introduction by JOHN MORLEY, and Portrait. Cr. 8vo. 7s. 6d.
—— THE RECLUSE. Fcp. 8vo. 2s. 6d.—Large Paper Edition. 8vo. 10s. 6d.
(*See also* GOLDEN TREASURY SERIES, p. 20.)

Poetical Collections and Selections.
(*See also* GOLDEN TREASURY SERIES, p. 20; BOOKS FOR THE YOUNG, p. 38.)

HALES (Prof. J. W.).—LONGER ENGLISH POEMS. With Notes, Philological and Explanatory, and an Introduction on the Teaching of English. Ext. fcp. 8vo. 4s. 6d.
MACDONALD (George).—ENGLAND'S ANTIPHON. Cr. 8vo. 4s. 6d.
MARTIN (F.). (*See* BOOKS FOR THE YOUNG, p. 38.)
MASSON (R. O. and D.).—THREE CENTURIES OF ENGLISH POETRY. Being Selections from Chaucer to Herrick. Globe 8vo. 3s. 6d.
PALGRAVE (Prof. F. T.).—THE GOLDEN TREASURY OF THE BEST SONGS AND LYRICAL POEMS IN THE ENGLISH LANGUAGE. Large Type. Cr. 8vo. 10s. 6d. (*See also* GOLDEN TREASURY SERIES, p. 20; BOOKS FOR THE YOUNG, p. 38.)
WARD (T. H.).—ENGLISH POETS. Selections, with Critical Introductions by various Writers, and a General Introduction by MATTHEW ARNOLD. Edited by T. H. WARD, M.A. 4 vols. 2nd Edit. Cr. 8vo. 7s. 6d. each.—Vol. I. CHAUCER TO DONNE; II. BEN JONSON TO DRYDEN; III. ADDISON TO BLAKE; IV. WORDSWORTH TO ROSSETTI.
WOODS (M. A.).—A FIRST POETRY BOOK. Fcp. 8vo. 2s. 6d.
—— A SECOND POETRY BOOK. 2 Parts. Fcp. 8vo. 2s. 6d. each.
—— A THIRD POETRY BOOK. Fcp. 8vo. 4s. 6d.
WORDS FROM THE POETS. With a Vignette and Frontispiece. 12th Edit. 18mo. 1s.

PROSE FICTION.

Prose Fiction.

BIKÉLAS (D.).—LOUKIS LARAS; or, The Reminiscences of a Chiote Merchant during the Greek War of Independence. Translated by J. GENNADIUS. Cr. 8vo. 7s. 6d.

BJÖRNSON (B.).—SYNNÖVE SOLBAKKEN. Translated by JULIE SUTTER. Cr. 8vo. 6s.

BLACK (William).—THE STRANGE ADVENTURES OF A PHAETON. Illustr. Cr. 8vo. 6s.
— A PRINCESS OF THULE. Cr. 8vo. 6s.
— THE MAID OF KILLEENA: and other Tales. Cr. 8vo. 6s.
— MADCAP VIOLET. Cr. 8vo. 6s.
— GREEN PASTURES AND PICCADILLY. Cr. 8vo. 6s.
— MACLEOD OF DARE. Illustr. Cr. 8vo. 6s.
— WHITE WINGS. Cr. 8vo. 6s.
— THE BEAUTIFUL WRETCH; THE FOUR MACNICOLS; THE PUPIL OF AURELIUS. Cr. 8vo. 6s.
— SHANDON BELLS. Cr. 8vo. 6s.
— YOLANDE. Cr. 8vo. 6s.
— JUDITH SHAKESPEARE. Cr. 8vo. 6s.
— THE WISE WOMEN OF INVERNESS: A Tale, and other Miscellanies. Cr. 8vo. 6s.
— WHITE HEATHER. Cr. 8vo. 6s.
— SABINA ZEMBRA. Cr. 8vo. 6s.

BOLDREWOOD (Rolf).—*Uniform Edition.* Cr. 8vo. 3s. 6d. each.
ROBBERY UNDER ARMS: A Story of Life and Adventure in the Bush and in the Goldfields of Australia.
THE MINER'S RIGHT.
THE SQUATTER'S DREAM.
A SYDNEY-SIDE SAXON.
A COLONIAL REFORMER.
— NEVERMORE. 3 vols. Cr. 8vo. 31s. 6d.

BURNETT (Frances Hodgson).-HAWORTH'S. Globe 8vo. 2s.
— LOUISIANA, and THAT LASS O' LOWRIE'S. Illustrated. Cr. 8vo. 3s. 6d.

CARMARTHEN (Marchioness of). — A LOVER OF THE BEAUTIFUL. Cr. 8vo. 6s.

CONWAY (Hugh). — A FAMILY AFFAIR. Cr. 8vo. 3s. 6d.
— LIVING OR DEAD. Cr. 8vo. 3s. 6d.

CORBETT (Julian).—THE FALL OF ASGARD: A Tale of St. Olaf's Day. 2 vols. Gl. 8vo. 12s.
— FOR GOD AND GOLD. Cr. 8vo. 6s.
— KOPHETUA THE THIRTEENTH. 2 vols. Globe 8vo. 12s.

CRAIK (Mrs.).—*Uniform Edition.* Cr. 8vo. 3s. 6d. each.
OLIVE.
THE OGILVIES. Also Globe 8vo, 2s.
AGATHA'S HUSBAND. Also Globe 8vo, 2s.
THE HEAD OF THE FAMILY.
TWO MARRIAGES. Also Globe 8vo, 2s.
THE LAUREL BUSH.
MY MOTHER AND I.
MISS TOMMY: A Mediæval Romance.
KING ARTHUR: Not a Love Story.

CRAWFORD (F. Marion).—*Uniform Edition.* Cr. 8vo. 3s. 6d. each.
MR. ISAACS: A Tale of Modern India.
DR. CLAUDIUS.
A ROMAN SINGER.
ZOROASTER.

CRAWFORD (F. Marion)—*continued.*
A TALE OF A LONELY PARISH.
MARZIO'S CRUCIFIX.
PAUL PATOFF.
WITH THE IMMORTALS.
GREIFENSTEIN.
SANT' ILARIO.
A CIGARETTE MAKER'S ROMANCE.
— KHALED: A Tale of Arabia. 2 vols. 12s.
— THE WITCH OF PRAGUE. 3 vols. Cr. 8vo. 31s. 6d.

CUNNINGHAM (Sir H. S.).—THE CŒRULEANS: A Vacation Idyll. Cr. 8vo. 3s. 6d.
— THE HERIOTS. Cr. 8vo. 3s. 6d.
— WHEAT AND TARES. Cr. 8vo. 3s. 6d.

DAGONET THE JESTER. Cr. 8vo. 4s. 6d.

DAHN (Felix).—FELICITAS. Translated by M. A. C. E. Cr. 8vo. 4s. 6d.

DAY (Rev. Lal Behari).—BENGAL PEASANT LIFE. Cr. 8vo. 6s.
— FOLK TALES OF BENGAL. Cr. 8vo. 4s. 6d.

DEFOE (D.). (*See* GLOBE LIBRARY, p. 20: GOLDEN TREASURY SERIES, p. 20.)

DEMOCRACY: AN AMERICAN NOVEL. Cr. 8vo. 4s. 6d.

DICKENS (Charles). — THE POSTHUMOUS PAPERS OF THE PICKWICK CLUB. With Notes and Illustrations. Edit. by CHARLES DICKENS the younger. 2 vols. Ext. cr. 8vo. 21s.

DILLWYN (E. A.).—JILL. Cr. 8vo. 6s.
— JILL AND JACK. 2 vols. Globe 8vo. 12s.

DUNSMUIR (Amy).—VIDA: Study of a Girl. 3rd Edit. Cr. 8vo. 6s.

EBERS (Dr. George).—THE BURGOMASTER'S WIFE. Transl. by C. BELL. Cr. 8vo. 4s. 6d.
— ONLY A WORD. Translated by CLARA BELL. Cr. 8vo. 4s. 6d.

"ESTELLE RUSSELL" (The Author of).—HARMONIA. 3 vols. Cr. 8vo. 31s. 6d.

FALCONER (Lanoe).—CECILIA DE NOEL. Cr. 8vo. 3s. 6d.

FLEMING (George).—A NILE NOVEL. Gl. 8vo. 2s.
— MIRAGE: A Novel. Globe 8vo. 2s.
— THE HEAD OF MEDUSA. Globe 8vo. 2s.
— VESTIGIA. Globe 8vo. 2s.

FRATERNITY: A Romance. 2 vols. Cr. 8vo. 21s.

"FRIENDS IN COUNCIL" (The Author of).—REALMAH. Cr. 8vo. 6s.

GRAHAM (John W.).—NEÆRA: A Tale of Ancient Rome. Cr. 8vo. 6s.

HARBOUR BAR, THE. Cr. 8vo. 6s.

HARDY (Arthur Sherburne).—BUT YET A WOMAN: A Novel. Cr. 8vo. 4s. 6d.
— THE WIND OF DESTINY. 2 vols. Gl. 8vo. 12s.

HARDY (Thomas). — THE WOODLANDERS. Cr. 8vo. 3s. 6d.
— WESSEX TALES: STRANGE, LIVELY, AND COMMONPLACE. Cr. 8vo. 3s. 6d.

HARTE (Bret).—CRESSY. Cr. 8vo. 3s. 6d.
— THE HERITAGE OF DEDLOW MARSH: and other Tales. Cr. 8vo. 3s. 6d.

LITERATURE.

Prose Fiction—*continued.*

"HOGAN, M.P." (The Author of).—HOGAN, M.P. Globe 8vo. 2s.
— THE HONOURABLE MISS FERRARD. Gl. 8vo. 2s.
— FLITTERS, TATTERS, AND THE COUNSELLOR, ETC. Globe 8vo. 2s.
— CHRISTY CAREW. Globe 8vo. 2s.
— ISMAY'S CHILDREN. Globe 8vo. 2s.

HOPPUS (Mary).—A GREAT TREASON: A Story of the War of Independence. 2 vols. Cr. 8vo. 9s.

HUGHES (Thomas).—TOM BROWN'S SCHOOL DAYS. By AN OLD BOY.—Golden Treasury Edition. 4s. 6d.—Uniform Edition. 3s. 6d. —People's Edition. 2s.—People's Sixpenny Edition. Illustr. Med. 4to. 6d.—Uniform with Sixpenny Kingsley. Med. 8vo. 6d.
— TOM BROWN AT OXFORD. Cr. 8vo. 3s.6d.
— THE SCOURING OF THE WHITE HORSE, and THE ASHEN FAGGOT. Cr. 8vo. 3s. 6d.

IRVING (Washington). (*See* ILLUSTRATED BOOKS, p. 12.)

JACKSON (Helen).—RAMONA. Gl. 8vo. 2s.

JAMES (Henry).—THE EUROPEANS: A Novel. Cr. 8vo. 6s.; 18mo, 2s.
— DAISY MILLER: and other Stories. Cr. 8vo. 6s.; Globe 8vo, 2s.
— THE AMERICAN. Cr. 8vo. 6s.—18mo. 2 vols. 4s.
— RODERICK HUDSON. Cr. 8vo. 6s.; Gl. 8vo, 2s.; 18mo, 2 vols. 4s.
— THE MADONNA OF THE FUTURE: and other Tales. Cr. 8vo. 6s.; Globe 8vo, 2s.
— WASHINGTON SQUARE, THE PENSION BEAUREPAS. Cr. 8vo. 6s., Globe 8vo, 2s.
— THE PORTRAIT OF A LADY. Cr. 8vo. 6s.; 18mo, 3 vols. 6s.
— STORIES REVIVED. In Two Series. Cr. 8vo. 6s. each.
— THE BOSTONIANS. Cr. 8vo. 6s.
— NOVELS AND TALES. Pocket Edition. 18mo. 2s. each volume.
CONFIDENCE. 1 vol.
THE SIEGE OF LONDON; MADAME DE MAUVES. 1 vol.
AN INTERNATIONAL EPISODE; THE PENSION BEAUREPAS; THE POINT OF VIEW. 1 vol.
DAISY MILLER, a Study; FOUR MEETINGS; LONGSTAFF'S MARRIAGE; BENVOLIO. 1 vol.
THE MADONNA OF THE FUTURE; A BUNDLE OF LETTERS; THE DIARY OF A MAN OF FIFTY; EUGENE PICKERING. 1 vol.
— TALES OF THREE CITIES. Cr. 8vo. 4s. 6d.
— THE PRINCESS CASAMASSIMA. Cr. 8vo. 6s.; Globe 8vo, 2s.
— PARTIAL PORTRAITS. Cr. 8vo. 6s.
— THE REVERBERATOR. Cr. 8vo. 6s.
— THE ASPERN PAPERS; LOUISA PALLANT; THE MODERN WARNING. Cr. 8vo. 3s. 6d.
— A LONDON LIFE. Cr. 8vo. 3s. 6d.
— THE TRAGIC MUSE. Cr. 8vo. 3s. 6d.

KEARY (Annie).—JANET'S HOME. Cr. 8vo. 3s. 6d.
— CLEMENCY FRANKLYN. Globe 8vo. 2s.
— — OLDBURY. Cr. 8vo. 3s. 6d.

KEARY (Annie).—A YORK AND A LANCASTER ROSE. Cr. 8vo. 3s. 6d.
— CASTLE DALY. Cr. 8vo. 3s. 6d.
— A DOUBTING HEART. Cr. 8vo. 3s. 6d.

KINGSLEY (Charles).—*Eversley Edition.* 13 vols. Globe 8vo. 5s. each.—WESTWARD HO! 2 vols.—TWO YEARS AGO. 2 vols.—HYPATIA. 2 vols.—YEAST. 1 vol.—ALTON LOCKE. 2 vols.—HEREWARD THE WAKE. 2 vols.
— *Complete Edition.* Cr. 8vo. 3s. 6d. each. —WESTWARD HO! With a Portrait.—HYPATIA.—YEAST.—ALTON LOCKE.—TWO YEARS AGO.—HEREWARD THE WAKE.
— *Sixpenny Edition.* Med. 8vo. 6d. each. — WESTWARD HO! — HYPATIA. — YEAST.—ALTON LOCKE.—TWO YEARS AGO. — HEREWARD THE WAKE.

KIPLING (Rudyard).—PLAIN TALES FROM THE HILLS. Cr. 8vo. 6s.
— THE LIGHT THAT FAILED. Cr. 8vo. 6s.
— LIFE'S HANDICAP: Being Stories of mine own People. Cr. 8vo. 6s.

LAFARGUE (Philip).—THE NEW JUDGMENT OF PARIS. 2 vols. Globe 8vo. 12s.

LEE (Margaret).—FAITHFUL AND UNFAITHFUL. Cr. 8vo. 3s. 6d.

LEVY (A.).—REUBEN SACHS. Cr. 8vo. 3s.6d.

LITTLE PILGRIM IN THE UNSEEN, A. 24th Thousand. Cr. 8vo. 2s. 6d.o

"LITTLE PILGRIM IN THE UNSEEN, A" (Author of).—THE LAND OF DARKNESS. Cr. 8vo. 5s.

LYTTON (Earl of).—THE RING OF AMASIS: A Romance. Cr. 8vo. 3s. 6d.

McLENNAN (Malcolm).—MUCKLE JOCK; and other Tales of Peasant Life in the North. Cr. 8vo. 3s. 6d.

MACQUOID (K. S.).—PATTY. Gl. 8vo. 2s.

MADOC (Fayr).—THE STORY OF MELICENT. Cr. 8vo. 4s. 6d.

MALET (Lucas).—MRS. LORIMER: A Sketch in Black and White. Cr. 8vo. 3s. 6d.

MALORY (Sir Thos.). (*See* GLOBE LIBRARY, p. 20.)

MINTO (W.).—THE MEDIATION OF RALPH HARDELOT. 3 vols. Cr. 8vo. 31s. 6d.

MITFORD (A. B.).—TALES OF OLD JAPAN. With Illustrations. Cr. 8vo. 3s. 6d.

MIZ MAZE (THE); OR, THE WINKWORTH PUZZLE. A Story in Letters by Nine Authors. Cr. 8vo. 4s. 6d.

MURRAY (D. Christie). — AUNT RACHEL. Cr. 8vo. 3s. 6d.
— SCHWARTZ. Cr. 8vo. 3s. 6d.
— THE WEAKER VESSEL. Cr. 8vo. 3s. 6d.
— JOHN VALE'S GUARDIAN. Cr. 8vo. 3s. 6d.

MURRAY (D. Christie) and HERMAN (H.). —HE FELL AMONG THIEVES. Cr.8vo. 3s.6d.

NEW ANTIGONE, THE: A ROMANCE. Cr. 8vo. 6s.

NOEL (Lady Augusta).—HITHERSEA MERE. 3 vols. Cr. 8vo. 31s. 6d.

NORRIS (W. E.).—MY FRIEND JIM. Globe 8vo. 2s.
— CHRIS. Globe 8vo. 2s.

PROSE FICTION—COLLECTED WORKS.

NORTON (Hon. Mrs.).—OLD SIR DOUGLAS. Cr. 8vo. 6s.
OLIPHANT (Mrs. M. O. W.).—A SON OF THE SOIL. Globe 8vo. 2s.
—— THE CURATE IN CHARGE. Globe 8vo. 2s.
—— YOUNG MUSGRAVE. Globe 8vo. 2s.
—— HE THAT WILL NOT WHEN HE MAY. Globe 8vo. 2s.
—— SIR TOM. Globe 8vo. 2s.
—— HESTER. Cr. 8vo. 3s. 6d.
—— THE WIZARD'S SON. Globe 8vo. 2s.
—— THE COUNTRY GENTLEMAN AND HIS FAMILY. Globe 8vo. 2s.
—— THE SECOND SON. Globe 8vo. 2s.
—— NEIGHBOURS ON THE GREEN. Cr. 8vo. 3s. 6d.
—— JOYCE. Cr. 8vo. 3s. 6d.
—— A BELEAGUERED CITY. Cr. 8vo. 3s. 6d.
—— KIRSTEEN. Cr. 8vo. 3s. 6d.
—— THE RAILWAY MAN AND HIS CHILDREN. 3 vols. Cr. 8vo. 31s. 6d.
PALMER (Lady Sophia).—MRS. PENICOTT'S LODGER: and other Stories. Cr. 8vo. 2s. 6d.
PATER (Walter).—MARIUS THE EPICUREAN: HIS SENSATIONS AND IDEAS. 3rd Edit. 2 vols. 8vo. 12s.
ROSS (Percy).—A MISGUIDIT LASSIE. Cr. 8vo. 4s. 6d.
RUSSELL (W. Clark).—MAROONED. Cr. 8vo. 3s. 6d.
ST. JOHNSTON (A.).—A SOUTH SEA LOVER: A Romance. Cr. 8vo. 6s.
SHORTHOUSE (J. Henry).—Uniform Edition. Cr. 8vo. 3s. 6d. each.
JOHN INGLESANT: A Romance.
SIR PERCIVAL: A Story of the Past and of the Present.
THE LITTLE SCHOOLMASTER MARK: A Spiritual Romance.
A TEACHER OF THE VIOLIN: and other Tales.
THE COUNTESS EVE.
—— BLANCHE, LADY FALAISE. Cr. 8vo. 6s.
SLIP IN THE FENS, A. Globe 8vo. 2s.
TIM: A STORY OF SCHOOL LIFE. Cr. 8vo. 6s.
TOURGÉNIEF.—VIRGIN SOIL. Translated by ASHTON W. DILKE. Cr. 8vo. 6s.
VELEY (Margaret).—A GARDEN OF MEMORIES; MRS. AUSTIN; LIZZIE'S BARGAIN. Three Stories. 2 vols. Globe 8vo. 12s.
VOICES CRYING IN THE WILDERNESS: A Novel. Cr. 8vo. 7s. 6d.
WARD (Mrs. T. Humphry).—MISS BRETHERTON. Cr. 8vo. 3s. 6d.
WORTHEY (Mrs.).—THE NEW CONTINENT: A Novel. 2 vols. Globe 8vo. 12s.
YONGE (Charlotte M.).—Uniform Edition. Cr. 8vo. 3s. 6d. each.
THE HEIR OF REDCLYFFE.
HEARTSEASE.
HOPES AND FEARS.
DYNEVOR TERRACE.
THE DAISY CHAIN.
THE TRIAL: MORE LINKS OF THE DAISY CHAIN.
PILLARS OF THE HOUSE. Vol. I.
PILLARS OF THE HOUSE. Vol. II.
THE YOUNG STEPMOTHER.
CLEVER WOMAN OF THE FAMILY.
THE THREE BRIDES.
MY YOUNG ALCIDES.
THE CAGED LION.

YONGE (Charlotte M.).—Uniform Edition. Cr. 8vo. 3s. 6d. each.
THE DOVE IN THE EAGLE'S NEST.
THE CHAPLET OF PEARLS.
LADY HESTER, and THE DANVERS PAPERS.
MAGNUM BONUM.
LOVE AND LIFE.
UNKNOWN TO HISTORY.
STRAY PEARLS.
THE ARMOURER'S PRENTICES.
THE TWO SIDES OF THE SHIELD.
NUTTIE'S FATHER.
SCENES AND CHARACTERS.
CHANTRY HOUSE.
A MODERN TELEMACHUS.
BYE WORDS.
BEECHCROFT AT ROCKSTONE.
MORE BYWORDS.
A REPUTED CHANGELING; or, Three Seventh Years Two Centuries Ago.
THE LITTLE DUKE, RICHARD THE FEARLESS.
THE LANCES OF LYNWOOD.
THE PRINCE AND THE PAGE.
THE TWO PENNILESS PRINCESSES: A Story of the Time of James I. of Scotland.
P'S AND Q'S: LITTLE LUCY'S WONDERFUL GLOBE.
—— THAT STICK. 2 vols. Cr. 8vo. 12s.

Collected Works; Essays; Lectures; Letters; Miscellaneous Works.

AN AUTHOR'S LOVE. Being the Unpublished Letters of PROSPER MÉRIMÉE'S "Inconnue." 2 vols. Ext. cr. 8vo. 12s.
ARNOLD (Matthew).—ESSAYS IN CRITICISM. 6th Edit. Cr. 8vo. 9s.
—— ESSAYS IN CRITICISM. Second Series. Cr. 8vo. 7s. 6d.
—— DISCOURSES IN AMERICA. Cr. 8vo. 4s. 6d.
BACON. With Introduction and Notes. by F. G. SELBY, M.A. Gl. 8vo. 3s.; swd. 2s. 6d.
(See also GOLDEN TREASURY SERIES, p. 20.)
BLACKIE (John Stuart).—LAY SERMONS. Cr. 8vo. 6s.
BRIDGES (John A.).—IDYLLS OF A LOST VILLAGE. Cr. 8vo. 7s. 6d.
BRIMLEY (George).—ESSAYS. Globe 8vo. 5s.
BUNYAN (John).—THE PILGRIM'S PROGRESS FROM THIS WORLD TO THAT WHICH IS TO COME. 18mo. 2s. 6d. net.
BUTCHER (Prof. S. H.).—SOME ASPECTS OF THE GREEK GENIUS. Cr. 8vo.
CARLYLE (Thomas). (See BIOGRAPHY.)
CHURCH (Dean).—MISCELLANEOUS WRITINGS. Collected Edition. 5 vols. Globe 8vo. 5s. each.—Vol. I. MISCELLANEOUS ESSAYS.—II. DANTE: AND OTHER ESSAYS.—III. ST. ANSELM.—IV. SPENSER.—V. BACON.
CLIFFORD (Prof. W. K.). LECTURES AND ESSAYS. Edited by LESLIE STEPHEN and Sir F. POLLOCK. Cr. 8vo. 8s. 6d.
CLOUGH (A. H.).—PROSE REMAINS. With a Selection from his Letters, and a Memoir by HIS WIFE. Cr. 8vo. 7s. 6d.
COLLINS (J. Churton).—THE STUDY OF ENGLISH LITERATURE. Cr. 8vo.
CRAIK (Mrs.).—CONCERNING MEN: and other Papers. Cr. 8vo. 4s. 6d.
—— ABOUT MONEY: and other Things. Cr. 8vo. 6s.
—— SERMONS OUT OF CHURCH. Cr. 8vo. 6s.

LITERATURE.

Collected Works; Essays; Lectures; Letters; Miscellaneous Works—*contd.*

DE VERE (Aubrey).—ESSAYS CHIEFLY ON POETRY. 2 vols. Globe 8vo. 12s.
—— ESSAYS, CHIEFLY LITERARY AND ETHICAL. Globe 8vo. 6s.
DRYDEN, ESSAYS OF. Edited by Prof. C. D. YONGE. Fcp. 8vo. 2s. 6d. (*See also* GLOBE LIBRARY, p. 20.)
DUFF (Rt. Hon. Sir M. E. Grant).—MISCELLANIES, POLITICAL AND LITERARY. 8vo. 10s. 6d.
EMERSON (Ralph Waldo).—THE COLLECTED WORKS. 6 vols. Globe 8vo. 5s. each.—I. MISCELLANIES. With an Introductory Essay by JOHN MORLEY.—II. ESSAYS.—III. POEMS.—IV. ENGLISH TRAITS; REPRESENTATIVE MEN.—V. CONDUCT OF LIFE; SOCIETY AND SOLITUDE.—VI. LETTERS; SOCIAL AIMS, ETC.
FITZGERALD (Edward): LETTERS AND LITERARY REMAINS OF. Ed. by W. ALDIS WRIGHT, M.A. 3 vols. Cr. 8vo. 31s. 6d.
GLOBE LIBRARY. Gl. 8vo. 3s. 6d. each:
BURNS.—COMPLETE POETICAL WORKS AND LETTERS. Edited, with Life and Glossarial Index, by ALEXANDER SMITH.
COWPER.—POETICAL WORKS. Edited by the Rev. W. BENHAM, B.D.
DEFOE.—THE ADVENTURES OF ROBINSON CRUSOE. With Introduction by HENRY KINGSLEY.
DRYDEN.—POETICAL WORKS. A Revised Text and Notes. By W. D. CHRISTIE, M.A.
GOLDSMITH.—MISCELLANEOUS WORKS. Edited by Prof. MASSON.
HORACE.—WORKS. Rendered into English Prose by JAMES LONSDALE and S. LEE.
MALORY.—LE MORTE D'ARTHUR. Sir Thos. Malory's Book of King Arthur and of his Noble Knights of the Round Table. The Edition of Caxton, revised for modern use. By Sir E. STRACHEY, Bart.
MILTON.—POETICAL WORKS. Edited, with Introductions, by Prof. MASSON.
POPE.—POETICAL WORKS. Edited, with Memoir and Notes, by Prof. WARD.
SCOTT.—POETICAL WORKS. With Essay by Prof. PALGRAVE.
SHAKESPEARE.—COMPLETE WORKS. Edit. by W. G. CLARK and W. ALDIS WRIGHT. *India Paper Edition.* Cr. 8vo, cloth extra, gilt edges. 10s. 6d. net.
SPENSER.—COMPLETE WORKS Edited by R. MORRIS. Memoir by J. W. HALES, M.A.
VIRGIL.—WORKS. Rendered into English Prose by JAMES LONSDALE and S. LEE.
GOLDEN TREASURY SERIES.—Uniformly printed in 18mo, with Vignette Titles by Sir J. E. MILLAIS, Sir NOEL PATON, T. WOOLNER, W. HOLMAN HUNT, ARTHUR HUGHES, etc. 4s. 6d. each.—Also a re-issue in monthly vols. 2s. 6d. net, from June, 1891.
THE GOLDEN TREASURY OF THE BEST SONGS AND LYRICAL POEMS IN THE ENGLISH LANGUAGE. Selected and arranged, with Notes, by Prof. F. T. PALGRAVE.
THE CHILDREN'S GARLAND FROM THE BEST POETS. Selected by COVENTRY PATMORE.

GOLDEN TREASURY SERIES—*contd.*

BUNYAN.—THE PILGRIM'S PROGRESS FROM THIS WORLD TO THAT WHICH IS TO COME.
BACON.—ESSAYS, and COLOURS OF GOOD AND EVIL. With Notes and Glossarial Index by W. ALDIS WRIGHT, M.A.
THE BOOK OF PRAISE. From the Best English Hymn Writers. Selected by ROUNDELL, EARL OF SELBORNE.
THE FAIRY BOOK: THE BEST POPULAR FAIRY STORIES. Selected by Mrs. CRAIK, Author of "John Halifax, Gentleman."
THE JEST BOOK. The Choicest Anecdotes and Sayings. Arranged by MARK LEMON.
THE BALLAD BOOK. A Selection of the Choicest British Ballads. Edited by WILLIAM ALLINGHAM.
THE SUNDAY BOOK OF POETRY FOR THE YOUNG. Selected by C. F. ALEXANDER.
THE SONG BOOK. Words and Tunes selected and arranged by JOHN HULLAH.
SCOTTISH SONG. Compiled by MARY CARLYLE AITKEN.
LA LYRE FRANÇAISE. Selected and arranged, with Notes, by G. MASSON.
DEUTSCHE LYRIK. The Golden Treasury of the best German Lyrical Poems. Selected by Dr. BUCHHEIM.
BALLADEN UND ROMANZEN. Being a Selection of the best German Ballads and Romances. Edited, with Introduction and Notes, by Dr. BUCHHEIM.
A BOOK OF GOLDEN THOUGHTS. By HENRY ATTWELL.
ADDISON.—ESSAYS. Chosen and Edited by JOHN RICHARD GREEN.
MATTHEW ARNOLD.—SELECTED POEMS.
SIR THOMAS BROWNE.—RELIGIO MEDICI, LETTER TO A FRIEND, &C., AND CHRISTIAN MORALS. Edited by W. A. GREENHILL, M.D.
BYRON.—POETRY. Chosen and arranged by MATTHEW ARNOLD.—Large Paper Edition. 9s.
COWPER.—SELECTIONS FROM POEMS. With an Introduction by Mrs. OLIPHANT.
—— LETTERS. Edited, with Introduction, by Rev. W. BENHAM.
DEFOE.—THE ADVENTURES OF ROBINSON CRUSOE. Edited by J. W. CLARK, M.A.
HARE.—GUESSES AT TRUTH. By Two Brothers.
HERRICK.—CHRYSOMELA. Edited by Prof. F. T. PALGRAVE.
HUGHES.—TOM BROWN'S SCHOOL DAYS.
KEATS.—THE POETICAL WORKS. Edited by Prof. F. T. PALGRAVE.
LAMB.—TALES FROM SHAKSPEARE. Edited by Rev. ALFRED AINGER, M.A.
LANDOR.—SELECTIONS. Ed. by S. COLVIN.
LONGFELLOW.—POEMS OF PLACES: ENGLAND AND WALES. Edited by H. W. LONGFELLOW. 2 vols.
—— BALLADS, LYRICS, AND SONNETS.
MOHAMMAD.—SPEECHES AND TABLE-TALK. Translated by STANLEY LANE-POOLE.
NEWCASTLE.—THE CAVALIER AND HIS LADY. Selections from the Works of the First Duke and Duchess of Newcastle. With an Introductory Essay by E. JENKINS.
PLATO.—THE REPUBLIC. Translated by J. LL. DAVIES, M.A., and D. J. VAUGHAN.
—— THE TRIAL AND DEATH OF SOCRATES. Being the Euthyphron, Apology, Crito and Phaedo of Plato. Transl. by F. J. CHURCH.

COLLECTED WORKS.

GOLDEN TREASURY SERIES—*contd.*
PLATO.—THE PHAEDRUS, LYSIS, AND PROTAGORAS. Translated by J. WRIGHT.
SHAKESPEARE.—SONGS AND SONNETS. Ed. with Notes, by Prof. F. T. PALGRAVE.
SHELLEY.—POEMS. Edited by STOPFORD A. BROOKE.—Large Paper Edit. 12s. 6d.
TENNYSON.—LYRICAL POEMS. Selected and Annotated by Prof. F. T. PALGRAVE.—Large Paper Edition. 9s.
— IN MEMORIAM. Large Paper Edit. 9s.
THEOCRITUS.—BION, AND MOSCHUS. Rendered into English Prose by ANDREW LANG.—Large Paper Edition. 9s.
WORDSWORTH.—POEMS. Chosen and Edited by M. ARNOLD.—Large Paper Edition. 9s.
CHARLOTTE M. YONGE.—A BOOK OF WORTHIES, GATHERED FROM OLD HISTORIES AND WRITTEN ANEW.
— A BOOK OF GOLDEN DEEDS OF ALL TIMES AND ALL COUNTRIES.
— THE STORY OF THE CHRISTIANS AND MOORS IN SPAIN.

GOLDSMITH, ESSAYS OF. Edited by C. D. YONGE, M.A. Fcp. 8vo. 2s. 6d. (*See also* GLOBE LIBRARY, p. 20; ILLUSTRATED BOOKS, p. 12.)

GRAY (Thomas).—WORKS. Edited by EDMUND GOSSE. In 4 vols. Globe 8vo. 20s.—Vol. I. POEMS, JOURNALS, AND ESSAYS.—II. LETTERS.—III. LETTERS.—IV. NOTES ON ARISTOPHANES AND PLATO.

HAMERTON (P. G.).—THE INTELLECTUAL LIFE. Cr. 8vo. 10s. 6d.
— HUMAN INTERCOURSE. Cr. 8vo. 8s. 6d.
— FRENCH AND ENGLISH: A Comparison. Cr. 8vo. 10s. 6d.

HARRISON (Frederic).—THE CHOICE OF BOOKS. Gl. 8vo. 6s.—Large Paper Ed. 15s.

HARWOOD (George).—FROM WITHIN. Cr. 8vo. 6s.

HELPS (Sir Arthur).—ESSAYS WRITTEN IN THE INTERVALS OF BUSINESS. With Introduction and Notes, by F. J. ROWE, M.A., and W. T. WEBB, M.A. 1s. 9d.; swd. 1s. 6d.

HOBART (Lord).—ESSAYS AND MISCELLANEOUS WRITINGS. With Biographical Sketch. Edited by Lady HOBART. 2 vols. 8vo. 25s.

HUTTON (R. H.).—ESSAYS ON SOME OF THE MODERN GUIDES OF ENGLISH THOUGHT IN MATTERS OF FAITH. Globe 8vo. 6s.
— Essays. 2 vols. Gl. 8vo. 6s. each. Vol. I. Literary; II. Theological.

HUXLEY (Prof. T. H.).—LAY SERMONS, ADDRESSES, AND REVIEWS. 8vo. 7s. 6d.
— ESSAYS SELECTED FROM ABOVE. Cr. 8vo. 1s.
— CRITIQUES AND ADDRESSES. 8vo. 10s. 6d.
— AMERICAN ADDRESSES, WITH A LECTURE ON THE STUDY OF BIOLOGY. 8vo. 6s. 6d.
— SCIENCE AND CULTURE, AND OTHER ESSAYS. 8vo. 10s. 6d.
— INTRODUCTORY SCIENCE PRIMER. 18mo. 1s.
— ESSAYS ON SOME CONTROVERTED QUESTIONS. 8vo.

JAMES (Henry).—FRENCH POETS AND NOVELISTS. New Edition. Cr. 8vo. 4s. 6d.
— PORTRAITS OF PLACES. Cr. 8vo. 7s. 6d.

KEATS.—LETTERS. Edited by SIDNEY COLVIN. Globe 8vo. 6s.

KINGSLEY (Charles).—COMPLETE EDITION OF THE WORKS OF CHARLES KINGSLEY. Cr. 8vo. 3s. 6d. each.
WESTWARD HO! With a Portrait.
HYPATIA.
YEAST.
ALTON LOCKE.
TWO YEARS AGO.
HEREWARD THE WAKE.
POEMS.
THE HEROES; or, Greek Fairy Tales for my Children.
THE WATER BABIES: A Fairy Tale for a Land Baby.
MADAM HOW AND LADY WHY; or, First Lesson in Earth-Lore for Children.
AT LAST: A Christmas in the West Indies.
PROSE IDYLLS.
PLAYS AND PURITANS.
THE ROMAN AND THE TEUTON. With Preface by Professor MAX MÜLLER.
SANITARY AND SOCIAL LECTURES.
HISTORICAL LECTURES AND ESSAYS.
SCIENTIFIC LECTURES AND ESSAYS.
LITERARY AND GENERAL LECTURES.
THE HERMITS.
GLAUCUS; or, The Wonders of the Sea-Shore. With Coloured Illustrations.
VILLAGE AND TOWN AND COUNTRY SERMONS.
THE WATER OF LIFE, AND OTHER SERMONS.
SERMONS ON NATIONAL SUBJECTS: AND THE KING OF THE EARTH.
SERMONS FOR THE TIMES.
GOOD NEWS OF GOD.
THE GOSPEL OF THE PENTATEUCH; AND DAVID.
DISCIPLINE, AND OTHER SERMONS.
WESTMINSTER SERMONS.
ALL SAINTS' DAY, AND OTHER SERMONS.

LAMB (Charles).—COLLECTED WORKS. Ed., with Introduction and Notes, by the Rev. ALFRED AINGER, M.A. Globe 8vo. 5s. each volume.—I. ESSAYS OF ELIA.—II. PLAYS, POEMS, AND MISCELLANEOUS ESSAYS.—III. MRS. LEICESTER'S SCHOOL; THE ADVENTURES OF ULYSSES; AND OTHER ESSAYS.—IV. TALES FROM SHAKESPEARE.—V. and VI. LETTERS. Newly arranged, with additions.
— TALES FROM SHAKESPEARE. 18mo. 4s. 6d. Globe Readings Edition. Globe 8vo. 2s.

LANKESTER (Prof. E. Ray).—THE ADVANCEMENT OF SCIENCE. Occasional Essays and Addresses. 8vo. 10s. 6d.

LIGHTFOOT (Bishop).—ESSAYS. 2 vols. I. THEOLOGICAL. II. MISCELLANEOUS. 8vo.

LODGE (Prof. Oliver).—THE PIONEERS OF SCIENCE. Illustrated. Ext. cr. 8vo.

LOWELL (Jas. Russell).—COMPLETE WORKS. 10 vols. Cr. 8vo. 6s. each.—Vols. I.—IV. LITERARY ESSAYS.—V. POLITICAL ESSAYS. —VI. LITERARY AND POLITICAL ADDRESSES. VII.—X. POETICAL WORKS.
— POLITICAL ESSAYS. Ext. cr. 8vo. 7s. 6d.

LUBBOCK (Rt. Hon. Sir John, Bart.).—SCIENTIFIC LECTURES. Illustrated. 2nd Edit. revised. 8vo. 8s. 6d.
— POLITICAL AND EDUCATIONAL ADDRESSES. 8vo. 8s. 6d.
— FIFTY YEARS OF SCIENCE: Address to the British Association, 1881. 5th Edit. Cr. 8vo. 2s. 6d.

LITERATURE.

Collected Works; Essays; Lectures; Letters; Miscellaneous Works—*contd.*

LUBBOCK (Rt. Hon Sir John, Bart.).—THE PLEASURES OF LIFE. New Edition. 60th Thousand. Gl.8vo. Part I. 1s.6d.; swd. 1s.—*Library Edition.* 3s. 6d.—Part II. 1s. 6d.; sewed, 1s.—*Library Edition.* 3s. 6d.—Complete in 1 vol. 2s. 6d.

MACMILLAN (Rev. Hugh).—ROMAN MOSAICS, or, Studies in Rome and its Neighbourhood. Globe 8vo. 6s.

MAHAFFY (Prof. J. P.).—THE PRINCIPLES OF THE ART OF CONVERSATION. Cr.8vo.4s.6d.

MASSON (David).—WORDSWORTH, SHELLEY, KEATS: and other Essays. Cr. 8vo. 5s.

MAURICE (F. D.).—THE FRIENDSHIP OF BOOKS: and other Lectures. Cr. 8vo. 4s. 6d.

MORLEY (John).—WORKS. Collected Edit. In 11 vols. Globe 8vo. 5s. each.—VOLTAIRE, 1 vol.—ROUSSEAU. 2 vols.—DIDEROT AND THE ENCYCLOPÆDISTS. 2 vols.—ON COMPROMISE. 1 vol.—MISCELLANIES. 3 vols.—BURKE. 1 vol.—STUDIES IN LITERATURE. 1 vol.

MYERS (F. W. H.).—ESSAYS. 2 vols. Cr. 8vo. 4s. 6d. each.—I. CLASSICAL; II. MODERN.

NADAL (E. S.).—ESSAYS AT HOME AND ELSEWHERE. Cr. 8vo. 6s.

OLIPHANT(T.L. Kington).—THE DUKE AND THE SCHOLAR: and other Essays. 8vo. 7s.6d.

OWENS COLLEGE ESSAYS AND ADDRESSES. By Professors and Lecturers of the College. 8vo. 14s.

PATER (W.).—THE RENAISSANCE; Studies in Art and Poetry. 4th Ed. Cr. 8vo. 10s.6d.
— IMAGINARY PORTRAITS. Cr. 8vo. 6s.
— APPRECIATIONS. With an Essay on "Style." 2nd Edit. Cr. 8vo. 8s. 6d.
— MARIUS THE EPICUREAN. 2 vols. Cr. 8vo. 12s.

PICTON (J. A.).—THE MYSTERY OF MATTER: and other Essays. Cr. 8vo. 6s.

POLLOCK (Sir F., Bart.).—OXFORD LECTURES: and other Discourses. 8vo. 9s.

POOLE (M. E.).—PICTURES OF COTTAGE LIFE IN THE WEST OF ENGLAND. 2nd Ed. Cr. 8vo. 3s. 6d.

POTTER (Louisa).—LANCASHIRE MEMORIES. Cr. 8vo. 6s.

PRICKARD (A. O.).—ARISTOTLE ON THE ART OF POETRY. Cr. 8vo. 3s. 6d.

RUMFORD.—COMPLETE WORKS OF COUNT RUMFORD. Memoir by G. ELLIS. Portrait. 5 vols. 8vo. 4l. 14s. 6d.

SCIENCE LECTURES AT SOUTH KENSINGTON. Illustr. 2 vols. Cr. 8vo. 6s. each.

SMALLEY (George W.).—LONDON LETTERS AND SOME OTHERS. 2 vols. 8vo. 32s.

STEPHEN (Sir James Fitzjames, Bart.).—HORAE SABBATICAE. Globe 8vo.

THRING (Edward).—THOUGHTS ON LIFE SCIENCE. 2nd Edit. Cr. 8vo. 7s. 6d.

WESTCOTT (Bishop). (See THEOLOGY, p. 36.)

WILSON (Dr. George).—RELIGIO CHEMICI. Cr. 8vo. 8s. 6d.
— THE FIVE GATEWAYS OF KNOWLEDGE 9th Edit. Ext. fcp. 8vo. 2s. 6d.

WHITTIER (John Greenleaf). THE COMPLETE WORKS. 7 vols. Cr. 8vo. 6s. each.—Vol. I. NARRATIVE AND LEGENDARY POEMS. —II. POEMS OF NATURE; POEMS SUBJECTIVE AND REMINISCENT; RELIGIOUS POEMS. —III. ANTI-SLAVERY POEMS; SONGS OF LABOUR AND REFORM.—IV. PERSONAL POEMS; OCCASIONAL POEMS; THE TENT ON THE BEACH; with the Poems of ELIZABETH H. WHITTIER, and an Appendix containing Early and Uncollected Verses.—V. MARGARET SMITH'S JOURNAL; TALES AND SKETCHES.—VI. OLD PORTRAITS AND MODERN SKETCHES; PERSONAL SKETCHES AND TRIBUTES; HISTORICAL PAPERS.—VII. THE CONFLICT WITH SLAVERY, POLITICS, AND REFORM; THE INNER LIFE, CRITICISM.

LOGIC. (*See under* PHILOSOPHY, p. 26.)

MAGAZINES. (*See* PERIODICALS).

MAGNETISM. (*See under* PHYSICS, p. 26.)

MATHEMATICS, History of.

BALL (W. W. R.).—A SHORT ACCOUNT OF THE HISTORY OF MATHEMATICS. Cr. 8vo. 10s. 6d.

MEDICINE.

(*See also* DOMESTIC ECONOMY; NURSING; HYGIENE; PHYSIOLOGY.)

ACLAND (Sir H. W.).—THE ARMY MEDICAL SCHOOL: Address at Netley Hospital. 1s.

ALLBUTT (Dr. T. Clifford).—ON THE USE OF THE OPHTHALMOSCOPE. 8vo. 15s.

ANDERSON (Dr. McCall).—LECTURES ON CLINICAL MEDICINE. Illustr. 8vo. 10s.6d.

BALLANCE(C. A.) and EDMUNDS(Dr. W.). LIGATION IN CONTINUITY. Illustr. Roy.8vo.

BARWELL (Richard, F.R.C.S.).—THE CAUSES AND TREATMENT OF LATERAL CURVATURE OF THE SPINE. Cr. 8vo. 5s.
— ON ANEURISM, ESPECIALLY OF THE THORAX AND ROOT OF THE NECK. 3s. 6d.

BASTIAN (H. Charlton).—ON PARALYSIS FROM BRAIN DISEASE IN ITS COMMON FORMS. Cr. 8vo. 10s. 6d.

BICKERTON (T. H.).—ON COLOUR BLINDNESS. Cr. 8vo.

BRAIN: A JOURNAL OF NEUROLOGY. Edited for the Neurological Society of London, by A. DE WATTEVILLE, Quarterly. 8vo. 3s.6d. (Part I. in Jan. 1878.) Vols. I. to XII. 8vo. 15s. each. [Cloth covers for binding, 1s. each.]

BRUNTON (Dr. T. Lauder).—A TEXT-BOOK OF PHARMACOLOGY, THERAPEUTICS, AND MATERIA MEDICA. 3rd Edit. Med. 8vo. 21s.—Or in 2 vols. 22s. 6d.
— DISORDERS OF DIGESTION: THEIR CONSEQUENCES AND TREATMENT. 8vo. 10s. 6d.
— PHARMACOLOGY AND THERAPEUTICS; or, Medicine Past and Present. Cr. 8vo. 6s.
— TABLES OF MATERIA MEDICA: A Companion to the Materia Medica Museum. 8vo. 5s.
— CROONIAN LECTURES ON THE CONNECTION BETWEEN CHEMICAL CONSTITUTION AND PHYSIOLOGICAL ACTION. Being an Introduction to Modern Therapeutics. 8vo.

BUCKNILL (Dr.).—THE CARE OF THE INSANE. Cr. 8vo. 3s. 6d.

CARTER (R. Brudenell, F.C.S.).—A PRACTICAL TREATISE ON DISEASES OF THE EYE. 8vo. 16s.

CARTER (R. Brudenell).—EYESIGHT, GOOD AND BAD. Cr. 8vo. 6s.
— MODERN OPERATIONS FOR CATARACT. 8vo. 6s.

CHRISTIE (J.).—CHOLERA EPIDEMICS IN EAST AFRICA. 8vo. 15s.

COWELL (George).—LECTURES ON CATARACT: ITS CAUSES, VARIETIES, AND TREATMENT. Cr. 8vo. 4s. 6d.

FLÜCKIGER (F. A.) and HANBURY (D.).—PHARMACOGRAPHIA. A History of the Principal Drugs of Vegetable Origin met with in Great Britain and India. 8vo. 21s.

FOTHERGILL (Dr. J. Milner).—THE PRACTITIONER'S HANDBOOK OF TREATMENT; or, The Principles of Therapeutics. 8vo. 16s.
— THE ANTAGONISM OF THERAPEUTIC AGENTS, AND WHAT IT TEACHES. Cr. 8vo. 6s.
— FOOD FOR THE INVALID, THE CONVALESCENT, THE DYSPEPTIC, AND THE GOUTY. 2nd Edit. Cr. 8vo. 3s. 6d.

FOX (Dr. Wilson). — ON THE ARTIFICIAL PRODUCTION OF TUBERCLE IN THE LOWER ANIMALS. With Plates. 4to. 5s. 6d.
— ON THE TREATMENT OF HYPERPYREXIA, AS ILLUSTRATED IN ACUTE ARTICULAR RHEUMATISM BY MEANS OF THE EXTERNAL APPLICATION OF COLD. 8vo. 2s. 6d.

GRIFFITHS (W. H.).—LESSONS ON PRESCRIPTIONS AND THE ART OF PRESCRIBING. New Edition. 18mo. 3s. 6d.

HAMILTON (Prof. D. J.).—ON THE PATHOLOGY OF BRONCHITIS, CATARRHAL PNEUMONIA, TUBERCLE, AND ALLIED LESIONS OF THE HUMAN LUNG. 8vo. 8s. 6d.
— A TEXT-BOOK OF PATHOLOGY, SYSTEMATIC AND PRACTICAL. Illustrated. Vol. I. 8vo. 25s.

HANBURY (Daniel). — SCIENCE PAPERS, CHIEFLY PHARMACOLOGICAL AND BOTANICAL. Med. 8vo. 14s.

KLEIN (Dr. E.).—MICRO-ORGANISMS AND DISEASE. An Introduction into the Study of Specific Micro-Organisms. Cr. 8vo. 6s.
— THE BACTERIA IN ASIATIC CHOLERA. Cr. 8vo. 5s.

LEPROSY INVESTIGATION COMMITTEE, JOURNAL OF THE. Edited by P. S. ABRAHAM, M.A. Nos. 2 and 3. 2s. 6d. each net.

LINDSAY (Dr. J. A.). — THE CLIMATIC TREATMENT OF CONSUMPTION. Cr. 8vo. 5s.

MACKENZIE (Sir Morell).—THE HYGIENE OF THE VOCAL ORGANS. Cr. 8vo. 6s.

MACLAGAN (Dr. T.).—THE GERM THEORY. 8vo. 10s. 6d.

MACLEAN (Surgeon-General W. C.).—DISEASES OF TROPICAL CLIMATES. Cr. 8vo. 10s. 6d.

MACNAMARA (C.).—A HISTORY OF ASIATIC CHOLERA. Cr. 8vo. 10s. 6d.

MERCIER (Dr. C.).—THE NERVOUS SYSTEM AND THE MIND. 8vo. 12s. 6d.

PIFFARD (H. G.).—AN ELEMENTARY TREATISE ON DISEASES OF THE SKIN. 8vo. 16s.

PRACTITIONER, THE: A MONTHLY JOURNAL OF THERAPEUTICS AND PUBLIC HEALTH. Edited by T. LAUDER BRUNTON, F.R.S., etc.; DONALD MACALISTER, M.A., M.D., and J. MITCHELL BRUCE, M.D. 1s. 6d. monthly. Vols. I.—XLVI. Half-yearly vols. 10s. 6d. each. [Cloth covers for binding, 1s. each.]

REYNOLDS (J. R.).—A SYSTEM OF MEDICINE. Edited by J. RUSSELL REYNOLDS, M.D., In 5 vols. Vols. I.—III. and V. 8vo. 25s. each.—Vol. IV. 21s.

RICHARDSON (Dr. B. W.).—DISEASES OF MODERN LIFE. Cr. 8vo.
— THE FIELD OF DISEASE. A Book of Preventive Medicine. 8vo. 25s.

SEATON (Dr Edward C.).—A HANDBOOK OF VACCINATION. Ext. fcp. 8vo. 8s. 6d.

SEILER (Dr. Carl). — MICRO-PHOTOGRAPHS IN HISTOLOGY, NORMAL AND PATHOLOGICAL. 4to. 31s. 6d.

SIBSON (Dr. Francis).—COLLECTED WORKS. Edited by W. M. ORD, M.D. Illustrated. 4 vols. 8vo. 3l. 3s.

SPENDER (J. Kent).—THERAPEUTIC MEANS FOR THE RELIEF OF PAIN. 8vo. 8s. 6d.

SURGERY (THE INTERNATIONAL ENCYCLOPAEDIA OF). A Systematic Treatise on the Theory and Practice of Surgery by Authors of various Nations. Edited by JOHN ASHHURST, jun., M.D. 6 vols. Roy. 8vo. 31s. 6d. each.

THORNE (Dr. Thorne).—DIPHTHERIA. Cr. 8vo. 8s. 6d.

WHITE (Dr. W. Hale).—A TEXT-BOOK OF GENERAL THERAPEUTICS. Cr. 8vo. 8s. 6d.

ZIEGLER (Ernst).—A TEXT-BOOK OF PATHOLOGICAL ANATOMY AND PATHOGENESIS. Translated and Edited by DONALD MACALISTER, M.A., M.D. Illustrated. 8vo.—Part I. GENERAL PATHOLOGICAL ANATOMY. 12s. 6d.—Part II. SPECIAL PATHOLOGICAL ANATOMY. Sections I.—VIII. and IX.—XII. 8vo. 12s. 6d. each.

METALLURGY.

(See also CHEMISTRY.)

HIORNS (Arthur H.).—A TEXT-BOOK OF ELEMENTARY METALLURGY. Gl. 8vo. 4s.
— PRACTICAL METALLURGY AND ASSAYING. Illustrated. Globe 8vo. 6s.
— IRON AND STEEL MANUFACTURE. Illustrated. Globe 8vo. 3s. 6d.
— MIXED METALS OR METALLIC ALLOYS. Globe 8vo. 6s.

PHILLIPS (J. A.).—A TREATISE ON ORE DEPOSITS. Illustrated. Med. 8vo. 25s.

METAPHYSICS.

(See under PHILOSOPHY, p. 25.)

MILITARY ART AND HISTORY.

ACLAND (Sir H. W.). (See MEDICINE.)

AITKEN (Sir W.).—THE GROWTH OF THE RECRUIT AND YOUNG SOLDIER. Cr. 8vo. 8s. 6d.

CUNYNGHAME (Gen. Sir A. T.).—MY COMMAND IN SOUTH AFRICA, 1874—78. 8vo. 12s. 6d.

MUSIC—PERIODICALS.

MILITARY HISTORY—continued.

"DAILY NEWS."—Correspondence of the War between Russia and Turkey, 1877, to the Fall of Kars. Cr. 8vo. 6s.
—— Correspondence of the Russo-Turkish War, from the Fall of Kars to the Conclusion of Peace. Cr. 8vo. 6s.

HOZIER (Lieut.-Col. H. M.).—The Seven Weeks' War. 3rd Edit. Cr. 8vo. 6s.
—— The Invasions of England. 2 vols. 8vo. 28s.

MARTEL (Chas.).—Military Italy. With Map. 8vo. 12s. 6d.

MAURICE (Lt.-Col.).—War. 8vo. 5s. net.
—— The National Defences. Cr. 8vo.

MERCUR (Prof. J.).—Elements of the Art of War. 8vo. 17s.

SCRATCHLEY — KINLOCH COOKE.— Australian Defences and New Guinea. Compiled from the Papers of the late Major-General Sir Peter Scratchley, R.E., by C. Kinloch Cooke. 8vo. 14s.

THROUGH THE RANKS TO A COMMISSION. New Edition. Cr. 8vo. 2s. 6d.

WILKINSON (S.). — The Brain of an Army. A Popular Account of the German General Staff. Cr. 8vo. 2s. 6d.

WINGATE (Major F. R.).—Mahdiism and the Egyptian Sudan. An Account of the Rise and Progress of Mahdiism, and of Subsequent Events in the Sudan to the Present Time. With 10 Maps. 8vo. 30s. net.

WOLSELEY (General Viscount).—The Soldier's Pocket-Book for Field Service. 5th Edit. 16mo, roan. 5s.
—— Field Pocket-Book for the Auxiliary Forces. 16mo. 1s. 6d.

MINERALOGY. (See Geology.)

MISCELLANEOUS WORKS.
(See under Literature, p. 19.)

MUSIC.

FAY (Amy).—Music-Study in Germany. Preface by Sir Geo. Grove.. Cr. 8vo. 4s. 6d.

GROVE (Sir George).—A Dictionary of Music and Musicians, A.D. 1450—1889. Edited by Sir George Grove, D.C.L. In 4 vols. 8vo. 21s. each. With Illustrations in Music Type and Woodcut.—Also published in Parts. Parts I.—XIV., XIX.—XXII. 3s. 6d. each; XV. XVI. 7s.; XVII. XVIII. 7s.; XXIII.—XXV., Appendix. Edited by J. A. Fuller Maitland, M.A. 9s. [Cloth cases for binding the volumes, 1s. each.]
—— A Complete Index to the Above. By Mrs. E. Wodehouse. 8vo. 7s. 6d.

HULLAH (John).—Music in the House. 4th Edit. Cr. 8vo. 2s. 6d.

TAYLOR (Franklin).—A Primer of Pianoforte Playing. 18mo. 1s.

TAYLOR (Sedley).—Sound and Music. 2nd Edit. Ext. cr. 8vo. 8s. 6d.
—— A System of Sight-Singing from the Established Musical Notation. 8vo. 5s. net.

NATURAL HISTORY.

ATKINSON (J. C.). (See Antiquities.)

BAKER (Sir Samuel W.). (See Sport.)

BLANFORD (W. T.).—Geology and Zoology of Abyssinia. 8vo. 21s.

FOWLER (W. W.).—Tales of the Birds. Illustrated. Cr. 8vo. 3s. 6d.
—— A Year with the Birds. Illustrated. Cr. 8vo. 3s. 6d.

KINGSLEY (Charles).—Madam How and Lady Why; or, First Lessons in Earth-Lore for Children. Cr. 8vo. 3s. 6d.
—— Glaucus; or, The Wonders of the Sea-Shore. With Coloured Illustrations. Cr. 8vo. 3s. 6d.—Presentation Edition. Cr. 8vo, extra cloth. 7s. 6d.

WALLACE (Alfred Russel).—The Malay Archipelago: The Land of the Orang Utang and the Bird of Paradise. Maps and Illustrations. Ext. cr. 8vo. 6s. (See also Biology.)

WATERTON (Charles).—Wanderings in South America, the North-West of the United States, and the Antilles. Edited by Rev. J. G. Wood. Illustrated. Cr. 8vo. 6s.—People's Edition. 4to. 6d.

WHITE (Gilbert).—Natural History and Antiquities of Selborne. Ed. by Frank Buckland. With a Chapter on Antiquities by the Earl of Selborne. Cr. 8vo. 6s.

NATURAL PHILOSOPHY. (See Physics.)

NAVAL SCIENCE.

ROBINSON (Rev. J. L.).—Marine Surveying, An Elementary Treatise on. For Younger Naval Officers. Illust. Cr.8vo. 7s.6d.

SHORTLAND (Admiral).—Nautical Surveying. 8vo. 21s.

THOMSON (Sir Wm.). — Popular Lectures and Addresses.—Vol. III. Navigation. Cr. 8vo. 7s. 6d.

NOVELS. (See Prose Fiction, p. 17.)

NURSING.
(See under Domestic Economy, p. 8.)

OPTICS (or LIGHT). (See Physics, p. 27.)

PAINTING. (See Art.)

PERIODICALS.

AMERICAN JOURNAL OF PHILOLOGY, THE. (See Philology.)

BRAIN. (See Medicine.)

ECONOMIC JOURNAL, THE. (See Political Economy.)

ECONOMICS, THE QUARTERLY JOURNAL OF. (See Political Economy.)

ENGLISH ILLUSTRATED MAGAZINE, THE. — Profusely Illustrated. Published Monthly. No. I. October, 1883. 6d. net.—Vol. I. 1884. 7s. 6d.—Vols. II.-VIII. Super royal 8vo, extra cloth, coloured edges. 8s. each. [Cloth Covers for binding Volumes, 1s. each.]

PHILOLOGY—PHILOSOPHY.

NATURE: A WEEKLY ILLUSTRATED JOURNAL OF SCIENCE. Published every Thursday. Price 6*d*. Monthly Parts, 2*s*. and 2*s*. 6*d*.; Current Half-yearly vols., 15*s*. each. Vols. I.—XLIII. [Cases for binding vols. 1*s*. 6*d*. each.]

HELLENIC STUDIES, THE JOURNAL OF. Pub. Half-Yearly from 1880. 8vo. 30*s*.; or each Part, 15*s*. Vol. XII. Part I. 15*s*. net. The Journal will be sold at a reduced price to Libraries wishing to subscribe, but official application must in each case be made to the Council. Information on this point, and upon the conditions of Membership, may be obtained on application to the Hon. Sec., Mr. George Macmillan, 29, Bedford Street, Covent Garden.

MACMILLAN'S MAGAZINE. Published Monthly. 1*s*.—Vols. I.-LXIII. 7*s*. 6*d*. each. [Cloth covers for binding, 1*s*. each.]

PHILOLOGY, THE JOURNAL OF. (*See* PHILOLOGY.)

PRACTITIONER, THE. (*See* MEDICINE.)

PHILOLOGY.

AMERICAN JOURNAL OF PHILOLOGY, THE. Edited by Prof. BASIL L. GILDERSLEEVE. 4*s*. 6*d*. each No. (quarterly).

AMERICAN PHILOLOGICAL ASSOCIATION, TRANSACTIONS OF. Vols. I.—XX. 8*s*. 6*d*. per vol. net, except Vols. XV. and XX., which are 10*s*. 6*d*. net.

CORNELL UNIVERSITY STUDIES IN CLASSICAL PHILOLOGY. Edited by I. FLAGG, W. G. HALE, and B. I. WHEELER. I. THE *CUM*-CONSTRUCTIONS: their History and Functions. Part I. Critical. 1*s*. 8*d*. net. Part II. Constructive. By W. G. HALE. 3*s*. 4*d*. net.—II. ANALOGY AND THE SCOPE OF ITS APPLICATION IN LANGUAGE. By B. I. WHEELER. 1*s*. 3*d*. net.

GILES (P.).—A SHORT MANUAL OF PHILOLOGY FOR CLASSICAL STUDENTS. Cr. 8vo.

JOURNAL OF SACRED AND CLASSICAL PHILOLOGY. 4 vols. 8vo. 12*s*. 6*d*. each.

JOURNAL OF PHILOLOGY. New Series. Edited by W. A. WRIGHT, M.A., I. BYWATER, M.A., and H. JACKSON, M.A. 4*s*. 6*d*. each No. (half-yearly).

KELLNER (Dr. L.).— HISTORICAL OUTLINES OF ENGLISH SYNTAX.

MORRIS (Rev. Richard, LL.D.).—PRIMER OF ENGLISH GRAMMAR. 18mo. 1*s*.

—— ELEMENTARY LESSONS IN HISTORICAL ENGLISH GRAMMAR. 18mo. 2*s*. 6*d*.

—— HISTORICAL OUTLINES OF ENGLISH ACCIDENCE. Fcp. 8vo. 6*s*.

MORRIS (R.) and BOWEN (H. C.).—ENGLISH GRAMMAR EXERCISES. 18mo. 1*s*.

OLIPHANT (T. L. Kington).— THE OLD AND MIDDLE ENGLISH. Globe 8vo. 9*s*.

—— THE NEW ENGLISH. 2 vols. Cr. 8vo. 21*s*.

PEILE (John).— A PRIMER OF PHILOLOGY. 18mo. 1*s*.

PELLISSIER (E.).—FRENCH ROOTS AND THEIR FAMILIES. Globe 8vo. 6*s*.

TAYLOR (Isaac).—WORDS AND PLACES. 9th Edit. Maps. Globe 8vo. 6*s*.

—— ETRUSCAN RESEARCHES. 8vo. 14*s*.

—— GREEKS AND GOTHS: A Study of the Runes. 8vo. 9*s*.

WETHERELL (J.).—EXERCISES ON MORRIS'S PRIMER OF ENGLISH GRAMMAR. 18mo. 1*s*.

YONGE (C. M.).—HISTORY OF CHRISTIAN NAMES. New Edit., revised. Cr. 8vo. 7*s*. 6*d*.

PHILOSOPHY.

Ethics and Metaphysics—Logic—Psychology.

Ethics and Metaphysics.

BALFOUR (Right Hon. A. J.).—A DEFENCE OF PHILOSOPHIC DOUBT. 8vo. 12*s*.

BIRKS (Thomas Rawson).—FIRST PRINCIPLES OF MORAL SCIENCE. Cr. 8vo. 8*s*. 6*d*.

—— MODERN UTILITARIANISM; or, The Systems of Paley, Bentham, and Mill Examined and Compared. Cr. 8vo. 6*s*. 6*d*.

—— MODERN PHYSICAL FATALISM, AND THE DOCTRINE OF EVOLUTION. Including an Examination of Mr. Herbert Spencer's "First Principles." Cr. 8vo. 6*s*.

CALDERWOOD (Prof. H.).—A HANDBOOK OF MORAL PHILOSOPHY. Cr. 8vo. 6*s*.

FISKE (John).—OUTLINES OF COSMIC PHILOSOPHY, BASED ON THE DOCTRINE OF EVOLUTION. 2 vols. 8vo. 25*s*.

FOWLER (Rev. Thomas). — PROGRESSIVE MORALITY: An Essay in Ethics. Cr. 8vo. 5*s*.

HARPER (Father Thomas).—THE METAPHYSICS OF THE SCHOOL. In 5 vols.—Vols. I. and II. 8vo. 18*s*. each.—Vol. III. Part I. 12*s*.

KANT.—KANT'S CRITICAL PHILOSOPHY FOR ENGLISH READERS. By J. P. MAHAFFY, D.D., and J. H. BERNARD, B.D. 2 vols. Cr. 8vo.—Vol. I. THE KRITIK OF PURE REASON EXPLAINED AND DEFENDED. 7*s*. 6*d*. —Vol. II. THE PROLEGOMENA. Translated, with Notes and Appendices. 6*s*.

KANT—MAX MÜLLER. — CRITIQUE OF PURE REASON BY IMMANUEL KANT. Translated by F. MAX MÜLLER. With Introduction by LUDWIG NOIRÉ. 2 vols. 8vo. 16*s*. each (sold separately).—Vol. I. HISTORICAL INTRODUCTION, by LUDWIG NOIRÉ, etc.—Vol. II. CRITIQUE OF PURE REASON.

MAURICE (F. D.).—MORAL AND METAPHYSICAL PHILOSOPHY. 2 vols. 8vo. 16*s*.

McCOSH (Rev. Dr. James).—THE METHOD OF THE DIVINE GOVERNMENT, PHYSICAL AND MORAL. 8vo. 10*s*. 6*d*.

—— THE SUPERNATURAL IN RELATION TO THE NATURAL. Cr. 8vo. 7*s*. 6*d*.

—— THE INTUITIONS OF THE MIND. 8vo. 10*s*. 6*d*.

—— AN EXAMINATION OF MR. J. S. MILL'S PHILOSOPHY. 8vo. 10*s*. 6*d*.

—— CHRISTIANITY AND POSITIVISM. Lectures on Natural Theology and Apologetics. Cr. 8vo. 7*s*. 6*d*.

—— THE SCOTTISH PHILOSOPHY FROM HUTCHESON TO HAMILTON, BIOGRAPHICAL, EXPOSITORY, CRITICAL. Roy. 8vo. 16*s*.

—— REALISTIC PHILOSOPHY DEFENDED IN A PHILOSOPHIC SERIES. 2 vols.—Vol. I. EXPOSITORY. Vol. II. HISTORICAL AND CRITICAL. Cr. 8vo. 14*s*.

PHILOSOPHY.
Ethics and Metaphysics—*continued.*

McCOSH (Rev. Dr. J.).—First and Fundamental Truths. Being a Treatise on Metaphysics. 8vo. 9s.
— The Prevailing Types of Philosophy: Can they Logically reach Reality? 8vo. 3s. 6d.
MASSON (Prof. David).—Recent British Philosophy. 3rd Edit. Cr. 8vo. 6s.
SIDGWICK (Prof. Henry).—The Methods of Ethics. 4th Edit., revised. 8vo. 14s.
— A Supplement to the Second Edition. Containing all the important Additions and Alterations in the Fourth Edition. 8vo. 6s.
— Outlines of the History of Ethics for English Readers. Cr. 8vo. 3s. 6d.
THORNTON (W. T.).—Old-Fashioned Ethics and Common-Sense Metaphysics. 8vo. 10s. 6d.

Logic.

BOOLE (George). — The Mathematical Analysis of Logic. 8vo. sewed. 5s.
CARROLL (Lewis).—The Game of Logic. Cr. 8vo. 3s. net.
JEVONS (W. Stanley).—A Primer of Logic. 18mo. 1s.
— Elementary Lessons in Logic, Deductive and Inductive. 18mo. 3s. 6d.
— Studies in Deductive Logic. 2nd Edit. Cr. 8vo. 6s.
— The Principles of Science: A Treatise on Logic and Scientific Method. Cr. 8vo. 12s. 6d.
— Pure Logic: and other Minor Works. Edited by R. Adamson, M.A., and Harriet A. Jevons. 8vo. 10s. 6d.
KEYNES (J. N.).—Studies and Exercises in Formal Logic. 2nd Edit. Cr. 8vo. 10s. 6d.
McCOSH (Rev. Dr.).—The Laws of Discursive Thought. A Text-Book of Formal Logic. Cr. 8vo. 5s.
RAY (Prof. P. K.).—A Text-Book of Deductive Logic. 4th Edit. Globe 8vo. 4s. 6d.
VENN (Rev. John).—The Logic of Chance. 2nd Edit. Cr. 8vo. 10s. 6d.
— Symbolic Logic. Cr. 8vo. 10s. 6d.
— The Principles of Empirical or Inductive Logic. 8vo. 18s.

Psychology.

BALDWIN (Prof. J. M.).—Handbook of Psychology: Senses and Intellect. 8vo. 12s. 6d.
CALDERWOOD (Prof. H.). — The Relations of Mind and Brain. 8vo. 12s.
CLIFFORD (W. K.).—Seeing and Thinking. Cr. 8vo. 3s. 6d.
HÖFFDING (Prof. H.).—Outlines of Psychology. Translated by M. E. Lowndes. Cr. 8vo. 6s.
JAMES (Prof. William).—The Principles of Psychology. 2 vols. Demy 8vo. 25s. net.
JARDINE (Rev. Robert).—The Elements of the Psychology of Cognition. 3rd Edit. Cr. 8vo. 6s. 6d.
McCOSH (Rev. Dr.).—Psychology. Cr. 8vo. I. The Cognitive Powers. 6s. 6d.—II. The Motive Powers. 6s. 6d.
— The Emotions. 8vo. 9s.

MAUDSLEY (Dr. Henry).—The Physiology of Mind. Cr. 8vo. 10s. 6d.
— The Pathology of Mind. 8vo. 18s.
— Body and Mind. Cr. 8vo. 6s. 6d.
MURPHY (J. J.).—Habit and Intelligence. 2nd Edit. Illustrated. 8vo. 16s.

PHOTOGRAPHY.

MELDOLA (Prof. R.).—The Chemistry of Photography. Cr. 8vo. 6s.

PHYSICS OR NATURAL PHILOSOPHY.
General—Electricity and Magnetism—Heat, Light, and Sound.

General.

ANDREWS (Dr. Thomas): The Scientific Papers of the late. With a Memoir by Profs. Tait and Crum Brown. 8vo. 18s.
EVERETT (Prof. J. D.).—The C. G. S. System of Units, with Tables of Physical Constants. New Edit. Globe 8vo. 5s.
FESSENDEN (C.).—Physics for Public Schools. Globe 8vo.
FISHER (Rev. Osmond).—Physics of the Earth's Crust. 2nd Edit. 8vo. 12s.
GUILLEMIN (Amédée).—The Forces of Nature. A Popular Introduction to the Study of Physical Phenomena. 455 Woodcuts. Roy. 8vo. 21s.
— The Applications of Physical Forces. With Plates and Illustrations. Roy. 8vo. 21s.
KEMPE (A. B.).—How to draw a Straight Line. Cr. 8vo. 1s. 6d.
LOEWY (B.).—Questions and Examples in Experimental Physics, Sound, Light, Heat, Electricity, and Magnetism. Fcp. 8vo. 2s.
— A Graduated Course of Natural Science. Part I. Gl. 8vo. 2s.—Part II.
MOLLOY (Rev. G.).—Gleanings in Science: A Series of Popular Lectures on Scientific Subjects. 8vo. 7s. 6d.
STEWART (Prof. Balfour).—A Primer of Physics. Illustrated. 18mo. 1s.
— Lessons in Elementary Physics. Illustrated. Fcp. 8vo. 4s. 6d.
— Questions. By T. H. Core. 18mo. 2s.
STEWART (Prof. Balfour) and GEE (W. W. Haldane).—Lessons in Elementary Practical Physics. Illustrated.—General Physical Processes. Cr. 8vo. 6s.
TAIT (Prof. P. G.).—Lectures on some Recent Advances in Physical Science. 3rd Edit. Cr. 8vo. 9s.
THOMSON (Sir Wm.).—Popular Lectures and Addresses.—Vol. I. Constitution of Matter. Cr. 8vo. 7s. 6d.

Electricity and Magnetism.

CUMMING (Linnæus).—An Introduction to Electricity. Cr. 8vo. 8s. 6d.
DAY (R. E.).—Electric Light Arithmetic. 18mo. 2s.
GRAY (Prof. Andrew).—The Theory and Practice of Absolute Measurements in Electricity and Magnetism. 2 vols. Cr. 8vo. Vol. I. 12s. 6d.
— Absolute Measurements in Electricity and Magnetism. Fcp. 8vo. 5s. 6d.

PHYSICS—PHYSIOLOGY.

GUILLEMIN (A.).—ELECTRICITY AND MAGNETISM. A Popular Treatise. Translated and Edited by Prof. SILVANUS P. THOMPSON. Super Roy. 8vo. 31s. 6d.

LODGE (Prof. Oliver).—MODERN VIEWS OF ELECTRICITY. Cr. 8vo. 6s. 6d.

MENDENHALL (T. C.).—A CENTURY OF ELECTRICITY. Cr. 8vo. 4s. 6d.

STEWART (Prof. Balfour) and GEE (W. W. Haldane).—LESSONS IN ELEMENTARY PRACTICAL PHYSICS. Cr. 8vo. Illustrated.—ELECTRICITY AND MAGNETISM. 7s. 6d.
—— PRACTICAL PHYSICS FOR SCHOOLS. Gl. 8vo.—ELECTRICITY AND MAGNETISM. 2s. 6d.

THOMPSON (Prof. Silvanus P.). — ELEMENTARY LESSONS IN ELECTRICITY AND MAGNETISM. Illustrated. Fcp. 8vo. 4s. 6d.

THOMSON (Sir Wm.).—PAPERS ON ELECTROSTATICS AND MAGNETISM. 8vo. 18s.

TURNER (H. H.).—EXAMPLES ON HEAT AND ELECTRICITY. Cr. 8vo. 2s. 6d.

Heat, Light, and Sound.

AIRY (Sir G. B.).—ON SOUND AND ATMOSPHERIC VIBRATIONS. Cr. 8vo. 9s.

CARNOT–THURSTON.--REFLECTIONS ON THE MOTIVE POWER OF HEAT, AND ON MACHINES FITTED TO DEVELOP THAT POWER. From the French of N. L. S. CARNOT. Edited by R. H. THURSTON, LL.D. Cr. 8vo. 7s. 6d.

CLAUSIUS(R.).—THE MECHANICAL THEORY OF HEAT. Translated by W. R. BROWNE. Cr. 8vo. 10s. 6d.

FERRERS (Rev. N. M.).—SPHERICAL HARMONICS AND SUBJECTS CONNECTED WITH THEM. Cr. 8vo. 7s. 6d.

JOHNSON (Amy).—SUNSHINE. Illustrated. Cr. 8vo.

JONES (Prof. D. E.).—HEAT, LIGHT, AND SOUND. Globe 8vo. 2s. 6d.

MAYER (Prof. A. M.).—SOUND. A Series of Simple Experiments. Illustr. Cr. 8vo. 3s. 6d.

MAYER (Prof. A. M.) and BARNARD (C.).—LIGHT. A Series of Simple Experiments. Illustrated. Cr. 8vo. 2s. 6d.

PARKINSON (S.).—A TREATISE ON OPTICS. 4th Edit., revised. Cr. 8vo. 10s. 6d.

PEABODY (Prof. C. H.).—THERMODYNAMICS OF THE STEAM ENGINE AND OTHER HEAT-ENGINES. 8vo. 21s.

PERRY (Prof. J.).—STEAM: An Elementary Treatise. 18mo. 4s. 6d.

PRESTON (T.).—THE THEORY OF LIGHT. Illustrated. 8vo. 12s. 6d.
—— THE THEORY OF HEAT. 8vo.

RAYLEIGH (Lord).—THEORY OF SOUND. 8vo. Vol. I. 12s. 6d.—Vol. II. 12s. 6d.

SHANN (G.).—AN ELEMENTARY TREATISE ON HEAT IN RELATION TO STEAM AND THE STEAM-ENGINE. Illustr. Cr. 8vo. 4s. 6d.

SPOTTISWOODE (W.).—POLARISATION OF LIGHT. Illustrated. Cr. 8vo. 3s. 6d.

STEWART (Prof. Balfour) and GEE (W. W. Haldane).—LESSONS IN ELEMENTARY PRACTICAL PHYSICS. Cr. 8vo. Illustrated.—OPTICS, HEAT, AND SOUND.
—— PRACTICAL PHYSICS FOR SCHOOLS. Gl. 8vo.—HEAT, LIGHT, AND SOUND.

STOKES (Sir George G.).—ON LIGHT. The Burnett Lectures. Cr. 8vo. 7s. 6d.

STONE (W. H.).—ELEMENTARY LESSONS ON SOUND. Illustrated. Fcp. 8vo. 3s. 6d.

TAIT (Prof. P. G.).—HEAT. With Illustrations. Cr. 8vo. 6s.

TAYLOR (Sedley).—SOUND AND MUSIC. 2nd Edit. Ext. cr. 8vo. 8s. 6d.

TURNER (H. H.). (See ELECTRICITY.)

WRIGHT (Lewis).—LIGHT. A Course of Experimental Optics. Illust. Cr. 8vo. 7s. 6d.

PHYSIOGRAPHY and METEOROLOGY.

ARATUS.—THE SKIES AND WEATHER FORECASTS OF ARATUS. Translated by E. POSTE, M.A. Cr. 8vo. 3s. 6d.

BLANFORD (H. F.).—THE RUDIMENTS OF PHYSICAL GEOGRAPHY FOR THE USE OF INDIAN SCHOOLS. Illustr. Cr. 8vo. 2s. 6d.
—— A PRACTICAL GUIDE TO THE CLIMATES AND WEATHER OF INDIA, CEYLON AND BURMAH, AND THE STORMS OF INDIAN SEAS. 8vo. 12s. 6d.

FERREL (Prof. W.).—A POPULAR TREATISE ON THE WINDS. 8vo. 18s.

FISHER (Rev. Osmond).—PHYSICS OF THE EARTH'S CRUST. 2nd Edit. 8vo. 12s.

GALTON (Francis).—METEOROGRAPHICA; or, Methods of Mapping the Weather. 4to. 9s.

GEIKIE (Sir Archibald).—A PRIMER OF PHYSICAL GEOGRAPHY. Illustrated. 18mo. 1s.
—— ELEMENTARY LESSONS IN PHYSICAL GEOGRAPHY. Illustrated. Fcp. 8vo. 4s. 6d.
—— QUESTIONS ON THE SAME. 1s. 6d.

HUXLEY (Prof. T. H.).—PHYSIOGRAPHY. Illustrated. Cr. 8vo. 6s.

LOCKYER (J. Norman).—OUTLINES OF PHYSIOGRAPHY: THE MOVEMENTS OF THE EARTH. Illustrated. Cr. 8vo, swd. 1s. 6d.

MELDOLA (Prof. R.) and WHITE (Wm.).—REPORT ON THE EAST ANGLIAN EARTHQUAKE OF APRIL 22ND, 1884. 8vo. 3s 6d.

PHYSIOLOGY.

FEARNLEY (W.).—A MANUAL OF ELEMENTARY PRACTICAL HISTOLOGY. Cr. 8vo. 7s. 6d.

FOSTER (Prof. Michael).—A TEXT-BOOK OF PHYSIOLOGY. Illustrated. 5th Edit. 8vo.—Part I. Book I. BLOOD: THE TISSUES OF MOVEMENT, THE VASCULAR MECHANISM. 10s. 6d.—Part II. Book II. THE TISSUES OF CHEMICAL ACTION, WITH THEIR RESPECTIVE MECHANISMS: NUTRITION. 10s. 6d.—Part III. Book III. THE CENTRAL NERVOUS SYSTEM. 7s. 6d.—Part IV. Book III. THE SENSES, AND SOME SPECIAL MUSCULAR MECHANISMS.—BOOK IV. THE TISSUES AND MECHANISMS OF REPRODUCTION.
—— A PRIMER OF PHYSIOLOGY. 18mo. 1s.

FOSTER (Prof. M.) and LANGLEY (J. N.). —A COURSE OF ELEMENTARY PRACTICAL PHYSIOLOGY AND HISTOLOGY. Cr. 8vo. 7s. 6d.

GAMGEE (Arthur).—A TEXT-BOOK OF THE PHYSIOLOGICAL CHEMISTRY OF THE ANIMAL BODY. Vol. I. 8vo. 18s. Vol. II.

PHYSIOLOGY—continued.

HUMPHRY (Prof. Sir G. M.).—THE HUMAN FOOT AND THE HUMAN HAND. Illustrated. Fcp. 8vo. 4s. 6d.

HUXLEY (Prof. Thos. H.).—LESSONS IN ELEMENTARY PHYSIOLOGY. Fcp. 8vo. 4s. 6d.
— QUESTIONS. By T. ALCOCK. 18mo. 1s. 6d.

MIVART (St. George).—LESSONS IN ELEMENTARY ANATOMY. Fcp. 8vo. 6s. 6d.

PETTIGREW (J. Bell).—THE PHYSIOLOGY OF THE CIRCULATION IN PLANTS IN THE LOWER ANIMALS AND IN MAN. 8vo. 12s.

SEILER (Dr. Carl).—MICRO-PHOTOGRAPHS IN HISTORY, NORMAL AND PATHOLOGICAL. 4to. 31s. 6d.

POETRY. (See under LITERATURE, p. 14.)

POLITICAL ECONOMY.

BASTABLE (Prof. C. F.).—PUBLIC FINANCE.

BÖHM-BAWERK (Prof.).—CAPITAL AND INTEREST. Trans. by W. SMART. 8vo. 12s. net.
— THE POSITIVE THEORY OF CAPITAL. By the same Translator. 12s. net.

BOISSEVAIN (G. M.).—THE MONETARY QUESTION. 8vo, sewed. 3s. net.

BONAR (James).—MALTHUS AND HIS WORK. 8vo. 12s. 6d.

CAIRNES (J. E.).—SOME LEADING PRINCIPLES OF POLITICAL ECONOMY NEWLY EXPOUNDED. 8vo. 14s.
— THE CHARACTER AND LOGICAL METHOD OF POLITICAL ECONOMY. Cr. 8vo. 6s.

CLARKE (C. B.). — SPECULATIONS FROM POLITICAL ECONOMY. Cr. 8vo. 3s. 6d.

CO-OPERATION IN THE UNITED STATES: HISTORY OF. Edited by H. B. ADAMS. 8vo. 15s.

DICTIONARY OF POLITICAL ECONOMY, A. By various Writers. Edited by R. H. INGLIS PALGRAVE. 3s. 6d. net. (Part I. July, 1891.)

ECONOMIC JOURNAL, THE. — THE JOURNAL OF THE BRITISH ECONOMIC ASSOCIATION. Edit. by Prof. F. Y. EDGEWORTH. Published Quarterly. 8vo. 5s. (Part I. April, 1891.)

ECONOMICS: THE QUARTERLY JOURNAL OF. Vol. II. Parts II. III. IV. 2s. 6d. each. —Vol. III. 4 parts. 2s. 6d. each.—Vol. IV. 4 parts. 2s. 6d. each.

FAWCETT (Henry).—MANUAL OF POLITICAL ECONOMY. 7th Edit. Cr. 8vo. 12s.
— AN EXPLANATORY DIGEST OF THE ABOVE. By C. A. WATERS. Cr. 8vo. 2s. 6d.
— FREE TRADE AND PROTECTION. 6th Edit. Cr. 8vo. 3s. 6d.

FAWCETT (Mrs. H.).—POLITICAL ECONOMY FOR BEGINNERS, WITH QUESTIONS. 7th Edit. 18mo. 2s. 6d.

FIRST LESSONS IN BUSINESS MATTERS. By A BANKER'S DAUGHTER. 2nd Edit. 18mo. 1s.

GILMAN (N. P.). — PROFIT-SHARING BETWEEN EMPLOYER AND EMPLOYEE. Cr. 8vo. 7s. 6d.

GOSCHEN (Rt. Hon. George J.).—REPORTS AND SPEECHES ON LOCAL TAXATION. 8vo. 5s.

GUIDE TO THE UNPROTECTED: IN EVERY-DAY MATTERS RELATING TO PROPERTY AND INCOME. Ext. fcp. 8vo. 3s. 6d.

GUNTON (George).—WEALTH AND PROGRESS. Cr. 8vo. 6s.

HORTON (Hon. S. Dana).—THE SILVER POUND AND ENGLAND'S MONETARY POLICY SINCE THE RESTORATION. 8vo. 14s.

HOWELL (George).—THE CONFLICTS OF CAPITAL AND LABOUR. Cr. 8vo. 7s. 6d.

JEVONS (W. Stanley).—A PRIMER OF POLITICAL ECONOMY. 18mo. 1s.
— THE THEORY OF POLITICAL ECONOMY. 3rd Ed. 8vo. 10s. 6d.
— INVESTIGATIONS IN CURRENCY AND FINANCE. Edit. by H. S. FOXWELL. 8vo. 21s.

KEYNES (J. N.).—THE SCOPE AND METHOD OF POLITICAL ECONOMY. Cr. 8vo. 7s. net.

MACDONELL (John).—THE LAND QUESTION. 8vo. 10s. 6d.

MARSHALL (Prof. Alfred).—PRINCIPLES OF ECONOMICS. 2 vols. 8vo. Vol. I. 12s. 6d. net.

MARSHALL (Prof. A. and Mary P.).—THE ECONOMICS OF INDUSTRY. Ext. fcp. 8vo. 2s. 6d.

MARTIN (Frederick).— THE HISTORY OF LLOYD'S, AND OF MARINE INSURANCE IN GREAT BRITAIN. 8vo. 14s.

PRICE (L. L. F. R.).—INDUSTRIAL PEACE: ITS ADVANTAGES, METHODS, AND DIFFICULTIES. Med. 8vo. 6s.

SIDGWICK (Prof. Henry).—THE PRINCIPLES OF POLITICAL ECONOMY. 2nd Edit. 8vo. 16s.

SMART (W.).—AN INTRODUCTION TO THE THEORY OF VALUE.

WALKER (Francis A.).—FIRST LESSONS IN POLITICAL ECONOMY. Cr. 8vo. 5s.
— A BRIEF TEXT-BOOK OF POLITICAL ECONOMY. Cr. 8vo. 6s. 6d.
— POLITICAL ECONOMY. 8vo. 12s. 6d.
— THE WAGES QUESTION. Ext. cr. 8vo. 8s. 6d. net.
— MONEY. New Edit. Ext. cr. 8vo. 8s. 6d. net.
— MONEY IN ITS RELATION TO TRADE AND INDUSTRY. Cr. 8vo. 7s. 6d.
— LAND AND ITS RENT. Fcp. 8vo. 3s. 6d.

WALLACE (A. R.).—BAD TIMES: An Essay. Cr. 8vo. 2s. 6d.

WICKSTEED (Ph. H.).—THE ALPHABET OF ECONOMIC SCIENCE.—I. ELEMENTS OF THE THEORY OF VALUE OR WORTH. Gl. 8vo. 2s. 6d.

POLITICS.

(See also HISTORY.)

ADAMS (Sir F. O.) and CUNNINGHAM (C.).—THE SWISS CONFEDERATION. 8vo. 14s.

BAKER (Sir Samuel W.).—THE EGYPTIAN QUESTION. 8vo, sewed. 2s.

BATH (Marquis of). — OBSERVATIONS ON BULGARIAN AFFAIRS. Cr. 8vo. 3s. 6d.

BRIGHT (John).—SPEECHES ON QUESTIONS OF PUBLIC POLICY. Edit. by J. E. THOROLD ROGERS. With Portrait. 2 vols. 8vo. 25s.
—Popular Edition. Ext. fcp. 8vo. 3s. 6d.
— PUBLIC ADDRESSES. Edited by J. E. T. ROGERS. 8vo. 14s.

BRYCE (Jas., M.P.).—THE AMERICAN COMMONWEALTH. 2 vols. Ext. cr. 8vo. 25s.

BURKE (Edmund).—LETTERS, TRACTS, AND SPEECHES ON IRISH AFFAIRS. Edited by MATTHEW ARNOLD, with Preface. Cr. 8vo. 6s.
— REFLECTIONS ON THE FRENCH REVOLUTION. Ed. by F. G. SELBY. Globe 8vo. 5s.

POLITICS—SOCIAL ECONOMY.

CAIRNES (J. E.).—POLITICAL ESSAYS. 8vo. 10s. 6d.
—— THE SLAVE POWER. 8vo. 10s. 6d.
COBDEN (Richard).—SPEECHES ON QUESTIONS OF PUBLIC POLICY. Ed. by J. BRIGHT and J. E. THOROLD ROGERS. Gl. 8vo. 3s. 6d.
DICEY (Prof. A. V.).—LETTERS ON UNIONIST DELUSIONS. Cr. 8vo. 2s. 6d.
DILKE (Rt. Hon. Sir Charles W.).—GREATER BRITAIN. A Record of Travel in English-Speaking Countries during 1866-67. (America, Australia, India.) 9th Edit. Cr. 8vo. 6s.
—— PROBLEMS OF GREATER BRITAIN. Maps. 3rd Edit. Ext. cr. 8vo. 12s. 6d.
DONISTHORPE (Wordsworth).—INDIVIDUALISM: A System of Politics. 8vo. 14s.
DUFF (Rt. Hon. Sir M. E. Grant).—MISCELLANIES, POLITICAL AND LITERARY. 8vo. 10s. 6d.
ENGLISH CITIZEN, THE.—His Rights and Responsibilities. Ed. by HENRY CRAIK, C.B. Cr. 8vo. 3s. 6d. each.
THE PUNISHMENT AND PREVENTION OF CRIME. By Col. Sir EDMUND DU CANE.
LOCAL GOVERNMENT. By M. D. CHALMERS.
COLONIES AND DEPENDENCIES: Part I. INDIA. By J. S. COTTON, M.A.—II. THE COLONIES. By E. J. PAYNE.
THE STATE IN ITS RELATION TO EDUCATION. By HENRY CRAIK, C.B.
THE STATE AND THE CHURCH. By Hon. ARTHUR ELLIOTT, M.P.
THE STATE IN ITS RELATION TO TRADE. By Sir T. H. FARRER, Bart.
THE POOR LAW. By the Rev. T. W. FOWLE.
THE STATE IN RELATION TO LABOUR. By W. STANLEY JEVONS.
JUSTICE AND POLICE. By F. W. MAITLAND.
THE NATIONAL DEFENCES. By Colonel MAURICE, R.A. [*In the Press.*
THE LAND LAWS. By Sir F. POLLOCK, Bart. 2nd Edit.
CENTRAL GOVERNMENT. By H. D. TRAILL.
THE ELECTORATE AND THE LEGISLATURE. By SPENCER WALPOLE.
FOREIGN RELATIONS. By S. WALPOLE.
THE NATIONAL BUDGET; THE NATIONAL DEBT; TAXES AND RATES. By A. J. WILSON.
FAWCETT (Henry).—SPEECHES ON SOME CURRENT POLITICAL QUESTIONS. 8vo. 10s. 6d.
—— FREE TRADE AND PROTECTION. 6th Edit. Cr. 8vo. 3s. 6d.
FAWCETT (Henry and Mrs. H.).—ESSAYS AND LECTURES ON POLITICAL AND SOCIAL SUBJECTS. 8vo. 10s. 6d.
FISKE (John).—AMERICAN POLITICAL IDEAS VIEWED FROM THE STAND-POINT OF UNIVERSAL HISTORY. Cr. 8vo. 4s.
—— CIVIL GOVERNMENT IN THE UNITED STATES CONSIDERED WITH SOME REFERENCE TO ITS ORIGIN. Cr. 8vo. 6s. 6d.
FREEMAN (Prof. E. A.).—DISESTABLISHMENT AND DISENDOWMENT. WHAT ARE THEY? 4th Edit. Cr. 8vo. 1s.
—— COMPARATIVE POLITICS and THE UNITY OF HISTORY. 8vo. 14s.
—— THE GROWTH OF THE ENGLISH CONSTITUTION. 5th Edit. Cr. 8vo. 5s.
HARWOOD (George).—DISESTABLISHMENT; or, a Defence of the Principle of a National Church. 8vo. 12s.
—— THE COMING DEMOCRACY. Cr. 8vo. 6s.

HILL (Florence D.).—CHILDREN OF THE STATE. Ed. by FANNY FOWKE. Cr. 8vo. 6s.
HILL (Octavia).—OUR COMMON LAND, AND OTHER ESSAYS. Ext. fcp. 8vo. 3s. 6d.
HOLLAND (Prof. T. E.).—THE TREATY RELATIONS OF RUSSIA AND TURKEY, FROM 1774 TO 1853. Cr. 8vo. 2s.
JENKS (Prof. Edward).—THE GOVERNMENT OF VICTORIA (AUSTRALIA). 8vo.
LOWELL (J. R.). (*See* COLLECTED WORKS.)
LUBBOCK (Sir J.). (*See* COLLECTED WORKS.)
MACDONELL (John).—THE LAND QUESTION. 8vo. 10s. 6d.
PALGRAVE (Reginald F. D.).—THE HOUSE OF COMMONS: Illustrations of its History and Practice. Cr. 8vo. 2s. 6d.
PALGRAVE (W. Gifford).—ESSAYS ON EASTERN QUESTIONS. 8vo. 10s. 6d.
POLLOCK (Sir F., Bart.).—INTRODUCTION TO THE HISTORY OF THE SCIENCE OF POLITICS. Cr. 8vo. 2s. 6d.
PRACTICAL POLITICS. Published under the auspices of the National Liberal Federation. 8vo. 6s.
ROGERS (Prof. J. E. T.).—COBDEN AND POLITICAL OPINION. 8vo. 10s. 6d.
ROUTLEDGE (Jas.).—POPULAR PROGRESS IN ENGLAND 8vo. 16s.
RUSSELL (Sir Charles).—NEW VIEWS ON IRELAND. Cr. 8vo. 2s. 6d.
—— THE PARNELL COMMISSION: THE OPENING SPEECH FOR THE DEFENCE. 8vo. 10s. 6d.
—*Popular Edition.* Sewed. 2s.
SELBORNE (Earl of). (*See under* THEOLOGY, p. 32.)
SIDGWICK (Prof. Henry).—THE ELEMENTS OF POLITICS. 8vo. 14s. net.
SMITH (Goldwin).—CANADA AND THE CANADIAN QUESTION. 8vo. 8s. net.
STATESMAN'S YEAR-BOOK, THE. (*See* STATISTICS.)
STATHAM (R.).—BLACKS, BOERS, AND BRITISH. Cr. 8vo. 6s.
THORNTON (W. T.).—A PLEA FOR PEASANT PROPRIETORS. New Edit. Cr. 8vo. 7s. 6d.
—— INDIAN PUBLIC WORKS, AND COGNATE INDIAN TOPICS. Cr. 8vo. 8s. 6d.
TRENCH (Capt. F.).—THE RUSSO-INDIAN QUESTION. Cr. 8vo. 7s. 6d.
WALLACE (Sir Donald M.).—EGYPT AND THE EGYPTIAN QUESTION. 8vo. 14s.

PSYCHOLOGY.
(*See under* PHILOSOPHY, p. 26.)

SCULPTURE. (*See* ART.)

SOCIAL ECONOMY.

FAWCETT (H. and Mrs. H.). (*See* POLITICS.)
HILL (Octavia).—HOMES OF THE LONDON POOR. Cr. 8vo, sewed. 1s.
HUXLEY (Prof. T. H.).—SOCIAL DISEASES AND WORSE REMEDIES: Letters to the "Times" on Mr. Booth's Schemes. Cr. 8vo. sewed. 1s. net.
JEVONS (W. Stanley).—METHODS OF SOCIAL REFORM. 8vo. 10s. 6d.
STANLEY (Hon. Maude).—CLUBS FOR WORKING GIRLS. Cr. 8vo. 6s.

SPORT—THEOLOGY.

SOUND. (See under PHYSICS, p. 27.)

SPORT.

BAKER (Sir Samuel W.).—WILD BEASTS AND THEIR WAYS: REMINISCENCES OF EUROPE, ASIA, AFRICA, AMERICA, FROM 1845—88. Illustrated. Ext. cr. 8vo. 12s. 6d.
CHASSERESSE (D.).—SPORTING SKETCHES. Illustrated. Cr. 8vo. 3s. 6d.
EDWARDS-MOSS (Sir J. E., Bart).—A SEASON IN SUTHERLAND. Cr. 8vo. 1s. 6d.

STATISTICS.

STATESMAN'S YEAR-BOOK, THE. Statistical and Historical Annual of the States of the World for the Year 1891. Revised after Official Returns. Ed. by J. SCOTT KELTIE. Cr. 8vo. 10s. 6d.

SURGERY. (See MEDICINE.)

SWIMMING.

LEAHY (Sergeant).—THE ART OF SWIMMING IN THE ETON STYLE. Cr. 8vo. 2s.

THEOLOGY.

The Bible—History of the Christian Church—The Church of England—Devotional Books—The Fathers—Hymnology—Sermons, Lectures, Addresses, and Theological Essays.

The Bible.

History of the Bible—
THE ENGLISH BIBLE; An External and Critical History of the various English Translations of Scripture. By Prof. JOHN EADIE. 2 vols. 8vo. 28s.
INTRODUCTION TO THE HISTORY OF THE CANON OF THE OLD TESTAMENT. By Prof. H. E. RYLE. Cr. 8vo.
THE BIBLE IN THE CHURCH. By Right Rev. Bp. WESTCOTT. 10th edit. 18mo. 4s. 6d.

Biblical History—
BIBLE LESSONS. By Rev. E. A. ABBOTT. Cr. 8vo. 4s. 6d.
STORIES FROM THE BIBLE. By Rev. A. J. CHURCH. Illust. Cr. 8vo. 2 parts. 3s. 6d. each.
BIBLE READINGS SELECTED FROM THE PENTATEUCH AND THE BOOK OF JOSHUA. By Rev. J. A. CROSS. Gl. 8vo. 2s. 6d.
THE CHILDREN'S TREASURY OF BIBLE STORIES. By Mrs. H. GASKOIN. 18mo. 1s. each.—Part I. Old Testament; II. New Testament; III. The Apostles.
A CLASS-BOOK OF OLD TESTAMENT HISTORY. By Rev. Dr. MACLEAR. 18mo. 4s. 6d.
A CLASS-BOOK OF NEW TESTAMENT HISTORY. By the same. 18mo. 5s. 6d.
A SHILLING BOOK OF OLD TESTAMENT HISTORY. By the same. 18mo. 1s.
A SHILLING BOOK OF NEW TESTAMENT HISTORY. By the same. 18mo. 1s.

The Old Testament—
SCRIPTURE READINGS FOR SCHOOLS AND FAMILIES. By C. M. YONGE. Globe 8vo. 1s. 6d. each: also with comments, 3s. 6d. each.— GENESIS TO DEUTERONOMY.— JOSHUA TO SOLOMON.—KINGS AND THE PROPHETS.—THE GOSPEL TIMES.—APOSTOLIC TIMES.
THE PATRIARCHS AND LAWGIVERS OF THE OLD TESTAMENT. By F. D. MAURICE. 7th Edit. Cr. 8vo. 4s. 6d.
THE PROPHETS AND KINGS OF THE OLD TESTAMENT. By the same. Cr. 8vo. 6s.

The Pentateuch—
AN HISTORICO-CRITICAL INQUIRY INTO THE ORIGIN AND COMPOSITION OF THE HEXATEUCH (PENTATEUCH AND BOOK OF JOSHUA). By Prof. A. KUENEN. Trans. by P. H. WICKSTEED, M.A. 8vo. 14s.

The Psalms—
THE PSALMS CHRONOLOGICALLY ARRANGED. By FOUR FRIENDS. Cr. 8vo. 5s. net.
GOLDEN TREASURY PSALTER. Student's Edition of the above. 18mo. 3s. 6d.
THE PSALMS. With Introduction and Notes. By A. C. JENNINGS, M.A., and W. H. LOWE, M.A. 2 vols. Cr. 8vo. 10s. 6d. each.
INTRODUCTION TO THE STUDY AND USE OF THE PSALMS. By Rev. J. F. THRUPP. 2nd Edit. 2 vols. 8vo. 21s.

Isaiah—
ISAIAH XL.—LXVI. With the Shorter Prophecies allied to it. Edited by MATTHEW ARNOLD. Cr. 8vo. 5s.
ISAIAH OF JERUSALEM. In the Authorised English Version, with Introduction and Notes. By the same. Cr. 8vo. 4s. 6d.
A BIBLE-READING FOR SCHOOLS. The Great Prophecy of Israel's Restoration (Isaiah xl.—lxvi.). Arranged and Edited for Young Learners. By the same. 18mo. 1s.
COMMENTARY ON THE BOOK OF ISAIAH: Critical, Historical, and Prophetical: including a Revised English Translation. By T. R. BIRKS. 2nd Edit. 8vo. 12s. 6d.
THE BOOK OF ISAIAH CHRONOLOGICALLY ARRANGED. By T. K. CHEYNE. Cr. 8vo. 7s. 6d.

Zechariah—
THE HEBREW STUDENT'S COMMENTARY ON ZECHARIAH, Hebrew and LXX. By W. H. LOWE, M.A. 8vo. 10s. 6d.

The New Testament—
THE NEW TESTAMENT. Essay on the Right Estimation of MS. Evidence in the Text of the New Testament. By T. R. BIRKS. Cr. 8vo. 3s. 6d.
THE MESSAGES OF THE BOOKS. Discourses and Notes on the Books of the New Testament. By Archd. FARRAR. 8vo. 14s.
THE CLASSICAL ELEMENT IN THE NEW TESTAMENT. Considered as a Proof of its Genuineness, with an Appendix on the Oldest Authorities used in the Formation of the Canon. By C. H. HOOLE. 8vo. 10s. 6d.
ON A FRESH REVISION OF THE ENGLISH NEW TESTAMENT. With an Appendix on the last Petition of the Lord's Prayer. By Bishop LIGHTFOOT. Cr. 8vo. 7s. 6d.
THE UNITY OF THE NEW TESTAMENT. By F. D. MAURICE. 2 vols. Cr. 8vo. 12s.
A COMPANION TO THE GREEK TESTAMENT AND THE ENGLISH VERSION. By PHILIP SCHAFF, D.D. Cr. 8vo. 12s.
A GENERAL SURVEY OF THE HISTORY OF THE CANON OF THE NEW TESTAMENT DURING THE FIRST FOUR CENTURIES. By Bishop WESTCOTT. Cr. 8vo. 10s. 6d.
THE NEW TESTAMENT IN THE ORIGINAL GREEK. The Text revised by Bishop WESTCOTT, D.D., and Prof. F. J. A. HORT, D.D. 2 vols. Cr. 8vo. 10s. 6d. each.—Vol. I. Text.—Vol. II. Introduction and Appendix.
SCHOOL EDITION OF THE ABOVE. 18mo, 4s. 6d.; 18mo, roan, 5s. 6d.; morocco, gilt edges, 6s. 6d.

THEOLOGY. 31

The Gospels—
THE COMMON TRADITION OF THE SYNOPTIC GOSPELS. In the Text of the Revised Version. By Rev. E. A. ABBOTT and W. G. RUSHBROOKE. Cr. 8vo. 3s. 6d.
SYNOPTICON: An Exposition of the Common Matter of the Synoptic Gospels. By W. G. RUSHBROOKE. Printed in Colours. In Six Parts, and Appendix. 4to.—Part I. 3s. 6d.—Parts II. and III. 7s.—Parts IV. V. and VI., with Indices, 10s. 6d.—Appendices, 10s. 6d.—Complete in 1 vol. 35s.
INTRODUCTION TO THE STUDY OF THE FOUR GOSPELS. By Bp. WESTCOTT. Cr. 8vo. 10s. 6d.
THE COMPOSITION OF THE FOUR GOSPELS. By Rev. ARTHUR WRIGHT. Cr. 8vo. 5s.

Gospel of St. Matthew—
THE GREEK TEXT, with Introduction and Notes by Rev. A. SLOMAN. Fcp. 8vo. 2s. 6d.
CHOICE NOTES ON ST. MATTHEW. Drawn from Old and New Sources. Cr. 8vo. 4s. 6d. (St. Matthew and St. Mark in 1 vol. 9s.)

Gospel of St. Mark—
SCHOOL READINGS IN THE GREEK TESTAMENT. Being the Outlines of the Life of our Lord as given by St. Mark, with additions from the Text of the other Evangelists. Edited, with Notes and Vocabulary, by Rev. A. CALVERT, M.A. Fcp. 8vo. 2s. 6d.
CHOICE NOTES ON ST. MARK. Drawn from Old and New Sources. Cr. 8vo. 4s. 6d. (St. Matthew and St. Mark in 1 vol. 9s.)

Gospel of St. Luke—
GREEK TEXT, with Introduction and Notes by Rev. J. BOND, M.A. Fcp. 8vo. 2s. 6d.
CHOICE NOTES ON ST. LUKE. Drawn from Old and New Sources. Cr. 8vo. 4s. 6d.
THE GOSPEL OF THE KINGDOM OF HEAVEN. A Course of Lectures on the Gospel of St. Luke. By F. D. MAURICE. Cr. 8vo. 6s.

Gospel of St. John—
THE GOSPEL OF ST. JOHN. By F. D. MAURICE. 8th Ed. Cr. 8vo. 6s.
CHOICE NOTES ON ST. JOHN. Drawn from Old and New Sources. Cr. 8vo. 4s. 6d.

The Acts of the Apostles—
GREEK TEXT, with Notes by T. E. PAGE, M.A. Fcp. 8vo. 3s. 6d.
THE CHURCH OF THE FIRST DAYS: THE CHURCH OF JERUSALEM, THE CHURCH OF THE GENTILES, THE CHURCH OF THE WORLD. Lectures on the Acts of the Apostles. By Very Rev. C. J. VAUGHAN. Cr. 8vo. 10s. 6d.

The Epistles of St. Paul—
THE EPISTLE TO THE ROMANS. The Greek Text, with English Notes. By the Very Rev. C. J. VAUGHAN. 7th Edit. Cr. 8vo. 7s. 6d.
THE EPISTLES TO THE CORINTHIANS. Greek Text, with Commentary. By Rev. W. KAY. 8vo. 9s.
THE EPISTLE TO THE GALATIANS. A Revised Text, with Introduction, Notes, and Dissertations. By Bishop LIGHTFOOT. 10th Edit. 8vo. 12s.
THE EPISTLE TO THE PHILIPPIANS. A Revised Text, with Introduction, Notes, and Dissertations. By the same. 8vo. 12s.

The Epistles of St. Paul—
THE EPISTLE TO THE PHILIPPIANS. With Translation, Paraphrase, and Notes for English Readers. By the Very Rev. C. J. VAUGHAN. Cr. 8vo. 5s.
THE EPISTLES TO THE COLOSSIANS AND TO PHILEMON. A Revised Text, with Introductions, etc. By Bishop LIGHTFOOT. 9th Edit. 8vo. 12s.
THE EPISTLES TO THE EPHESIANS, THE COLOSSIANS, AND PHILEMON. With Introduction and Notes. By Rev. J. Ll. DAVIES. 2nd Edit. 8vo. 7s. 6d.
THE FIRST EPISTLE TO THE THESSALONIANS. By Very Rev. C. J. VAUGHAN. 8vo, sewed. 1s. 6d.
THE EPISTLES TO THE THESSALONIANS. Commentary on the Greek Text. By Prof. JOHN EADIE. 8vo. 12s.

The Epistle of St. James—
THE GREEK TEXT, with Introduction and Notes. By Rev. JOSEPH MAYOR. 8vo.

The Epistles of St. John—
THE EPISTLES OF ST. JOHN. By F. D. MAURICE. 4th Edit. Cr. 8vo. 6s.
— The Greek Text, with Notes, by Bishop WESTCOTT. 2nd Edit. 8vo. 12s. 6d.

The Epistle to the Hebrews—
GREEK AND ENGLISH. Edited by Rev. FREDERIC RENDALL. Cr. 8vo. 6s.
ENGLISH TEXT, with Commentary. By the same. Cr. 8vo. 7s. 6d.
THE GREEK TEXT, with Notes, by Very Rev. C. J. VAUGHAN. Cr. 8vo. 7s. 6d.
THE GREEK TEXT, with Notes and Essays, by Bishop WESTCOTT. 8vo. 14s.

Revelation—
LECTURES ON THE APOCALYPSE. By F. D. MAURICE. 2nd Edit. Cr. 8vo. 6s.
THE REVELATION OF ST. JOHN. By Rev. Prof. W. MILLIGAN. Cr. 8vo. 7s. 6d.
LECTURES ON THE REVELATION OF ST. JOHN. By Very Rev. C. J. VAUGHAN. 5th Edit. Cr. 8vo. 10s. 6d.

THE BIBLE WORD-BOOK. By W. ALDIS WRIGHT. 2nd Edit. Cr. 8vo. 7s. 6d.

History of the Christian Church.

CHURCH (Dean).—THE OXFORD MOVEMENT, 1833—45. 8vo. 12s. 6d. net.
CUNNINGHAM (Rev. John).—THE GROWTH OF THE CHURCH IN ITS ORGANISATION AND INSTITUTIONS. 8vo. 9s.
CUNNINGHAM (Rev. William).—THE CHURCHES OF ASIA: A Methodical Sketch of the Second Century. Cr. 8vo. 6s.
DALE (A. W. W.).—THE SYNOD OF ELVIRA, AND CHRISTIAN LIFE IN THE FOURTH CENTURY. Cr. 8vo. 10s. 6d.
HARDWICK (Archdeacon).—A HISTORY OF THE CHRISTIAN CHURCH: MIDDLE AGE. Edited by Bp. STUBBS. Cr. 8vo. 10s. 6d.
—— A HISTORY OF THE CHRISTIAN CHURCH DURING THE REFORMATION. 9th Edit., revised by Bishop STUBBS. Cr. 8vo. 10s. 6d.

THEOLOGY.
History of the Christian Church—*contd.*

HORT (Dr. F. J. A.).—Two Dissertations. I. On MONOΓΕΝΗΣ ΘΕΟΣ in Scripture and Tradition. II. On the "Constantinopolitan" Creed and other Eastern Creeds of the Fourth Century. 8vo. 7s. 6d.

KILLEN (W. D.).—Ecclesiastical History of Ireland, from the Earliest Date to the Present Time. 2 vols. 8vo. 25s.

SIMPSON (Rev. W.).—An Epitome of the History of the Christian Church. 7th Edit. Fcp. 8vo. 3s. 6d.

VAUGHAN (Very Rev. C. J.).—The Church of the First Days: The Church of Jerusalem, The Church of the Gentiles, The Church of the World. Cr. 8vo. 10s. 6d.

WARD (W.).—William George Ward and the Oxford Movement. 8vo. 14s.

The Church of England.

Catechism of—
A Class-Book of the Catechism of the Church of England. By Rev. Canon Maclear. 18mo. 1s. 6d.
A First Class-Book of the Catechism of the Church of England. By the same. 18mo. 6d.
The Order of Confirmation. With Prayers and Devotions. By the same. 32mo. 6d.

Collects—
Collects of the Church of England. With a Coloured Floral Design to each Collect. Cr. 8vo. 12s.

Disestablishment—
Disestablishment and Disendowment. What are they? By Prof. E. A. Freeman. 4th Edit. Cr., 8vo. 1s.
Disestablishment; or, A Defence of the Principle of a National Church. By Geo. Harwood. 8vo. 12s.
A Defence of the Church of England against Disestablishment. By Roundell, Earl of Selborne. Cr. 8vo. 2s. 6d.
Ancient Facts and Fictions concerning Churches and Tithes. By the same. Cr. 8vo. 7s. 6d.

Dissent in its Relation to—
Dissent in its Relation to the Church of England. By Rev. G. H. Curteis. Bampton Lectures for 1871. Cr. 8vo. 7s. 6d.

Holy Communion—
The Communion Service from the Book of Common Prayer. With Select Readings from the Writings of the Rev. F. D. Maurice. Edited by Bishop Colenso. 6th Edit. 16mo. 2s. 6d.
Before the Table: An Inquiry, Historical and Theological, into the Meaning of the Consecration Rubric in the Communion Service of the Church of England. By Very Rev. J. S. Howson. 8vo. 7s. 6d.
First Communion. With Prayers and Devotions for the newly Confirmed. By Rev. Canon Maclear. 32mo. 6d.
A Manual of Instruction for Confirmation and First Communion. With Prayers and Devotions. By the same. 32mo. 2s.

Liturgy—
An Introduction to the Creeds. By Rev. Canon Maclear. 18mo. 2s. 6d.
An Introduction to the Thirty-Nine Articles. By same. 18mo. [*In the Press.*
A History of the Book of Common Prayer. By Rev F. Procter. 18th Edit. Cr. 8vo. 10s. 6d.
An Elementary Introduction to the Book of Common Prayer. By Rev. F. Procter and Rev. Canon Maclear. 18mo. 2s. 6d.
Twelve Discourses on Subjects connected with the Liturgy and Worship of the Church of England. By Very Rev. C. J. Vaughan. Fcp. 8vo. 6s.
A Companion to the Lectionary. By Rev. W. Benham, B.D. Cr. 8vo. 4s. 6d.

Judgment in the Case of Read and Others v. the Lord Bishop of Lincoln. Nov. 21, 1890. By his Grace the Archbishop of Canterbury. 8vo. 1s. 6d. net.

Devotional Books.

EASTLAKE (Lady).—Fellowship: Letters addressed to my Sister-Mourners. Cr. 8vo. 2s. 6d.

IMITATIO CHRISTI. Libri IV. Printed in Borders after Holbein, Dürer, and other old Masters, containing Dances of Death, Acts of Mercy, Emblems, etc. Cr.8vo. 7s.6d.

KINGSLEY (Charles).—Out of the Deep: Words for the Sorrowful. From the Writings of Charles Kingsley. Ext. fcp. 8vo. 3s. 6d.
—— Daily Thoughts. Selected from the Writings of Charles Kingsley. By His Wife. Cr. 8vo. 6s.
—— From Death to Life. Fragments of Teaching to a Village Congregation. Edit. by His Wife. Fcp. 8vo. 2s. 6d.

MACLEAR (Rev. Canon).—A Manual of Instruction for Confirmation and First Communion, with Prayers and Devotions. 32mo. 2s.
—— The Hour of Sorrow; or, The Office for the Burial of the Dead. 32mo. 2s.

MAURICE (F. D.).—Lessons of Hope. Readings from the Works of F. D. Maurice. Selected by Rev. J. Ll. Davies, M.A. Cr. 8vo. 5s.

RAYS OF SUNLIGHT FOR DARK DAYS. With a Preface by Very Rev. C. J. Vaughan. D.D. New Edition. 18mo. 3s. 6d.

SERVICE (Rev. J.).—Prayers for Public Worship. Cr. 8vo. 4s. 6d.

THE WORSHIP OF GOD, AND FELLOWSHIP AMONG MEN. By Prof. Maurice and others. Fcp. 8vo. 3s. 6d.

WELBY-GREGORY (Hon. Lady).—Links and Clues. 2nd Edit. Cr. 8vo. 6s.

WESTCOTT (Rt. Rev. Bishop).—Thoughts on Revelation and Life. Selections from the Writings of Bishop Westcott. Edited by Rev. S. Phillips. Cr. 8vo. 6s.

WILBRAHAM (Francis M.).—In the Sere and Yellow Leaf: Thoughts and Recollections for Old and Young. Globe 8vo. 3s. 6d.

THE FATHERS—SERMONS, LECTURES, ETC. 33

The Fathers.

DONALDSON (Prof. James).—THE APOSTOLIC FATHERS. A Critical Account of their Genuine Writings, and of their Doctrines. 2nd Edit. Cr. 8vo. 7s. 6d.

Works of the Greek and Latin Fathers: THE APOSTOLIC FATHERS. Revised Texts, with Introductions, Notes, Dissertations, and Translations. By Bishop LIGHTFOOT.—Part I. ST. CLEMENT OF ROME. 2 vols. 8vo. 32s.—Part II. ST. IGNATIUS TO ST. POLYCARP. 3 vols. 2nd Edit. 8vo. 48s.

THE APOSTOLIC FATHERS. Abridged Edit. With Short Introductions, Greek Text, and English Translation. By same. 8vo. 16s.

THE EPISTLE OF ST. BARNABAS. Its Date and Authorship. With Greek Text, Latin Version, Translation and Commentary. By Rev. W. CUNNINGHAM. Cr. 8vo. 7s. 6d.

Hymnology.

BROOKE (S. A.).—CHRISTIAN HYMNS. Gl. 8vo. 2s. net.—CHRISTIAN HYMNS AND SERVICE BOOK OF BEDFORD CHAPEL, BLOOMSBURY. Gl. 8vo. 3s. net.—SERVICE BOOK. Gl. 8vo. 1s. net.

PALGRAVE (Prof. F. T.). — ORIGINAL HYMNS. 3rd Edit. 18mo. 1s. 6d.

SELBORNE (Roundell, Earl of).—THE BOOK OF PRAISE. 18mo. 2s. 6d. net.
—— A HYMNAL. Chiefly from "The Book of Praise."—A. Royal 32mo, limp. 6d.—B. 18mo, larger type. 1s.—C. Fine paper. 1s. 6d. —With Music, Selected, Harmonised, and Composed by JOHN HULLAH. 18mo. 3s. 6d.

WOODS (Miss M. A.).—HYMNS FOR SCHOOL WORSHIP. 18mo. 1s. 6d.

Sermons, Lectures, Addresses, and Theological Essays.

ABBOT (F. E.).—SCIENTIFIC THEISM. Cr. 8vo. 7s. 6d.
—— THE WAY OUT OF AGNOSTICISM; or, The Philosophy of Free Religion. Cr. 8vo. 4s. 6d.

ABBOTT (Rev. E. A.).—CAMBRIDGE SERMONS. 8vo. 6s.
—— OXFORD SERMONS. 8vo. 7s. 6d.
—— PHILOMYTHUS. A discussion of Cardinal Newman's Essay on Ecclesiastical Miracles. Cr. 8vo. 3s. 6d.
—— NEWMANIANISM. Cr. 8vo. 1s. net.

AINGER (Canon).—SERMONS PREACHED IN THE TEMPLE CHURCH. Ext. fcp. 8vo. 6s.

ALEXANDER (W., Bishop of Derry and Raphoe).—THE LEADING IDEAS OF THE GOSPEL. New Edit. Cr. 8vo.

BAINES (Rev. Edward).—SERMONS. With a Preface and Memoir by Bishop BARRY, Cr. 8vo. 6s.

BARRY (Bishop).—FIRST WORDS IN AUSTRALIA: Sermons. Cr. 8vo. 5s.

BATHER (Archdeacon).—ON SOME MINISTERIAL DUTIES, CATECHISING, PREACHING, Etc. Edited, with a Preface, by Very Rev. C. J. VAUGHAN, D.D. Fcp. 8vo. 4s. 6d.

BETHUNE-BAKER (J. F.).—THE INFLUENCE OF CHRISTIANITY ON WAR. 8vo. 5s.
—— THE STERNNESS OF CHRIST'S TEACHING, AND ITS RELATION TO THE LAW OF FORGIVENESS. Cr. 8vo. 2s. 6d.

BINNIE (Rev. W.).—SERMONS. Cr. 8vo. 6s.

BIRKS (Thomas Rawson).—THE DIFFICULTIES OF BELIEF IN CONNECTION WITH THE CREATION AND THE FALL, REDEMPTION, AND JUDGMENT. 2nd Edit. Cr. 8vo. 5s.
—— JUSTIFICATION AND IMPUTED RIGHTEOUSNESS. A Review. Cr. 8vo. 6s.
—— SUPERNATURAL REVELATION; or, First Principles of Moral Theology. 8vo. 8s.

BROOKE (S. A.).—SHORT SERMONS. Cr. 8vo.

BROOKS (Bishop Phillips).—THE CANDLE OF THE LORD: and other Sermons. Cr. 8vo. 6s.
—— SERMONS PREACHED IN ENGLISH CHURCHES. Cr. 8vo. 6s.
—— TWENTY SERMONS. Cr. 8vo. 6s.
—— TOLERANCE. Cr. 8vo. 2s. 6d.
—— THE LIGHT OF THE WORLD. Cr. 8vo. 3s. 6d.

BRUNTON (T. Lauder).—THE BIBLE AND SCIENCE. Illustrated. Cr. 8vo. 10s. 6d.

BUTLER (Archer).—SERMONS, DOCTRINAL AND PRACTICAL. 11th Edit. 8vo. 8s.
—— SECOND SERIES OF SERMONS. 8vo. 7s.
—— LETTERS ON ROMANISM. 8vo. 10s. 6d.

BUTLER (Rev. Geo.).—SERMONS PREACHED IN CHELTENHAM COLL. CHAPEL. Cr. 8vo. 7s. 6d.

CALDERWOOD (Rev. Prof.).—THE RELATIONS OF SCIENCE AND RELIGION. Cr. 8vo. 5s
—— THE PARABLES OF OUR LORD. Cr. 8vo.

CAMPBELL (Dr. John M'Leod).—THE NATURE OF THE ATONEMENT. Cr. 8vo. 6s.
—— REMINISCENCES AND REFLECTIONS. Edited by his Son, DONALD CAMPBELL, M.A. Cr. 8vo. 7s. 6d.
—— THOUGHTS ON REVELATION. Cr. 8vo. 5s.
—— RESPONSIBILITY FOR THE GIFT OF ETERNAL LIFE. Compiled from Sermons preached 1829—31. Cr. 8vo. 5s.

CANTERBURY (Edward White, Archbishop of).—BOY-LIFE: ITS TRIAL, ITS STRENGTH, ITS FULNESS. Sundays in Wellington College, 1859—73. Cr. 8vo. 6s.
—— THE SEVEN GIFTS. Primary Visitation Address. Cr. 8vo. 6s.
—— CHRIST AND HIS TIMES. Second Visitation Address. Cr. 8vo. 6s.
—— A PASTORAL LETTER TO THE DIOCESE OF CANTERBURY, 1890. 8vo, sewed. 1d.

CARPENTER (W. Boyd, Bishop of Ripon).—TRUTH IN TALE. Addresses, chiefly to Children. Cr. 8vo. 4s. 6d.
—— THE PERMANENT ELEMENTS OF RELIGION. 2nd Edit. Cr. 8vo. 6s.

CAZENOVE (J. Gibson).—CONCERNING THE BEING AND ATTRIBUTES OF GOD. 8vo. 5s.

CHURCH (Dean).—HUMAN LIFE AND ITS CONDITIONS. Cr. 8vo. 6s.
—— THE GIFTS OF CIVILISATION: and other Sermons and Letters. Cr. 8vo. 7s. 6d.
—— DISCIPLINE OF THE CHRISTIAN CHARACTER; and other Sermons. Cr. 8vo. 4s. 6d.
—— ADVENT SERMONS, 1885. Cr. 8vo. 4s. 6d.
—— VILLAGE SERMONS. Cr. 8vo.

CLERGYMAN'S SELF-EXAMINATION CONCERNING THE APOSTLES' CREED. Ext. fcp. 8vo. 1s. 6d.

CONGREVE (Rev. John).—HIGH HOPES AND PLEADINGS FOR A REASONABLE FAITH, NOBLER THOUGHTS, AND LARGER CHARITY. Cr. 8vo. 5s.

THEOLOGY.

Sermons, Lectures, Addresses, and Theological Essays—*continued*.

COOKE (Josiah P., jun.).—RELIGION AND CHEMISTRY. Cr. 8vo. 7s. 6d.

COTTON (Bishop).—SERMONS PREACHED TO ENGLISH CONGREGATIONS IN INDIA. Cr. 8vo. 7s. 6d.

CUNNINGHAM (Rev. W.).—CHRISTIAN CIVILISATION, WITH SPECIAL REFERENCE TO INDIA. Cr. 8vo. 5s.

CURTEIS (Rev. G. H.).—THE SCIENTIFIC OBSTACLES TO CHRISTIAN BELIEF. The Boyle Lectures, 1884. Cr. 8vo. 6s.

DAVIES (Rev. J. Llewelyn).—THE GOSPEL AND MODERN LIFE. Ext. fcp. 8vo. 6s.
— SOCIAL QUESTIONS FROM THE POINT OF VIEW OF CHRISTIAN THEOLOGY. Cr.8vo. 6s.
— WARNINGS AGAINST SUPERSTITION. Ext. fcp. 8vo. 2s. 6d.
— THE CHRISTIAN CALLING. Ext.fp.8vo. 6s.
— ORDER AND GROWTH AS INVOLVED IN THE SPIRITUAL CONSTITUTION OF HUMAN SOCIETY. Cr. 8vo. 3s. 6d.
— BAPTISM, CONFIRMATION, AND THE LORD'S SUPPER. Addresses. 18mo. 1s.

DIGGLE (Rev. J. W.).—GODLINESS AND MANLINESS. Cr. 8vo. 6s.

DRUMMOND (Prof. Jas.).—INTRODUCTION TO THE STUDY OF THEOLOGY. Cr. 8vo. 5s.

ECCE HOMO: A SURVEY OF THE LIFE AND WORK OF JESUS CHRIST. Globe 8vo. 6s.

ELLERTON (Rev. John).—THE HOLIEST MANHOOD, AND ITS LESSONS FOR BUSY LIVES. Cr. 8vo. 6s.

FAITH AND CONDUCT: AN ESSAY ON VERIFIABLE RELIGION. Cr. 8vo. 7s. 6d.

FARRAR (Ven. Archdeacon).—WORKS, *Uniform Edition*. Cr. 8vo. 3s. 6d. each. Monthly from December, 1891.
SEEKERS AFTER GOD.
ETERNAL HOPE. Westminster Abbey Sermons.
THE FALL OF MAN: and other Sermons.
THE WITNESS OF HISTORY TO CHRIST. Hulsean Lectures, 1870.
THE SILENCE AND VOICES OF GOD: Sermons.
IN THE DAYS OF THY YOUTH. Marlborough College Sermons.
SAINTLY WORKERS. Five Lenten Lectures.
EPHPHATHA; or, The Amelioration of the World.
MERCY AND JUDGMENT.
SERMONS AND ADDRESSES DELIVERED IN AMERICA.
— THE HISTORY OF INTERPRETATION. Bampton Lectures, 1885. 8vo. 16s.

FISKE (John).—MAN'S DESTINY VIEWED IN THE LIGHT OF HIS ORIGIN. Cr. 8vo. 3s. 6d.

FORBES (Rev. Granville).—THE VOICE OF GOD IN THE PSALMS. Cr. 8vo. 6s. 6d.

FOWLE (Rev. T. W.).—A NEW ANALOGY BETWEEN REVEALED RELIGION AND THE COURSE AND CONSTITUTION OF NATURE. Cr. 8vo. 6s.

FRASER (Bishop).—SERMONS. Edited by JOHN W. DIGGLE. 2 vols. Cr. 8vo. 6s. each.

HAMILTON (John).—ON TRUTH AND ERROR. Cr. 8vo. 5s.
— ARTHUR'S SEAT; or, The Church of the Banned. Cr. 8vo. 6s.
— ABOVE AND AROUND: Thoughts on God and Man. 12mo. 2s. 6d.

HARDWICK (Archdeacon).—CHRIST AND OTHER MASTERS. 6th Edit. Cr. 8vo. 10s.6d.

HARE (Julius Charles).—THE MISSION OF THE COMFORTER. New Edition. Edited by Dean PLUMPTRE. Cr. 8vo. 7s. 6d.
— THE VICTORY OF FAITH. Edited by Dean PLUMPTRE. With Notices by Prof. MAURICE and Dean STANLEY. Cr. 8vo. 6s.6d.

HARPER (Father Thomas).—THE METAPHYSICS OF THE SCHOOL. Vols. I. and II. 8vo. 18s. each.—Vol. III. Part I. 12s.

HARRIS (Rev. G. C.).—SERMONS. With a Memoir by C. M. YONGE. Ext. fcp. 8vo. 6s.

HUTTON (R. H.). (*See* COLLECTED WORKS, p. 21.)

ILLINGWORTH (Rev. J. R.).—SERMONS PREACHED IN A COLLEGE CHAPEL. Cr.8vo. 5s.

JACOB (Rev. J. A.).—BUILDING IN SILENCE: and other Sermons. Ext. fcp. 8vo. 6s.

JAMES (Rev. Herbert). — THE COUNTRY CLERGYMAN AND HIS WORK. Cr. 8vo. 6s.

JEANS (Rev. G. E.).—HAILEYBURY CHAPEL: and other Sermons. Fcp. 8vo. 3s. 6d.

JELLETT (Rev. Dr.).—THE ELDER SON: and other Sermons. Cr. 8vo. 6s.
— THE EFFICACY OF PRAYER. Cr. 8vo. 5s.

KELLOGG (Rev. S. H.).—THE LIGHT OF ASIA AND THE LIGHT OF THE WORLD. Cr. 8vo. 7s. 6d.

KINGSLEY (Charles). (*See* COLLECTED WORKS, p. 21.)

KIRKPATRICK (Prof.).—THE DIVINE LIBRARY OF THE OLD TESTAMENT. Cr. 8vo. 3s. net.

KYNASTON (Rev. Herbert, D.D.).—CHELTENHAM COLLEGE SERMONS. Cr. 8vo. 6s.

LEGGE (A. O.).—THE GROWTH OF THE TEMPORAL POWER OF THE PAPACY. Cr.8vo. 8s.6d.

LIGHTFOOT (Bishop).—LEADERS IN THE NORTHERN CHURCH: Sermons. Cr. 8vo. 6s.
— ORDINATION ADDRESSES AND COUNSELS TO CLERGY. Cr. 8vo. 6s.
— CAMBRIDGE SERMONS. Cr. 8vo. 6s.
— SERMONS PREACHED IN ST. PAUL'S CATHEDRAL. Cr. 8vo. 6s.
— SERMONS ON SPECIAL OCCASIONS. 8vo. 6s.
— A CHARGE DELIVERED TO THE CLERGY OF THE DIOCESE OF DURHAM, 1886. 8vo. 2s.
— ESSAYS ON THE WORK ENTITLED "SUPERNATURAL RELIGION." 8vo. 10s. 6d.
— ON A FRESH REVISION OF THE ENGLISH NEW TESTAMENT. Cr. 8vo. 7s. 6d.

MACLAREN (Rev. A.).—SERMONS PREACHED AT MANCHESTER. 11th Ed. Fcp. 8vo. 4s. 6d.
— SECOND SERIES. 7th Ed. Fcp. 8vo 4s. 6d.
— THIRD SERIES. 6th Ed. Fcp. 8vo. 4s.6d.
— WEEK-DAY EVENING ADDRESSES. 4th Edit. Fcp. 8vo. 2s. 6d.
— THE SECRET OF POWER: and other Sermons. Fcp. 8vo. 4s. 6d.

SERMONS, LECTURES, ETC. 35

MACMILLAN (Rev. Hugh).—BIBLE TEACHINGS IN NATURE. 15th Edit. Globe 8vo. 6s.
—— THE TRUE VINE; or, The Analogies of our Lord's Allegory. 5th Edit. Gl. 8vo. 6s.
—— THE MINISTRY OF NATURE. 8th Edit. Globe 8vo. 6s.
—— THE SABBATH OF THE FIELDS. 6th Edit. Globe 8vo. 6s.
—— THE MARRIAGE IN CANA. Globe 8vo. 6s.
—— TWO WORLDS ARE OURS. Gl. 8vo. 6s.
—— THE OLIVE LEAF. Globe 8vo. 6s.
—— THE GATE BEAUTIFUL: and other Bible Teachings for the Young. Cr. 8vo. 3s. 6d.

MAHAFFY (Prof. J. P.).—THE DECAY OF MODERN PREACHING. Cr. 8vo. 3s. 6d.

MATURIN (Rev. W.).—THE BLESSEDNESS OF THE DEAD IN CHRIST. Cr. 8vo. 7s. 6d.

MAURICE (Frederick Denison).—THE KINGDOM OF CHRIST. 3rd Ed. 2 vols. Cr. 8vo. 12s.
—— EXPOSITORY SERMONS ON THE PRAYERBOOK, AND THE LORD'S PRAYER. Cr.8vo. 6s.
—— SERMONS PREACHED IN COUNTRY CHURCHES. 2nd Edit. Cr. 8vo. 6s.
—— THE CONSCIENCE: Lectures on Casuistry. 3rd Edit. Cr. 8vo. 4s. 6d.
—— DIALOGUES ON FAMILY WORSHIP. Cr. 8vo. 4s. 6d.
—— THE DOCTRINE OF SACRIFICE DEDUCED FROM THE SCRIPTURES. 2nd Edit. Cr.8vo. 6s.
—— THE RELIGIONS OF THE WORLD. 6th Edit. Cr. 8vo. 4s. 6d.
—— ON THE SABBATH DAY; THE CHARACTER OF THE WARRIOR; AND ON THE INTERPRETATION OF HISTORY. Fcp. 8vo. 2s. 6d.
—— LEARNING AND WORKING. Cr. 8vo. 4s.6d.
—— THE LORD'S PRAYER, THE CREED, AND THE COMMANDMENTS. 18mo. 1s.
—— THEOLOGICAL ESSAYS. Cr. 8vo. 6s.
—— SERMONS PREACHED IN LINCOLN'S INN CHAPEL. 6 vols. Cr. 8vo. 3s. 6d. each. Monthly, from Oct. 1891.

MILLIGAN (Rev. Prof. W.).—THE RESURRECTION OF OUR LORD. 2nd Edit. Cr.8vo. 5s.

MOORHOUSE (J., Bishop of Manchester).—JACOB: Three Sermons. Ext. fcp. 8vo. 3s.6d.
—— THE TEACHING OF CHRIST: its Conditions, Secret, and Results. Cr. 8vo. 3s. net.

MYLNE (L. G., Bishop of Bombay).—SERMONS PREACHED IN ST. THOMAS'S CATHEDRAL, BOMBAY. Cr. 8vo. 6s.

NATURAL RELIGION. By the Author of "Ecce Homo." 3rd Edit. Globe 8vo. 6s.

PATTISON (Mark).—SERMONS. Cr. 8vo. 6s.

PAUL OF TARSUS. 8vo. 10s. 6d.

PHILOCHRISTUS: MEMOIRS OF A DISCIPLE OF THE LORD. 3rd. Edit. 8vo. 12s.

PLUMPTRE (Dean).—MOVEMENTS IN RELIGIOUS THOUGHT. Fcp. 8vo. 3s. 6d.

POTTER (R.).—THE RELATION OF ETHICS TO RELIGION. Cr. 8vo. 2s. 6d.

REASONABLE FAITH: A SHORT ESSAY. By "Three Friends." Cr. 8vo. 1s.

REICHEL (C. P., Bishop of Meath).—THE LORD'S PRAYER. Cr. 8vo. 7s. 6d.
—— CATHEDRAL AND UNIVERSITY SERMONS. Cr. 8vo. 6s.

RENDALL (Rev. F.).—THE THEOLOGY OF THE HEBREW CHRISTIANS. Cr. 8vo. 5s.

REYNOLDS (H. R.).—NOTES OF THE CHRISTIAN LIFE. Cr. 8vo. 7s. 6d.

ROBINSON (Prebendary H. G.).—MAN IN THE IMAGE OF GOD: and other Sermons. Cr. 8vo. 7s. 6d.

RUSSELL(Dean).—THE LIGHT THAT LIGHTETH EVERY MAN: Sermons. With an Introduction by Dean PLUMPTRE, D.D. Cr.8vo. 6s.

SALMON (Rev. George, D.D.).—NON-MIRACULOUS CHRISTIANITY: and other Sermons. 2nd Edit. Cr. 8vo. 6s.
—— GNOSTICISM AND AGNOSTICISM: and other Sermons. Cr. 8vo. 7s. 6d.

SCOTCH SERMONS, 1880. By Principal CAIRD and others. 3rd Edit. 8vo. 10s. 6d.

SERVICE (Rev. J.).—SERMONS. Cr. 8vo. 6s.

SHIRLEY (W. N.).—ELIJAH: Four University Sermons. Fcp. 8vo. 2s. 6d.

SMITH (Rev. Travers).—MAN'S KNOWLEDGE OF MAN AND OF GOD. Cr. 8vo. 6s.

SMITH (W. Saumarez).—THE BLOOD OF THE NEW COVENANT: An Essay. Cr. 8vo. 2s.6d.

STANLEY (Dean).--THE NATIONAL THANKSGIVING. Sermons Preached in Westminster Abbey. and Edit. Cr. 8vo. 2s. 6d.
—— ADDRESSES AND SERMONS delivered in America, 1878. Cr. 8vo. 6s.
—— THE ATHANASIAN CREED. Cr. 8vo. 2s.

STEWART (Prof. Balfour) and TAIT (Prof. P. G.).—THE UNSEEN UNIVERSE, OR PHYSICAL SPECULATIONS ON A FUTURE STATE. 15th Edit. Cr. 8vo. 6s.
—— PARADOXICAL PHILOSOPHY: A Sequel to the above. Cr. 8vo. 7s. 6d.

STUBBS (Rev. C. W.).—FOR CHRIST AND CITY. Sermons and Addresses. Cr. 8vo. 6s.

TAIT (Archbp.).—THE PRESENT CONDITION OF THE CHURCH OF ENGLAND. Primary Visitation Charge. 3rd Edit. 8vo. 3s. 6d.
—— DUTIES OF THE CHURCH OF ENGLAND. Second Visitation Addresses. 8vo. 4s. 6d.
—— THE CHURCH OF THE FUTURE. Quadrennial Visitation Charges. Cr. 8vo. 3s. 6d.

TAYLOR (Isaac).—THE RESTORATION OF BELIEF. Cr. 8vo. 8s. 6d.

TEMPLE (Frederick, Bishop of London).—SERMONS PREACHED IN THE CHAPEL OF RUGBY SCHOOL. Ext. fcp. 8vo. 4s. 6d.
—— SECOND SERIES. Ext. fcp. 8vo. 6s.
—— THIRD SERIES. 4th Edit. Ext. fcp.8vo. 6s.
—— THE RELATIONS BETWEEN RELIGION AND SCIENCE. Bampton Lectures, 1884. 7th and Cheaper Edition. Cr. 8vo. 6s.

TRENCH (Archbishop). — THE HULSEAN LECTURES FOR 1845—6. 8vo. 7s. 6d.

TULLOCH (Principal).—THE CHRIST OF THE GOSPELS AND THE CHRIST OF MODERN CRITICISM. Ext. fcp. 8vo. 4s. 6d.

VAUGHAN (C. J., Dean of Landaff).—MEMORIALS OF HARROW SUNDAYS. 8vo. 10s.6d.
—— EPIPHANY, LENT, AND EASTER. 8vo. 10s.6d.
—— HEROES OF FAITH. 2nd Edit. Cr. 8vo. 6s.
—— WORDS FROM THE GOSPELS. 3rd Edit. Fcp. 8vo. 4s. 6d.

THEOLOGY.
Sermons, Lectures, Addresses, and Theological Essays—*continued.*

VAUGHAN (Dr. C. J.).—Life's Work and God's Discipline. Ext. fcp. 8vo. 2s. 6d.
— The Wholesome Words of Jesus Christ. 2nd Edit. Fcp. 8vo. 3s. 6d.
— Foes of Faith. 2nd Edit. Fcp. 8vo. 3s. 6d.
— Christ Satisfying the Instincts of Humanity. 2nd Edit. Ext. fcp. 8vo. 3s. 6d.
— Counsels for Young Students. Fcp. 8vo. 2s. 6d.
— The Two Great Temptations. 2nd Edit. Fcp. 8vo. 3s. 6d.
— Addresses for Young Clergymen. Ext. fcp. 8vo. 4s. 6d.
— "My Son, Give Me Thine Heart." Ext. fcp. 8vo. 5s.
— Rest Awhile. Addresses to Toilers in the Ministry. Ext. fcp. 8vo. 5s.
— Temple Sermons. Cr. 8vo. 10s. 6d.
— Authorised or Revised? Sermons on some of the Texts in which the Revised Version differs from the Authorised. Cr. 8vo. 7s. 6d.
— Lessons of the Cross and Passion; Words from the Cross; The Reign of Sin; The Lord's Prayer. Four Courses of Lent Lectures. Cr. 8vo. 10s. 6d.
— University Sermons, New and Old. Cr. 8vo. 10s. 6d.
— Notes for Lectures on Confirmation. 14th Edit. Fcp. 8vo. 1s. 6d.

VAUGHAN (Rev. D. J.).—The Present Trial of Faith. Cr. 8vo. 9s.

VAUGHAN (Rev. E. T.)—Some Reasons of our Christian Hope. Hulsean Lectures for 1875. Cr. 8vo. 6s. 6d.

VAUGHAN (Rev. Robert).—Stones from the Quarry. Sermons. Cr. 8vo. 5s.

VENN (Rev. John).—On some Characteristics of Belief, Scientific, and Religious. Hulsean Lectures, 1869. 8vo. 6s. 6d.

WARINGTON (G.).—The Week of Creation. Cr. 8vo. 4s. 6d.

WELLDON (Rev. J. E. C.).—The Spiritual Life: and other Sermons. Cr. 8vo. 6s.

WESTCOTT (Rt. Rev. B. F., Bishop of Durham).—On the Religious Office of the Universities. Sermons. Cr. 8vo. 4s. 6d.
— Gifts for Ministry. Addresses to Candidates for Ordination. Cr. 8vo. 1s. 6d.
— The Victory of the Cross. Sermons Preached in 1888. Cr. 8vo. 3s. 6d.
— From Strength to Strength. Three Sermons (In Memoriam J. B. D.). Cr. 8vo. 2s.
— The Revelation of the Risen Lord. 4th Edit. Cr. 8vo. 6s.
— The Historic Faith. Cr. 8vo. 6s.
— The Gospel of the Resurrection. 6th Edit. Cr. 8vo. 6s.
— The Revelation of the Father. Cr. 8vo. 6s.
— Christus Consummator. Cr. 8vo. 6s.
— Some Thoughts from the Ordinal. Cr. 8vo. 1s. 6d.
— Social Aspects of Christianity. Cr. 8vo. 6s.
— Essays in the History of Religious Thought in the West. Globe 8vo. 6s.

WICKHAM (Rev. E. C.).—Wellington College Sermons. Cr. 8vo. 6s.

WILKINS (Prof. A. S.).—The Light of the World: An Essay. 2nd Ed. Cr. 8vo. 3s. 6d.

WILSON (J. M., Archdeacon of Manchester).—Sermons Preached in Clifton College Chapel. Second Series. 1888—90. Cr. 8vo. 6s.
— Essays and Addresses. Cr. 8vo. 4s. 6d.
— Some Contributions to the Religious Thought of our Time. Cr. 8vo. 6s.

WOOD (Rev. E. G.).—The Regal Power of the Church. 8vo. 4s. 6d.

TRANSLATIONS.
From the Greek—From the Italian—From the Latin—Into Latin and Greek Verse.

From the Greek.

AESCHYLUS.—The Supplices. With Translation, by T. G. Tucker, Litt.D. 8vo. 10s. 6d.
— The Seven against Thebes. With Translation, by A. W. Verrall, Litt. D. 8vo. 7s. 6d.
— Eumenides. With Verse Translation, by Bernard Drake, M.A. 8vo. 5s.

ARATUS. (*See* Physiography.)

ARISTOPHANES.—The Birds. Trans. into English Verse, by B. H. Kennedy. 8vo. 6s.

ARISTOTLE ON FALLACIES; or, The Sophistici Elenchi. With Translation, by E. Poste, M.A. 8vo. 8s. 6d.

ARISTOTLE.—The First Book of the Metaphysics of Aristotle. By a Cambridge Graduate. 8vo. 5s.
— The Politics. By J. E. C. Welldon, M.A. 10s. 6d.
— The Rhetoric. By same. Cr. 8vo. 7s. 6d.
— On the Constitution of Athens. By E. Poste. Cr. 8vo. 3s. 6d.

BION. (*See* Theocritus.)

HERODOTUS.—The History. By G. C. Macaulay, M.A. 2 vols. Cr. 8vo. 18s.

HOMER.—The Odyssey done into English Prose, by S. H. Butcher, M.A., and A. Lang, M.A. Cr. 8vo. 6s.
— The Odyssey. Books I.—XII. Transl. into English Verse by Earl of Carnarvon. Cr. 8vo. 7s. 6d.
— The Iliad done into English Prose, by Andrew Lang, Walter Leaf, and Ernest Myers. Cr. 8vo. 12s. 6d.

MELEAGER.—Fifty Poems. Translated into English Verse by Walter Headlam. Fcp. 4to. 7s. 6d.

MOSCHUS. (*See* Theocritus).

PINDAR.—The Extant Odes. By Ernest Myers. Cr. 8vo. 5s.

PLATO.—Timæus. With Translation, by R. D. Archer-Hind, M.A. 8vo. 16s. (*See also* Golden Treasury Series, p. 20.)

POLYBIUS.—The Histories. By E. S. Shuckburgh. Cr. 8vo. 24s.

SOPHOCLES.—Œdipus the King. Translated into English Verse by E. D. A. Morshead, M.A. Fcp. 8vo. 3s. 6d.

THEOCRITUS, BION, and MOSCHUS. By A. Lang, M.A. 18mo. 4s. 6d.—Large Paper Edition. 8vo. 9s.

VOYAGES AND TRAVELS.

XENOPHON.—THE COMPLETE WORKS. By H. G. DAKYNS, M.A. Cr. 8vo.—Vol. I. THE ANABASIS AND BOOKS I. AND II. OF THE HELLENICA. 10s. 6d.
[Vol. II. in the Press.

From the Italian.

DANTE.—THE PURGATORY. With Transl. and Notes, by A. J. BUTLER. Cr. 8vo. 12s. 6d.
—— THE PARADISE. By the same. 2nd Edit. Cr. 8vo. 12s. 6d.
—— THE INFERNO. By the same. Cr. 8vo.
—— DE MONARCHIA. By F. J. CHURCH. 8vo. 4s. 6d.
—— THE DIVINE COMEDY. By C. E. NORTON. I. HELL. Cr. 8vo. 6s.

From the Latin.

CICERO.—THE LIFE AND LETTERS OF MARCUS TULLIUS CICERO. By the Rev. G. E. JEANS, M.A. 2nd Edit. Cr. 8vo. 10s. 6d.
—— THE ACADEMICS. By J. S. REID. 8vo. 5s. 6d.
HORACE: THE WORKS OF. By J. LONSDALE, M.A., and S. LEE, M.A. Gl. 8vo. 3s. 6d.
—— THE ODES IN A METRICAL PARAPHRASE. By R. M. HOVENDEN, B.A. Ext. fcp. 8vo. 4s. 6d.
—— LIFE AND CHARACTER: AN EPITOME OF HIS SATIRES AND EPISTLES. By R. M. HOVENDEN, B.A. Ext. fcp. 8vo. 4s. 6d.
—— WORD FOR WORD FROM HORACE: The Odes Literally Versified. By W. T. THORNTON, C.B. Cr. 8vo. 7s. 6d.
JUVENAL.—THIRTEEN SATIRES. By ALEX. LEEPER, LL.D. Cr. 8vo. 3s. 6d.
LIVY.—BOOKS XXI.—XXV. THE SECOND PUNIC WAR. By A. J. CHURCH, M.A., and W. J. BRODRIBB, M.A. Cr. 8vo. 7s. 6d.
MARCUS AURELIUS ANTONINUS.— BOOK IV. OF THE MEDITATIONS. With Translation and Commentary, by H. CROSSLEY, M.A. 8vo. 6s.
SALLUST.—THE CONSPIRACY OF CATILINE AND THE JUGURTHINE WAR. By A. W. POLLARD. Cr. 8vo. 6s.—CATILINE. 3s.
TACITUS, THE WORKS OF. By A. J. CHURCH, M.A., and W. J. BRODRIBB, M.A. THE HISTORY. 4th Edit. Cr. 8vo. 6s.
THE AGRICOLA AND GERMANIA. With the Dialogue on Oratory. Cr. 8vo. 4s. 6d.
THE ANNALS. 5th Edit. Cr. 8vo. 7s. 6d.
VIRGIL: THE WORKS OF. By J. LONSDALE, M.A., and S. LEE, M.A. Globe 8vo. 3s. 6d.
—— THE ÆNEID. By J. W. MACKAIL, M.A. Cr. 8vo. 7s. 6d.

Into Latin and Greek Verse.

CHURCH (Rev. A. J.).—LATIN VERSION OF SELECTIONS FROM TENNYSON. By Prof. CONINGTON, Prof. SEELEY, Dr. HESSEY, T. E. KEBBEL, &c. Edited by A. J. CHURCH, M.A. Ext. fcp. 8vo. 6s.
GEDDES (Prof. W. D.).—FLOSCULI GRÆCI BOREALES. Cr. 8vo. 6s.
KYNASTON (Herbert D.D.).—EXEMPLARIA CHELTONIENSIA. Ext. fcp. 8vo. 5s.

VOYAGES AND TRAVELS.

(See also HISTORY; SPORT.)

APPLETON (T. G.).—A NILE JOURNAL. Illustrated by EUGENE BENSON. Cr. 8vo. 6s.
"BACCHANTE." THE CRUISE OF H.M.S. "BACCHANTE," 1879—1882. Compiled from the Private Journals, Letters and Note-books of PRINCE ALBERT VICTOR and PRINCE GEORGE OF WALES. By the Rev. Canon DALTON. 2 vols. Med. 8vo. 52s. 6d.
BAKER (Sir Samuel W.).—ISMAILIA. A Narrative of the Expedition to Central Africa for the Suppression of the Slave Trade, organised by ISMAIL, Khedive of Egypt. Cr. 8vo. 6s.
—— THE NILE TRIBUTARIES OF ABYSSINIA, AND THE SWORD HUNTERS OF THE HAMRAN ARABS. Cr. 8vo. 6s.
—— THE ALBERT N'YANZA GREAT BASIN OF THE NILE AND EXPLORATION OF THE NILE SOURCES. Cr. 8vo. 6s.
—— CYPRUS AS I SAW IT IN 1879. 8vo. 12s. 6d.
BARKER (Lady).—A YEAR'S HOUSEKEEPING IN SOUTH AFRICA. Illustr. Cr. 8vo. 3s. 6d.
—— STATION LIFE IN NEW ZEALAND. Cr. 8vo. 3s. 6d.
—— LETTERS TO GUY. Cr. 8vo. 5s.
BOUGHTON (G. H.) and ABBEY (E. A.).— SKETCHING RAMBLES IN HOLLAND. With Illustrations. Fcp. 4to. 21s.
BRYCE (James, M.P.). — TRANSCAUCASIA AND ARARAT. 3rd Edit. Cr. 8vo. 9s.
CAMERON (V. L.).—OUR FUTURE HIGHWAY TO INDIA. 2 vols. Cr. 8vo. 21s.
CAMPBELL (J. F.).—MY CIRCULAR NOTES. Cr. 8vo. 6s.
CARLES (W. R.).—LIFE IN COREA. 8vo. 12s. 6d.
CAUCASUS: NOTES ON THE. By "WANDERER." 8vo. 9s.
CRAIK (Mrs.).—AN UNKNOWN COUNTRY. Illustr. by F. NOEL PATON. Roy. 8vo. 7s. 6d.
—— AN UNSENTIMENTAL JOURNEY THROUGH CORNWALL. Illustrated. 4to. 12s. 6d.
DILKE (Sir Charles). (See POLITICS.)
DUFF (Right Hon. Sir M. E. Grant).—NOTES OF AN INDIAN JOURNEY. 8vo. 10s. 6d.
FORBES (Archibald).—SOUVENIRS OF SOME CONTINENTS. Cr. 8vo. 6s.
—— BATTLES, BIVOUACS, AND BARRACKS. Cr. 8vo. 7s. 6d.
FULLERTON (W. M.).—IN CAIRO. Fcp. 8vo. 3s. 6d.
GONE TO TEXAS: LETTERS FROM OUR BOYS. Ed. by THOS. HUGHES. Cr. 8vo. 4s. 6d.
GORDON (Lady Duff). — LAST LETTERS FROM EGYPT, TO WHICH ARE ADDED LETTERS FROM THE CAPE. 2nd Edit. Cr. 8vo. 9s.
GREEN (W. S.).—AMONG THE SELKIRK GLACIERS. Cr. 8vo. 7s. 6d.
HOOKER (Sir Joseph D.) and BALL (J.).— JOURNAL OF A TOUR IN MAROCCO AND THE GREAT ATLAS. 8vo. 21s.
HÜBNER (Baron von).—A RAMBLE ROUND THE WORLD. Cr. 8vo. 6s.
HUGHES (Thos.).—RUGBY, TENNESSEE. Cr. 8vo. 4s. 6d.
KINGSLEY (Charles).—AT LAST: A Christmas in the West Indies. Cr. 8vo. 3s. 6d.

VOYAGES AND TRAVELS—BOOKS FOR THE YOUNG.

VOYAGES AND TRAVELS—*continued.*

KINGSLEY (Henry).— TALES OF OLD TRAVEL. Cr. 8vo. 3s. 6d.

KIPLING (J. L.).—BEAST AND MAN IN INDIA. Illustrated. 8vo. 21s.

MACMILLAN (Rev. Hugh).—HOLIDAYS ON HIGH LANDS; or, Rambles and Incidents in Search of Alpine Plants. Globe 8vo. 6s.

MAHAFFY (Prof. J. P.).—RAMBLES AND STUDIES IN GREECE. Illust. Cr. 8vo. 10s. 6d.

MAHAFFY (Prof. J. P.) and ROGERS (J. E.).—SKETCHES FROM A TOUR THROUGH HOLLAND AND GERMANY. Illustrated by J. E. ROGERS. Ext. cr. 8vo. 10s. 6d.

MURRAY (E. C. Grenville).—ROUND ABOUT FRANCE. Cr. 8vo. 7s. 6d.

NORDENSKIÖLD. — VOYAGE OF THE "VEGA" ROUND ASIA AND EUROPE. By Baron A. E. VON NORDENSKIÖLD. Trans. by ALEX. LESLIE. 400 Illustrations, Maps, etc. 2 vols. 8vo. 45s.—*Popular Edit.* Cr. 8vo. 6s.

—— THE ARCTIC VOYAGES OF ADOLPH ERIC NORDENSKIÖLD, 1858—79. By ALEXANDER LESLIE. 8vo. 16s.

OLIPHANT (Mrs.). (*See* HISTORY.)

OLIVER (Capt. S. P.).—MADAGASCAR: AN HISTORICAL AND DESCRIPTIVE ACCOUNT OF THE ISLAND AND ITS FORMER DEPENDENCIES. 2 vols. Med. 8vo. 52s. 6d.

PALGRAVE (W. Gifford.)—A NARRATIVE OF A YEAR'S JOURNEY THROUGH CENTRAL AND EASTERN ARABIA, 1862-63. Cr. 8vo. 6s.

—— DUTCH GUIANA. 8vo. 9s.

—— ULYSSES; or, Scenes and Studies in many Lands. 8vo. 12s. 6d.

PERSIA, EASTERN. AN ACCOUNT OF THE JOURNEYS OF THE PERSIAN BOUNDARY COMMISSION, 1870-71-72. 2 vols. 8vo. 42s.

ST. JOHNSTON (A.).—CAMPING AMONG CANNIBALS. Cr. 8vo. 4s. 6d.

SANDYS (J. E.).—AN EASTER VACATION IN GREECE. Cr. 8vo. 3s. 6d.

STRANGFORD (Viscountess). — EGYPTIAN SEPULCHRES AND SYRIAN SHRINES. New Edition. Cr. 8vo. 7s. 6d.

TAVERNIER (Baron): TRAVELS IN INDIA OF JEAN BAPTISTE TAVERNIER. Transl. by V. BALL, LL.D. 2 vols. 8vo. 42s.

TRISTRAM. (*See* ILLUSTRATED BOOKS.)

TURNER (Rev. G.). (*See* ANTHROPOLOGY.)

WALLACE (A. R.). (*See* NATURAL HISTORY.)

WATERTON (Charles).—WANDERINGS IN SOUTH AMERICA, THE NORTH-WEST OF THE UNITED STATES, AND THE ANTILLES. Edited by Rev. J. G. WOOD. Illustr. Cr. 8vo. 6s.—*People's Edition.* 4to. 6d.

WATSON (R. Spence).—A VISIT TO WAZAN, THE SACRED CITY OF MOROCCO. 8vo. 10s. 6d.

YOUNG, Books for the.

(*See also* BIBLICAL HISTORY, p. 30.)

ÆSOP—CALDECOTT.—SOME OF ÆSOP'S FABLES, with Modern Instances, shown in Designs by RANDOLPH CALDECOTT. 4to. 5s.

ARIOSTO.—PALADIN AND SARACEN. Stories from Ariosto. By H. C. HOLLWAY-CALTHROP. Illustrated. Cr. 8vo. 6s.

ATKINSON (Rev. J. C.).—THE LAST OF THE GIANT KILLERS. Globe 8vo. 3s. 6d.

AWDRY (Frances).—THE STORY OF A FELLOW SOLDIER. (A Life of Bishop Patteson for the Young.) Globe 8vo. 2s. 6d.

BAKER (Sir Samuel White).—TRUE TALES FOR MY GRANDSONS. Illustrated by W. J. HENNESSY. Cr. 8vo. 3s. 6d.

—— CAST UP BY THE SEA: OR, THE ADVENTURES OF NED GRAY. Illustrated by HUARD. Cr. 8vo. 6s.

BUMBLEBEE BOGO'S BUDGET. By a RETIRED JUDGE. Illustrated by ALICE HAVERS. Cr. 8vo. 2s. 6d.

CARROLL (Lewis).—ALICE'S ADVENTURES IN WONDERLAND. With 42 Illustrations by TENNIEL. Cr. 8vo. 6s. net.

People's Edition. With all the original Illustrations. Cr. 8vo. 2s. 6d. net.

A GERMAN TRANSLATION OF THE SAME. Cr. 8vo. 6s. net.

A FRENCH TRANSLATION OF THE SAME. Cr. 8vo. 6s. net.

AN ITALIAN TRANSLATION OF THE SAME. Cr. 8vo. 6s. net.

—— ALICE'S ADVENTURES UNDER-GROUND. Being a Facsimile of the Original MS. Book, afterwards developed into "Alice's Adventures in Wonderland." With 27 Illustrations by the Author. Cr. 8vo. 4s. net.

—— THROUGH THE LOOKING-GLASS AND WHAT ALICE FOUND THERE. With 50 Illustrations by TENNIEL. Cr. 8vo. 6s. net.

People's Edition. With all the original Illustrations. Cr. 8vo. 2s. 6d. net.

People's Edition of "Alice's Adventures in Wonderland," and "Through the Looking-Glass." 1 vol. Cr. 8vo. 4s. 6d. net.

—— RHYME? AND REASON? With 65 Illustrations by ARTHUR B. FROST, and 9 by HENRY HOLIDAY. Cr. 8vo. 6s. net.

—— A TANGLED TALE. With 6 Illustrations by ARTHUR B. FROST. Cr. 8vo. 4s. 6d. net.

—— SYLVIE AND BRUNO. With 46 Illustrations by HARRY FURNISS. Cr. 8vo. 7s. 6d. net.

—— THE NURSERY "ALICE." Twenty Coloured Enlargements from TENNIEL'S Illustrations to "Alice's Adventures in Wonderland," with Text adapted to Nursery Readers. 4to. 4s. net.

People's Edition. 4to. 2s. net.

—— THE HUNTING OF THE SNARK, AN AGONY IN EIGHT FITS. With 9 Illustrations by HENRY HOLIDAY. Cr. 8vo. 4s. 6d. net.

CLIFFORD (Mrs. W. K.).—ANYHOW STORIES. With Illustrations by DOROTHY TENNANT. Cr. 8vo. 1s. 6d.; paper covers, 1s.

CORBETT (Julian).—FOR GOD AND GOLD. Cr. 8vo. 6s.

CRAIK (Mrs.).—ALICE LEARMONT: A FAIRY TALE. Illustrated. Globe 8vo. 4s. 6d.

—— THE ADVENTURES OF A BROWNIE. Illustrated by Mrs. ALLINGHAM. Gl. 8vo. 4s. 6d.

—— THE LITTLE LAME PRINCE AND HIS TRAVELLING CLOAK. Illustrated by J. McL. RALSTON. Cr. 8vo. 4s. 6d.

—— OUR YEAR: A CHILD'S BOOK IN PROSE AND VERSE. Illustrated. Gl. 8vo. 2s. 6d.

—— LITTLE SUNSHINE'S HOLIDAY. Globe 8vo. 2s. 6d.

—— THE FAIRY BOOK: THE BEST POPULAR FAIRY STORIES. 18mo. 4s. 6d.

—— CHILDREN'S POETRY. Ex. fcp. 8vo. 4s. 6d.

—— SONGS OF OUR YOUTH. Small 4to. 6s.

BOOKS FOR THE YOUNG—ZOOLOGY.

DE MORGAN (Mary).—THE NECKLACE OF PRINCESS FIORIMONDE, AND OTHER STORIES. Illustrated by WALTER CRANE. Ext. fcp. 8vo. 3s. 6d.—Large Paper Ed., with Illustrations on India Paper. 100 copies printed.

FOWLER (W. W.). (*See* NATURAL HISTORY.)

GREENWOOD (Jessy E.).—THE MOON MAIDEN: AND OTHER STORIES. Cr. 8vo. 3s. 6d.

GRIMM'S FAIRY TALES. Translated by LUCY CRANE, and Illustrated by WALTER CRANE. Cr. 8vo. 6s.

KEARY (A. and E.).—THE HEROES OF ASGARD. Tales from Scandinavian Mythology. Globe 8vo. 2s. 6d.

KEARY (E.).—THE MAGIC VALLEY. Illustr. by "E.V.B." Globe 8vo. 4s. 6d.

KINGSLEY (Charles).—THE HEROES; or, Greek Fairy Tales for my Children. Cr. 8vo. 3s. 6d.—*Presentation Ed.*, gilt edges. 7s. 6d.

MADAM HOW AND LADY WHY; or, First Lessons in Earth-Lore. Cr. 8vo. 3s. 6d.

THE WATER-BABIES: A Fairy Tale for a Land Baby. Cr. 8vo. 3s. 6d.—New Edition. Illustr. by LINLEY SAMBOURNE. Fcp. 4to. 12s. 6d.

MACLAREN (Arch.).—THE FAIRY FAMILY. A Series of Ballads and Metrical Tales. Cr. 8vo. 5s.

MACMILLAN (Hugh). (*See* p. 35.)

MADAME TABBY'S ESTABLISHMENT. By KARI. Illust. by L. WAIN. Cr. 8vo. 4s. 6d.

MAGUIRE (J. F.).—YOUNG PRINCE MARIGOLD. Illustrated. Globe 8vo. 4s. 6d.

MARTIN (Frances).—THE POET'S HOUR. Poetry selected for Children. 18mo. 2s. 6d.
—— SPRING-TIME WITH THE POETS. 18mo. 3s. 6d.

MAZINI (Linda).—IN THE GOLDEN SHELL. With Illustrations. Globe 8vo. 4s. 6d.

MOLESWORTH (Mrs.).—WORKS. Illust. by WALTER CRANE. Globe 8vo. 2s. 6d. each.
"CARROTS," JUST A LITTLE BOY.
A CHRISTMAS CHILD.
CHRISTMAS-TREE LAND.
THE CUCKOO CLOCK.
FOUR WINDS FARM.
GRANDMOTHER DEAR.
HERR BABY.
LITTLE MISS PEGGY.
THE RECTORY CHILDREN.
ROSY.
THE TAPESTRY ROOM.
TELL ME A STORY.
TWO LITTLE WAIFS.
"US": An Old-Fashioned Story.
CHILDREN OF THE CASTLE.
—— A CHRISTMAS POSY. Illustrated by WALTER CRANE. Cr. 8vo. 4s. 6d.
—— SUMMER STORIES. Cr. 8vo. 4s. 6d.
—— FOUR GHOST STORIES. Cr. 8vo. 6s.
—— NURSE HEATHERDALE'S STORY. Illust. by LESLIE BROOKE. Cr. 8vo. 4s. 6d.

"MRS. JERNINGHAM'S JOURNAL" (Author of).—THE RUNAWAY. Gl. 8vo. 2s. 6d.

OLIPHANT (Mrs.).—AGNES HOPETOUN'S SCHOOLS AND HOLIDAYS. Illust. Gl. 8vo. 2s. 6d.

PALGRAVE (Francis Turner).—THE FIVE DAYS' ENTERTAINMENTS AT WENTWORTH GRANGE. Small 4to. 6s.

—— THE CHILDREN'S TREASURY OF LYRICAL POETRY. 18mo. 2s. 6d.—Or in 2 parts, 1s. each.

PATMORE (C.).—THE CHILDREN'S GARLAND FROM THE BEST POETS. Globe 8vo. 2s.; 18mo, 2s. 6d. net.

ROSSETTI (Christina).—SPEAKING LIKENESSES. Illust. by A. HUGHES. Cr. 8vo. 4s. 6d.

RUTH AND HER FRIENDS: A STORY FOR GIRLS. Illustrated. Globe 8vo. 2s. 6d.

ST. JOHNSTON (A.).—CAMPING AMONG CANNIBALS. Cr. 8vo. 4s. 6d.
—— CHARLIE ASGARDE: THE STORY OF A FRIENDSHIP. Illustrated by HUGH THOMSON. Cr. 8vo. 4s. 6d.

"ST. OLAVE'S" (Author of). Illustrated. Globe 8vo.
WHEN I WAS A LITTLE GIRL. 2s. 6d.
NINE YEARS OLD. 2s. 6d.
WHEN PAPA COMES HOME. 4s. 6d.
PANSIE'S FLOUR BIN. 4s. 6d.

STEWART (Aubrey).—THE TALE OF TROY. Done into English. Globe 8vo. 3s. 6d.

TENNYSON (Hon. Hallam).—JACK AND THE BEAN-STALK. English Hexameters. Illust. by R. CALDECOTT. Fcp. 4to. 3s. 6d.

"WANDERING WILLIE" (Author of).—CONRAD THE SQUIRREL. Globe 8vo. 2s. 6d.

WARD (Mrs. T. Humphry).—MILLY AND OLLY. With Illustrations by Mrs. ALMA TADEMA. Globe 8vo. 2s. 6d.

WEBSTER (Augusta).—DAFFODIL AND THE CROÄXAXICANS. Cr. 8vo. 6s.

WILLOUGHBY (F.).—FAIRY GUARDIANS Illustr. by TOWNLEY GREEN. Cr. 8vo. 5s.

WOODS (M. A.). (*See* COLLECTIONS, p. 16.)

YONGE (Charlotte M.).—THE PRINCE AND THE PAGE. Cr. 8vo. 3s. 6d.
—— A BOOK OF GOLDEN DEEDS. 18mo. 4s. 6d.; Globe 8vo, 2s.—Abridged Edition. 18mo. 1s.
—— LANCES OF LYNWOOD. Cr. 8vo. 2s. 6d.
—— P's AND Q's; and LITTLE LUCY'S WONDERFUL GLOBE. Illustrated. Cr. 8vo. 3s. 6d.
—— A STOREHOUSE OF STORIES. 2 vols. Globe 8vo. 2s. 6d. each.
—— THE POPULATION OF AN OLD PEAR-TREE; or, Stories of Insect Life. From E. VAN BRUYSSEL. Illustr. Gl. 8vo. 2s. 6d.

ZOOLOGY.

Comparative Anatomy—Practical Zoology—Entomology—Ornithology.

(*See also* BIOLOGY; NATURAL HISTORY; PHYSIOLOGY.)

Comparative Anatomy.

FLOWER (Prof. W. H.).—AN INTRODUCTION TO THE OSTEOLOGY OF THE MAMMALIA. Illustrated. 3rd Edit., revised with the assistance of HANS GADOW, Ph.D. Cr. 8vo. 10s. 6d.

HUMPHRY (Prof. Sir G. M.).—OBSERVATIONS IN MYOLOGY. 8vo. 6s.

LANG (Prof. Arnold).—TEXT-BOOK OF COMPARATIVE ANATOMY. Transl. by H. M. and M. BERNARD. Preface by Prof. E. HAECKEL. Illustr. 2 vols. 8vo. Part I. 17s. net.

PARKER (T. Jeffery).—A COURSE OF INSTRUCTION IN ZOOTOMY (VERTEBRATA). Illustrated. Cr. 8vo. 8s. 6d.

ZOOLOGY.

Comparative Anatomy—*continued.*

PETTIGREW (J. Bell).—THE PHYSIOLOGY OF THE CIRCULATION IN PLANTS, IN THE LOWER ANIMALS, AND IN MAN. 8vo. 12s.

SHUFELDT (R. W.).—THE MYOLOGY OF THE RAVEN (*Corvus corax Sinuatus*). A Guide to the Study of the Muscular System in Birds. Illustrated. 8vo. 13s. net.

WIEDERSHEIM (Prof. R.).—ELEMENTS OF THE COMPARATIVE ANATOMY OF VERTEBRATES. Adapted by W. NEWTON PARKER. With Additions. Illustrated. 8vo. 12s. 6d.

Practical Zoology.

HOWES (Prof. G. B.).—AN ATLAS OF PRACTICAL ELEMENTARY BIOLOGY. With a Preface by Prof. HUXLEY. 4to. 14s.

HUXLEY (T. H.) and MARTIN (H. N.).—A COURSE OF PRACTICAL INSTRUCTION IN ELEMENTARY BIOLOGY. Revised and extended by Prof. G. B. HOWES and D. H. SCOTT, Ph.D. Cr. 8vo. 10s. 6d.

THOMSON (Sir C. Wyville).—THE VOYAGE OF THE "CHALLENGER": THE ATLANTIC. With Illustrations, Coloured Maps, Charts, etc. 2 vols. 8vo. 45s.

THOMSON (Sir C. Wyville).—THE DEPTHS OF THE SEA. An Account of the Results of the Dredging Cruises of H.M.SS. "Lightning" and "Porcupine," 1868-69-70. With Illustrations, Maps, and Plans. 8vo. 31s.6d.

Entomology.

BUCKTON (G. B.).—MONOGRAPH OF THE BRITISH CICADÆ, OR TETTIGIDÆ. In 8 Parts Quarterly. 8s. each net.—Part I. Jan. 1890. Vol. I. 33s. 6d. net.

LUBBOCK (Sir John).—THE ORIGIN AND METAMORPHOSES OF INSECTS. Illustrated. Cr. 8vo. 3s. 6d.

SCUDDER (S. H.).—FOSSIL INSECTS OF NORTH AMERICA. Map and Plates. 2 vols. 4to. 90s. net.

Ornithology.

COUES (Elliott).—KEY TO NORTH AMERICAN BIRDS. Illustrated. 8vo. 2l. 2s.

—— HANDBOOK OF FIELD AND GENERAL ORNITHOLOGY. Illustrated. 8vo. 10s. net.

FOWLER(W. W.). (*See* NATURAL HISTORY.)

WHITE (Gilbert). (*See* NATURAL HISTORY.)

INDEX.

	PAGE		PAGE		PAGE
ABBEY (E. A.)	37	ATTWELL (H.)	20	BERNARD (J. H.)	25
ABBOT (F. E.)	33	AUSTIN (Alfred)	14	BERNARD (M.)	12
ABBOTT (Rev. E.)	3, 13, 30, 31, 33	AUTENRIETH (Georg)	7	BERNERS (J.)	11
ACLAND (Sir H. W.)	22	AWDRY (F.)	38	BESANT (W.)	4
ADAMS (Sir F. O.)	28	BACON (Francis)	19, 20	BETHUNE-BAKER (J. F.)	33
ADAMS (Herbert B.)	28	BAINES (Rev. E.)	33	BETTANY (G. T.)	6
ADDISON	4, 20	BAKER (Sir S. W.)	28, 30, 37, 38	BICKERTON (T. H.)	22
AGASSIZ (L.)	3	BALCH (Elizabeth)	12	BIGELOW (M. M.)	12
AINGER (Rev. A.)	4, 16, 20, 33	BALDWIN (Prof. J. M.)	26	BIKÉLAS (D.)	17
AINSLIE (A. D.)	14	BALFOUR (Rt. Hon. A. J.)	25	BINNIE (Rev. W.)	33
AIRY (Sir G. B.)	2, 27	BALFOUR (F. M.)	5, 6	BIRKS (T. R.)	6, 25, 30, 33
AITKEN (Mary C.)	20	BALFOUR (J. B.)	6	BJÖRNSON (B.)	17
AITKEN (Sir W.)	23	BALL (V.)	38	BLACK (W.)	4
ALBEMARLE (Earl of)	3	BALL (W. Platt)	6	BLACKBURNE (E.)	3
ALDRICH (T. B.)	14	BALL (W. W. R.)	22	BLACKIE (J. S.)	9, 14, 19
ALEXANDER (C. F.)	20	BALLANCE (C. A.)	22	BLAKE (J. F.)	2
ALEXANDER (T.)	8	BARKER (Lady)	2, 8, 37	BLAKE (W.)	3
ALEXANDER (Bishop)	33	BARNARD (C.)	27	BLAKISTON (J. R.)	8
ALLBUTT (T. C.)	22	BARNES (W.)	3	BLANFORD (H. F.)	9, 27
ALLEN (G.)	6	BARRY (Bishop)	33	BLANFORD (W. T.)	9, 24
ALLINGHAM (W.)	20	BARTHOLOMEW (J. G.)	3	BLOMFIELD (R.)	9
AMIEL (H. F.)	3	BARTLETT (J.)	7	BLYTH (A. W.)	11
ANDERSON (A.)	14	BARWELL (R.)	22	BÖHM-BAWERK (Prof.)	28
ANDERSON (Dr. McCall)	22	BASTABLE (Prof. C. F.)	28	BOISSEVAIN (G. M.)	28
ANDREWS (Dr. Thomas)	26	BASTIAN (H. C.)	6, 22	BOLDREWOOD (Rolf)	17
APPLETON (T. G.)	37	BATESON (W.)	6	BONAR (J.)	28
ARCHER-HIND (R. D.)	36	BATH (Marquis of)	28	BOND (Rev. J.)	31
ARNOLD, M.	8, 14, 19, 20, 21, 30	BATHER (Archdeacon)	33	BOOLE (G.)	26
ARNOLD (Dr. T.)	9	BAXTER (L.)	3	BOUGHTON (G. H.)	37
ARNOLD (W. T.)	9	BEESLY (Mrs.)	9	BOUTMY (E.)	12
ASHLEY (W. J.)	28	BENHAM (Rev. W.)	5, 20, 32	BOWEN (H. C.)	25
ATKINSON (J. B.)	2	BENSON (Archbishop)	32, 33	BOWER (F. O.)	6
ATKINSON (Rev. J. C.)	1, 38	BERLIOZ (H.)	3	BRIDGES (J. A.)	19

INDEX.

	PAGE		PAGE		PAGE
Bright (H. A.)	9	Clarke (C. B.)	9, 28	Dillwyn (E. A.)	17
Bright (John)	28, 29	Clausius (R.)	27	Dobson (A.)	4
Brimley (G.)	19	Clifford (Ed.)	3	Donaldson (J.)	33
Brodie (Sir B. C.)	7	Clifford (W. K.)	19, 26	Donisthorpe (W.)	29
Brodribb (W. J.)	13, 37	Clifford (Mrs. W. K.)	38	Dowden (E.)	4, 13, 15
Brooke (Sir J.)	3	Clough (A. H.)	14, 19	Doyle (Sir F. H.)	14
Brooke (S. A.)	13, 14, 21, 33	Cobden (R.)	29	Doyle (J. A.)	10
Brooks (Bishop)	33	Cohen (J. B.)	7	Drake (B.)	36
Brown (A. C.)	26	Colenso (J. W.)	32	Drummond (Prof. J.)	34
Brown (J. A.)	1	Coleridge (S. T.)	14	Dryden	20
Brown (Dr. James)	4	Collier (Hon. John)	2	Du Cane (E. F.)	29
Brown (T. E.)	14	Collins (J. Churton)	19	Duff (Sir M.E.Grant)	20,29,37
Browne (J. H. B.)	11	Colquhoun (F. S.)	14	Dunsmuir (A.)	17
Browne (Sir T.)	20	Colvin (Sidney)	4, 20	Düntzer (H.)	4, 5
Browne (W. R.)	27	Combe (G.)	8	Dupré (A.)	7
Brunton (Dr. T. Lauder)	22, 33	Congreve (Rev. J.)	33	Dyer (L.)	1
Bryce (James)	9, 28, 37	Conway (Hugh)	17	Eadie (J.)	4, 30, 31
Buchheim (C. A.)	20	Cook (E. T.)	2	Eastlake (Lady)	32
Buckland (A.)	5	Cooke (C. Kinloch)	24	Ebers (G.)	17
Buckley (A. B)	9	Cooke (J. P.)	7, 34	Edgeworth (Prof. F. Y.)	28
Bucknill (Dr. J. C.)	22	Corbett (J.)	4, 17, 38	Edmunds (Dr. W.)	22
Buckton (G. B.)	40	Corfield (W. H.)	11	Edwards-Moss (Sir J. E.)	30
Bunyan	4, 19, 20	Corry (T. H.)	6	Eimer (G. H. T.)	6
Burgon (J. W.)	14	Cotterill (J. H.)	8	Elderton (W. A.)	9
Burke (E.)	28	Cotton (Bishop)	34	Ellerton (Rev. J.)	34
Burn (R.)	1	Cotton (C.)	12	Elliot (Hon. A.)	29
Burnett (F. Hodgson)	17	Cotton (J. S.)	29	Ellis (T.)	2
Burns	14, 20	Coues (E.)	40	Emerson (R. W.)	4, 20
Bury (J. B.)	9	Courthope (W. J.)	4	Evans (S.)	14
Butcher (Prof. S. H.)	13,19,36	Cowell (G.)	23	Everett (J. D.)	26
Butler (A. J.)	37	Cowper	20	Falconer (Lance)	17
Butler (Rev. G.)	33	Cox (G. V.)	9	Farrar (Archdeacon)	5, 30, 34
Butler (Samuel)	14	Craik (Mrs.)14, 17, 19, 20, 37, 38		Farrer (Sir T. H.)	29
Butler (W. Archer)	33	Craik (H.)	8, 29	Faulkner (F.)	7
Butler (Sir W. F.)	4	Crane (Lucy)	2, 39	Fawcett (Prof. H.)	28, 29
Byron	20	Crane (Walter)	39	Fawcett (M. G.)	5, 28
Cairnes (J. E.)	29	Craven (Mrs. D.)	8	Fay (Amy)	24
Caldecott (R.)	12, 38, 39	Crawford (F. M.)	17	Fearnley (W.)	27
Calderwood (Prof. H.)	8, 25, 26, 33	Creighton (Bishop M.)	4, 10	Fearon (D. R.)	8
		Crichton-Browne (Sir J.)	8	Ferrel (W.)	27
Calvert (Rev. A.)	31	Cross (J. A.)	30	Ferrers (N. M.)	27
Cameron (V. L.)	37	Crossley (E.)	2	Fessenden (C.)	26
Campbell (J. F.)	37	Crossley (H.)	37	Finck (H. T.)	1
Campbell (Dr. J. M.)	33	Cumming (L.)	26	Fisher (Rev. O.)	26, 27
Campbell (Prof. Lewis)	5, 13	Cunningham (C.)	28	Fiske (J.)	6, 10, 25, 29, 34
Capes (W. W.)	13	Cunningham (Sir H. S.)	17	Fison (L.)	1
Carles (W. R.)	37	Cunningham (Rev. J.)	31	Fitch (J. G.)	8
Carlyle (T.)	3	Cunningham (Rev. W.)	31, 33, 34	Fitz Gerald (Caroline)	14
Carmarthen (Lady)	17	Cunynghame (Sir A. T.)	24	Fitzgerald (Edward)	14, 20
Carnarvon (Earl of)	36	Curteis (Rev. G. H.)	32, 34	Fitzmaurice (Lord E.)	5
Carnot (N. L. G.)	27	Dahn (F.)	17	Fleay (F. G.)	13
Carpenter (Bishop)	33	Dakyns (H. G.)	37	Fleischer (E.)	7
Carr (J. C.)	2	Dale (A. W. W.)	31	Fleming (G.)	17
Carroll (Lewis)	26, 38	Dalton (Rev. J. N.)	37	Flower (Prof. W. H.)	39
Carter (R. Brudenell)	23	Dante	3, 13, 37	Flückiger (F. A.)	23
Cassel (Dr. D.)	9	Davies (Rev. J. Ll.)	20, 31, 34	Forbes (A.)	4, 37
Cautley (G. S.)	14	Davies (W.)	5	Forbes (Prof. G.)	3
Cazenove (J. G.)	33	Dawkins (W. B.)	1	Forbes (Rev. G. H.)	34
Chalmers (J. B.)	8	Dawson (G. M.)	9	Foster (Prof. M.)	6, 27
Chalmers (M. D.)	29	Dawson (Sir J. W.)	9	Fothergill (Dr. J. M.)	8, 23
Chapman (Elizabeth R.)	14	Dawson (J.)	1	Fowle (Rev. T. W.)	29, 34
Chasseresse (Diana)	30	Day (L. B.)	17	Fowler (Rev. T.)	4, 25
Cherry (R. R.)	12	Day (R. E.)	26	Fowler (W. W.)	24
Cheyne (C. H. H.)	2	Defoe (D.)	4, 20	Fox (Dr. Wilson)	23
Cheyne (T. K.)	30	Deighton (K.)	15	Foxwell (Prof. H. S)	28
Christie (J.)	23	Delamotte (P. H.)	2	Framji (D.)	10
Christie (W. D.)	20	Dell (E. C.)	12	Frankland (P. F.)	1
Church (Prof. A. H.)	6	De Morgan (M.)	39	Fraser (Bishop)	34
Church (Rev. A. J.)	4, 30, 37	De Vere (A.)	20	Fraser-Tytler (C. C.)	14
Church (F. J.)	20, 33	Dicey (A. V.)	12, 29	Frazer (J. G.)	1
Church (Dean)	3,4,13,19,31,33	Dickens (C.)	5, 17	Frederick (Mrs.)	8
Clark (J. W.)	20	Diggle (Rev. J. W.)	34	Freeman (Prof. E. A.)	2, 4, 10, 29, 32
Clark (L.)	2	Dilke (Ashton W.)	19		
Clark (S.)	3	Dilke (Sir Charles W.)	29	French (G. R.)	13

INDEX.

	PAGE
FRIEDMANN (P.)	3
FROST (A. B.)	38
FROUDE (J. A.)	4
FULLERTON (W. M.)	37
FURNISS (Harry)	38
FURNIVALL (F. J.)	14
FYFFE (C. A.)	10
FYFE (H. H.)	9
GAIRDNER (J.)	4
GALTON (F.)	1, 27
GAMGEE (Arthur)	27
GARDNER (Percy)	1
GARNETT (R.)	14
GARNETT (W.)	5
GASKELL (Mrs.)	12
GASKOIN (Mrs. H.)	30
GEDDES (W. D.)	13, 37
GEE (W. H.)	25, 27
GEIKIE (Sir A.)	4, 9, 27
GENNADIUS (J.)	17
GIBBINS (H. de B.)	10
GIBBON (Charles)	3
GILCHRIST (A.)	3
GILES (P.)	25
GILMAN (N. P.)	28
GILMORE (Rev. J.)	13
GLADSTONE (Dr. J. H.)	7, 8
GLADSTONE (W. E.)	13
GLAISTER (E.)	2, 8
GODFRAY (H.)	3
GODKIN (G. S.)	5
GOETHE	4, 14
GOLDSMITH	4, 12, 14, 20, 21
GOODALE (Prof. G. L.)	6
GOODFELLOW (J.)	11
GORDON (General C. G.)	4
GORDON (Lady Duff)	37
GOSCHEN (Rt. Hon. G. J.)	28
GOSSE (Edmund)	4, 13
GOW (J.)	1
GRAHAM (D.)	14
GRAHAM (J. W.)	17
GRAND'HOMME (E.)	8
GRAY (Prof. Andrew)	26
GRAY (Asa)	6
GRAY	4, 14, 21
GREEN (J. R.)	9, 10, 12, 20
GREEN (Mrs. J. R.)	4, 9, 10
GREEN (W. S.)	37
GREENHILL (W. A.)	20
GREENWOOD (J. E.)	39
GRIFFITHS (W. H.)	23
GRIMM	39
GROVE (Sir G.)	9, 24
GUEST (E.)	10
GUEST (M. J.)	10
GUILLEMIN (A.)	26, 27
GUIZOT (F. P. G.)	5
GUNTON (G.)	28
HALES (J. W.)	16, 20
HALLWARD (R. F.)	12
HAMERTON (P. G.)	2, 21
HAMILTON (Prof. D. J.)	23
HAMILTON (J.)	34
HANBURY (D.)	6, 23
HANNAY (David)	4
HARDWICK (Archd. C.)	31, 34
HARDY (A. S.)	17
HARDY (T.)	17
HARE (A. W.)	20
HARE (J. C.)	20, 34
HARPER (Father Thos.)	25, 34
HARRIS (Rev. G. C.)	34
HARRISON (F.)	4, 5, 21

	PAGE
HARRISON (Miss J.)	1
HARTE (Bret)	17
HARTIG (Dr. R.)	6
HARTLEY (Prof. W. N.)	7
HARWOOD (G.)	21, 29, 32
HAYES (A.)	14
HEADLAM (W.)	36
HELPS (Sir A.)	21
HEMPEL (Dr. W.)	7
HERODOTUS	36
HERRICK	20
HERTEL (Dr.)	8
HILL (F. Davenport)	29
HILL (O.)	29
HIORNS (A. H.)	23
HOBART (Lord)	21
HOBDAY (E.)	9
HODGSON (Rev. J. T.)	4
HOFFDING (Prof. H.)	26
HOFMANN (A. W.)	7
HOLE (Rev. C.)	7, 10
HOLIDAY (Henry)	38
HOLLAND (T. E.)	12, 29
HOLLWAY-CALTHROP (H.)	38
HOLMES (O. W., junr.)	12
HOMER	13, 36
HOOKER (Sir J. D.)	6, 37
HOOLE (C. H.)	30
HOOPER (G.)	4
HOOPER (W. H.)	2
HOPE (F. J.)	9
HOPKINS (E.)	14
HOPPUS (M. A. M.)	18
HORACE	13, 20
HORT (Prof. F. J. A.)	30, 32
HORTON (Hon. S. D.)	28
HOVENDEN (R. M.)	37
HOWELL (George)	28
HOWES (G. B.)	40
HOWITT (A. W.)	1
HOWSON (Very Rev. J. S.)	32
HOZIER (Col. H. M.)	24
HÜBNER (Baron)	37
HUGHES (T.)	4, 15, 18, 20, 37
HULL (E.)	2, 9
HULLAH (J.)	2, 20, 24
HUME (D.)	4
HUMPHRY (Prof. Sir G. M.)	28, 39
HUNT (W.)	10
HUNT (W. M.)	2
HUTTON (R. H.)	4, 21
HUXLEY (T.)	4, 21, 27, 28, 29, 40
IDDINGS (J. P.)	9
ILLINGWORTH (Rev. J. R.)	32
INGRAM (T. D.)	10
IRVING (J.)	9
IRVING (Washington)	12
JACKSON (Helen)	18
JACOB (Rev. J. A.)	34
JAMES (Henry)	4, 18, 20
JAMES (Rev. H. A.)	34
JAMES (Prof. W.)	26
JARDINE (Rev. R.)	26
JEANS (Rev. G. E.)	34, 37
JEBB (Prof. R. C.)	4, 10, 13
JELLETT (Rev. J. H.)	34
JENKS (Prof. Ed.)	29
JENNINGS (A. C.)	10, 30
JEVONS (W. S.)	4, 26, 28, 29
JEX-BLAKE (Sophia).	8
JOHNSON (Amy)	27
JOHNSON (Samuel)	13
JONES (H. Arthur)	15
JONES (Prof. D. E.)	27

	PAGE
JONES (F.)	7
KANT	25
KARI	39
KAVANAGH (Rt. Hn. A. M.)	4
KAY (Rev. W.)	31
KEARY (Annie)	10, 18, 39
KEARY (Eliza)	39
KEATS	4, 20, 21
KELLNER (Dr. L.)	25
KELLOGG (Rev. S. H.)	34
KEMPE (A. B.)	26
KENNEDY (Prof. A. B. W.)	8
KENNEDY (B. H.)	36
KEYNES (J. N.)	26, 28
KIEPERT (H.)	9
KILLEN (W. D.)	32
KINGSLEY (Charles)	4, 8, 10, 11, 12, 13, 15, 18, 21, 24, 32, 37, 39
KINGSLEY (Henry)	20, 38
KIPLING (J. L.)	38
KIPLING (Rudyard)	18
KIRKPATRICK (Prof.)	34
KLEIN (Dr. E.)	6, 23
KNIGHT (W.)	14
KUENEN (Prof. A.)	30
KYNASTON (Rev. H.)	34, 37
LABBERTON (R. H.)	3
LAFARGUE (P.)	18
LAMB.	4, 20, 21
LANCIANI (Prof. R.)	2
LANDAUER (J.)	7
LANDOR	4, 20
LANE-POOLE (S.)	20
LANFREY (P.)	5
LANG (Andrew)	2, 12, 21, 36
LANG (Prof. Arnold)	39
LANGLEY (J. N.)	27
LANKESTER (Prof. Ray)	6, 21
LASLETT (T.)	6
LEAF (W.)	13, 36
LEAHY (Sergeant)	30
LEA (M.)	18
LEE (S.)	20, 37
LEEPER (A.)	37
LEGGE (A. O.)	10, 34
LEMON (Mark)	20
LESLIE (A.)	38
LETHBRIDGE (Sir Roper)	10
LEVY (Amy)	18
LEWIS (R.)	13
LIGHTFOOT (Bp.)	21, 30, 31, 33, 34
LIGHTWOOD (J. M.)	12
LINDSAY (Dr. J. A.)	23
LOCKYER (J. N.)	3, 7, 27
LODGE (Prof. O. J.)	21, 27
LOEWY (B.)	26
LOFTIE (Mrs. W. J.)	2
LONGFELLOW (H. W.)	20
LONSDALE (J.)	20, 37
LOWE (W. H.)	30
LOWELL (J. R.)	15, 21
LUBBOCK (Sir J.)	6, 8, 21, 22, 40
LUCAS (F.)	15
LUPTON (S.)	7
LYALL (Sir Alfred)	4
LYTE (H. C. M.)	10
LYTTON (Earl of)	18
MACALISTER (D.)	23
MACARTHUR (M.)	10
MACAULAY (G. C.)	36
MACCOLL (Norman)	14
M'COSH (Dr. J.)	25, 26
MACDONALD (G.)	16
MACDONELL (J.)	29

INDEX. 43

Name	Page	Name	Page	Name	Page
Mackail (J. W.)	37	Moulton (L. C.)	15	Poole (R. L.)	11
Mackenzie (Sir Morell)	23	Mudie (C. E.)	15	Pope	4, 20
Maclagan (Dr. T.)	23	Muir (M. M. P.)	7	Poste (E.)	27, 36
Maclaren (Rev. Alex.)	34	Müller (H.)	6	Potter (L.)	22
Maclaren (Archibald)	39	Mullinger (J. B.)	11	Potter (R.)	35
Maclean (W. C.)	23	Murphy (J. J.)	26	Preston (T.)	27
Maclear (Rev. Dr. G. F.)	30, 32	Murray (D. Christie)	18	Price (L. L. F. R.)	28
M'Lennan (J. F.)	1	Murray (E. C. G.)	38	Prickard (A. O.)	22
M'Lennan (Malcolm)	18	Myers (E.)	15, 36	Prince Albert Victor	37
Macmillan (Rev. H.)	22, 35, 38	Myers (F. W. H.)	4, 15, 22	Prince George	37
Macmillan (Michael)	5, 15	Mylne (Bishop)	35	Procter (F.)	32
Macnamara (C.)	23	Nadal (E. S.)	22	Propert (J. L.)	2
Macquoid (K. S.)	18	Nettleship (H.)	13	Radcliffe (C. B.)	3
Madoc (F.)	18	Newcastle (Duke and Duchess)	20	Ramsay (W.)	7
Maguire (J. F.)	39	Newcomb (S.)	3	Ransome (C.)	13
Mahaffy (Prof. J. P.) 2, 11, 13, 22, 25, 35, 38		Newton (Sir C. T.)	2	Rathbone (W.)	8
Maitland (F. W.)	12, 29	Nichol (J.)	4, 13	Rawlinson (W. G.)	2
Malet (L.)	18	Noel (Lady A.)	18	Rawnsley (H. D.)	15
Malory (Sir T.)	20	Nordenskiöld (A. E.)	38	Ray (P. K.)	26
Mansfield (C. B.)	7	Norgate (Kate)	11	Rayleigh (Lord)	27
Markham (C. R.)	4	Norris (W. E.)	18	Reichel (Bishop)	35
Marriott (J. A. R.)	5	Norton (Charles Eliot)	3, 37	Reid (J. S.)	37
Marshall (Prof. A.)	28	Norton (Hon. Mrs.)	15, 18	Remsen (I.)	7
Marshall (M. P)	28	Oliphant (Mrs. M. O. W.)		Rendall (Rev. F.)	31, 35
Martel (C.)	24	4, 11, 13, 19, 20, 39		Rendu (M. le C.)	9
Martin (Frances)	3, 39	Oliphant (T. L. K.)	22, 25	Reynolds (H. R.)	35
Martin (Frederick)	28	Oliver (Prof. D.)	6	Reynolds (J. R.)	23
Martin (H. N.)	40	Oliver (Capt. S. P.)	38	Reynolds (O.)	11
Martineau (H.)	5	Oman (C. W.)	4	Richardson (B. W.)	11, 23
Martineau (J.)	5	Ostwald (Prof.)	7	Richey (A. G.)	12
Masson (D.) 4, 5, 15, 16, 20, 22, 26		Otté (E. C.)	11	Robinson (Preb. H. G.)	35
Masson (G.)	7, 20	Page (T. E.)	31	Robinson (J. L.)	24
Masson (R. O.)	16	Palgrave (Sir F.)	11	Robinson (Matthew)	5
Maturin (Rev. W.)	35	Palgrave (F. T.)		Rochester (Bishop of)	5
Maudsley (Dr. H.)	26	2, 15, 16, 20, 21, 33, 39		Rockstro (W. S.)	4
Maurice (Fredk. Denison)		Palgrave (R. F. D.)	29	Rogers (J. E. T.)	11, 28, 29
8, 22, 25, 30, 31, 32, 35		Palgrave (R. H. Inglis)	28	Romanes (G. J.)	6
Maurice (Col. F.)	5, 24, 29	Palgrave (W. G.)	15, 29, 38	Roscoe (Sir H. E.)	7
Max Müller (F.)	25	Palmer (Lady S.)	19	Roscoe (W. C.)	15
Mayer (A. M.)	27	Parker (T. J.)	6, 39	Rosebery (Earl of)	4
Mayor (J. B.)	31	Parker (W. N.)	40	Rosenbusch (H.)	9
Mayor (Prof. J. E. B.)	3, 5	Parkinson (S.)	27	Ross (P.)	19
Mazini (L.)	39	Parkman (F.)	11	Rossetti (C. G.)	15, 39
M'Cormick (W. S.)	13	Parsons (Alfred)	12	Routledge (J.)	29
Meldola (Prof. R.)	7, 26, 27	Pasteur (L.)	7	Rowe (F. J.)	16
Mendenhall (T. C.)	27	Pater (W. H.)	2, 19, 22	Rücker (Prof. A. W.)	7
Mercier (Dr. C.)	23	Paterson (J.)	12	Rumford (Count)	22
Mercur (Prof. J.)	24	Patmore (Coventry)	20, 39	Rushbrooke (W. G.)	31
Meredith (G.)	15	Patteson (J. C.)	5	Russell (Dean)	35
Meredith (L. A.)	12	Pattison (Mark)	4, 5, 35	Russell (Sir Charles)	29
Meyer (E. von)	7	Payne (E. J.)	10, 29	Russell (W. Clark)	4, 19
Miall (A.)	5	Peabody (C. H.)	8, 27	Ryland (F.)	13
Michelet (M.)	11	Peel (E.)	15	Ryle (Prof. H. E.)	30
Mill (H. R.)	9	Peile (J.)	25	St. Johnston (A.)	19, 38, 39
Miller (R. K.)	3	Pellissier (E.)	25	Sadler (H.)	2
Milligan (Rev. W.)	31, 35	Pennell (J.)	2	Saintsbury (G.)	4, 13
Milton	13, 15, 20	Pennington (R.)	9	Salmon (Rev. G.)	35
Minto (Prof. W.)	4, 18	Penrose (F. C.)	1, 3	Sandford (M. E.)	5
Mitford (A. B.)	18	Perry (Prof. J.)	27	Sandys (J. E.)	38
Mivart (St. George)	28	Pettigrew (J. B.)	6, 28, 40	Sayce (A. H.)	11
Mixter (W. G.)	7	Phillimore (J. G.)	12	Schaff (P.)	30
Mohammad	20	Phillips (J. A.)	23	Schliemann (Dr.)	2
Molesworth (Mrs.)	39	Phillips (W. C.)	23	Schorlemmer (C.)	7
Molloy (G.)	26	Picton (J. A.)	22	Scott (D. H.)	6
Monahan (J. H.)	12	Piffard (H. G.)	23	Scott (Sir W.)	15, 20
Montelius (O.)	1	Plato	20	Scratchley (Sir Peter)	24
Moore (C. H.)	2	Plumptre (Dean)	35	Scudder (S. H.)	40
Moorhouse (Bishop)	35	Pollard (A. W.)	37	Seaton (Dr. E. C.)	23
Morison (J. C.)	3, 4	Pollock (Sir Fk., 2nd Bart.)	5	Seeley (J. R.)	11
Morley (John)	3, 4, 16, 22	Pollock (Sir F., Bart.)	12, 22, 29	Seiler (Dr. Carl)	23, 28
Morris (Mowbray)	4	Pollock (Lady)	2	Selborne (Earl of)	12, 20, 32, 33
Morris (R.)	20, 25	Pollock (W. H.)	2	Sellers (E.)	2
Morshead (E. D. A.)	36	Poole (M. E.)	22	Service (J.)	32, 35
				Sewell (E. M.)	11

INDEX.

	PAGE		PAGE		PAGE
Shairp (J. C.)	4, 15	Tanner (H.)	1	Ward (A. W.)	4, 13, 20
Shakespeare	13, 15, 20, 21	Tavernier (J. B.)	38	Ward (H. M.)	6
Shann (G.)	8, 27	Taylor (Franklin)	24	Ward (S.)	16
Sharp (W.)	5	Taylor (Isaac)	25, 35	Ward (T. H.)	16
Shelley	15, 21	Taylor (Sedley)	24, 27	Ward (Mrs. T. H.)	19, 39
Shirley (W. N.)	35	Tegetmeier (W. B.)	8	Ward (W.)	5, 32
Shorthouse (J. H.)	19	Temple (Bishop)	35	Warington (G.)	36
Shortland (Admiral)	24	Temple (Sir R.)	4	Waters (C. A.)	28
Shuchhardt (Carl)	2	Tennant (Dorothy)	38	Waterton (Charles)	24, 38
Shuckburgh (E. S.)	11, 36	Tenniel	38	Watson (E.)	5
Shufeldt (R. W.)	40	Tennyson	14, 16, 21	Watson (R. S.)	38
Sibson (Dr. F.)	23	Tennyson (Frederick)	16	Webb (W. T.)	16
Sidgwick (Prof. H.)	26, 28, 29	Tennyson (Hallam)	12, 39	Webster (Mrs. A.)	39
Sime (J.)	9, 10	Thompson (D'A. W.)	6	Welby-Gregory (Lady)	32
Simpson (Rev. W.)	32	Thompson (E.)	10	Welldon (Rev. J. E. C.)	36
Skeat (W. W.)	13	Thompson (S. P.)	27	Westcott (Bp.)	30, 31, 32, 36
Skrine (J. H.)	5, 15	Thomson (A. W.)	8	Westermarck (E.)	1
Slade (J. H.)	8	Thomson (Sir C. W.)	40	Wetherell (J.)	25
Sloman (Rev. A.)	31	Thomson (Hugh)	12	Wheeler (J. T.)	11
Smart (W.)	28	Thomson (Sir Wm.)	24, 26, 27	Whewell (W.)	5
Smalley (G. W.)	22	Thorne (Dr. Thorne)	23	White (Gilbert)	24
Smetham (J. and S.)	5	Thornton (J.)	6	White (Dr. W. Hale)	23
Smith (A.)	20	Thornton (W. T.)	26, 29, 37	White (W.)	27
Smith (C. B.)	16	Thorpe (T. E.)	7	Whitham (J. M.)	8
Smith (Goldwin)	4, 5, 29	Thring (E.)	8, 22	Whitney (W. D.)	8
Smith (H.)	16	Thrupp (J. F.)	30	Whittier (J. G.)	16, 22
Smith (J.)	6	Thudichum (J. L. W.)	7	Wickham (Rev. E. C.)	36
Smith (Rev. T.)	35	Thursfield (J. R.)	4	Wicksteed (P. H.)	28, 30
Smith (W. G.)	6	Todhunter (I.)	5, 8	Wiedersheim (R.)	40
Smith (W. S.)	35	Torrens (W. M.)	5	Wilbraham (F. M.)	32
Somerville (Prof. W.)	6	Tourgénief (I. S.)	19	Wilkins (Prof. A. S.)	2, 13, 36
Southey	5	Tout (T. F.)	11	Wilkinson (S.)	24
Spender (J. K.)	23	Tozer (H. F.)	9	Williams (G. H.)	9
Spenser	20	Traill (H. D.)	4, 29	Williams (Montagu)	5
Spottiswoode (W.)	27	Trench (Capt. F.)	29	Williams (S. E.)	13
Stanley (Dean)	35	Trench (Archbishop)	35	Willoughby (F.)	39
Stanley (Hon. Maude)	29	Trevelyan (Sir G. O.)	11	Wills (W. G.)	16
Statham (R.)	29	Tribe (A.)	7	Wilson (A. J.)	29
Stebbing (W.)	4	Tristram (W. O.)	12	Wilson (Sir C.)	4
Stephen (C. E.)	8	Trollope (A.)	4	Wilson (Sir D.)	1, 3, 13
Stephen (H.)	13	Truman (J.)	16	Wilson (Dr. G.)	4, 5, 22
Stephen (Sir J. F.)	11, 13, 22	Tucker (T. G.)	36	Wilson (Archdeacon)	36
Stephen (J. K.)	13	Tulloch (Principal)	35	Wilson (Mary)	13
Stephen (L.)	4	Turner (C. Tennyson)	16	Wingate (Major F. R.)	24
Stephens (J. B.)	16	Turner (G.)	1	Winkworth (C.)	5
Stevenson (J. J.)	2	Turner (H. H.)	27	Wolseley (Gen. Viscount)	24
Stewart (A.)	39	Turner (J. M. W.)	12	Wood (A. G.)	16
Stewart (Balfour)	26, 27, 35	Tylor (E. B.)	1	Wood (Rev. E. G.)	36
Stewart (S. A.)	6	Tyrwhitt (R. St. J.)	2, 16	Woods (Rev. F. H.)	1
Stokes (Sir G. G.)	27	Vaughan (C. J.)	31, 32, 35, 36	Woods (Miss M. A.)	17, 33
Story (R. H.)	3	Vaughan (Rev. D.)	20, 36	Woodward (C. M.)	8
Stone (W. H.)	27	Vaughan (Rev. E. T.)	36	Woolner (T.)	16
Strachey (Sir E.)	20	Vaughan (Rev. R.)	36	Wordsworth	5, 14, 16, 21
Strachey (Gen. R.)	9	Veley (M.)	19	Worthey (Mrs.)	19
Strangford (Viscountess)	38	Venn (Rev. J.)	26, 36	Wright (Rev. A.)	31
Strettell (A.)	16	Vernon (Hon. W. W.)	13	Wright (C. E. G.)	8
Stubbs (Rev. C. W.)	35	Verrall (A. W.)	13, 36	Wright (J.)	21
Stubbs (Bishop)	31	Verrall (Mrs.)	1	Wright (L.)	27
Sutherland (A.)	9	Wain (Louis)	39	Wright (W. Aldis)	8, 15, 20, 31
Symonds (J. A.)	4	Waldstein (C.)	2	Wurtz (Ad.)	7
Symonds (Mrs. J. A.)	5	Walker (Prof. F. A.)	28	Wyatt (Sir M. D.)	2
Symons (A.)	16	Wallace (A. R.)	6, 24, 28	Yonge (C. M.)	5, 6, 8, 10, 11, 19, 21, 25, 30, 39
Tait (Archbishop)	35	Wallace (Sir D. M.)	29		
Tait (C. W. A.)	11	Walpole (S.)	29	Young (E. W.)	8
Tait (Prof. P. G.)	26, 27, 35	Walton (I.)	12	Ziegler (Dr. E.)	23

MACMILLAN AND CO.

BEDFORD STREET, COVENT GARDEN, LONDON.

J. PALMER, PRINTER, ALEXANDRA STREET, CAMBRIDGE.

3/60/12/91

www.ingramcontent.com/pod-product-compliance
Lightning Source LLC
Chambersburg PA
CBHW051859300426
44117CB00006B/462